Unrevolutionary Mexico

Unrevolutionary Mexico

The Birth of a Strange Dictatorship

Paul Gillingham

Yale UNIVERSITY PRESS NEW HAVEN AND LONDON

Published with assistance from the Mary Cady Tew Memorial Fund.

Yale University Press books may be purchased in quantity for educational, business, or promotional use. For information, please e-mail sales.press@yale.edu (U.S. office) or sales@yaleup.co.uk (U.K. office).

Set in Scala type by IDS Infotech Ltd., Chandigarh, India.
Printed in the United States of America.

Library of Congress Control Number: 2020945160
ISBN 978-0-300-25312-2 (hardcover : alk. paper)

A catalogue record for this book is available from the British Library.

This paper meets the requirements of ANSI/NISO Z39.48-1992 (Permanence of Paper).

10 9 8 7 6 5 4 3 2 1

For Snježana

Contents

Acknowledgments

I would like to start in literal terms by thanking very much the people in those villages, towns, and cities that I visited while researching this book. In metaphorical terms, Oxford University, the Instituto de Investigaciones Dr. José Luis Mora, the Colegio de México, the University of North Carolina Wilmington, the University of Pennsylvania, Columbia University, and Northwestern University have all provided bases, colleagues, and resources over the years. I am particularly grateful for the training I was given at Oxford University's Latin American Centre and St. Antony's College, and latterly the very generous welcome and support offered by the members of the history department of Northwestern University.

The research funding without which there is no book was afforded by Oxford and Northwestern Universities and by grants from the Arts & Humanities Research Board, the Past & Present Society, the Institute for Historical Research, and the Andrew W. Mellon Foundation. Marcel Anduiza, Diana Ávila Hernández, Felipe Cole, and Jayson Porter were excellent research assistants. The maps were painstakingly created by Kelsey Rydland of Northwestern University Libraries. Publishers I have worked with in the past provided training and uniformly accomplished editors; some extracts from that work appear here courtesy of Duke University Press and the University of Arizona Press. The book was brought out in its plump form thanks to the enthusiasm of my agent, Alison MacKeen, and my editor at Yale University Press, Jaya Chatterjee. Their reputation rightly precedes them both.

As for my professional village, I am extremely grateful for the ideas, support, and criticism offered over the years by a large number of fellow Latin Americanists. I am indebted to those who have been generous in sharing documents as well as interests, among them Sergio Aguayo, Barry Carr, Ben Fallaw, Heather Fowler-Salamini, Renata Keller, Michael Lettieri, Andrew Paxman, Jayson Porter, Thom Rath, and Ben Smith. The blind readers of Yale University Press offered careful, knowledgeable, and meticulous comments that I greatly appreciated.

I would like to offer particularly warm thanks to Ben Smith for the educational and entertaining experience of editing books together and complaining; Ipek Yosmaoğlu, Josh and Ilias Cox for their unflinching hospitality; Pablo Piccato for his personal and professional welcome to New York; and above all Alan Knight, who first interested me in Mexican history as an undergraduate, whose support has been generous and critical—pun intended—ever since, and whom I have almost certainly plagiarized at points of this book.

Finally, I'd like to thank all of my family—which includes, of course, Oscar Altamirano—for their enthusiasm; and in particular my son, Alastair, who has taught me as much as, probably more than, I have taught him. The book, though, is dedicated to my wife, Snježana, for so many reasons.

Abbreviations

CIDOSA	Compañía Industrial de Orizaba, SA
CIVSA	Compañía Industrial Veracruzana, SA
CNC	Confederación Nacional Campesina
CNOP	Confederación Nacional de Organizaciones Populares
CNT	Confederación Nacional de Trabajadores
COCM	Confederación de Obreros y Campesinos de México
CROM	Confederación Regional Obrera Mexicana
CTM	Confederación de Trabajadores Mexicanos
DFS	Dirección Federal de Seguridad
DGIPS	Dirección General de Investigaciones Políticas y Sociales
FPPM	Federación de Partidos del Pueblo Mexicano
ISI	Import Substitution Industrialization
LNCUG	Liga Nacional Campesina Ursulo Galván
PAN	Partido Acción Nacional
PNR	Partido Nacional Revolucionario
PP	Partido Popular
PRI	Partido Revolucionario Institucional
PRM	Partido de la Revolución Mexicana
SEP	Secretaría de Educación Pública
STFRM	Sindicato de Trabajadores Ferrocarrileros de la República Mexicana

Introduction

"There's nowhere like Mexico"—*como México no hay dos*—is a nationalist catchphrase: sometimes jingoistic, sometimes ironic, always accurate.[1] In the first place Mexico enjoys the fundamental distinction of housing one of the few great social and political revolutions; in the Americas only Cuba compares.[2] Among twentieth-century revolutions the Mexican is further distinguished by its lack of either a vanguard party or a universalist ideology.[3] The revolutionary credo was instead firmly individualist and crowd-sourced, justified in the nationalist language of the times with its obedience to the "idiosyncrasy" of the Mexican rather than the dangerous "exotic doctrines" of the Twenty Years' Crisis and the Cold War, and over the years it—and the constitution it informed and sometimes followed—proved slippery, pragmatic, and profoundly flexible.[4] Even Marxist guerrillas rejected imported ideologies: Lucio Cabañas lectured his followers that "the way to make a revolution will not be taught by Cuba . . . China, the Soviet Union, or any other country," while the ideological hodgepodge of *jaramillismo* blended Marxism, anarchism, Maoism, Zapatismo, and Methodism.[5] Evangelicals were likewise creatively syncretic: the Luz del Mundo congregation mixed revolutionary nationalism with elements of Judaism, Catholicism, and Protestantism.[6] Unlike other revolutions, moreover, there were no significant, self-conscious iterations like the fall of France's July Monarchy, "its cycle bitterly comparable to the cycle of the First Republic with its own Girondins, Jacobins, and Thermidorians and even a second Bonaparte," or the subsequent fall of the Second Empire.[7] In Mexico national revolution was a strict one-off, the aim of subsequent elites being precisely to eulogize and avoid apocalyptic popular mobilization, and after 1924 would-be repeat runs played in provincial theaters as contained tragedies or one-act farces.[8]

As for what came next, the revolution's successor regime was standard enough in its Tocquevillian search for central power, but wholly exceptional for its time and place: a dictatorship that was formally civilian, collective, and punctiliously electoral. It did not, in fact, look much like a dictatorship at all, if our preconceptions are of unambiguous, institution-trashing tyranny, the gaudy one-man shows of a Duvalier—take your pick as to which one—a Somoza—take your pick once more—or a Trujillo. Mexico's strange dictatorship was further exceptional in its record-breaking longevity: seventy-one years of rule by the same party. After 1940 there were neither caudillos nor top-level assassinations. Mexico was not the United States, where the major progressive leaders of the postwar period—Martin Luther King, JFK, RFK, Malcolm X, and Harvey Milk—were all murdered. There was extensive repressive violence in the countryside, but it was quite successfully downplayed, hidden even, from the chattering classes inside and outside Mexico, who for years quibbled over how democratic or dictatorial each successive government or election was. The system was, in absolute terms, neither of the above, neither fish nor fowl, an enduring mixture of both democratic and authoritarian elements. Such distinguishing ambiguity became common in the hybrid regimes of the post–Cold War period but during the Cold War was exceptional, characterizing a genuinely idiosyncratic power structure that Mexicans met with a mixture, often in the same person, of resistance, resigned tolerance, and acceptance. Theirs was a *dictablanda,* a punning neologism combining *dictadura,* dictatorship, with *blanda* (soft) in place of *dura* (hard). It was a system that ran on a complex blend of political monopoly fostered by election rigging, *no reelección,* and a broad governing coalition; a qualified level of cultural control, ranging from the nationalism of school programs to the censorship of the national newspapers; strategic payoffs from a mixed economy, access to which relied on the benevolence of governmental gatekeepers; and, in some times and some places, considerable violence, whether repressive, riotous, or rebellious. As has been said elsewhere, a system of bread and circuses and guns.[9]

This is a balancing act of definition, as is clear from debate as to whether the concept of dictablanda overprivileges violence, underprivileges violence, or, according to one innovative commentary, does both at the same time. That is perhaps only appropriate for a regime that was itself a balancing act.[10] If it is accepted that naming things, classifying regimes with nouns—as opposed to chronological adjectives, whether Cold War, midcentury, or postrevolutionary—is generally worthwhile, affording comparison and debate over the concrete features of different political entities, then it is probably worth considering which noun best fits Mexico in the first decades after the revolution. Two arguments have been advanced against the idea of Mexico as a dictablanda: that the term is straightforwardly inadmissible and that it is admissible but misleading. One critique holds the classification technically inadmissible as it applies only to military regimes; but while the definition was first widely applied to General Dámaso Berenguer's government in the Spain of the early 1930s a dictablanda is not by definition exclusively military. Daniel Cosío Villegas applied it to the civilian regime of General Porfirio Díaz, an instance of the term's potential for thought-provoking comparison.[11] Another critique suggests the term is ethically inadmissible due to its self-justifying usage by another general, Agustín Pinochet; but if sociological terms are rejected because they are used by unpleasant historical actors, then democracy, in light of the Democratic People's Republic of Korea, or the German Democratic Republic, also needs ditching.[12]

As for the proposal that dictablanda is a historically misleading idea, if we register that the term as defined—and chronologically specified, as it has been, to the period between the midforties and the midsixties—actually encompasses quite a lot of violence, then it is worth considering some alternatives which have captured facets of the state and prospered. That the only meaningful party in Mexico was the PRI makes that country to a certain extent *priista* is self-evident, and the idea of the priista state is useful; but it is also particular rather than comparative, and overlooks recent scholarship that establishes just how much the party could be an adornment to rather than a bulwark of the state. As Rogelio Hernández Rodríguez shows, the executives who really counted, the presidents and governors, did not come up through the party's ranks. Regional party apparatchiks did not control governors; quite the opposite.[13] While Joy Langston takes a more traditional view of the party's power, she also points out that the party had no assets of its own. As John Womack has rhetorically asked, who paid whose rent—the PRI that of the Interior Ministry, which actually ran the country, or vice versa? The party had no inputs into policy-making and, while highly centralized, little continuity in its top personnel, who served at the president's pleasure. The Kuomintang or Communist Party of the Soviet Union it was not.[14] At the local level, meanwhile, Ben Smith has likewise found that "surprisingly, political backing and party activism were not terribly important"; *presidentes municipales*—mayors, the politicians that most Mexicans cared most about—were, for good or ill, self-starters.[15] The perfect dictatorship, on the other hand, is evocative but not very accurate. The Mexican population was not drugged into submission in any *Brave New*

World, locked into the impenetrable false consciousness of *The Matrix,* or monitored into submission in Airstrip One. Finally, biological metaphors—dairy products, marine animals or charitably inclined bogeymen—while also evocative, are also not much use for comparison.[16] Conceptualizing Mexico between the early 1940s and the early 1960s as a dictablanda, in short, seems useful for its balance of precision and comparison until an equally specific and less flawed alternative term can be proposed.

This book is about how that first exceptional political phenomenon, the revolution, grew into the second, the dictablanda. That path is not obvious: the groundbreaking edited volume of Gil Joseph, Anne Rubenstein, and Eric Zolov focused on the politics of culture for reasons both methodological and of available data, postulating that "cultural history provides the best and *sometimes the only* window onto crucial aspects of the post-1940 Mexican experience."[17] The more recent and more overtly political historiography of the period after 1940 is concentrated elsewhere in terms of chronology, in particular toward the 1960s, their sweep long and their clout global, their distinguishing feature the Cold War and 1968.[18] Recent Anglophone political histories of the period concentrate elsewhere in terms of people too, privileging the dissident glamor of students, guerrillas, journalists, strikers, and the spies who watched them all.[19] Rubén Jaramillo exerts greater charm than the dour, domino-shuffling President Adolfo Ruiz Cortines, as he probably did in real life. The upshot of these choices, however, is an understanding of the intervening years, the 1940s and 1950s, that is thinner and that still tends toward the particular and the cupular. The early political histories of Blanca Torres and Luis Medina were largely constrained by the limited sources available at the time, in the main newspapers, government reports, and memoirs.[20] Their insights have been notably developed by the work of subsequent scholars, among others Luis Aboites, Jorge Alonso, Tiziana Bertaccini, Heather Fowler-Salamini, Rogelio Hernández Rodríguez, Soledad Loaeza, Aurora Loyo, Stephen Niblo, Thom Rath, Ariel Rodríguez Kuri, Elsa Servín, and Ben Smith.[21] We now know much more about the silent majorities of taxpayers (or evaders), party members, businessmen great and small, Catholics, elections, pliant union bosses both male and female, and assorted middle classes and what went wrong when their interests diverged too far from those of the state-builders of the time, in particular in 1952, the last substantial electoral challenge for several decades. Yet we still know less about what happened when things went right, for those state-builders at least, when, and how, Mexico reached the relative stability of the mature PRI: by no means a golden age, but perhaps, in Beatriz Magaloni's wording, a "golden parenthesis."[22]

Dating the end of the revolution is comparatively straightforward. For all the rhetoric of subsequent presidents, the period of dramatic change in social structures and the social foundations of political power came at the end of the 1930s or beginning of the 1940s. The black-and-white of the revolution gave way to the Kodachrome of modern Mexico—literally, as some of the first color film was shot there in 1937—the father of agrarian reform, Andrés Molina Enríquez, died, and, more to the point, President Lázaro Cárdenas departed office, taking with him much of revolutionary policy and personnel. The change began before that—1938 is an evident inflection point, the oil expropriation both a peak and a last swagger of the revolutionary left—and continued after the traditional expiry date of 1940, with the centrist president Manuel Avila Camacho declaring his faith, ending socialist education, ditching the Cardenistas who initially populated his cabinet, appointing conservatives to governorships and the Supreme Court, winding down agrarian and labor reform, and introducing the usefully totalitarian law of *disolución social,* a more or less carte blanche to jail dissidents.[23] Yet the successor regime did not spring to life fully formed, as once held, from the foundation of the corporate Partido de la Revolución Mexicana (PRM) and the social contract—stability for reform—of the pax cardenista. Its creation was, as Alan Knight put it, a "cumulative, piecemeal process, whose full significance only became clear over time, with the benefit of hindsight."[24]

Just how cumulative and piecemeal that process was is evident in any social or regional history of the Avila Camacho *sexenio,* the six-year presidential term in office. Hal Jones's argument that World War II brought peace to Mexico works best on the turf of elite, *capitalino* politics, where violent polarization among revolutionaries and with the Right was indeed replaced by a blander, old-school project of national unity and a porfirian modus vivendi—of both civilians and soldiers—with the church hierarchy, a positive "accomplice of the government's social project."[25] (Although full acceptance of the argument necessitates overlooking the near-coup of 1948, the reelection maneuverings of Miguel Alemán before the 1952 and 1958 elections, the violence necessary to win the former election against a revitalized Left, the dealings with old-fashioned regional strongmen in winning the latter, and even a 1944 presidential assassination attempt, albeit the last confirmed one for fifty years.)[26] Other metrics are less convincing. The military was distinctly not out of politics. They had installed eighteen presidents by force since Independence; it was nowhere written that they would not continue the tradition.[27] The general responsible for modernizing the army, Joaquín Amaro, was a serial malcontent who was not above considering coups himself.[28] Workers were untamed, for all the divide and rule union creation of the wartime years and the patriotic pact with labor; there were more strikes in 1944 than at any other point between 1938 and 1993.[29] Grassroots Catholics had not followed their bishops, and sinarquista militants were numerous and well drilled, in 1944 capable of marching in columns out of nowhere to occupy Tacámbaro, Michoacán, with five thousand men in green shirts.[30] (Like some other colored-shirt enthusiasts of the era—Ireland's Blueshirts, Britain's Blackshirts—they exalted violence without committing all that much of it.) Rural violence, put largely out of sight and out of mind in the bigger crisis, endured, with the army summarily executing holdup men on the highways, unsure whether to call them bandits or rebels (they sometimes chose both—Eric Hobsbawm would have been delighted).[31] Teachers, excellent quantitative measures of a state's presence outside a capital, were absent—and with them much of the state, as Bernard Fall would argue in Vietnam—in large numbers across large swathes of the country.[32] When Abel Quezada drew a cartoon summarizing the presidencies he represented Avila Camacho with an empty box labeled "six years of nothing."[33] Even considering the possibility that Avila Camacho was a more gifted politician than his reputation and dull public persona suggested—a positive trope with midcentury presidents, applicable also to Lázaro Cárdenas and Adolfo Ruiz Cortines—the put-down still reflects an underlying verity, in that the sexenio, and the war it encompassed, did not decisively redefine Mexico (as both its predecessor and successor did). Instead it left, in 1946, considerable uncertainty as to the country's future course, and considerable instability outside of the capital.[34]

This book argues that both uncertainty and instability decreased dramatically, in a clear rupture, over the decade that straddles the midcentury, 1945 to 1955, during which a new and very different regime coalesced. To classify that regime and its historical path as exceptional in modern Latin America is not to dismiss some similarities between the violently repressive governments of the later 1960s and 1970s and the more overt dictatorships of Brazil or the Southern Cone, or indeed the military's involvement in civilian government, a lot greater than once thought.[35] The United States exercised more influence over Mexican foreign policy during the Cold War than was always visible, and there were politicians at the highest level who were notably close to the gringos' embassy and even their CIA station.[36] The masked cooperation played out in particular over Cuba: frontstage Mexico defied the United States to support Castro while backstage helping the Americans to spy on the Cubans and implementing unspoken sanctions of their own on oil and food sales.[37] As for economic exceptionalism, the Mexican miracle of postwar development looks less miraculous when removed from the rhetoric of presidential *informes* and considered in comparative quantitative terms, whether of equity—among the lowest in the world—or GDP growth. Mexico was the world's twenty-seventh largest economy when the great postwar capitalist boom began and the twenty-seventh when it ended.[38] A relatively rich country grew, in short, at the same rate as its global peers and enjoyed less success in distributing the rewards of that growth than most. Diplomats by 1960 deemed it less revolutionary state than plutocracy, run by a readily perceived oligarchy.[39] And yet caveats read, Mexico remains exceptional not just in the Americas but in the twentieth-century world tout court.[40]

The pivotal period in the creation of this strange dictatorship at a national level was the time of the rise and fall of Miguel Alemán, encompassing his final steps from the Secretaría de Gobernación, the interior ministry he had steered to a whole new level of power, to his final replacement by a Ruiz Cortines consolidated, in the wake of devaluation and midterm elections, as his own man rather than the puppet he was intended to be. The analytical focus is on causation rather than phenomenology, aiming to trace the most salient political changes in the shift from a revolutionary to an authoritarian state rather than to describe the main features of contemporary society. As such, it does not devote chapters to women, businessmen, clerics or any other single social group, although their stories run through the entire history. *Agraristas* are the most important of these groups, the story of the end of large-scale land reform and colonization of agrarian organizations too imbricated in every facet of the time's history to be excised and presented discretely. Rather than actor-centered, the framework is one of a multiregional social history of politics, examining the political evolution of two states in particular: Guerrero and Veracruz. Within that framework it examines the five most salient areas for gauging the balance of force and consent in the dictablanda: elections, violence, economic development, cultural control, and civil–military relations.

The rationale for selecting Guerrero and Veracruz was one of the contrasts between the two regions, whose paths from Independence onward diverged markedly. That contrast was intended to provide not a complete topography of political practice but rather an outline of its main contours. In 1950 Guerrero had the lowest literacy rate, the second-lowest average rural salary, and the second-highest murder rate in Mexico; men from Guerrero lost the presidential elections of 1940 and 1946. Veracruz, on the other hand, was one of the wealthiest, most urban, and industrialized states, and her elites dominated central government for most of the forties and fifties.[41] Veracruz was described by one contemporary as "the most important state in the Republic"; Guerrero was perceived as an unruly frontier of secondary economic importance until the tourism and forestry booms of the later 1940s.[42] Despite these divergences, though, the two states had two important things in common in the mid-1940s: their port cities were major networking hubs where federal politicians gathered, meddled promiscuously in local politics, acquired properties, and cut far-reaching deals with domestic and international businessmen, providing en route insights into national as well as regional developments; and, most important of all, they were both in a condition of profound crisis.[43]

To chart the dramatic changes of the midcentury the book is divided into a narrative and an analysis drawing on that narrative. The histories of each state between 1880 and 1945, unfolded in chapters 1 and 2, form a necessary baseline for the decade at the center of the argument, 1945–55, its course in each state explored in chapters 3 and 4. The periodization reflects the political cycles of the two regions, cycles that in turn reflect the autonomy of provincial governments, what Rogelio Hernández Rodríguez has called "the enormous power of the states," their administrations at times distinctly out of step with presidential periods and philosophies.[44] In both states 1945 was a critical year, as newly technocratic governors made their first struggling attempts to wield power in unpromising conditions.[45] Stories told, a second, thematic section investigates five questions central to any understanding of the period and its implications for the subsequent development of the Mexican state. The first two straddle histories of force and consent: chapter 5 analyzes the salience and representative weight of elections, while chapter 6 considers the management and decline of criminal and political violence. The following two focus on the mechanisms and limits of consent: the material rewards and costs of development and corruption, the minimal demands of a state at times positively Hapsburg in its unintended laissez-faire, and the significance of the cultural tools of that state in fostering and constraining the power of federal government and bureaucracy.[46] A final chapter returns to the question of force, and in particular the salience and cost of the military's guarantees of civilian, single-party rule against the tide of militarism rising across the rest of Latin America.

"In the matter of hiding their light under a bushel," a contemporary diplomat observed, "the PRI have nothing to learn from the Kremlin."[47] This book attempts to counter the smoke and mirrors of the politics of the time by triangulating vastly divergent stories of traditional, top-down sources—government reports, circulars, and instructions, diplomatic impressions, the reports of a generally tamed national press—with the grassroots versions of popular protests, voluminous letters and telegrams of complaint, the critiques of more oppositional provincial journalists, and the immensely revealing correspondence of the *agentes municipales,* the smallest cogs in the machinery of government, whose unenviable lot it was to try to enforce distant policy in a recalcitrant countryside. Research at that close-up level focused on six places: in Guerrero, the villages of Ixcateopan and San Jerónimo and the town of Ometepec, and in Veracruz the village of Soledad de Doblado and the towns of Chicontepec and San Andrés Tuxtla. They were chosen as communities that collectively encompassed a wide spectrum of different ethnic, ecological, and economic variables. San Jerónimo and Soledad de Doblado are mestizo villages on rich coastal plains with long histories of agrarian conflict; San Andrés Tuxtla and Ometepec are market towns where powerful rancher societies dominated indigenous villages and forged early links to export markets; Chicontepec and Ixcateopan are both remote and relatively impoverished *municipios* in the mountains.[48] In the middle of these stories of domination and resistance lie the polyvalent reports of the intelligence services, which can be profitably used both as windows on the federal government's priorities and *mentalité* and as detailed chronicles, rather than reliable analyses, of grassroots reactions to that government. These three groups of archives between them depict both political designs and realities, actions and reactions, the interlocking worlds of rulers, middlemen, and ruled in a holistic approximation to the actual—rather than the would-be—mechanisms of the state.

No single group of sources has been systematically privileged at the expense of the others: governors' reports are only partly fictional, the protests of dissident peasants can be tactical perjury, and the conclusions of Gobernación agents can be manipulated, purchased, or downright wrong. The evidence of village-level political correspondence and national intelligence reports was nonetheless central to the final analysis. Spies can be false friends, and in Mexico the amateurism and political bias of the early Dirección General de Investigaciones Políticas y Sociales (DGIPS) and Dirección Federal de Seguridad (DFS) should be constantly held in mind in using their output.[49] Failing to do so can only derail analysis. Thus Aaron Navarro concludes that the security services' "lasting ties to the bureaucratic and political agenda of the PRI . . . [were] the foundation of the PRI's electoral dominance over the decades after

World War II" and that they were able to dedicate themselves to the job wholeheartedly because they sheltered under the security umbrella of the United States.[50] This bypasses both the significance of softer and less institutionalized tools of domination as well as the still-primitive nature of the contemporary DFS and DGIPS. A state with a starting total of forty-two DFS agents, which could spare only fifteen DGIPS agents to oversee the contested 1952 federal elections throughout the country, and which preferred to draw political intelligence from party operatives rather than its own spies, is no police state.[51] (At its inception there were about as many DGIPS agents in Mexico as there were FBI agents in wartime Ecuador.)[52] Even after the expansion of the 1950s there may have been in 1961 as few as thirty-six DGIPS inspectors—who showed up for work, as opposed to flashing badges—in the country, and even they didn't always show up for work; in a request for replacements the director noted that one agent hadn't come to the office in five years, while another two were just "not competent."[53] Yet some others were competent, were interested in the same questions we are, and had the advantages of being on the spot to try and solve them. Sometimes they came up with answers, and those answers provide critical insights into the transmission belts of power between people, bosses, bureaucrats, and the far-off central government.

Ultimately, the sources impose intrinsic limits on any interpretation. The mere existence of constant flows—and periodic floods—of protest correspondence undercuts the more unequivocal conclusions regarding the dictatorial repressiveness or unadulterated authoritarianism of midcentury Mexico. In "proper," fully-fledged authoritarian systems people do not write such letters, and when they do it is with the revolutionary exultation of a hidden transcript unmasked as a regime crumbles.[54] There are few equivalents in the archives of the Uruguayan, Argentine, or Chilean dictatorships. Across Mexico, in contrast, peasants, workers, townsmen, villagers, bureaucrats, and political bosses, *caciques,* frequently made no attempt whatsoever to conceal their transcripts of power. Yet just as the state's protestations often fell on deaf ears, so too were these protests regularly ignored by the politicians and bureaucrats in Mexico City. The letters and telegrams were systematically forwarded to the very provincial authorities whose abuses the dissident authors censured, leading, as some requests for anonymity show, to sometimes unpleasant personal consequences.[55] Force and physical fear were unmistakably strong, everyday presences in Mexican politics in the 1940s and 1950s; a counterfactual history where Priistas hesitated overlong before resorting to force would not contain a PRI at all, its predecessor having fallen at the first fence of the 1940 presidential election, which most people believed the opposition won. Cultural hegemony was long a dominant framework in historical work on modern Mexico, and the early priista state was indeed to some extent hegemonic.[56] So, however, are the overwhelming majority of modern states; Mao, Stalin, and Hitler all took some diehard believers with them to their graves. The Mexican combination of revolutionary heritage with stark economic inequality and longevity with measured violence may suggest that the country's politics were more hegemonic, in the brute sense of subjectively consensual against objective odds, to the point of distinction.[57] Such a proposition, however, begs more questions of causation (and detail) than it resolves. It is some of those questions that this book seeks to explore on the exceptional path from revolutionary to unrevolutionary Mexico.

1 • Archipelagos of Power

Guerrero

A Geographical Expression

In 1949 Alejandro Wladimir Paucic, an irascible Croatian engineer, gave his new map of Guerrero to the governor, General Baltasar Leyva Mancilla.[1] Paucic was an odd man out in the state bureaucracy, a would-be encyclopedist whose liking for precisely ordered information sat uncomfortably with the slapdash cynicism of his political masters. He found relief in filing acerbic descriptions of them for posterity; politics, he noted, was "a demagogue's trade for easy and rapid self-enrichment at the expense of the sheep."[2] Delivering the first complete map of the state must have given him a more innocent pleasure. Only a couple of years earlier *National Geographic* had described the state's northwest as "a vast, mountainous tract known as *Región inexplorada.*"[3] No prior governor had known in full the territory he (theoretically) ruled; earlier cartographers had left large tracts entirely blank.[4] Such ignorance reflected not just the modest administrative ambitions of the men who governed Guerrero but also the state's state-thwarting topography. Guerrero is predominantly mountainous, straddling the east–west axis of the Sierra Madre del Sur, whose peaks are joined in the north by a volcanic range that spills southward out of the state of Mexico. The baking flatlands of the narrow Balsas River valley, the mountain-bound plains of the northwest, and a strip of tropical coastline do little more than punctuate the sierra. Until well after the revolution no one in Guerrero managed the engineering works that drew railways and roads across the mountains and deserts of Porfirian Mexico: the difficulties were pronounced, the rewards, given the territory's unruly villagers and unreliable caciques, uncertain. For all its proximity to Mexico City, the state

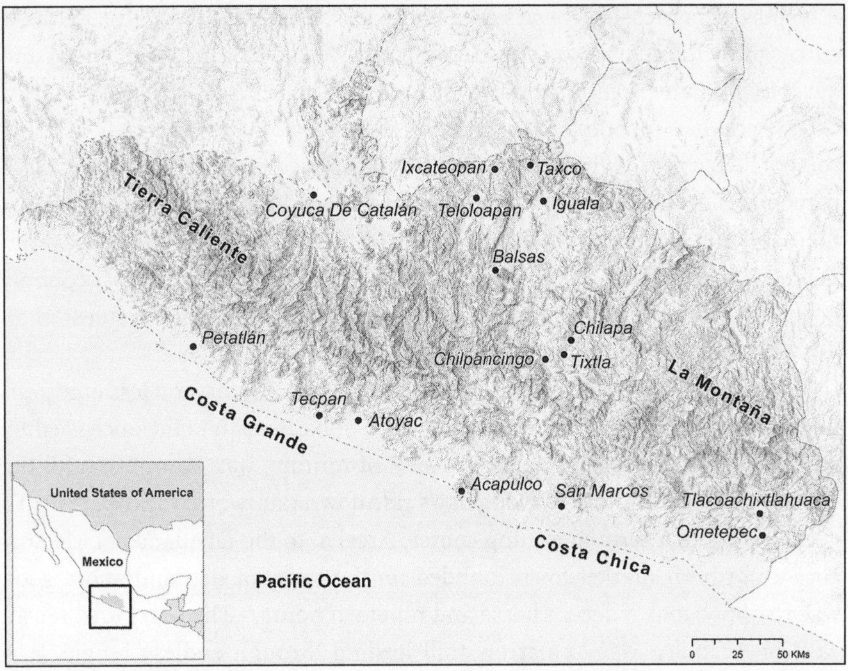

The state of Guerrero. Created by Kelsey Rydland, Research Services, Northwestern University Libraries.

was to outsiders a frontier; or, as Paucic in his brighter moments might have seen it, a blank canvas.

Another way of seeing Guerrero might be, in the words of another Austro-Hungarian, as not so much a state as a geographical expression.[5] Communications, the main determinants of development, were for most of the period 1880–1945 restricted to mule tracks and the sea roads that led to and from Acapulco, the routes and—the odd steamship aside—technologies of the sixteenth century. The railways that linked other regions of Mexico to national and international markets barely grazed the north of Guerrero, reaching the northern town of Iguala in 1892 and coming to a terminal halt at the Balsas River, thirty miles farther south, in 1900. From the Iguala railway station to the state capital Chilpancingo—a dusty valley enclosing wooden or adobe huts, a skyline of five two-story buildings and a couple of church spires—was a two-day ride down a cart road, the state's only highway until the late 1920s.[6] Even mule tracks were scarce, one governor remarked, explaining that it was "proverbial that the state generally lacks means of communication."[7] Assorted transport schemes—highways and railroads, shipping down the Balsas—successively foundered; freight costs from the fertile lowlands remained ruinously high.[8] One project, a highway from Acapulco across the sierra to Mexico City, would have opened up the interior; it was opposed for precisely that reason by the narrow Acapulco elites, who had parlayed isolation into enduring if parochial monopolies.[9] Until that road was pushed through in the late 1920s the overland journey from Acapulco to Mexico City lasted fifteen days on horse- or muleback.[10] The irony was striking: while Mexico's export economy boomed its finest natural port, to Alexander von Humboldt "the finest of all those on the coast of the great ocean," lay more or less useless.[11]

Bottlenecks for trade inside the state were likewise tight, and less epic journeys equally slow. From the northern village of Ixcateopan to the once-wealthy town of Taxco, devastated by the collapse of mining, was 20 miles; until the late 1940s, however, it took a long day's ride down rain-worn, rocky paths.[12] To get from another *serrano* mining center, Arcelia, to the farmlands of Teloloapan, a northern market town founded on the rarity of flat land and a good water supply, took a decent horse and nineteen hours.[13] The coast road northwest of Acapulco was "a narrow trail leading through endless jungle."[14] A Gobernación agent dispatched in 1932 to the main town of the southern coast, Ometepec, was told to "take a motorcar to Acapulco, from there eight hours by boat to the Barra de Tecoanapa and from there seven hours on horseback, alternatively five days on horseback from Tierra Colorada."[15] The state government levied an extraordinary tax in the mid-1920s to fund a road network; of the sixty thousand pesos collected, however, five thousand built a five-kilometer track over the mountain from Chilpancingo to Tixtla and the rest disappeared.[16] The Acapulco road aside, there was no real advance in communications until the national infrastructure program of the 1940s, before which the state's only paved road crossed the border from Morelos and promptly ran out, as the railroad once had, in Iguala.[17] There were only two bridges into Michoacán along the entire 426 miles of the Río Balsas.[18] The low level of much more than local trade inside the state is evident in the census counts of muleteers, the main transport agents until the late 1930s. In 1895 there were only three muleteers working the northern district of Aldama, while in Morelos, a district in the indigenous eastern highlands, there were none at all.[19] And there was more than geography to such introversion. Banditry, the *alcabala*—an often arbitrary state and municipal tax—and a lack of internal demand all further discouraged trade between the state's different regions.[20]

Acapulco from the west, c. 1885. Charles Fletcher Lummis. Image courtesy of Princeton University Library. Department of Rare Books and Special Collections.

Yet while Guerrero consistently collected less taxes than almost any other state—the 1940 tax paid per capita was the lowest in Mexico—that does not invariably signify endemic poverty.[21] During the Porfiriato there was, rather, a widespread perception of imminent prosperity. Marie Robinson Wright rhapsodized about "great mining possibilities," "very fertile" soil, and "excellent timber" and dreamed of selling Acapulco's lemons to the world. The French traveler Louis Lejeune noted mature forests and extensive rangelands and imagined a hacienda that would give him "real coffee, real rum, real milk, good hammocks for the siesta, good horses, good steaks" and go into profit within the year. Alfonso Luis Velasco concluded that Guerrero had "a great future as a farming region," lacking only "railroads, good local roads, [and] an active and vigorous population mixed with that which already lives there and made up of immigrants." William Niven, prospector and eccentric archaeologist, immersed himself for a decade in mining and transport schemes, convinced that Guerrero would one day make him rich. He was wrong, as, fatally, were others: the venture capitalist who visited Niven's mine promptly died of malaria, the American Beltran Stephens was robbed, killed, and mutilated near Chilpancingo, and in 1899 two French prospectors were lynched after shooting their Indian guides dead (they had refused to cross a river in flood).[22] Some men, such as the cotton and cattle magnate Carlos Miller, did not err; their success substantiated Wright's airy assertion of Guerrero's "enormous possibilities of wealth."[23]

Some historians agree with these Porfirian adventurers in countering the traditionally bleak evaluation of the state economy.[24] It is clear that Porfirian modernization was sporadic and limited; that agriculture in many regions remained heavily subsistence-oriented; and that the key mining sector declined across the nineteenth century. Yet there were also, as Teresa Pavía Guzmán argues, overlooked success stories in commercial agriculture and stockbreeding.[25] As early as 1840 the hill town of Igualapa was producing over twenty tons a year of excellent tobacco. Cotton production, which had declined after Independence under the pressure of cheap imports, recovered sufficiently by midcentury to harvest two thousand tons a year in Tlapa, an upland town at the confluence of two small rivers; by 1907 extensive cultivation in the coastal districts of Galeana and Abasolo gave Guerrero the third highest cotton yield in Mexico. The abortive railroad got far enough to drive a northern sugar boom: as early as 1889 the sugar harvest—further favored by tax breaks on cane cultivation—was worth nearly half a million pesos a year. Cattle ranching was favored ecologically (by the vigorous growth of guinea grass for feed) and logistically (by the animals' ability to export themselves on their own four hooves). All the state's borderlands, including la Montaña, where archaic transhumant haciendas of goats survived until the revolution, reared appreciable quantities of livestock for export.[26] An extensive soap and vegetable oil industry prospered in the late century, processing sesame and cotton seed in factories that ranged from Florencio Salgado's steam-driven colossus in Teloloapan, employing 140 workers in 1910, to the small soap factory run by Florentino Juárez for Ixcateopan's local market.[27] The wealth that exports to other states created has perhaps been underestimated because it may not always have registered beyond the bounds of provincial entrepreneurs' (secretive) bookkeeping. It certainly did not flow to Chilpancingo, smaller than any other state capital bar Tlaxcala, whose underfunded administrations relied heavily on federal subsidies and troops.[28] Along the peripheries, though, on the borders shared with Michoacán, the Estado de México, Morelos, Puebla, and the Pacific Ocean, *guerrerenses* shared in at least some of the export-led growth of the period.

Between 1880 and 1940 Guerrero's population followed national trends and approximately doubled from 349,000 to 733,000 people. There was, however, no generalized shift toward urban living. Guerrero did not share in the urban boom of the period, which saw Monterrey's population quintuple and Mexico City grow from 250,000 to 1.8 million people; only Iguala, stimulated by the rail connection, really took off.[29] The most notable change of the twentieth century in guerrerense demographic patterns, the dramatic expansion of Acapulco, did not begin until the mid-1940s. Guerrero's towns remained local market centers and administrative hubs; they were not all that urban. Professionals, industrial, and service workers were few, clustered in the main towns, and like most other townspeople they tended to continue farming small plots of agricultural land.[30] According to a 1922 estimate some 80 percent of the population of Iguala, the state's most modern city, worked in agriculture.[31] The townsmen of 1920s Taxco appeared, to the Italian Appelius, to have "a little of the cattle dealer and a little of the bandit captain."[32] By 1957 Frank Sinatra could suggest that Acapulco Bay was perfect for a flying honeymoon—if, he left out, you flew through Mexico City first—but until the 1940s the port was still a place of dirt tracks, open sewers and absent street cleaners, just one more of the towns in a state that lacked many of the basic structures of urban life.[33]

The overwhelming majority of Guerrero's population in 1940 were still farmers. They were scattered, much as they had been sixty years earlier, in settlements of a few hundred people, politically and commercially dominated by the nearest large village or market town, the *cabecera municipal,* or county seat. Three of the state's four indigenous groups—the Nahua, Tlapanec, and Mixtec—were dispersed across much of the state; only the Amuzgo all lived in the same place, concentrated in the foothills of the Costa Chica, jostling up against the *afromestizos* of the lowlands.[34] The distances between such places loomed large in the minds and practices of villagers. In a revealing comment, one mayor called the villages he administered in the late nineteenth century *patrias,* fatherlands, the term usually reserved for the nation as a whole.[35] (And neighboring villages did bolster their disputes with claims to the sort of threatening cultural differences that nationalists adduce.) For such villagers travel to Mexico City remained an indulgence of the wealthy, a gamble for the enterprising or a last resort for the desperate. While the revolution did increase mobility, particularly to the north and the United States, most guerrerenses stayed put. Despite their growth and their revolution, in 1940 they remained in some ways a static population, with low levels of in-migration and out-migration, living in a far-flung archipelago of isolated rural settlements.[36]

The contours of life in those settlements varied greatly from place to place, shaped as they were by the overlapping *longue durée* determinants of altitude, environment, and communications. Even the fundamental measures of life

Taxco in the 1920s. Hugo Brehme. DeGolyer Library, Southern Methodist University, Mexico Photographs, Manuscripts, and Imprints.

varied enormously: the basic unit of maize, the *carga,* could be as little as one hundred liters in the north and as much as three hundred liters in the east.[37] From the early Porfiriato onward Guerrero's population could be clearly grouped into four quite distinct regions though: the remote subtropical borderlands of the northwest, the Tierra Caliente; the better-communicated, semiarid uplands of the north and center; the heavily indigenous eastern highlands of la Montaña; and the dry tropical strip and foothills of the coasts. These regions had quite distinct paths through the stuttering arrival of capitalism, the revolution, and the time of the would-be centralizers.

Tierra Caliente

Tierra Caliente was formed by the northwestern borderlands with Michoacán, divided into the districts of Mina and Montes de Oca and increased by the 1906 addition of the municipios of Zirándaro and Pungarabato.[38] While Porfirians saw the entire state as remote, Tierra Caliente was the backwater of a backwater, cut off from the rest of the state by the Sierra Madre, described by a French traveler as "a little-explored and even little-known region." The plains and fertile valleys with their wet summers and dry winters struck visitors with their agricultural potential; as Adolfo Dollero put it, the country was "very rich, and in the main unexploited." Abundant water was on tap from the Balsas River system. There was "an infinity of gold mines" in the sierra, barely touched by primitive mining techniques. The forests of the uplands contained "oaks of seven to eight feet in diameter, straight and clean up to 80 or 100 feet, pines of 70 to 175 feet and spruce of the highest quality." The only obstacles to wealth, the men concluded, were the burning heat, which seduced peon and master into chronic torpor, the shortage of wage laborers, and, above all, the lack of a railroad. Once the latter was built it would bring capital investment, commercial agriculture, and modernization. In anticipation, the Mirabaud-Rothschild group were already preparing "significant investments in this new region."[39]

Yet as is often the case frontierdom lay in the eye of the beholder, and these travelers overlooked the strong rancher economy that already existed and was already articulated with that of neighboring Michoacán. Tax receipts single out Mina as one of the wealthiest districts in Guerrero: in 1882 it paid more than any other district, and its 1943 contribution to the treasury was double the combined revenues of all three districts of la Montaña.[40] It was an economy founded above all on livestock—in 1892 there were fifty-five thousand head of cattle spread across the region—as a lack of transport discouraged the spread of cash crops like sugar, tobacco, or cotton, all of which had been cultivated during the colonial period.[41] Sesame, however, was a low-volume, high-value commodity, and as early as 1907 nearly a fifth of Mexican production came from large estates around Ajuchitlán.[42] As the Río Balsas curved north and west the main crop became maize, cultivated commercially, particularly in Coyuca de Catalán, by sharecroppers on haciendas of up to fifteen thousand hectares. This was by no means the "near virgin" frontier that authors like Velasco (a publicist for colonization schemes, after all) liked to imagine. The Balsas valley had actually been farmed since the dawn of agriculture in Mesoamerica; it was there that maize was first domesticated.[43] What Porfirian travelers saw was, in reality, a poorly communicated but extensively farmed country, and it produced appreciable, if perhaps stealthy, wealth for the rural bourgeoisie who dominated it.[44]

Such wealth was expressed in the squares, arcades, and public buildings of Ajuchitlán, a place of "riches and civilization" that was home to large numbers of servants, seamstresses, silversmiths, and tailors.[45] Wealth was also clear in the region's multiplying large farms: the 8 haciendas and 70 ranches of 1871 had increased, by 1900, to 48 haciendas and 281 ranches. Such holdings were the results of early colonization—unsuccessfully resisted by the indigenous villagers, whose 1827 manifesto demanded the expulsion of all Spaniards and Englishmen and the installation of an Indian monarchy—and of expansion when *desamortización,* the disentailment of Church and indigenous land, was convincingly implemented in the 1880s.[46] Medium and large landowners dominated local mestizo society and pushed the indigenous inhabitants toward the less productive hill country. By 1900 only one of Ajuchitlán's 11,799 inhabitants owned up to speaking Nahuatl; at the same time five of the region's 23 pueblos had ceased to exist.[47]

Those landless peasants who remained could work as peons or sharecroppers on the new haciendas and ranches. The sharecropping system was common to much of the rest of Mexico: the landowner provided land, tools, animals, seed, credit, and various hacienda products, such as cheese or aguardiente, in exchange for clientship and the agreed proportion of the harvest. In this proportion, however, labor relations in Tierra Caliente stood out. In some regions of Guerrero these rents, key measures of tenants' bargaining power, were comparatively low: on the prerevolutionary Costa Chica, the coast to the south of Acapulco, the sharecrop rent was 4 percent of the harvest, and fruit, firewood, and zacate grass were held in common.[48] Across most of the north rents ranged from 20 to 30 percent of harvest.[49] In Tierra Caliente, by contrast, sharecropping rates were above 50 percent. Such high rates reflect reliable harvests and accessible markets. Taken together with labor control mechanisms such as widespread tenant indebtment they also indicate a high level of landowner domination. This system enabled considerable capital accumulation by such landowners as Ignacio Chávez, whose hacienda measured approximately fifteen thousand hectares, or Carlos Pérez, whose accounts show an annual income of eight hundred cargas of maize in sharecropping rents from seven ranches. It also fueled resentment and widespread mobilization in the decade of the 1910s, when Tierra Caliente became the center of Zapatismo in Guerrero.[50]

Theirs was an ephemeral revolution: the local zapatista chieftain, Jesús H. Salgado, was killed in 1919, and the movement rapidly disintegrated. The landowners, meanwhile, followed their counterparts on the Costa Chica and mobilized as Maderistas. Such early adoption of revolution may have been opportunistic, but it was also legitimizing, and it combined with close alliances to the state governments of the 1920s to facilitate a marked landowner revanchism in the region. By the mid-1920s *hacendados* had returned to town halls, particularly in the richest zones. Dissidence in municipal elections could be overcome by state violence: thus in the 1923 municipal elections in the village of Totolapan the three opposition leaders were killed, while in 1925 all thirty-two members of the opposition were jailed until the polls closed.[51] In the early 1930s this local landowning elite went on to colonize both the Partido Nacional Revolucionario (PNR) and the increasingly powerful peasant union, the Liga de Comunidades Agrarias (powerful enough to be known simply as la Liga). The agrarista delegates for Coyuca de Catalán in 1933 came from the Brugada and Gómez families, owners of some fourteen thousand and eight thousand hectares, respectively; the federal deputies for Mina in the mid-1930s were the hacendados Salvador González of Zirándaro and Rufino Salgado of Arcelia.[52]

In this context it is unsurprising that land reform was sporadic, halting, and sabotaged. The federal government granted the first five *ejidos*, the collective landholdings of the revolution, in the aftermath of the 1923 De la Huerta rebellion, rewards for peasant militiamen; they were administered, however, under the terms of Governor Rodolfo Neri's 1922 law, whereby the affected landowner chose which land he would surrender.[53] The loyalists on the ensuing ejidos, such as Poliutla or Santa Fe in Ajuchitlán, predictably complained that they had been presented with wastelands. Even under a governor who was both agrarista and native son, General Adrián Castrejón (1929–33), the thirty-two ejidal grants in Tierra Caliente constituted only an estimated 10 percent of the total area distributed across the state.[54] The absentee-owned latifundia of the Guerrero Land and Timber Company, covering an estimated 150,000 hectares, survived well into the 1940s. The Porfirian dynasties endured and got ahead in state politics: José Inocente Lugo, a major landowner in Ajuchitlán, was twice governor (1911–13 and 1935–37). The advantages of their endurance became clear in the later 1930s, when the Depression ended and the prices of cattle, maize, and sesame all rose rapidly.[55] What had seemed to earlier travelers a geographical frontier turned out instead to be a metaphorical frontier for the revolutionary state, one colonized by Porfirian hacendados.

The North and Center

The north and the center were the most urbanized and densely populated parts of Guerrero. The districts of Hidalgo, Alarcón, and Aldama in the north, and Bravos and Guerrero in the center held most of the state's significant towns, such as Iguala, Teloloapan, Taxco, Huitzuco, and Chilpancingo. By 1910 the north alone housed one-third of the state's population.[56] It was not that agricultural land was any richer or more abundant there than in the rest of the state; most was quite dry hill country, leavened only by narrow fertile valleys such as those surrounding Iguala and Teloloapan. Yet these lands were comparatively accessible from Mexico City, and their rich mineral deposits had once drawn migrants far beyond the major centers like Taxco. The strong colonial mining sector provided seasonal employment and local markets for food, which in turn drove the early insertion of the region into a market economy. Villagers were trading maize, cattle, poultry, salt, and sugar with the miners as early as the mid-seventeenth century. While the sector declined precipitously and permanently in the nineteenth century, the legacy of early development endured.[57] Even before the economic expansion of the later Porfiriato the north was among the wealthiest of the state's regional economies: in 1882 the district of Hidalgo paid as much tax as Acapulco.[58]

Although the railway in Guerrero never reached the coast, it did connect these northern farmers to national markets, stimulate the expansion of cane cultivation and the production of soap and oil, and shift the major regional trading center from Tepecoacuilco to Iguala. Trains brought national newspapers, Remington typewriters, and White sewing machines to the region's towns.[59] More than the railway, though, it was desamortización that decisively changed the socioeconomic makeup of the region. In 1877 there were 79 ranches, 13 haciendas, and 103 pueblos listed for Aldama and Hidalgo; by 1901 there were only 67 pueblos left, the rest gone under to expanding haciendas and more than 70 new ranches, homes to a powerful and concentrated northern rancher elite.[60] The effects of this redistribution of land were complex and varied markedly from municipio to municipio. The social mobility it enabled is unmistakable. In Ixcateopan Florentino Juárez began life as a field hand and ended up owning six hundred hectares; in Teloloapan Pedro Mójica started out as a herdsman, bought seven pesos of land in a desamortización sale, sold maize surpluses for several years, and ended up with a small ranch, seventy head of cattle, and four or five peons.[61] But desamortización also allowed the formation of latifundia, such as the Montufar family's thirty-six thousand hectares in Hidalgo.[62]

Given such a range of stories, it is unsurprising that the overall social impact of such tenure shifts should be debated. Attacking the traditional view that equates land privatization with immiseration, Ian Jacobs argued that implementation was slow and incomplete, frequently leaving villagers who resisted in possession of communal lands, and that the sudden influx of land on to the open market stimulated the formation of a dynamic class of capitalist smallholders. In Alarcón and Hidalgo 18 out of 34 communities held onto their corporate holdings across the Porfiriato even as a new village elite emerged.[63] Yet 15 of those 18 surviving communities were concentrated in just two municipios, Taxco and Tepecoacuilco, and these had the longest histories of trading with the mines and negotiating contacts with the wider world. In more remote municipios the evidence of dispossession and impoverishment is clear. "Various cases," reported the Teloloapan *jefe político* in 1885, "are being brought before this *jefatura política* concerning denunciations of indigenous community lands in this District, made by individuals who are not residents of the said localities."[64] In Ixcateopan the new concentration of landholding was pronounced: only 6 of the municipio's 16 communities preserved any communal lands, and at the turn of the century only 49 men in the entire municipio described themselves as ranchers. Cadastral surveys, even those taken long after the revolution, paint this new village elite as a narrow oligarchy, firmly entrenched in power, holding down an extensive new village poor.[65] And Ixcateopan was not an extreme case: of 53 northern villages surveyed by Jacobs, in 22 not a single villager owned land, the villages reduced to dormitories for field hands.[66] In such villages desamortización, whose "principal purpose," its liberal legislators claimed, was "to favor the most disadvantaged classes," achieved quite the opposite.[67]

The rewards for the new dynasties could be considerable because booming Iguala and the region's several other appreciable towns made the north Guerrero's strongest market. Many were used to trading outside their districts even before the railway arrived; Hidalgo produced a quarter of Guerrero's maize and sold it across the state, while Aldama traded with wealthy Toluca, the capital of the Estado de México. Landowners doubled as merchants, industrialists, and even bankers: Miguel Montufar produced copious quantities of mezcal and represented the Banco Nacional de México; the Hacienda Atlixtac refined sugar; the Salgado brothers made sesame oil and cane alcohol in Teloloapan. Most of these landowners were either new to the region or newly rich, and their fortunes were inextricably bound to political influence. Emigdio Pastrana, whose Hacienda de Xilocintla was the largest estate in northern Guerrero, was eight times mayor of Tepecoacuilco. Alberto Rivera, with twenty thousand hectares in Hidalgo, was five times local deputy, twice mayor of Iguala, and twice jefe político.[68] Both Florencio Salgado and his father, Cipriano, owners of some thirteen thousand hectares around Teloloapan, were jefes of Aldama.[69] The *jefatura* had substantial power over desamortización petitions, and incumbents took full advantage. Cipriano Salgado expropriated extensive common lands from the villages of Santo Tomás, Ahuatepec, and Totoltepec. Perfecto Beltrán acquired the Hacienda de Tilapa thanks to a rental agreement he found in Aldama's district archives, and later added forty-eight mining concessions in Arcelia.[70] Such concentrated economic and political domination was reproduced in microcosm in the more isolated villages; in Ixcateopan five families monopolized the irrigated lands, owned the village shops, ran the petty industries of aguardiente and soap production and shuffled municipal power among themselves.[71]

By 1910 the north and center were scattered with unmistakable symbols of modern life and a qualified public prosperity: paved plazas, telephones, bandstands, and town clocks.[72] Porfirian development, for all its shortcomings, had created a middle class of ranchers, teachers, merchants, and lawyers. The extent to which such men were affected by the economic slump of 1907–9 is unclear. The rancher ideologue Francisco Figueroa identified the principal economic root of rebellion as a heavy tax burden on the poor, not the middle classes. The main grievance of men like the Figueroa brothers was instead political. While they had some successes in local contests—a Figueroa was mayor of Huitzuco four times between 1890 and 1910—the strategic positions in regional government, the jefaturas and the governorship, remained out of reach. That these places were filled by carpetbaggers (the governors from 1885 to 1904 were all from out of state, as were nearly half the *jefes políticos* in 1889) was added insult. Liberal ideology, frustrated ambition, and the repressive consequences of lost feuds drew them to Maderismo in 1910. Like other rancher risings, those of northern Guerrero started out as family affairs: fully half the Figueroas' initial group were kin. Soon, however, the politically dispossessed were joined in revolt, if in little else, by the materially dispossessed. By 1912 peasant risings were pullulating, above all around the fringes of the north and center, and in 1914 Zapatistas briefly occupied Chilpancingo. By the end of 1916, though, Silvestre Mariscal's *carrancista* army controlled the towns; in 1918 Mariscal was replaced by Francisco Figueroa, and by the end of October the region was more or less pacified.[73]

The consequences of the revolution in the north were nothing if not unintended. Neither the Figueroas' stated goals—*sufragio efectivo,* "a real vote," and municipal autonomy—nor their unstated ambition—the creation of a traditional *cacicazgo*—was realized. The early 1920s saw instead a fierce struggle for control of the state between them and the Neris of Chilpancingo, a dynasty of caciques whose power predated even the Porfiriato, in the course of which Governor Rodolfo Neri (1921–24) used tactical land reform to create an agrarista counterweight to the Figueroas and the federal army. By the time Rómulo Figueroa had fought and lost his rebellion against the central government, nominally as a Delahuertista, Neri had distributed over one hundred thousand hectares, the ejidal grants disproportionately concentrated in the Figueroas' northern heartlands. His successors in the 1930s made similarly instrumental expropriations and broke many of the largest landowners, such as the Frisbies of Atlixtac, breaking at the same time their grip on northern politics.[74] Yet the landowners were not replaced by agraristas, and agrarian reform did not politically stabilize the north and center. By the early 1940s there were, rather, overlapping layers of the discontented. The typical conflicts surrounding ejido formation had splintered and weakened the peasantry. Religious violence was deadlier here than anywhere else in Guerrero. Many of the middle class were alienated by endemic electoral fraud and cronyism: in 1933, for example, Governor Guevara replaced all of the northern and all but three of the central *ayuntamientos* with appointed municipal councils.[75] He simultaneously toppled all but three of Iguala's *comisariado ejidales,* the collective farms' head administrators.[76] Reactions to the new politics, an incompetent authoritarianism, were unambiguous; in 1940 the dissident presidential candidate, Juan Andreu Almazán—a guerrerense, a conservative, a businessman, and a former Zapatista—polled 70 percent in Iguala and 95 percent in Chilpancingo.[77]

La Montaña

The eastern highlands were partitioned on paper by the three districts of Alvarez, Morelos, and Zaragoza, and on earth by the Sierra Madre, whose watershed divides la Montaña in two: the north, a more densely populated area linked since the colony with Puebla, and the south, traditionally linked to the Costa Chica and Oaxaca. Four-fifths of the rocky land was unfit for cultivation, and of the remaining fifth a large majority was dedicated to slash-and-burn plots of maize. Only the valleys around Chilapa, Tlapa, and Huamuxtitlán were developed for commercial agriculture, with much of their produce crossing the state border to the railroad in Puebla.[78] The richest district was northeastern Zaragoza, where irrigated estates gave substantial sugar harvests: in the mid-1880s the villagers of Huamuxtitlán alone produced 46 tons of sugar and 880 barrels of aguardiente per year. Cane cultivation was the business of a narrow elite; livestock, on the other hand, used 30 percent to 40 percent of the region's land and was a business in which small and medium Nahua and Mixtec producers could coexist alongside Guillermo Acho, the livestock baron whose herds of goats numbered an estimated 400,000. Lumber could have been a greater resource than either cane or cattle, the region's woodlands ranging from cloud forest on the heights of the sierra down through pine, oak, and finally tropical deciduous forests. Until the late 1930s, however, they went unlogged due to the lack of roads. (Even in the 1940s there were only three dirt roads in all of la Montaña, and in the absence of bridges they became unreliable in the rains.)[79] To catalogue commercial resources further would miss the point: the overwhelming majority of people were subsistence farmers with toeholds in the capitalist economy, and theirs was the poorest region in Guerrero.

That poverty only increased between 1880 and 1945.[80] Porfirian land concentration did not bypass la Montaña, and the richer lands of Chilapa and the northeast were increasingly divided among small to medium haciendas of a few thousand hectares.[81] In Olinalá a handful of rancher families suborned the jefe político and used disentailment to take over the commons and peasant holdings, set up sugar estates, and leave 80 percent of the municipio's workingmen as landless peons.[82] Close to Tlapa the two plantations of the colony had become five sugar haciendas by 1886. Some fought back: in 1884 a Nahua named Pascual Claudio drew up the Plan Socialista de Xochihuehuetlán and led the hundred men of his Ejército del Pueblo in a rebellion demanding "Industria, Tierra y Armas." Across most of la Montaña, however, the marginal quality of the land and the internal cohesion of the villages enabled indigenous peoples to comply de jure with the legislation, privatizing and dividing communal lands, while maintaining de facto communal ownership.[83] Immiseration was not, however, solely rooted in dispossession. Neither was it the product of complete isolation from capitalist markets; small indigenous producers had a long history of selling livestock, corn, and the products of cottage industries such as textile weaving and Olinalá lacquer work. They were adaptable, and when cheap manufactures made homespun textiles unprofitable, artisans rapidly switched to weaving palm, and when high-end lacquer work fell from fashion *laqueros* switched to cheaper gourds.[84] Three phenomena, however, defied any coping strategies save outmigration. The population grew dramatically in the twentieth century: by midcentury there remained only a third of a hectare of agricultural land per person in Zaragoza, the little available wage labor could not absorb the landless, and peon wages fell below subsistence levels.[85] The widespread violence of the armed revolution and the Cristiada further increased the pressure on the poor. Petty trade, finally, was decreasingly profitable as the mestizo and Spanish merchants of the market towns consolidated monopolies in both agricultural and artisanal production.

These merchants owned the high ground of the regional economy, the supply of trade goods and credit. When many small-scale stockbreeders, *ganaderos,* lived at or near subsistence levels, credit mechanisms such as prior purchase gave buyers substantial leverage. Tlapa's merchants got cattle at 30 to 40 percent of market value by paying in advance or bartering for food or trade goods. A similar price-fixing went on in palm weaving, by the mid-twentieth century the primary economic activity in Morelos and Alvarez. Anybody could weave the plaited palm strips from which hats were made, but from the 1890s onward the mere handful of buyers in Tlapa and Chilapa could dictate prices. These were low enough to provoke unsuccessful state intervention in the mid-1940s; the absence of other sources of cash in the regional economy, however, kept production high, with Tlapa making an estimated 1.6 million hats in 1936. People wove palm constantly, an ethnographer later noticed; they wove while walking, haggling, and even while getting drunk. Such running to stand economically still reinforced secular, overlapping class and ethnic conflicts: expressed in the four sackings of Tlapa in eighty years, in endemic cattle rustling, and in the everyday practices of Spanish elites which included banning Indians from the main square of Tlapa, or instituting, as did the Porfirian mayordomo of the Rancho Santa Rosa, a local droit de seigneur.[86] The revolution brought some Mexicans into the ranks of the merchant class; it did not fundamentally change the sharp inequalities which characterized la Montaña. They had been, wrote one man from Malinaltepec in 1943, "victims of extortion since the time of porfirismo."[87]

If the fundamentals of the economic system remained and poverty increased, what did the revolution change? Even here there was limited reform, and some Porfirian land seizures were reversed. The municipio of Ahuacotzingo, for example, had been taken over by a handful of cane-growing ranches and haciendas in the Porfiriato. In the 1920s and 1930s some of them were expropriated for redistribution; the beneficiaries, the new *ejidatarios,* collectively received some seventeen thousand hectares. While this was a distinctly partial economic restoration, it did restore large areas to indigenous political control, as the ejidal leadership was usually chosen by the village elders, the *principales.* Ejidal grants could also serve as an incentive to continued popular mobilization; the Ahuacotzingo ejidos won thirteen extensions to their lands in the late 1930s. Yet the ejidos rarely received irrigated land; the 1950 agrarian census classified 93 percent of ejidal land as *tlacolol,* hillside swidden plots. Of the seventeen thousand hectares granted by Cárdenas only forty-two were the coveted *tierras de riego,* irrigated lands, and even the fortunate got only *temporal,* the seasonal rainland.[88] Land reform did not, moreover, solve the frequent armed boundary clashes between neighboring villages. And other social reforms bypassed the region entirely. La Montaña at the end of the nineteenth century supposedly had more public schools than villages (some of them undoubtedly the products of local politicians' modernizing imaginations).[89] By the late 1920s fewer than twenty remained.[90]

The main shift after the revolution was political, as the mobilization of the 1910s proved enduring. La Montaña had been firmly zapatista; piecemeal forces in 1912, they had taken the region's cities in 1915 before fading before carrancista counteroffensives and surrendering in 1918.[91] In the 1920s another guerrilla war was fought in la Montaña, this time between the government troops, agrarian militias, and numerous Cristeros, and only the miraculous downing of a telegraph line saved the bishop of Chilapa and nine other priests from being shot.[92] Later the region was pacific, but sinarquista to the point of recruiting even "local government elements"; in 1934 Lázaro Cárdenas rebuked the governor for turning a blind eye to public religious processions in Chilapa, the seat of Guerrero's diocese.[93] Federal agencies such as Chilapa's secondary school were pointedly rejected; villages like Huamuxtitlán closed their schools and refused point-blank to send their sons for military service; and support for General Almazán—an oligarch with a distinctly shady reputation, but a local man—was overwhelming.[94] Such resistance had little impact on municipal politics, where the division of political labor common to most of the contemporary indigenous populations of Mexico—namely government by principales at the hamlet or small village level, and government by mestizos in the cabeceras and above—survived. Neither could it prevent the consolidation of cacicazgos when they were legitimized and armed by the state. Angel Salgado, for example, dominated Cualac and parts of Huamuxtitlán and Olinalá in the late thirties and forties and was held responsible for numerous killings and substantial cattle rustling. As leader of the village Frente Zapatista he received Mausers and political backing from the military zone commanders.[95] The state's mounted police, the *montada,* was another violent agency directed against peasants, and agraristas in particular; the head of the montada was actually arrested in 1942 after a series of extrajudicial killings of ejidatarios.[96] Yet while the "weapons of the strong" consistently outgunned popular resistance, people in la Montaña could always respond with a mass, delegitimizing opt-out from formal politics. Urged by the sinarquista newspaper not to become "election fodder," they listened; in the 1940 election for Chilapa's federal deputy fewer than ten people voted for the government.[97]

The Coasts

The coasts of Guerrero were divided into four districts: Galeana (the Costa Grande, north of Acapulco), Tabares (Acapulco), and Allende and Abasolo (the Costa Chica, to the south). They formed a single trading system which hinged on Acapulco, in this period a different world from the boomtown of the late 1940s; one visitor, on the eve of the revolution, could not find a hotel.[98] While the port declined in the late nineteenth century to only a few thousand people, enjoying, *National Geographic* found, "an evil reputation for its climate . . . and a most flourishing graveyard," it recovered to some extent in the 1900s and even if ramshackle sat at the hub of a diverse, sophisticated economy.[99]

352 THE NATIONAL GEOGRAPHIC MAGAZINE

Photo by Goldman

Round Hut of Negros, South of Acapulca, Guerrero

The Negros in this region have crowded out the Indians. This is the same kind of house that their ancestors built in Africa

Afromestizos and ethnographers (with revealingly poor spelling). *National Geographic* 1904. E. A. Goldman/National Geographic Image Collection.

There was a long tradition of plantation agriculture and afromestizo labor on the floodplains of the coasts, where cotton yields were some of the largest in Mexico: at the industry's prerevolutionary peak there were eight cotton gins on the Costa Chica alone. The forty-five thousand bales a year these produced fed the textile mills of Atoyac, Aguas Blancas, Mexico City, and Puebla. In the 1920s farmers began replacing cotton with palm trees and sesame, a change driven by falling prices, revolutionary violence, and the erosion of haciendas by ejidos.[100] Yet the coasts were never a monoculture. Cattle were always important; even in 1940, when lengthy rural instability had decimated herds, the Costa Grande and Acapulco were home to an estimated sixty thousand head. The hardwood forests of cacao, cedar, brazilwood, and Spanish elm were exploited, at first sporadically and later, as communications improved, intensively; by 1940 there were five sawmills in Acapulco alone. Commercial agriculture stretched beyond the predominant crops of cotton and palm trees, the dried coconut kernels used as a source of oil. Lime trees came to the valleys of the Papagayo and Sabana Rivers; coffee bushes grew up in the Atoyac foothills. There was, finally, a growing cluster of factories around Acapulco, which by 1940 included textiles, oil, soap, soft drinks, and chemicals. The largest of these, the El Ticuí mill in Atoyac, employed two hundred workers. The net effect was striking: economic growth in the coastal districts between 1882 and 1943 may have been as much as 3,000 percent.[101]

The region's historiography centers on peasant resistance and is at times nationalist to the point of xenophobia; it reflects, however, two central themes of the coasts.[102] A tradition of periodic and intensive peasant mobilization stretches back to Independence, when the contribution of the coastal militias was rewarded with numerous municipios. There is simultaneously a parallel and intertwined tradition of xenophobia. Militia rebellions broke out against Spaniards in 1827 and 1829; the killers of an English cotton trader in 1838 wore "death to foreigners" devices on their hats.[103] A century later the first act of the workers who seized El Ticuí was to try to lynch the factory's Spanish manager, while the lyrics of a 1934 *corrido* to that factory's murdered union organizer accuse the governor of selling the pueblo to "the cruel Spaniards" and concludes that "this beloved patria / lacks independence."[104] The Vidales brothers' 1926 revolutionary manifesto had among its slogans "death to the Spaniards," called for the repeal of Clause 13 of the 1821 Plan de Iguala (which specified that the lives and properties of the Spanish resident in Mexico would be inviolate), and explained that this was essential to the country's "complete economic emancipation." Here was the rational base of such enduring attitudes: a seemingly high level of monopolization of local resources.[105]

Yet the actual extent of foreign ownership is questionable. The historiography claims that the entire economy of the coasts was effectively divided between three Spanish companies, namely, B. Fernández y Compañía, P. Uruñuela Compañía y Sucursales, and Alzuyeta y Compañía. These must have relied heavily on native agents, for census data record no more than a handful of foreigners in the region. Renato Ravelo confirms as much in describing two to three hundred rich merchants and hacendados subordinate to the Spanish.[106] There were only 160 foreigners resident in the entire state in 1895. In 1900 there was only one Spaniard in Atoyac and three in Ometepec; there were only 39 Spaniards in Acapulco itself. These men occupied admittedly strategic positions in local society. One of the Omepetec Spanish was the

Alzuyeta's agent, while the other two foreigners were Antonio Reyna, the long-term Ecuadorian jefe político, and the American Carlos Miller, the region's dominant hacendado.[107] At a lower level, the main shopkeeper in Coyuca in the 1920s was Spanish.[108] The sheer scarcity of foreigners, however, strongly suggests that the colonial nature of local property structures has been exaggerated and that an important component of such descriptions is the ethnic mislabeling of class conflicts.

A second and related question concerns the disappearance in such narratives of any middle class, whether urban or rancher. Schematic elite / subaltern dichotomies utterly ignore, for example, the numerous *costeños* who described themselves on census forms as "agricultores," a classification that encompassed smallholders and petty ranchers. The painstaking agronomist Moisés de la Peña found "a numerous and wealthy" population in the sierra around Atoyac; in the 1900 census over 1,500 men in Atoyac registered as ranchers or smallholders. The same census found 250 ranchers in Ometepec, where families such as the Añorves and the Aguirres prospered alongside hacendados and achieved local political dominance on the basis of comparatively modest landholdings.[109] There is, finally, the question of where some of the largest holdings in the region fit into this picture of Spanish monopolization, which accounts for neither the American-owned Miller empire, nor the Compañía Americana Washington in Acapulco, nor the tens of thousands of hectares of timberland interests of the American Roberto Silberg or the Maderas Papanoa company.

The dominance of the leading families was, moreover, neither long-established nor secure. The Uruñuela and Alzuyeta houses were founded in the 1820s, but their landholdings by the 1920s were unexceptional. The principal commercial house, Fernández y Compañía, dated to the early 1900s. This was the very model of a modern monopoly, owning sixty thousand hectares of the Costa Grande and founding, with assorted partners, both El Ticuí and La Especial, the main oil and soap factory. The Fernández family controlled dockers, warehouses, local mafiosi, and much of local government; they also enjoyed useful links with foreign governments, as Rafael Fernández, although Spanish, served for many years as British vice-consul.[110] But while the armed revolution temporarily consolidated their power, the pent-up political demands which came in its wake provided serious challenges. The state's politicians became an unreliable source of support or control, bitterly divided as they were between the revolutionary factions of the Figueroas, Neris, Adrián Castrejón, and Hector F. López (though the latter, having spent much of his career in Michoacán, had not much of a faction). In a newly competitive environment the Fernándezes and their allies faced electoral, agrarian, and violent conflict. Their hold on local politics was shaken by the Partido Obrero de Acapulco (POA), an alliance of workers and agraristas under middle-class leadership that by 1923 had won the municipios of Acapulco, Atoyac, Coyuca, Tecpan, and La Unión. The Acapulco masses elected the party's founder, Juan Escudero—the "Lenin of Guerrero"[111]—mayor of Acapulco twice; Amadeo Vidales and Valente de la Cruz were mayors of Tecpan in 1923 and 1925, respectively. The POA also organized agrarian petitioners, and between 1922 and 1923 nineteen ejidos gained provisional grants in Tabares.[112] When the Fernándezes responded to such inroads with violence they met with violence: thus the rebel followers of De la Cruz in 1925 began by sacking the Fernández hacienda in San Luis, while the Vidalistas in 1926 began by destroying the Fernández factories in Aguas Blancas and Atoyac.[113] Uncertain of civilian political allies, the dominant families formed close alliances with the federal military garrisons. It was federal troops who killed the Escuderos and who threw De la Cruz and his followers out of office. The coasts became an arena for violent competition between armed agraristas, "genuine caciques in their respective villages," and the axis of conservative militias, or *guardias blancas*, and soldiers.[114]

Gobernación reports from the 1930s detail the complexity and armed power of this axis. In Tecpan, for example, Hermenegildo Pérez headed the guardias blancas, who operated in league with the lieutenant commanding the town garrison. One of his sons led the San Luis guardias blancas; others occupied strategic bureaucratic posts such as tax collector and judge. For operations like the February 1936 attack on the local agrarian committee's offices—which killed two agraristas—the Pérezes could muster thirty armed men. Links with the military stretched far beyond the junior officer level. The commanding officer of the 80th Battalion, which garrisoned most of the coast, was heavily implicated in organizing the anti-agrarista terror; the Acapulco garrison commander, General Santiago Nogueda, was a local landowner and ex-mercenary whose son led the Atoyac guardias blancas.[115] The clergy supplied ideological and practical support: on the Costa Grande Father Herrera preached condemnations of agrarismo and told parishioners how to vote, while in Acapulco Father Florentino Díaz was implicated in the Escudero assassination.[116] Rural power structures multiplied in the period, however, and some of them—agrarian committees, teachers, and the popular militia of the *defensas rurales*—were sometimes beyond the influence of regional elites. By

1940, moreover, landowners were politically in retreat across the coasts: the Costa Grande was "efficiently controlled by the Liga de Comunidades Agrarias," and even the deeper-entrenched elites of the Costa Chica were starting to cede ground to peasants. In 1939 Ometepec elected its first agrarista mayor; in 1940 the agrarista Antonio Molina became the district's federal deputy.[117]

The Political Culture of *Guerrero Bronco*

If geographical fragmentation is the main feature of the state's political economy, violence is traditionally seen as the main feature of its political culture. From its foundation through the *guerra sucia* of the 1960s and 1970s, the 1995 Aguas Blancas massacre, the 2014 Ayotzinapa disappearances, and the drug wars of the twenty-first century Guerrero has appeared on the mental radar of both Mexicans and foreigners as a zone of perennial conflict. Repetition has refined the image of *Guerrero bronco,* savage Guerrero, into a trope of algebraic neatness: isolation, due to the barren mountain ranges that divide and encircle the state, has since Independence ensured poverty, caciquismo, and endemic violence. In such Hobbesian conditions, this version goes, guerrerenses have become quick to violence by nature and get a bad press from most comers: "primitive and ignorant," according to Ernest Gruening, heirs to "ancestral backwardness," according to one of their own senators, to "problems of ethnic origin and culture," according to their federal deputies, victims of "a cultural deficit" and a "mortal educational deficit" according to Governor Baltasar Leyva Mancilla.[118] According to a governmental plaque in Ixcateopan, the state harbors "the dark currents of still-isolated peoples and cultures"; the law there, according to one 1940s hack, "was represented by the rifle, the .45 and the machete"; and what criminology statistics existed, claimed another contemporary, gave Guerrero "a very poor championship: that of murders, not just in the Mexican Republic, but in the entire world."[119]

There are both constants and undoubtable continuities in this image of all-pervasive violence; guerrillas, guardias blancas, and defensas sociales, the community gunmen of the revolution, are precedent and memory for the community gunmen of the twenty-first century, the *autodefensas.* But there is also a marked pulp fiction side to the trope. Guerrero was not among the most violent states of the revolution, and other states such as Veracruz or Morelos were just as violent in the midcentury; but we do not hear of *Morelos bronco.* Guerrero is characterized as bronco, on the other hand, by scholars, pressmen, and politicians, a preconception that also infuses more popular sources such as corridos and travel guides, the former emphasizing guerrerense violence, the latter the state's "literally unexplored" territory, and the threats to travelers intrepid enough to explore it.[120] The essentialization and cultural determinism inherent to Guerrero bronco have been variously criticized. A 1926 Gobernación report stressed the honest nature of the state's population and blamed the entire local government hierarchy for the state's chronic instability; in 1949 De la Peña denied that "there should be, as is falsely purveyed, a marked inclination to theft on behalf of the population"; an increasingly sophisticated regional historiography routinely challenges the embedded assumption that Guerrero is violent by natural law or Act of God.[121] The trope endures, however, for three reasons. The incidence of rebellion, guerrilla warfare, political assassination, homicide, and battery confirms that Guerrero is in fact an intensely violent place. Moreover, the cross-class appeal of the state's dangerous reputation leads few guerrerenses to downplay this. Violent traditions are graphically celebrated in the corrido; as the 1934 corrido of the dead agrarista David Flores runs, "The coward Rosalío / Went on humiliating David / And before killing him / They tortured him." While some corridos condemn violence, many express a certain self-satisfaction in violent self-representation. As one local doctor put it, "The costeño likes to be seen as a son of a bitch."[122] The drive to uphold such a (potentially useful) perception could, moreover, itself generate physical aggression: on the unlikely turf of the Chilapa seminary costeños and *terracalentanos* used to brawl in defense of their collective reputations as hard men.[123] And there is, finally, the tactical utility of Guerrero bronco to regional and national elites.

Political elites in Guerrero, as elsewhere in modern Mexico, confronted a tension implicit in the informal rules of political practice. They were permitted and even encouraged to play local politics by hardball rules, which allowed the everyday use of corruption and violence. They could not, however, transgress the softball discourse of their federal overseers overly frequently or explicitly.[124] Failure to reconcile these contradictory codes of practice could result in abrupt unemployment: between January 1946 and January 1947 the governors of Guanajuato, Oaxaca, and Chiapas were all fired after their repressive violence was judged excessive.[125] To those in the grasp of this conundrum the essentialization of Guerrero as naturally violent was extremely useful. It cast elite violence as inevitable, justified, and defensive rather than incompetent or aggressive; it also enabled state leaders to claim indispensability in mediating between a little-known, unruly population and a distant center. (As with the "productive inefficiency" of bureaucratic practice, a measured level of incompetence probably reinforced local elite positions.)[126] Moreover, this image of predetermined violence backed the systematic attempts of local worthies to depoliticize bloodshed, providing narratives of crime, women, and alcohol to explain away homicides which peasants claimed were political murders. When in early 1945 Gobernación called Governor Rafael Catalán Calvo to account for political violence on the Costa Chica, he explained at some length that "the events . . . have their origin, very remote of course, in personal questions and interests . . . as regrettably the majority of the inhabitants of this zone are uncivilized people, whether ejidatarios or ranchers, they cannot be kept in line by the judicial authorities."[127] Race was central to such explanations, "uncivilized" a code word for Indian or afromestizo; a cousin to "savage," another term that the newspapers and government reports of the Porfiriato used to describe the "hordes" of the coast and the highlands beyond.[128] By both reifying and depoliticizing a guerrerense culture of violence, politicians, caciques, generals, and landowners all attempted to escape any responsibility for beatings, woundings, and murders.

Yet attempts to pin down the reality of violence behind the trope of Guerrero bronco run into problems both quantitative (how many people were killed) and qualitative (why people were killed). It is one-sided to register the depoliticization of violence as a tool of the dominant classes without simultaneously acknowledging the existence of the opposite procedure, the politicization of honest apolitical violence by the ruled. Homicides denounced as political by a protesting peasantry to a distant Gobernación could in fact be rooted in cantina quarrels, family vendettas, or ill-judged romance, and elite protestations of innocence could, at least occasionally, be worth the flimsy telegram paper on which they were printed. On November 15, 1944, for example, the agrarista candidate for local deputy Luis Camacho was shot dead as he walked home from the billiard hall through the unlit streets of Tlapa. The agrarista leadership immediately cabled Miguel Alemán to accuse local deputy Jesús Rodríguez Maldonado of the homicide, alleging that Rodríguez had killed Camacho to clear the path to the state legislature for his own nephew, Caritino Maldonado. When Gobernación investigated, however, their inspector found that Camacho had followed the local custom of *rapto,* bride capture, and had seven months earlier made off with Maria González Rodríguez from Ometepec. Her mother had also followed local custom and, in the absence of the requisite marriage and formal reconciliation, had Camacho killed.[129] Taken alone, such a report might be read as another case of a morally flexible Gobernación inspector being squared; both Camacho's ex-wife and his son, however, supported the inspector's version.[130] Similar competing interpretations surround other deaths from the same hotly fought election.[131] When attributing meaning to violence offered political gain it is hardly surprising that all social groups should have struggled to establish their meaning with the referees of Gobernación, and that perjury should have frequently marked such struggles.

Beyond attempting to extract meaning by triangulating the contradictory discourses of conflicting classes on violence, the question of quantifying that violence is similarly testing. Contemporary federal agents wrestled with the problem with frustratingly inconclusive results. Reports of gunrunning into the small port of Zihuatanejo in 1926, for example, proved false. In the late 1930s a series of denunciations from local agraristas of landowner arms smuggling reached Mexico City. One such memorandum from the Costa Chica specified that arms shipments were arriving through the Barra de Tecoanapa, a river mouth traditionally used for coastal trade, in preparation for a landowner-backed revolt against the Cárdenas government.[132] It was an unusually disturbing story given the simultaneous rebellion of Saturnino Cedillo in San Luis Potosí and the local networks of the opposition presidential candidate, General Almazán, who was not just guerrerense but also linked by marriage with the fiercely conservative ranchers of Ometepec.[133] Cedillo expected Almazán and other right-wing generals to join his revolt after the 1940 elections (as did Cárdenas).[134] Guerrero would have been an ideal site to launch a national almazanista rising: poorly communicated yet physically close to the capital, politically unstable, and "probably the state most riddled with Almazanismo in the entire Republic."[135] Yet the agent who investigated found that while villagers talked a lot about guns and killings no arms or munitions had actually arrived. Red herrings seemed to shoal along the coasts: a 1940 Gobernación spy sighed, "I have gathered more rumors about gun-running in Guerrero than in any other state."[136] Nine years later the rumors ran on: nefarious arms dealers were, the local press reported, shipping half a million cartridges to a secret landing place on the coast.[137]

Rebellions were difficult to hide, although the authorities tried manfully enough (and met with some success, at the time). Everyday violence, from intimidation, jailings, and beatings to woundings and homicides, occurred in a murkier world. There was a fundamental reporting problem: victims or their relatives were scared of perpetrators and unimpressed by law enforcement. There was also a fundamental registering problem: well-connected gunmen did not go far enough in the judicial process to leave much archival trace.[138]

What prefabricated crime statistics exist are consequently deeply flawed. In the absence of precise indices of violence one is left with the rough gauges of rebellions, political assassinations, and the homicides reported to *registros civiles* across Guerrero.[139] These are eloquent. The period 1920–30 was marked by six substantial rebellions, those of Obregón, Figueroa / De la Huerta, Valente de la Cruz (twice), the Vidales brothers, and the Cristeros. It was, as one traveler had it, "a permanent state of insurrection," or, as a Gobernación agent entitled his report, "a state [. . .] of anarchy."[140] The 1930s were characterized by multiple killings, such as the 1934 street fighting between the workers of the Confederación Regional Obrera Mexicana (CROM) and agraristas in Arcelia, which killed four men, including the head of the local mining union; the 1935 religious killings in Yextla, when anticlerical agraristas interrupted Mass and were beaten, shot, and dismembered; the 1935 Coyuca de Catalán gunfight in which seven men—including Vicente Bedolla, leader of the peasant league—were killed in a bullring; or Rubén Figueroa's 1940 attack on an Iguala polling booth, which killed four men and a child.[141] In 1938 alone twenty-six peasant leaders were reported murdered.[142] Voluminous correspondence from peasants to Gobernación attests to the daily attrition, catalogued in summary lists of the dead like that from the tiny settlement known only as Kilómetro 30, Acapulco, where nine people were murdered in less than a year.[143] Among the surprising features of this violence were that, in contradiction to what are assumed to be national patterns, it continued with vigor through the 1940s, driven by the social, economic, and political mobility (both upward and downward) that the armed revolution created and land reform sustained.

Present Porfirians, Absent Party Men

The violent struggle for control of the state's resources was a long-standing one.[144] The immediate roots of postrevolutionary conflict lay, however, in the fluidity of land tenure enabled by the legislation of the Restored Republic and realized in the Porfiriato. Between 1871 and 1901 the number of haciendas—above all on the coasts and in Tierra Caliente—doubled, and the number of ranches—most notably in the north—trebled.[145] As the Independence era dynasties—the Alvarez, Bravo, and Jiménez—lumbered toward extinction, both hacendados and ranchers moved into the political spaces opened by their crumbling fiefdoms and an increased, but still remarkably loose, central control. Entire agricultural, commercial, and political systems were monopolized by upwardly mobile families like the Fernándezes of Acapulco, who held sixty thousand hectares along the Costa Grande, the Pérezes of Coyuca de Catalán, or the Millers of Cuajinicuilapa, who owned up to ninety thousand hectares of the Costa Chica.[146] Municipios without haciendas or substantial indigenous populations, meanwhile, were often dominated by a handful of rancher families who reproduced in microcosm the aggrandizing success of the hacendados. In Ixcateopan, for example, the Juárez and Jaimes families owned a quarter of the municipio's lands and dominated local industry, trade, and the town hall.[147] The state's formal political system revolved around carpetbagger governors and jefes políticos whose appointments were often consecrations of cacicazgos rather than genuine exercises of central authority. With the exception of the modernizing Francisco Arce administration, such governments were characterized by minimal aspirations, budgets, and cognitive capacity; puny political operations backed by a weighty military presence (commanded, for much of the 1890s, by Victoriano Huerta) in Chilpancingo.[148] The informal political system—islands of capitalism run by a monopolizing agricultural and mercantile elite, spreading outside their initial stomping grounds—was, by contrast, both powerful and resilient.

The armed revolution did little to unseat these landowners and merchants. Between 1910 and 1920 Guerrero was divided into periodically stabilized fiefs, among which actual fighting was localized and relatively low intensity: above the skirmishing the state was run by the Figueroas in the north, Jesús H. Salgado in Tierra Caliente, Julián Blanco in the center and on the Costa Chica, and Silvestre Mariscal on the Costa Grande.[149] These new caudillos, ephemeral warlords all, were gone by 1923, when the wrong choice of sides in the De la Huerta rebellion ended the Figueroas' first period as regional strongmen. With them went some vulnerable members of the elite, notably both Mexican and foreign absentee landlords. Locally resident landowners, however, tended to endure: either preemptively joining the broad churches of Maderismo and Carrancismo (the Añorves, Regueras, and Aguirres on the Costa Chica; the Leyvas of Chilpancingo; Eucaria Apreza in Chilapa; José Inocente Lugo, Salvador González, and the Jaimeses in Tierra Caliente) or successfully co-opting the regional revolutionaries (the Spanish merchant triad of Acapulco, who paid 6,000 pesos a month in protection money to Silvestre Mariscal).[150] Business prospects were good enough to attract buyers for some of the largest estates: in 1912 the American Lewis Lamm felt sanguine enough to invest in Guillermo Acho's forty thousand hectares in la Montaña.[151] Certain municipios were heavily affected: in the north Ixcapuzalco, for example, was razed and temporarily abandoned.[152] Overall, however, Guerrero was in a different world to that of conflict zones such as Chihuahua or Morelos, where six bitterly hostile campaigns, the burning or reconcentration of entire villages, and the Spanish influenza epidemic of 1918 reduced the population by some 40 percent between 1910 and 1921.[153] The armed revolution in consequence settled little, and much of the Porfirian elite lived to fight popular mobilization another day.

That mobilization was based on the profound (and overlapping) class and ethnic divisions laid bare in the 1910s. While ranchers, many hacendados, and a skeletal urban middle class had joined the fighting in a timely way as Maderistas, Figueroistas, or Constitucionalistas, the villagers whom they dominated in peacetime became—where possible—Zapatistas. They became briefly dominant under Salgado in Tierra Caliente and parts of the north, and put up widespread resistance along the coasts and across la Montaña; but zapatista influence was in the end constrained by the movement's intrinsic parochialism, by its national decline after 1915, by intercommunity divisions, and by the summary assassinations of entire leaderships. On the Costa Chica, for example, the principales of Igualapa were summoned to a meeting in Ometepec and executed en masse; in 1917 the local *jefe militar* organized a dance for the Zapatistas of San Nicolás and Cuajinicuilapa, gave them aguardiente, and shot them while they slept it off.[154] During the De la Huerta revolt, however, the positive feedback of toppling elites and tactical agrarian reform gave an organized peasantry new vigor. In the north over twenty presidential resolutions redistributed sizeable areas in Huitzuco, Teloloapan, and Taxco, the heartlands of figueroismo; along the Costa Grande the Vidales brothers' intelligent guerrilla campaign gained them ejidos, the construction of the Acapulco–Mexico City highway, and substantial political leverage.[155] A newly active peasantry was joined in some regions, notably Acapulco, by cross-class opposition to established elites. There was simultaneously an influx of opportunist converts to agrarismo, such as the *tinterillo* Nabor Ojeda or the terracalentano landowner Salvador González. (Ojeda didn't discover his agrarista beliefs until the 1920s, after campaigning against the Zapatistas; González defended his lands with death threats to agronomists, including a young Rubén Figueroa.)[156] The net result was a powerful and enduring agrarista movement.

Guerrero's agraristas staked ambitious claims to political representation. In 1937 agrarian leaders claimed control of "85% of the electoral volume of the said state" and asked Cárdenas for six of the nine local deputyships and sixty-four of the municipios.[157] That formally elected posts should be requested as appointments was increasingly the norm, reflecting recent lessons. The agrarista candidate for governor in 1936, David Arizmendi, was reported to have won the most votes; he also enjoyed powerful support in the federal congress and the services of a committed group of election fixers. Nevertheless the federal government overruled him in favor of the rancher elite's candidate, General Alberto Berber, in the PNR primaries.[158] With the exception of the Castrejón administration agraristas never dominated state politics. All governors, including opponents of land reform like Gabriel Guevara, made tactical use of agraristas; land reform was often, as Ojeda noted, "a simple instrument for securing political ends."[159] Even under Cárdenas, though, agraristas were left with the scraps of regional political power. At a local and occasionally regional level they could be influential players in the violently competitive elections that were the revolution's legacy. Substantial control at the state level escaped them; it was vested in shifting coalitions of landowners, *licenciados,* violent entrepreneurs, and the (generally despised) "professional politicians," men who rose through unions, the bureaucracy, elected office, and federal contacts. The politicians whom they backed, particularly in the later 1930s, provoked outrage across classes and regions. Analyzing Almazán's 1940 election victory in Guerrero, a Gobernación agent concluded that "the hostility of the population against the current regime [was] decisive, a hostility that reflects the hatred awakened by a succession of dreadful local governments."[160] Lifting from the Gettysburg Address, the schoolteacher Macrina Rabadán summed up Guerrero's political system—at a governor's banquet—as "government of the bandits, by the bandits, for the bandits."[161]

Accusations of kleptocratic misrule aside, it is difficult to impose a coherent single interpretation on Guerrero's political history in this period. Ian Jacobs's classic study hazards a tentative conclusion of successful centralization, based on the frequency with which the president fired governors, the ease with which Mexico City purged town halls, and the success with which the PRM overturned their loss of the 1941 gubernatorial election.[162] That the federal administration should have to depose the state governor regularly was not, however, an indicator of successful central control. Toppling governors was rightly seen as a two-edged sword: while it restored federal control and gained the center temporary political capital, it also rewarded popular mobilization and civic disobedience. Drastic presidential intervention was as much an admission of powerlessness as an expression of central authority.[163] It did not inculcate greater caution in future guerrerense politicians; both governors elected in the course of the 1950s were fired.[164] As for ayuntamientos, just as they could be purged from Mexico City so they could be installed, against central diktat, from Chilpancingo. The municipal elections of 1932, 1938, and 1940 all saw governors impose their clients at the expense of ruling party slates.[165] Many of those ayuntamientos relied on what Ben Fallaw dubbed the *voto morado,* the bloc Catholic vote secured by the efforts of priests and lay associations, especially those of women such as the Damas Católicas and the Hijas de María Inmaculada. Finally, the successful rigging of the second 1941 gubernatorial election in favor of the PRM candidate Catalán Calvo was a pale reflection of the defeat Berber had inflicted on the party in the 1940 federal elections, when he flooded Chilpancingo with several hundred gunmen, and his chief of police killed a PRM congressman, or in the first gubernatorial contest, in which he had imposed his murderous half brother Francisco Carreto.[166] This was hardly the behavior of a politician nervous about federal opinion or sanction.

Three final questions must be considered in gauging the reality of revolutionary centralization. The first is secure electoral domination. Voting patterns from the second half of the twentieth century suggest that the PRI eventually went some way to attaining this in Guerrero. For all the demonstrations and guerrilla movements of the sixties and seventies, between 1964 and 1982 the state trailed only the other southern states of Chiapas, Quintana Roo, and Tabasco in the size of the PRI vote.[167] Yet in the 1940s guerrerenses did not toe the party line. In the absence of trustworthy vote counts, Gobernación was convinced that the party lost the 1940 presidential election in Guerrero; most likely the defeat was repeated in 1946.[168] Voters in municipal elections proved similarly unreliable, as did the state politicians who were supposed to manage them. In 1944 some half of all municipal elections were protested; in 1945 the state legislature actually annulled the PRM victory in Acapulco.[169] Such protests verged on collective bargaining by riot, beyond which the only escalation was into armed rebellion, two of which actually broke out in the north in 1946 and 1947.[170] Such violence is the second metric of centralization, or rather its absence; the continuity of high levels of violence in the 1930s and 1940s defied central rule and rhetoric. Finally, an effective degree of centralization would have permitted the low-cost implementation of federal policies. Yet in Guerrero federal initiatives, from land reform to literacy, met with resistance—sometimes popular, sometimes governmental, and sometimes both at the same time—ranging from foot-dragging to noncompliance and overt obstructionism. When challenged, governors blamed subordinates or guerrerenses themselves, pleaded weakness, or just filed false reports. They were, for all the hostility of federal agents, regularly successful at evading the queries and instructions of a distant center.[171]

In 1945, then, there were few signs of stabilization or of that elusive abstraction, the postrevolutionary settlement. There were striking structural continuities between Porfirian and postrevolutionary economies. Cardenismo by no means passed without trace, as some of the largest (and especially the absentee) landowners were gone, and much of the land that could be profitably redistributed had in fact gone to ejidos. With them came some of the quotidian but life-changing benefits of petty social reform, such as communal corn mills, sewing machines, basketball courts. Yet most ejidatarios remained at subsistence level, and much of the peasantry did not have an ejidal parcel.[172] Neither the state's wealth nor the equity of its distribution was greatly increased: in 1935 indigenous peons in Ometepec were being paid twelve centavos for a twelve-hour day, half the twenty-five centavos a day that had prevailed across most of the state in the Porfiriato.[173] As for the intertwined questions of violence and effective administration, the former increased while the latter decreased. Mexico City seemed blithely unaware of provincial realities; when seeking lands to grant workers repatriated from the United States they looked to Guerrero's coasts, already rife with agrarian conflicts. (The only one created, with twenty or so returnees from Detroit, rapidly disappeared.)[174] Their ignorance was perhaps unsurprising, for there was no revolutionary equivalent of the neatly penned monthly reports that Porfirian *prefectos* filed for each region, and it was impossible to get a budget statement out of even the largest towns.[175] The post, once reliable enough for the Alvarez family to use in organizing rebellions, was now so unreliable that the Secretaría de Educación Pública (SEP) reverted to hand delivery.[176] Ten years after the cardenista education drive had begun, vast numbers of villages remained without *maestros*.[177] Between 1942 and 1943 only one out of six school inspectors bothered to visit any schools.[178] The social contract that some have glimpsed in land reform, an exchange of obedience and order for land, was unfulfilled; Guerrero's Liga considered withdrawing from the PRM in 1939.[179] In a time of rapid yet unpredictable change central questions of who would dominate local politics, economies, and societies remained unresolved. There was no neat ending in 1940. In that year there wasn't much government in evidence, whether federal or regional. Guerrero remained an archipelago of state—and church, for that matter—power. Or, as in the late nineteenth century, more a geographical expression than anything else.

2 • A Rich Place, a Poor State

Veracruz

The Political Economy of a Central State

The 1918 register of directors of the Interoceanic Railway of Mexico (Acapulco to Veracruz) Ltd holds several surprises. First, the railway was English, owned by four men living in the home counties.[1] Second, despite that it worked: the railway cost £300,000 in 1888 and was valued at £2.7 million ten years later. Finally, the scale and diversity of the directors' other investments were impressive: George William Houghton of Kent, for example, also sat on the boards of oil, timber, railroad, petroleum, and land corporations in Argentina, Cuba, and Mexico.[2] He was on the board of five other sizeable Mexican companies, and yet Houghton was, compared to the English oil magnate Weetman Pearson or the French industrialist Thomas Braniff, a small fish, for Veracruz, always cosmopolitan, attracted an extraordinary volume of foreign investment and immigration during the Porfiriato.[3] The combination of rich sedimentary soils, multiple rivers draining the altiplano, and generous rainfall made much land in Veracruz, from the temperate foothills of the Sierra Madre down to the tropical coastal plains, highly productive; Veracruz yielded more maize per hectare than any other state.[4] More important, Veracruz held several of the winning numbers in the contemporary commodity lottery, including sugar, coffee, tobacco, and later, crucially, oil.[5] In a prewar period characterized by the international mobility of capital—1914 saw the highest gross foreign investment ever in developing countries, unsurpassed until the century's end—Veracruz became wealthier and more cosmopolitan than ever.[6] By the 1890s there were some five thousand foreigners resident in the state, a fifth of all Mexico's naturalized citizens lived there, and the port harbored nineteen

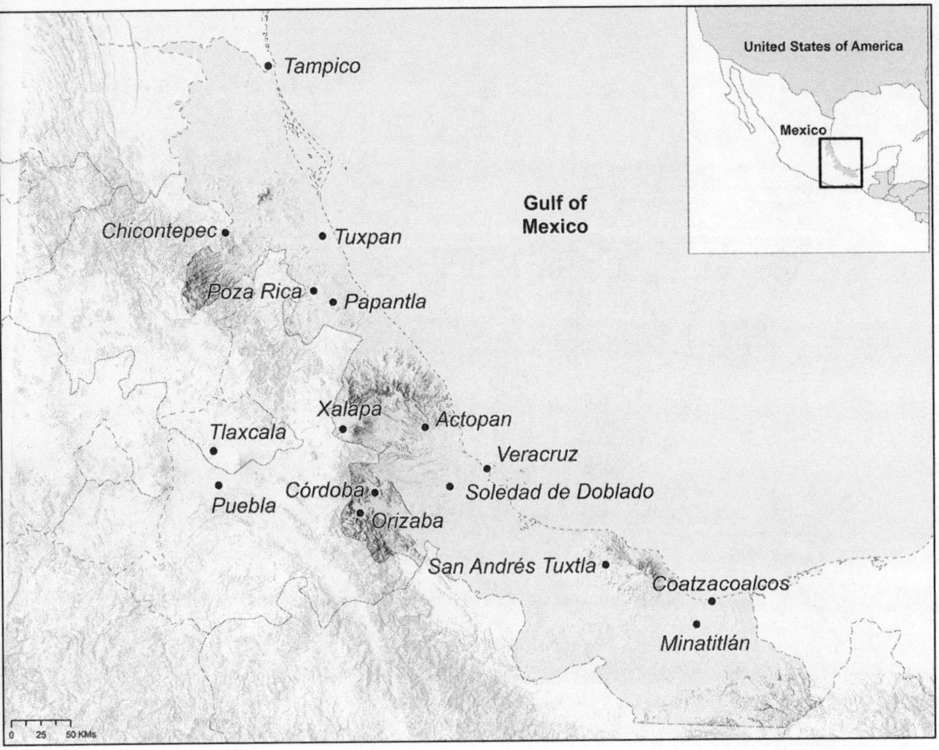

The state of Veracruz. Created by Kelsey Rydland, Research Services, Northwestern University Libraries.

consulates.[7] By 1910 the cross-pollination of natural resources, foreign capital, extensive railways, and political modernizers bent on land reform and industrialization had resulted in vigorous, if skewed, economic growth.

The railroads catalyzed booms in both commercial agriculture and manufacturing, favored by rising commodity prices, a growing domestic market for manufactures, and state intervention that ranged from the dogged promotion of desamortización to tax breaks, tariff barriers, and the three regiments of *rurales,* paramilitary police, deployed along the tracks of the Ferrocarril Mexicano.[8] Yet with booms came the inevitable corollaries of busts. Veracruz's largest sugar refinery, San Cristóbal, changed hands four times in its first ten years of existence, and suffered clear capital depreciation in the process.[9] Such microeconomic indicators were matched by clear macroeconomic signals of decline. Enrique Cárdenas traces a 20 percent fall in exports out of Veracruz during the last five years of the nineteenth century.[10] The booms were ephemeral for

Metlac Ravine on the Ferrocarril Mexicano. Abel Briquet. Digital image courtesy of the J. Paul Getty Trust's Open Content Program.

several reasons. Even when price trends in tropical commodities were uncommonly benign, producers were still subject to the vagaries of harvests. The coast was prone to hurricanes, the river basins, above all the Papaloapan, to flooding; the harvest in any part of the state was vulnerable to locusts, which the local politician Porfirio Pérez Olivares remembered blotting out the sun in his natal Soledad de Doblado.[11] In 1896 the north's maize crop failed; in 1898 the sugar yield for the entire state plummeted to just over thirteen hundred tons.[12] Industrialists, whose attempts to export generally did not prosper, faced more predictable obstacles. The national consumer market on which they depended was broad—perhaps as many as five million Mexicans by 1895—yet notably shallow, and a single bad maize harvest could cut textile consumption to the point of crisis. Their factories were large, modern, and capital-intensive: the four plants of the Compañía Industrial de Orizaba, SA (CIDOSA), employed between them six thousand workers who drew on the power of eighteen turbines to run one hundred thousand spindles. But they were also run well below capacity by a highly unproductive workforce. Despite far lower wages, it cost 19 percent more to produce a piece of cloth in Orizaba, the "Manchester of Mexico," than in Manchester itself.[13] Veracruz's importance in the Atlantic economy, finally, was challenged by the emergence of rival trade routes and their associated production zones: the rail lines to the northern border in the 1880s, and in the 1890s the port of Tampico, closer to the United States and naturally favored by the deepwater river mouth of the Río Pánuco.[14]

Between 1900 and 1940 the state economy continued to grow, however, both in absolute terms and relative to the rest of Mexico. This was in part due to the emergence of the oil industry. In 1887 there were 226 known petroleum sources along the Veracruz coast and a primitive refinery near the port.[15] Between 1900 and 1910 exploitation began in earnest. On the back of discoveries such as Potrero del Llano no. 4, which produced 100,000 barrels a day when it was drilled in 1910, or Cerro Azul no. 4, which in 1911 was the world's most productive well at 250,000 barrels a day, annual production rose from 5,000 barrels in 1900–1901 to 8 million in 1910–11 and 193 million in 1921.[16] Quantifying the effects of this bonanza on the *veracruzano* economy is complex. The oil companies were slow to contribute to the state treasury: what little taxes they did pay were purely federal prior to 1922, although in subsequent years

Río Blanco, Orizaba. Charles Betts Waites, 1905. DeGolyer Library, Southern Methodist University, Mexico Photographs, Manuscripts, and Imprints.

Cervecería Moctezuma, Orizaba. Charles Betts Waites, 1905. DeGolyer Library, Southern Methodist University, Mexico Photographs, Manuscripts, and Imprints.

their payments constituted up to 20 percent of Veracruz's total revenues.[17] However, their infrastructural projects—pipelines, rail links, the refinery that Pearson opened in 1908 in Minatitlán—formed a major source of employment.[18] A timely one, moreover, given the simultaneous winding down of rail, port, and factory construction.[19] In places, above all in the north, the new industry was built through land seizures, fraud, forced labor, violence, and environmental destruction.[20] After the revolution, though, oil workers' salaries became mainstays holding up aggregate demand. Even in the mid-1940s, when output had fallen off substantially, the industry employed some fifteen thousand people, who were paid generously—the average salary was six times the state minimum—and spent generously.[21] In a rare excursion to Poza de Cuero the social butterfly Salvador Novo wrung his hands at the 2 million pesos of Christmas bonuses that disappeared in a couple of nights' hedonism while the workers lived in wooden huts. But such conspicuous consumption, combined with remittances to the workers' villages, pumped an estimated 70 million pesos into the Veracruz economy in 1945.[22]

The oil companies rode out the armed revolution well, for all their protests.[23] For the economy as a whole, in fact, the destruction caused by the revolution was relatively minor and localized. The agricultural sector was the hardest hit. Cattle rustling more than halved the state's herds in ten years; cane fields, such as those of El Modelo in central Veracruz, were burned; in Tlacotalpan the destruction of the sugar mills pushed the ancient town into permanent decline.[24] Yet most industrial plants survived intact and continued production; both of the textiles giants, CIDOSA and its rival, the Compañía Industrial Veracruzana, continued paying dividends, the latter at a higher level during than after the revolution.[25] Oil output rose by well over 2,000 percent. Data from the state's census and treasury confirm the surprisingly low destructive impact of the revolution on Veracruz. In sharp contrast to the contraction of the national population, the state population grew between 1910 and 1921, while the state treasury's tax receipts, adjusted for inflation, were 160 percent those of 1910.[26] Over the medium term the revolution constituted a positive stimulus to growth. Admittedly it caused leading industrialists to run their plant into the ground rather than to maintain and modernize. Yet factories such as Río Blanco had always been white elephants: overlarge and underproductive, they were uncompetitive internationally and had been domestically constrained by a shallow market. That market actually expanded in Veracruz as a result of revolutionary land and labor reform: real wages in one textile mill nearly doubled across the 1920s.[27] The revolution's capricious redistribution of comparative advantage also strongly favored Veracruz's agricultural sector, despite the state's radical peasant movements. In both sugar and cattle Porfirian Veracruz had played second fiddle to the leading regional producers, Morelos and Chihuahua, respectively. Revolutionary violence in those states was far greater than the skirmishing and protection rackets in Veracruz, however, and Chihuahua's cattle ranches did not recover until the 1940s; the Morelos sugar plantations never fully recovered. Producers from Veracruz invaded their markets; in sugar the timing was lucky, as World War I removed European beet farmers from competition and stimulated sharp price rises. By 1918 Mexican sugar sold at four times its 1910 price, and Veracruz was the country's main production zone.[28]

Business confidence revived in the late 1910s and early 1920s. In 1917 the San Cristóbal refinery found a buyer, while the state's industrialists formed a series of pressure groups to negotiate with the new government. Industrial profits increased significantly between 1918 and 1925.[29] In the countryside of the center a generation of hard-faced men who looked as though they had done well out of the revolution began to take over haciendas from the Porfirian elite and find new ways to make them profitable.[30] This was by no means a period of peaceful or stable reconstruction. The 1923 rebellion of Adolfo de

Table 2.1: The revolution and shifting zones of agricultural production, 1900–1940

State	Head cattle, 1902	Head cattle, 1924	Head cattle, 1940
Chihuahua	396,023	120,230	685,282
Veracruz	392,858	206,656	743,018

State	Tons sugar, 1907	Tons sugar, 1921	Tons sugar, 1940
Morelos	42,655	Not listed	30,252
Veracruz	23,172	47,600	145,476

Sources: A. Peñafiel, *Anuario estadística de la República Mexicana 1907* (Mexico City: Departamento de la Estadística Nacional, 1912); Departamento de la Estadística Nacional, *Anuario estadístico 1923–1924* (Mexico City: Departamento de la Estadística Nacional, 1925); Secretaría de la Economía Nacional, Departamento de la Estadística Nacional, *Anuario estadístico de los Estados Unidos Mexicanos 1940* (Mexico City: Secretaría de la Economía Nacional, 1942).

la Huerta brought a short-lived civil war over the presidential succession to Veracruz; agrarian reform and the resistance it provoked generated high levels of everyday violence. The economy suffered repeated external shocks before 1929, such as the permanent reduction in the price of sugar that occurred in 1921. The tobacco industry went into crisis in 1923, laying off half its workforce; the textile factories worked a mere 187 days in 1929.[31] The oil industry suffered from wells that ran dry, a dramatic fall in demand during the Depression, and the emergence of Venezuela as a rival producer. Between 1929 and 1944 the value of industrial production fell by 11 percent.[32] The impression of a capitalist economy in crisis was reinforced by the political polarization of the period; the socialist governor Adalberto Tejeda called for workers' administrations in factories.[33] Yet this was a global crisis, and relative to the rest of Mexico and much of the rest of the world the Veracruz economy was resilient.[34] Minimum salaries in the mid-1930s were the second highest in the country, considerably higher than those of the Distrito Federal or Monterrey.[35] The state budget grew relatively steadily between 1920 and 1940, and between 1930 and 1940 it grew much faster than the national budget. Internal migration statistics suggested that the charms of Veracruz were not just the *diluvio de estrellas, palmera y mujer* of Agustín Lara's eponymous ballad, but also the compelling arguments of raw economics: by 1940 there were 136,000 immigrants in the state.[36] This was no dull compulsion, though; as labor power increased so, notably, did living conditions.[37]

World War II abruptly ended Veracruz's long-running economic growth. The state budget dropped a third between 1940 and 1946; minimum salaries fell from second to ninth place relative to other states.[38] Regional elites considered it the worst crisis in the state's modern history, something beyond their control; Gobernación's agent in the port of Veracruz considered it a consequence of their years of misrule.[39] Beyond the effects of the oil expropriation, the explosive rural violence, and the maladministration of the late thirties and early forties, however, the war provided an external explanation for economic decline. Foreign trade, which had boomed for a short period under the stimulus of wartime commodity prices, collapsed completely in the space of six months in 1942. In March the New York & Cuba Mail Steamship Company stopped its service to Veracruz, cutting off communications with the United States. In June German submarines sank two Mexican tankers, and by October the Argentine shipping service linking Veracruz to South America had also stopped. The three tramp steamers confiscated by the government from

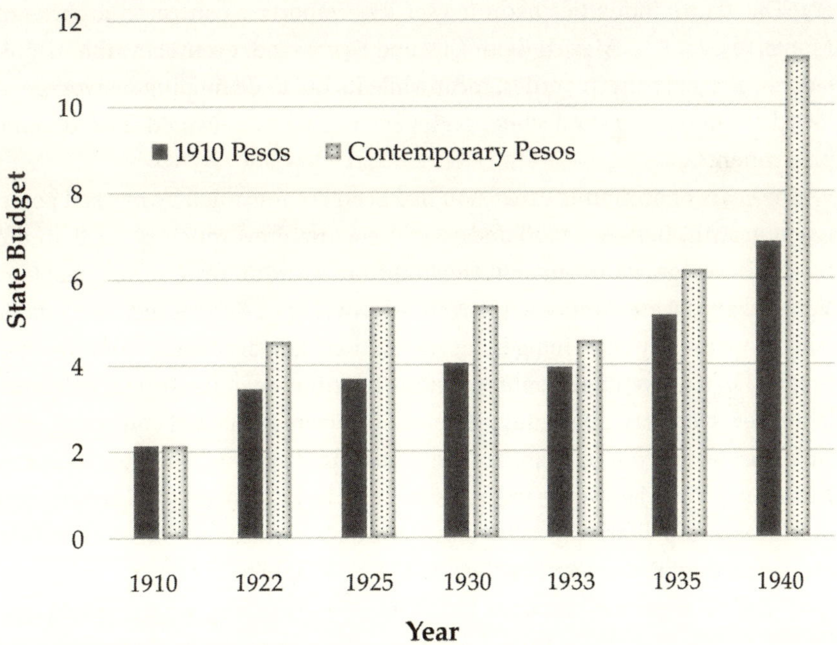

Veracruz's budget, 1910–40, in millions of current and 1910 pesos. Data from De la Peña, *Veracruz económico*, 2:484–86; deflated using wholesale price index Mexico City 1886–1978, INEGI Estadísticas Históricas CD-ROM.

Axis nationals proved no substitute, and the bulk of international trade was rerouted by land to the U.S. border.[40]

As the state economy contracted and the cost of food doubled, so the population's heavy dependence on purchased food became increasingly threatening. There was, wrote one Veracruz education inspector, "a terrible hunger" on its way.[41] Food shortages were widespread in 1942, 1944, and 1945; in April 1945 teachers, dockworkers, artisans, and employees all struck in protest against steep increases in the cost of living.[42] There was no quick postwar recovery: the state budget did not return to its 1940 level until 1951.[43] Poor harvests of maize, rice, and wheat in 1946 provoked the state government to attempt a 20 percent increase in production by decree, but flooding destroyed much of the south's harvests for 1945 and 1947, while the livestock industry grappled from 1947 onward with the *fiebre aftosa,* foot-and-mouth disease.[44] Successive years of low demand had inevitable effects on the consumer industry, and in 1947 the second-largest textile factory, Santa Rosa, dropped its second shift and put 800 workers on the street.[45] The generous federal spending of two successive veracruzano presidents helped an eventual but partial recovery. The state's industries became ever less important compared to those of Monterrey, Puebla, Mexico (both City and State), and, eventually, the maquiladoras of the northern border; meanwhile its rail and shipping networks followed its industry into decline, and Veracruz never regained its economic preeminence.

The years of economic expansion had been accompanied by marked population growth. Between 1878 and 1940 Veracruz grew much faster than the national average, its population trebling from 543,918 to 1,619,338 people.[46] Veracruzanos were similar to guerrerenses in at least one respect: both states had comparatively large indigenous populations that declined steeply over the first half of the twentieth century. Yet the distribution of the two states' populations evolved very differently. Whereas Guerrero remained something of a rural backwater even in 1945, Veracruz urbanized rapidly generations earlier. By the mid-Porfiriato veracruzanos were relatively literate, highly mobile, and notably cosmopolitan. One of wealthy Orizaba's early magazines was, in fact, called just that, *El Cosmopolita,* the boast given weight by the city's art nouveau town hall, designed by Gustave Eiffel, its steel parts forged in Belgium and hauled up the mountain from Veracruz.[47] A large number of veracruzanos were employed outside agriculture for they were, above all, an urban group by Mexican standards: in 1910 there were twenty-four settlements in Veracruz of more than 4,000 inhabitants and four important cities.[48]

The state's urbanization stretched well back into the nineteenth century. Orizaba, although still close to a colonial town in structure and appearance, had running water, street lighting, and sidewalks in the wealthier neighborhoods as early as 1865; the southern market town of San Andrés Tuxtla had street lighting in 1869, well before its boom years arrived; by 1881 so did northern Chicontepec, something of a hub for mule trains but no less remote for that.[49] The railways brought a new tempo to the reshaping of towns and cities. The port of Veracruz, for example, expanded from 10,000 inhabitants in 1878 to nearly 50,000 in 1910.[50] In the process it lost its town walls and acquired breakwaters, docks, a sewage system, drinking water, electrical street lighting, and a tram company. Such urban transformations stretched beyond the port. There were similar tram systems established in Córdoba and Orizaba, and projected for more provincial Acayucán and Tlacotalpan; electric street lighting in the up-and-coming port of Tuxpan and the marshy oil town of Minatitlán; and two small factories and piped drinking water in Soledad de Doblado, in 1900 still a village of 480 palm-roofed huts.[51] Soledad, twenty miles inland from the port, its tropical savanna land hugging the line of the Ferrocarril

Table 2.2: Selected population indicators, Veracruz, 1895–1940

Population indicators	1895	1910	1940
% economically active population in agriculture	61	*	58
% population over five years old speaking an indigenous language	21	18	9
% population over ten years old literate	15	24	40

* no data available
Source: Instituto Nacional de Estadística y Geografía.

Table 2.3: Populations of selected major towns, Veracruz, 1900–1940

Selected major towns	1900	1910	1940
Coatzacoalcos	2,937	5,095	13,740
Orizaba	32,393	35,263	47,910
Papantla	4,067	5,465	6,644
San Andrés Tuxtla	8,415	10,132	10,154
Veracruz	29,164	48,633	77,101
Xalapa	20,388	23,640	39,530

Source: Instituto Nacional de Estadística y Geografía.

Mexicano, was marked for development. But few places in central and much of southern Veracruz were far from a railway by the 1900s. Even Zongólica, cabecera of the most remote of the central cantons in the Sierra Madre, was only fifteen miles from a rail line, helping its indigenous smallholders to follow the dictates of international commodity prices, swap their traditional maize cultivation for coffee, or sell their lands to French immigrants.[52]

The outcome of such widespread communications was a comparatively decentralized state, scattered with large towns and small to medium-sized cities. This was the decisive peculiarity of Veracruz, and it was only increased by the communications advances of the 1930s, when city halls, agrarian radicals, bureaucrats, and businessmen set up their own road making fiefdoms and created a web of motorways without a center, or indeed a completed coastal road.[53] (The quality of those roads was distinctly patchy, with the key highway between Veracruz and Xalapa still unpaved in 1938, while the road between Veracruz and Córdoba was, Rand McNally judged, impassable.)[54] It fostered a population that, across class and rural / urban divisions, was politically sophisticated, used to both thinking and moving outside the *patria chica*, the

Soledad de Doblado before the Porfirian takeoff. Paul-Émile Miot, c. 1867.

The railway arrives at Soledad de Doblado, 1909. Anonymous. Wikimedia Commons.

cherished homelands of provincial Mexicans. With this mobility came a growing degree of cultural homogenization. In Veracruz, unlike Guerrero, few villages were islands. Yet the sheer length of the state preserved substantial diversity, as did its dramatic altitudinal and ecological divisions, and there were at least three very different regions in the state: the center, north, and south.[55]

The Center

Central Veracruz is defined to the east by the shifting lines of dunes and wetlands where the Gulf begins and marked to the west, sometimes a mere fifty miles inland, by the uneven edges of the Sierra Madre del Sur. The northern boundary follows a spur of hills that almost meets the sea in the canton of Misantla; the southern boundary crosses the Río Papaloapan as it meanders west-north-west across the lowlands from Oaxaca. The zone compresses extreme ecological diversity into a narrow strip of land. A traveler arriving by sea on a clear day would first sight the snowcapped volcano of the Pico de Orizaba, nearly six thousand meters high, and shortly afterward,—if a norther, the feared gale, weren't blowing—make landfall in Veracruz.[56] The port was a poor one—not so much a port as "a disagreeable anchorage among shallows," sniffed Humboldt—but it was the only one for over a hundred miles in each direction, and its mere existence, the direct (if steep) road to Mexico City, and the quality of soil drew early and intensive settlement in the *tierra templada,* the temperate hill country between one thousand and two thousand meters above sea level.[57] Travelers raved about this part of the country. To the enchanting Fanny Calderón, the first Spanish ambassador's Scottish wife, it was an approach to Paradise "after leaving Purgatory, typified by Vera Cruz," a metaphor repeated by the Austrian botanist Karl Heller; a place where the air was "soft and balmy," the heat "that of a July day in England," the trees "loaded with the most delicious tropical fruits," and where "flowers of every color fill[ed] the air with fragrance."[58] Yet the tierra templada was a relatively narrow band, and most of central Veracruz consisted of coastal lowlands, relatively fertile, well-watered land that could serve equally well for sugar as for grazing.

These lands had been intensively cultivated in pre-Hispanic times. During the colony and the early Independence period, on the other hand, they were left largely unpopulated.[59] Immigrants, whether mestizo or European, proved vulnerable to disease: smallpox, cholera, typhoid, malaria, and the incurable yellow fever. Isolated snapshots of mortality illustrate the health risks that curtailed widespread settlement in the lowlands. In the mid-nineteenth century the American diplomat Brantz Mayer counted 1,017 deaths in the four hospitals of the port in a single year, the equivalent of a rate of 156 deaths per 1,000 population; Heller claimed that two-thirds of newly arriving Europeans were dead inside a year.[60] It took the railroad and modern vaccines to alter the grim cost-benefit calculus of profit and death. In the 1890s the smallpox vaccine was made obligatory, and its administration was monitored municipio by municipio in the jefes políticos' reports to the governor.[61] They met such threats as the 1885 cholera and smallpox epidemics energetically, ordering town dwellers to clean, disinfect, and whitewash their houses, while suspected carriers of disease—both humans and vessels—were quarantined. The draining of swamps, above all, was noted to have a positive effect on public health (as it should have had, given the mosquito's then unrealized role as a vector for both malaria and yellow fever).[62] In the wake of the government's quarter of a million peso campaign against yellow fever no cases were reported in 1908.[63] By then a friend of the midwestern flaneur Charles Flandrau could flippantly write off the risks of a jaunt to the port as "some yellow fever and a great deal of smallpox—but who minds smallpox when you're having a good time?"[64] Such changed attitudes reflected the Porfirian reclamation of tropical lowlands as habitable and profitable places. As a consequence, the population of the center did not just grow across the nineteenth century; it also moved downhill.

The center was the mainstay of the state's economy, supplemented by the towns of Papantla, San Andrés Tuxtla, and Coatzacoalcos in the frontier zones of the north and south. Tax records show the preeminence of the central zone: in the 1888 cadastral survey the center's rural land was valued at 72 percent and its urban land at 89 percent of the state total, while in 1894 its population paid more than three-quarters of Veracruz's direct taxes. (They produced virtually all the state's coffee and sugar.)[65] Theirs were thick, exceptionally fertile soils; the river lowlands around Soledad de Doblado were deemed of supreme quality by an agrarian engineer, "a pleasure to plough" according to one peasant.[66] Many of these lands came on the open market during the Porfiriato. A combination of the high demand for land and a comparative lack of indigenous communities—typically the most successful opponents of desamortización—facilitated early and comprehensive land reform. Some villages, such as Tenango in Orizaba or Chicuasen in Actopan, redistributed their communal lands in the late 1850s and early 1860s. By the mid-1890s 70 percent of the central municipios had begun some form of privatization, and the majority of the rest had not encompassed communal land in the first place. Fierce competition for land in such a favored region did not favor latifundia; its profitability instead sustained numerous ranches and small to medium-sized haciendas.[67]

The owners of such estates were not just a rural bourgeoisie. They were also key actors in simultaneous, widely distributed urban development. By 1910 there were seventeen towns of over four thousand inhabitants in central Veracruz. These tended to be more than overgrown villages: a 1904 economic survey of one of those towns, Perote, listed multiple local industries, including a textile mill, a distillery, three sawmills, an oil factory, and a soft drinks factory. Even some of the villages had diverse, economically sophisticated populations. Paso del Macho, another railway stop, was home to a mechanic, five telegraphists, and forty-six shopkeepers; more people there spoke French than Nahuatl.[68] As the Porfiriato drew to a close, the reports of jefes políticos and the governor lovingly detailed the spread of paved roads, telephones, and schools.[69] Such small-town modernization combined with the booming of the principal cities and the rapid spread of commercial agriculture to produce a complex society. On its commanding heights stood the coalition of domestic politicians and foreign merchant financiers who owned banks, railroads, industries, and major plantations. Immediately below them came a more domestic grande bourgeoisie of merchants, financiers, and industrialists, whose rural holdings gave them an overlap with a relatively extensive group of hacendados and ranchers. The landowners, in turn, dominated much of the trade and industry outside the principal cities; the textiles factory in Perote, La Claudina, to give one example, was founded by the hacendado of Los Molinos.[70] A diverse middle class was simultaneously capable of dramatic social mobility, most notably in the early Porfiriato: the technocratic Teodoro Dehesa spent eight years as a shopkeeper's apprentice before spending nineteen years as governor.[71] The advanced division of labor lent yet greater diversity to the lower classes, who ranged from mestizo smallholders, indigenous coffee pickers, and women coffee sorters through cane cutters to construction workers, dockers, and the pickers, spinners, and weavers of the huge textile mills.

Class relationships were phrased, by regional elites at least, in terms of a progressive paternalism. The relatively minor violence of 1910 and 1911 went well with their narrative: Governor Dehesa and *El Correo de Sotavento* both interpreted the relative calm as a vote of confidence in "thirty years of patient and persevering efforts toward peace and progress."[72] Breaches of that peace such as Luis Mier y Terán's killing of nine middle-class rebels in Veracruz in 1879, or Apolinar Castillo's repression of the Xacatla indigenous rising, or the 1906 massacre of textile workers at Río Blanco were nationally resonant but abnormal.[73] Resistance was fragmentary, locally modulated, and above all contained: exemplified not by any muralist's vision of liberty reclaimed, but by the constant breaches of factory floor rules—a revealing collection, which barred everything from fornication to practice bullfighting—in the Santa Rosa mill.[74] This demands explanation, especially given that both the north and the south of the state were zones of serial rebellion during the Porfiriato. The composition of the population was almost certainly the key variable. The industrial / urban workforce was largely migrant and enjoyed some of the highest salaries in Porfirian Mexico; their principal concerns, for all the anarchist agitators who moved among them, were questions of pay, status, and working conditions. The Río Blanco strikers complained of Frenchmen, fines, bans on newspaper reading, and the price gouging of the company store; the Orizaba railwaymen, quiescent despite their strategic leverage, complained of late salaries and the unjust dismissal of two colleagues in what seems to have been their one and only Porfirian work stoppage.[75] Rebellion was more likely to come from the countryside, where two status groups—ranchers and Indian communities—had the potential to rapidly mobilize armed peasants. Yet very few indigenous

Picking over coffee in Coatepec, Mexico. Charles Betts Waites. DeGolyer Library, Southern Methodist University, Mexico Photographs, Manuscripts, and Imprints.

communities actually remained in central Veracruz by the Porfiriato. On fertile lands they were scarce by the beginnings of the nineteenth century; by the end of the nineteenth century their communities were disappearing even in the remote and chilly highlands of the *tierra fría*.[76]

The ranchers of central Veracruz, meanwhile, enjoyed a good Porfiriato and were not much prone to revolt either before or after 1910. Cándido Aguilar, a ranch administrator near Córdoba, had rancher, Maderista, and Magonista networks and yet was incapable of starting an effective rising; as late as May 1911 he had only twenty-two followers.[77] His experience was emblematic of the course of the revolution in the zone. Organization would be largely exogenous, as would be violence: the main military clashes in central Veracruz stemmed from the 1914 U.S. landings and the 1923 De la Huerta rebellion. Some popular mobilization spilled over from Puebla into the uplands, as when Perote was raided by two thousand Zapatistas. Other rebels encroached from the extremes of the state, as when Félix Díaz—the old dictator's nephew, overlooked even by him for decades, a clown prince—established his headquarters in the Sierra de Misantla.[78] For most of the 1910s, however, the significant military presence surrounding the port, federal until 1914, Constitutionalist thereafter, kept an uneasy semblance of peace. Across most of the center the popular experience of the revolution was defined by occasional jacquerie, sabotage—burning cane fields was common and popular—a high level of rural insecurity, and expanding numbers of worker and peasant organizations, most of which aimed at revolutionary advances without revolutionary violence.

Such organizations changed the face of village and state politics in the 1920s and 1930s. The revolution could be an almost abstract set of events in subsistence communities with few articulations to the outside world; in one isolated fishing hamlet near Veracruz, for example, the revolution was something that happened to other people.[79] In the towns and cities, on the other hand, the alliance between workers and Constitutionalists opened new political spaces for anarcho-syndicalists, libertarians, communists, feminists, and the unions they formed. The Casa del Obrero Mundial moved its headquarters to Orizaba in 1915; the Federación de Sindicatos Obreros del Distrito Federal held their national conference in Veracruz in 1916; in its aftermath the first tenants' union was created.[80] Women formed feminist labor associations: the unions of both the port's tortilla makers and Córdoba's coffee sorters had *por los derechos de la mujer* as their official motto.[81] Unions emerged outside the major cities and industries: in 1919 the woodcutters of the valley joined the textile workers in a union in Perote. Urban radicalism was contagious, as leaders returned to the countryside to disseminate their beliefs. This was not always by choice: in Perote the textile mill was shut down (a reaction to its workers' unionization), and the workers became hacienda peons, increasing their political networks and influence. Some men, on the other hand, set out as self-conscious proletarian missionaries. In Soledad de Doblado a young tobacco worker named José María Caracas came home after studying anarchism with the Spanish activist Pedro Junco in Veracruz, formed a peasants' union, and obtained the second ejidal grant in the state. In 1915 Orizaba's Federación de Obreros y Campesinos constituted fifteen peasant unions. By the early 1920s there was, in some places, an oversupply of leadership cadres competing for recruits.[82] It was a period of extraordinary mobility for budding local leaders of all stripes; elite politicians stood in urgent need of popular constituencies, and men like Ursulo Galván, a carpenter, communist, and future senator, could deliver them.

In exchange these grassroots leaders negotiated government support for rapid social change. Labor legislation brought down working hours and collective contracts upped wages. The seasonal cane cutters on El Modelo negotiated near-trebled wages during the 1920s.[83] The new labor relationships stretched beyond the proletariat and the peasantry and ran along lines of both class and gender: prostitutes were at the center of the port's rent strike, which culminated in government-controlled rents and low-cost workers' housing.[84] That mobilization touched even the world of unpaid household labor, with the tenant newspaper publishing a call for women's liberation headlined *La esclava del esclavo*.[85] It was the peasantry, however, who formed the most enduringly radical sector, who enjoyed the most powerful state alliance in their partnership with Tejeda, and who obtained the most dramatic benefits from revolutionary reform. Between 1920 and 1940 most of the best land in central Veracruz was redistributed to over eight hundred ejidos, some 60 percent of the state's total.[86] Much of this reform came in the twenties, before the rest of Mexico: between 1925 and 1926 the peasants of Soledad de Doblado sent in no fewer than twenty-nine petitions, while in La Antigua eight of the eventual twelve ejidos were formed by 1927.[87] Parallel to control of the land came, as always, the intertwined control of violence and elections. Peasant militias were armed to combat the De la Huerta and Escobar rebellions; the guns served equally well to defend the ayuntamientos that they won. And agraristas contested local elections vigorously well before the 1929 break between the Liga and the Communist Party. Peasants ran La Antigua from 1923 onward; the dominance of Ursulo Galván (himself a local deputy) in Cardel was so marked that next to no one bothered to vote in the 1925 municipal elections.[88] Elections could even be adjudged clean, as in Misantla that same year. More often the contests were deemed flawed by the monitors dispatched from Mexico City, fraudulent and violent yet at the same time animated and competitive.[89] The men elected were sometimes the leaders of a new, and frequently popular, political class.

These new men did not survive the 1930s, whether literally—virtually all the first-generation peasant leaders had been murdered by the decade's end—or figuratively, as dominant politicians. The center's agraristas were clearly the most successful in the state, and yet the reversal of their fortunes began as soon as Tejeda finished his second period as governor. At the end of 1932 the militias (numbering between twenty thousand and fifty thousand men, according to wildly varying estimates) were disarmed by the military. In early 1933 the new regime purged strategic agrarista municipios, including that of the port; by mid-1933 the Liga was under attack from without, as the Confederación Campesina Mexicana expanded, and from within, as it splintered in three.[90] The PNR excluded agraristas from slates across central Veracruz in 1935; when they ran as independents they were threatened, denied credentials and "the liberty to vote."[91] A profoundly violent landowner revanchism gathered force across the mid-1930s and early 1940s; its victims ranged from rank-and-file ejidatarios to Manlio Fabio Altamirano, the Liga's gubernatorial candidate in 1936. In extreme cases the ascendant conservatives killed an entire generation of municipal leaders. In Soledad de Doblado the landowner / bandit Gonzalo Lagunes, whose family owned sizeable estates across the center, was accused of the improbable feat of killing several ejidos' presidents in a single evening.[92] Soledad was ruled by an appointed junta for much of the decade, one of several militant lowland municipios where such bypassing of elections became close to a norm. The effect was to demoralize the majority of peasants in the region, a demoralization only increased by the governor's takeover of the Liga in 1937. Their marginalization grew further under Governor Miguel Alemán, a fresh-faced labor lawyer who had risen rapidly from the petty bureaucracy to the Superior Court of the Distrito Federal and thence to the senate; in 1940 the Confederación Nacional Campesina (CNC) did not even enter the elections for his replacement.[93] By then one of the most radical popular movements in Mexico had delivered lands to the center's peasantry and then stalled amid violence tantamount, in many areas, to a civil war. In the cities, meanwhile, support for the PRM was grudging and unreliable; the port railway men backed Almazán in 1940, while the textile workers of Santa Rosa went further and plotted an armed almazanista rising.[94] Popular engagement in politics and substantial reform made central Veracruz one of the (less acknowledged) "laboratories of the revolution."[95] By 1940 the experimenters had not, however, created either peace or any clear consensus on what a new Mexico should look like.[96]

The South

The south was both the largest and the least populated zone of Veracruz: a frontier still in the mid-1940s, when some inland settlements such as Playa Vicente could be reached only by river for most of the year. Four cantons—Cosamaloapan, Los Tuxtlas, Acayucán, and Minatitlán—covered nearly thirty thousand square kilometers that stretched from the Papaloapan basin to the state border with Tabasco.[97] It was a flat, well-watered country, broken only on the coast by the hills surrounding the San Martín volcano; rich arable land, complemented by extensive tropical forests and floodplain grazing. The pre-Porfirian population, outside the scattered cabeceras where mestizos and immigrants lived, was predominantly indigenous—Nahua, Popoloca, and Zapotec—and relatively small. In 1878 a mere seventy-eight thousand people, or some 15 percent of the state population, lived in the south.[98] As late as 1900 a cabecera such as Sayula could be home to a mere half a dozen mestizo families.[99] Disease and indigenous resistance both helped limit settlement; San Andrés Tuxtla lost some 40 percent of its population during the 1833 cholera epidemic, which at its height killed over two hundred people a day in the market town.[100] But it was the absence of communications, above all, that qualified the attractions of the south.

The state government and the regional bourgeoisie both promoted steamer services; there was a riverboat on the Papaloapan River as early as 1855, and in 1880 the state was subsidizing a bimonthly coastal service from Minatitlán up to Veracruz.[101] Yet the strategic first rail connection (from Córdoba) lagged behind those of the center by over twenty years, and stopped almost as soon as it entered the south in Tierra Blanca. Feeder lines did not reach the region's main towns—Acayucán, Coatzacoalcos, and San Andrés Tuxtla—until the very end of the Porfiriato.[102] For a narrow corridor across the Isthmus of Tehuantepec the 1900s was a time of rapid change. The railway from the Pacific port of Salina Cruz to Coatzacoalcos began service, the Coatzacoalcos River was dredged, and Mexico's first modern oil refinery opened fifteen miles upstream in Minatitlán.[103] The speculative concessions of survey companies carved up the Coatzacoalcos hinterland among three pueblos and seven private estates, among whose owners William Randolph Hearst, José Yves Limantour, and Weetman Pearson figured prominently.[104] The expansion of commercial agriculture, however, both anticipated the railway and spread beyond its immediate reach. Cattle, plantain, rice, and cotton had all been well established across the south as early as the 1850s: regional production of cotton between 1858 and 1859 was over one thousand tons, processed in steam-driven plants in places as far-flung as Playa Vicente, a small village on the border with Oaxaca.[105] As cotton declined in the late nineteenth century it was more than replaced in the south's economy by sugar cane, tobacco, and tropical hardwoods; by 1899 clear-cutting in the Coatzacoalcos valley was generating a fifth of the state's timber production.[106] The steep rise in sugar cultivation, especially in the northernmost canton of Cosamaloapan, sustained three major refineries by 1910.[107] The greatest profits, however, lay in the tobacco of Los Tuxtlas, where by 1894 some forty thousand hectares were under cultivation.[108] The war in Cuba catalyzed the industry's expansion yet further, and in 1895 growers sowed three times as much as in the previous year.[109] Producers exported across the world. The cigars of Octaviano Carrión, the town's largest grower, were awarded a gold medal by the khedive of Egypt at Cairo's 1895 Concours International du Commerce. The wealth brought by the newfound connections to global markets made of San Andrés a boomtown, a strange place where the hardware store sold pianos alongside Smith & Wesson revolvers, the tailors imported cashmere from England, and the grocers sold wine and cognac from France.[110] In 1900 there were 154 merchants and shopkeepers in town, or roughly one for every two ranchers.[111]

The names of their businesses were impregnated with a Porfirian faith in progress: the cigar factory was La Vencedora, the pharmacy Moderna, the cantina El Renacimiento, and the groceries La Esperanza and La Nirvana.[112] It was a faith far from universal. In 1906, the same year these companies were recorded in the *plano mercantil,* a florid map of downtown surrounded by adverts (and a bust of Socrates), a former millworker called Hilario Salas built a coalition of dispossessed native people and disenchanted middle-class radicals and led a thousand men in simultaneous attacks on Acayucán, Coatzacoalcos, and Minatitlán.[113] Both shopkeepers' prosperity and this short-lived anarchist rebellion had a single local root in desamortización. During the key decade of 1885 to 1895 surveyors, local officials, and aspirational farmers imposed the privatization of communal lands on unwilling and recalcitrant communities across the south. It came earliest in the most commercially promising cantons, Cosamaloapan and Los Tuxtlas; by 1891, however, even Minatitlán's municipal landholdings were completely privatized.[114] Commercial farmers were distinctly favored over local communities in the process—the San Andrés community representatives of the Sociedad Agrícola were bypassed in favor of the *junta divisionista*—and by the advantages of literacy, money, and municipal power. In San Andrés the Artigas, Carrión, and Turrent families quickly came to dominate the privatized lands; in Soteapan Manuel Romero Rubio, the powerful interior minister, took over seventy thousand hectares from the villagers that he subsequently leased to the Aguila Oil Company.[115] The histories of desamortización have been revised in the north and center of Veracruz to downplay the scope, homogeneity, and popular reception of the process.[116] That revisionism is difficult to apply to the south, where between 1890 and 1907 the number of haciendas, averaging over ten thousand hectares each, more than doubled from 48 to 111.[117] With such land concentration came, as one frank jefe político put it, the extinction of Indian communities; sometimes, as in the case of the villagers who followed Salas, they fought back.[118]

There was more to resistance than outright rebellion. (And resistance was not an automatic response; not all indigenous people were against privatization.)[119] The recalcitrant had several tools to hand. Communities went to court to defend their claims to communal lands; in Zaragoza and Oteapan indigenous villages successfully continued a de facto communal ownership behind a façade of disentailment.[120] Urban protesters could, at least occasionally, be both militant and effective. In San Andrés tobacco workers struck in 1896, tarring and feathering scabs and eventually forcing a settlement; the same year a young artisan mounted the ayuntamiento's podium during the patriotic revelries of the *fiestas patrias* to denounce local government.[121] A broad gamut of everyday practices, ranging from the determined regionwide evasion of the vaccination program to endemic cattle rustling, formed a more continuous, half-hidden challenge to the claims of the expanding Porfirian state.[122] And resistance stretched beyond the indigenous peasantry and their worker allies to encompass local worthies. In Santiago Tuxtla the Carvajal family, liberal ranchers who had fought against Maximilian, became first Magonistas and later Maderistas.[123] In the market town of Acayucán Miguel Alemán González, the local shopkeeper, vigorously conspired with other members of the local middle class while rehearsing with the town band.[124] The chronicler of the Partido Liberal Mexicano (PLM) in the region even lists Manuel Turrent, distinctly local aristocracy, as an anarchist sympathizer.[125] In the south, as on a national level, the Porfiriato incurred increasing opposition as it aged.

Yet widespread resistance did not translate into revolutionary gains. The south of Veracruz was one of the first areas to rise in 1910: by autumn the PLM's troops were mustering in the Sierra de Soteapan while the well-reported activities of the bandit Santanón ("social," according to Cándido Padua and Heather Fowler-Salamini, just bandit according to León Medel) were causing the governor national embarrassment.[126] By the end of April 1911 larger towns such as Cosamaloapan and Catemaco were falling to Maderista forces, and the administrators of the ancien régime were being toppled; in Catemaco the local boss fled while revolutionaries dragged his secretary behind a horse. There was little Maderista stabilization. The orozquista rebellion of February 1912 led to raids on San Andrés and Playa Vicente; in October 1912 Félix Díaz's short-lived and incompetent Veracruz coup attracted locals if few others.[127] Such divisions endured across the decade, undermining the revolutionary groups and denying any single force the cohesion to dominate the region. Even the Huerta coup, that great unifier, failed to weld together a broad front in the south. Huertismo's local manifestation was typically draconian: numerous peasants were taken for the hated draft, the *leva,* while summary shootings and hangings became commonplace. Yet when the three main leaders—Miguel Alemán González, Pedro Carvajal, and

Hilario Salas—signed a joint manifesto against Huerta, Carvajal promptly had Salas assassinated.[128] What revolutionary stabilization there was came from outside with Cándido Aguilar's seaborne invasion of July 1914.[129] With it came the insertion of relatively conservative Aguilar clients, many of them allied to the Porfirian landowners, in key regional positions of power and the removal of radical local authorities. In 1922, for example, the army forced the mayors of both Acayucán and San Andrés into exile.[130] There was, as a consequence, very little of the early land reform that characterized the center of Veracruz in the 1910s and early 1920s. In San Cristóbal the sugar refinery actually expanded, illegally, onto peasant lands in 1921, and then recruited the government to persuade the true owners to leave the cane five years in situ. In San Andrés Tuxtla, despite a 1912 petition for the restoration of communal lands, there was no land reform until 1923.[131] When the Liga was founded that year the cantons of Acayucán and Minatitlán—half of the south—did not even manage to send delegates.[132]

Such failure characterized the history of the south's popular movements. The inroads peasant politicians made upon the region's formal structures of power were confined to agrarian committees whose petitions went largely unanswered, occasional deputyships, and isolated ayuntamientos.[133] Porfirian elites survived well: in San Andrés Tuxtla landowners accused of leading roles in the De la Huerta rebellion were still running the municipio's government and bureaucracy in 1925, and families like the Turrents and Carrións remained among the state's political elites across the twentieth century.[134] The economic rewards of such endurance were considerable: in 1945 eight of the state's ten latifundia of twenty-five thousand hectares or more were to be found in the south.[135] Even at the height of Tejeda's power agraristas were frequently presented with rigged elections against which their protests failed.[136] Federal teachers, their natural allies, were few and far between, and frequently run out of town by the local authorities.[137] Organized labor might have been politically potent—the Minatitlán refinery's thirty-four hundred oil workers made it one of Mexico's larger industrial complexes—but it was quickly demobilized.[138] The watershed 1932 gubernatorial elections met with indifference in the oil town; by the mid-1930s the area's leading politician was Amado Trejo, the Aguila Oil Company's representative.[139] Other unions were similarly politically quiescent: the CROMista sugar workers, for example, formed *sindicatos blancos,* employers' stooges who accepted wage reductions and pay in vouchers for the company store.[140] By 1940 the classic formula of the demoralized—"the revolution has not arrived"—circulated freely.[141]

Popular political failure was, perhaps, overdetermined. The relatively small populations dispersed across the vast expanses of the south favored petty guerrilla warfare but not mass civilian politics. The main local leaders were not straightforward social revolutionaries; more traditional liberals like Alemán senior seem to have fought on primarily political grounds and were opposed to both Tejeda and his socialist followers. Even the south's most successful revolutionary, General Heriberto Jara of Minatitlán, a middle-class bookkeeper in a textile mill who was a labor radical by conviction—reading to cigar workers, helping draft Article 123 of the Constitution, later becoming a prominent defender of the Soviet Union—had his dose of opportunism and ambiguity, fostering tactical alliances with landowners and a powerful dislike for the region's main Tejedista, Primitivo Valencia.[142] Radical leadership, often imported and in low supply, was hard hit by the attrition common to peasant movements in the period. Juan Rodríguez Clara was killed in 1923; Francisco Moreno in 1925; Primitivo Valencia in 1929.[143] The opposition strategies of traditional elites—fictitious land sales, co-option of individual revolutionaries, the formation of spurious revolutionary parties, the forging of conservative-leaning alliances with national elites—were diverse and effective.

Most, if not all, of these obstacles could be found elsewhere in Veracruz, or indeed elsewhere in Mexico. The south was distinguished, however, by the violent balkanization of labor and peasant constituencies. In its milder incarnations such organizational division neutered reform movements and held back local economic growth: in Cosamaloapan, for example, the divisions between the Confederación de Trabajadores de México (CTM) of the millworkers and the Liga of the field hands generated insecurity, repelled investment, and allowed the business elite to continue running local politics. In its most severe forms it caused an extraordinary level of interpeasant violence, as in Los Tuxtlas where coalitions of ejidos led by Juan Paxtián and Nicolás Parra fought it out in the "age of terror" of the 1930s.[144] In such a context complaints concerning murders instigated by the landowning and business elite, such as the 1940 killing of the Catemaco fishermen's union secretary, paled beside the constant denunciations of peasant leaders' massed paramilitary raids and the razed hamlets they left behind them.[145] Land reform came slowly to such a divided set of petitioners and was successfully resisted by long-standing landowners: on the rich tobacco lands of Caleria, one of the ejidos opposed to Paxtián, ejidal ownership was still contested even as the agrarian reform was being legislated out of existence in the early 1990s.[146]

The North

The north of Veracruz is an etiolated strip of coastal plain that stretches from the mountains above Misantla to the port of Tampico in Tamaulipas, narrowing down to twenty miles in places before pushing deep into the mountains of the Huasteca in the canton of Chicontepec. The region was largely covered by forest across the period, and even in the logging boom of the mid-1940s there remained some seven hundred thousand hectares of tropical forest.[147] Northerners were overwhelmingly indigenous. Over 90 percent of the population across the nineteenth century was formed by Nahuas, Otomís, Totonacs, and Téenek, scattered in small, fiercely autonomous settlements across the five cantons of Chicontepec, Papantla, Ozuluama, Tantoyuca, and Tuxpan. It might have been a rich country: sugar, cotton, tobacco, and coffee all grew well, and the maize yields from the hills of the Sierra Papanteca to the flatlands of the Río Cazones were some of the highest in Veracruz.[148] Yet while there was an abundant supply of fertile agricultural land, the north was badly communicated and in capitalist terms poor; in 1894 its contribution to the state revenues was a mere 12 percent of the whole.[149] Until the oil fields came into production in the 1900s regional industry remained overwhelmingly small scale and artisanal.[150] Islands of wealth did form where communications made exports cost-effective. Tuxpan enjoyed a coastal steamer link with Veracruz; Papantla was within range of the roads to the altiplano. Such zones, apt for commercial agriculture, saw an aggressive wave of hacienda expansion in the 1830s which clearly foreshadowed the Porfiriato in both cronyism—Guadalupe Victoria took an entire coastal municipio, Tecolutla, for his hacienda—and resistance—the first of serial peasant uprisings started in Papantla in 1836.[151] Even the poorest municipios of the north were notably richer than their equivalents in Guerrero's la Montaña. The municipio of Chicontepec had considerably higher tax revenues in the mid-Porfiriato than the entire guerrerense district of Morelos; and while Morelos completely lacked muleteers, Chicontepec was home to fifteen of them whose mule trains took aguardiente, tobacco, and hardwoods to the coast or into Hidalgo and returned with manufactures.[152] The "exuberance of [Chicontepec's] lands," the jefe político Leonardo Chagoya noted in 1890, could have sustained such cash crops as rubber, vanilla, and chicle. It did not, he explained, because the local peasants "lacked the inclination" to cultivate them.[153] In Texcatepec, he lamented, "as the majority of the vecinos of the municipio are Indians, by nature indolent and very given to drunkenness, all these and yet more sources of wealth that the municipio contains are not properly exploited, and for this reason the same municipio is remarkable for its poverty."[154]

Chagoya did not share their regrettable lack of ambition. In the aftermath of the 1885 state diktat that divided Chicontepec's municipal lands into eleven large *condueñazgos,* collective landholdings, he promptly appropriated fifteen hundred hectares in Tzimpiasco from their indigenous owners. His subordinates followed suit. Three of the councilors from the 1890 ayuntamiento, Félix Montiel, Crescencio Sánchez, and Benito Zenil, were the most prominent of the men accused of similar land grabs. Benjamín del Rosal, who later bought some of their lands, was three times mayor. Such men, the literate mestizo minority, used their traditional role as brokers to good effect: Enrique Llorente, for example, persuaded the natives of Pemuxtitla to give him power of attorney by claiming that foreigners had invaded.[155] Yet privatizers were not invariably outsiders: in 1890s Papantla successful Totonac vanilla farmers and caciques like Simón Tiburcio were critical in overturning the condueñazgos that had hitherto protected community ownership. By the turn of the century some areas had witnessed large-scale shifts in land tenure. Perhaps a third of Papantla's lands, long-coveted for plantations and costly on the open market, had been turned from condueñazgos into the haciendas owned by Totonac worthies and merchant families such as the Tremaris, the Zorillas, and the Zardonis.[156] But two-thirds remained in the hands of Totonac smallholders, and relatively successful elite land grabs constituted the exception in the north, where desamortización largely failed. The 1874 state law establishing condueñazgo, a legal framework for collective ownership, had in itself been a recognition of defeat, the impossibility of a blanket imposition of private property. Local extensions to the deadline of the 1889 law (decreeing subdivision of communal holdings within two years) were still being awarded as late as 1905.[157] In 1900 private properties in the north were still restricted to a narrow corridor along the Río Pánuco, a handful of cattle haciendas on the Tamaulipas border, and some small ranches in the southern Huasteca.[158] While most privatization in Veracruz occurred between 1885 and 1895, in the north the governor's reports sketch a losing struggle to redistribute communal lands that continued down to the revolution.[159]

Behind this Porfirian failure lay a tradition of indigenous resistance, rooted in the realization that cattle ranching and plantations were antithetical to their livelihoods as shifting forest cultivators.[160] Between 1819 and 1906 there were seven rebellions in the Huasteca and Papantla—basically one a decade, barring the time of the French intervention—many of which lasted several years.

They had a common agrarian base: the 1836 Papantla rising, which spread as far as the State of Mexico, was a reaction to hacienda expansionism; the 1847 Papantla rising centered on the rents that haciendas attempted to charge longtime Totonac residents; the 1891 Papantla rising—stifled by a brutal counterinsurgency and outbreaks of smallpox and yellow fever—was sparked by the arrival in town of hated land surveyors during the Corpus Christi celebrations.[161] Intertwined with the periodic explosions of agrarian violence was a bitter struggle for control of the basic practices of everyday life. In Papantla the jefe político banned the Totonacs' traditional dress, fiestas, and public assemblies, made the use of shoes obligatory, and placed an extraordinary tax on firewood.[162] In Tantoyuca the jefe político stopped Téenek from carrying machetes in town and enforced the wearing of trousers; in 1891 he jailed or fined one in ten of the municipio's population.[163] Such measures amounted to a permanent cultural offensive against the indigenous, its foot soldiers happily marrying profit to ideology. It was met, and to some extent defused, by a broad spectrum of defensive strategies. The idleness Chagoya bemoaned in Texcatepec, for example, reads as a typical weapon of the weak given that the same allegedly indolent Indians organized an armed rising in the 1890s.[164] "Indolence" or "ignorance" were classic elite shorthand for the passive resistance found in Chiconamel and Tantoyuca, where *comuneros* refused to attend public meetings at which they were to receive the titles to individual plots. Indigenous villages engaged as well in very active resistance, which ranged from appeals to courts or central government to violence. In Chicontepec, one of the relative success stories of desamortización, the survey company was forced from the canton in 1892.[165] Surveyors could be escorted by rurales, but the landowners who succeeded in obtaining former indigenous lands had no such protection and faced daily threats. The combination of everyday resistance and violence was too much for many of them, who opted for selling the land back to its original occupants. In 1884 Bernardo Estopier sold 50,000 hectares in Papantla back to ninety-six Huastecs; in Chicontepec both Llorente and the jefe político Chagoya ended up selling their estates back to their original indigenous owners in the 1900s.[166]

Oil men were far more successful than hacendados in both getting control of indigenous land and (at least partially) proletarianizing its inhabitants. By 1906 Weetman Pearson owned over 270,000 hectares in the north and had leased a further 100,000 hectares; the American Edward Doheny, owner of oil fields from Los Angeles to Lake Maracaibo, controlled a similar amount through his Huasteca Petroleum Company. The rate of land accumulation increased in the 1920s as established wells began to run dry. By the 1930s oil companies either leased or owned outright most of the land in the region, some 2 million hectares.[167] Many indigenous people became oil workers or provided food and laundry services to the camps. Many others used piecework in the oil fields to subsidize their former livelihoods as peasants. The cultural conversions that the oil companies performed across the north, persuading indigenous villagers to supply first their land and then their labor, were in part forcibly imposed. Oil companies possessed the same violent capabilities as hacendados and until the revolution had far more reliable backing from Mexico City in exercising them. When literate trickery failed, violence could follow: thus Eufrosina Flores, after a long struggle, capitulated and sold Cerro Azul when company thugs murdered her husband. Land obtained, a second phase of violence often ensued when drilling began, and the company guards or guns for hire would burn homes, kill leading resisters, and in extreme cases deport people en masse. Yet oil companies may also have been more successful than the hacendados because their greater resources allowed them to purchase some consent alongside their use of force: Eufrosina Flores was eventually paid 200,000 pesos by the Huasteca and moved to Los Angeles.[168]

The oil boom coincided with the armed revolution to make the 1910s a decade of rapid and far-reaching change in the north. The region fragmented politically under maderismo and remained a shifting patchwork of anarchic local movements until the fall of President Venustiano Carranza in 1919. There was—as in much of Guerrero—an initial flurry of discrete rancher revolts as declining power brokers mobilized opportunistically and the dominant mobilized preemptively; there wasn't that much sociologically to tell between the two sides. Wealthy mestizo leaders recruited indigenous villages en masse to become petty warlords; indigenous autonomy and violent potential could also push local leaders to assassinate—as again in Guerrero—entire cohorts of principales. The strategic prizes of the ports and oil fields further complicated an already chaotic war. The region became a front line between Carrancistas and Villistas in 1914 and 1915; between 1915 and 1920 an influx of oil money sustained the rancher Manuel Peláez's private army, regional but powerful enough to maintain a large exclusion (and extortion) zone around the main oil fields. (His mercenaries did not come cheap, costing El Aguila alone $15,000 a month.) Outside the oil camps and district capitals there were no fixed or secure positions, and local populations suffered arbitrary violence from all sides. In early 1917 Peláez burned the strategic small town of Tamiahua, where the eponymous lagoon drained into the sea, while the Carrancistas took the village of Amatlán, twenty miles inland, and hanged all its menfolk.[169] The intertwined experiences of revolution and oil boom varied greatly according to place; yet as a broad rule of thumb the phenomena of fighting, forced migration, and environmental degradation were at their worst in the Huasteca.[170] The Papantla district's only oil field closed in 1911, and it is no coincidence that revolutionary violence there was less pronounced.[171] Population statistics mark the difference: while between 1890 and 1930 the Totonac population declined by 10 percent, that of the Téenek dropped some 65 percent.[172]

In the span of a generation many northerners moved from work in milpas or haciendas to oil refineries, the state façade of the Porfiriato folded, and the ecology of much of the region was dramatically reshaped. One constant was the strong drive of indigenous populations, like the Zapatistas in Morelos, to stay in the same place, and the fighting that choice demanded.[173] The north was throughout the revolutionary period a zone of endemic resistance. Some of it was channeled through the new labor organizations. Oil workers were quick to form unions and quick to strike: in 1914 the three thousand men crewing well no. 4 at Potrero del Llano walked out for higher wages.[174] That oil workers were often also peasants pushed unions rapidly into the countryside: by 1920 some sixty rural unions had formed in the Pánuco area alone.[175] Villages in the north were among the first to petition for the restitution of ejidos: in Chicontepec, for example, peasants lodged at least five petitions between 1917 and 1918.[176] Some resistance centered on sabotaging the economy of the powerful. Cattle rustling—*abigeato*—was a lucrative economic activity; it was also a material and symbolic attack on the locally dominant, and by the early 1940s it was sufficiently widespread to tie up five flying columns of soldiers in the Huasteca alone.[177] The cooperatives introduced by Cardenismo, antidotes to the traditional exploitation of the *acaparadores,* provincial middlemen, were well received.[178] There was, finally, a deep well of antipathy to the state itself. Some of it centered on defense of profound religious faith (if not always the Church). Many northern villagers sympathized with the Cristeros, while in the 1940s Sinarquistas recruited strongly and launched campaigns of civil disobedience, particularly in the Huastec zones.[179] Sometimes resistance ended in violence. In August 1935 agraristas in the Papantla region launched a jacquerie that lynched local officials and toppled six ayuntamientos.[180] For all the shifts of the revolutionary period the north in the early 1940s was still recognizable as the isolated frontier of the nineteenth century, a place where villages fought for their right to be left alone and where, as cattlemen complained, "the government of Veracruz . . . has not been able to make tranquility reign."[181]

Political Culture and National Power

Men from Veracruz thought they were special. Politicians, journalists, and provincial intellectuals repeatedly stressed their homeland's peculiarities and the leading position in Mexican national life that they (at least publicly) attributed to the "exceptional quality of the veracruzano, our state's essential treasure."[182] (Such men did not generally use the term *jarocho,* which was a reification of a different kind: at best a happy-go-lucky, *danzón*-shuffling, tropical idler, at worst a violent opponent of civilization.) Governors' reports from the midcentury collectively endowed their subjects with "high culture," "patriotism and nobility," "glorious traditions," and "that lucid intelligence of the veracruzanos."[183] To be veracruzano, editorialized the *Diario de Xalapa,* was an honor and a responsibility; part of the responsibility lay in assuming the white man's burden and enlightening the rest of the country. The state's elites had traditionally believed that they ran the better parts of Mexico's economy and political system. Veracruz, proclaimed her newspapermen and administrators, had "set the pace in all of history's epochs, in relation to the other states of the Republic," and had "led the way in . . . so many other questions of national importance"; was "the cradle of the Reforma," "the national banner of the country's politics," and "a lighthouse that illuminates the paths of the Patria."[184] Adolfo Ruiz Cortines gave a saltier version: in Veracruz, he told one governor, "no hay pendejos," there are no dickheads.[185]

These self-confident projections were part instrumentalist rhetoric, part wishful thinking, and part true. Veracruz repeatedly served as an alternative capital to the country: liberals drew up the Reform laws there, and Carranza set up his first government in the port. At the same time the workingmen and -women of the docks, textile mills, railways, and oil refineries formed the advance guard of the national labor movement. (They were quite literally ahead of the times: in 1911 Veracruz had its own time zone in miniature, running twelve minutes ahead of the capital.)[186] In Guerrero revolutionary generals inhabited the governors' palaces for decades after the revolution; in Veracruz they were quickly elbowed aside by civilians and licenciados. Journalists were vibrant and many: *El Dictamen,* founded in 1868, had been joined as early as 1878 by at least thirty other state newspapers.[187] Between 1920 and 1940 a buoyant export economy and a proven popular military capacity gave veracruzano elites unusual autonomy in national politics, allowing state leaders to implement policies distinctly out of step with federal aims. While President Calles was struggling to bury agrarian reform, Governor Tejeda was redistributing 240,000 hectares; conversely while President Cárdenas was promoting land reform, Governor Miguel Alemán redistributed a mere 95,000.[188] The tensions between national and regional systems ended in an effective merger when Veracruz became one of only three states—alongside Sonora and the Distrito Federal—to capture the federal government. And veracruzano dominance went deeper than Alemán's and Ruiz Cortines's spells in Los Pinos. The two men were responsible for running much of the Avila Camacho campaign in 1940, Alemán as director and Ruiz Cortines as a member of the national committee; Alemán as secretario de Gobernación was subsequently responsible for running much of the country.[189] This newly powerful Gobernación was, barring the brief tenancy of Hector Pérez Martínez, run by a series of veracruzanos from 1940 to 1958; six of Alemán's cabinet were veracruzanos, as were his commanders of the Presidential Guards and the Mexico City Military Zone. His hated informal inner court contained yet more.[190] For a good fifteen years of the midcentury, half-joking advice held that it was best to forget about a career in public office unless you came from the Universidad Nacional Autónoma de México, Alemán's alma mater, or from his state, Veracruz.[191]

This elite success story was not founded on consensus: the long sweep of Veracruz, part coast, part forest, and part sierra, was difficult for any single faction to dominate. National politicians took advantage of a high level of competition between those factions, archetypal *camarillas*, and attempted to exert everyday control through the politics of divide and rule and a heavy military presence. Cándido Aguilar's career illustrates the strategy's potential and pitfalls. Aguilar was rewarded with a senatorship for abandoning his patron Tejeda in the presidential succession maneuvering of 1933.[192] By March 1937, however, he controlled many of the state's agrarian organizations and unions, had installed a client as governor, and played a key role in the unification of the agraristas.[193] Seeking a counterweight to such concentrated power, in April Cárdenas sent the forceful and ambitious General Alejandro Mange to command the 26th Military Zone in Veracruz, where he began disarming aguilarista defensas rurales. So far—from a cardenista perspective at least—so good, even if Mange was a dedicated Callista. But in containing Aguilar's regional capabilities Cárdenas fostered two fresh and enduringly powerful cacicazgos, those of Mange himself and of Miguel Alemán. The two men were natural enemies, but the general's dominance of much of Veracruz nevertheless survived Alemán's passage from governor to interior minister to president; it survived, in fact, until a long-postponed retirement in 1959. Such longevity was eloquent testimony to the difficulty of controlling the state, and to the center's reliance on military cacicazgos to counterbalance civilian power there.[194]

A similar dissensus characterized relationships between the state's rulers and ruled. Peasants and workers in 1920s Veracruz were powerful beyond the Mexican norm, the former thanks to their organization, leadership, and the arms they had obtained in defending the regime in 1923, and the latter—particularly dockers, oil workers, and railway men—through their influence over strategic resources. They had negotiated an alliance with the state government during the eight years of tejedista rule that had encouraged as much regional stability as could be expected during the locally intense experiences of land reform and conservative rebellion. (The latter even furnished excuses for agrarista exclusion of opponents; in 1929 Tejeda deposed 142 of Veracruz's 181 ayuntamientos.) But Tejeda fell hard in 1933. Within nine months the peasant militia was disarmed, and the Tejedistas had lost control of local governments, the legislature, the Liga, and the state PNR. In 1936 Tejeda went into the euphemized exile of a diplomatic posting in France, and by 1940 Gobernación was dismissing the remaining Tejedistas as a fringe movement.[195] Tejeda's removal coincided with, and to a great extent caused, a general fragmentation of state politics. No single leader inherited his power, and the ensuing competition between regional and federal heavyweights for influence encouraged the fission of popular organizations. In such conditions of instability and opportunity violent entrepreneurs flourished; whether old landowners like the Lagunes or the Armentas, or new landowners such as Manuel Parra, their power won with *pistoleros,* the professional gunmen of the postrevolutionary period, or agrarista caciques such as Juan Paxtián, often equally handy with a gun. Veracruz became a Machiavellian environment of highly aggressive geographical and organizational fiefdoms; less autonomous, perhaps, but also less governable.

By the early 1940s Veracruz was a failing state. Jorge Cerdán's conservative governorship, arranged between Aguilar and Alemán, was violently incompetent. It failed in the most basic tasks: tax revenues fell off steeply, in part due to the mounting corruption of supervisors and collectors, seventeen of whom would be arrested for accepting bribes when Cerdán left office.[196] Only half of the state's municipios had the money to cover essential services, including village secretaries and teachers.[197] While the CTM increasingly dominated elections it also became increasingly unrepresentative of Veracruz's workers. Labor, far from being a disciplined bulwark of any emerging corporate state, was in reality in chaos. Between 1941 and 1942 both the CTM and the CROM split and the Confederación de Obreros y Campesinos de México (COCM) grew rapidly; five distinct unions competed for the allegiance of the dockworkers alone.[198] As the formal political system splintered and weakened, the informal political system, the deals cut between pistoleros, elites, and military, expanded.[199] Corruption started at the top of the hierarchy: the Aguilar family ran Orizaba's illegal gambling clubs, Alemán and the mayor of Veracruz sold off the city park to line their pockets, and General Mange used the comparative advantage of command to build businesses and extort rents across the state.[200] Amid the economic disaster of the war food supplies to the cities periodically broke down: in 1944 the mayor of Orizaba made a pilgrimage to Mexico City to beg the central government for maize.[201] Against such a backdrop it was, perhaps, a paradoxical time for Miguel Alemán to begin Veracruz's dominance of the national government.

3 • Peasants, Presidents, and Carpetbaggers

The End of Peasant Government: The 1945 Elections

"The greatest problem of a ruler," Miguel Alemán was fond of saying, "is the succession"; Guerrero between 1944 and 1945 lived up to his axiom.[1] Part of what Mexican politicians revealingly called the *problema electoral* was structural. Guerrero's elections were traditionally violent: as one commentator put it, "Guerrero is a giant bonfire that goes up at the slightest electoral spark."[2] The 1945 gubernatorial election was the first genuine contest in nearly a decade, and under recent constitutional reforms the winner would govern for six rather than four years. The outcome would consequently be pivotal in defining relations between peasants and other political groups after Cardenismo. There was also a conjunctural side to the tension in 1944. A powerful governor might control his state's competing elites, discourage popular mobilization, and generally manage the inevitable turbulence of elections. But Governor Rafael Catalán Calvo was a carpetbagger, and a notably weak one. Before his imposition from Mexico City he had been outside Guerrero since the revolution, and he lacked the local networks of his predecessors. Yet Catalán Calvo also lacked patrons in Mexico City. By 1944, consequently, his control of the state was minimal. Many of the basic cogs of the governmental machine, such as mayors and teachers, opposed him.[3] He was ignored by state PRM leaders, who drew up the slates for the strategic 1944 municipal elections without consulting him.[4] The state's military commander backed his clients against the governor's men across conflict zones such as the Costa Chica.[5] As the campaigning season began, the front-runners, far from seeking Catalán Calvo's support, attacked him vigorously in public speeches.[6] Guerrero was a microcosm of President Avila Camacho's Mexico: a supposedly centralized system without much of a center.[7]

If the governor didn't run Guerrero, who did? In the absence of much central authority the unintended polyarchy of the recent past intensified. Four groups competed and colluded in locally mediated balances of power: the peasantry, the state elites, the military, and the federal government. The state expansion of the 1930s had multiplied the sites of rural political influence, layering an increased federal bureaucracy and a numerous, politically ambitious teaching profession onto preexisting electoral, military, and cacical networks.[8] The balance sheet by the mid-1940s was accordingly confused. The agraristas had lost leaders and influence under Governor Berber: in addition to the killings he was accused of masterminding, the general gerrymandered district boundaries to hitch the agrarista heartlands of the Costa Grande to the landowner-dominated northern town of Coyuca de Catalán.[9] Under Catalán Calvo peasant politicians had to some extent rebounded. At a federal level one of two senators and two of six deputies were agraristas, while in the state legislature agraristas like Mauro Reyes rubbed shoulders with conservative landowners like Luis Bedolla. At a municipal level agraristas consolidated old strongholds such as Petatlán and made advances in traditional landowner municipios like Ometepec, where every mayor between 1939 and 1945 was an agrarista.[10] Yet their longer-term prospects were darkening. The Liga's share of the 1943 state legislature fell to three of the nine seats; yet more foreboding, the secretary-general of the Liga ceased to be elected in 1945 and was instead appointed by the governor.[11] Where peasant leaders made advances they were systematically opposed by General Matías Ramos Santos, the commander of the 27th Military Zone who, as former secretary-general of the PNR, had better federal contacts than anyone else in the state.[12] Ramos did largely as he pleased, excluding agraristas from the army's strategically key rural reserves, militias who held the high ground in local conflicts, and defying Catalán Calvo to the point where the governor asked Gobernación for help.[13] The state's political hierarchies were sufficiently blurred, and the federal government a sufficiently distant referee, for even minor players to enjoy considerable autonomy: in 1943 the cacical teacher Angel Cirineo Martínez tried to install an independent as federal deputy for Acapulco.[14] The PRM was far from uncontested dominance: when party leaders cut the governor out of the selection process for the strategic Acapulco ayuntamiento, he in turn nullified their victory and installed a municipal council.[15]

To Guerrero's agraristas the astute as well as just solution was clear: an agrarista governorship that would reflect the fact that the vast majority of guerrerenses were peasants, a fact the Liga repeatedly brought to the government's attention when haggling over their *cuota de poder*.[16] They had a governor in waiting in the person of the costeño Senator Nabor Ojeda, their leader, who had been a vital ally to Mexico City in getting rid of Berber and in getting the improbable Catalán Calvo into office in his place.[17] Ojeda had the experience—one of the Liga's first secretaries-general, a member of the national leadership of the Confederación Campesina Mexicana, allegedly a handy gunman—and the backing, with not just the state's agraristas but also the Federación de Organizaciones Populares, a considerable faction of the CTM and various PRM leaders behind him.[18] As politicking began in spring 1944 he was backed by a majority of the state's ayuntamientos and by the main party committees of the coasts and center.[19] The president had promised the state's agraristas a fair election; that would return Ojeda.[20]

By June 1944 it was evident that Ojeda's main rival would be General Baltasar Leyva Mancilla, a career military officer who, in a Gobernación inspector's verdict, "although a native of [Guerrero], has been outside the state for many years, and as such does not have popular backing."[21] Leyva Mancilla had indeed not spent much time in Guerrero since primary school, and his rise to power had come through fighting with the federal army on the right side of the De la Huerta, Cristero, and cedillista rebellions.[22] Yet he never left the dense networks of the state's narrow political elite. Some connections were blood ties: his father, Pablo, had been a minor Porfirian luminary, making it as high as finance secretary; his half brother had been secretario de Gobernación in the 1930s; and the Martínez Adame family, longtime heavyweights in the region—Arturo was at the time a senator—were cousins. Others were alliances by marriage: his sister had married a Carreto, the family seen as the power behind the throne of the tottery Governor Berber, and his niece was married to Alfredo Córdoba Lara, the onetime bootblack who had become the state's main union leader. Leyva Mancilla's own wife was a Neri, the family who had built on prerevolutionary power to become the state's dominant clan for most of the 1920s. Finally, he had numerous fictive kin in a large group of compadres that included rising guerrerense politicians such as Nicolás Wences García and Caritino Maldonado.[23]

While Baltasar Leyva Mancilla was attacked as yet another carpetbagger, he was much more than that, a man emblematic of an emerging generation who had feet in the camps of both state and national power.[24] To his extensive regional networks he could add critical central backing. He was offered a clear run at the governorship by Alfredo Córdoba Lara, who drove all the way to

Nabor Ojeda's primary campaign, a parade, 1944. Archivo General de la Nación, Mexico City, Dirección de Investigaciones Políticas y Sociales, box 782, file 118.

Chihuahua to convince him to accept.[25] Córdoba Lara did not control a majority of Guerrero's workers' movement, which was minuscule anyway, but he was national labor leader Fidel Velázquez's man in Acapulco and a talented election fixer.[26] Leyva Mancilla was at first dubious, citing his lack of local knowledge; he may also have been discouraged by some of his family's previous experiences in state politics, which had killed three of his brothers.[27] Both his longtime military patron, General Antonio Guerrero, and Córdoba Lara reassured him that the president, whom General Guerrero immediately phoned, would support him.[28] Leyva Mancilla had an "old and brotherly friendship" with Avila Camacho, and he and his brother had fought in the Brigada Serdán, a regiment recruited from the president's hometown of Teziutlán in Puebla.[29] In addition to Avila Camacho and Velázquez, Leyva Mancilla was backed by Ezequiel Padilla, the guerrerense foreign minister, and by key party figures, among them Teófilo Borunda, leader of the Sector Popular, and General Sánchez Taboada, soon to be secretary-general.[30] The majority of the state legislature and bureaucracy had swung to Leyva Mancilla early on as rumors of his presidential support spread. He had rich and violent backers in the conservative landowners who campaigned with him in Iguala and on the Costa Grande and who included Rosalio Radilla—held responsible for numerous killings, notably those of the martyred Escudero brothers—and other hard men of the coasts such as the Venturas, the Lunas, the Guerreros, and Nicolás Torreblanca.[31] Finally and far less predictably Adrián Castrejón and Gabriel Guevara, ex-governors bound hitherto only by mutual loathing, were both Leyva men.[32] Castrejón, an agrarista himself, was promised the regional military command in exchange for undermining Ojeda's peasant base, a reflection of the marked central interest in the election.[33] The eclectic breadth of this coalition betrayed the main reason for Leyva Mancilla's candidacy: to stop Ojeda and with him Guerrero's agrarian movement.

They succeeded. The key moment came with the party primary election of November 1944, which the Leyvistas rigged through bureaucratic shenanigans, economic pressure, and violent intimidation. All three of the party sector conventions shut out Ojeda's supporters: the Sector Popular quite literally, its leaders employing the state police to keep Ojedistas out. The CTM held their meeting without advance publicity and packed it with apocryphal unions; the CNC followed instructions from Mexico City and never met at all.[34] Those slow to take the hint were told in no uncertain terms of the costs. Ejidatarios in la Montaña were told to sign up to the Leyva campaign or lose their land and schools (the extent to which the latter was much of a threat is open to question).[35] Mine workers in the north were turned away by the federal work inspector when they needed him to do paperwork; traffic police warned truck drivers not to transport Ojedistas.[36] Sometimes things turned violent. Pistoleros shot and killed the party delegate in Cuautepec, Telésforo Guerrero, when he refused to sign blank electoral forms. A Castrejón aide was accused of murdering two of the three directors of the Las Cruces ejido.[37] When the PRM declared Leyva Mancilla the winner of the primaries Ojeda protested loudly and withdrew his candidacy, but without following through on his threat to disobey the party.[38] His supporters clearly abstained in the final election, which an unopposed Leyva Mancilla won with, Gobernación inspectors observed, assorted tricks and "a very low number of voters." In Chilpancingo they watched as one of the polling booths had its ballot boxes filled by the very men manning it; in Acapulco the board of elections failed to hold a meeting as they fell short of a quorum. The Liga temporized for three weeks and then professed loyalty to the new regime.[39]

The Liga's reluctance was not just down to Ojeda's defeat; agraristas were also shut out of the coinciding municipal and legislative elections. Peasants did not keep a single local deputyship, and they held on to only three of the state's seventy-two ayuntamientos, the coastal strongholds of San Marcos, Tecpan,

Table 3.1: The Liga's claims to municipal power and state government resistance, 1944 elections

Municipio	% of ayuntamiento seats claimed by Liga	% of ayuntamiento seats awarded to Liga	Agrarista control?
Acapulco	29	0 (elections annulled)	No
Ajuchitlán	57	0	No
Alcozauca	60	0	No
Alpoyeca	60	0	No
Apaxtla	57	14	No
Arcelia	43	0	No
Atenango del Río	80	20	No
Atoyac	57	0	No
Ayutla	57	0	No
Azoyu	57	0 (elections annulled)	No
Chichihualco	60	0 (elections annulled)	No
Chilapa	43	0	No
Chilpancingo	14	7	No
Ciudad Altamirano	57	0	No
Coahuayutla	60	0 (elections annulled)	No
Cocula	60	10	No
Copala	60	0 (elections annulled)	No
Copalillo	60	0 (elections annulled)	No
Copanatoyac	60	0	No
Coyuca de Benítez	57	0	No
Coyuca de Catalán	43	0	No
Cualac	60	10	No
Cuautepec	60	0	No
Cuetzala	80	0	No
Cutzamala	57	0 (elections annulled)	No
Florencio Villareal	60	0 (elections annulled)	No
Huamuxtitlán	43	0	No
Huitzuco	43	0	No
Iguala	57	0	No
Igualapa	60	10	No
Ixcateopan	60	0	No
Mártir de Cuilapan	60	0 (elections annulled)	No
Mochitlán	80	0 (elections annulled)	No
Olinalá	60	0 (elections annulled)	No
Ometepec	43	0	No

Petatlán	57	0	No
Pilcaya	60	0	No
Quechultenango	60	0	No
San Jerónimo	60	0 (elections annulled)	No
San Luis Acatlán	57	7	No
San Marcos	57	57	Yes
San Miguel Toto- lápan	57	0	No
Taxco	29	0	No
Tecoanapa	57	14	No
Tecpan*	57	21	Yes
Teloloapan	43	0	No
Tepecoacuilco	57	0	No
Tetipac	57	0	No
Tixtla	50	0	No
Tlacoachistlahuaca	60	60	Yes
Tlacotepec	57	0	No
Tlalchapa	80	0	No
Tlapa	43	0	No
Xalpatlahuac	60	20	No
Xochihuehuetlán	60	0	No
Xochistlahuaca	60	0	No
Zirándaro	57	14	No
Zitlala	60	0	No

*Tecpan is counted as an agrarista ayuntamiento as the minority of agrarista representatives included the mayor.

Sources: Comparison of Liga list 1944 municipal election victories in Liga to Avila Camacho, December 20, 1944, and state-government recognized results in Catalán Calvo to Gobernación, January 2, 1945, AGN/DGG/2/311M(9)/5B/75.

and Tlacoachistlahuaca, none of which was all that important (and none of which lasted past the summer anyway).[40] They did not get any *regidores,* town councilors, at all in the vast majority of Guerrero's towns and villages. Neither were the new municipal elites centrists, but rather landowners and pistoleros, widely held to be Panistas and Sinarquistas.[41] In Coyuca de Catalán the new mayor was Luis Brugada, a hardline landowner; in Cuetzala, the pistolero Malaquías Rabadán, one of a large family of caciques; in Coyuca de Benítez, the *abigeo*—cattle rustler—Luis Otero; in zapatista Igualapa, one of the Ometepec landowners, Higinio Morga.[42] Those ayuntamientos who refused to recognize the results—Teloloapan in the north, not even agrarista, Ciudad Altamirano in the Tierra Caliente—watched as the Leyvista winners were installed by soldiers.[43] The results caused protests in 49 percent and outbreaks of violence in 17 percent of Guerrero's municipios.[44] They wiped out most of the political gains peasants had made since the revolution.

The Leyva Mancilla Sexenio

Hegemony this was not. The crushing victory known as a *carro completo*—a whitewash, or full house—was rather too complete, and when combined with postelectoral persecution turned distinctly counterproductive for Leyva Mancilla. His supporters jailed, fired, and exiled losing agraristas;[45] someone killed Ojeda's campaign director, Francisco Hernández Solís, and someone else attacked Ojeda's family house.[46] With a sympathetic president such embarrassments might be glossed over, as long as they did not last too long. But Guerrero's electoral cycles were as unsynchronized with national cycles as could be, and Leyva Mancilla faced five years serving a president who had not appointed him and who had good reason to dislike him. Ideologically, he and Miguel Alemán were quite close; politically they were distanced. Like many other generals, Leyva Mancilla had sympathized with the precandidature of Alemán's early military rival, Miguel Henríquez Guzmán; of the governor's key backers one, the zone commander Adrián Castrejón, had led the national Frente Zapatista in opposition; another, the foreign minister Ezequiel Padilla, ended up actually being the opposition candidate in the presidential race.[47] There were even reports of a conspiracy to kill Alemán while he campaigned in Guerrero.[48] Nabor Ojeda, on the other hand, had declared early for Alemán, and was an important organizer in the peasant leagues of both his and Alemán's state.[49] When Alemán took office Leyva Mancilla was consequently threatened on two fronts, at home by a bitterly resentful peasant party and away by an executive unenthusiastic at best.

Anxious to keep his head below the parapet, the governor tried conciliation in the December 1946 municipal elections. Compromise slates readmitted some agraristas into local government, and the elections passed uneventfully.[50] It was a successful piece of political adjustment, but it was overlooked by the men at Gobernación; they were more interested in a series of risings in Veracruz, Morelos, Michoacán, San Luis Potosí, and above all Guerrero that broke out between November 25 and 27, 1946. It was the run-up to Alemán's assumption of power, and the rebels claimed to be acting in the name of Ezequiel Padilla, the ex–foreign minister who had lost the election. The government had feared that something was up, and when Padilla retreated to California after the elections they were concerned enough to follow him and enlist U.S. help in doing so. The losing candidate, however, disappeared amid alarming rumors: rebels were massing to take the Sonoran towns of Naco and Cananea, they had purchased planes in the United States, an armed revolution was imminent. On the twenty-fifth the U.S. authorities reported that they had found Padilla again; that he was driving in a small convoy en route to Arizona was no reassurance, though, and so the government dispatched troops to Cananea and Melchor Ortega, the leader of Padilla's party, to Los Angeles to dissuade him from any subversion.[51] The precautions turned out to be unnecessary. It is unclear whether the skirmishes were planned by Padilla—an indecisive man—as the sort of multitudinous rural movements that had added up to national rebellions in the past, or whether they were the independent initiatives of the locally disenchanted. Whatever the case, 1910 it was not. In its early days the government took the violence seriously, and it was successfully hushed up, staying out of the reports of papers, diplomats, and, later, historians.[52] Yet while there were isolated casualties—five men attacked the guard at Poza Rica, leading to two deaths and a host of arrests of Petróleos Mexicanos (PEMEX) workers; the municipal police in Panindícuaro, Michoacán, attacked the army barracks and killed a soldier—1946 was essentially a rebellion stillborn.[53] There was, however, one seeming guerrilla *foco,* and that, to Governor Leyva Mancilla's embarrassment, lay in Guerrero, in the northern municipios of Teloloapan and Iguala, Padilla's heartland. In that "mountainous region, propitious for rebellion," a Gobernación agent reported, a strange coalition of political outs had ridden into the sierra with pistols, shotguns, and what other weapons they could lay their hands on, "hoping that outbreaks of armed risings would spread in other parts of the Republic."[54] There were between three and five hundred of them, led by regional elites—doctors, licenciados, businessmen, and a hotelier from the defeated campaign—among them, allegedly, ex-governors Carlos Carranco Cardoso and Urbano Lavín.[55] (On the coast the mayor of San Jerónimo claimed to have fought off a nighttime attack by two hundred Padillistas, but it was in reality the two sides of a local feud seizing their opportunity, and the lack of any casualties makes the estimates of their numbers improbable.)[56] When Alemán assumed the presidency on December 1 it became evident that there would be no national rebellion, and the rebels ceased even minor skirmishing.[57] By the middle of the month it was clearly all over bar the formalities of demobilizing the rebels and prosecuting the leaders.

It was here that Leyva Mancilla and Castrejón behaved strangely. Unlike most provincial rebellions, the padillista risings could not be blamed on the state leadership: the grievance was national rather than local, and the governor did not seem to have ignored any prior intelligence.[58] On hearing the first reports the governor fired off a telegram in code, requested an extra battalion of infantry, while maestros and peasants asked for arms to defend the revolution.[59] In the aftermath, however, regular troops and the Teloloapan defensas rurales hunted the rebels for two weeks without success. The only recorded shoot-out was suspiciously bloodless. None of the movement's leaders were captured; they were, rather, complained one *maestro rural,* getting off scot-free, and the leaders J. Encarnación Cuevas and Alberto Salgado would be pardoned.[60] This was Castrejón's milieu; he came from Apaxtla, at the center of the uprising.[61] He and the governor were accused of cutting deals with and even supplying arms to the Padillistas; which, together with his inability to contact the rebels or arrest their leaders, provoked suspicion in Mexico City.[62] It was a poor beginning to relations with the new president.

While the Padillistas were vanishing, a different problem arrived with a shipment of cattle from Brazil which, landing in Veracruz, infected local livestock with foot-and-mouth disease. The federal response was undermined by a lack of personnel to enforce quarantine decrees, and cattlemen illegally removing their animals from the infected zone spread the disease quickly.[63] By February 21 the cabinet, assured of U.S. aid, took the standard decision to shoot all sick animals, but it was too late, and by the end of 1947 all central Mexico from Jalisco to Oaxaca was infected.[64] Guerrero was the last state to be declared a foot-and-mouth zone, and Leyva Mancilla, forewarned, reacted well. Before the disease arrived he went on a preemptive tour with a veterinarian and local deputies to explain the imminent threat and the government's countermeasures of quarantine, transport control, vaccination, and the *rifle sanitario,* the compulsory slaughter of diseased herds. By March 1947 he had formed a state foot-and-mouth commission, recruited veterinary students, divided the state into four zones, inspected the borders with infected states, and ordered disinfectant tanks for border municipios; in the budget he set aside 82,000 pesos for the Agriculture Department to fund the campaign. At the peak of the epidemic there were 149 municipal committees and nearly a thousand men from state and federal agencies working in the campaign. This competent administration may have been responsible for avoiding the extremes of resistance encountered in other states: in Senguio, Michoacán, a mob lynched a vet and his seven-man military escort.[65]

It could not, however, overcome the social problems inherent to the eradication campaign across Mexico. The shooting of livestock caused inevitable resistance, but it was a resistance exacerbated by official ineptitude—all the five-hundred-odd cattle of Palo Blanco, Tierra Colorada, were slaughtered after a federal veterinarian misdiagnosed a case of foot-and-mouth, while in Apaxtla all the cattle, sick and healthy, were shot at once—and by the sometimes colonial attitudes of the campaign personnel. In Atenango del Río one Doctor Klimerk attempted to slaughter sixty-two animals without having the cash to pay indemnity, and when the villagers refused he returned with soldiers. (For the state veterinarians, whose local knowledge gave them greater sensitivity, it was a positive disadvantage working with soldiers, who appropriated food from the villagers and made themselves generally unwelcome.) There was also corruption: in Petatlán General Javier Altamirano swindled locals when buying their livestock.[66] Peasant and ganadero livelihoods suffered from more than the loss of cattle, into the bargain, as uncertainty drove livestock prices down dramatically, and for want of paperwork producers were often unable to sell animal products before they rotted.[67] The simultaneous increase in the state tax on cattle was extraordinarily ill-considered.[68] It was unsurprising that rural populations should, as a *comité de orientación* pamphlet put it, "consider those in charge of the campaign as enemies," issue commissioners with death threats, and believe the loss of value and killing of their animals part of a nefarious United States conspiracy.[69] It was also unsurprising that Gobernación should be preoccupied, dispatching a DFS agent disguised as a traveling salesman to monitor the situation.[70] It was unfortunate for Leyva Mancilla, however, for the worst-affected areas of his state were also the least stable: the Costa Chica and Tierra Caliente.

The Balsas Rebellion and Other Woes

Tierra Caliente was the richest cattle country in the state, with nearly a quarter of a million head in the 1940s.[71] It had also been deeply divided since the revolution, and many of its elites had backed Padilla in the election and the ensuing rising. By August 1947 troops were hunting two new armed groups, who were reinforced in mid-September by cattlemen, miners, reservas rurales, and Padillistas from the region's villages.[72] In the early morning of September 22 they attacked and disarmed the platoon that garrisoned the town of Balsas and seized the train. About one hundred poorly armed men then came down from the sierra, sending foot soldiers ahead by train to capture the next stop, Cocula, and leaving horsemen to demand money and arms from local merchants. The rebels left the train at the Ingenio San Martín outside Cocula to join up with other groups for the attack; their coconspirators never arrived. The rebels were perhaps disheartened by now; according to assorted local accounts they had intended to capture the governor and Castrejón, who had been in nearby Apipilulco for a banquet the day before. These luminaries escaped, thus foiling the rebels (according to one unlikely account, they fled vigorously pumping a push-pull railway cart). The attack on Cocula was, at any rate, a total failure: a platoon of regulars and another of agraristas held them off for several hours until reinforcements of defensas rurales arrived. The rebels retreated to the sierra, where they were hunted by cavalry, infantry, and planes, and by September 26 they were reported to have completely dispersed.[73]

This was a rebellion, even if ill-planned, unconvincing, and in "Parched Country So Hot that Few Upland Mexicans Ever Visit It," and one with several disturbing facets for the federal government.[74] Even as the British embassy accepted the defense secretary's claim that the train assault was the work of bandits and cattle rustlers, it noted that such events were "generally symptomatic of something worse" and that the government "might be hard put to cope with simultaneous outbreaks elsewhere."[75] The Balsas rebellion came three weeks after the massacre at Senguio and at the same time as reports of arms dumps in the Sierra de Puebla.[76] In Jonacatepec, Morelos, leaflets circulated calling for an armed rising.[77] The rebellion evinced, moreover, an impressive degree of cross-class collaboration against the government. Many of the foot soldiers were ejidatarios, whom four sinarquista chiefs had worked hard to convince that Cárdenas would aid a rising against the injustice of the rifle sanitario. Among the suspected leaders were landowners such as General Salvador González's brother, Padillistas like Dario Tabares and Urbano Lavín, and even, it was rumored, the zapatista colonel Amelio Robles, notorious for both his military skill and transgender identity.[78] And finally there were, as in the padillista risings, suspicions, sedulously encouraged by Ojeda, of state government complicity.[79] Once again the movement was centered on Castrejón's patria chica, the familial stomping grounds, involving even a relative of the zone commander, and once again the leaders escaped arrest; only five foot soldiers were ever taken, and the general ordered his subordinate officers not to disarm peasants.[80] There was no apparent link between Leyva Mancilla and the rebels; yet as governor and a close ally of Castrejón he was, inevitably, tainted by association.[81]

Two risings in a year and no heads to show for them was a feeble record for Leyva Mancilla, especially in the light of Alemán's initial promise as a "new broom."[82] The president had fired four governors, those of Chiapas, Oaxaca, Jalisco, and Tamaulipas, in the first four months of 1947; this was nearly as many as Avila Camacho had fired in his entire six years.[83] That the most common cause for dismissal was state violence would not have reassured the governor of Guerrero, for letters and telegrams continued filling the in trays of the Presidency and Gobernación with reports of the beatings and killings carried out by the state government's men. In the Abasolo district petty government officials murdered several agraristas and helped provoke a popular rising that killed the Leyvista mayor of Igualapa.[84] And reports of local politicians' violence were not confined to the coasts. Sometimes the accusations stretched beyond the local level: the state deputy Nicolás Wences García, a close ally of the governor, was accused of dragging a *señorita* behind his horse, of seizing ejidatarios' parcels, and of orchestrating multiple killings in and around Coyuca de Catalán.[85] The Venturas of Copala, Leyva Mancilla's clients—his wife's nephews—prevented ejidatarios from working their lands and continued killing their opponents, who included the Agriculture Department engineer's guides and two boys gathering turtle eggs.[86] Castrejón was widely accused of indiscriminately arming petty caciques across the state; Leyva Mancilla of not just tolerating but creating conflicts such as the Yextla sawmill dispute. Here his government interrupted negotiations between a logging company and an ejido in order to claim jurisdiction over the forests in question and sell the rights, cutting out the ejidatarios and giving rise to armed clashes between peasants from fifteen communities and the loggers.[87] The net result was a state that relied heavily on the military and that had, if anything, grown less stable under Leyva Mancilla. It was symbolic that a year after the Balsas rebellion eleven died in fighting between soldiers and alleged bandits near Acapulco, while, in an apparently unrelated incident, veterans of that rebellion shot up the Balsas train.[88]

Alemán was accordingly receptive to requests such as that of the ejidatarios who asked him "to remove this yoke that is killing us and doing away with the best of our state, which is this Government which General Baltasar Leyva Mancilla directs."[89] In May 1948 the national president of the Liga asked Alemán to investigate the continuing lack of constitutional guarantees and "political gangsterism" in eleven municipios across Guerrero.[90] The Secretaría de la Defensa Nacional, worried by the volume of complaints against Castrejón, had replaced him in March with General Miguel Z. Martínez, so the main target of the investigation would be the governor.[91] (And Martínez himself had some experience in investigation, having been inspector general of the Mexico City police when Alemán was interior minister.)[92] Such statewide investigations were veiled warnings; they had preceded the overthrows of Governors López, Guevara, and Berber.[93] In June three Gobernación agents toured the major towns and the coasts. Their reports were not definitive; they did not directly link Leyva Mancilla to sins of commission, whether in terms of corruption or political violence. They were, however, a long catalogue of sins of omission. There were numerous accusations of corruption. The state treasury officials had base reputations: the tax collectors for Chilapa and for Guerrero, respectively, had been dismissed and arrested for sizeable fraud. Their boss, the state treasurer Jesús Martínez, had come to his job poor and now owned a fleet of trucks and a series of mezcal distilleries. In Iguala the tax collector (a nephew of the governor) threatened tax increases for those who did not patronize his petrol station. When an agrarian bureaucrat came to investigate, the state police murdered him, riddling his truck with bullets. Insecurity in the north and on the coasts was attributed to Leyva Mancilla's inaction or even support for the violent: arms permits and guns had been freely distributed, the civil authorities connived at the work of pistoleros, many of whom worked in the police, and the governor's allies in San Marcos had even attacked and killed federal troops. The governor was seen at best as well meaning but weak, controlled by a dishonest camarilla; at worst, as in the north and la Montaña, he was personally blamed by all classes for the state's problems.[94]

Election Rigging and Political Endurance

The threat from Mexico City left Leyva Mancilla facing an interesting decision. Guerrero's ayuntamientos for 1949 and 1950 would be elected in December 1948, and as they would oversee the next gubernatorial campaign it was in his interest to return to the politics of the carro completo, packing local government with Leyvistas in order to increase his influence in the succession. Yet to do so would generate violent and controversial elections, after which the losers would inevitably protest to the federal government. In his favor he was aware of Alemán's antipathy toward his main rival, Ojeda, and of the president's national weakness in the troubled autumn of 1948. An obstinate man, he seems to have weighed the options and decided to go ahead and exclude the agraristas. It was long rumored that the municipal elections would install only his clients, a proposition opposed by state leaders including Castrejón, Ruffo Figueroa, Catalán Calvo, and Ojeda.[95] Preparations began early, as did protests: at an early August meeting with the secretary-general of the PRI, General Sánchez Taboada, Ojeda was told that forty-five thousand guerrerense peasants did not need and could not have PRI credentials.[96] For the October 10 PRI primaries electoral registers went unpublished, the whereabouts of voting booths unpublicized, and in over twenty municipios ojedista slates were denied the registration they needed to compete.[97]

Agraristas were excluded from both the PRI municipal committees and the resulting slates. It was a repeat of the 1944 shutout from local government: in Acapulco over twenty ejidos were without a single representative on the PRI slate; in Huitzuco the PRI selected two Sinarquistas and no agraristas.[98] As the December 5 elections approached a violently repressive campaign against the Ojedistas—who had decided to compete with the PRI in the *constitucionales,* the constitutional elections, as an undeclared opposition party—took shape. In municipios including Ajuchitlán, Atoyac, Copala, and Teloloapan Ojedistas were jailed; in others, including Tepecoacuilco and Arcelia, they were killed.[99] Numerous complaints from the ejidos of the Costa Grande detailed a series of military and paramilitary raids in November and December that killed peasants, including several ejidal commissioners, and interrupted the harvest.[100] The elections were marked by apathy and low turnout in the towns and dissuaded, disqualified, or ignored voters in the countryside; the transfer of power was "a day," *La Verdad de Acapulco* remarked dismissively, "of authentic Mexican democracy."[101]

The Ojedistas did not accept the results, and by late December the police and army were being reinforced in the contested municipios, which included most of the state's cities.[102] When the ayuntamientos were handed over on January 1 the Ojedistas formed parallel, "legitimate" local governments in about a quarter of Guerrero's municipios, heavily concentrated in the north of the state.[103] Most of these were in private homes; in Ajuchitlán, however, an armed crowd seized the town hall, killed one of the councilors, and settled in for a siege.[104] Gobernación had been steadily losing patience with the governor during the electoral period, and by the end of the first week of January he felt on the brink of disaster, close to joining the governors of Guanajuato and Chiapas in being fired for electoral violence.[105] So he told his local allies to proceed with "extreme tact and serenity" and requested Gobernación arbitration in the worst-hit places.[106] Federal inspectors accordingly visited Ajuchitlán, Apaxtla, Cutzamala, Iguala, Teloloapan, and Tepecoacuilco, the Ojedistas in most cases retiring peacefully from town halls, at times agreeing that a *consejo municipal* would replace the unwanted ayuntamiento.[107] There was an old tradition of violence surrounding transfers of municipal power, and indeed two of the candidates for Taxco in 1948 had previously taken municipal governments by assault.[108] Such attacks could be straightforward grabs for local power, but they could also be convoluted games in which victory involved demonstrating a governor's basic inability to control his territory. Such was the case in the 1948 municipal elections: the sheer scale of protests and Leyva Mancilla's need to call in Gobernación constituted a distinct political defeat. Nabor Ojeda (as was his wont) called for a federal investigation and the governor's arrest.[109] Gobernación concluded that the state government was weak, the PRI severely divided, and the opposition profiting.[110] Even Chilpancingo—Leyva Mancilla's stronghold—was unreliable, the local Partido de Acción Nacional (PAN) having gained significant strength.[111]

Against this turbulent background the president's tour in late February and early March 1949 assumed unusual import. Such royal processions were epoch-making events for villagers and townsmen, once-in-a-generation opportunities to request or protest in the presence of a man culturally constructed, with great effort, as all-powerful and paternally *simpático*. For presidents, intensive touring had been since Cárdenas's time both a public relations exercise and a useful way to increase a sometimes-patchy presidential cognitive capacity. Leyva Mancilla took this ritualized inspection seriously, appropriating 100,000 pesos from the budget to prepare the state and issuing instructions to prevent ojedista demonstrators from coming into contact with Alemán's motorcade.[112] Despite his efforts, however, the tour was a disaster, and far from seeing a state enjoying order, development, and unity, the official alemanista virtues, the president was confronted with Guerrero bronco. On February 21, just days before he arrived, the car of the union leader and state deputy Elpidio Rosales went off the road and into a gulley outside Acapulco. All of the passengers escaped unhurt bar Rosales, who was found with no serious injury besides a crushed skull. The Acapulco public prosecutor thought it was murder, but his investigation was quickly stopped. Public opinion and the Rosales family made their own judgment, though, finding the culprit in the dead man's rival union boss and federal candidate for Acapulco, Alfredo Córdoba Lara.[113] He was the governor's main ally in Guerrero; he had made Leyva Mancilla's candidacy; and Leyva Mancilla was now trying to repay him with the lucrative deputyship for Acapulco. Any hope that Alemán might pass through Acapulco ignorant of events was undone by Rosales's widow, who cornered the president and accused Córdoba Lara of murder.[114] When Alemán went on to tour the Costa Grande he was stopped by ejidatarios in Tecpan shouting slogans against General Martínez, and lectured by the maestro rural Miguel Aroche Parra on regional caciquismo and military violence.[115] The CNC launched an investigation into Martínez, whose botched attempt to arrest Aroche Parra only generated further metropolitan press coverage. Peasants set off on a protest caravan to Mexico City; the DFS's man in Chilpancingo filed a series of hostile reports, and so did the press, who by the end of the month were reporting Leyva Mancilla's imminent departure.[116]

Yet he didn't go, seeing out his term in office—one of a mere handful of guerrerense governors to do so—and doing so with some credit. Part of his turnaround was the lack of any evident unifying replacement. Part of it was sheer luck; as the president oversaw a major devaluation in the summer of 1948 he was too weak to risk firing any governors at all, much less military ones. And part was judgment, in particular Leyva Mancilla's adept balancing of technocracy, political reform, public relations, and corruption.

Despite his tense relations with Alemán, Leyva Mancilla had a certain affinity with the president. Both spoke of progress, modernization, and the tacit conservatism of "the constructive revolutionary movement." Leyva Mancilla realized that any of that construction would require major tax reform, lecturing his legislature in his first report that "the transformation of the idea of the State, the astonishing growth in its functions and the unlimited panorama of public services" were all impossible without taxpayers and a competent treasury, neither of which had marked Guerrero's history to date.[117] State governments across Mexico shared this problem and met with substantial resistance in addressing it: between 1940 and 1955 there were major tax protests in at least fourteen cities. Many governors retreated, but Leyva Mancilla was not among them. While foreswearing neither brown envelopes nor the community labor of *faenas* (supposedly voluntary, in reality often forced) he did fire his corrupt state treasurer, commission an urban cadastral survey to increase property taxes in the towns and cities, chase up the historically ineffectual rural taxmen, and push through unpopular but lucrative tax increases, such as those on alcohol.[118] He met with considerable resistance but also, in relative terms, considerable success: he increased the state's budget by 240 percent, far outperforming his fellow technocrat Adolfo Ruiz Cortines in Veracruz, and even the fast-growing federal budget.[119]

The new revenues were spent on the tools of the state, communications, electrification, irrigation, education, hospitals, and public health. There were more bureaucrats, policemen—the key mounted police grew from seven to eleven detachments—and technocrats such as Moisés de la Peña, who formulated an exhaustive economic survey, and Alejandro Paucic with his map and archive. Twenty-two percent of the budget went to public works and economic development, funding projects that included irrigation systems for over ten thousand hectares of land on the Costa Grande, the completion of the Cotolipa hydroelectric plant, regional air strips, twelve hundred kilometers of feeder roads, and a major upgrade of the road between Iguala and Ciudad Altamirano. Electric streetlights replaced gas lamps, and electric lightbulbs paraffin lanterns; hundreds of kilometers of telephone lines stretched into regions of the state ignored since the Porfiriato; road workers were backed by bulldozers. The state cofunded hospitals in Acapulco, Chilapa, Chilpancingo, Ometepec,

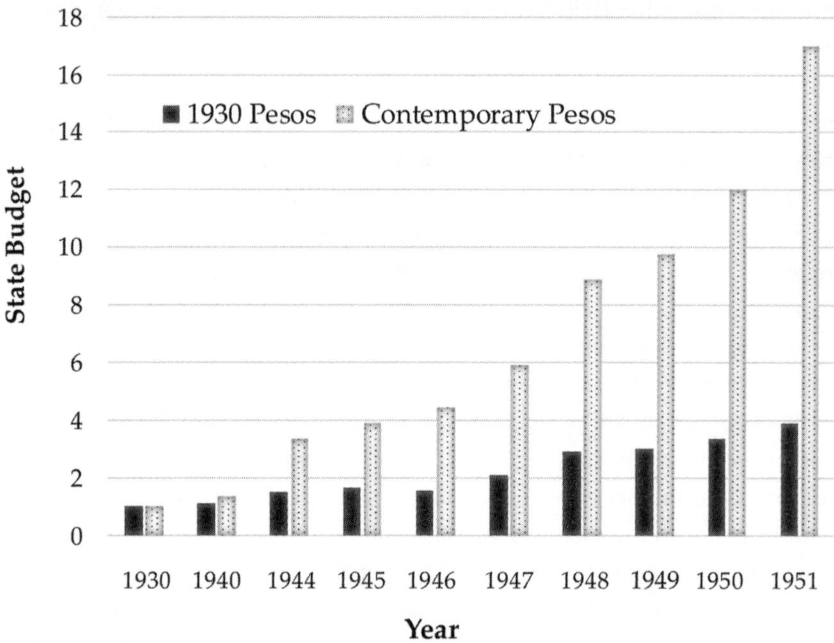

Guerrero's budget, 1930–51, in millions of contemporary and 1930 pesos. Data from governors' reports; De la Peña, *Guerrero Económico,* 2:599–622; deflated using wholesale price index Mexico City 1886–1978, INEGI Estadísticas Históricas CD-ROM.

and Tlapa, and allied with the Dirección de Cooperación Interamericana de Salubridad Pública to destroy the mosquitoes that made malaria one of the main killers from the coasts to the highlands. The state's education department oversaw the doubling of schools and the tripling of maestros. Leyva Mancilla even claimed record-breaking land grants, overseeing—so the statistics said—the distribution of half a million hectares.[120] All amounted to a track record of development that, for all its flaws, was indeed revolutionary; and the governor made sure that the governed—and perhaps more important, the politicians in both municipios and Mexico City—knew all about it with the new official newspaper that he printed at the new government printworks.[121]

Leyva Mancilla was also to some extent a political reformer. In formal terms he commissioned a rewrite of the state constitution and electoral law, eliminating some striking anomalies.[122] Informally he followed broader elite trends in political violence, seemingly eschewing it himself while covering up that of his friends, such as Córdoba Lara (held responsible for various murders, including that of Rosales) and family, such as his son Francisco (who was widely believed to have killed the panista lawyer Ricardo Sámano).[123] After his initial intransigence he became more politically adept as his term developed, and had the nous to defer to the center's selection of congressmen in the 1949 elections. Many of the leading members of Leyva Mancilla's camarilla, among them Alfredo Córdoba Lara, Leopoldo Ortega Lozano, Alejandro Castañón, José Ventura Neri, Benigno Leyva Neri, Leopoldo Castro García, and Dario Arrieta, sought congressional seats; the party nominated none of them, preferring a collection of veteran politicians. Only one, Nicolás Wences García, was a Leyvista, and he was balanced by the inclusion of the secretary-general of the Liga, Rafael Jaimes Silva, as *suplente*—understudy, a common steppingstone for career advancement—for Acapulco.[124] For Leyva Mancilla to accept these decisions, which bypassed the traditional bartering of seats between federal and state governments, was to make a public demonstration of submission. He did so, beating a tactical retreat; in PRIspeak, he got in line.

Less publicly acknowledgeable, Leyva Mancilla also provided guarantees for big business, much of which was owned by politicians, and for the graft that business had made possible. Rubén Figueroa, installed as federal deputy in 1940, got a trucking concession on the Mexico City–Acapulco route; Adrián Castrejón's construction company won a 1½-million-peso contract to build the biggest irrigation project on the Costa Grande, one of whose dams watered one of his orchards.[125] The greatest opportunities lay in Acapulco, where the postwar influx of visitors fueled an extraordinary boom; as early as 1947 there were some seventy hotels with a capitalization of over 200 million pesos.[126] Farsighted politicians had seen it coming and formed consortia to dispossess ejidatarios and seize state lands. It sometimes made for strange bedfellows: according to Juan Andreu Almazán—an unreliable source, but in this case telling a story that does him no favor—he had teamed up with ex–Secretary of War Joaquín Amaro, ex-President Pascual Ortiz Rubio, Luis Montes de Oca, at the time the director of the Banco de México, and Lázaro Cárdenas to illegally acquire beachfront communal lands and develop them for tourism.[127] Maximino Avila Camacho privatized the island that lay between the beaches of Caleta and Caletilla (and almost wholly covered it with his mansion). Less than six weeks into his presidency Miguel Alemán expropriated the waterfront lands of the ejidos El Jardín and Garita de Juárez; he remained heavily involved in the port's development, visiting frequently and instructing the dictatorial head of the Material Improvements Junta, Melchor Perusquía, as to expropriations.[128] Manuel Suárez, the president's favorite contractor, ended up building houses and a golf course on the lands of the Icacos ejido.[129] These were not the only victims; some fourteen ejidos lost land around the bay to the new hoteliers, who as "workers' representatives" took over the CTM convention in 1948.[130] Córdoba Lara, their leader, became an important businessman and real estate owner in Acapulco, as did Leyva Mancilla himself. Among outside investors, the winners were some of the president's closest associates and the Alemán family itself. By the 1950s he and relatives such as his uncle General Juan Valdés owned some of the best real estate in Acapulco.[131] Luxury housing in Acapulco was not just an investment but also a tool for further advancement: in just two months at the end of his sexenio Alemán hosted executives from, among others, Anaconda Copper, Industrial Rayon Corp, Monsanto, B.F. Goodrich, Bank of America, and Sears Roebuck.[132] Whatever the ebb and flow of their political relationship, the president and the governor sustained a profitable business relationship.

Leyva Mancilla did not list such deals among his achievements. When asked to sum up his time in office the governor preferred instead to fall back on his contribution to Mexican nationalism, namely, the 1949 disinterment of Cuauhtémoc, the last Mexica emperor. It was, admittedly, something out of the usual run of bad statuary and worse rhetoric; told of a village tradition that placed Cuauhtémoc beneath the parish church of Ixcateopan—a small municipio near the epicenter of the padillista risings—Leyva Mancilla pushed past the scholarly objections of the Instituto Nacional de Antropología e Historia (INAH) and had the church excavated at speed. To scholarly wonder there was actually a tomb there, and from the pages of Octavio Paz to the tabloids the discovery was hailed as a landmark in Mexican history. The state legislature awarded Leyva Mancilla a special medal commemorating the "more than usual patriotism" and "unlimited aid" that he had given in drumming up funds, recruiting a suitable archaeologist—the *indigenista* Eulalia Guzmán—and ordering the dig.[133] When the tomb was opened he obtained national prominence overnight. When INAH declared it a fraud he became even more prominent in his aggressive defense of the bones' authenticity. In Guerrero he ordered ceremonies, produced commemorative books, and commissioned murals; in Mexico City he importuned politicians and dispatched vitriolic letters to the national press.[134] Nationalist ritual enabled Leyva Mancilla to play statesman and to cultivate a domestic popularity he had never before had. By March 1950 Gobernación were reporting that he would actually be missed and that—in something of a dramatic reversal of sentiment—the "popular masses . . . wish [the new governor] might have the qualities of the departing governor, whose work they recognize as meritorious."[135]

So, by this stage, did Los Pinos. Alemán invited him to join the presidential tour of the southeast, promoted him and made him Oficial Mayor of the Secretaría de la Defensa Nacional.[136] Leyva Mancilla was allowed to exert marked influence over the succession and subsequent regional politics: he was replaced by his private secretary, Alejandro Gómez Maganda, while another of his secretaries, Leopoldo Castro García, took over the state's PRI, and Leyvistas took up the portfolios of Gobernación, Hacienda, and the Procuradoría. By 1954 Leyva Mancilla was being described as something like a caudillo: "he will," the relevant letter fretted, "convert the state of Guerrero into a private political estate, become owner boss and lord; he is arming his devoted followers, pulling strings in the principal places of the state, that he might continue to rule in a very hushed way."[137] This was impossible; the Figueroa and Alemán families were too powerful for Guerrero to be a one-man show. After a decade out of state Leyva Mancilla did, however, return to Guerrero politics in the 1960s, heading the state PRI, representing the state as senator, and maneuvering a longtime client, Caritino Maldonado, into the governor's palace. Backstage he remained central to regional politics until his death, becoming, as one tribute put it, "the true patriarch of guerrerense politicians."[138] Yet Leyva Mancilla was a patriarch who had learned the necessity of being at times also a satrap, bending to the center's imperatives and giving them at least some modernizing substance.

Centralization and Demobilization: The Lessons of the 1940s

Baltasar Leyva Mancilla was not the only guerrerense to learn where the boundaries of the possible lay in 1940s politics. The 1945 gubernatorial election had, for all its messiness, suggested the inevitability of centralized dominant party rule; the 1950 election seemed to confirm it. All four precandidates had made their careers in the federal bureaucracy or the military; three of them had spent most of their lives in Mexico City, and none of them had substantial connections to the world of popular politics. Donato Miranda Fonseca had trained as a lawyer and worked as a federal bureaucrat and judge before winning election to congress and subsequently the senate. Raúl Caballero Aburto was a hitherto unpolitical career military officer from Ometepec who taught cavalry command at the Escuela Superior de Guerra. Ruffo Figueroa—nephew of Andrés Figueroa, Avila Camacho's defense secretary—was a career bureaucrat who had been secretary-general of the Federación de Sindicatos de los Trabajadores al Servicio del Estado, the powerful national bureaucrats' union, before being elected first deputy and then senator. Finally, Alejandro Gómez Maganda was a dilettante. He had dropped out of both the Escuela Normal de Maestros or the Escuela Vocacional del Colegio Militar, he had been fired from bureaucratic and diplomatic jobs, and his election as mayor of Acapulco had been nullified. He was a bad writer into the bargain and, Gobernación noted pruriently, "very keen on alcohol and sex," but he was also a friend of both Alemán and Cárdenas.[139] There was no agrarista candidate: Guerrero's peasantry was deeply divided, Nabor Ojeda was discouraged at an early stage, and his followers' attempted campaign was notably half-hearted.[140] The candidates were a new political generation, with little or no experience of the armed revolution but a firm grasp of the increasingly centralized and bureaucratic paths to power.

The anatomy of the campaign was revealing. Donato Miranda Fonseca was an early front-runner in the undeclared competition, backed in rumor by an imposing coalition of governor, state bureaucracy, the CTM, CNC, and the Confederación Nacional de Organizaciones Populares (CNOP), the catchall grouping for anyone who was neither peasant nor worker.[141] Compared to the six months of intense, disorganized, and violent campaigning of 1944, the succession of 1950 was compressed and rigorously controlled. Telegram campaigns in favor of Ojeda and Figueroa in January failed to launch an open campaign season. The party delayed the *convocatoria,* the party's call for candidates, far past the expected date; in late April, when the PRI had chosen candidates for the eleven other gubernatorial contests for 1950, the Regional Committee was instructing municipal cadres to "insist to our campesinos and the other sectors of this organism by all means you possess that they dampen all agitation of a political nature that they might attempt to develop in your municipio and wait until the Central Executive Committee of our Party issues the convocatoria that indicates the lines that we shall have to follow."[142]

Various organizations and leaders publicly announced that they would accept the center's choice of governor. The federal bureaucrats, in March, awaited orders from their national organization; Iguala's health and road workers stated in April that they "would not adopt any political position" until otherwise instructed; the Liga called for peasant unity and discipline in the PRI; Córdoba Lara's CTM agreed in their Acapulco congress to "cede to the National Executive Committee the power of determining the organization's political stance."[143] The trappings of a competitive election—tours, speeches, advertising, and conventions—were entirely absent. The candidates, adroitly kept anxious by recurrent rumors of a *tapado,* a kept-under-wraps alternative to any of the established contenders, confined themselves to occasional (and deniable) attempts by their allies to blacken their opponents' reputations.[144] The guerrerense political classes waited impatiently for the governor to return from Mexico City with "the resolution of the political case." There had still been no convocatoria at the end of June, when—revealingly enough, in Mexico City—Leyva Mancilla summoned Miranda Fonseca, Figueroa, and Gómez Maganda "to inform them that the President of the Republic had resolved the politico-electoral case of Guerrero," and that Gómez Maganda would be the next governor.[145]

This was the most unpopular choice available. Despite professing socialism, Gómez Maganda was loathed by the agraristas, who held him responsible for various political killings during the Guevara campaign.[146] Neither the CTM nor the CNC backed him.[147] Ex-governor Catalán Calvo described him with classical flourish as "an unhealthy mind in an unhealthy body"; the Sociedad Guerrerense del DF, a club that gathered the state's elite diaspora, cabled Alemán to plead that he back another person.[148] But presidential decisions were not subject to appeal. Castrejón, another opponent, was told by Leyva Mancilla over the phone that "it was expected of him, as a revolutionary and a soldier, that he obey in a disciplined fashion the presidential decision." The presidential appointment was not even an open secret: it was published on June 27 in the government newspaper, the *Diario de Guerrero*.[149] The *cargada*, the stampede of politicians to endorse the chosen one, followed immediately. Figueroa and Miranda Fonseca offered their support in the same meeting where they discovered they had lost; the secretaries of the Liga and the CTM signaled their immediate agreement; on June 28 the local deputies set off to declare their allegiance to Gómez Maganda in Mexico City, four days before the convocatoria was even issued. A lengthy round of politically charged meals ensued: breakfast with Castrejón on June 30, a "Unity Banquet" on July 5, and the Acapulco Hotel Owners' Association banquet on July 10.[150] Underneath such froth lay a greatly strengthened ritual imperative to publicly demonstrate unconditional obedience and unity. It was obeyed, after the merest flicker of resistance from Caballero's followers, across the board. Nabor Ojeda made the underlying compact unusually explicit in a series of letters to Alemán and Sánchez Taboada. As he had promised the president, he wrote, "I and my friends and organizations left you in complete liberty that you might, as a friend and our Jefe, decide whatever you felt pertinent." He offered to meet ceremonially with Gómez Maganda, and ordered his followers to turn out for his rallies. In return he asked that "my friends and organizations be taken into account in your Government and that of our state."[151] Under the new, closely choreographed conditions the party conventions were a brief formality; by the end of July Gómez Maganda had been nominated by all sectors, and on December 3 he was duly elected unopposed.

Alejandro Gómez Maganda's election demonstrated the substantial increase in presidential power that Alemán had achieved. The 1952 presidential election gave more signs of central control: while Henriquismo in Guerrero attracted a strange coalition of outs—led by ex-Governor Berber and including his old enemies Nabor Ojeda and María de la O—the leadership disintegrated in early 1952 and utterly failed to challenge the PRI.[152] Yet the little that Gómez Maganda served of his sexenio qualified that centralization as largely electoral. Any deep political centralization would involve presidential control of the everyday actions of regional politicians. But despite the repeated warnings of Ruiz Cortines, Guerrero under Gómez Maganda adopted once more the appearance of a banana (or, more accurately, copra and tourist) republic.[153] Progressive taxation policies were replaced by governmental pilfering, administered by the same Jesús Martínez whom Leyva Mancilla had jailed for corruption. In Acapulco hotel owners were exempted from property taxes for ten years while residents were charged extraordinary taxes for everyday services such as water, electricity, and paving. Gómez Maganda, frequently absent from the state, publicly lied about his administrative achievements, inventing nonexistent agrarian reforms while occupying the legislature's time with absurdist measures such as the declaration of his wife a "favorite daughter" of the state.[154]

Most damaging of all, what little progress Leyva Mancilla's government had made toward obtaining a legitimate monopoly of violence was rapidly reversed. The early months of the Gómez Maganda government saw two notable political assassinations, the killings of the mayor of San Jerónimo and the peasant leader Samuel Diego in a restaurant next to Acapulco's army barracks.[155] By mid-1952 a violent crime wave gripped Acapulco: yet while Gobernación asked Gómez Maganda to enforce gun control (and the DFS sent five agents to Acapulco alone) he authorized the opening of one of Mexico's only gun shops. The countryside was no quieter, with numerous reports in the Mexico City press of cattle rustling and murders such as the May 1953 assassination of Crispín Ocampo and the July 1953 attack on the La Poza ejido which killed four. The governor considered draconian responses such as the deportation of felons to the Islas Marías penal colony and the death penalty; simultaneously, however, he was accused of providing professional hitmen such as El Patotas ("Big Foot") and El Chante ("The House") with police badges.[156] On May 21, 1954, Ruiz Cortines broke both federal and state constitutions by petitioning congress for the governor's dismissal and personally appointing his successor.[157] It was, all in all, a convincing demonstration of the fragility of administrative modernization, of the highly personalist nature of regional government, and of the embryonic quality of the state.

And yet there were, for all that, two salient changes. The first was the demilitarization, partial but unmistakable, of the very top of state politics. The end of the 1940s saw the end of fierce competition between military and civilian authorities. This trend was, perhaps, related to the simultaneous and more marked phenomenon of popular demobilization. Elections still had assorted functions, but by the end of the 1940s competitively selecting popular representatives was not often one of them. Public opinion was quite clear on this; as a Gobernación inspector reported in 1949, "Everybody states that when the electoral struggle begins they will follow the instruction whatever it be, as a very clear disillusionment holds sway among the masses regarding the free competition of political parties across the Republic. Nobody wants to risk themselves in the knowledge that in the long term the reprisals of the winner are inevitable and that they might even have to leave the state."[158]

Little was left to chance, however, and traditional methods of controlling an already feeble opposition continued. In Xochihuehuetlán villagers took Ruiz Cortines at his inaugural word regarding political liberties and elected a panista ayuntamiento only to find, two weeks after taking office, that an army platoon had come to arrest them en masse.[159] Such blunt measures were complemented by new, legislative obstacles to daily formal opposition; one of Gómez Maganda's first laws authorized the police to prevent unlicensed political demonstrations and increased the budget for such activities.[160] Most noteworthy of all was the 1950 PRI national congress's rubber-stamping of the hierarchy's decision to change the party statutes and end primary elections.[161] These had been, as Ojeda once told the president, the real elections, sites of sometimes genuine mass political competition under the umbrella of the PRI.[162] With their passing went open—as opposed to enduring backstage—electoral opposition for a generation.

This demobilization was more than merely electoral; it was a deeper, everyday process that reached to the bottom of (onetime) grassroots organizations such as unions, ejidos, and the Liga. As early as the first half of the 1940s there were, Bustamante has found, "clear signals of disenchantment" among agraristas in Tierra Caliente. This was rooted, in part, in the satisfaction of some demands (such as basic land reform) and the perceived improbability of satisfying others (such as further land reform). It was also rooted in the strategic murders of their leaders, whether union bosses like Elpidio Rosales, agraristas like Francisco Hernández Solís, or Panistas like Ricardo Sámano. Surviving popular leaders, meanwhile, often generated disillusionment as they dug themselves into sinecures. As early as 1942 the Liga identified ejidal caciquismo as an emerging problem, as presidents of comisariados ejidales doggedly stayed in their posts after their terms ended.[163] In Ajuchitlán Gustavo Torres fixed the elections and led the ejido ("a Russian concentration camp") for six consecutive years; in Atoyac Crispín Ocampo was treasurer, secretary-general, and president of Corral Falso for at least thirteen years.[164] In extreme cases ejidos could be administered by agraristas' enemies, as in San Jerónimo, where the president of the comisariado ejidal in 1946 was Nicolás Torreblanca, a prominent and violent landowner.[165] At a state level, the late 1940s saw the co-option of once-combative organizations into the party mainstream. The Liga lost its independence in 1945, when the leadership came under the governor's control, and by 1950, far from promoting agrarista politicians, it was actively undermining Nabor Ojeda.[166] The fractious and divided union movement lost its principal independent when Rosales was killed, and came increasingly under the control of Córdoba Lara, who remained secretary-general of the CTM until his death in 1962.[167] Bussed-in rent-a-crowds grew across the period: Gómez Maganda claimed an audience of ten thousand for a rally in Chilapa.[168] Authentic mobilization, however, took place increasingly outside the sites of formal politics: in resource conflicts, "weapons of the weak" resistance, and, decades later, in urban protests and guerrilla movements.

In contrast to the instability and lack of definition of postrevolutionary Guerrero, the years between 1945 and 1954 saw the solidification of the economic and political structures that prevailed for much of the rest of the century. The state economy was profoundly transformed by the Acapulco boom: in the five years from 1947 to 1952 the state budget, a rough indicator of wealth, climbed from twenty-first to twelfth place in the national rankings.[169] The new riches combined with the high costs of extensive land tenure to attract the more prescient members of the elite toward tourism and the marketing of harvests rather than their production. The Fernández family moved from agribusiness into Acapulco real estate and tourism, while Nicolás Torreblanca struggled to control the copra harvest of the Costa Grande.[170] A parallel shift occurred in politics as old career paths through the military or popular organizations grew obsolete before the encroachment of the Mexico City bureaucracy. At a state level, it was emblematic that the Figueroa family fortunes should be restored by Ruffo, a lifelong bureaucrat; at a municipal level, an entire generation of the Aguirres of Ometepec, powerful ranchers since the mid-nineteenth century, chose bureaucratic careers and were eventually repaid with a governorship.[171] This was another facet of the broad process of centralization of the later 1940s, when the president and party apparatchiks achieved unprecedented levels of control over politics in Guerrero. Even in

1952, as Henriquismo threatened elsewhere, a DFS man could report that "in this state the political situation is completely dominated by the PRI," while the DGIPS predicted "no electoral problem" in the presidential contest; claims that earlier agents could never have made.[172]

Within the state, political mobility decreased and enduring hierarchies formed. In villages the new ruling classes drew from a blend of Porfirian survivals, revolutionary arrivals and a rural technocracy of maestros, small-town lawyers, and bureaucrats. At a regional level two highly influential groups coalesced, centered on Leyva Mancilla's camarilla and a rehabilitated Figueroa family, competing for control of the levers of an increasingly sophisticated and ambitious governmental machine. The army remained essential to rural systems of domination, but their marked political autonomy had declined and Castrejón, the state's last great military cacique, died in 1954 after his presidential hopes proved nonstarters.[173] The president chose impressively technocratic senators, those key checks on regional politicians, for the 1952–58 session: Emigdio Martínez Adame, a lawyer, experienced bureaucrat, and economist, and Alfonso G. Alarcón, a former interim governor, doctor, and noted academic.[174] Most important of all, a politically radical peasantry was convincingly defeated. Nabor Ojeda's 1944 campaign was the last agrarista claim to the governorship, and his majority was overcome by a numerically slight but broad elite coalition backed by the president. There were no peasant politicians in the 1950 election, and while campesinos firmly disliked both front-runners the new political reality was barely protested.[175] The unnecessarily high costs of completely excluding peasants had been, however, firmly demonstrated in the first four turbulent years of Leyva Mancilla's governorship, and the 1949 and 1952 federal elections redistributed some compensatory congressional seats. The governor also intensified agrarian reform, redistributing five hundred thousand hectares among sixteen thousand peasants; this was more than 10 percent of the national total for the sexenio, even if most of the land given away was of marginal quality.[176] Nabor Ojeda obtained a *colonia militar*—the shady land grant for soldiers present or past, a classic payoff for ambitious generals and regional caciques—while his son went on to head the state's CNC.[177] The political history of the Alemán years in Guerrero handed out uneven lessons in the costs and benefits of violence: while power brokers were reminded of the benefits of consent, peasants were shown the costs of force. A certain stability ensued, a dynamic equilibrium of coercion and conciliation that was notable even if ephemeral.

4 • Party, Peace, and Caciquismo

The Nationalization of State Politics

In Veracruz, politics was bigger business than in the rest of provincial Mexico. There were more politicians, for starters, than in other states; 198 municipios meant about three times as many elected positions were up for grabs in Veracruz as in Guerrero. There were more voters, and more organization too; the contenders for mayor in Orizaba drew union-marshaled crowds of four or five thousand to their rallies, twice as many as gubernatorial candidates could muster in Guerrero.[1] The leading rural caciques had a similarly impressive *poder convocatorio,* the ability to raise a crowd: Rafael Cornejo Armenta, the pistolero who killed would-be governor Manlio Fabio Altamirano, reportedly brought five thousand men down to the port for one presidential campaign stop.[2] Moreover, Veracruz's cities and even the larger market towns were more creditworthy than entire states. The Banco Hipotecario Urbano y de Obras Públicas lent Orizaba 1.1 million pesos in 1945, and San Andrés Tuxtla 2 million in 1946; both sums were greater than the credit Governor Leyva Mancilla managed to wheedle for all of Guerrero in 1947.[3] Even without the fragmentation of politics of the mid-1930s the size and complexity of this system would have favored pluralism. Unlike in Guerrero, however, the fragmentation of authority in Veracruz was clearly a federal goal, reflecting not just regional infighting but also national politicians' aspirations to checks and balances. Inside the state four networks fought vigorously for local and regional dominance, namely, the peasant leagues; the unions; the conservative alliances of soldiers, landowners, and pistoleros; and, interwoven with all three, the so-called professional politicians who manned the electoral and bureaucratic apparatus of the state. The Mexico City elites' main aim was to ensure that no single professional politician stitched together enough of these groups to recapture the autonomy and power of the Tejeda years.

A 1945 letter from the Liga Nacional Campesina Ursulo Galván (LNCUG) illustrates how well divide and rule worked. The Ursulo Galván was historically the most militant and independent-minded of the two main peasant leagues, and its leaders were proposing a new party for the upcoming presidential election, the Partido Nacional Campesino Independiente. How independent that party might be was clear in their requests for the PRI candidate's permission to go ahead. "We will not," the would-be founders promised, "do anything about this before speaking with Licenciado Alemán."[4] The other agrarian organization, the CNC-affiliated Liga, was already campaigning for Alemán, who as governor had seized control of their leadership. Such clientelist loyalty didn't pay off: by 1945 the Liga was without any seats in the state congress.[5] At a municipal level long-established popular gains were slipping away, even in the heartlands of peasant militancy, as the bloody attrition of the 1930s continued. Between 1940 and 1945 gunmen sent by Manuel Parra's lieutenant Crispín Aguilar killed scores of local peasant politicians.[6] Regional leaders who might have organized resistance were likewise killed: Parra's men shot the federal deputies Salvador González and Carolino Anaya in 1942 and 1943, respectively.[7] And peasant losses in the period went beyond leaders and political posts. Land grants under Governor Cerdán were a quarter of those under Tejeda, and the new property rights often proved insecure.[8] In the port hinterlands the violent loss of municipal power was followed by cattlemen's repossession of ejidal pastureland.[9] It was, a Gobernación agent reported, a time of anarchy and an "absolute lack of constitutional rights" in the countryside.[10] In the Sierra Madre and the Huasteca peasants reacted by signing up with sinarquista recruiters, who targeted ejidatarios, indigenous peasants, and smallholders.[11] Across the rest of the state most, however, chose to wait out the storm.[12]

For workers too the early 1940s was a time of division. Unionized labor was a powerful, geographically concentrated political resource: in Orizaba the CROM and the CTM controlled some ten thousand workers, while in Veracruz the dockworkers alone numbered three thousand. The CTM's regional incarnation, the Federación de Trabajadores de Veracruz, had begun the decade in a position of strength, overriding governor and party to install their own Veracruz ayuntamiento.[13] The CTM was aggressively expanding into the countryside through its cane worker subsidiary and through strategic alliances with rural heavyweights like Juan Paxtián in Los Tuxtlas.[14] But the centrist state leadership was unrepresentative of much of the quite radical CTM rank and file: drawn in part from the smaller nonindustrial unions (President Fernando "Sífilis" Suárez, for example, came from the hotel agents' union, with all of fifty members) and closely linked to the regional bourgeoisie, they increasingly alienated the labor aristocracy of railway men and oil workers.[15] The heavyweight unions threatened secession from the late 1930s onward; by the early 1940s they were actually leaving. The Poza Rica chapter of the oil workers voted to secede in 1940; the entire union followed in 1944. The powerful groups who controlled the transport bottlenecks of the economy, the docks and trains, likewise left the fold. The longshoremen abandoned the CTM in late 1939; powerful dissident sectors of the Sindicato de Trabajadores Ferrocarrileros de la República Mexicana (STFRM) followed their lead in 1944.[16] Such divisions were encouraged by Governor Cerdán, who systematically excluded CTM bosses from political office and violently encouraged desertion.[17]

As a result, by 1942 both the state CTM and the CROM had fractured, with powerful dissident groups first jostling for the recognition of their national committees and then joining the independent COCM.[18] The remaining Cetemistas under cane worker cacique Vidal Muñoz Díaz compounded their problems by backing the wrong horse in the union's national elections, opposing the unstoppable Fidel Velázquez.[19] The CTM's chaotic decline in Veracruz was difficult to check: when leaders proclaimed their resurgence in the 1945 Tuxpan regional congress they needed soldiers to protect them from dissident oil workers.[20] Yet to write the union history of the period in terms of the CTM's fortunes would be teleological. Even in 1940 Cetemistas were a minority in Xalapa and Veracruz; in Orizaba they were nearing extinction.[21] The state's labor politics were of a multipolar world, where cacical and bureaucratic repression coexisted with meaningful worker influence. Which tendency predominated depended heavily on location: thus in 1940 the Minatitlán oil workers were dominated by a single faction, while in Poza Rica Chapter 30 the same union averaged seventy-five general assemblies a year and changed its committee between competing groups every six months.[22] Even Orizaba's textile workers, their radical years firmly in the past, disciplined by emergency war legislation, pistoleros, and the closed shop, were capable of moments of startling autonomy. In 1944 Catholic workers celebrated an illegal open-air Mass attended by twenty-five hundred people.[23] Such independent-minded unions were not necessarily model worker democracies: Manuel Moreno, the rail worker boss, personally executed rivals, accepted employers' bribes, and, when ousted by reformers, tried to regain his position by storming union headquarters.[24] Yet compared to labor conditions under the later, more monolithic CTM, it was advantageous for workers to have the CTM as only one of four major confederations—the CTM, CROM, COCM, and the Confederación Proletariana Nacional—all with statewide access to places on ayuntamientos.[25] CTM weakness certainly did not decrease labor's overall cuota de poder, its acknowledged share of political positions: in 1945 the unions controlled five seats in the state congress, several federal deputyships, and one of the two senate seats.[26]

If peasant and worker experiences of the early 1940s were, respectively, disastrous and mixed, those of the conservative alliance of army and violent entrepreneurs were of success and expansion. (The distinction between categories is flimsy: army officers were often violent entrepreneurs themselves, and the word "pistolero" was applied to foot soldiers and bosses alike.) A rough typology of those elite pistoleros might consist of three classes: those who fought to defend / extend ancestral lands, such as the Lagunes and Armenta dynasties; those who fought to defend / extend a single industrial center, such as Antonio Domínguez, the longtime cacique of the Tuzamapán refinery; and the few who fought to defend / extend an entire regional network of producers and industrialists, such as Manuel Parra of Almolonga and Crispín Aguilar of Actopan. Their power rested in part on reliable repressive violence: the cane field ambush, the backstreet shoot-out, the factory floor execution. Aguilar was believed responsible for hundreds of deaths of men, women, and children, many disappeared to a "private cemetery" in the hills; Gobernación could name ninety-four of his victims from the period 1939–45 alone.[27] Their power also rested on a certain degree of popular recruitment.[28] Newspapers and corridos attributed a basic mafioso-like legitimacy to some pistoleros, who provided poorer clients like smallholders with some of the protection of the state in stateless places.[29] They obtained, finally, practical and political cover from the military in exchange for money, lands, and services.[30] The highest-ranking officers supplied pistoleros with arms, soldiers, commissions as policemen, the benefits of a blind eye, and at times even a public defense. Manuel Parra's impunity was guaranteed beyond the fluctuations of state politics by his close contacts with the Avila Camacho family and by his business partnership with defense secretary General Pablo Quiroga, who ordered local garrisons to support him unconditionally.[31] Crispín Aguilar received a written apologia in *El Dictamen* from the zone commander Alejandro Mange, who described him as a distinguished agrarian leader.[32] The diversity, institutionalization, and local monopolies of violence enjoyed by pistolero networks made them in many localities more statelike than the civilian administration. (Which they frequently colonized.)[33] The first half of the 1940s was the peak of the pistoleros' power, as they, their military allies, and associated profiteers enjoyed a neutered agrarista opposition and a failing state government.

Such conditions favored Miguel Alemán, as rival regional networks checked each other's progress and competed for the favorable decisions of the federal government. Even before becoming secretario de Gobernación Alemán had outdistanced his elite rivals. While Cándido Aguilar is sometimes seen as preserving his dominance at this point, with Cerdán and Alemán his subordinates, Gobernación agents from 1939 preferred Alemán as the "boss and lord" of Veracruz, and reported a breakdown of relations between him and Aguilar.[34] Aguilar's base—some of the sugar workers and some peasant leagues in central Veracruz—was far weaker than the alemanista alliance, which comprised the rest of the agrarian organizations, the unions, the increasingly powerful CNOP (founded in 1943 with Alemán's backing), and the emerging avilacamachista machine in the federal government (whose chief engineer was Alemán's long-term patron Gonzalo N. Santos).[35] While Aguilar claimed control of the floundering governor Cerdán, it was Alemán who actually controlled the state apparatus: his successful nominations included senators, interim governor Fernando Casas Alemán, interior minister Adolfo Ruiz Cortines, eleven of the fourteen state deputies, and the mayors of all the strategic cities. It was, furthermore, Alemán who sustained Cerdán against General Arturo Campillo Seyde, the Avila Camacho family's preferred candidate.[36] Cándido Aguilar did not disappear in the early 1940s: he nearly became leader of congress, while his nephew Silvestre was the state's subsecretario de Gobernación.[37] But Alemán was in a different league, remaking Gobernación as a veracruzano fief—his subsecretario was Fernando Casas Alemán, his chief of staff Adolfo Ruiz Cortines—and using its powers, including intelligence, to tighten his grip on state politics.[38] In 1944 Alemán installed the doggedly loyal Ruiz Cortines as governor. This might have been a difficult election to manage: the state was in a deep recession accompanied by violent instability; the 1936 and 1940 elections had been complex, dirty, and difficult to rig; and both Mange and Aguilar—the state's other two power brokers—were hostile. Yet Alemán got Ruiz Cortines elected without significant opposition, and went on to dash the senatorial hopes of Tejeda and Aguilar a year later.[39] Such elections were emblematic of a two-way traffic between federal and state governments that came to bypass the regional elites' usual mediation between provincial populations and Mexico City. It was, in effect, a nationalization of state politics. As one mayor explained, "The people of Veracruz didn't choose me; the President did."[40] The definitive election of the period, in consequence, was not state-level, but rather the presidential contest of 1946.

This was widely billed as a democratic election to bring a political reformer to Los Pinos. The president, Alemán himself, and regional leaders such as Vidal Díaz Muñoz inveighed against prevailing electoral practice and promised a fresh start of, in Alemán's words, "the greatest political honesty and the most austere civic responsibility."[41] The simultaneous state elections—for federal representatives and ayuntamientos—would be genuinely competitive and not, Alemán promised, the imposition of predetermined single-party slates. Yet the defining characteristic of the 1946 federal elections was just that. Díaz Muñoz had already experimented in his patria chica, Los Tuxtlas, with electoral pacts between the three elements of the newborn PRI, the CTM, CNC, and CNOP, that excluded all other factions. He went on to broker a carro completo for the entire state in 1946, excluding swathes of the political classes, including teachers, cattlemen, dissident agraristas, and even the railway men and the independent unions whose membership outnumbered that of his CTM.[42] Nineteen forty-six was, even before such an aggressive move, a pivotal moment for each of the state's networks. For all concerned the mechanics of the presidential election and the role individual actors played in the campaign would define the well connected for at least the next six years. For the military / pistolero network, the prospect of a yet-more-powerful Alemán threatened their regional dominance; for agraristas and Aguilaristas, already on their back foot, the question was mere survival. The adoption of the carro completo, with its explicit rejection of power sharing, increased the inevitable tension surrounding the election. This tension centered on two parallel struggles: one, the elbowing for places on the Alemán bandwagon, the other, a quest to derail it.

The campaign began in May 1945, and by mid-June a headlong cargada was running across Veracruz for Alemán. The Liga (marshaled by Nabor Ojeda) nominated Alemán on June 10, followed over the next two weeks by the oil workers and the Sector Popular.[43] The state was gripped, newspapers reported, by a political turbulence, *agitación*, paralleled only in Jalisco, the home state of Alemán's early rival General Miguel Henríquez Guzmán.[44] This agitación—never a positive phenomenon in Mexican political discourse—was not, however, caused by overwhelming home support for Alemán. He was, after all, held responsible for much of the course of veracruzano politics during nearly a decade of state failure.[45] It was instead a product of considerable early opposition. Cándido Aguilar's peasant constituencies, concentrated in the central sierra but stretching down to the port hinterlands and to a handful of municipios in the deep south, were eloquently silent.[46] Cerdán's followers, concentrated in the port, were from henriquista elements of the regional bourgeoisie, represented by the Malpica family's *El Dictamen;* they favored first Javier Rojo Gómez and later Henríquez Guzmán. More threateningly, General Mange was a leading member of an influential group of officers (including Adrián Castrejón, Agustín Mora, Manuel Palafox, and Antonio Romero) who resolutely opposed civilian rule on principle and Alemán in particular. Mange—claiming that "a whoreson wimp can't control the military, nor be president"—even launched a statewide tour to promote Henríquez's candidacy.[47]

Such military opposition, in Alemán's home state, linked closely to national and local groups, might have seriously threatened his candidacy. Mange was, however, quickly driven to submission by a series of maneuvers beyond even his long reach. Alemán had secretly met with Lázaro Cárdenas in Acapulco in May, before launching his campaign, to negotiate the ex-president's support. Cárdenas was widely expected to back Henríquez Guzmán; in Acapulco, however, he agreed instead to endorse Alemán and to swing the army behind him. Avila Camacho subsequently retired some twenty-three hundred officers, including nearly five hundred generals, and reshuffled many others in a purge softened by continuing salaries for the newly retired.[48] From Veracruz Mange watched the national henriquista campaign fold; by the end of June its leaders, Senators Adrián Morales Salas and Antonio Mayés Navarro, had declared for Alemán, as had the most important henriquista general, Governor Marcelino García Barragán of Jalisco.[49] Finally his garrison commander and fellow Henriquista Agustín Mora was posted away, and Mange bowed to the inevitable.[50] In early July he wrote to Avila Camacho to congratulate him on the purge and to promise that he would have no contacts with the remaining army dissidents nor attend the politically charged banquet they were planning.[51] The state band began rehearsing its director's new tune, the "Miguel Alemán March."[52] Finally in October Cándido Aguilar—who had initially used violence to enforce his clients' neutrality—declared for Alemán, ending any lingering possibility of a contested election in Veracruz.[53]

There remained islands of opposition, impervious to the inevitable, who became supporters of the rival Partido Democrático Mexicano and its candidate Ezequiel Padilla. Padillistas formed an eclectic alliance that spanned conservative elites, particularly the losers of agrarian reform; sinarquista strongholds such as the heavily indigenous municipios of the Sierra Madre; and disappointed Henriquistas of all stripes.[54] Opposition attempts to campaign across the state met the usual obstacles: absent permits and reluctant notaries, the ubiquitous ninety-nine-peso fines, the destruction of election material, arrests, campaign office raids, beatings, and the occasional shoot-out.[55] By the standards of 1936 and 1940, however, the campaign was almost sleepy, and even the enthusiastic muckraking of Gobernación Inspector Migoni could dredge up only rumors of political murder.[56] The Alemán camarilla was, if anything, a victim of its own success: the existence of a clear winner almost a year before election day created severe strains within the campaign as local factions and turncoat state elites fought for the limited patronage on offer. As early as the autumn of 1945 Alemán had to send a special representative to Veracruz to unite his anarchic campaign there, riven between old loyalists, opportunist newcomers, and the port's ayuntamiento, recent converts from a supposedly diehard Henriquismo.[57]

This infrapolitical squabbling combined with a sense of inevitability and its corollary, a perception of the futility of elections, to produce notable voter apathy. The state press stressed the need for electoral reform, to abolish the "great carnivalesque farces that we have come to call elections, when they do everything but elect through public and democratic contests."[58] In the absence of reform, and with the memory of 1940 to deter them, veracruzanos decided early on to abstain: the numbers registering for the vote were, the electoral roll commission found, extremely low.[59] This was blamed in part on the state government's lack of promotion of the registration campaign, and on April 11, 1946, Ramón Beteta, the presidential campaign manager and crony, told Ruiz Cortines that Veracruz had fallen below the national average of registered voters and demanded urgent action.[60] Coercive measures were ordered: state bureaucrats were reminded that failing to register could be punished under current electoral law with the loss of the vote, fines of up to 300 pesos, and six-month jail sentences.[61] By May, however, only 35 percent of eligible voters had registered—the same proportion as in far-off Chiapas—and on election day at least fourteen municipios were still without any electoral roll at all, while a further thirty-one—ranging from the major industrial centers of Orizaba and Córdoba to the remote mountain communities of Zongolica—were deemed "defectively registered."[62]

Such statistics reflected more than the logistical difficulties of voter registration. They revealed, for all the state's efforts to get out the vote, a fundamental lack of consent, clues to which seep through the chaos and half truths of the election result files. A list of raw election data from sixty-one municipios reveals clear patterns of disenfranchisement and disenchantment. Election day found voters in some municipios too keen to be true: in Martínez de la

Torre, for example, over four times the estimated electorate turned up to vote. In others, voters seemed remarkably single-minded: in over half the sampled polls Alemán took every single vote. (In less-easily rigged Xalapa, by contrast, a quarter of voters went for the uninspiring Padilla.) And in others, perhaps those with the least savvy election managers, next to no one bothered voting in the first place. In independent-minded Papantla only 7 percent of the estimated electorate voted; in Ayahualulco, 12 percent; in Ixhuacán, 8 percent. Even the municipios clustered around Acayucán, Alemán's patria chica and one place sure to benefit from his presidency, were markedly apathetic, with less than a third of the estimated electorate turning out. Statewide, Padilla, General Calderón, and José Castro officially won token handfuls of votes; Miguel Alemán won the presidency.[63]

The Alemán Presidency Playing at Home

The Alemán victory substantially reinforced his camarilla's control of Veracruz. While his lieutenant Ruiz Cortines had easily taken the governorship in 1944, the Alemanistas had from the outset faced the downside of divide and rule, namely, serious problems of governance. Ruiz Cortines's eight-point manifesto stressed security, administrative, and tax reform, "social credit," and public / private sector cooperation in development projects.[64] His covert aims could be read between the lines: the removal of agraristas and their potential allies, the Aguilaristas, from state politics, and the erosion of the informal parallel state of pistoleros, landowners, and the military. With Alemán in the presidency the camarilla could accelerate their essential project, that of creating a new and civilian governmental machine while dismantling its rusty predecessor.

The informal network of violent entrepreneurs was not rusty. It was, rather, an impressively codified system of territorial domination whose key players, the leading regional pistoleros and the military, held regular summits to maintain their boundaries, businesses, and a profitable stability. (Rather like the five families of the New York Mafia; there are not that many paths to Rome in organized crime.) From 1937 until 1942 it had been an effective dyarchy, run between General Alejandro Mange and Manuel Parra, that covered a patchwork of much of the south and center. (Why no such system emerged in the north is an open question; lower land values, poor communications, more cohesive indigenous communities, and the absence of a single long-lasting commander in the north's 19th Military Zone may be partial answers.) Heriberto Jara, former commander of the 26th Zone, had maintained some semblance of a balance of power in the countryside by arming agraristas while tolerating their opponents' violence.[65] Mange, who had a history of energetic alliances with local bosses against agraristas, upset what balance there was, setting out from the start to disarm agrarista militias and redirect the sequestered army rifles to Parra's men. He failed to prevent arms shipments from the coast from reaching Almolonga; he visited Parra, with whom he had a "regular and frequent" correspondence, and was observed meeting with other pistolero luminaries such as Gonzalo Lagunes.[66] The resulting shift in power gave Parra an unusual ascendancy, backed by a paramilitary force of some five hundred men.[67]

Yet Parra died—a natural death—in 1943, and the onetime consensus on hierarchy and spheres of influence was undone by rivalries such as that between the Armentas of Plan de las Hayas and Crispín Aguilar of Actopan. By 1945 there was a pistolero civil war under way as the different groups competed to replace Parra as the acknowledged head of the system. Yet even as bands sent by Rafael Cornejo Armenta invaded Actopan, notably collegial practices still obtained at the highest level of the pistolero / military alliance.[68] As with any mafia, fighting between the main families was bad for everyone's business. General Mange tried to stop the hostilities: in April 1945 he summoned Aguilar and the other leaders—Manuel Viveros from Almolonga, Rafael Cornejo Armenta, the Campomanes brothers from Ursulo Galván—to a sit-down in his headquarters. The zone commander complained that their feuding had given General Reyes Esquivel in Martínez de la Torre "a very bad impression" of them, and told them to visit Reyes and explain themselves. They went to Xalapa, rented a Flecha Roja bus, and traveled together to meet the general in Perote. There they explained to him "that they were slandered in the sense that they were killers and bandits but that that was not true" and that they were both unified and prepared to pacify the countryside. The pistoleros then returned to Xalapa, accompanied by Lieutenant-Colonel Sebastián Contreras Barreras, and tried to report their meeting to General Josué Benignos, the chief of state police.[69] Or at least such was the cover story; Gobernación's agents suspected it to be an elaborate smoke screen behind which Mange and the pistoleros had been planning their henriquista campaign.[70] Whichever version happened to be true, the matter-of-fact way in which Veracruz's gunmen sat down together and talked business with the state's military and police leaders revealed their accepted, normalized role inside the state's ruling classes, entitled, whatever their foibles, to a substantial cuota de poder.

Ruiz Cortines had claimed some early victories in defusing rural violence. In certain villages, such as Coatepec and Xico, he had pressured armed groups into handing in their weapons.[71] He had instructed mayors to collect unlicensed weapons, as part of the gun control campaign that the military was supposed to implement. As a result he reported a 26 percent decrease in crime over the first nine months of his term.[72] This, however, was the wishful thinking that characterizes much gubernatorial reporting. The disarmament campaign, known as *despistolización,* was a notorious, long-running failure: the *Diario de Xalapa* claimed that it had resulted in all of eleven confiscations in 1945, while the police report for 1948 registered only sixteen arrests for carrying unlicensed guns.[73] The governor was, in reality, initially impotent in the face of a wave of rural killings. The uncertainty and opportunity afforded by Parra's early death, the change of governor, and the presidential election all fostered violent competition across 1944 and 1945 as pistoleros fought it out with each other and with agraristas to redraw the boundaries of their territories.[74] Ruiz Cortines was bitterly criticized for his inaction—many of the culprits were, after all, household names—but it took time to reorganize the state police and a new level of central support to make any inroads into pistolero power.[75] In 1947 the state's new mounted police, equipped with jeeps and led by a new commander, Antioco Lara Salazar, began to arrest low-ranking gunmen in regional sweeps that captured 220 wanted men in the first eight months of the year.[76] In December they progressed to the elites when Crispín Aguilar was arrested by the army and jailed for two years. Mange, under concerted pressure from Mexico City, had finally abandoned his allies, triggering a critical shift in regional power relationships.[77] In tandem with an energetic judicial campaign came a series of high-level extrajudicial killings. Three of the Armenta brothers were assassinated by Miguel Alemán's agents; José Aguilar, Crispín's brother, was killed by the state police; the army connived at the eventual murder of Crispín himself, who was shot dead in Actopan soon after his release in 1950.[78] If not quite the liquidation of pistoleros that the state press proclaimed, it was a decisive end to their ambitions to state-sized power.[79] Rafael Cornejo Armenta symbolized the change neatly; after reportedly threatening to kill Alemán in revenge for his brothers' deaths he reflected, threw his support behind Ruiz Cortines, and tried to retire to life as a provincial hotelier.[80] Instead, like all his brothers he met a violent end, shot in the back on his way home from a game of billiards.[81]

The civilian administration was easier to purge. Credible excuses for dismissal were not hard to find: the customary inaugural purge of ayuntamientos, fifteen of which were dismissed in 1945, was followed by a wholesale reshuffle of tax inspectors, a mass arrest of tax collectors, and finally by a mass arrest of mayors in 1948 on charges of pilfering federal taxes.[82] Ruiz Cortines linked such anticorruption measures with a program of administrative modernization and state expansion that was phrased in the rhetorics of technocracy and liberal citizenship. "Empiricism and intuition," he told the legislature, were insufficient bases for good government, which required "research and the application of scientific methods" to rule according to "social and economic planning."[83] He formed, as a consequence, a department of technical studies to plan development projects, spent 154,000 pesos on Moisés de la Peña's exhaustive economic survey, and demanded monthly reports in a variety of fields from the statistics department.[84] Such advances in cognitive capacity would, however, be wasted without a contractarian response by the veracruzanos, whose enjoyment of civic rights would have to be matched by their fulfillment of obligations. For the bureaucracy this signified increased salaries, and such benefits as social security, life insurance, pensions, and housing loans in exchange for a new degree of administrative probity. For the population at large the new social pact would trade heightened obedience, the payment of taxes, and a certain degree of voluntarism—channeled through the Juntas de Mejoramiento Moral, Cívico y Material into public works and social reform projects—for a new morality in government, a drive to enforce law and order and to promote development. The rhetoric, at least, was a dress rehearsal for the Ruiz Cortines presidency: the exchange of wanton kleptocracy for austere technocracy.[85]

Yet state expansion required hard cash as well as moralizing speeches, and Ruiz Cortines inherited an exchequer emptied by his predecessor's administrative incompetence and comprehensive tax exemptions. Cerdán's list of industries enjoying near-total tax breaks ranged from hotels and cinemas to commercial maize producers; organizations ranging from ejidos to PEMEX had for years refused outright to pay taxes; in compensation, revenues had been routinely inflated by 10 percent on paper to lessen the impression of state penury. The mean state tax burden per capita in 1946 was ten pesos, paltry next to those of other wealthy states such as Sonora (thirty-eight), Tamaulipas (nineteen), or Chihuahua (twenty-three).[86] Ruiz Cortines may not have had the necessary policy autonomy to rebuild the tax base, constrained as he was either by the agreements of the Alemán camarilla, or by his need to pander to Veracruz's business community, who protested against any tax increases on principle. He may have considered tax increases counterproductive

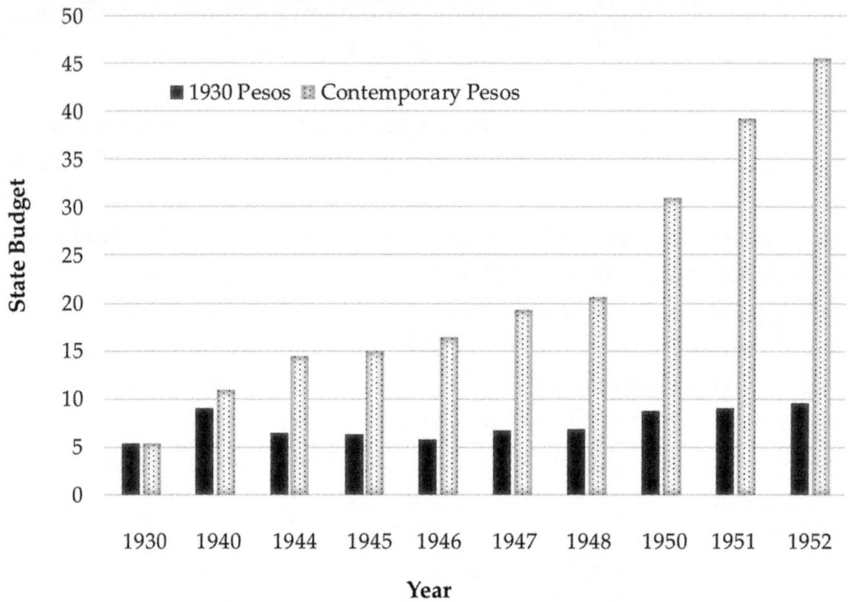

Veracruz's budget, 1940–53, in millions of contemporary and 1930 pesos. Data from governors' reports; De la Peña, *Veracruz económico,* 2:507; deflated using wholesale price index Mexico City 1886–1978, INEGI Estadísticas Históricas CD-ROM.

in a period marked by recession and the natural disasters of hurricanes, flooding, and the foot-and-mouth epidemic.[87] Whatever the reason, his tax policy was secretive, timid, and regressive. While exemptions were abolished and tax collectors disciplined, he allowed the Chamber of Commerce to set their own tax rates, suppressed De la Peña's conclusions advocating tax increases, and left the public finances much as he had found them, neither transparent, equitable, nor adequate.[88] While the federal budget, adjusted for inflation, increased by 197 percent between 1945 and 1953, the state budget rose only 153 percent; the 1950 budget fell nearly 40 percent short of De la Peña's estimate of the 50 million pesos the state should raise.[89]

In place of wholesale tax reform Ruiz Cortines found funds in long-term loans, in generous federal subsidies, and in the euphemized stealth taxation of "popular cooperation." Half the cost of the state baseball team and two-thirds of its paving and sewage costs were raised through the voluntary contributions of the Juntas de Mejoramiento in 1947; the legislature even codified a leverage principle in development fundraising by passing a law guaranteeing 34 percent of the costs of any public works project once the community concerned had raised the first 66 percent.[90] It was a short-term policy, much of whose costs would fall on the lower classes (who could be co-opted as unpaid labor as part of the community contribution, or encouraged to contribute financially by coercive municipal elites), which relied on a finite quantity of popular and presidential goodwill and enthusiasm for development, and which left the problem of an inadequate tax base unresolved. When Ruiz Cortines moved on to Gobernación in 1948 he left a state treasury that in real terms had yet to recover its 1940 level of revenue. Future governors would follow the same course; the state government abandoned another attempt to raise taxes in 1965.[91] Yet the political effect, equally short term, was to allow Ruiz Cortines the conjuring trick of delivering public services and infrastructural development without appreciable increases in direct taxation.

The development program promoted by Ruiz Cortines and his two immediate successors rested on the four pillars of public health, communications, policing, and education.[92] Parts of industrial Veracruz impressed visitors as distinctly unhealthy; the oil camp at Poza Rica, for example, was described by Egon Kisch in 1943 as "a flooded landscape [where] squalid children with swollen bellies escorted by dogs roll around in the liquid rubbish or deposit what adults likewise deposit there."[93] The statewide lack of sewage systems was a fundamental problem: in 1945 only Veracruz, Orizaba, and Xalapa had sewage systems, which halved the death rate from waterborne diseases like dysentery and typhoid.[94] The provision of sanitation and potable water was consequently promoted in cooperation with any partners the government could find. In Banderilla the community contributed half the cost; in the oil fields PEMEX cooperated with the government's sanitary brigades; in frontier areas such as the Huasteca army sappers installed the pipework for communal water supplies.[95] Public health campaigns were among the least controversial and most effective manifestations of the expanding state, and agents such as soldiers and maestros were heavily involved in both education and sanitation projects. Teachers played key roles in draining swamps, showing films, and distributing quinine and the highly effective DDT in the antimalarial campaign, a multifaceted program that began in 1956 and was coordinated by brigades operating out of Coatzacoalcos, Minatitlán, Veracruz, and Tuxpan. Such measures combined with vaccination programs covering hundreds of thousands of veracruzanos improved public health substantially in a relatively short period. By the late 1940s smallpox had almost vanished, polio was a rarity, and malaria had been nearly eradicated in the port area. The inauguration

Photograph by Alexander Wetmore

ERODED TRAILS SERVE AS HIGHWAYS

An occasional bullock cart is driven over this road near Tres Zapotes, but for the most part it is traversed by natives on foot or riding mules or steers. Along such trails natives drive pigs to market, or carry chickens or bundles of wood for fuel. When a man and his wife travel together, the wife usually walks and carries the burdens, while the husband rides.

Highway near San Andrés Tuxtla, 1939. "An occasional bullock cart is driven over this road near Tres Zapotes, but for the most part it is traversed by natives on foot or riding mules or steers." Alexander Wetmore, "Discovering the New World's Oldest Dated Work of Man," *National Geographic Magazine* 76, no. 2 (August 1939). National Geographic Image Collection.

of three new hospitals gave Veracruz a total of sixteen, increasing the number of beds to over two thousand.[96] The success of combined sanitation, vaccination, education, and treatment was reflected in the principal indicators: infant mortality, for example, dropped 36 percent between 1940 and 1950.[97]

In the early 1940s surfaced roads remained a novelty in Veracruz. The first modern highway between Veracruz and Mexico City was completed in 1940; by 1945 it had been joined by only two others, those connecting Teziutlán,

Puebla, to Poza Rica and Ciudad Valles, San Luis Potosí, to Tampico, totaling some thirteen hundred kilometers of all-weather roads. Networks of feeder roads to these highways were still in planning, and key interregional roads to connect the north and south to the center had been vetoed as unjustifiably expensive. The south was still without a single tarmacadam road in 1945; when a tuxtleco commission asked Cárdenas's communications secretary, Múgica, to fund a coastal highway linking San Andrés Tuxtla to Veracruz they were told that only a local boy in the presidency would build such a white elephant. With Alemán's presidential win they got both local boy and road, part of an extraordinary 102-million-peso communications plan. This massive infrastructural investment—equivalent to five times the roads budget for 1940–45, and some seven times the state's budget for 1945—was half funded by federal grants, the state's half coming from loans, local extraordinary taxes, and a bond issue.[98] Like other contemporary development projects, road construction was also supported by cooperation with other agencies, notably the military and PEMEX, and by the supposedly voluntary labor of neighboring communities. Some funding was undoubtedly diverted, via inflated contracts, to political ends: noting that Henríquez Guzmán was the contractor for the Poza Rica highway, the Mexico City wit Salvador Novo suggested that the work had proved time consuming enough to push him out of the presidential race. (Henríquez was not the only road-building would-be president; Almazán's Constructora Anáhuac built most of the Pan-American Highway from Hidalgo to the border.)[99] Yet the program was both effective and extremely popular, and by the 1950s the north and south of Veracruz were connected by all-weather highways with the center and neighboring states. The trucks that could ply such a network would add up to, De la Peña projected, the "democratization of transport."[100] They certainly aided village entrepreneurs like Porfirio Pérez Olivares, whose business—shipping papaya from Soledad to La Merced, Mexico City's main market—expanded dramatically when he began using trucks in place of the railroad.[101]

The third pillar of the development program, policing, was described by Ruiz Cortines as "among the most important and urgent tasks and among the least satisfactory."[102] Police modernization in Veracruz dated to 1937, when the Organic Law of Policing had established a state police responsible directly to the governor.[103] The law aspired to remove policing from the hardball world of municipal politics, where local police or agrarista militias were generally little more than the dominant faction's hard men. Paltry funding and gubernatorial negligence had, however, kept the state police force toothless: tiny,

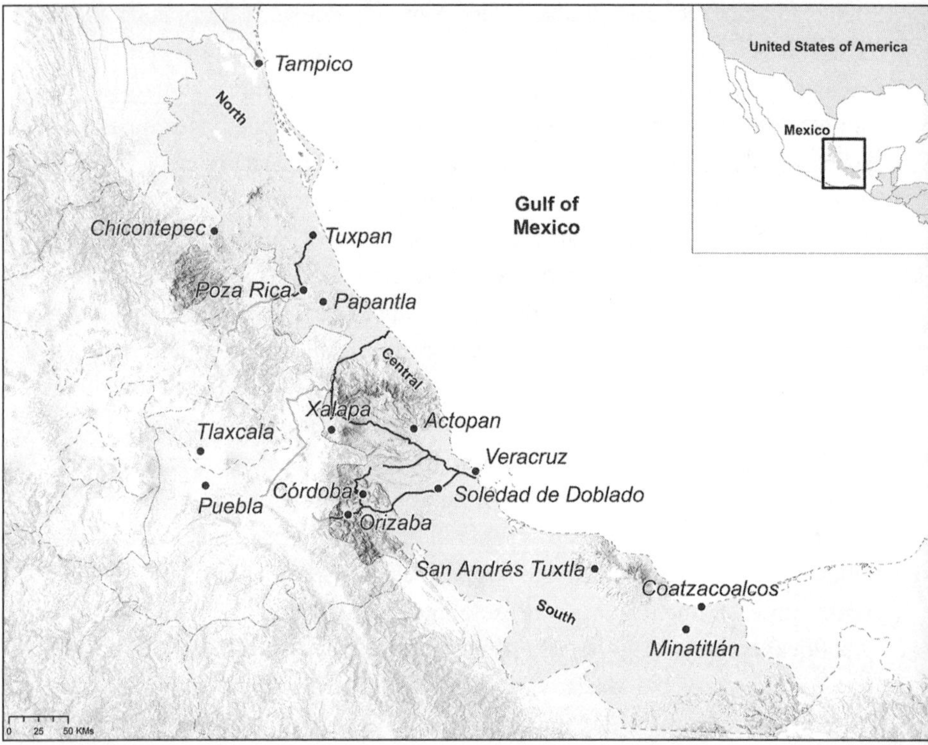

The Veracruz highway network, 1940. Created by Kelsey Rydland, Research Services, Northwestern University Libraries.

unreformed, and unrepentantly corrupt. The military, who filled the vacuum as the state's violent agency in the countryside, was deemed authoritarian by even the conservatives of the Cattlemen's Union, those who benefited the most from army operations.[104] They were also markedly compromised in Veracruz by the depth of their associations with pistoleros. The ambitious lieutenant-colonel Contreras, for example, influenced the state police commander to have many of the guardias blancas of the western highlands made police commanders in the mid-1940s.[105] None of this changed overnight; local police commands continued to be strategic posts for local heavies and the military continued to play a key role in policing. Yet civilian policing was both expanded a great deal and professionalized in the Alemán sexenio. Police recruits were vetted for criminal records; they were better paid and better equipped with uniforms, jeeps, rifles, and submachine guns. They were also far more numerous: eight regional detachments in 1949 grew to fifteen in

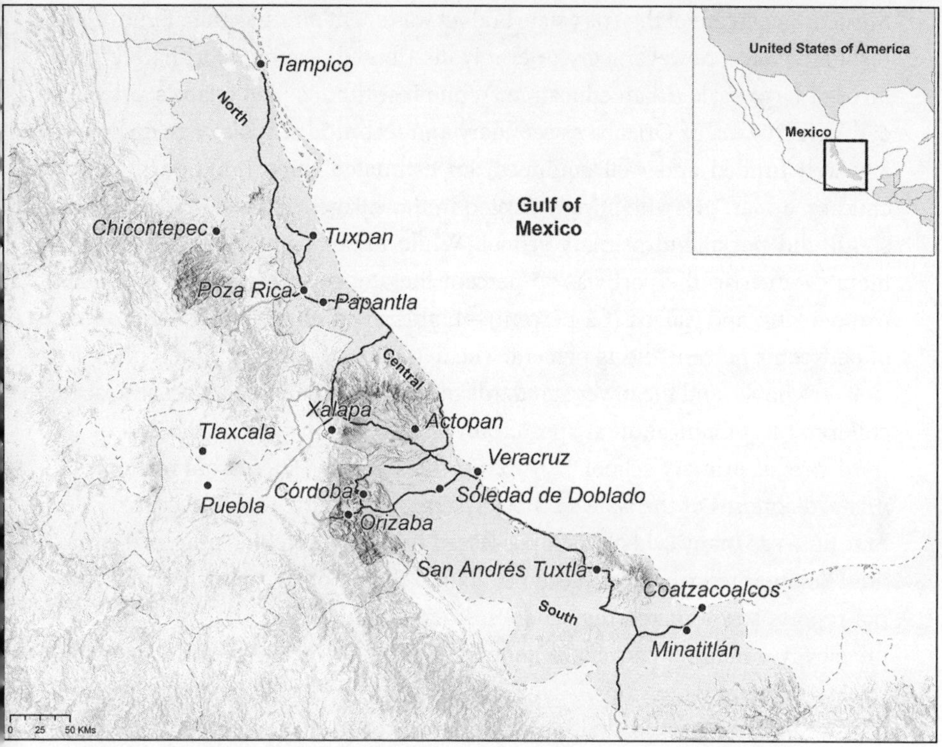

The Veracruz highway network, 1950. Created by Kelsey Rydland, Research Services, Northwestern University Libraries.

1950 and thirty-seven in 1953.[106] Rising arrest rates reflected the new efficiency in everyday policing: in the first eight months of 1948 the state police made over seven hundred arrests.[107] By the late 1940s the police had taken over many of the functions formerly monopolized by the military. Many of the mass arrests of pistoleros were police operations, and while the army was still deployed to take over strongholds such as Actopan or Alto Lucero it was the state police who then garrisoned them.[108] Their position at the sharp end of state expansion was a dangerous one, and the contemporary press records regular killings of police commanders in remote villages.[109] Backed by the modernization of other components of the justice system—notably the Ministerio Público and the prison service—police reform was, however, one of the alemanista administration's clear successes.

In education, on the other hand, their record was more ambiguous. Veracruz had a long tradition of good public education, backed by the largest subsidies in

Mexico; 43 percent of the 1945 state budget was spent on education. Educational resources were, however, very unevenly distributed, leading to a sharp bias in favor of large-scale urban education. While institutions like Xalapa's Universidad Veracruzana or Orizaba's secondary and technical schools were exceptionally well funded and well equipped, an estimated three hundred thousand children a year, overwhelmingly located in the villages of the sierra and the far south, did not attend primary school. While urban populations were highly literate—in 1930 the port was 77 percent literate, closely followed by Orizaba (69 percent) and Xalapa (64 percent)—highland communities tended to rates of between 5 percent and 15 percent. The demands of the agricultural cycle, the lack of schools, and the lower standards of those that did exist all drove peasant children out of education at speed; only 10 percent made it to the end of the third year of primary school.[110] Ruiz Cortines and his successors made pessimistic diagnoses of the state's school system, estimating that Veracruz needed four times as many schools as it possessed if it was to provide universal education. Yet their reforms were piecemeal rather than root-and-branch. Gubernatorial reports stress increasing school numbers and teacher salaries; they detail the slowly emerging packets of benefits for the low-paid maestros, including social security and pensions. They evade, however, the key indicators of registration, attendance, and graduation of students, for the simple reason that these statistics were disheartening. Governors repeatedly called for popular and institutional cooperation from communities, unions, peasant leagues, and businesses to expand schooling. Such stopgap improvisations were, however, no replacement for the larger budget De la Peña proposed in 1945, and which could be achieved only by politically costly tax hikes. Education remained underfunded and biased toward the urban constituencies of labor and the middle classes, a revealing microcosm of much contemporary development: materially impressive—the number of schools did rise by some 50 percent—but fundamentally inequitable.[111]

A final if unprogrammed component of development, one that went with the turf of a Gulf state, was disaster management. Hurricanes and their associated floods were regular events, and the main river basins—the Papaloapan in the south and the Tuxpan and Pánuco in the north—were severely affected in 1945, 1947, and 1952.[112] Each event provoked a bitter politics of disaster relief; a governor, keen to project his control of the state, might, for example, downplay the gravity of the damage while ejidatarios and farmers bombarded Mexico City with requests for emergency aid.[113] The most expensive natural disaster of the period, the 1946 foot-and-mouth outbreak, was similarly politically complex.

The initial response was slow: cattlemen suspected a "false alarm, whose unspeakable motives come from Texan stockbreeders"; many moved their animals out of a quarantine zone whose borders the regional government was incapable of enforcing; infected corpses were burned next to the Veracruz slaughterhouse, and cattle coming in for slaughter were not routinely checked for the disease. "It should," the Agriculture Department commented, "have been easy to contain [the epidemic]," but it was not until January 7, 1947, that Ruiz Cortines realized the ramifications of the problem.[114] He then requested army assistance in policing the borders of the quarantine zone.[115] It was too late, and the federal government soon declared all Veracruz north of the Tehuantepec railway an infected zone. The rifle sanitario threatened livelihoods from the coastal cattle empires down to ejidatarios such as Román Ramírez, who begged the president not to slaughter his yoke of oxen, the only patrimony he possessed.[116] Some invested in the popular veterinary medicine of desperation: improvised emetics, snake oil vaccines, lime juice or Picot's grape salts in drinking troughs, the rubbing down of infected animals with butter.[117] Others in the rainy season of 1947 chose to resist, hiding animals from the veterinarians or refusing to allow the slaughter.[118] The foot-and-mouth campaign in Veracruz was simultaneously another victim of budgetary anemia. In the critical first year Ruiz Cortines set aside only 100,000 pesos to fund the eradication effort, while the army attributed mounting desertions to a lack of federal payments for expenses or tents. Caught between poverty and popular refusal, the state and federal agencies were often powerless: only a thousand head were actually killed in the first nine months of the epidemic, and even the priority vaccinations in centers of infection were slow. In late 1947, with nearly a quarter of Veracruz's cattle believed infected, the foot-and-mouth commission issued new instructions privileging vaccination over slaughter. In 1948 fresh cases of the disease spread across the south of Veracruz; it was not until 1950 that outbreaks were rapidly and efficiently controlled.[119] The flawed campaign may have been a learning experience for state and national elites, as the next serious agricultural threat, the 1948 arrival of the black fly—an insect that destroyed coffee and citrus plants—attracted immediate and intensive countermeasures costing 5 million pesos in two years.[120]

Foot-and-mouth was to some extent a demonstration—in Veracruz as elsewhere—of the state's still-limited leverage. That resistance did not stretch to large-scale violence, however, also revealed the tightening political grip of Alemán's camarilla. The formal policies of the period were locally mediated and had distinctly mixed outcomes. Regional policymakers ran into problems of unforeseen obstacles and unintended consequences. The postwar agricultural recession, for example, was aggravated by a hurricane in 1947, a devaluation in 1948, and a 1949 drought that decimated the maize harvest. "It seemed," Ruiz Cortines gloomily remarked, "as if the New World [was] putting them to the test."[121] Yet in the infrapolitical world of informal policy, where the demobilization of peasant and labor militants, the elimination of Cándido Aguilar, and the extension of central civilian control were paramount aims, the Alemanistas proved increasingly effective.

Their opponents were widely distributed both territorially, across a string of municipios from Papantla down to Tierra Blanca, and organizationally, in the committee rooms of unions and in political parties new and old. In 1946 pockets of dissident LNCUG agraristas still belonged to the Partido Comunista Mexicano and claimed ayuntamientos from the deep south of Oluta and Tierra Blanca up to the port hinterlands of Ursulo Galván; the party itself requested control of the port Treasury.[122] Cándido Aguilar still dominated many highland municipios, his networks radiating out from Córdoba to cover much of the Sierra Madre from the Puebla border down past Paso del Macho to Soledad de Doblado; the general's reach also extended southward to the Oaxaca border municipios of Tierra Blanca and Jesús Carranza, and he was attempting to capture the agroindustrial centers of Cosamaloapan and San Andrés Tuxtla.[123] On aguilarista turf, a snitch told Ruiz Cortines, the only governor recognized was Cándido Aguilar.[124] In other areas the dominance of the PRI and its regional leaders was equally notional, as direct control got lost in enduring local conflicts and the traditions of resistance they fostered. A 1946 military tour of the Huasteca found several ayuntamientos and petty garrisons neutered by internal divisions and by the greater firepower of abigeos.[125] In Papantla, meanwhile, the vanilla broker Raúl del Cueto's entire PRI slate for 1946 was arrested for electoral fraud yet ended up forming the town's government anyway.[126] Finally, long-standing problems of political control were further complicated by the marked independence of many of Veracruz's numerous, rancorously divided unions. The sum of these different types of opposition was sufficient to subvert everyday control of the state. Beneath the Alemanistas' command of the strategic heights—congressional and senatorial seats, judgeships, governorships—a diverse municipal and labor opposition mined the walls of government.

One response was an electoral offensive centered on the municipal elections of 1946 and 1949 and the state congressional elections of 1947. Mexico City intended from the start to strengthen the Xalapa government's tenuous hold over local politics by weeding peasant militants and Aguilaristas out of town halls. This was no secret; there were, as Porfirio Pérez Olivares remembered, instructions straight from the president to purge Aguilar's men.[127] Both before and after the elections the governor's confidential agents—locally knowledgeable men such as General Marcelino Absalón Pérez in the San Andrés region, or Telésforo Contreras in the Papaloapan basin—toured towns and villages reviewing local candidates and trying to engineer unified alemanista slates. Their reports paint early priista electoral management as ambitious, ad hoc, and often amateurish. The governor's men did not always know who was who: thus two reports on the micropolitics of Manlio Fabio Altamirano, a strategic municipio bordering Veracruz, alternately described the mayoral candidate Luis de la Hoz as aguilarista and alemanista. Small-town electoral pacts, moreover, did not always stand the test of time: in Cosamaloapan, Chacaltianguis, and Tlacotalpan, for example, Absalón Pérez left in August with agreements that local actors would follow the party diktat in choosing candidates for the ayuntamientos, only to discover the elections returning aguilarista slates in November.[128] Such agents did succeed in overseeing a new level of exclusion of agraristas and dissident union leaders from local government. In the southern 11th and 14th districts, which included Aleman's hometown, coalitions of ranchers, smallholders, and shopkeepers overturned twenty years of ejidatario dominance.[129] In Veracruz and Xalapa the railway men were denied their traditional seats in city hall.[130] Alemán's electoral fixers were incapable, however, of managing a quick victory over the Aguilaristas, who brought together a broad and strange coalition of pistoleros, local businessmen, and agraristas. The governor's men did make some tactical gains: in Córdoba, for example, the aguilarista labor leader José Zúñiga Acevedo was overruled in favor of the banker Saúl Marenco.[131] Yet across the Sierra Madre Aguilar hung on to long-standing possessions, while in the south his clients captured numerous ayuntamientos which they were never supposed to take.[132] At the same time he was alleged to be preparing a takeover of the Liga, or the formation of a new national agrarian organization; Aguilar was not going quietly into any political night.[133]

Perhaps alerted by these unexpected reverses, the Alemanistas became more aggressive in managing the 1947 legislative elections. They fixed single candidacies in both north and south; in the center, where opposition candidates competed in all districts bar the port, the desire for legitimacy was subordinated to the will to power. In Misantla the unofficial candidate disappeared without distributing ballot papers. In Xalapa, Coatepec, and Orizaba federal agents watched one set of candidates win the elections and a second, supposedly official set of candidates be declared winners. And in Córdoba and Paso del Macho aguilarista lieutenants, attempting to crudely rig the poll, had the poll crudely rigged against them. The regional cadres of the PRI itself were clearly divided: in Córdoba the party committee was aguilarista, causing the party delegate—the future president Adolfo López Mateos—to duck the problem of choosing sides by staying away from the elections which he was supposed to monitor. Even the Alemanistas were less than unified: the continued court intrigues between Ruiz Cortines and Fernando López Arias caused a clumsy last-minute change of candidate in Coatepec.[134] All the losing candidates ran against the PRI in the constitucionales, and July 6 in central Veracruz saw heated, dirty elections marked by beatings, stabbings, a homicide in Orizaba, and parallel *juntas computadoras* in five districts. The results returned an impeccably alemanista congress.[135] The exercise had, however, been untidy and delegitimizing. In November several CTM power brokers led by Vidal Muñoz Díaz left the PRI for the Partido Popular (PP), the new left-wing party; Cándido Aguilar, meanwhile, was appeased in Mexico City with control of a new agrarian agency, the Comisión Coordinadora de Asuntos Campesinos.[136] This open competition, schism, and enforced tolerance of elite dissidence clearly marked the boundaries, still narrow by later standards, of the Alemán group's autonomy.

These boundaries were, however, rapidly expanding. Both the condition of the state economy (recession) and the political cycle determined highly contested municipal elections in 1949. The 1948 and 1949 devaluations had brought steep increases in the cost of basic foodstuffs; the military took to the streets to control the crowd in Orizaba.[137] The July 1949 elections to the federal congress were so tightly controlled that in Xalapa the PAN and the PP were reported to have received no votes at all. Reports of widespread abstention were commonplace. The electoral monopoly was paralleled in the gubernatorial elections, publicly announced as "resolved" in favor of Marco Antonio Muñoz in July 1949, nearly a year before they were to take place.[138] At a contentious time the only remaining space for political competition lay at the municipal level, where, moreover, 1946 had demonstrated how distant the Alemanistas were from grassroots dominance. The PP, the PAN, and even the Sinarquistas all began campaigning early in the year, and by late summer Veracruz was "fizzing like an Alka Seltzer." The port of Coatzacoalcos, a lucrative place to control, attracted twenty-one candidates for the internal elections.[139] Some Priistas, such as the newspaper editor Rubén Pabello Acosta, proposed opening up the municipal elections to greater competition.[140] The Alemanistas, now led by interim governor Angel Carvajal, decided instead to rig the contests as much as possible. A small minority of dissident victories were allowed, such as that of a left-wing railway man in Tierra Blanca; in a key shift, however, Aguilar clients—from southern municipios such as Emiliano Zapata to rich central municipios such as Soledad de Doblado—were excluded from local government.[141] The PRI even tried to overturn the results in Aguilar's hometown, Fortín, before conceding the general that and a handful of other highland municipios.[142] Nearly a third of the results were challenged; the ruthlessness of the party line extended even to protest, however, with the unprecedented announcement that rebels against the electoral decisions of the PRI would be expelled.[143]

At the same time as they clamped down on local elections, the Alemán camarilla decapitated the principal dissident unions of oil workers and railway men. Alemán had begun his relations with independent labor by sending the army to break an oil workers' strike in Poza Rica in December 1946, occupying installations, and arresting leaders on the excuse of a supposed padillista conspiracy.[144] In 1949 the army returned: in April soldiers pushed through a minority takeover of Minatitlán's Chapter 10 of the Sindicato de Trabajadores Petroleros de la República Mexicana, and in August General Gastelum led soldiers to occupy the Poza Rica union offices, beat workers, and break up dissident meetings, thus fulfilling Alemán's order to push through *charro* leader Salvador Jonguitud's takeover of the (traditionally radical) Chapter 30. (Jonguitud was a pawn of the long-running PEMEX cacique Ingeniero Jaime Merino, the boss of the Poza Rica camp.)[145] The rail workers had lost their brief independence earlier, when in 1948 their national leader, Luis Gómez Z., was jailed by the government and the union was taken over at gunpoint by Jesús Díaz de León. By 1949 Díaz de León had put former leader Manuel Moreno—an assistant mechanic who holidayed in New York and who had shot dead the secretary of the port ayuntamiento in 1940—in charge of Veracruz's four STFRM chapters.[146] Such appointments were mileposts in the national process of violently forcing unions into the party's arms, a process well advanced by 1952, when the STFRM's VII Convention made PRI membership mandatory for continued employment.[147] They also had immediate effects on labor militancy: the twenty-three strikes of 1949 shrank to a mere three in 1952.[148] Neutering the unions was, in the end, a more effective way of regulating workers' political behavior than the complex business of election rigging. Many of the key positions in city politics—the Veracruz treasury, the Orizaba ayuntamiento—were recognized union monopolies; controlling the unions was consequently a sure and subtle means of dominating much of urban life.

The newfound political control was not total. The oil workers' union continued to be riven by conflict for several years; several Poza Rica leaders were henriquista organizers in 1952, just as they had been Padillistas in 1946.[149] The 1952 municipal elections were marked by enduring dissent. The conventions that replaced primary elections were widely protested as fraudulent, and in a handful of municipios—Atoyac, Manlio Fabio Altamirano, and Ixhuatlán de Córdoba—the party had to recognize dissident Priistas' electoral victories.[150] Yet overall there was a clear trend toward increasingly sophisticated electoral management, in which repression and co-option permitted the uncontested top-down selection of candidates. The 1950 local congressional elections generated none of the public debate and overt competition of 1947. There were, quite simply, no primaries at all, none of the telling vote counts formerly published in the papers, and little of the heated participation of 1947.[151] These were the types of election satirized by the *Diario de Xalapa* as offering a "very difficult choice": Ortega-Contreras or Contreras-Ortega.[152] Gubernatorial elections, stage-managed since 1936, reached a new level of bureaucratization when the little-known technocrat Marco Antonio Muñoz was installed in 1950. (They also reached a new level of cynicism, as numerous organizations came out first for Alemán's uncle, Juan Valdés, and then equally passionately for Muñoz.)[153] The contrasting fates of the Aguilars clearly illustrated the new rules. Cándido, the family chieftain, was expelled from the PRI in November 1950 for harboring presidential ambitions.[154] He formed the Partido de la Revolución in April 1951 and launched a vacillating campaign which tacked between incendiary attacks on Henríquez Guzmán and Ruiz Cortines before opting to back the former.[155] These were, as political gossip predicted, the sputtering of a "spent cartridge"; after an ineffectual campaign Aguilar was arrested and exiled to Cuba.[156] His municipal strongholds were purged and his life, he claimed, was saved only by the governor, who removed him from General Mange's clutches.[157] Silvestre, his nephew and lieutenant, took the road more traveled by; he got in line in 1949, abandoning Cándido and leading Muñoz's gubernatorial campaign. He was rewarded with a profitable sinecure—Head of Forestry—and returned as federal deputy for Huatusco in 1949 before retiring to a long-lived cacicazgo in Córdoba.[158] After initial uncertainty surrounding the official party's future there was, by the early 1950s, a distinctly delineated new order, which could be perceived by veracruzanos of all classes. Juan Matías Valdés, a distant, semiliterate relative of Miguel Alemán, put it as well as anyone. "I know," he told the president, "that the PRI is the one who puts [people in power] and has the last word."[159]

Closing Down Politics, Opening Up for Business

Political practice in Veracruz changed radically across the Alemán years. Many of the main players from the revolutionary period and the reaction of the 1930s—Cándido Aguilar, Adalberto Tejeda, Vidal Díaz Muñoz, and the leading rural caciques—disappeared. The 1952 killing of Rafael Armenta Cornejo marked the end of the era of the more baronial pistoleros.[160] Later that year women voted in municipal elections for the second time, without the earnest warnings that had attended their first trips to the polling booth.[161] (Where they turned out in some strength, and in Sayula elected a woman mayor, but without visibly changed voting patterns very much.)[162] The party elites ended the intense electoral competition that once characterized the primaries, and enforced an increasingly ceremonial, consensual approach to elections that rewarded the obedient and excluded the dissident. The diversity that had characterized many of Veracruz's municipal governments, where communists, Aguilaristas, independent unionists, and even Sinarquistas all routinely held seats, came to an end. As the channels of political mobility narrowed, so the levels of political violence fell. That these were related phenomena was clear to Porfirio Pérez Olivares, who returned to Soledad politics in 1949, explaining that "the eternal enemies, the landowners, had lost strength, as the ruling situation was nothing like that of years before; and even though they continued to take part in the rough and tumble, they went about it in a very different way than in that other epoch full of sad and bitter memories."[163] The new politics was far from unchallenged, as Pérez Olivares discovered when he was shot in his cantina a week before taking office.[164] By 1953, however, the Alemanistas had gone a long way toward bringing the four violently competing networks of the mid-1940s inside a single, centrally brokered *pax priista*.

In the horse trading that this entailed, rural populations enjoyed an end to the intense violence of pistolero rule but suffered steep declines in land grants and political autonomy. If 1949 press reports are accurate, military veterans received almost as much land in a single grant in the Huasteca as did ejidatarios during the whole sexenio.[165] Dead peasant leaders were increasingly deployed as totems by the state's politicians: José Cardel's bones were moved to the top of Macuiltépetl, where, alongside Hilario Salas and Ursulo Galván—dead of cancer in the Rochester Clinic—they could receive periodic visits from the governor and his retinue.[166] Agraristas' living descendants could trade the political capital generated by the dead for good jobs: thus Galván's widow was on the executive committee of the Liga, which Ferrer Galván—an engineer whose "sole merit," according to Gobernación, was being Ursulo's son—took over in the late 1940s. Such leaders monopolized the shrinking cuota de poder left to peasants, moving smoothly between bureaucratic and electoral sinecures, and taking over as gatekeepers controlling peasants' access to the governor. Appointed from above—in Galván Junior's case, with neither experience nor political following—they were accountable more to their party patrons than to their constituents, whose interests they frequently overlooked. In Orizaba's 1949 elections for federal deputy, for example, Galván endorsed a candidate whom the local branch of the Liga called an enemy.[167] Agraristas had already been largely excised from state and federal congresses by 1945; they had, on the other hand, retained control over a number of municipios from which they were now progressively eliminated. The cumulative effect of twenty years of steady losses, even in the agrarista strongholds of the central coastal plain, was "mistrust, apathy, and marked dissent," as peasants complained that "even if they vote for a candidate whom they like, a different one is imposed, causing disillusion and loss of the will to exercise their civic rights."[168] Peasants made a comeback at the municipal level later in the 1950s, but they never recovered their former power at any higher level.[169]

Labor passed through a similar process of political neutering. Genuine alliances with agraristas might have produced stiffer local resistance to centralization; but the Liga had long been divided, at odds with both the grassroots and the leaderships of the CROM and the CTM.[170] The blunt coercion used against independent unions involved gunmen, the army, and the courts. The compliant, on the other hand, enjoyed political power, appreciable funds, and a certain local autonomy. Orizaba's most powerful union, Eucario León's Confederación Nacional de Trabajadores (CNT), controlled both ayuntamiento (León's brother, Primitivo, was mayor in 1951) and the town's seats in state and federal congresses. The CNT leaders were rich, taking in a million pesos a year in dues alone (and undoubtedly rents from businesses such as gambling and prostitution). In July 1948 León and other union leaders personally oversaw the assassination of four workers who had sued them for unjust dismissal.[171] The ensuing national scandal forced General Mange and the state government to send in the army for a series of spectacular arrests inside union headquarters; but the men arrested were immediately, quietly released; León was able to welcome the governor to Orizaba in October and go on to be the CROC's national leader.[172] And yet such violence was (as Gobernación observed) in part generated by the intense competition between Orizaba's rival unions for recruits. While it attested to the leaders' impunity, it also evinced their perception of grassroots workers as something more than stooges without choice or power. The elite strategy of violence was consequently paralleled by one of economistic co-option. The CNT funded a flagship secondary school in Ciudad Mendoza which, at a cost of half a million pesos, provided workers' children with carpentry, metalworking, a theater seating two thousand people, and a twenty-five-meter swimming pool.[173] The southern oil workers, another group with leaders of long-standing cacical tendencies, were similarly reported to enjoy "the best of everything" in PEMEX's exclusive schools and hospitals.[174] The labor aristocracy had proved to be the most independent minded of the working class; they were, as a consequence, the targets of simultaneous political repression and wide-ranging perks as the state cut into their onetime autonomy.

While Alemán's men followed broadly similar, stick-and-carrot approaches to peasants and labor, they adopted distinctly different policies in controlling the conservative soldiers and pistoleros. Between 1947 and 1952 the pistoleros were divided from their erstwhile military allies and eliminated as rivals to the expanding state. Some individuals survived; in the south the Colonna brothers preserved their arms and their alliance with Mange throughout the 1950s.[175] The majority of the bosses, however, were ushered off the stage, undermined, imprisoned, their henchmen eliminated through jail or extrajudicial execution, their own assassinations connived at or contrived. The military's wide-ranging political autonomy had rested, traditionally, on their management of such allies; on being the least unreliable agency for state violence in the countryside; and on their leaders' rent seeking, which led all ranks to use provincial command as the starting point for business empires. The first two pillars were greatly eroded in the period. While in 1947 the state deployed army units to arrest Crispín Aguilar, in 1952 it was the state police who occupied Plan de las Hayas after Armenta's death.[176] Astute army leaders realized they were less necessary and consequently of lesser political clout; it was noticeable that the 1952 Henríquez campaign found no takers among Mange's general staff. Yet the third pillar, the dense local networks that officers constructed, continued working in their favor to preserve extensive economic power. Such networks gave army leaders local constituents and business partners, generally influential, who would reliably (and quite often successfully) complain about attempts to transfer their military cronies out of state. They strengthened, simultaneously, officers' claims to the local knowledge that made them effective mediators for the center. Finally, the army was still periodically essential in policing the limits of the state, whether against electoral dissidents such as Cándido Aguilar; against labor, as during the 1958 rail strike; or against anachronistic rebellion, as in the 1961 Celestino Gasca fiasco. The Alemán presidency inculcated a new level of political realism in survivors like Mange, who accepted the Faustian bargain of demilitarization, bartering overall political quiescence for considerable local license.[177]

The real winners, though, were the members of the catchall political grouping which the PRI (misleadingly) called the Sector Popular. The businessmen and the state employees who formed its spine tended toward dominance by the mid-1940s: they already held, for example, a two-thirds majority in the state congress of 1945.[178] While more research is needed on the extent to which the petit bourgeoisie had ever really slipped from local power structures, lists of ayuntamiento and *junta de mejoramiento* members from the late 1940s detail their increasing control of local politics. Artisans, shopkeepers, merchants, petty bureaucrats, and the ubiquitous teachers elbowed peasants in particular out of their way: thus in Chicontepec, Tejeda's hometown and a place with a lengthy tradition of agrarista militancy, the 1949 ayuntamiento was formed—despite futile ejidatario protests—by three shopkeepers, a silversmith, a leatherworker, three teachers, two señoritas, and a rancher.[179]

One of the principal objections such people had held to joining the party, its onetime anticlericalism, was long buried. The new generation tacitly sanctioned very public displays of Catholic faith and power, in something of a return to the Porfirian modus vivendi. In 1950 the devout exhumed the body of Tejeda's church opponent Bishop Rafael Guizar y Valencia and, when found to be remarkably well preserved, made it the object of a miracle cult whose celebrations included lying in state in the cathedral, mass pilgrimages, and attempts at beatification.[180] Other political duties and taboos still required observance. State employees paid periodic extraordinary assessments to the PRI, in election years at least, and most years were election years at one level or another. Chicontepec's teachers, hardly the richest, paid up to fifteen pesos each toward a 1949 campaign fund, their contributions enforced by threats of summary dismissal.[181] And the boundaries of the politically possible were closely policed. The PAN was systematically repressed, from tiny indigenous municipios in the Sierra de Puebla to big towns such as Orizaba, where the 1949 candidate for deputy stood down when formally refused permission to use campaign posters.[182] For the trained, the well connected, or the entrepreneurial, however, debating the niceties of electoral procedure could seem quixotic in the face of the many incentives to cooperation. These ranged from bureaucrats' perks—life insurance, housing loans, pensions—to the opportunities, both competitive and rent seeking, opened by the rapid development and rural stabilization of the Alemán years. By 1950 political environments ranging from small fishing hamlets all the way up to the governor's palace were dominated by strong coalitions of businessmen and bureaucrats.[183]

The late 1940s and early 1950s saw a clear restructuring and expansion of state capacities in Veracruz. Peasants, workers, and the caciques who had struggled to dominate both groups were pressured into different versions of the same transaction: the more or less conscious surrender, like latter-day Tocquevillian aristocrats, of political autonomy in exchange for basic security and economistic gains within the confines of the state. The "rising level of conflict and dissidence within 'official' organizations" that David Skerritt identifies in the same period was, in reality, a subplot of the main story, the incorporation and / or repression of already established dissidents within increasingly dominant and ambitious, and decreasingly open and responsive, party structures.[184] In facing down regional actors the Alemán group was favored by the grim precedents of the 1930s and 1940s and by the federal largesse they could pump into developing Veracruz. As across Mexico, the center also controlled access to the booming postwar economy, acting as a gatekeeper for everything from village trucker permits through the fortunes there to be made with logging concessions or PEMEX contracts.[185] Local leaders who accepted the adverse dictates of electoral managers could hope for future handouts as paid-up party faithful, for whom the circulation of elites held out promises to all but the irredeemably *quemado,* the burnouts who, like Vidal Díaz Muñoz, found themselves in the end untouchables even in their patrias chicas.[186] The dividends of economic recovery and development—ranging from public works projects through cattle trucks for campesinos to a Nestlé factory—meanwhile helped sugar the pill for some of the ruled.[187] It was no peaceful hegemony. Military caciques and municipal power struggles persisted. The democratic railway movement of the late 1950s emerged from the Pacific Line and was led by Demetrio Vallejo from Coatzacoalcos.[188] Postwar Veracruz was, however, a more stable and less violent world than that of the late 1930s and early 1940s. And those attributes, after the experiments of agrarista revolution and Hobbesian pistolerismo, appealed to people across a wide range of places and classes.

5 • Elections, Fraud, and Democracy

Unseen Elections

The 1948 election was the epitome of fraud trumping popularity. The winning candidate bussed in voters, bought votes, stuffed the ballot boxes, and found, some six days after the polls closed, yet more votes from citizens who cast those votes in alphabetical order to give him a final majority of eighty-seven. He bought or scared notaries and judges so that no one registered his opponents' protests, and he blocked their access to the ballot boxes with "armed unshaven pistoleros."[1] He had clearly listened when the president told him at the outset of his career that "when the election is over you have to sit on the ballot boxes."[2] The president was FDR; the winning candidate, LBJ; the election, a senatorial primary in Texas, the key step en route to Johnson's own presidency.

Yet cynicism about midcentury elections was not confined to the rottener boroughs of the United States. Elections in modern Mexico, until the PRI began to lose or barter them away, were not taken very seriously either. Despite being entitled *Democracy in Mexico,* Pablo González Casanova's landmark analysis of Mexican politics devoted all of four paragraphs to "the ceremony of elections."[3] Even Priistas were tempted more to satirize than to analyze them: Rubén Pabello Acosta, a journalist and state deputy, began his coverage of the 1952 presidential elections with "the story . . . [of] a gringo who, wanting to boast to a poor Mexican . . . told him: 'In the United States the winner is definitively known the day after the elections are done.' Our rustic fellow countryman immediately replied: 'That's nothing, mister. In Mexico we know who's going to win a year before the election is held.' "[4] This was a threadbare joke, common in the (supposedly well-drilled) provincial press of the 1940s and less common in the (genuinely well-drilled) national papers. Yet even their comments could be barbed:

between 1949 and 1951 assorted writers described Mexico as dogged by bad governments, legitimized by a constitution and a promise of effective suffrage that were equally illusory. "It is said," wrote one columnist, "that [Mexico] is run along strictly democratic lines. Excuse me while I laugh!"[5]

Electoral nihilism was nothing new; similar world-weary sketches of democratic failure cropped up in Porfirian newspapers (likewise less well drilled than generally believed).[6] "Effective suffrage," wrote one journalist in 1893, "does not exist in Mexico."[7] Such statements reflected an elite commonplace—publicly expressed after 1910 in the works of Emilio Rabasa, Francisco Bulnes, and José Yves Limantour—that conceded the charge of top-down electoral fraud and attributed ultimate responsibility for the same to ordinary Mexicans, whom they depicted as culturally incapable of grappling with fair elections.[8] "No one," wrote Limantour, "can argue in good faith, no matter how giddy a jacobin they may be, that, given the condition in which the people found themselves at the end of the last century, it was possible to govern them in accordance with the letter and the spirit of the reigning institutions."[9] There had, Rabasa argued, never been a free election in Mexico; the revolutionaries' promise of "a real vote," Limantour explained, ignored "the real needs of a people who lack the indispensable enlightenment and mentality to assimilate democratic values."[10] Porfirio Díaz had called the Mexicans of the nineteenth century "unprepared for the exercise of the extreme principles of democratic government"; his followers extended that judgment well into the twentieth.[11]

Two phrases recur in condemnations of an imagined national incapacity for free elections: civic education (lack thereof) and apathy (excess thereof). Together they formed an effective pair of discursive pincers. If an election was contested with the rough and tumble of early electoral life, it was held up against an aseptic ideal of democratic practice to conclude that citizens had once more displayed their ignorance. If, on the other hand, citizens foresaw an overly manipulated contest and did not turn out, then their apathy had sabotaged the political process. Against the backdrop of this orthodoxy Mexicans—whether struggling to vote or abstaining—could be unfailingly represented as inherently incapable of democracy. This was a useful justification for the tutelary attitudes of developmentalist authoritarians and was, as such, sometimes reproduced by the revolutionaries. Both President Carranza and would-be president Pablo González issued manifestos in 1919 which explicitly linked a Mexican lack of *educación democrática* with a need to restrict political campaigning.[12] Calles's December 1928 manifesto counterintuitively invoked democracy as an end that justified the immediate suppression of competitive politics.[13] The combination of such Orwellian inversions of meaning and the volume of denunciations of electoral fraud undoubtedly influenced the corporatist vision of elections in Mexico as nothing more than celebrations of patronage and legitimizing political theater. Even their role in elite recruitment was seen as minor; Peter Smith rated the postrevolutionary electoral network as less influential than administrative or executive paths to the cabinet.[14] That the few elections to have been studied in detail were also the most clumsily rigged presidential contests—1929, 1940, 1952, and 1988—only reinforced the assumption that Mexico lacked "meaningful electoral competition" until the 1980s.[15]

Yet the black legend of Mexican elections as perennially irrelevant is unsustainable. Peasants competed vigorously in the municipal elections of post-Independence Guerrero and Oaxaca; despite his best efforts, Santa Anna's rigging of congressional elections repeatedly went awry. The 1835 centralist reforms remedied some of this, abolishing elected governors, replacing state legislatures with small administrative councils, and disenfranchising the majority of Mexicans through property thresholds.[16] Renewed popular mobilization in the wars of the 1860s brought renewed competitiveness to provincial elections; in Puebla, for example, Benito Juárez was denied his choice of governor and forced to accept pluralist legislatures and ayuntamientos in the early 1870s.[17] To Daniel Cosío Villegas the narrow margins that characterized two of Juárez's three presidential victories demonstrated the competitiveness of even these elections.[18] Some Mexicans continued to take municipal elections seriously under Porfirio Díaz, and when independent candidates won a majority they could end up bargaining their way into at least some power. This was not what Limantour described as "complete electoral inertia," and in its aftermath the 1920s and 1930s saw a return to more representative contests in which local and regional parties—the Partido Obrero de Acapulco, the Confederación Social Campesina Domingo Arenas in Tlaxcala, the Liga de Comunidades Agrarias in central Veracruz, the Partido Socialista Chiapaneco—won elections in the teeth of fierce opposition from traditional and national elites.[19] Such successes catalyzed a frenzied multiplication of parties; by the time of the 1929 presidential race, some 1,250 registered political organizations would start out in support of the presumed Callista candidate, Aaron Sáenz, leaving a mere 550 other parties uncommitted.[20] For more than a century after Independence Mexican political history was marked by the rise and fall of tides of popular mobilization that brought with them the surges of competitive elections. Such elections were frequently fraudulent and violent. They could simultaneously be broadly representative, the arenas of what Gonzalo N. Santos called "a real gunman's democracy."[21]

The formation of the PNR did not immediately push these teeming local parties into extinction, and it—and its successor the PRM—struggled to impose a central diktat on regional elections. For the first decade or so of the national party's life governors across the country defied orders and ran their own candidates against the center's picks. In 1932, 1938, and 1940 the governors in turn of Guerrero ignored explicit instructions from Gobernación and rigged elections against good party men at municipal, legislative, and gubernatorial levels. The Partido Revolucionario Chihuahuense, a PNR affiliate, ran candidates against the central PNR's chosen. In Yucatán's 1938 local elections the governor ignored the party and installed his own slates, while in Sonora the PNR outright lost the 1936 gubernatorial elections. In Tabasco the 1939 gubernatorial primaries were so fraudulent that the party annulled them and then failed to run any candidate at all. In Oaxaca Cárdenas managed to control gubernatorial elections, but only in exchange for allowing opposition wins at municipal and congressional levels.[22] It was not until the mid-1940s that party cadres sidelined their regional competitors, such as Veracruz's Partido Socialista de las Izquierdas. With their passing a provincial multiparty system ended.

Electoral competition did not. It was displaced inside the newborn PRI, whose internal elections became ferocious contests between hugely diverse politicians: peasant radicals, communist workers, right-wing ranchers, crypto-Catholics, labor caciques, and crony capitalists.[23] Such men competed among themselves, one dissident complained, as though they "weren't compañeros and members of the same party."[24] The *internas* or *primarias* were "the important political fight[s]," the "ones that count, without a doubt," their results—sometimes—an "expression of the people."[25] Primary campaigns generally took up three-quarters of the electoral season, and turnouts regularly eclipsed those of the later constitucionales.[26] These contests made the 1940s a key transition period during which a party leadership of authoritarian ambition coexisted with an eclectic membership and a powerful tradition of popular mobilization. It ended in February 1950, when the PRI's National Assembly quietly changed the party statutes and abolished primaries.[27]

Election Rigging and Popular Representation

The formal parameters of electoral life were set by three overlapping codes: the party statutes, the federal electoral code, and individual states' laws, which varied markedly. In Veracruz municipal governments served three years; in Guerrero only two. Despite the provisions of Article 41 of the Constitution—which specified that suffrage should be "universal, free, secret and direct"—the ballot in Veracruz's municipal elections between 1925 and 1940 was not even formally secret; in Guerrero, on the other hand, by 1946 the vote was at least supposed to be confidential.[28] Tracing the arcana of regional variation over time would be an encyclopedic task, as reforms were frequent. Five federal electoral laws were passed between 1942 and 1951, and some of their provisions starkly contradicted both party statutes and state laws.[29] State laws, in turn, were not invariably constitutional: thus Guerrero's 1946 electoral law empowered the governor (wary of the PAN's potential strength) to veto the electoral participation of any party by refusing a state registration, a straightforward breach of Article 121.[30] Beyond the confines of the law, variation in regional political cultures also affected the practice of elections. In 1948 San Luis Potosí was so rigorously controlled that no one knew, three weeks before polling day, that legislative elections were under way at all.[31] In central Veracruz, on the other hand, the 1947 legislative elections were bitterly fought over several months.[32] Yet even if federal, state, and municipal elections varied substantially, broad patterns of electoral practice remained stable across the period. While the dates and periodicity of elections varied substantially, all elections began with the convocatoria, the party's call for candidates, which was the starting gun for a complex, two-phase campaign race.

Until 1950 the first phase of that race centered on the primaria, the primary election. The convocatoria triggered the registration of contenders and the revision of the electoral rolls. The primary to choose a candidate followed in short order: before 1945 and after 1950 party rules specified voting in corporate conventions, while the PRI initially ran primary elections with individual voting at polling stations distributed on a geographical basis. A result was determined within a week of election day by the junta computadora, a board of elections who took charge of totaling and certifying valid the count from all the polling stations; their decision then required confirmation by regional and national party leaderships. It was "very rare that a PRM slate was seen to lose," as the party's backing was "a guarantee of triumph," and the primaries that anointed that slate were usually the central focus of competition.[33] This was expressed both in the proportion of the overall electoral process primaries occupied—commonly some 75 percent of the electoral season—and by their turnouts which (even in manipulated accounts) frequently surpassed those of the constitucionales. In disputed elections competition spilled outside the party as losing Priistas seceded to run at the head of independent, fly-by-night parties. The second phase of constitucionales and the recognition of results put an end to contests at all bar municipal levels, where postelectoral haggling

Endurance on the primary election trail. Archivo General de la Nación, Mexico City, Dirección de Investigaciones Políticas y Sociales, box 782, file 118.

was endemic. An election was a long haul: the 1946 party statutes specified six months' advance notice for state and legislative elections and nine months for presidential elections.[34] Informally, it could be even longer; after just five months of Alemán's presidency one group launched a manifesto proposing his successor.[35]

Mexicans frequently depicted elections as rites of appointment, predetermined by coteries of the influential clustered around presidents, governors, or regional strongmen, the "grandes electores."[36] At the highest level, what might be called an informal senate composed of ex-presidents had to sign off on the incumbent president's choice of successor.[37] At a gubernatorial and senatorial level, the presidential inner circle was believed to decide most contests in advance. Congressional elections were more of a gray zone, their outcomes a barometer of the relative influence of regional and national elites. Mayoral elections, finally, were swayed in major towns and cities by federal power brokers and governors, while in lesser towns and villages local deputies were often seen as kingmakers. Widespread popular belief in such straightforward powers of appointment shines through the begging letters sent to the prominent. "My backers esteem me," begins one of the many such missives President Alemán received from long-lost relatives in the Veracruz backwoods, "and proposed me for the presidency of this village of San Juan Evangelista I want as a poor man you to recommend me to all those who surround you. . . . I was very close to your father and I helped him in what I could and you are my blood and he always said that if he could he would give me a cozy job. . . . I am the eldest brother of the dead Próspero Gómes Alemán and . . . I always saw you as family and for that reason I want you with your power to give me [the mayor's job] . . . you don't know me but I love you and please answer favorably and forgive me my spelling."[38] Six similar letters to Alemán wangled another distant relative, Juan Matías Valdés, a councilman's job; across the border in Loma Bonita, Oaxaca, an Alemán cousin running for mayor was described as "behaving honorably . . . despite this relationship." Clientelist faith in kinship was well founded.[39]

Yet the apparent simplicity of central control was belied by the intense effort elites invested in managing elections.[40] It was not haphazard that Priistas conceptualized elections as problems; the problema electoral offered a complex series of interests to be reconciled and conflicts to be resolved, and in that process the machinations of rival factions and the levers of popular mobilization all counted. Behind the problem lay a centuries-long fixation with the *municipio libre*—its roots ran back to both the Spanish *comunidad* and the indigenous *altépetl*—only strengthened by the rhetoric of revolutionary democracy, immovably lodged in public discourse. Government documents were mechanically stamped with the Maderista slogan "sufragio efectivo"; the second point of the so-called Alemán doctrine, disseminated in primary schools, was that the "government is and must be considered as essentially democratic."[41] Leaders ritually promised to live up to these words. Assurances of real contests were given by Cárdenas to Almazán in 1939, by Avila Camacho to all the presidential precandidates in 1945, by Alemán to the congressional aspirants of 1949, and by Ruiz Cortines, in his inauguration speech, to the country as a whole.[42] Avila Camacho promised guerrerenses clean gubernatorial elections in 1941 and 1945 before overseeing the energetic manipulation of both contests; gubernatorial statements of respect for the self-determination of their municipios were political clichés.[43] Yet it was all "eye-wash," concluded a scathing report from the U.S. embassy.[44] Elections were bypassed completely on occasion. When a tropical storm spoiled the 1940 municipal elections in the port of Veracruz they were never rerun; some villages, above all in indigenous zones, complained repeatedly of being denied even the slightest pretense of elections; even some market towns were ruled for long periods by appointed councils.[45] In 1948 Olinalá, Guerrero, had not had a municipal election in eight years.[46] Yet such authoritarian practice constituted a clear breach of the moral schema of local politics, and ordinary

Mexicans complained bitterly. "Even if we are peasants," wrote one group of ejidatarios to Gobernación, "we know our obligations to the right to vote and be voted for, and we hate dirty tricks and professional politicians."[47] State authorities sometimes reacted and sacked ayuntamientos installed through flawed or imaginary elections.[48] For elites, elections were a necessary evil, their favorable outcomes likely but not guaranteed, their manipulation, consequently, a vital dark art.

Election riggers practiced that art at five sites: the convocatoria, the primarias, the constitucionales, the junta computadora that tallied vote counts to declare a victor, and the *comisión dictaminadora* in congress who ratified or denied that victory. In some races foreknowledge of official preference was enough to suppress competition: of the four gubernatorial elections held in Veracruz and Guerrero between 1944 and 1951, three were single-candidate beauty parades. (Real beauty parades could be much more competitive, detonating explosive mixtures of politics, aspiration, and sexual jealousy.)[49] Other elections required more intensive management. "Undesirable" candidates for ayuntamientos were sometimes straightforwardly denied the chance to register, their disenfranchisement enforced by "the terrorism often exercised by municipal bodies."[50] Where such blunt measures were impossible, election riggers could go to the opposite extreme and flood the registry with spurious candidacies, allowing the chosen one to control more than his share of the polling stations and lending his victory a cosmetic touch of competition. Once rivalries were demarcated, the next step was the mustering of support from the party sectors: for municipal and legislative elections this stemmed from individual ejidos, union chapters, and the *organizaciones populares,* the catchall sector for everyone else, while gubernatorial and presidential elections required the candidate to be anointed at statewide or nationwide conventions. Well-engineered conventions covered top-down manipulation with a façade of popular democracy, and they were frequently held without warning. *Madrugando* the opposition—"getting up earlier than them," that is to say, ambushing—allowed party leaders to flood a provincial cinema or sports ground with stooge delegates and impose candidates before dissidents could muster their own delegates. When surprise was lost convention fixers took to more labor-intensive methods: the creation of phony collective organizations, the intimidation of what unions and peasant leagues actually existed, the forgery of nominations from far-off ejidos. Finally, the police could always physically bar stubborn dissidents from the convention hall.[51] These public demonstrations of elite preference thinned the ranks of candidates notably; the absence of such clear signaling in lower-level elections helped make these messier and more competitive.

When primaries were really competitive the electoral alchemy of mobilization, demobilization, and fraud became critical. Deputies, mayors, bureaucrats, peasant and union leaders, corrido singers, and reporters were all energetically deployed to guide—*orientar*—the electorate while slandering their opponents. (A corrido circulated about Ojeda called him Guerrero's Satan; in Veracruz an "Open Letter from Victoriano Huerta to Ezequiel Padilla" attributed an imaginative range of sins to the latter.)[52] Campaign rallies were fleshed out by *acarreados,* "the peasants and the unemployed who lend themselves to come to any [political] event in favor of any candidate under the incentive of a Sunday out, to drink copiously and to earn themselves one or two pesos to animate any of these farces."[53] They were transported by dragooned bus drivers, who fumed about losing hours of work "to go like flocks of sheep to shout and applaud a man [they] didn't even know."[54]

Acarreados were more than a lumpen electorate, though; they included bureaucrats, teachers, and unionized workers, whose participation as muralist backdrops or voting fodder was often coerced by threats to livelihoods that ranged from losing wages to losing ejidal lands.[55] If he did not attend an Alemán rally, one bureaucrat told a Padillista, "he would be suspended from work for eight days, which would be miserable for his family."[56] (Such men did not always make docile backdrops: the acarreados shipped to Mexico City for Ruiz Cortines's swearing-in as candidate began leaving halfway through his acceptance speech.)[57] Regional leaders reviewed the party municipal committees, weeding out less reliable election riggers, and attempted to deny dissidents their quota of polling station representatives.[58] As the party cadres arranged the institutional conditions for official victory, they disrupted the day-to-day operations of their opponents. Heavies raided campaign offices and stole their banners, posters, and records.[59] The trucks that were essential to campaigning were denied, by dint of fining drivers who transported dissidents.[60] Public notaries, required under some electoral laws to certify the assemblies that constituted parties, were generally prominent in the local PRI and often refused to do so for their opponents.[61] While only a minority of elections was ever seriously violent—during the most contested local elections of the 1940s only 17 percent of municipios in Guerrero, and 5 percent of those in Veracruz, actually reported violence—threats, beatings, and stabbings were common enough: the 1950 Veracruz gubernatorial election was singled out as unprecedented precisely because it never made the crime pages.[62]

When the outcome was still in question on election day rigging peaked. Ayuntamientos mislaid electoral rolls, party agents refused to distribute ballot papers or voter credentials, and those dissidents who were not disenfranchised could always be outnumbered by squads of hired voters who voted early and often. In Taxco's 1948 primaries, for example, the bulk of the electorate was formed by 450 acarreados who "went from polling booth to polling booth . . . there were those who voted up to three times in a single booth."[63] Policemen, soldiers, and pistoleros could arrest dissidents or drive voters away, in clashes that were only occasionally lethal.[64] The violent theft of ballot boxes was less risky and more commonplace: during Coatepec's 1949 municipal primary, for example, Elías Forzan, "seeing himself lost," had the ballot boxes stolen by a gang armed with knives and clubs.[65] He then saw himself win.

When primaries were close enough to end in such open, delegitimizing fraud, the losers often seceded and ran against the party in the ensuing constitucionales. In such cases the electoral engineering of the primary season was repeated and intensified. *Orientaciones*—"orientations" that ranged from categorical hints to categorical orders—became more frequent and less coded, and ran increasingly through the conduits of the state. In June 1946 Mexico's mayors were instructed to "cooperate, as much as is possible, so that all the inhabitants of your municipio, registered or not, go to the ballot boxes to deposit their vote in favor of our candidate, señor Licenciado don Miguel Alemán."[66] The repression of "undesirable" campaigns became more authoritarian once these left the party fold. Local authorities refused to allow opposition candidates to hold rallies and destroyed their posters; agents distributing opposition election material were frequently arrested. (Even when, as in the case of Poza Rica's Henriquistas, they were sticking up posters at 4 am.)[67] Local authorities openly sanctioned ballot box theft: during Xalapa's 1944 congressional election, a policeman stopped a group carrying away a ballot box and, informed that they had the governor's blessing, replied "if that's the case, take it, I'll protect you."[68] Regional governments threatened state employees with dismissal for supporting the opposition. In 1940 the state government fired 27 Chilpancingo bureaucrats for voting for Almazán.[69] In 1947 Culiacán's public transport workers were warned that they would lose their concession if they did not switch sides; three councilors who failed to do so were fired.[70] (Inside the PRI, ballot papers recorded individual voters' decisions, requiring their names as well as those of their chosen candidates.)[71] Perhaps the greatest change was the increase in the frequency and intensity of violence between primaries and constitucionales. Violence could erupt in an unplanned escalation of polling day rivalries, or it

"Mexicans Hold a 'Free' Election for Presidente at the Cost of 100 Killed." *Life* (July 22, 1940). Robert Capa © International Center for Photography/Magnum Photos.

could be a more deliberate phenomenon; in extremis party gunmen undertook the purposive, theatrically violent occupation of public space for the entire day, something that happened once in Mexico City—in 1940—and many times in the unsung streets and squares of the provinces.[72]

Such blanket clampdowns were not always rational, for even after polling day there remained assorted bureaucratic ways to alter unwelcome results. Local officials, seeing the voting run against the official candidate, could refuse to install the junta computadora.[73] The party delegate collecting the vote packets could insert votes for the official candidate before they came anywhere near the junta; during Coatepec's 1947 primaries for local deputy a federal agent watched as Ferrer Galván's 74 votes in polling booth no. 1 were inflated by the party representative to 269.[74] If the balance of local forces left dissidents controlling both vote packets and junta computadora, then electoral fixers could conjure up a second junta computadora, complete with a second set of votes, party documentation, and photos to prove their physical existence. The 1947 legislative election in Paso del Macho was, for example, convincingly (if crookedly) won on election day by Anselmo Sandoval, an aguilarista cacique. The local PRI tackled their problema electoral with a parallel count committee, which the mayor denounced as fraudulent; it worked nonetheless to get Alfonso Mendivil the seat.[75]

If an undesirable candidate navigated the multiple sites for manipulation of both primary election and constitucional, there remained the simple veto that the legislature could exert over election results. Dissident victories could get as far as a certificate of a majority of votes, presented ceremonially before congress, only to be overturned by the deputies of the comisión dictaminadora. In Sayula the 1952 municipal primaries elected Saturnino Dodero, whose victory was subsequently blocked by the local deputy, who gave the party committee signed instructions from the governor to select Juan Vidaña. Undeterred, Dodero seceded and won the constitucional by 997 votes to 103. When congress met to ratify the elections, the local deputy barred Dodero's representatives from the session and awarded Vidaña victory.[76] This was not unusual practice; when Ferrer Galván was declared (despite vote inflation) to have lost Veracruz's 7th district by a factor of some 20 to 1 the Liga protested and the result, already public, was changed in his favor.[77] Finally, municipal elections that were strongly contested were almost universally characterized by assorted breaches of electoral law, and as such could always be annulled or vetoed by the state legislature or governor to make way for an appointed council. "Annulling constitucionales is nothing new in the dirtiness of national politics," declared Acapulco's *Trópico* in the aftermath of the 1944 municipal elections, in which nearly one in five of the winning slates was replaced by appointed councils.[78] There were, in conclusion, multiple procedural safety nets which protected party brokers from unwanted election results.

So far, so top down. This broad panoply of methods to manipulate elections chimes with the stereotypical image of swaggering priista domination: an image made literature by Carlos Fuentes, cartoon by Abel Quezada, memoirs by Gonzalo N. Santos, film by *La ley de hérodes,* and political science by Frank Brandenburg. Yet the lack of grassroots agency in such depictions does not square with the intensity that elites invested in rigging elections. Popular mobilization threatened in reality to alter the outcome of an election at three stages: during the cognitive/managerial process of *auscultación*—the revealingly ubiquitous metaphor of a doctor taking the electorate's pulse—across the long haul of a contested campaign, and inside the games of bluff and barter that began when election day ended.

For a start, the preferences established higher up the political ladder were not plucked from thin air, clientelism or rent seeking alone. The detailed biographies that spies and party agents drew up on precandidates and the painstaking tours of governors' representatives and local deputies give substance to the notion of auscultación: the search, through a certain amount of popular consultation, for genuinely popular, or at least broadly acceptable candidates.[79] (The researchers' methodologies were admittedly ad hoc: one agent counted the numbers of corridos each candidate for a governorship had inspired.)[80] Before a convocatoria had been issued, the ambitious encouraged their supporters to write in to central government promoting them as men (and increasingly women) of the people. Guerrero's teachers' union suggested that its members write "a little letter or a simple note to the diverse organs of the Party . . . as well as to the Interior Minister, with a copy to the person whom you are supporting, in which you make clear your recognition of him whose work has earned it. . . . One must have faith in the zeal of our National Government, which in a shrewd way gauges the mood of the people."[81] The ensuing letters were phrased in terms of an explicit quid pro quo: the promotion of would-be candidates in exchange for their track record of delivering state benefits—development projects, land grants, soft loans—for their would-be constituents. Gobernación agents and state power brokers applied similar litmus tests of popularity in their attempts to make sense of provincial politics. "My aim," wrote one of San Andrés Tuxtla's local worthies to the governor, introducing his recommendations for municipal slates, "is to procure that the Ayuntamientos be represented as well as possible, by honest people, who have the backing of the Municipio's inhabitants to the end of getting some public work done."[82] Gobernación reports on candidates came to conclude with a section headed "Popular Acceptance."[83] Taking this seriously was, as an eloquent dissident from Tierra Blanca, Veracruz, put it, in the best interests of the power brokers themselves, as "even admitting that the official party does not dare to play fair for fear of some probability that power will be taken from it, its own interest in enduring should counsel it to install better-chosen elements in public office."[84] Revolutionary orthodoxy, enduring even as it was betrayed, held that elected officials should have some record of satisfying popular goals.

Some did. Elections were very frequent; the states ran an average of more than one election a year, and the more frequent elections are, the more difficult they are to rig. Grassroots resistance exercised decisive influence over municipal elections in particular. In this respect priista Mexico might be compared to the Kuomintang's regime in Taiwan, where single-party national dictatorship—leavened with a token opposition eloquently dubbed the outsiders, *dangwai*—coexisted with competitive local primary elections.[85] From a federal perspective, the insignificance of most municipal governments made what Robert Dahl termed "the cost of toleration" of defeats lower than the "cost of suppression"; meanwhile, for most voters, municipal contests counted more and were more verifiable than state or federal elections.[86] Popular election monitoring worked: "The irregularities in the voting for deputies," noted Gobernación during Taxco's 1948 primaries, "were the greater, as more attention was paid to the municipal elections."[87]

Nor were electoral managers invariably powerful enough to impose the party's solutions. In 1947 a Gobernación agent visiting electoral hotspots reported Catholic locals getting their way in the face, quite literally, of party higher-ups. In Guanajuato the sinarquista merchants and hacendados of San Luis de la Paz straightforwardly defied the agent, the governor's representative, and the garrison commander, and rigged the 1947 election against a priista popular front spanning rival Sinarquistas, agraristas, miners, teachers, and a lonely communist.[88] In Zinapécuaro, Michoacán, the PRI's central representative watched helplessly (he'd been threatened with the jailhouse) as the PRI's municipal representative destroyed his own party's ballots and filled in those of the opposition.[89] And it was not just Catholics who defied their betters. During the 1946 Veracruz municipal elections two of the governor's fixers toured sixteen southern municipios in an attempt to manage the forthcoming contests. They were seemingly successful in 38 percent of the municipios, where local politicians agreed to follow the party line. In 44 percent of cases, however, local Priistas either continued faction fighting or rejected the suggested candidates.[90] In the aftermath of the elections, moreover, the governor's men faced further disappointment; half the municipal committees that had agreed to follow the party line reneged and returned dissident slates. The sum of electoral outcomes, in short, matched the party operators' goals in less than a quarter of cases.

Thus burned, the party elites accordingly approached Veracruz's 1949 municipal elections warily: they issued the convocatoria one rather than the statutory six months in advance, and held public meetings with local deputies "to end the campaigns of diatribe and insults prevalent on other occasions."[91] Yet a sample of twenty-two results from these elections reinforces the impression of the partial, patchwork, and negotiated nature of provincial electoral control. Here six cases were strongly contested, with rival factions claiming victory.[92] While none of the dissidents were allowed to win outright, frantic backstage negotiations ensued: in this case, the party's list of winning slates was delayed three times, and when released three weeks late it identified only the presidentes municipales since "the pulling and pushing of electoral accommodation was still under way."[93] Popular leaders, or, indeed, caciques—discerning the two is difficult, at times semantic—who toed the line stood to earn compensatory electoral posts, bureaucratic jobs, the promise of outright victory next time. The losers of the 1947 congressional primaries for Orizaba and Córdoba were generously rewarded for accepting rigged defeats: within a couple of years one had made federal deputy, the other workers' leader on the PRI's regional committee.[94] Guerrero's teachers, having backed the unusually detested Gómez Maganda for governor, wrote to Gobernación announcing that they "had determined that two of our most zealous and hardworking leaders should take part in the next Government."[95] Embracing co-optation could be an individual's self-serving sellout; it could also be a roundabout but effective path to popular representation.

The other path was to continue resistance after the elections. Protests to Gobernación and the Presidency commonly marked both the immediate aftermath of polling day and the formal transfer of power. Local traditions and national precedents of popular violence in response to electoral fraud underwrote such letters. Two postelectoral massacres—León, Guanajuato, and Tapachula, Chiapas—marked the acceptable limits of hardball provincial practice. The foreknowledge that central government would fire politicians who used massacres to manage local politics lent ordinary Mexicans a powerful lever for postelectoral haggling. To avoid "bloody clashes," wrote an agrarista dissident in Ajuchitlán, Gobernación should override the state government's recognition of his opponents, dispatch an inspector, and recognize his slate.[96] In the tiny serrano municipio of Rafael Delgado, Veracruz, dissidents in the 1946 village elections threatened to be "ready for any sacrifice," warning that "the bloodshed . . . that has occurred in different parts of the Republic and recently in Tapachula, Chis., should we believe be a reason for this pueblo to be heard."[97] Similar threats came from Demetrio Vallejo's CTM chapter in Coatzacoalcos, who protested at their defeat in the 1946 municipal elections by telling the governor that he "[would] be responsible if the pueblo use their force and sovereignty, as in León, Guanajuato, to have their will respected."[98]

Such brinkmanship signals were directed horizontally, at local rivals, as well as vertically to state and national governments, and were made flesh in the crowds that physically denied imposed ayuntamientos access to town halls. In 1947 the newly elected ayuntamientos of Apaxtla, Coahuayutla, Cocula, and Tixtla, Guerrero, all met with enough popular resentment to dissuade their members from turning up to take power; in Guasave, Sinaloa, a shoot-out achieved the same end.[99] When such controversial ayuntamientos did move into the town hall dissidents could form a parallel government and appeal for investigation and recognition from Mexico City. In 1939 there were parallel ayuntamientos in nearly all of San Luis Potosí's municipios; in 1948 excluded agraristas formed parallel ayuntamientos in nearly a quarter of Guerrero's municipios.[100] Sometimes the two phenomena coalesced, and dissidents would seize the *palacio municipal* to install their own government. In Ajuchitlán, Guerrero, gunmen in the town hall opened fire on agraristas protesting the rigged 1948 elections, and "the indignation of the Pueblo provoked, they hurled themselves through the doors and windows with sticks, stones, machetes, billhooks, daggers, pistols, shotguns and other arms, and stormed the hall."[101] The authorities could read such popular violence as revolt and choose repression: the Ajuchitlán agraristas (who had formed a similar parallel ayuntamiento four years earlier) ended up languishing in jail for months without trial.[102] The choice of repression could trigger formal rebellion: in 1962 soldiers bloodily repulsed Genaro Vásquez's attempted seizure of Iguala's city hall, driving him into the mountains.[103] (Rubén Jaramillo took the same path a decade earlier in Morelos, heading for the sierra preaching revolution after his exclusion from the gubernatorial elections.)[104] Yet authorities could also recognize violence as collective bargaining by riot, influential practice in Mexico since colonial times, and negotiate a compromise.[105] Postelectoral resistance was a risky strategy, but one with three realistic aims: an immediate veto on opponents' entry to government, seats on a compromise municipal council, and a greater sensitivity to future demands.

The critical questions are How frequently were elections competitive? and How frequently did popular mobilization decisively influence their outcome? Both are difficult to answer. By the mid-1940s the inevitability of party triumph in federal elections was so ingrained that when one PRM candidate lost he blew his brains out on the podium of congress, complaining that trying to change the party's decision was "as futile as trying to melt the snow from the top of Popocatépetl with a single match."[106] The (sometimes literally) warring factions of earlier state congresses had vanished, replaced by the homogeneity of the carro completo. Of the ten legislatures elected in Guerrero and Veracruz between 1940 and 1952, only one, the 1942–44 guerrerense congress, was overtly divided. In such contexts it is a fair assumption that the auscultación stage was the main point at which public opinion could influence results. But local contests were a different matter. "Municipal elections," fretted a leading Priista in Veracruz, "excite the citizens too much and in many places give rise to fights and divisions."[107] Such fights, divisions, and protests were logical only if Mexicans entered these elections believing they might somehow win.[108] And

Table 5.1: Municipal election protests in Guerrero, 1944–52

Year	% primary elections/conventions protested	% constitucionales protested	% municipalities reporting violence	% protested elections overall
1944	11	47	17	49
1946	1	8	0	8
1948	19	33	8	36
1950	—	8	1	8
1952	—	13	1	13

Source: AGN/DGG-2.311M (9) series.

Table 5.2: Municipal election protests in Veracruz, 1943–52

Year	% primary elections/conventions protested	% constitucionales protested	% municipalities reporting violence	% protested elections overall
1943	5	9	0.5	12
1946	3	13	1	13
1949	18	24	4.5	31
1952	—	17	1	17

Source: AGN/DGG-2.311M(26) series.

the high rates of protests across the 1940s and early 1950s—when on average a fifth and in some years as many as half of the elections examined were protested—suggest that a lot of Mexicans voted for their mayors and councilors in the belief that these elections were competitive.

Were they right? Some municipal elections were indeed taken by dissident or opposition candidates, the PAN winning the first such uphill struggle in 1946 in Quiroga, Michoacán. In 1949 the PRI's imposition of Aniceto de los Santos, an abigeo, in Sayula was overturned in favor of the popular candidate Gelasia Ceballos.[109] In 1952 the state government awarded Cuetzala del Progreso to the PP and sent policemen to evict recalcitrant local Priistas from town hall, while independent slates won three ayuntamientos in Veracruz. Across the 1950s state governments in Oaxaca faced the stark choice of sending in troops or acknowledging PAN victories across much of the Mixteca.[110] Yet overt upsets were comparatively rare.[111] By far the most common result of popular mobilization was a more subtle exercise of power, as dissidents became veto players who barred the unpopular from power.[112] Just how frequently such blackballing worked is difficult to quantify. The most historically visible mechanisms of veto are annulled elections or the gubernatorial appointment of a municipal council or both. Yet these can signify radically different outcomes. Annulled elections could represent a successful popular veto; they could also mean a popular victory being overturned. Municipal councils could be vehicles for compromise; in Atzacán a council smoothed over the violent competition between the Liga and local union chapters for peasant recruits.[113] They could, on the other hand, be petty, often enough military, dictatorships, installed to override local representation: agrarista strongholds such as Ursulo Galván and Villa Cardel, or San Jerónimo, were repeatedly ruled by appointed councils.[114] Between 1943 and 1949 Salinas, San Luis Potosí, was ruled by one Colonel Quintero; at one point or another across the 1940s the state government of Puebla appointed military officers to head such councils in every major town outside the capital.[115] Such equifinality—superficially identical results covering very different processes and actual outcomes—muddies the interpretive waters.

Yet it is clear that while state and national elites aspired to thorough electoral control, they found it too costly to establish universally. Veracruz authorities struggled for a decade to root out municipal clients of the Aguilarista cacicazgo; in Guerrero the campaign against local agraristas was abandoned half finished, the attempt almost costing the governor his job. Even that archetypal cacique Gonzalo N. Santos was incapable of complete electoral domination, negotiating compromises with the serially unruly in what Wil Pansters has dubbed "inclusive subordination," the "negotiation with dissident groups and their incorporation, in some form, into local administrations."[116] In 1945 his candidate for local deputy in the Huasteca, his patria chica, was driven out by locals in a (Santos-like) hail of bullets; in 1948 Gobernación believed him incapable of controlling at least three of the state's nine electoral districts.[117] Moreover, the repression Santos employed to defend his electoral preeminence was unsustainable. In 1952 his arrest of a PAN/Sinarquista candidate detonated a "civic insurgency"; in 1959 his bitter enemy Salvador Nava, a right-wing Catholic, became mayor of the state capital.[118] The widespread efficacy of local mobilization—whether to install the genuinely popular or to veto the genuinely unpopular—was demonstrated by the opposition's focus on local elections. As early as 1948 the PAN ran several hundred municipal campaigns; the municipio, Efraín González Luna told the PAN convention, was Mexico's "political wellspring."[119]

That belief eventually paid off. The end-of-century democratic transition began in villages and towns: between 1979 and 1987 opposition parties won more than half of Mexico's 236 most important municipios, foreshadowing and helping drive later victories at gubernatorial and senatorial levels.[120] Yet those victories did not come out of the blue. From the late 1950s on the PAN won major cities such as San Luis Potosí, Hermosillo, Monclova, and Mérida, and minor, generally serrano, villages. Elsewhere the PRI had from the start been a fig leaf covering autonomous parties, such as the Charistas—partisans of the popular cacique Heliodoro Charis—who dominated Juchitán, Oaxaca, from the 1940s to the mid-1960s, or the popular representatives who ran Zinacantán, Chiapas, until the 1970s.[121] At times Priistas campaigned vigorously against their own party; even the Panista Nava was a member of the PRI's Sector Popular.[122] In the Mixteca Baja Panistas with strong electoral showings dominated the compromise Juntas de Administración Civil or, in smaller municipios, simply superseded the official priista town councils with undeclared authorities of their own exercising the real power.[123] Both party and people knew that such representation was underpinned by the threat of collective bargaining by riot; the sort of large-scale, widespread riots that broke out in the municipios of Zacatecas in 1958, Chihuahua and Baja California in 1959. (Where someone upped the ante by planting a time bomb in the governor-elect's office.)[124] That collective bargaining by riot worked is clear in its subsequent, long-lasting ubiquity. In 1982, thirty-five out of a sample of fifty protests at municipal election results involved forcible town hall seizures.[125] The commonplace that competitive elections were absent from Mexico's towns and villages until those years is wrong. More accurate is the national division of power advanced by Adolfo Ruiz Cortines: federal legislators and governors for the presidency, local legislators for the governors, and municipal governments for the pueblo.[126]

Taking Mexicans Away from Elections, and Elections Away from Mexicans

Alemán came to office promising democratization. President Avila Camacho had invoked wartime necessity to justify the suppression of political competition ("in the face of the war to which Nazi-fascist aggression has driven us, internal controversies—no matter how respectable—must go silent").[127] But the war had not brought peace to provincial Mexico, and as it ended a pent-up demand for reform emerged. In September 1944 the leader of congress "made a frontal attack on the PRM," criticizing "the one-party system in Mexico, and the gangster methods used at election times, which make democracy a farce."[128] In the same year Guerrero's governor lamented the weakness, dependence, and caciquismo of the state's municipios, and proposed redrawing local boundaries to create a lesser number of stronger, genuinely autonomous municipios libres.[129] By the end of 1945 the PAN were demanding electoral reform while persistent rumors predicted a comprehensive liberalization of the political system.[130] The tipping point came in January 1946 at León, Guanajuato, when the army machine-gunned a crowd of Catholic militants who were protesting fraudulent elections; at their national convention soon after the PRM abolished itself and arose from the ashes as the Partido Revolucionario Institucional, the PRI.[131] That party's founding statement declared that it "accepted absolutely and without reservation the democratic system of government" in the opening sentence (the revolution came in second); Alemán, taking the oath as the PRI's candidate, vowed "to struggle in the polls for a democratic triumph, without deals, tricks or violence, respecting the verdict of the pueblo even if this is adverse."[132]

This rhetoric was read in the remotest villages as an offer "to change with the new Party the hateful procedures of electing Representatives by naming between camarillas."[133] In the cities "public opinion [was] marked by optimism and confidence," as a regime that the playwright Rodolfo Usigli called a "manufacturer and salesman of wholesale hope" took power; the hope was, Cándido Aguilar remembered, that "democracy would take root" under Alemán.[134] Early developments seemed to substantiate the rhetoric. The PAN won their first municipio, in Michoacán, and four seats in congress. Alemán fired the governors of Chiapas and Oaxaca for postelectoral violence during his second month in office. These were, the British ambassador wrote, "milestone[s] on Mexico's march to democracy." Manuel Gómez Morín was "very hopeful" about the new government; his party, at their 1947 convention, expressed support for President Alemán, and even the Sinarquistas were enthused.[135] There was a Latin America–wide *apertura democrática*—democratic spring—in the midforties that left all major countries formal—if ill-defined—democracies; Mexico was an exemplar.[136] Invited to address the U.S. Congress in 1947, Alemán lectured his hosts on the need to protect democracy across the region.[137]

As in the rest of Latin America, however, Mexico's was a brief, quickly reversed transition. Mobilization varied greatly from the start: while some Mexicans were experiencing competitive local elections in 1946 and 1947, others were asking plaintively, "Why are elections held?" or "Why vote, if the results are going to be the same whether we vote or not?"[138] By the early 1950s belief in Alemán's promises of reform had faded across Mexico, the opposition—dissident Priistas, the PAN, the PP, and the Sinarquistas—disenchanted by the combination of promises of reform, primaries, presidential denunciations of caciquismo, and tightening central control of elections. In Otatitlán, Veracruz, less than 10 percent of the villagers voted in the 1949 municipal elections, and the winner received thirty votes, representing 1 percent of the population.[139] In Matamoros, Tamaulipas, a Gobernación agent made three tours of the 1951 municipal elections and counted a total of fifty-five voters at the only four polling booths (out of twenty plus) that had any voters at all.[140] In Morelos the Partido Agrario–Obrero Morelense did not run gubernatorial candidates after Jaramillo's defeats in 1946 and 1952, concluding that "por las buenas no se puede."[141] Municipal election protests declined in Guerrero in the early 1950s. Shifting elite practices catalyzed popular disenchantment, with press statements phrased as communiqués transmuting elections into political cases to be resolved from on high. In 1949 readers of the *Diario de Xalapa* in Coatepec were informed, two weeks before the primaries, that their new mayor would be Elías Forzán; in 1953 *El Dictamen* let the citizens of Soledad de Doblado know that their new mayor would be Enrique Domínguez; progovernment newspapers in Guerrero and Veracruz announced the results of the 1950 and 1951 gubernatorial elections before the campaign season even began.[142] Such news constituted straightforward official denials of the relevance of elections.

There had always been pronounced cyclical and geographical variation in the intensity of election rigging, popular mobilization, and popular representation. Municipal elections that preceded either a presidential or gubernatorial contest were less competitive than local contests at other times, as reliable village apparatchiks were installed to oversee the grassroots management of the important election. This passed, the inevitable purges orchestrated by the incoming president or governor, largely clientelist in rationale, could be presented as political reform in a useful piece of window dressing. Conflictual regions could show clear boom and bust patterns of electoral manipulation: thus Guerrero's local elections under Leyva Mancilla very visibly alternated between the high-cost, total imposition of Leyvistas and more conciliatory compromise formulae. Yet the changes in the practice of Mexican elections in the late 1940s went beyond cyclical variation. A handful of far-reaching institutional changes made elections abruptly less competitive, for all the façade of a tolerated opposition and a Federal Electoral Commission, and made Mexicans more cynical about the value of their vote.[143]

The central change was the end of primary elections. Primaries are a universal demand of dissidents fighting party fixers. In the United States Theodore Roosevelt instituted them in his 1912 presidential run; in safe congressional districts of the 1940s they were "not a successful alternative to two-party competition," but they were nonetheless "real election[s]," two-thirds of them close calls.[144] In Lyndon Johnson's Texas, Democratic primaries were the only elections that counted, "the crucial election[s] in a one-party state";[145] overall about half of all U.S. congressional districts were such one-party states, a pattern particularly prevalent in the South.[146] In Mexico primaries were introduced by centrist party leaders desperate for legitimation in a struggle against popular dissatisfaction, elite reformism, and looming military subversion. They briefly fostered intense and overt competition in provincial politics. But PRI leaders got more grassroots democracy than they bargained for and might well have abolished primaries sooner had the devaluation of 1948 not profoundly shaken the government. Instead, severely weakened, Alemán promised further reform; "most unusually" congress held an extraordinary session in January 1949 to draw up a new electoral law mandating primaries for all parties. Ten months later the government had made a remarkable recovery, and in December Alemán felt strong enough to launch a "systematic anti-Communist campaign" and to pass legislation banning primaries.[147] The PRI then changed its statutes in the national convention of February 2–3, 1950, which sat for two brief mornings and acclaimed the return to bloc convention voting as "new waves of light, principles of the purest democracy."[148] This was something of a U-turn: five years earlier, founding the party, they had condemned the same procedures as antidemocratic.[149]

The new level of central control went far beyond bloc voting; across the late 1940s and 1950s priista elites placed further procedural restrictions on internal and external electoral competition.[150] Party regulations were progressively tightened to decrease the length of electoral seasons. While the PRM statutes had specified that the convocatoria for presidential elections be issued at least a year before election day, the PRI statutes of 1946 reduced that to nine months, and the reformed 1950 statutes removed any deadline whatsoever, specifying that convocatorias be issued "when convenient."[151] New electoral laws hindered dissident and opposition campaigns by requiring the notarization of their assemblies and protests; notaries, generally prominent in the local party, frequently refused to do it.[152] In Acapulco in 1948 all notaries had their licenses revoked bar one, Alfredo Díaz Garzón, who happened to be the cousin and campaign manager of the PRI's candidate. (He unsurprisingly refused to certify the opposition's denunciations of fraud.)[153] Legal obstacles to opposition campaigning increased while checks on fraud decreased: in Guerrero Governor Gómez

Maganda increased the state police budget and authorized policemen to break up unlicensed political meetings, while simultaneously instructing his presidentes municipales to use cardboard boxes as ballot boxes.[154] The opposition frequently came up with innovations to increase the representativeness or probity of elections—the PP proposed proportional representation, the Padillistas suggested following Colombia's lead and marking voters' thumbs with indelible ink—which the government rejected.[155] Detailed, questionable results were no longer made public: the *Diario de Xalapa,* which had traditionally printed vote tallies for congressional elections, ceased doing so in 1950.[156] Outside the PRI key parties were banned under the provisions of the 1946 electoral law, which gave Gobernación the power to register and deregister parties, placing them on or taking them off the ballot. They used it in 1948 to deregister the Sinarquistas and in 1949 the communists. Subsequent reforms in 1951 and 1954 raised the bar for obtaining or keeping the registry, requiring that parties have seventy-five thousand certified members, construct civic centers, and maintain a substantial presence in at least two-thirds of the states.[157] In February 1954 Gobernación used the new law to abolish General Henríquez Guzmán's left-leaning Federación de Partidos del Pueblo Mexicano (FPPM).[158] With its passing went the only real national opposition for a generation. Until the 1980s the PAN never got beyond 10 percent in a presidential election, and seemed at times not to seek much more; when the British ambassador asked the party leader, Manuel Gómez Morín, whether he aspired to a two-party system the answer was, "Good Heavens no, that would mean shooting and violence at every election!"[159] By 1959 less than 10 percent of city dwellers believed they could influence local or national politics.[160] At a national level the British embassy was right: the PRI had become "the steamroller in Mexican politics."[161]

The token space allotted to the surviving opposition parties of the 1950s was no substitute for the disorderly competitiveness of primaries. In some places such parties may have paradoxically reduced the effective choices of voters, siphoning internal competition out of the PRI and legitimating a party monoculture without establishing a competitive external alternative. In Veracruz 75 percent of the (unusually hard-fought) 1964 municipal elections were multiparty affairs: the opposition won all of 3 percent of them. Inside the PRI, on the other hand, popular inputs unequivocally counted in those same elections, even in the absence of primaries: 9 percent of candidates were publicly vetoed before polling day, and a further 7 percent of eventual victories were annulled.[162] The electoral reforms of 1963, which offered the PAN a handful of congressional seats through proportional representation, were table scraps designed to check disturbing levels of abstentionism. (Notably fewer Mexicans in the North, Mexico City, and the Center West bothered voting; the PAN's deputies themselves abstained from taking their congressional seats in 1958.) However, in the long run—a very long run, if a week is a long time in politics—those seats grew into real power, as opposition parties capitalized on a persistent democratic culture and governments incrementally upped their numbers.[163]

In the interim, what endured? The diverse noncompetitive functions of elections retained a very real importance. For rulers, elections had four functions. They institutionalized the circulation of elites. They deterred elite exits and reinforced the idea that the party was the path to power, irrespective of true beliefs or constituencies. They provided politicians with critical intelligence: brief and stage-managed as tour visits were, they gave the candidates local knowledge, a quick look at local talent, and a better idea of the minimum of services they could deliver to keep the peace. Finally, elections channeled most opponents into a fundamentally loyal opposition.[164] For the ruled, meanwhile, elite aspirations to legitimacy made campaign seasons times of opportunity and social mobility, times when they could negotiate political or material gains in exchange for collaboration in mounting the spectacle of an election. Campaigns were essential channels of communication between villagers and their distant rulers, many of whom appeared only in the run-up to an election. Elections remained, as they had been even in Porfirian times, conjunctures when elites might be temporarily generous—with benefits ranging from barbecues to land grants—in purchasing some grudging compliance from the ruled.

Yet elections had once been far more than this. They had seen the election, at least occasionally, of dissidents; the veto, more commonly, of unacceptable official candidates; and the exchange of electoral discipline in the most important contests for representation in secondary positions. The democratic functions of primaries should not be exaggerated. They had not offered direct popular representation at any level beyond the municipal, and there only sporadically. Elections such as the 1948 Taxco primary, "irregular in all aspects" with "votes [that were] fictitious and exaggerated," were commonplace.[165] When Porfirio Pérez Olivares ran for mayor in Soledad de Doblado, he remembered that "there was no Convention like there is nowadays, instead the Party resolved the case internally and on 20 September 1949 I received a credential as the PRI's official candidate."[166] Dissidents, moreover, were not automatically democrats: Nabor Ojeda, Cándido Aguilar, and Vidal Díaz Muñoz, to name but a few, were election fixers of considerable experience. Yet primaries had provided sites for intense, contestatory mobilization, for many of the practices of meaningful electoral life, for unpredictable results, and for official defeats. Even the black farce of the 1948 Taxco primary had some representative impact, causing the party quietly to replace the official candidate for mayor.[167] Primaries, for all their flaws, regularly permitted the contestation and participation that are the principal elements of Robert Dahl's minimum definition of polyarchy, rule by the many.[168]

Even after their abolition, though, local elections remained more than period pieces, weary reruns of old Porfirian plays. The "largely democratic culture" identified by Fagen and Tuohy in 1960s Xalapa, or Booth and Seligson in northern industrial towns of the late 1970s persisted.[169] It translated into a handful of overt opposition wins in three types of municipio: northern cities, strongly Catholic cities, and serrano villages. There was also the outlier of Juchitán, the Oaxacan city that fell into none of the above categories and that kept the PRI out of town until the 1970s (at which point the *juchitecos* elected an opposition mayor).[170] It was expressed in the reduced, but still noteworthy tradition of electoral protests, particularly strong at the municipal level, where the early 1950s return of the bloc vote—in which small groups of centrally marshalled Priistas barred themselves in cinemas, theaters, and other public spaces, forcibly excluded dissidents, and declared themselves representative party conventions—provoked "a flood of protests."[171] It shines through Gobernación's potted biographies of later priista mayors; while some had lurid entries in the "criminal record" and "popular acceptance" rubrics, others would undoubtedly have won free and fair elections. They did not live up at all to the PAN leader's billing as "the greatest rogues, the most violent of men, those who have distinguished themselves as killers."[172] Neither did they live up to the stereotype of puppets imposed from on high: by the 1960s only a quarter of mayors had direct support from outside their municipios, while nearly half had no links to party or state or federal administrations.[173] A democratic culture was expressed in the vigorous participation of newly enfranchised women, whether in the ranks of the PP, whose women aggressively demanded the right to vote against the PRI in Paso del Macho, or inside the PAN, whose women took over the majority of Iguala's polling stations in 1948 and managed the (disallowed) victory of a panista woman as mayor.[174] The prospect of such difficult-to-manage mobilization—doubling the electorate overnight—may even have been one more good reason to abolish primaries.[175] Finally, a long-term belief in the benefits of elections emerged repeatedly in the work of provincial journalists, ranging from the sly asides of the *Diario de Xalapa* through the straightforward *Trinchera de Culiacán*—which described the PRI as "a dagger to the hopes of democracy"—to the irate guerrerense columnist who demanded that "a real vote" be removed from government correspondence.[176]

Primaries, above all, were eloquent of that which endured—culture—and that which had been lost—much, but not all, of the practice. They became totemic to reform-minded Priistas such as Carlos Madrazo, Jesús Reyes Heroles, and Luis Donaldo Colosio. In 1957 Cárdenas proposed their resurrection as part of democratizing the PRI.[177] When primaries were fleetingly reintroduced for mayoral elections—in Sonora in 1961, in ten states in 1965—dissidents formed new parties within the PRI and long-term abstainers turned out to vote, believing that these were genuinely unpredictable, representative contests; many voters weren't even party members.[178] Madrazo gambled his tenure as head of the PRI on that enthusiasm, and on the locally popular candidates who won open elections; but the gamble failed and he was ousted on November 17, 1965, within a year of taking over, after the final straw of a struggle with Governor Leopoldo Sánchez Celis over municipal elections in Culiacán. Hardline Priistas were unusually forthcoming in their postmortems of the chaos, *desorientación,* divisions, and "vulgar squabbles" into which this "wrong direction" had plunged the party. Primaries had not only divided party members; they had opened the door for opposition wins in major towns like Santa Bárbara, Chihuahua, and Taxco, Guerrero, and they had been subject to wholesale cancellations in Oaxaca. They were, Senator Carlos Loret de Mola judged, "good in theory, a disaster in practice"; their abolition, *Excélsior* tentatively criticized, meant more "democracia dirigida."[179]

Mexico went through what our contemporaries would call a democratic transition in the second half of the 1940s. For four years Mexicans experienced genuine if flawed elections. Notwithstanding the ubiquity of election rigging, they went to the ballot boxes to choose between slates of highly diverse PRI candidates, their choices sometimes influential, and occasionally decisive in determining the results. The radically opposed factions inside the early revolutionary party exemplified Gramsci's dictum: "Even if no other legal parties exist, other parties do in fact always exist."[180] The representation such "organic parties" obtained through the primaries of a heterodox PRI, whose electoral managers were at times out of their depth, was comparable at times to that of a (corrupt and unbalanced) multiparty system.

Like many recent transitions, Mexico's provoked heady optimism, subsequent confusion, and the eventual disillusionment of a competitive authoritarian ending. Between the 1950s and the late 1970s Mexico was a country in which numerous elections gave near-uniform results: victories for the PRI, and—unlike predominant-party democracies like Japan or India—the requisite supermajorities, rooted in both formal and informal electoral manipulation, to block all but incremental institutional change. As in contemporary competitive authoritarian states, elections remained "arenas of contestation through which oppositions [could] legally—and legitimately—challenge incumbents," who "[were] forced to sweat."[181] Independent local majorities running campaigns as Priistas in name alone quite often did not have to sweat to have their power rubber-stamped. Overt opponents, though, had to sweat blood to win a minority of local contests and, more feasibly, to veto the winners of others. Yet even at the PRI's peak mobilizations mattered. As one village protester put it, "We don't have arms, but we do have balls." That didn't help him much: soldiers beat him with rifle butts, his *compañeros* retreated sullenly to the general store, and the election stayed stolen.[182] But enough others had the same attributes to form jostling, angry crowds beneath a soft authoritarian surface. Their efforts and their memories constituted a recessive gene in the Mexican body politic; one that was sporadically expressed across the entire period, and one that reemerged, critically, in the protracted transition of the late twentieth century.[183]

6 • Law and Order in *México Profundo*

The Anatomy of Violence

It was once a truism that in 1940 the lead of the revolution was transmuted (by the philosophers' stone of cardenismo) into a golden age of political stability and economic development. Yet in reality rural Mexico remained markedly violent long after that traditional watershed. In 1950 Ometepec, for example, had a homicide rate high enough to place it among the twenty most violent municipios in Antioquia, Colombia, itself the third most violent department during the Violencia.[1] The idea that Mexican and Colombian provinces might be compared in terms of violence during the 1940s and 1950s was once counterintuitive. The metanarrative of modern Colombian history has always revolved around a peculiarly high degree of violence, making violence "a privileged historical referent . . . one of the poles of attraction for . . . social investigation."[2] One of the main assumptions of modern Mexico historiography was the polar opposite: the comparatively low salience of violence in sustaining priista rule. Recent studies have changed that, stressing both the continuity and scope of violence after the revolution, whether among pistoleros, guerrillas, students, or soldiers.[3] It was minimized at the time, perhaps because it was concentrated in the *México profundo* of the countryside, populated by unmetropolitan types with racial bents for assault and battery and worse: homicidal blacks, savage Indians, and even, in Paz's prose, those violent bastards the mestizos.[4] The Amuzgos of the Costa Chica were, an SEP inspector established in 1949, "opposed to civilization" and "in a deplorable state of backwardness," while the neighboring Afromestizos were even worse, "chaotic, vicious individualists" for whom "criminality is a pleasure."[5] The certainties of racialist thinking contrasted with the marked uncertainties that metropolitan elites—politicians, journalists, generals, spies, and diplomats—held regarding provincial reality. Early Priistas were unsure as to precisely how violent the countryside remained, but they often suspected the worst, and kept their suspicions as quiet as possible; and quite often they were right.[6]

Yet for contemporary historians, with the advantages of intelligence materials in particular, qualitative data on violence are straightforward and copious. It is there in the reports of DGIPS agents, more prolix than their (more thuggish) counterparts in the DFS; in political correspondence at the lowest levels of Mexican government, and in particular that of the *comisarios municipales*—the administrators of villages outside the county seat, often thankless jobs—and comisariados ejidales; in state judicial archives; in the voluminous protests countrymen sent to the Presidency and Gobernación; in those provincial newspapers which resisted censorship, such as Ignacio de la Hoya's magnificently plainspoken *La Verdad de Acapulco;* and in the work of contemporary ethnographers such as Gonzalo Aguirre Beltrán, Paul Friedrich, and Marcos Muñoz. (Some of whom had a clear elective affinity for caciquismo; Friedrich was told, "You could be a leader here, Paul, you could order killings").[7] Such data are detailed and comprehensive enough even to suggest regional differences in the quality of violence. In both Guerrero and Veracruz, for example, the cultural norms that partly regulated violence were looser than in contemporary Naranja, Michoacán, where (despite the villagers' very violent reputations) Friedrich found homicide confined to the shooting of men, and where sadistic, performative violence was highly unusual.[8] Reports from Guerrero and Veracruz, on the other hand, denounce attacks on whole families, both incidental, from house sieges or burnings, and deliberate, when women and children were killed in reprisal for male family members' political or business dealings.[9] In Zilacatipán, Pompeyo Rodríguez stood up to the local caciques and had his family "completely exterminated"; in Paso del Macho the Lagunes gang took Juan Gutiérrez's ranch away and decimated his family.[10] A similar logic of deterrence encouraged violent theatrics such as burying alive or postmortem mutilation, public performances that remain visible in the archives decades later.[11]

Quantitative data, on the other hand, are more complicated, suffering from four major problems. First, there is no valid baseline for postrevolutionary levels of violence, as neither federal nor *registro civil* numbers cover the 1920s. We might well assume they were higher on a national scale—a society in arms, an embryonic central state, multiple rebellions, a civil war, and the stories all these phenomena generated—but in some regions violence was undoubtedly greater during the agrarian reforms of the 1930s than during the reconstruction of the 1920s. Second, the historical dataset we possess does not cover the entire period, and some of the missing judicial data, such as that covering Guerrero in the late 1970s, or Veracruz in the mid-1940s, coincide with times of unusually intense violence. The lack of a census in 1980 puts an accurate calculation of the rate for that particular data point out of reach, just as agrarian violence in the Huasteca returned dramatically; the CNC estimated that over five hundred peasants there were murdered in the second half of the seventies.[12] Third, official crime statistics were far from comprehensive to start with. The 112 homicide arrests in Veracruz in 1948 reflect a mere fraction of the murders actually committed.[13] In Guerrero in 1950 the Procuradoría recorded 276 murder cases; the Registro Civil, 715 murders.[14] At the other extreme, there are a couple of years when, perhaps under political pressure, the conviction rate edged above 100 percent, as prosecutors claimed to have won more cases than they had actually brought to court.[15]

The main difficulty, however, lay with neither absent policemen nor aspirational prosecutors but with terrified victims. Fear of reprisal and mistrust of local government meant that homicides in particular went routinely unreported. A 1948 protest from the eastern highlands of Guerrero pinned 20 murders on the Salgado brothers—well-connected cattle rustlers—and explained the rationale for victim underreporting: "There was no investigation by any Authority of these killings, it was kept quiet and the very mourners knew . . . who they were and said nothing to avoid the same fate. . . . Generals and representatives of the Sr. Gobernador have come and have left Huamuxtitlán with a few thousand pesos in their pockets and they go and mislead the Governor that all is quiet and that there are no such troubles."[16] "It is customary," one veracruzano told the president, "that anyone who sees anything and tells tales to the Authorities is murdered."[17] In some cases official homicide counts actually decline as violence peaks; and no one was using household surveys to collect alternative statistics in 1940s Mexico.[18] On a national level the murder rate found in civil registry statistics between 1940 and 1960 is consistently twice as high as that of the courts. The civil registry, moreover, did not capture all violent deaths either. Reviewing the Cuajinicuilapa, Guerrero, registro civil for 1948, Aguirre Beltrán found that only 30 percent of all deaths were recorded; Veronique Flanet obtained a similar estimate of reporting frequency twenty years later in Jamiltepec, Oaxaca.[19] "It is important," Moisés de la Peña noted in the late 1940s, "to point out that the data on recorded presumed crimes does not represent anything but a minimal part of the real number of crimes committed."[20] The consequent omissions of reporting inject a tangible unreality into governmental accounts of crime.[21]

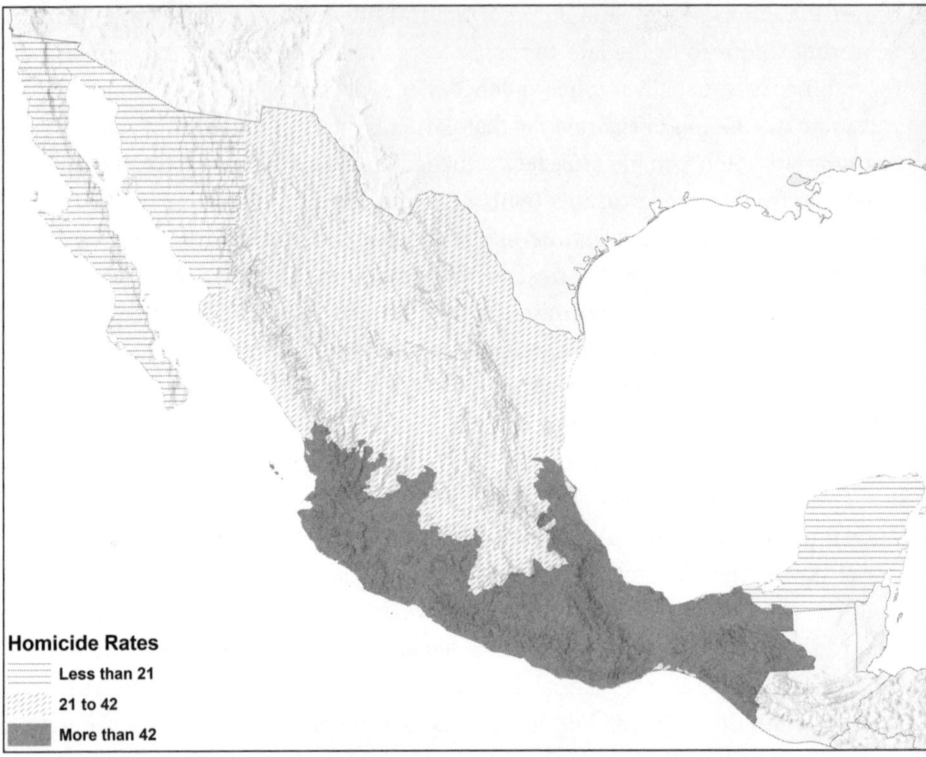

The national distribution of homicide, 1950–54. Created by Kelsey Rydland, Research Services, Northwestern University Libraries, based on data from the Escuela e Instituto de Salubridad y Enfermedades Tropicales, AQC-14.

Yet this is a standard problem: using police or military statistics as an index of the real level of violence is highly suspect in many societies.[22] Colombian statistical records are similarly variable: the Ministry of Justice homicide rate for the Violencia in Antioquia is roughly half that calculated by the department's governor.[23] There is something of a paradox in that the more significant a society's homicide rate is, the more difficult it becomes to measure accurately. (And the less politically convenient: an instance of Campbell's Law, which holds that the more politically charged a statistic is, the less likely it is to be accurate.)[24] Judicial statistics are especially imperfect: they make Guerrero one of the least violent states in 1940s Mexico. Yet they still have multiple, critical applications. If we assume either constant or rising reporting rates since 1940—which, given the growing "degree of stateness" across the period, is a justifiable assumption[25]—then the finding of a long-term decline

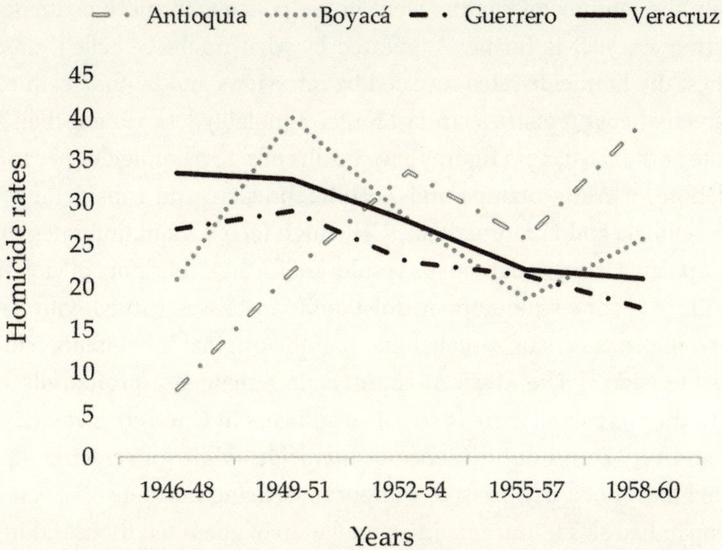

Homicide rates per 100,000 population, selected Mexican states and Colombian departments, 1948–60. Created by the author. Data from Ministerio de Justicia, *Cinco años de criminalidad aparente, 1955–1959*, vol. 2 (Bogotá, 1961), reproduced in James D. Henderson, *When Colombia Bled: A History of the Violencia in Tolima* (University of Alabama, 1985), 254; Pablo Piccato, https://ppiccato.shinyapps.io/judiciales/ INEGI, Estadísticas históricas de México CD-ROM (Mexico City, 2000).

in the national homicide rate from the 1940s onward is reliable. Second, while the data are flawed they can still reveal just how much gender mattered: in any given year, men were between ten and fifteen times as murderous as women. Third, both judicial and registro civil statistics reveal coherent and dramatic geographical variation. Cities were far safer than the countryside, while the Pacific Coast and the South were far more dangerous than the other regions. Finally, acknowledging the crude quality of both Mexican and Colombian statistics should not bar their comparison.

Such an exercise reveals broadly similar official rates of homicide—that is, those entering the judicial system—in Guerrero, San Luis Potosí, and Veracruz in Mexico, and all bar the most violent Colombian departments between 1946 and 1960.[26] The proposal that statistics from these very distinct contexts are meaningfully comparable is strongly reinforced by the nonjudicial statistics, which in the more conflictual zones of both countries report rates roughly twice as high. The accuracy of reporting, in other words, seems similar enough; the families of victims went to the police with more or the less the same frequency. It is further supported by what might be called grassroots statistics: the homicide rates revealed by interviews and by the death records of individual civil registries. In la Montaña (notably less violent than Tierra Caliente or the coast) 1953 figures gave results of c. 100 homicides per 100,000 population for Ahuacotzingo and Xochihuehuetlán, and considerably above that for Olinalá and Huamuxtitlán.[27] The high forced migration rates that can be extrapolated from ejidal census results are further indicators of violence. In Tulapan, in a zone where opportunist agrarian bosses battled with peculiar ferocity, the 1952 census revealed that half the original inhabitants had abandoned the ejido.[28] The Mexican countryside remained a profoundly violent place in the 1940s and early 1950s: army officers in Guerrero stressed the intense and very common incidence of homicide, while in Veracruz an agent reported that "not a day [passed] without underhand murders."[29] Even sleepy Ixcateopan had seven murders in a population of about ten thousand in 1947, and was visited by an outsider in the unmistakable uniform of the pistolero (city trousers and a *tejano* hat).[30] As a man from nearby Xalostoc put it, fellow villagers were "not very murderous, although they were always killing each other."[31] Both government and grassroots statistics reinforce the qualitative evidence that the priista state was not born of any pax cardenista.[32]

Table 6.1: Homicide rates in selected Mexican and Colombian municipios, 1949–53

Municipio and Year	Homicides per 100,000 population
Ometepec, Guerrero, 1950	129
Cuajinicuilapa, Guerrero, 1948	397
Huamuxtitlán, Guerrero, 1953	203
Caucasia, Antioquia, 1949–53	840
Dabeiba, Antioquia, 1949–53	670
San Luis, Antioquia, 1949–53	189
Anzá, Antioquia, 1949–53	478

Sources: Libros de defunciones, Ometepec registro civil; Marcos Muñoz, "Mixteca-Nahua-Tlapaneca," in *Memorias del Instituto Nacional Indigenista*, vol. 10 (Mexico City, 1963); Paul Friedrich, *The Princes of Naranja: An Essay in Anthrohistorical Method* (Austin, 1986); Gonzalo Aguirre Beltrán, *Cuijla: esbozo etnográfico de un pueblo negro* (Mexico City, 1995 [1958]); Instituto Nacional de Estadística y Geografía; Mary Roldán, *Blood and Fire: La Violencia in Antioquia, Colombia, 1946–1953* (Durham, 2002).

Homicide was merely one point on a broad spectrum of violence. At one end of this spectrum lay the everyday violence of intimidation, jailings, fights, and beatings; at the other end were full-fledged (if failed) rural rebellions such as the 1946 padillista risings or the 1947 Balsas rebellion. In the middle lay rapes, riots (particularly common after contested elections), individual murders, small-scale massacres, forced migrations, and peasant jacqueries, such as the lynching of a vet and seven soldiers by a mob in Senguio, Michoacán, during the campaign against foot-and-mouth disease.[33] The marked diversity of violent behavior may be conceptualized in various manners. A common framework attempts to divine the goals of the perpetrators, dividing their acts into social, economic, and political categories.[34] This tripartite conceptualization often breaks down in practice, however, due to frequent contests over the meaning of violent acts and frequent overlaps of all three categories.[35] In midcentury Mexico at least Pierre Bourdieu's concept of the ready interconvertibility of different forms of social capital—symbolic, economic, and political—may offer more analytical insight.[36] Violence during the revolutionary and immediate postrevolutionary periods constituted a key commodity, as it could be readily traded for any and all of these forms of social capital. Why that should have been so—why Mexico remained highly violent—is the subject of the basic sociological section of this analysis, a synchronic sketch of violence in the 1940s. What changed (and what did not) across that decade and the first half of the 1950s will form the ensuing history.

A History of Justice

"Neither the Federal Army nor the state police," reported an agent in 1945, "can guarantee the lives and properties of the inhabitants of the various regions."[37] This was nothing new; the Mexican state was traditionally weak in both the specialization and the separation from social life of its violent agencies. The image of Porfirian policing was one of growing institutionalized sophistication, whether modernist, in the case of the uniformed, literate gendarmes of Mexico City, or rooted in a romanticized frontier mythology in the case of the rurales. Police numbers expanded to some three thousand gendarmes and twenty-four hundred rurales by 1910. Yet behind the window dressing of uniforms, parades, and news management both urban and rural forces were low-paid, lacking in training, and characterized by high rates of turnover and desertion. Some worked a second job to get by: in Mexico City Alberto Brusco was simultaneously a policeman and a carpenter.[38] Their deployment, moreover, was distinctly uneven. Wealthy Mexico City neighborhoods, state capitals, mines, plantations,

An officer of the Mexican *Rurales* no. 207. DeGolyer Library, Southern Methodist University, Mexico Photographs, Manuscripts, and Imprints.

factories, and railroads all drew concentrations of police.[39] Veracruz in 1893 spent 115,000 pesos (7 percent of its budget) on the state police, funding garrisons and secure jails in the principal towns; by 1910 they were federally complemented by the 1st, 6th, and 9th corps of rurales.[40] If policing success is measured by numbers jailed (preferable, after all, to a bald application of the *ley fuga,* the informal death penalty of shot-while-trying-to-escape), then such places were increasingly subject to state control. Mexico City court sentences rose from 3,836 in 1879 to 14,929 in 1910, while in the canton of Veracruz the jefe político reported 4,653 prisoners jailed in 1890.[41] Yet outside strategic centers public order was a far more haphazard, patchwork affair. Everyday policing in much of the Mexican countryside was in the hands of untrained municipal policemen or the unhappy everymen of the *ronda,* the night watch. They were ineffective, their reports full of unchallenged bandits, untouchable caciques, unenforced arrest warrants, and easy jailbreaks. Even the jefes políticos of such zones were unsafe: Colonel José Almazán, the prefect of Taxco, "imprudently" confronted a mob in 1886 and became another of the several jefes murdered in Porfirian Guerrero.[42] As the dictatorship aged, the rurales were deployed more widely in small garrisons outside the central states. Yet in such regions as Guerrero, or southern Veracruz, where cattle rustling, banditry, and revolt were endemic, the army remained the mainstay of state attempts to manage violence.[43]

When the central state collapsed in 1914 the limited civilian policing of the Porfiriato was replaced by the de facto justice of soldiers, revolutionaries, and community defense forces. The Mexico City police were outgunned by the invading provincial armies; the rurales were abolished by the revolutionaries.[44] When the large-scale fighting stopped, the countryside remained divided between army garrisons, militias, and gunmen, who dominated local societies and negotiated formal recognition as state agents even as they subverted that state's authority. Governmental weakness, newly fluid property rights, and a society in arms favored the spread of violent entrepreneurship, defined by Vadim Volkov as "a set of organizational solutions and action strategies enabling organized force (or organized violence) to be converted into money or other valuable assets on a permanent basis."[45] The ease with which violence could be converted into economic capital made it ubiquitous; in 1926 a Gobernación agent found that even federal agents—an education ministry inspector, a post inspector—were killed just for their pistols. "Everywhere [in Guerrero]," he reported, "there are killings, thefts, rapes, breaches of the peace, and all sorts of abuses without the responsible being punished, in some cases through ineptitude, in others through the lack of armed force to make oneself respected and in many others, finally, through the complicity of the very authorities, from the humblest comisario to the Governor."[46]

The authorities' complicity was frequently voluntary, but it was also a structural imperative rooted in the poverty of state budgets. Regional elites, lacking autonomous forces, relied on those suppliers of violence who existed and were, consequently, doubly unable to control them, implicated as sometime allies, incapable of mounting violent opposition to their transgressions. By 1938 Juan Paxtián had seven homicide charges and several arrest warrants pending in San Andrés Tuxtla, but when finally sought by Colonel Cano he was protected by General Jara and behind him President Cárdenas.[47] Neither Guerrero nor Veracruz established an effective state police until the late 1940s: in 1935 Guerrero spent 1.5 percent and Veracruz 2 percent of their respective budgets on policing.[48] In 1945, the governor complained, Veracruz still lacked the finances to field a professionally equipped force that would cover the whole state.[49] Even large towns and small cities could have next to no police force. In 1947 law and order among the forty thousand citizens of Ciudad Madero, Tamaulipas, was in the hands of eight men.[50] Where police coverage did exist, meanwhile, it could be so flawed that public opinion preferred its absence. In Chicontepec in 1946 "most of the town's classes" asked for the state police to be withdrawn, while in Las Choapas in 1948 it was the masons who requested the removal of the local police.[51] And in Paso del Macho in 1943 the villagers removed them all by themselves by lynching the commander and four of his men.[52]

Such rejection was generally founded on police incompetence or criminal behavior or both; in Paso del Macho the commander was accused of a senseless double homicide. Municipal police appointments were made on factional grounds, from the smallest hamlets to the major cities. Investigations into the Acapulco and Veracruz police in 1945 reported presidentes municipales transforming local heavies into policemen and using them to guard their personal properties and run extortion and protection rackets.[53] The state police were not much more Weberian. Two of the nationally significant political assassinations of the 1940s—those of the Guerrero agrarista Feliciano Radilla and the Tampico newspaper editor Vicente Villasana—were committed by commanders of the respective states' police forces.[54] The drug trade in Baja California was fostered and even sponsored by the police, while in Sinaloa policemen themselves grew poppy and protected the governor's investment in its trafficking. As that might suggest, oversight left something to be desired; in 1955 the inspector general of police in Córdoba, Juan José Gómez, was rumored to be

"Juan Paxtián." Miguel Covarrubias, Archivo Miguel Covarrubias, Sala de Archivos y Colecciones Especiales, Dirección de Bibliotecas, Universidad de las Américas Puebla.

on the run in Mexicali.[55] The answer to *quis custodiet ipsos custodes* was senior policemen, military officers, and politicians, all of whom were, all too often, part-time crooks themselves.

Alongside political violence and venality, the police were also regularly reported for incompetence in even minor duties. One Ixcateopan policeman tried to break up a small street fight and ended up being beaten up himself.[56] The police in Soledad de Doblado were described as "useless . . . because the sergeant leaves the station daily at four in the afternoon and goes to sleep in the *casa de asignación* of the horizontal Rosa Pérez, madam of the local brothel."[57] There were, moreover, frequent failures of coordination between state and municipal police and the army, bringing consequences from simple inefficiency to armed clashes. The state police could enter Jesús Carranza (to investigate a series of municipal police murders) only with a strong armed escort; in Ometepec, three state policemen came to make an arrest and were killed by the municipal police.[58] The Veracruz state police ignored army orders to account for the arms and munitions they had been issued, and their paymaster was arrested in 1945 for stealing 10,000 pesos from their budget.[59] Before the reforms of the late 1940s conditions of police work above the municipal level—low salaries, violence, nonexistent benefits—offered few incentives to efficiency, and fewer still to heroics. The job was, rather, one for unemployed violent professionals and the desperate. The 1950 Veracruz police regulations offer clues to the quality of earlier recruits: henceforth, the reform specified, policemen should be literate, without criminal records, and over five foot three.[60]

The other central component of order enforcement, the courts, were more in evidence than the police but were neither institutionally neutral nor efficient; in 1940 Guerrero's prosecutors obtained 46 convictions from 638 cases.[61] The judicial system at all levels was subject to intense political bias. At the village level judges and agentes del ministerio público (investigating magistrates) were usually recruited from (or subsequently by) the dominant local faction. Ideal candidates possessed "considerable experience in the use of small arms."[62] Ometepec's *agente del ministerio público* in 1945 was Luis Añorve of the extensive and locally powerful Añorve rancher clan.[63] Guerrero's supreme court was controlled throughout the 1930s and 1940s by Rodolfo Neri, ex-governor and leader of one of the state's major political dynasties.[64] The practical implications of this overlap crop up in numerous denunciations of politically manipulated verdicts. A 1942 senatorial investigation found Teloloapan suffering from "heavily-armed individuals who carry out all sorts of attacks and against whom nothing can be done because they are the very municipal authorities and the local Judge."[65] Justice in Veracruz was, a Gobernación agent reported, likewise completely politicized.[66] (Although jarocho courts may have been the scenes of stitch-ups, they were more industrious than those of Guerrero, processing numerous offenders each year and averaging a conviction rate of 58 percent in 1940–45.)[67] Even the federal attorney general's office was accused of political corruption, Silvestre Aguilar's influence allegedly causing the misfiling of thousands of judicial complaints and engineering impunity for thousands of criminals.[68] If disappearing key documents failed, the *amparo*–a wide-ranging writ of habeas corpus—remained an effective instrument for circumventing the prosecution of political gunmen. Four months after confessing to the assassination of the agrarian leader Feliciano Radilla, José Antonio Nogueda Radilla was freed with an amparo from one of Guerrero's district judges, and was still free two years later in time to be accused of killing another costeño agrarista, Isaac García Espinosa.[69] The facts of cases like this, widely known, were fundamental pieces of what Pablo Piccato has called "the Mexican disjuncture of truth and justice."[70]

The judiciary's political corruption blurred with its economic corruption. An investigating magistrate's post could be a lucrative franchise; the seriousness of the investigation to be manipulated or derailed only increased the profit margin. In 1944, for example, a long-standing land dispute between Jicayán de Tovar and

Table 6.2: Conviction rates in homicide cases, *fuero común*, 1940–50

Year	% conviction in homicide cases, national	% conviction in homicide cases, Guerrero	% conviction in homicide cases, Veracruz
1940	37	10	48
1941	40	14	49
1942	40	33	57
1943	46	—	—
1944	44	—	—
1945	37	—	—
1946	37	15	44
1947	37	14	50
1948	40	29	37
1949	44	38	60
1950	43	27	46

neighboring communities in the Costa Chica's foothills led to the burning and total destruction of Jicayán.[71] The agente del ministerio público arrested twenty-one people from Metlatónoc, took over 2,000 pesos in bribes to declare them innocent, and then arrested a further group and repeated the process. "He," recalled a Tlapa hacendado, "had found his milk cow."[72] In Cuajinicuilapa a gang of local worthies was arrested for the murder of Martiniano Vázquez. With eyewitnesses and confessions against them, they were nevertheless released by the agente del ministerio público for 800 pesos.[73] This was cheap; a *suspensión provisional* for homicide in Acapulco's district court cost 3,000 pesos.[74]

Three powerful reasons favored such overt corruption. The judiciary's low and declining salaries were a perverse incentive; in Guerrero a *juez de primera instancia,* qualified to oversee civil but not criminal cases, earned one-third of a governor's salary in 1883, but only one-sixth of a governor's salary by 1940.[75] Judicial salaries decreased, moreover, in the more violent and less well-monitored frontier zones. Honest prosecution of the well connected and violent was risky and wholly unrewarding. "Death threats," reported one Gobernación inspector, "... are very common among the evildoers of [Guerrero's] settlements, and it is for this reason that crimes occur with such frequency, as the criminals know that there is no authority that will punish them."[76] "Justice here," wrote one tuxtleco, "is expensive and above all dangerous for those who demand it"; but he could not ignore the killing by police of his eleven-year-old son.[77] And there were, finally, minimal sanctions for corruption. Investigating magistrates were rarely dismissed, and when accused of malpractice they were usually transferred to other towns.[78] If official investigations of the judiciary are interpreted, consequently, as the tip of a particularly big iceberg, then judicial corruption was ubiquitous: in 1945 the judges of Coyuca de Catalán, Taxco, and Tlacotepec were all under investigation.[79] The weight of the law was reserved, so peasants, journalists, and academics concurred, for the poor. "Justice," concluded De la Peña, "is extremely slow, and venality, although energetically repressed, is a social cancer. . . . [T]he poor man has a long wait for sentencing, which sometimes takes years."[80] Or, as a Teloloapan field hand put it, "You see that here it's like with the flies; a big fly goes through a load of cobwebs with no problem; but the mosquitos, the little flies, they end up stuck there, and then that's justice."[81]

The failure of the state's formal mechanisms for violence management was reflected in a variety of means by which Mexicans opted out of using the police and courts. Many crimes, including homicides, went unreported: when Copala's agrarista gunmen were arrested in 1948 they were accused of several murders, none of which had left traces in the Acapulco police archive.[82] Local societies frequently fell back on homegrown justice. In la Montaña's indigenous villages a traditional and (according to ethnographers, at least) legitimate justice was imparted wherever possible by the principales.[83] Ranchers did likewise: in Ometepec the mayor held informal petty court sessions on Sundays in front of the town hall, settling cases as grave as rape with fines and secular sermons.[84] (That victims might have seen formal court going as a waste of time is suggested by the national average of successful prosecutions for rape across the 1940s, 1 per 100,000.)[85] In San José de Gracia, Michoacán, the victim was asked to suggest penalties which, if considered proportional to the crime, were imposed.[86] In Naranja, Michoacán, the "grassroots judge" tried "to judge in accordance with local mores, to distribute compensations and punishments over as wide a field as possible, and to protect fellow villagers from state and national law."[87] Such normative systems may have worked in some places to deal with a broad range of crime, spanning domestic violence, assault, theft, and rape. In other places they led to lynchings, regular and accepted enough to have their own macabre codes and practices; collective murders as choreographed in village squares as on the Orient Express, but without any mystery as to whodunit.[88] Homegrown justice could not, however, reliably manage large-scale violence, as its operatives were generally outgunned. Both state and local actors consequently dealt with high levels of rural violence by contracting locally specific protection arrangements with one or more of the four main violent agencies: the army, the defensas rurales, the police, and the pistoleros. The numbers and autonomy of such violent operators produced a "market of violence," defined by Georg Elwert as an "arena . . . of long-term violent interaction, unrestrained by overarching power structures and mitigating norms, where several rational actors employ violence as a strategy to bargain for power and material benefits."[89]

As the second and third most violent states in midcentury Mexico, Guerrero and Veracruz are useful places to study that market of violence;[90] and in Crispín Aguilar, "el patrón" of Actopan, held responsible for the deaths of hundreds of men, women, and children, some disappeared into a secret burial ground in the hills above his hometown, there is a useful case study.

Crispín Aguilar: The Rise and Fall of the Pistoleros, a Case Study

The most powerful—if not necessarily capable—of the violent were soldiers, the men of the regular army, and the reserves, variously called defensas rurales or defensas sociales. This is not to say there was a strict military / civilian separation in the conduct of violence: the division between civilian gunmen and the men of the reserves could be a question of mere semantics or apparel, foreshadowing the magical transformation of autodefensa vigilantes into army reservists in the twenty-first century. State, nonstate, and criminal actors were not at all universally opposed, and local gunmen moved fluidly in and out of the militias and police, sometimes controlling them, sometimes battling them ferociously. The right badge could transmute the men whom vox populi condemned as pistoleros and abigeos—cattle rustlers, small-town thugs, bandits or hitmen, Rafael Bernal's "fabricators of fucking corpses"—into state-backed enforcers of law and order.[91] The violent entrepreneurs who were such men's capos, also deemed pistoleros—a term with the all-encompassing reach of mafioso, similarly covering everything from foot soldier up to crime organization boss—could find further protection under the useful veneer of state or party authority. In Naranja Gonzalo "Bones" González was variously village judge, mayor, and main gunman of the Scarface faction.[92] Further up the ladder, the two men accused of orchestrating regional reigns of terror in Veracruz in the early 1940s both held party appointments: Manuel Parra was secretary of the federal cattlemen's union, part of the sector popular, while Juan Paxtián was the CTM's regional secretary for campesino affairs.[93] In the deep south Mario Colonna was a member of the Presidential Guard.[94] Successful violent entrepreneurs, whatever their formal label, colonized a state whose elites acquiesced for factional advantage, rural control, private gain, or combinations of all three. Where monopolies of violence obtained they were local and generally illegitimate; by Weber's criterion there was not much state at all. (A conclusion with which several Gobernación agents, who described Guerrero and Veracruz as anarchies, would have wholeheartedly agreed.)[95]

By Ernst Gellner's definition of statehood—"the state exists where specialized law-enforcing agencies, such as police forces and courts, have separated out from the rest of social life"—on the other hand, a very limited entity was there.[96] Police forces did after all exist, as did courts, at least in some places; but they were not much separated from the rest of society. The *credencialmania* of the violent in fact reflects quite accurately the salient but low degree of stateness of Mexico in the 1940s. Local authorities counted but were often overridden by hard men with police, army, Presidential Guard, and intelligence credentials, some genuine, some forged, which issuing agencies such as the DGIPS tried to control without much success.[97] The state was meaningful enough to make such documents tactically useful, a resource worth struggling or paying large sums to obtain. One pistolero, gunned down in a bar, was an inspector with identity cards from Gobernación, the Oficina de Reglamento, the government of the Distrito Federal, and the Tribunal Superior de Justicia del Estado de México.[98] As Bernal's fictional pistolero García puts it, "For a career as a pimp, for armed robbery and other pursuits, it's necessary to be part of some police force or other."[99] At the same time badges were meaningless enough to distribute them indiscriminately to just about anybody with the cash in hand. In many places the state was one more private protection agency; and one whose pistolero competitors sometimes did a better job.[100] Their operations were polyvalent: they could look like alliances with the state, exercising what Wil Pansters has called "parainstitutional violence."[101] They could also, and particularly for the ejidatarios or workers on the losing side, seem characteristic of nothing so much as a Hobbesian state of nature. And at times their operations seemed like the workings of their very own rough-and-ready statelets, where the pistoleros, in a recurrent description, were the "lords of lives and livelihoods."[102]

Both regional and federal elites represented violence and caciquismo as ruptures in the state's control, driven by powerful traditions of rural feud and petty authoritarianism. Alemán delivered a succinct version of this official line during his chaotic 1949 tour of Guerrero. "The caciquismo which exists in various regions of the Republic," he told the press, "is a problem with colonial roots, characteristic of our country, and whose influence the Federal Government tries to reduce to avoid damage to lives and livelihoods; but without ceasing to recognize that its extinction will come about only through the education of future generations."[103] Such structural explanations were useful to elites of all levels in two ways. Their strong cultural determinism gave the state's provincial managers, both military and civilian, a ready-made excuse for failure to control their domains. Guerrero's military commander in 1926 did nothing to control the intense violence of the Costa Chica, "under the pretext that the costeña people kill themselves for purely personal reasons, whose main cause is long-standing quarrels."[104] Essentializing guerrerenses, veracruzanos, or any other Mexicans as inherently violent—often either explicitly or implicitly because of their race—helped to depoliticize violence. This was desirable because political violence is a delegitimizing phenomenon for any state to recognize, signifying either the extremes of popular refusal or the incapacity of elites to achieve their ends by more stately means, and Mexican leaders naturally tended to deny the political nature of violence and their deep involvement in its commission. Yet violence was, in reality, profoundly political, and much of it was less a rupture with the state's control than a foundation stone of what tenuous control existed. Provincial Mexico could be rather like the Italy of the sixteenth century, where "justice was frequently an absent figure and governments were too new and too insecure to dispense with force and emergency measures. Terror was a means of government. *The Prince* taught the art of day-to-day survival."[105] And *The Prince* was in fact widely read: in Naranja the leading politicians quoted it regularly—there was a copy in the schoolhouse, and it was believed that Cárdenas had memorized it—and in revolutionary Mexico City it was advertised as one of the three "intellectual foundations of the modern world," critical to understanding "the age in which you live."[106]

Crispín Aguilar's career is a case study in the blunter politics of that age. Veracruz was a wealthy state: the revolution had largely destroyed its rivals in sugar and livestock production, Morelos and Chihuahua, leaving veracruzanos dominant in both industries. Agraristas, however, exercised a powerful selective pressure on the state's agrocapitalists, and so across the 1920s and 1930s a new generation of tough arrivistes took over Porfirian haciendas and found new ways of making them profitable.[107] They may have been pistoleros but they were no backwoodsmen, and they clustered and reached their greatest power in the heartlands of commercial agriculture: the sugar estates of central Veracruz, the cattle ranches of the south, the copra plantations of the Costa Grande of Guerrero. Many—like Artemio Cruz, himself a veracruzano—rose quickly in provincial high society.[108] When Crispín Aguilar finally came to trial he called several well-known xalapeños as character witnesses while *El Dictamen,* the grand old dame of provincial newspapers, defended him in a front-page column.[109] The Armenta dynasty was nothing less than "the family of founders and colonizers of the whole region" of Plan de las Hayas.[110] The pistoleros' blend of violence and capitalist enterprise allowed them to found substantial businesses: Juan Paxtián accumulated several thousand head of cattle through industrial-scale rustling, while Manuel Parra's Hacienda de Almolonga was worth 5 million pesos when he died.[111] In building such businesses—struggling to control resources, deter agraristas, demobilize labor—the leading pistoleros also built impressive violent corporations. By 1940 Paxtián, Parra, and the Armentas controlled several hundred foot soldiers each.[112]

But Parra was the most successful of all, arriving in Veracruz in 1929 and making the Hacienda Almolonga the headquarters of a regional power which stretched over twenty-five municipios.[113] At its base was violence: Parra was backed by a paramilitary force, the Mano Negra, which Gobernación estimated at five hundred men, he imported arms from "his" coast and he enjoyed links with defense secretaries—one, Pablo Quiroga, became a business partner—and zone commanders.[114] He was accused of the killings of thousands of agraristas, ranging from smallholders to the 1936 governor-elect, Manlio Fabio Altamirano.[115] Yet Parra was more than a simple hitman; he enjoyed a certain mafioso-like legitimacy. The "Corrido de Manuel Parra" approvingly cites his tolerance of religion (in a powerfully anticlerical state), his protection of small cattle ranchers from banditry, and the discernment of his violence, reminding listeners that "he only hits those who rob."[116] At least two of his local bosses were themselves agraristas, who considered Parra's organization as "a sort of police force in the center of the state, whose function was to maintain the order lost during the tejedista years."[117] Parra was also extremely well connected at both national and regional levels. He was a reliable ally to national politicians seeking counterbalances to Veracruz's agrarian radicals, from Calles through Cárdenas to Avila Camacho.[118] His relations with state elites were horizontal and mutualist, not hierarchical and clientelist. Governor Miguel Alemán reportedly "didn't take any important step without first consulting Parra"; the zone commander, General Mange, maintained a "regular and frequent correspondence" with the head of the Mano Negra, whom he also armed.[119]

Crispín Aguilar was Parra's lieutenant and a key player in this complex system of rural domination, which he joined after fighting the Delahuertistas in the agrarista 86th Battalion.[120] By the late 1930s Aguilar was boss of the wealthy cane and cattle zone of Actopan, Parra's most reliable and used hitman and a ganadero of some standing in Xalapa society.[121] His power continued to grow across the first half of the 1940s, and by 1947 he controlled the defensas rurales of at least three central municipios.[122] On the way up he killed scores of village and state-level agraristas, including the mayors of Villa Cardel, Ursulo Galván, and Actopan (inheriting the latter job himself); he colonized the village governments, police forces, and defensas rurales of both the coast and the foothills to the north and west of the port of Veracruz.[123] He also planned joint enterprises with other members of Parra's network, such as the Cuban émigré Antonio Eguía and Ernesto Pardo, Parra's doctor.[124] But Pardo's political and business acumen was not matched by his preventive medicine, and in 1943 Manuel Parra died unexpectedly of a heart attack, sparking a pistolero civil war and sending Aguilar's career into crisis. The violent competition was aggravated by the subsequent change of governor and presidential election campaigns.[125] These were Hobbesian times, in which Parra's network disintegrated into a war of all against all, fueled by "a perpetual and restless desire of power after power that ceaseth only in death . . . because [they could not] assure the power and means to live well . . . without the acquisition of more."[126] The ensuing state of nature lasted for five years as pistolero killed pistolero. Popular opinion enjoyed the show of self-destruction: "They did away with themselves," crowed one corrido.[127] In reality, however, the mass extinction of the Veracruz pistoleros was less suicide than state achievement.

On a federal level, President Miguel Alemán's administration forced General Mange to abandon his former allies; on a regional level, Governor Adolfo Ruiz Cortines first reformed the state police—kitting them out with new arms, jeeps, and commanders—and then sent them against the pistoleros.[128] In 1947 the state's new mounted police, equipped with jeeps and a gung-ho general, Antioco Lara Salazar, began to arrest low-ranking gunmen in regional sweeps that captured 220 wanted men in the first eight months of the year.[129] In December they arrested Crispín Aguilar himself, who was sentenced in 1948 to eight years in jail.[130] While Aguilar was in prison in Allende his colleagues and rivals continued to kill each other; meanwhile an energetic judicial campaign was supplemented with high-level extrajudicial killings. In March 1949 Aguilar gunmen shot Pardo and Eguía, once business partners, now enemies who had testified against him, on a bus in Villa Cardel.[131] Three of the Armenta brothers were assassinated by agents working for Miguel Alemán; José Aguilar, Crispín's brother, was killed by men dressed as state police.[132] In early 1950 Aguilar was released into a changed world, where his former gunmen were rumored to have turned against him, and where he was not expected to last long. On April 6 he returned to Actopan, where on the eighth he left his house for the drinking, cockfights, and horse races of the *sábado de gloria*. He began drinking with two bodyguards in the main square, defiant, singing "*traigo mi .45*" and firing shots in the air. The local garrison arrested him and, after a struggle, let him go with neither pistol nor bodyguards; Aguilar went back to drinking. In the early evening he set off down the Calle de San Francisco with his fourteen-year-old son Gonzalo and Eleuterio López. The streetlights went out and the municipal police—led by the López brothers, once his clients—opened fire. Gonzalo Aguilar was killed almost instantly, by mistake they claimed; Crispín Aguilar was hit in the chest and stomach and stumbled as far as the door of his house, where he died.[133]

The López brothers made full confessions: they had plotted to kill Crispín Aguilar before he killed them, and their father, the manager of the electricity plant, had turned off the streetlights to aid the ambush. It was notable, however, that soldiers both disarmed *el patrón* and passed down the street where he was shot immediately before the ambush.[134] That Aguilar's filmic death was seized as an opportunity by the state to retake lost territory is beyond question; Actopan was immediately flooded with army units, and the following months saw the disintegration of the rest of the Aguilar network in shootings and arrests.[135] Two years later Aguilar's great rival, Rafael Cornejo Armenta, was similarly murdered in his hometown, and his network dismantled by the state police.[136] These deaths were turning points in regional history. They also exemplified three tangible changes in the quality and quantity of violence in midcentury Mexico. State violence was in the process of institutionalization and partial demilitarization; entrepreneurial violence was decentralized; and across much of the countryside violence began to decrease.

Demilitarization, Deniability, and the Centralization of Violence

Violence in the Mexican countryside had always fluctuated, ebbing and flooding to the short-term rhythms of the agrarian, ceremonial, and political cycles. Agrarian conflict—between landowners and agraristas, rival peasant factions, or rival communities—and the lumbering army and police responses it drew followed a seasonal cycle.[137] It began in March, as countrymen began to clear plots and plant for the main spring / summer maize crop, harvested at the end of the year. (Only scarce irrigated land supported the second fall / winter crop, correspondingly rare.) "Every year," Catalán Calvo told the president, "when agricultural work begins in this state, the tensions which have existed for a long time between peasants due to land disputes are heightened, which owe in great part to the lack of boundaries, to vices which emerged with the implementation of previous agrarian policies and to the scarcity of workable land in relation to the high numbers of peasants."[138] Simultaneously the lengthening dry season brought hard dirt roads, fordable streams, and a greater visibility across plain and woodland which facilitated regional counterinsurgencies in conflict zones such as the Costa Chica.[139] The heightened violence that ensued continued throughout the rainy season, fed, perhaps, by the traditional subsistence pressures of the summer months, as maize stores ran short and disease increased. When the harvest came in the winter men left the dangerous fields and returned to a short-lived, relative time of plenty which was also a season of relative peace.

The rainy season's intensified violence was further determined by the longer rhythms of the formal political cycle, which scheduled most of the major contests for the summer months. The informal political cycle, although linked to the tides of favor and influence that ran through elections, was less metronomic. Manuel Parra's fatal 1943 heart attack, which sparked a five-year pistolero succession struggle, was wholly unpredictable. Such times of uncertainty

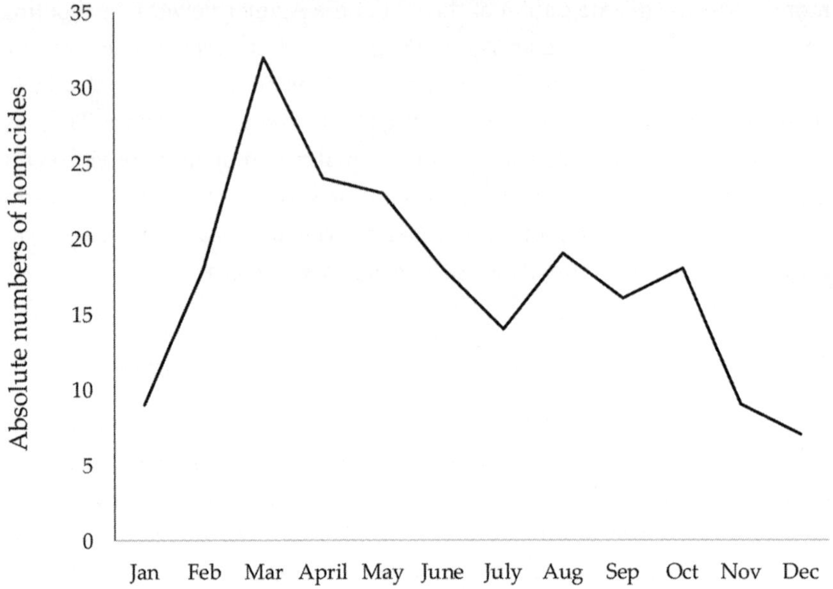

The seasonal distribution of homicide, Ometepec 1940–52. Created by the author. Data of total number homicides from Libros de defunción > 9 months coverage (1940, 1944, 1945, 1947, 1949, 1950, 1951, 1952), ORC. N=132.

were also times of opportunity and social mobility that fostered local competition and drew in violent entrepreneurs on the lookout for new markets. Violence also fluctuated in response to the internal rhythms of feud, whereby local tensions would erupt in a cluster of related killings that would in turn be followed by a period of relative détente and regrouping.[140] Such clusters may have had some correlation with the ceremonial calendar: as Aguilar's murder demonstrated, the combination of crowds, alcohol, and opportunity made festive killing a notable phenomenon.[141] The greatest change, however, was not a fluctuation but a long-term trend: the marked decline in homicide rates that began in the late 1940s and early 1950s and continued until the War on Drugs of the twenty-first century.

The demilitarization of state violence was due in part to a hard-won increase in civilian control over both the regular army and its anarchic reserves. Yet military power could never have been curtailed without the simultaneous construction of a viable alternative source of state violence, namely, police forces, functioning courts, and penitentiary systems. This could be seen even in such

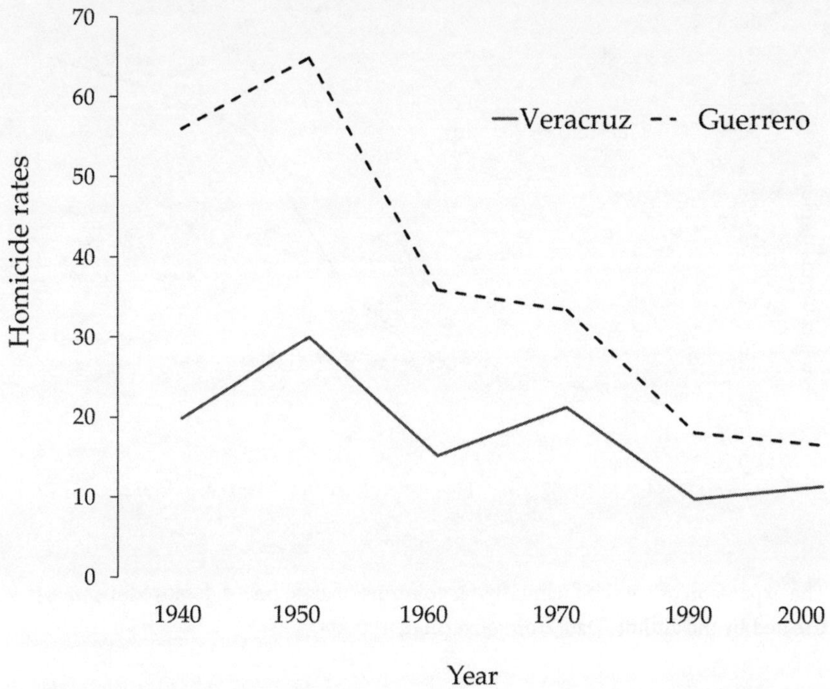

Official homicide rates per 100,000 population in Guerrero and Veracruz, 1940–2000. Created by the author. Data from Pablo Piccato, https://ppiccato.shinyapps.io/judiciales/ and INEGI census data.

unlikely places as San Luis Potosí, where Gonzalo N. Santos reformed the state police and warned judges against "amiguismo."[142] Even at a municipal level frequent denunciations of brutal incompetence and politicization were interspersed with indicators of an embryonic professionalization. In Ixcateopan the poorest townsmen refused in 1948 to continue with the customary amateur policing of the ronda; similar protests in Jamiltepec, Oaxaca, led to the establishment of a paid police force.[143] In 1951 the hapless Governor Gómez Maganda reorganized Guerrero's state police into a force of nearly six hundred better-paid, better-equipped policemen who covered some thirty of the state's municipios and reported directly to the governor.[144] The governments of both Guerrero and Veracruz deployed increasing numbers of rural flying columns in the second half of the 1940s, taking over some of the policing roles formerly monopolized by the army. Such state police forces grew notably in size and sophistication during the Alemán sexenio, underpinned by major increases in

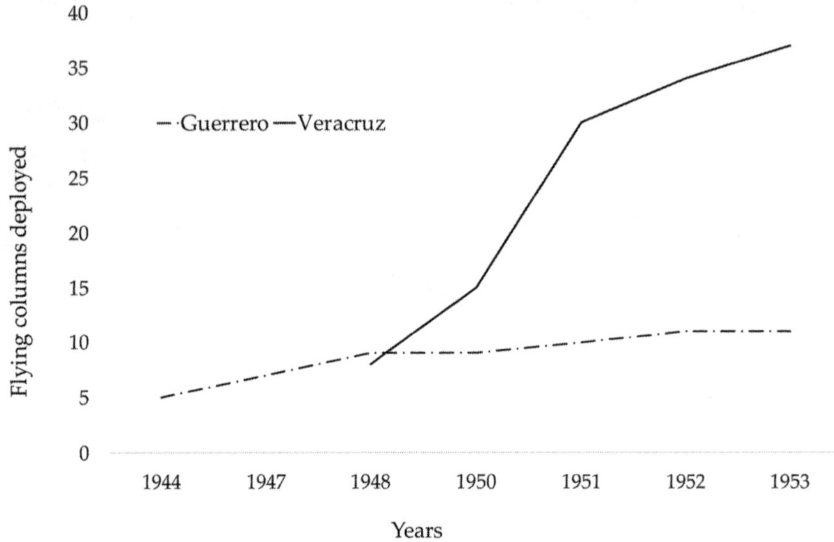

The expansion of rural policing: flying columns of state police deployed, 1944–53. Created by the author. Data from governors' reports.

funding. Veracruz's program of police reform between 1945 and 1953 encompassed new commanders, expanded recruitment, training, salaries, and pensions, the provision of Mausers, submachine guns, trucks, and jeeps to the policemen, and the creation of an elite detective force. The new force under General Antioco Lara Salazar had notable successes: a roundup of outstanding arrest warrants led to a series of large-scale police operations that resulted in 452 arrests in 1948 and 840 in 1949. The subsequent rate of arrest warrant completion trebled.

With more criminals inside to deal with, the courts in both states processed sharply increased volumes of cases: in Guerrero the numbers of convictions leapt from 241 in 1952 to 421 in 1953, and never fell back. (Given the meeting of a long-standing tradition of police torture with a new political will to convict, this was unsurprising.)[145] It was a more than equal opportunity increase: the proportion of women convicted also rose. Meanwhile the construction of new jails such as Perote's San Carlos penitentiary and the improvement of existing buildings made custodial sentencing more effective than in the early 1940s.[146] (When escape was an easy way out, as evinced by the 114 trials for jailbreak in Veracruz in 1943 alone.)[147] Even in Veracruz the new police were far from omnipresent, as the flying columns were overwhelmingly concentrated in the center of the state.[148] In Guerrero, which lagged far behind, even the main cities continued to lack effective full-time police coverage: in 1952 the DFS noted that booming Acapulco was policed by all of 17 officers and 36 men, making it "completely impossible to provide effective security to society and repress criminality."[149] Such complaints endured: in 1964 *Novedades* counted 18 visible *judiciales,* the federal police, and 150 wholly invisible beat cops.[150] Marked impunity endured, in that relatively few homicides ever made it to court. So did extralegal violence in the perceived cause of rough-and-ready justice, seen to be done through the ley fuga or lynching.[151] But for all the caveats there had been a leap in civilian police capacities which enabled a return to the Porfirian division of labor, with strategic centers under civilian police control while state peripheries remained largely militarized. The comparison was made explicit in recurrent proposals to resurrect the rurales, complete with charro uniforms.[152] Now that presidents and governors were able to control at least some of the countryside without recourse to the army, the generals' bargaining power and the autonomy it once bought were correspondingly reduced.

A younger generation of more educated and urban provincial politicians, less hard-bitten and with better police than their predecessors, simultaneously severed some of the traditional links between politicians and pistoleros. The

Table 6.3: Conviction rates in homicide cases, *fuero común,* 1950–60

Year	% conviction in homicide cases, national	% conviction in homicide cases, Guerrero	% conviction in homicide cases, Veracruz
1950	43	27	46
1951	43	24	48
1952	46	26	57
1953	100.3	67	75
1954	80	57	86
1955	89	69	103
1956	84	65	93
1957	85	59	112
1958	83	72	74
1959	81	64	86
1960	82	60	81

police, courts, military, intelligence, and hired assassins were all used by the new men against the old guard of gunmen. When governors proved recalcitrant in abandoning such useful allies they were pressured by the center: in 1952 DFS agents forced Gómez Maganda to fire the pistoleros whom he had recruited into the Acapulco police force, then took the two most prominent individuals into custody and executed them.[153] In Veracruz the result was the mass extinction of the leading violent entrepreneurs, in Guerrero a curtailing of their formal political careers. Alfredo Córdoba Lara, for example, was forced by General Sánchez Taboada to resign his candidacy for Acapulco's deputyship due to his implication in the murder of the union leader Pillo Rosales; he led, however, the state's branch of the CTM until his death in 1962.[154] Many gunmen continued their work inside the broad church of the state security services. As the "Corrido a la trágica muerte de Crispín Aguilar" had it, "[to spear] the bulls from Jaral, the horses from there."[155] The Armenta brothers were killed by men working for central government; a rash of Presidential Guard credentials protected pistoleros from the south of Veracruz to the Costa Grande; and Miguel Alemán was guarded by such men as Miguel Portilla, his driver, whose nickname in Xalapa was "el Asesino."[156] But Alemanista politicians were more sensitive to public opinion than their predecessors: they increased press and public relations spending and achieved a far greater distance in their relations with grassroots violence, "trying out," one journalist observed, "new methods of elimination that were not our classic 'preventive killings.' "[157]

Their search for deniability was exemplified in the changing fashions of assassination. When Governor Berber tried to kill the agrarista Nabor Ojeda in 1941 he had his car machine-gunned; when the union leader Pillo Rosales was killed he was hit over the head and his car driven into a ravine in a failed attempt to feign accidental death.[158] Obvious murders were being superseded by suspicious suicides and contrived car crashes.[159] There was, furthermore, a clear difference between the modus operandi of late 1940s governors such as Leyva Mancilla or Muñoz and their predecessors such as Berber or Cerdán; the former were never directly linked to political assassinations. This change was in part a genuine decentralization of informal state violence, encouraged by Alemán when he fired the governor of Tamaulipas for conniving at the killing of the newspaper editor Villasana.[160] It quite possibly also represented a substitution of suggestion for former, explicit command; a case of "kill them in cold blood" being paraphrased by "will no one rid me of this turbulent Priista?"[161]

Tales of Demise

Crispín Aguilar was killed in the midst of a bloody campaign of extermination of Veracruz's violent entrepreneurs; while ex-clients pulled the trigger, policemen and soldiers set him up. He died at the end of a decade less violent, on most indicators, than the late 1930s, but considerably more violent than the "national unity" propaganda of Avila Camacho and the early PRI let on. In 1950, the year Aguilar died, the regional homicide rate rose; thereafter it dropped sharply, mirroring a national decline that was noteworthy above all in the countryside, where the murder rate fell 24 percent between 1950 and 1954.[162] This closes a neat narrative for the history of violence and order in Veracruz, whereby gunmen capitalists are critical in first containing and then destroying radical agrarismo, and are then discarded by the first generation of Priistas, who manage to rule a weary countryside with less bloodshed than their predecessors.

It is a slightly over-neat story. Across Mexico the evidence for the tenacious continuity of violent practices by rulers and ruled between 1940 and 1955 outweighs that suggesting any sudden rupture. While the relative murder rate declined, the absolute rate—from the more accurate registro civil data—remained extremely high by global standards at 36 per 100,000 in 1955. Across the first five years of the 1950s Guerrero's homicide rate, again by registro civil, was 75 per 100,000; that of Veracruz, 74.[163] Of the forty-one countries publishing data on homicide in 1953, Mexico was—by over 400 percent—the most murderous; about as many people were murdered in a day there as in a year in Costa Rica.[164] In Italy homicide rates in the homelands of the mafia—the actual Mafia in Sicily, the 'Ndrangheta in Calabria, and the Camorra in Campania—fell below 6 per 100,000 in the late 1940s and stayed there for the next thirty years.[165] In Mexico their counterparts the pistoleros endured, not least in Veracruz: one of the leading pistoleros of the 1950s was José Antonio Arredondo, aka el Jarocho.[166] Mario Colonna, one of the major gunmen of south Veracruz, was not killed until the 1960s; el Animal, a legendary guerrerense gunman, survived and was wheeled out to a place of honor when Priistas came to the coast on campaign; Aristeo Prado, dubbed Michoacán's "last *valiente*," survived until the early 1980s.[167] Reformed police forces and courts fluctuated in their effectiveness, and were imbricated from the start with narcotraffickers: vox populi in the 1960s had the state attorney general and a commander of state police running the Veracruz drug trade.[168] (As, rather more importantly, they did in Sinaloa, where the state police became far bigger than

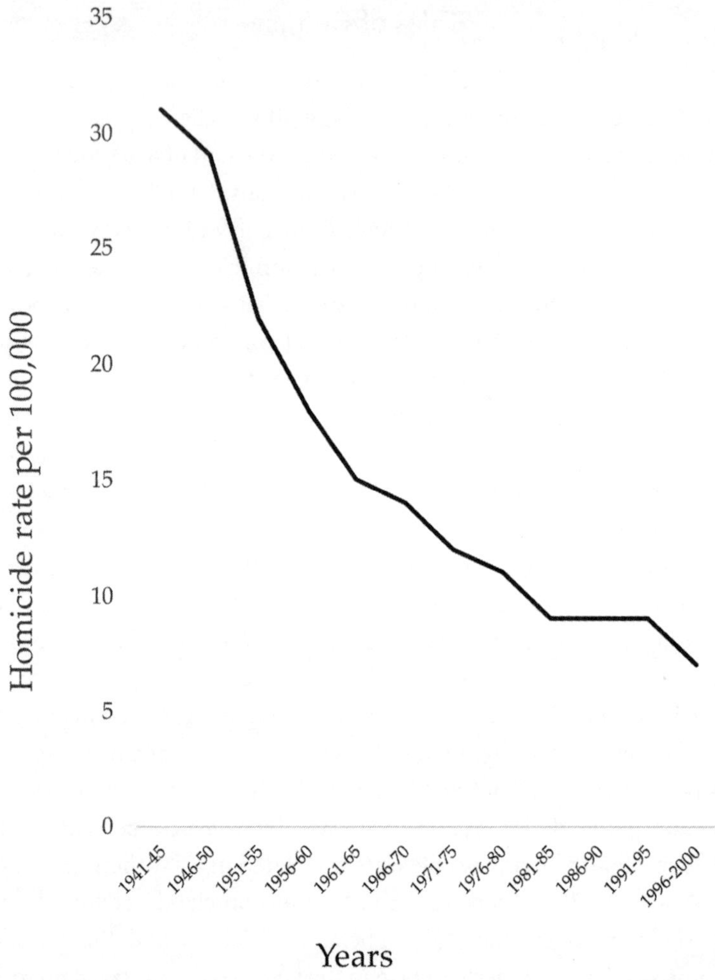

Official homicide rates per 100,000 population in Mexico, 1940–2000. Created by the author. Data from Pablo Piccato, https://ppiccato.shinyapps.io/judiciales/ and INEGI, Estadísticas históricas de México CD-ROM (Mexico City, 2000).

the entire federal judicial police force, and in Durango, where the first opium-trading families all contained policemen.)[169] Soldiers, meanwhile, remained essential to provincial schemes of order. The army's early 1940s role, that of part police force, part counterinsurgency force, would be reprised—particularly in Chihuahua and Guerrero—in the 1960s, as open guerrilla warfare spread in selected regions. As a 1967 CIA appraisal summarized it, "Rural unrest is frequently manifested in violent outbreaks. . . . Peace is maintained by the Mexican Army, which is both brutally effective and politically astute. The army has dispatched units to scenes of unrest where, after publicizing an imminent 'training maneuver,' they have used a hillside for massive firing practice, blasting all standing objects to rubble."[170] Across the Mexican countryside actual violence, the possibility of violence, and the decisive memory of violence past all continued powerfully to shape everyday lives.

Yet the late 1940s and early 1950s were nonetheless pivotal. The incidence of violence in the three states sampled may have been broadly comparable to all but the most violent Colombian departments. But the political management of violence in the two countries was not comparable at all.[171] As the violencia gathered momentum the Colombian government deprofessionalized the police, replacing Liberals with conservative peasant recruits, the *chulavitas;* encouraged the formation of paramilitaries, the *contrachusmas,* and the work of political assassins, the *pájaros;* and militarized the countryside.[172] The net effect was to create a vigorous free market of violence. In Mexico the first generation of Priistas pursued very different policies: they created professional police forces, engineered the moderation of pistolero violence, and reduced the army's operational autonomy. Courts began to work, at least by the metric of conviction rates: they soared in 1953 and did not fall back.[173] By the mid-1950s, as a result, markedly fewer Mexicans were using violence as an everyday political or business tool, and state regulation was slowly closing the free market of violence that had obtained since 1910.[174] Violence in Mexico decreased while violence in Colombia increased.

These phenomena varied from region to region: in Guerrero the homicide rate rose in the 1940s, dropped in the 1950s, and rebounded in the 1960s. Across most of Mexico, however, a long-term decline in violence had clearly begun by the 1950s, a decline that was steepest in the México profundo of the countryside and that continued for the rest of the twentieth century. State violence was critical in establishing the rule of the PRI over a disorderly countryside. The Priistas' subsequent, generally adroit management of both state and nonstate violence was central to that rule's endurance.

7 • Development, Corruption, and the Demands of the State

The Infrapolitics of Development

The governments of the 1920s and 1930s purchased limited but strategic consent with the material incentives of social reform and the political incentives of jobs for the boys (and a minority of women) of all classes. Politicians in city and countryside cut those offerings under Avila Camacho and—after the postwar democratic spring—continued cuts between 1945 and 1953. Alemán believed agrarian reform to be fundamentally damaging to Mexico's rural economy. "Almost always," he wrote from retirement, "after every grant, production falls."[1] He took office after several years of severe food shortages—in 1944 Mexico had to import 162,000 tons of maize—and, applying that logic, redistributed less land in his sexenio than any president until Carlos Salinas.[2] Political mobility also declined, in part through the generational effect of revolutionary veterans being replaced by younger, more middle-class cadres, and in part because of a deliberate exclusion of agraristas from state governments.[3] The changing face of Mexico's political class was evident at all levels. The youthful governor Marco Antonio Muñoz, born just as Huerta fell in August 1914, had been a lawyer and a bureaucrat all his life.[4] Seven of the eighteen state congressmen elected under Leyva Mancilla were teachers, as were five of the ten members of the state's PRI executive committee; by contrast, in 1945 there were no agrarista representatives in the state congresses of Guerrero and Veracruz.[5] (Though teachers were not necessarily bookish technocrats: the teacher-caciques of Naranja, Michoacán, or Chamula, Chiapas, or the Purépecha municipios of Michoacán, or Atliaca, or Texistepec, were all practiced in violence, often enough murder, in extreme cases mass forced migration.)[6] In place of the incentives of the revolution the Alemán administration intensified

Avila Camacho's offer of an intertwined package of economic, social, and infrastructural development programs that, brokered by the federal government, aimed to buy grassroots consent while increasing the state's leverage over local societies in government by petty apparatchik, a *licenciadocracia*.[7]

This radical shift in state priorities was predicated on rapid and stable economic growth. Macroeconomic policy centered on import substitution industrialization, stimulated by a series of measures that the government had taken piecemeal in wartime and later elaborated more programmatically. Tax breaks, cheap credit, and a guaranteed supply of cheap labor and raw materials favored industry, protected from foreign competition by Mexico's refusal to enter the General Agreement on Tariffs and Trade and by the 1949 end to the wartime trade agreement with the United States. The state bank Nacional Financiera SA (NAFINSA) credits trebled between 1945 and 1953 and were increasingly channeled to a handful of key industries; foreign investment, above all in electricity generation and manufacturing, rose from 12 percent to 22 percent of total private investment between 1947 and 1951.[8] The resulting growth was dramatic: GDP adjusted for inflation rose 63 percent between 1945 and 1953.[9]

At a macroeconomic level both Guerrero and Veracruz did well in the period, which saw increased federal subsidies, direct investment, and funds for agricultural modernization channeled to the provinces. Growth was very unevenly distributed across regions, economic sectors, and classes. The economies of agrarian states like Guerrero generally grew slower than those of the industrial zones; export sectors aside, it was the countryside's role to supply cheap food to the urban workforce, and while small farmers and ejidatarios received ploughs, improved seed types, fertilizers, and pesticides, they simultaneously suffered the effect of tight price controls. Ejidatarios were also prey to the concentration of credit in large-scale commercial agriculture, further stimulated by the fact that the Banco Ejidal by the 1940s was drawing some 80 percent of its funds from private investors, including the United States giant Anderson Clayton, with little interest in publicly owned lands.[10] Commercial banks were likewise skewed toward large concerns for reasons of bottom lines; the U.S. tycoon William Jenkins, by 1954 the majority shareholder in Bancomer, was unlikely to invest in microcredit.[11] Guerrero's economy, however, was stimulated by the spectacular expansion of Acapulco's tourist industry and (if state budgets are taken as a rough indicator) outperformed that of Veracruz. Economic growth in Veracruz, meanwhile, centered on new crops, such as pineapple cultivation in the south, on the expansion of heavy industry—a cement plant opened in Orizaba in 1945, 80 million pesos went into a steelworks—and on new light manufacturing, such as the Nestlé plant that opened in 1951.[12] The provision of consumer goods expanded dramatically, providing what were presented as the consolation prizes of capitalism in uncertain times, such as copies of the Kinsey Report on credit at the Librería Universidad in Mexico City.[13] The advertising of an Acapulco furniture emporium made the compact ironically clear: "The gringos are preparing a new war. . . . There will be mountains of the massacred. . . . The atom bombs will rain down . . . but don't you worry, come to the Modern Warehouses at Alvaro Obregón no. 22 and take your furniture away today!"[14]

Alemanista development offered more fundamental material rewards than new furniture. Infrastructural development was presented as a stimulus to further growth and as a social good in its own right; the 1952 presidential informe argued that "all the construction and the material improvements achieved have a profound human meaning."[15] (Some churchmen agreed; one threatened to excommunicate striking miners.)[16] At the end of the Alemán presidency the federal government claimed to have spent 7.8 billion pesos on roads, railways, airports, docks, telecommunications, electrification, and irrigation.[17] Endemic graft meant that some of that money left behind only the mirage of development. Yet while politicians' claims of pharaonic public works must be deflated for corrupt implementation and systematic statistical exaggeration, the administration's record remains impressive. The 2.3 billion pesos of federal money spent on road construction fundamentally changed provincial life: in both Guerrero and Veracruz the main interregional highways were largely completed by the end of the sexenio, while networks of feeder and local roads doubled between 1945 and 1955.[18] In Guerrero alone over twelve hundred kilometers of dirt roads were constructed in the period; even the Costa Chica highway, a traditionally low priority for the federal government, was at least under way by 1952, while dirt tracks carved across the hills connected Ometepec to the surrounding villages.[19]

Road construction was a complex political phenomenon, and its benefits at the village level were both ambiguous and class-mediated. Other infrastructure programs, such as the provision of public drainage or drinking water, afforded more universal benefits. Between 1950 and 1953, 31 towns in Veracruz, including most of the district capitals, received piped drinking water; nationwide, 310 communities received drinking water systems in the sexenio.[20] Even remote villages, given astute campaigning and good luck, obtained rapid infrastructural development in these years; Ixcateopan parlayed the discovery of Cuauhtémoc's bones into new roads, drinking water, and an electricity generator.[21]

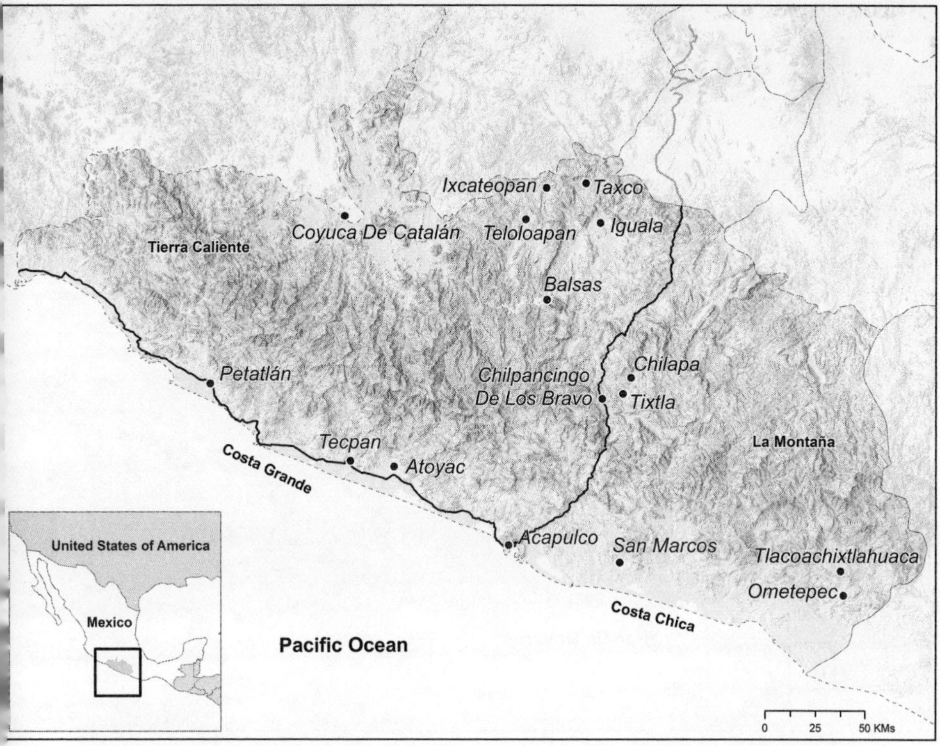

The Guerrero highway network, 1940. Created by Kelsey Rydland, Research Services, Northwestern University Libraries.

Table 7.1: The provision of new infrastructure in selected towns and villages, 1945–53.

Place and Infrastructure	Local roads	School buildings	Hospital buildings	Drinking water	Sewage	Electricity	Telephone lines
Chicontepec	x					x	
Ixcateopan	x			x		x	x
Ometepec	x	x	x				x
Perote	x	x	x	x			
San Andrés Tuxtla	x	x	x	x			
Soledad de Doblado	x			x		x	

Source: Assorted governors' reports.

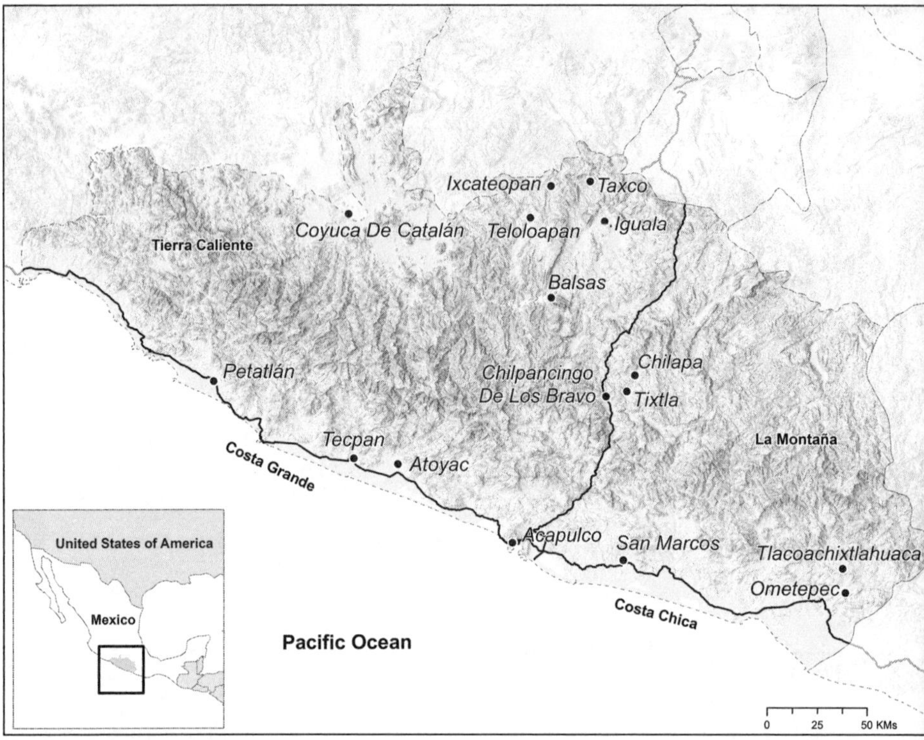

The Guerrero highway network, 1950. Created by Kelsey Rydland, Research Services, Northwestern University Libraries.

Public hygiene stretched far beyond large-scale projects of sewage works and drinking water; in 1952 the Ministry of Health ordered Ixcateopan's cantina owners to dig trench latrines.[22] Such measures formed part of an intensive public health campaign, whose other prophylactic policies were vaccination and vector eradication. Sanitary brigades cooperated with teachers and the army, particularly on the coasts, to drain swamps, hand out doses of quinine, and spray mosquito breeding grounds with DDT, all of which led to a 75 percent reduction in malaria fatalities across the 1950s.[23] There were 354,000 smallpox vaccinations in 1952 in Veracruz alone.[24] At the same time hospitals were built in most of the major cities and in strategically placed market towns. Even Chicontepec, traditionally overlooked in development plans, acquired a health center, while *misiones culturales*—small teams of development workers—brought trained doctors to more remote villages.[25] A profound and very old mistrust of state meddling obstructed some doctors' work; in 1947 smallpox immunization near Teloloapan was suspended due to "the systematic opposition of the inhabitants of the region," while in northern Veracruz the injections were popularly believed to be a sterilization campaign.[26] Health care was traditionally a key political resource for rural elites, ranging "from those who use invisible little globules to those who use spider liver with ant brains, vulgar witchdoctors, passing through those who cure by spiritism, and those who use the same remedies for any disease or recommend drugs which worked on one occasion."[27] In Petatlán the local doctor was ex-governor Berber's son; in Ixcateopan one of the once-dominant Juárez family competed with the former mayor Rodolfo Quintana.[28] There was good money in malpractice; in San Luis San Pedro, for example, local practitioners charged twenty pesos for three placebo laxatives, and fifty pesos for pointless (but psychologically powerful) injections.[29] It also bolstered their political power in multiple ways, ranging from the age-old leverage of medical care on credit to the lucrative new business of selling military service exemption certificates. These men, while often unpopular, resisted the new competition from state-sponsored professionals; Ixcateopan's amateur medics made life so difficult for the doctor who came with the misión cultural that he was transferred out.[30] In Ometepec and Tlapa the leaders of sanitary brigades similarly became entangled in local political webs and were dismissed.[31] Yet enough of the new doctors remained to have a dramatic impact on public health; a sharp reduction in the incidence of infectious and parasitic disease brought national mortality rates down from 23 to 16 deaths per 1,000 between 1940 and 1950.[32]

Alemanista education policy was similarly subject to the entrenched interests and tensions of local societies. The cardenista education crisis had continued, in Guerrero at least, through the first half of the 1940s; school inscriptions fell a further 16 percent between 1940 and 1944, some schools shut permanently, and even the secondary schools, carefully looked after by the SEP, struggled. In 1945 only one of the state's four *secundarias,* in forward-looking Iguala, was working at anything near full capacity, while that of Chilapa, with only seventy-nine pupils, had the lowest attendance of any such school in the entire country.[33] In Veracruz, traditionally the state that spent the highest proportion of its budget on education, the early 1940s was likewise a time of crisis, as the maestros were caught up in Cerdán's war against the CTM.[34] In 1944 De la Peña's study found maestros whose low pay caused any who could to take other jobs, pronounced shortages of teachers and buildings, and cooperative schools, formally sustained by state subsidies and peasant cooperation, that in reality opened only when villagers delivered food in harvest time.[35]

There was, moreover, an appreciable sector of the profession who were more petty caciques than teachers, maestros who went beyond union and local politics to rustle cattle, set up cantinas, skim subordinates' salaries, and rent out public goods such as schoolhouse lands and sewing machines.[36]

Yet there were also signs of educational development stretching beyond buildings, benches, blackboards, and salaries. Politicians, bureaucrats, and maestros had all learned the difficulty, if not the impossibility, of imposing unwanted education policy on a recalcitrant countryside in the 1930s. In the 1940s a new and officially promoted hegemonic caution, an acknowledged willingness to adapt teaching to local demands and mores, emerged on various levels. It spread across Mexico: Mary Kay Vaughan's conclusions stress similar if earlier shifts in Puebla and Sonora.[37] After long rifts between parents and maestros, Guerrero's education director wrote to his inspectors, "We understand that education is a very intimate cooperation between us and the parents of our pupils." After 1941 the SEP required that inspectors include a section on parent–teacher relationships in their reports. At the same time, revealingly, the mandatory labor social section disappeared.[38] The introduction of fifty bilingual maestros to Guerrero in 1946 was part of a similar outreach to indigenous, strongly Catholic populations alienated by the experience of cardenista education.[39] Such cultural shifts in the educational bureaucracy were combined, under Alemán, with notable increases in funding. At the federal level the average proportion of the budget spent on education rose from 13.2 percent under Avila Camacho to 15.5 percent.[40] State budgets rose in parallel, carrying with them the key indicators of numbers of functioning schools and numbers of school inscriptions. Guerrero's 592 schools in 1945 had grown to 764 by 1951; in Veracruz enrollments rose from 120,000 in 1944 to 175,000 in 1950.[41] Even allowing for healthy skepticism toward such upbeat statistics, Mexicans by 1953 were clearly both healthier and better educated than they had been in 1945.

Development programs fulfilled assorted political roles. Some prominent political outs, notably Cardenistas, were too weighty to be ignored; they won developmentalist fiefs and the patronage powers that went with them to compensate for growing electoral marginalization. Presidents allowed Cárdenas himself effective control over the resource politics of large regions of Michoacán and Guerrero through his chairmanship of the Tepalcatepec and later Balsas development commissions.[42] At the same time Alemán created the Tepalcatepec commission for Cárdenas, he created a new agency for Cándido Aguilar, the Comisión Coordinadora de Asuntos Campesinos, which enabled him to promote agricultural colonies for his clients in the south of Veracruz.

In Guerrero Nabor Ojeda was given extensive fertile lands near Cuajinicuilapa and the resources to develop them with his followers.[43] In Morelos Rubén Jaramillo was angling for a similar deal in the run-up to his death.[44] Such patronage was moreover not just rural, but also central to the squatter movements that grew up around the booming cities: in Acapulco, for example, the *colonias populares* took over much of the port's services and eventually government in their localized quest for electricity, sewage, and running water.[45] Schools, doctors, piped water, agricultural credit, ploughs, seeds, and machinery were limited resources that were used instrumentally to purchase grassroots consent. In conflict zones the army brokered infrastructural and health projects in what seems to have been tantamount to "hearts and minds" programs. On the Costa Chica the controversial Colonel Monroy, under investigation by the military *procurador,* was defended by a wide range of locals who cited his "vigorous work in pacification and progress" and listed the schools and roads he had helped build.[46] Such letter-writing campaigns, boasting of developmentalist credentials, were defensive bulwarks for local commanders under fire.[47] Other political actors, from mayors to presidents, made equally sure that their developmentalist claims, real or imaginary, reached as big an audience as possible. In Ixcateopan the outgoing mayor's report dwelled heavily on the public works he had overseen; from Los Pinos Alemán organized an Exposición Objectiva that attracted millions of visitors to showcase the development projects of his first three years.[48] Development was, like its first cousin nationalism, a bivalent resource for local politicians, petty bureaucrats, and caciques; successful projects enabled their authors to demonstrate administrative ability and popular legitimacy to superiors, while simultaneously proving their worth to their inferiors.

Voluminous correspondence (particularly at election time, when budgets rose at least 10 percent) suggests the efficacy of this strategy.[49] Development worked to cultivate grassroots consent, even when it affected other Mexicans in another part of Mexico. Cinema audiences in the capital could not hope to benefit from projects in the distant countryside whose results the newsreels brought them; they applauded them warmly nonetheless. Carefully noting the response to the screening of the 1948 informe, a Gobernación agent reported that he "could see that a favorable reaction took hold of the audience; a reaction that translated into murmurs of surprise, as the *señor Presidente* went on enumerating the public works that had been completed and that went parading across the screen: dams, irrigation canals, highways, railways, schools, etc."[50] Yet while development projects apparently won universal and uncritical grassroots backing in the city, they did not, ironically enough, in the provinces themselves, where village archives reveal a complex and selective popular approach to top-down development initiatives. The public spending in the provinces outpaced that of the center, but many projects were unpopular, causing alienation, direct opposition, and the everyday resistance of noncompliance, botched work, and endemic grumbling. Peasants and townsmen opposed some of the development plans of their masters for two main reasons: because they expropriated their labor, and because they attempted to change the use of basic resources that local societies struggled hard to control.

The forced labor that country people called *faenas, fáginas,* or *tequio,* and that politicians euphemized as *cooperación,* donation, was a long-standing mechanism by which the state compensated for its equally long-standing inability to collect taxes. The yawning gap between the state's development plans and the money available to fund them was to some extent filled by a tripartite arrangement: the federal or state government or both would apportion some of the materials for the road, drinking water, irrigation canals, or drainage system in question; local worthies would "voluntarily" come up with extraordinary financial contributions to supplement that of the state; and at the same time coerce the locally powerless into "donating" their labor. Some were willing volunteers; in some indigenous societies tequio could be long-accepted and legitimate practice, while in Veracruz De la Peña found an "anxious interest" of mestizo villagers to be included in new road schemes that verged on "psychosis."[51] Yet he may also have been talking to the village capitalists and power brokers, for a dense correspondence from both states also reveals substantial everyday resistance to development projects and the corvée labor they demanded. Peasants had always built evident local, community goods—churches, bandstands, or schools—with some degree of acceptance, enthusiasm even, but highways, irrigation canals for the wealthy, or telegraph wires for the government were a lot less of an evident community good, and they did not go along readily.

Three common means were employed to coerce peasants to turn peons of the state. Municipal authorities could use discretionary fines to enforce attendance; thus the ayuntamiento of Xochistlahuaca put the indigenous villagers of Cozoyoapan—who lived literally enough on the wrong side of the tracks, separated from the mestizo cabecera by a single street—to work for three months during the rainy season of 1949 on the track to Ometepec and fined them four pesos for every day they failed to show up.[52] Other authorities used the threat of jail as an incentive; as one villager from Pachivia remembered, "The school, the town hall, the church, the electricity . . . if you don't cooperate you'll go to jail, if you don't cooperate for the school, for the church, you'll go to jail, and with a good thrashing."[53] Finally, the more draconian rulers followed Porfirian precedent and arrested their workforce at the outset; in Teloloapan in 1949 the ayuntamiento built the drinking water system by systematically arresting fifteen people every Sunday and punishing their supposed misdemeanors with five days' work digging pipes.[54] The army too was heavily involved in drumming up free labor for development. Leyva Mancilla's last report detailed twelve hundred kilometers of dirt roads built under his government "with the valuable cooperation of the 27th Military Zone," which translated into local commanders ordering villagers to work alongside their soldiers.[55] Such strong-arm tactics could not be enforced everywhere, and in more urban settings—Acapulco or Orizaba—were replaced by extraordinary and regressive taxes; in Cosamaloapan the prisoners even got paid for their work.[56] The application of forced labor varied according to geography, ethnicity, and class, and impoverished indigenous peasants in remote areas with local army garrisons were far more likely to be recruited and for more time than richer peasants, mestizos, or the inhabitants of cabeceras. Yet faenas were ubiquitous across the Mexican countryside. In Tamiahua, Veracruz, the soldiers of the 19th Military Zone forced the villagers to work without pay on the Tuxpan–Tampico highway; the cacique of Huachinango, Puebla, similarly coerced locals into opening a road for the Compañía Mexicana de Luz y Fuerza Motriz SA; in Coaxcatlán, San Luis Potosí, the mayor arbitrarily jailed villagers in order to use them as road workers.[57] And faenas built a lot more than roads: between 1947 and 1948 villagers across the municipio of Ixcateopan cut and put up telegraph poles, built or performed substantial maintenance on nine schools, paved various streets in the cabecera, and rebuilt its Parque Hidalgo.[58]

Faenas provoked varied, intense, and knowing protests. Pressed road workers across Guerrero reminded the president that their employment was unconstitutional: "Article 5 of our MEXICAN POLITICAL CONSTITUTION," one letter instructed him, "runs thus: No one can be obliged to deliver their labor without just remuneration and without their full consent."[59] Resistance ran far beyond letters to Mexico City. In Pachivia Andrés Morales and Guillermo Espinoza refused for months to come and work on the new road, ignored repeated summons to town hall to explain themselves and, when they did turn up, "expressed themselves in a very incorrect fashion" before smugly producing an amparo from the district judge in Acapulco. In March 1947 the regional cacique Alberto Salgado was called on to intervene; he brokered a deal by which they would end their resistance in exchange for constructing a token stretch of four meters of highway; they refused to honor it, however, and they were blamed when the road was not completed.[60] In the Ixcateopan area, at least, such outright serrano noncompliance was commonplace; in 1948 the locals of Xalostoc refused to work on school and street repairs, while villagers in Pachivia, Simatel, and Tecociapan likewise refused to follow instructions to cut and bring in one telephone pole for every five villagers. The travails of their would-be overseers, set down in the phonetic spelling of municipal correspondence, are petty epics of frustration, rejection, and impotence.[61] In general, however, villagers eventually did the work, in part due to the strength of the political consensus regarding development. Electoral dissidents like Ojeda would not side with the recalcitrant opponents of roads or telephones; they were, rather, key brokers in delivering such benefits and as such formed part of a powerful developmentally minded coalition.

Yet the means by which authorities got countrymen to cooperate were distinctly open to negotiation. One of the simplest, most cost-effective methods to make forced labor actually work was to sweeten the pill with payments in kind of food, alcohol, and cigarettes. In El Potrero, Ixcateopan, the *comisario municipal* had none of his colleagues' problems in getting the telegraph poles cut and transported; he deployed a picnic. "I did not forget," he boasted in his report, "to bring nibbles, and mezcal, cigarettes, the people carried all [the poles] for me."[62] In other cases it seemed enough to remove the harsher coercive measures, such as fines for nonattendance, and reduce the demands of work; easiest of all, were it not for the permanent poverty of most municipios, was to actually pay the workers something. Forced labor endured at least into the mid-1950s, and the statistics of roads built testify to its success in delivering development on the cheap.[63] (Though those statistics were questionable at all levels; of the one hundred kilometers of roads claimed by the cacique of Miahuatlán, Oaxaca, only twenty existed, and at the national level there is an evident gap between the road system claimed by the government and that mapped by Rand McNally.)[64] But the benefits often gravitated to the well-off. In some municipios the public works turned out to be on the lands of village council members, while in others the enthusiasm of local worthies for new roads was closely connected to their truck monopolies.[65] That politicians still used such Porfirian practices to mobilize unwilling country people—at the same time as they vigorously hawked the *leyenda negra* of the Porfiriato—was too great an incongruity not to provoke resistance and delegitimizing. When *Novedades* reported the press-ganging of Indians on the Costa Chica they called it "a slavery similar to that which existed in the time of the Colony."[66]

Such bad press combined with the impermanent, resisted nature of the involuntarily voluntary to undercut the local manifestations of the state even as its infrastructure expanded.

Mexicans also resisted the plans of outsiders to expropriate or control the most basic resources: the crops they planted, the water they used, the forests they relied on for firewood, building materials, and the regulation of the municipal ecology. Some inroads into their control of these resources were central to state policy; in La Antigua, for example, the Agriculture Department tried (unsuccessfully) to convince peasants to exchange their mixed agriculture, predicated on reliable subsistence yields, for the commercial monoculture of extensive tomato growing.[67] Other resource conflicts were caused by the frequent failure of the state to act as an honest broker between the conflicting claims of crony capitalists and local societies. In San Jerónimo the public lands of the riverbank, long used by villagers for washing clothes, were granted to a well-connected local, who fenced off the river and got the police to evict the women. In this case the state eventually served as a referee: the women destroyed the fence twice, sent a delegation to Mexico City to protest, and successfully reclaimed their riverbank.[68] Yet similar bitter struggles over the everyday politics of resource use are ubiquitous in the nonofficial provincial press, and they do not all have happy endings.

One of the most frequent sites of conflict was in forestry, which had boomed in tandem with the expanding road network from the mid-1930s onward; the price of timber rose some 800 percent between 1937 and 1947.[69] The logging of Mexico's forests was seen by contemporaries as intensely politicized and corrupt, the timber companies favored by laws that enabled them to obtain concessions to operate even on ejidal land.[70] It was also shortsightedly destructive. A journalist visiting Rodríguez Clara, Veracruz, in 1937 noted that

> everywhere [lie] enormous trunks of red cedar, palo blanco, and *guanacaxtle* which probably belonged to trees hundreds of years old and which now go to the U.S., to Europe, where they will form part of the regalia of the lords and multi-millionaires. The way the forests are being exploited here is terrible. Not a single tree, no matter how distant, escapes the axe of the concessionary and the exporter. Not a single one is being planted. Trees which took centuries to grow will never be replaced. . . . Meanwhile, the electric saws work incessantly. . . . The Marxists' cliché springs unwanted to mind: "Mexico, a colonial country." But couldn't Mexico be a colony of itself?[71]

The devastation was not confined to the hardwoods of the tropical coasts and south, where states such as Tabasco and Chiapas had long been targeted by mahogany merchants; the greatest development in the lumber industry came in the softwood forests of Guerrero and Veracruz. Some of the logging was selective in what was theoretically a sustainable approach; other was straightforward clear-cutting. In extremis, the damage was irreversible, even had there been the will to reforest: around el Cofre de Perote, for example, sheet erosion set in on the cleared lands and replanting was ruled out as impossible.[72]

A few villages launched successful cross-class defenses of their forests. In 1949 a broad coalition of Ixcateopan's villagers petitioned the government to revoke a timber concession. An Estado de México logging company was opening a road "to devastate by mechanical means our hills, diminishing thereafter the rains through uncontrolled logging. . . . The majority of the village does not agree [with the logging], and protests against these activities which wound our sovereignty and our economic interests. . . . [T]he rights of man . . . are based on his agriculture."[73] A popular appreciation of the ecological consequences of climate change and soil erosion was a commonplace in such complaints; in the same year a protest from the *vecinos* of Iguala noted that if the government continued to turn a blind eye to deforestation, "very soon we will find ourselves with an even hotter climate and, what's worse, with a shortage of rain."[74] Despite serious obstacles—the president had approved the concession, the governor backed it, and the mayor was a poor political player—the Ixcateopan campaigners faced down threats of arrest and stopped the logging, enabling successive generations to profit from a flourishing business producing "rustic furniture."[75] Their story was exceptional, though; neighboring Ixcapuzalco had its woods quickly decimated, and in 1951 a total logging ban was imposed.[76]

Timber companies offered sops to local communities—free medical care, reforestation of roadsides—but fundamentally they relied on privately contracting the repressive services of the state.[77] Some politicians recognized the dangers of the logging boom as well as peasants. The governments of Guerrero and Veracruz instituted reforestation schemes; in 1951 Alemán created a *subsecretaría* for forestry in the Agriculture Department, proclaimed a blanket logging ban in several states, and canceled seventy-eight logging permits.[78] The bans, *vedas,* had some impact: on the basis of statistics of lumber transported by rail, more reliable than the government's numbers, commercial logging did in fact decrease between 1949 and 1955.[79] Yet forestry policies were systematically attenuated by the incestuous relationship between political and bureaucratic elites and big business and by excluded villagers' petty illegal logging. The governor of Guerrero proclaimed his concern for the state's forests but was rumored to be on the take from the logging companies, who purchased ejidatarios' timber at less than half the going rate in other states.[80] In Veracruz copious government files depict an administration that tried to control logging but was outgunned by the timber companies and their cronies in the federal forestry administration.[81] The timber industry was one of the largest in midcentury Mexico; by 1955 annual production was estimated at 1 billion pesos, a value comparable to that of textile manufacturing.[82] It was also a microcosm of the inequity of Alemanista economic development, as companies paid off bureaucrats and politicians for permission to ecologically devastate local communities, themselves often shut out from a traditional resource by the new fortress conservation, while offering little in return. It was, as such, perhaps appropriate that the first guerrilla attack of the 1960s should have come at Ciudad Madera in Chihuahua, a Porfirian company town where Alemán allowed well-connected loggers—from Mexico City friends like the financier Carlos Trouyet, from Chihuahua two former governors and a zone commander—latifundia totaling over a million hectares.[83]

Development in the Alemán years was represented as a continuation of revolutionary goals; economic growth was a priority, Alemán argued, so that there would "be more to redistribute."[84] Total federal public investment for his sexenio, adjusted for inflation, was 250 percent that of the Cárdenas presidency.[85] The president ran Mexico, *Excélsior* reported approvingly, like a corporation.[86] The cultural organs of the state were used to stress the universal and generous dividends paid by such sober management, in implicit contrast to the racier rhetoric and lesser economic growth of more revolutionary governments. The new political clichés of technocratic development were highly contagious, infecting the speeches of governors who lectured that "governments should speak in numbers and the truth."[87] (The politics of development were often more significant than the politics of elections; the front page of the San Andrés Tuxtla paper for December 19, 1946, was saturated with news of the highway commission, while four column inches at the bottom announced the PRI's win in the local elections.)[88] Some of the social dividends of the Alemanista corporation were relatively universal; multiple indicators depict rapid improvement in public health, while the provision and acceptance of education, freed from the controversies of the 1930s, expanded substantially. Others were strategically, sectorally targeted. The PRI's key foot soldiers, the bureaucrats and the teachers, received almost annual improvements in benefit packages that included health insurance, soft housing loans, and generous pensions; in Veracruz a 1950 law granted 100 percent state pensions to all maestros and state employees after thirty-five years of service.[89] (The PRI's real soldiers, the senior army commanders, likewise lobbied for and obtained generous benefit packages.) By 1952 such payoffs were already being criticized for "smothering" the nation.[90] And other benefits, most importantly those of economic development, went only to some Mexicans. In the villages, shopkeepers, truck owners, and other entrepreneurs enjoyed new opportunities; in the cities the new industrial workers lived notably wealthier lives than they had in the provinces they left behind. Starting out in a General Motors plant, Lorenzo Ramírez earned four times as much as he ever had before, while taking advantage of paid holidays, a pension scheme, and corporate team-building diversions like baseball.[91] Yet for country people in places like the Ramírezes' village in Puebla, the 1940s was a time of uncertainty and widespread hardship as rural real wages dropped over 40 percent. By the early 1950s the Gini coefficient for Mexico was 0.59, the beginning of a long period in Latin America during which only Brazil consistently registered a less equitable distribution of national income than Mexico.[92]

The Pros and Cons of Corruption

Not all strategic payoffs were formally announced, and development and corruption came closely intertwined, the one providing raw materials for the other. Corruption was in fact the party's (official) raison d'être: alongside electoral fraud, it was the central public justification for the 1946 abolition of the PRM and its replacement by the PRI, in what was far more than a mere rebranding exercise. The PRI was explicitly presented as an institutional new broom: in bidding farewell to the old party, its president's speech opened by proclaiming that it was "necessary to undertake a crusade against everything that stands for corruption and apostasy."[93] Alemán then—ironically—took a quantum leap forward in the systematic practice of corruption in all its forms, while his successor, the accountant—fittingly enough—Adolfo Ruiz Cortines, gained substantial legitimacy from reining it in. This was the defining period of Mexico's modern political system.[94] Corruption was central to it, and it remained central to political culture and practice across the rest of the century.[95]

Corruption was protean and polyvalent. At times it was a delegitimizing phenomenon, distilled in the fascinated revulsion against mythical figures like Alemán's "amigotes": Finance Minister Ramón Beteta, with his mansion and his "bejeweled American wife," or Jorge Pasquel, with his estates in Kenya and his

£4,000 sprees in Harrods.[96] Across his term Alemán and his camarilla by one estimate appropriated more than the entire external debt.[97] Without knowing many details—and details are rarely known, corrupters aspiring to the furtive—everyday Mexicans knew enough: in 1948 a historically inclined demonstrator suggested that the great looter Santa Anna was back from the beyond.[98] At other times, however, corruption was a critical source of stability, above all in civilian–military relations. As Obregón famously put it, "No Mexican general can resist a cannonade of 50,000 pesos."[99] Corruption could buy off the powerful; it could form deep alliances; it could be weaponized against political enemies (whether the accusations were true or not). It could also alienate those out of power, whether due to class, geography, or faction, and delegitimize an entire government. One of the most important questions in explaining the emergence and survival of the early PRI is precisely the balance between these stabilizing and destabilizing effects.[100]

There were three main types of corruption. The first was structural corruption, defined as regular, systematized payoffs to strategically placed actors; to all intents and purposes, rents and off-books salaries. The government supplemented the puritanically low declared wages of generals, for example, by paying several thousand pesos a month to each divisional general.[101] Even under Ruiz Cortines and his newly tight budget the generous individual payoffs continued.[102] The federal deputies of a rubber-stamp congress received a quiet 15,000 pesos a month to top up their pay.[103] For journalists, the frequency of payments comes through in the sheer number of slang terms for them: *embutes, igualas, sobres, rayas, chayotes,* and *la talis*. Some newspapers were nothing more than reminders to pay up. In Aguascalientes one weekly was never publicly sold, but rather sent out to local bureaucrats and politicians.[104] The governors who corrupted journalists were themselves in turn corrupted by the private sector, most notoriously by the rents they drew from drug organizations for monopoly control of their plazas. This was common knowledge to the extent of appearing in the newspapers: articles in 1947 accused the governor of Sinaloa, Pablo Macías Valenzuela, of providing coordination and airplanes to the state's traffickers.[105] Union leaders drew salaries from the private sector in return for peaceful labor relations. Policemen charged monthly tariffs to truck owners and bus companies to let them pass inspection points unhindered.[106] In extremis a town's entire public administration could be on the payroll: Jaime Merino, the cacique of Poza Rica, was accused of drawing on PEMEX funds to pay "the Commander of the 7th Battalion and his personnel, the Municipal President and his staff, the Police Commander and his staff, the President of the local CTM branch, the Federal Deputy for the 3rd Electoral District, the administrator of the 'Poza Rica' market, the Director and Administrator of *El Heraldo* . . . the Forestry Agent of the Region, Traffic Police Officers, the drivers of the Film Commission, the Basketball and Baseball teams . . . and others."[107]

The second type was the discretional corruption of one-off payments for services rendered: bribes. The spectrum of services for sale was broad, and it was not just public officials who were for sale. The National Committee of Employers paid the national union leaders for curbing workers' demands: in 1953 they fixed a dispute in the textile sector by giving Fidel Velázquez 100,000 pesos, Luis Morones 75,000 pesos, and Eucario León another 75,000 pesos.[108] The majority of transactions, however, tended toward illicit legal aid. Compromising documents could disappear or be misfiled, a practice common enough to have its own term, the *carpetazo*.[109] (They could also be purchased.)[110] Municipal books could be cooked; judgments in court cases could turn improbably favorable. One gang arrested for murder on Guerrero's Costa Chica got out of jail (relatively) free, despite damning confessions and eyewitness testimony, by clubbing together to pay the agente del ministerio público 800 pesos, or seven months' wages.[111] This was a good deal; ten years later a suspensión provisional for an individual homicide in the Acapulco district court cost 3,000 pesos, or nine months' wages.[112] In Iguala the sale of amparos was reportedly so common that, one wisecrack held, the prudent bought them before committing the relevant crimes.[113] The inner workings of justice were the epitome of the higher-up tolerance of discretional corruption, not just in terms of the legal exemptions for sale, but also in the minimal sanctions for the vendors if caught: when investigating magistrates were accused of taking bribes they were usually transferred rather than fired.[114]

The third and most influential form of corruption was graft. Midcentury Mexico was in some ways a gatekeeper state: fiscally weak, cash poor, bureaucratically understaffed, and yet imbued with a certain power through its ability to regulate access to the territory's natural and human resources, overcoming preexisting or artificially created bottlenecks.[115] Governments' regulatory scope and power grew markedly under Alemán as key tools of import substitution industrialization, namely, trade controls and tariffs, were used to build a new series of gates to the wealth of the postwar boom.[116] Control of those gates was central to stability at all levels of the state, from the municipality up to PEMEX or the Secretaría de Comunicaciones y Obras Públicas.[117] Those to be corrupted could be allowed through, or just given their own gates to exploit: as Aaron Saenz poignantly requested, "Don't give me anything, but put me where there is something."[118] Some of the most successful grafters received quite literal gates in the form of customs agencies: the "repulsively coarse-grained" Jorge Pasquel, for example, was given a Veracruz customs agency that was seen as the foundation of his ostentatious wealth.[119] But graft manifested itself across an extremely broad range of activities. Straightforward theft and embezzlement of government revenues were a structural constant. There was always a 20 percent surge in government spending in the last three months of any sexenio as the outgoing cashed in before losing their jobs, following the dictum "El año de Hidalgo, chinga su madre el que deje algo."[120] In the interim there were also tax farming, permit trading, and price gouging in noncompetitive public contracts.

Embezzlement was the most straightforward of grafting activities. It could be done circuitously by payroll padding, a practice with tradition. General Jacinto B. Treviño, a vocal critic of the PRI's corruption—"The Revolution is not . . . robbery. . . . Not *la mordida*. Not the crowning of a handful of politicians who have got rich trafficking in the poverty of the pueblo"[121]—had himself been spectacularly found out during the revolution, when drawing salaries for 21,300 troops he turned out to have a tenth of them actually on hand.[122] It could be done more directly by the resale of public goods. It could also be done by public contracts to the private companies of public figures: roads in Tamaulipas were built by Constructora de Tamaulipas SA, whose director was not just the nephew of the governor but also head of the state's Departamento de Obras Públicas.[123] Or it could be done by straightforward appropriation from treasuries at all levels of government. In the municipio of San Andrés Tuxtla, for example, "extraordinary expenses" took up to 15 percent of monthly spending.[124] In Villa Lerdo Pedro Martínez, aka La Changa, "The Joke," removed 7,890 pesos from the local treasury.[125] In Coatepec 250,000 pesos vanished from the tobacco workers' social security funds.[126] In Michoacán an open letter begged the government to undertake some basic public works, such as drinking water, instead of "accumulating monies"; meanwhile in Naranja it was the ejidal administrators who accumulated monies, an estimated 30,000 pesos worth of graft a year.[127] The governor of Coahuila, Ignacio Cepeda Dávila, was accused of taking 2 million pesos from the state budget under cover of funding to a nonexistent state university.[128] Presidents like Cárdenas or Ruiz Cortines might be personally puritanical; their peers, and their regimes, were not and could not be.

Tacit tax farming, embezzlement's kissing cousin, was also commonplace, and while being a collector meant being "a figure of fear, mistrust and hatred who was depicted as ill-educated, exploitative, and inveterately corrupt" it also meant relatively unregulated opportunity in what Ben Smith has called the "black fiscal economy."[129] In Guerrero Governor Leyva Mancilla's brother was a tax collector who owned a two-thousand-nine-hundred-hectare hacienda outside Chilpancingo; so too was his nephew, who threatened tax increases for truckers who failed to patronize his petrol station.[130] In Puebla federal taxmen dealing with William Jenkins could expect a good night on the town before a goodnight payoff.[131] When small fish met with crusading governors taxmen lost their jobs in waves: at the beginning of Ruiz Cortines's gubernatorial term seventeen taxmen were arrested for accepting bribes, while the eve of his presidency was another testing time for Veracruz taxmen, who once again lost their jobs in numbers.[132] At the same time, though, Ruiz Cortines's barely euphemized exchange of philanthropic commitments through municipal Juntas de Mejoramiento—Civic Development Juntas—for tax freezes was an effective admission of defeat in the cause of honest revenue raising. (A model the federal authorities followed with William Jenkins.)[133] Effective taxation was undermined by the fact that it was not just tax collectors who levied taxes; state representatives of all levels engaged in the less formal taxation of demanding money to allow businesses across the spectrum of legitimacy to function, either through the granting of a permit or license or the turning of a blind eye.

This was eminently doable because the Mexican economy was an intensely permit-rich zone, and at the same time the puritanical paternalism of the revolution's rhetoric and maximalist legislation, satirized by Malcolm Lowry—"Do you like this garden . . . that is yours? See to it that your children do not destroy it!"—placed gambling, prostitution, gun ownership, and even new bars firmly outside the law.[134] In Sinaloa one federal agent observed primly how "he saw perfectly clearly that the municipal authorities allow . . . illegal gambling, houses of pleasure, cockfights etc., which yield them fantastic pecuniary gains, given that all the town councilors of these ayuntamientos are the owners of expensive luxury automobiles and toss around fistfuls of cash."[135] Prohibition as ever made vice more lucrative: prostitutes in Chihuahua were effectively taxed more than doctors or lawyers, and while those taxes were not prescribed in the state's fiscal law—"to spare blushes," one observer remarked sardonically—they were charged (with some local and clientelist variation) at the municipal level; in 1943 a "first class" brothel in Parral paid between 150 and 300 pesos a month to avoid having its doors closed.[136] Unionized workers in the Palmolive-Colgate factory had to pay their leader, Luis Araiza, under the threat of being pushed out of the union and hence their jobs.[137] Paying for benign ignorance or the right to work was a business cost for both licit and illicit parts of the private sector.

The impact of all these practices was once hypothesized (counterintuitively) as positive, "a certain amount of corruption a welcome lubricant easing the path to modernization," according to Samuel Huntington, boosting the efficiency of government in countries with weak states and embryonic civic cultures, facilitating economic development and political stability.[138] That proposal gained wide acceptance: thus for Alan Riding corruption was oil for a rusty machine, working "like a piece rate for government employees (a bureaucrat may be more helpful when paid directly)" and "enabl[ing] entrepreneurs to overcome cumbersome regulations."[139] Such propositions are unsupported by convincing evidence and form part of a broader justification for supporting unsavory regimes during the Cold War. The majority of economists concur that corruption in reality hinders development, costing a private sector more than taxation, as "the imperative of secrecy makes bribes more distortionary than taxes."[140] The reigning belief is that corruption is a top-down, not bottom-up, phenomenon, which leads to both economic inefficiency and political destabilization.[141]

In the case of Mexico the economic conclusion is reasonable. The two decades after World War II have been described as a Golden Age, when astute economic management and canny investment (both public and private) produced sustained and miraculous growth. Yet Mexico's booming growth was not all that miraculous once set against Mexico's booming population or global comparatives. In comparative terms, GDP per capita actually stagnated across the midcentury; this was, after all, the time that Eric Hobsbawm defined as "a sort of Golden Age" across the globe, "some twenty-five or thirty years of extraordinary economic growth and social transformation, which probably changed human society more profoundly than any other period of comparable brevity."[142] In 1950 Mexico ranked twenty-seventh in the world in terms of GDP per capita; in 1973, after the end of the professed miracle, it remained twenty-seventh in the world. Inequality meanwhile increased.[143] The public funds lost to embezzlement, bribery, systematic tax evasion, and graft might have made both the scope and quality of development greater, while genuinely competitive tenders for public works would have lowered the cost of infrastructure, freeing up funds for more public investment. Alemán's building program was impressive, but so too was the waste it involved as contractors took the money and ran, at times without leaving any trace behind. In Coatzacoalcos the president's preferred contractor, Manuel Suárez, took a $4.5 million contract to supply drinking water and street paving but left behind "unpaved sand dunes."[144] In the first three years of Alemán's term the cost of road building trebled, rising from 33,000 to 97,000 pesos per kilometer; it was, his private secretary said in private, a crashing failure.[145] It is difficult to see how such inefficiencies stimulated economic growth.

The political conclusion, on the other hand, is unsustainable because corruption in midcentury Mexico demonstrably did have some stabilizing effects (if not always those proposed by modernization theorists). This is not to say that there were none of the predictable destabilizing impacts. When the weight of accusations of corruption grew unsustainable mayors, governors, and cabinet members tottered and fell. Alemán himself came near to falling in the autumn of 1948 as living standards plunged due to the sharp devaluation of the peso. Economic crisis and growing poverty were objectively not caused by corruption, but the subjective idea that they were proved graspable and morally satisfying. The placards in the demonstration of August 21, 1948, made the links explicit: "DOWN WITH THE MONOPOLIES. DEATH TO THE HUNGER-MONGERS. DOWN WITH THE POLITICIANS RICH AT THE COST OF THE PEOPLE'S POVERTY," demanded the oil workers; "RUIZ GALINDO MILLIONAIRE THANKS TO THE WORKERS' HUNGER," said the residents of the Colonia DM Nacional. Emboldened by popular outrage, some of the generals who had never been enthusiastic about Alemán plotted a coup. Rumors of an attempted assassination ran rife, given weight by their detail and by a wound to the president's hand; reportedly held back by Cárdenas and Avila Camacho, a large party of generals went to see Alemán, officially to pledge their support, in reality to pressure for drastic changes in the general staff and the appointment of five generals to the cabinet. They left with the seeming belief that the army would run the country from behind the throne, having gotten promises for all they wanted from the president.[146] But they left him still president, and Alemán must have felt relieved; he had, one report said, told the generals he believed they had come for his head.[147]

But in the toppling of corrupt politicians there was, once the crisis passed, political capital for those who had pushed them out, legitimacy for their replacements, and a certain reinforcement of the entire political system, its apparent capacity for self-correction demonstrated. This was the logic behind the foundation of the PRI (and its initial popular acceptance), and the logic behind the durable popularity of the dour Adolfo Ruiz Cortines, who made, in the British ambassador's words, "an end to graft and corruption in the government and administration" the "most significant feature of [his] policy."[148] And there were two rather less kosher stabilizing effects of corruption. Its proceeds were critical to prevent the elite exits that threaten such broad governing coalitions. The starkest example of that came precisely in the wake of the near-coup of 1948, when the institutional payoff to the army of an increased budget was accompanied by the uninstitutional payoffs of lucrative sinecures for top generals in a restructured command system. Commanding *zonas militares* had been lucrative; commanding the new *regiones militares,* which grouped several zones under a single officer, had yet greater revenue-raising potential. The flip side of the consent thus purchased, the force that was the other pillar of the dictablanda, lay in the power that records of that corruption gave the civilian leadership; for top-level graft, embezzlement, and extortion could always be weaponized against the corrupt and used to end their careers. The—quite literally—varying fortunes of General Antonio Ríos Zertuche are a case in point. He was one of the key movers in the 1948 crisis; the faction of northern generals discussing Alemán's overthrow met at his house. In October, the military having held off, he was given a colonia militar on former lands of the El Aguila oil company at Palma Sola, lands which gave him the additional bonus of forests that he duly clear-cut. Crisis past, *La Prensa*—one of whose directors worked in the presidential press office—revealed the extent of his profiteering and he was duly fired.[149] A substantial bribe one year became a powerful weapon another. In the short term, corruption bought off threatening dissidents; in the long term, it gave corrupters a threat to keep those ex-dissidents in line. The balance of the two phenomena were central to the larger balancing act of the new state's leaders.

The Demands of the State

If the weak civilian state of the 1940s relied heavily on elite corruption, to general disadvantage, its weakness also held some advantages for the ruled. The autonomy and power of an elite can be assessed by considering the assorted capacities of their state: the cognitive capacity of the leadership and bureaucracy, their penetration of local societies, success in extracting or appropriating resources, ability to regulate and change social relationships, and the persuasive power of the common cultural framework they project. Mexican state-builders enjoyed qualified success in piecing together a convincing nationalist story of heroism, altruism, and social justice. They did not lack ambition in the other tasks of state formation; modernizing agents of the state such as Leyva Mancilla at times seemed to dream of symmetrical social Brasilias built on the blank maps of their territories. A steady stream of correspondence to village governments in the 1940s carried instructions which, if obeyed, would have implied an impressive degree of social control. Modernizing politicians told peasant smallholders when (and sometimes what) to sow and when to harvest, instructed them under pain of arrest to attend night school and to send their sons off as army conscripts, hectored them to abandon their *vicios tradicionales* of gambling and drinking, and ordered them to report—and subsequently asphyxiate—vampire bats.[150] The Veracruz government demanded detailed annual statistical reports from the smallest settlements; in Guerrero the governor proposed the reconcentration of scattered populations into larger, better-controlled communities.[151] At the top of this would-be ordered state with its highfalutin high modernism sat the president, portrayed by party faithful, hacks, and intellectuals as the holder of exceptionally concentrated political power. Between the midforties and the midfifties, however, as revolution gave way to dictablanda, two realities undercut this projection of a strong central state: routine bureaucratic failure in the most basic tasks outside Mexico City, and noteworthy constraints on presidential political autonomy.

"The first and fundamental consideration of a ruler," said Ruiz Cortines, "is to know fully the territory that he will govern."[152] Yet the cognitive capacity of the federal bureaucracy was frequently remarkably low. In dealing with provincial complaints the presidency sometimes forwarded the letters to the wrong state government; thus in a fit of absent-mindedness Ometepec was once believed to be in Oaxaca, while Zirándaro was thought to belong to Michoacán.[153] Even a rapidly growing bureaucracy could not provide accurate information for the entire territory; Guerrero's 1950 agrarian census surveyed only half of the land in the districts of Alvarez and Zaragoza.[154] In addition to the difficulties inherent in ruling a large, complex territory, Mexicans of all classes had strong incentives to avoid or distort the truth in reporting to both their superiors and the public. Political reporting from the provinces was the scene of pitched battles of representation between local factions, who systematically painted their rivals in Manichaean terms as disciples of the public enemy of the moment. Socioeconomic reports from the villages were likewise unreliable, as peasants collaborated to evade taxes by consistently undervaluing their land; in northern Guerrero some contributors claimed that their land produced maize once every ten years, while in Veracruz villagers traditionally reported only a half or a third of their real maize harvests.[155]

Meanwhile politicians at all levels engaged in routine misreporting and refusals to disclose information. The agronomist De la Peña, despite powerful official backing, was unable to extract budget statements from even Guerrero's cities; Governor Gómez Maganda claimed to have implemented purely imaginary land grants; the statistical blizzards of presidential informes routinely gave agricultural production figures that were "considerably higher than estimates coming from other official sources."[156] The intention was clearly, as one wag put it, not so much to inform as to chloroform congressmen.[157] Skeptics sneered; Agriculture Secretary Marte Gómez "knew how to make such marvelous, eloquent statistics that the hungriest, after reading them, would be full up and burping chicken."[158] Naïve (or innumerate) book-cookers sometimes claimed success rates above 100 percent, whether for loan repayments or winning prosecutions.[159] But politicians were right to bet on a residual popular faith in statistics, and Gobernación agents listening in on postinforme gossip in the capital's cafés found that the statistics claiming increased production "caused the best impression."[160] The less politically desirable consequence of such mutual misleading was the sheer difficulty of ruling the vaguely comprehended provinces. Alemanista politicians took the problem seriously: both Guerrero and Veracruz invested heavily in De la Peña's work (as did Campeche, Chiapas, Chihuahua, Oaxaca, and Zacatecas); Veracruz set up a Department of Statistics to prepare monthly reports on demography, justice, the economy, and social policy; the Federal Law of Statistics established one-thousand-peso fines and jail terms for late or faulty statistics reports from petty bureaucrats.[161] Alemán founded the DFS and expanded the DGIPS in large part to give the presidency a verification system for the unreliable reports of underlings. Yet in their early days even these were far from well-oiled intelligence machines. The DGIPS archive was from the outset a mess: a 1944 investigation into file theft found that "nobody . . . bar those who work in the archive can readily track down a file, as their placings are quite complicated."[162] Inside Mexico City Alemán's knowledge of events, obtained from snitches and wide-ranging wiretaps, was impressive. In the provinces he and his government were often in the dark.

One thing every Mexican politician knew was the immense difficulty of collecting taxes. Taxation since Independence provoked evasion and revolt in a long-term cycle akin to collective bargaining by riot: in Guerrero the 1840s rebellions against Santa Anna, the minor crisis of 1891–93, the major crisis of 1910–11 and the overthrows of Governors López and Guevara were largely catalyzed by attempts to raise tax rates.[163] It was not a uniquely guerrerense problem: in Oaxaca broad coalitions, stretching from women market vendors through students to the *vallistocracia,* the planter elite of the valleys, brought down tax-raising governors in 1947 and 1952.[164] This entrenched, secular resistance created enduring practices—perhaps even a culture—of low, poorly enforced formal taxation rife with exemptions. Tax evasion, editorialized the *Diario de Xalapa,* was Mexico's "lifelong curse . . . the civic education which we have from the dawn of time."[165] In 1945 only 60 percent of Veracruz's population paid their taxes, and the collection rate of unpaid back taxes was 3 percent.[166] In such conditions paying taxes was not a rational choice. There was more to low revenues than calculation, poverty, or memories of successful popular refusal; a profound mistrust of government further encouraged Mexicans not to pay up. That the government could give only to the extent that it received was a mantra of governors' reports, yet the rulers' side of the social contract of taxation often went unfulfilled even when taxes were dutifully paid.[167] Complaints of vanishing tax payments were rife at the municipal level, possibly because the material returns on taxation were most easily monitored in the intimate environment of the patria chica. In 1949 the villagers of El Higo wanted to secede from Tempoal and form their own municipio, as they paid 600 pesos a month in taxes to the cabecera yet still lacked a school, a slaughterhouse, drinking water, electricity, and even a square.[168] Taxation was, moreover, one more weapon in the armory of discretionally observed constitutional provisions that dominant village factions turned on their rivals; in Ixcateopan ex-mayor Rodolfo Quintana was denounced for tax evasion by the village council that succeeded him.[169] The politicization of tax enforcement created the impression, as one governor said, that "tax is an unjustifiable punishment, and that to evade it by all means possible is legitimate and even admirable."[170] Finally, the revenue collection system was fundamentally flawed. The lucrative opportunities for corruption afforded both state and federal tax collectors had a double impact: money was siphoned out of the revenue system at the lowest level, while simultaneously the jobs were political plums awarded to clients rather than to the bureaucratically able. Such problems were particularly marked in Guerrero and Veracruz; in 1940 the former paid the lowest tax per capita of any state in the federation while the latter, for all its wealth, still contributed less than the national average.[171] It was, however, a distinctly national problem. The percentage of GDP Mexicans paid to their government declined sharply across the 1940s, and by 1950, with revenues running at 6.9 percent of GDP, they paid some of the lowest taxes in Latin America.[172]

Development economists suggest that a state should appropriate between 20 percent and 30 percent of GDP to meet even minimal goals, and while many states fall short of this target, Mexico's shortfall was exceptional.[173] Politicians in the late 1940s and early 1950s consequently made diverse attempts to increase the tax base. The governors of both Guerrero and Veracruz passed frequent legislation—Ruiz Cortines decreed sixteen treasury reforms in his first year of government—that aimed to expand the range of activities taxed, to raise rates, to update old and inaccurate cadastral surveys, and to centralize and modernize revenue collection.[174] In many places the endemic negotiation of tax contributions continued in a variety of guises. The San Andrés Tuxtla ayuntamiento offered a 50 percent reduction and no penalties to those who paid their back taxes by the end of 1945; in Ixcateopan a tax inspector imposed drastic increases on the municipal wealthy that were then bargained down in a village meeting.[175] As Ruiz Cortines noted, the long-standing expectation of such haggling constituted a perverse incentive to pay taxes late or not at all; yet his solution, allowing the grande bourgeoisie and middle classes to suggest their own rates, similarly acknowledged the state's continuing need to negotiate taxation from a position of hereditary weakness.[176] The Alemán sexenio did see a clear increase in the coercion of both treasury officials and taxpayers: in Veracruz there were several wide-ranging purges of tax collectors, in Guerrero the state treasurer was jailed for corruption, and in both states some nonpayers had their properties sequestered. Politicians made a consolidated attempt to engineer a cultural change in the beliefs and practices surrounding taxation, using speeches, media, and informes to stress the link between payment of taxes and delivery of state services.[177] Their efforts were in part successful. Even after negotiation veracruzanos paid 30 percent more commercial tax in 1946; Ixcateopan's elites paid up to 400 percent more property tax in 1951; the national budget more than doubled in real terms between 1945 and 1953, growing significantly faster than GDP.[178] Such new levels of revenue, when combined with the old-fashioned informal taxation of forced labor, funded the accelerated modernization programs of the period. Yet the Alemanistas had not dealt with the fundamental problem of taxation in Mexico—its institutionalization as a legitimate state appropriation—and they left the problem of a part-voluntaristic, continually negotiated tax system to future generations; in 1979 Mexico still paid only 9.2 percent of GDP in tax.[179]

The grassroots noncompliance that sabotaged taxation also sabotaged the state's efforts at social regulation, and the two most ambitious projects of social engineering of the 1940s—adult literacy and conscription—failed. Under the terms of the decree of August 21, 1944, the literacy campaign of *alfabetización* was projected as a massive mobilization of teachers, bureaucrats, chambers of commerce, union, peasant, party, and army leaders so that "every Mexican who knows how to read and write will teach an illiterate to read and write."[180] Each village was instructed to form a campaign committee and a literacy center, to which the SEP supplied copious literacy textbooks. The complex syntax of bureaucratic justification made the instrumental purpose of the campaign quite clear: "foreseeing the vital need to transform the country's semicolonial economy into one that was fully developed as much in agricultural as in industrial and commercial terms, for which it was necessary to create a complete feeling of national identity and a clear spirit of National Unity, and being necessary for all of these reasons to provide our Pueblo with a basic cultural preparation, the need to undertake a National Literacy Campaign became imperative."[181]

Yet across Mexico both would-be teachers and their pupils refused to cooperate, and the upbeat statistics of national and state leaders are given the lie by voluminous correspondence and piles of unused, moldering exercise books in village archives. Almost a year after the campaign's launch only eleven municipios in Guerrero had formed the mandatory committees.[182] Three years into the campaign only half of Veracruz's municipios reported results, many of which were confirmations of failure: Paso del Macho had sixteen pupils, none of whom had learned to read, San Andrés Tuxtla had five centers and two hundred pupils but no instructors and no success stories, and even Orizaba was unable to report a single *alfabetizado*.[183] (The comparison with revolutionary Cuba, where enthusiastic volunteers allegedly taught seven hundred thousand adults to read and write inside a year, is eye-watering.)[184] Watching Avila Camacho's brainchild emerge stillborn, governments at all levels tried coercion. By the end of 1945 fines were being imposed on illiterates who avoided classes; in Pachivia the comisario municipal was nearly lynched as a consequence; and by 1946 the municipal police were being used to round up pupils. Correspondence from Ixcateopan's comisarios municipales chart the two principles which motivated such resistance.[185] One was the demands of the agricultural cycle; the other was a serrano attitude to the cosmetic expectations of an encroaching state. One villager summed it up when the police came to take him to school, saying that "no motherfucker ordered him around, that he obeyed no one and that the President could go straight to hell."[186]

Servicio Militar Nacional was conceptualized, in terms similar to those of the literacy campaign, as a policy with benefits both material (a larger, conscript army for wartime) and instrumental, serving to "Mexicanize . . . the Mexicans."[187] The Ley de servicio militar of November 1942 required all eighteen-year-olds to register on a draft list, after which they would enter in a municipal lottery that would select a small number of conscripts for integration into the army, leaving the rest to undergo a year's Sunday training before passing into the ranks of the reserves. Thom Rath has charted the eloquently many local riots and armed revolts provoked when conscription began in wartime.[188] Even as the specter of active overseas service receded, however, vigorous everyday resistance—encouraged by endemic corruption in the conscription process—continued to dog the recruiting officers. The pistolero fiefs of Actopan and Alto

Lucero refused point-blank to send conscripts; in 1948 Actopan had yet to send a single recruit.[189] Indigenous villages likewise tended to blanket noncompliance. In Mixtla de Altamirano, Veracruz, the authorities fled when the recruiting officer arrived; with the help of the remaining villagers he tenaciously drew up a draft list only to find that the names he had been given were all ineligible old men.[190] In Soteapan the conscription lottery of the *sorteo* was broken up by armed men.[191] Even Mexicans in less conflictual municipios were capable of a near-total sabotage of the recruitment process. In Ixcateopan the 1944 draft list registered only seventy men, of whom thirty-five provided medical exemption certificates; twenty-seven were eventually approved for the sorteo, which selected twelve men, five of whom immediately tried evasion.[192] Only two hundred men attended the 1949 sorteo in Xalapa, which covered the inhabitants of twenty-eight municipios.[193] Among the few who were drafted desertions were commonplace.[194] The state lacked the coercive power to punish such recalcitrance, and as evaders and deserters were seen to go unpunished resistance seems to have solidified. In 1945 only one of the Ixcateopan conscripts actually went on active service, and in 1947 only four of the eight men drawn were delivered by the municipal defensa social.[195] In 1950 the state admitted defeat and ended active conscript service, replacing it with Sunday morning training (which was also evaded).[196] At the same time the literacy campaign was wound down. Both policies were, revealingly, legacies from previous administrations; both failed in an uneven struggle that pitted limited, corrupt, or ineffectual state agents against strenuous popular resistance. Alemán—yet more revealingly—did not initiate any direct social engineering of similar scope.

Mexico's state grew and became more powerful across the midcentury. Tax collection became slightly less ramshackle, even if it grew much slower than the economy, and the increased revenues of that rapidly growing economy helped fund a notable expansion of state capacities ranging from the provision of health care, welfare, and education to intelligence gathering. At the core of this new state three critical areas of political weakness endured. The presidency had not obtained the exaggerated policy autonomy once assumed to have characterized the Golden Age of the PRI. Alemán struggled to impose himself on the military, and never managed to break free of the informal senate which he inherited from past presidencies; Ruiz Cortines was openly defied by Muñoz, who refused to accept presidential instructions to fire key members of his cabinet.[197] Both relied on the stabilizing political effects of corruption: Alemán to buy off the generals, Ruiz Cortines to garner popularity through attacking it (while continuing to buy off the generals). The transmission belts of power running between Los Pinos and the provinces were very frayed. Most important of all, grassroots consent continued to be an elusive and expensive commodity for Mexican politicians. Gómez Maganda tried to apply a purposive, libertarian gloss to the fundamental difficulties of bending provincial populations to their leaders' will: "Thousands and thousands of Mexicans don't pay taxes; don't report whether they work or not; are outside the prejudices of church marriage; don't ask permission to sow, or to build their house; if they don't help Authority, are outside Authority. When we complain of our plagues, of poverty, of illness and ignorance, we forget that in exchange we enjoy liberties of which other peoples never dreamed."[198] In his absurdity there may have been some insight; that a more effective, a more powerful Mexican state might never have worked. Grassroots resistance and the cupular constraints exemplified by Cárdenas combined to thwart some of the authoritarian, banana-republican dreams of early Priistas from Alemán to Alejandro Gómez Maganda. Incapable of doing as they pleased, whether it entailed introducing the death penalty or refusing to give up the golden goose of the presidency, such men contributed to a more stable and institutional Mexico, in many ways in spite of themselves.

8 • Talking about a Revolution

Of Heroes and Bores: The Modern Synthesis of Nationalism

The postrevolutionary Mexican state has been described as a democracy with adjectives, but also as authoritarian with adjectives—variously liberal, inclusive, bureaucratic, semi, competitive, and soft—a "perfect dictatorship" or a dictablanda.[1] Such portmanteau labels often verged on the self-contradictory; it was, the British ambassador concluded, "an undemocratic form of democracy."[2] But they reflect the widespread perception (academic and popular) that the Mexican way of doing politics after the revolution was exceptional; *como México no hay dos.* This idea of exceptionalism was rooted in the reality that Mexico differed substantially from other Latin American regimes in the scope and violence of its revolution, the subsequent balance of force and consent employed by its elites, and the long-running political stability these delivered. The extreme violence of 1910–20 inculcated more than one generation of politicians with a healthy respect for the high costs (for both rulers and ruled) of failed authoritarian systems. Mexico's politicians for most of the twentieth century were, moreover, in hock to the memories of both the popular revolutionaries and the constitutional constituents of 1917; these meshed in a revolutionary discourse which, as the motor of the state's claim to legitimacy, demanded periodic servicing. Most important of all, Mexican elites long after 1910 lacked the muscle to rule without a substantial degree of popular consent: the impracticality of dropping the *pan* and applying pure *palo* to unruly provincials had been amply demonstrated by Huerta's defeat, by the Cristiada, and—to an admittedly lesser extent—by the failures of cardenista reform. From an elite perspective, the soft nature of Mexican authoritarianism was not optional, but rather a pragmatic, half-improvised response to the constraints they faced.

Replacing overt repression with what Pierre Bourdieu called "the gentle, hidden violence [of] man's exploitation by man whenever overt, brutal exploitation is impossible" required considerable time, multiple concessions to the resistance of the ruled, and hard work.[3] Midcentury federal and state politicians consequently devoted considerable resources to engineering grassroots consent. They struggled on two fronts: that of the material and ideological incentives to submission that were summed up as progress, modernization, or development, and that of cultural control, the attempt to convince Mexicans that progress, modernization, and development were indeed happening, that they were part of a powerful national narrative, and to edit reality to that narrative's outlines. This was—compared to earlier, root-and-branch attempts at social engineering—a modest program; a tacit recognition, perhaps, of the limits of state power. Just how salient this cultural project actually was in sustaining that power is central to interpretations of the sui generis Mexican state.

At the center of elite aspirations to cultural control lay the cohesive, long-running nationalist campaigns of generations of rulers. Mexico's nation-builders were favored by an exceptional collection of preexisting foundation myths.[4] At Independence they already possessed the raw materials that most other Latin Americans lacked. When Padre Morelos invoked Anáhuac as the new polity's ancestor he was at least in the right place, speaking to people with some of the right genes and surrounded by concrete—or stone, at least—proof of some links; whereas the man in Buenos Aires who in 1816 laid claim to Moctezuma, or his compatriot who wrote a national anthem proclaiming Argentina the Inka patria were somewhere between optimistic and delusional.[5] The serial political disintegration of the post-Independence period over, by the late nineteenth-century speeches, songs, place-names, funerals, monuments, civic ceremonies, novels, textbooks, and even the labels on beer bottles were being used to project an affectively powerful national identity, rooted in the double legitimacies of the pre-Hispanic past and the Wars of Independence, and reinforced in the provinces by the popular, patriotic liberalism that had emerged in the local guerrilla wars against the French.[6] Politicians, writers, and designers told with some success a secular story of being Mexican, and it was one of centuries of heroism and sacrifice that had culminated, against heavy odds, in independence and a leading place among the modern nations.

The revolution added further mythic layers: the prolific hero cults of dead leaders, the economic nationalism of land and oil expropriation, and finally, with increasing strength as events receded, the reification of the revolution as "a being on the march, an essence independent of the very revolutionaries, a material of progress and patriotism that, with or without revolutionaries, continues to work."[7] Such reification had begun under Plutarco Elias Calles and had been substantially developed by Lázaro Cárdenas; it reached its peak in the later 1940s, in a series of initiatives designed to flatten the complex, contradictory, and faction-ridden past into a single highway toward the "constructive stage of the revolution."[8] The ranks of those officially commemorated as part of the nationalist mainstream swelled each year. In 1931 Venustiano Carranza was incorporated into the pantheon, in 1942 the six living presidents, some literally mortal enemies, appeared together in a much-disseminated photo, and in 1950 the apparatchik (and onetime villain) Calles was honored at his tomb.[9] The calendar, already packed with commemorative dates, had a further layer of meaning superposed as the federal government dedicated whole sections of time to remembering nationalist symbols: thus 1950 was the year of Cuauhtémoc, February 1951 was the month of the national flag, and 1953 was the year of Hidalgo.[10] By the midcentury there had emerged, as in evolutionary biology, a modern synthesis, a powerful grafting together of three big ideas: the power and glamor of the pre-Hispanic empires, indigenous, Rousseauian even, yet *culto;* the self-sacrificial, but ultimately triumphant anticolonialism of the mestizo rebels for independence; and the apotheosis of that independence, the democracy, equality, and social justice of the revolution. The party organ *El Nacional* put it neatly: "Our party, following the march of progress of Mexico, has a record of positive affirmation: it was insurgent in the struggle for Independence, Republican and Federalist in our process of patriotic integration, liberal in the stage of the Reforma, and revolutionary since the movement of 1910. The Partido de la Revolución is, in reality, the same that has been fulfilling the desires of the pueblo across the different stages of our history."[11]

Yet even as politicians claimed legitimating ownership of the past they censored its unsettling radicalism. In Cuautla, Morelos, Alemán and Ruiz Cortines attended the 1950 commemoration of Emiliano Zapata's death and declared that the agrarian problem had been resolved, the majority of Mexican land redistributed, and the government's developmentalist program would have been Zapata's priority had he lived.[12] (This contrasted with the outside world's appreciation of Zapata the unwavering revolutionary, present from street names in Sarajevo to guerrilla murals in Belfast.) The official press recast Cuauhtémoc, that epitome of bloody resistance to oppression, the archetypal indigenous underdog, as a sort of historical teacher's pet, a "constructive myth without negative angles . . . a perennial lesson for youth."[13] The first Mexicans had found inspiration, the party secretary wrote in a compellingly execrable poem, in the last emperor's cheeriness while being burned:

May you be praised, Lord, for your smile,
Because it flourished above the flames,
And kindled your fire for the people.[14]

Pancho Villa, meanwhile—irredeemably radical, a loose cannon in both reality and ideology—was "a non-person for official Mexico," the sole missing name from the letters of gold on the wall of congress, the only distinguished corpse missing from the Monumento de la Revolución (his skull even missing from his Parral grave), and later down the line prominently missing from the Insurgentes metro line, where the stations of Zapata, Guerrero, the *Niños Héroes,* and Juárez are joined not by Villa but by the impersonal masses of the División del Norte.[15] As Priistas watered down the rebellious past they invented new traditions—Tree Day, Flag Day, Soldier Day, the sop to the Right that was Mother's Day—characterized by the consensual blandness of *mexicanidad,* mexicanness. To it they added the discourses of democracy and development, a "bourgeois-democratic" revolution to which the Marxist Left could also subscribe.[16] The aim was to depoliticize Mexican national identity in favor of a fuzzy national narrative that imposed the obligations of unity, discipline, and mexicanidad—the tautological abstraction of being Mexican, possession of which made one Mexican—while surrendering as few ideological hostages to fortune as possible.

The Nuts and Bolts of Nationalism

The increasingly anodyne nature of Mexican nationalism, at times strikingly banal, was partly compensated by the sheer increase in volume enabled by the spreading communications technologies of printing presses, radios, gramophones, cinemas, the first televisions, the various organizations of the state that deployed them, and the private media subsidized for their sympathies. While comparatively few Mexicans ever saw what we see as the staples of the visual culture of the revolution, the murals and monuments, and "memes need carriers," the numbers of carriers, the nuts and bolts of nationalism, soared across the 1940s and 1950s.[17] Diego Rivera's work had already been widely reproduced in the 1930s, in the strategically key teachers' magazine *El Maestro Rural* (and the less key domestic tourism magazine *Mapa*), and such circulation possibilities increased dramatically in the immediate postwar period.[18] Cheap printing presses came to Mexico in large numbers and a press boom began that lasted until the end of the 1950s: in the mid-

1940s eight new papers emerged in Oaxaca and twenty in Veracruz, while the citizens of San Luis Potosí enjoyed three cultural magazines (whether that talented prose stylist Gonzalo N. Santos subscribed to *Letras Potosinas: Vocero de la cultura* is unfortunately unknown).[19] In Teloloapan a mimeographed weekly appeared, *El Periquillo,* dealing with the "social and ideological problems" of the nearby villages and seeking foreign correspondents for each municipio.[20] The print boom reached across generations: by the late 1940s the comic *Pepín* claimed a circulation of 300,000, each issue running to 64 pages.[21] One of the newspapers founded on the back of *Pepín*'s profits, *El Sol de Guadalajara,* had a Goss cylindrical press that could spit out 25,000 copies an hour.[22] By the end of the 1950s there were 955 newspapers in Mexico, and nearly one in two families had a subscription.[23]

Radio sets, meanwhile, were already ubiquitous. By the late 1930s it was commonplace, Robert Marett reported, "to hear a wireless blaring forth from the door of a humble adobe hut in some quite remote village," while in the oil camps every house had "a radio of the very latest model."[24] Those that didn't still listened, as the party gave out sets to unions and rural community centers, while village shops used them to get customers through the doors.[25] In Tres Zapotes the biggest shop held two competitive advantages: customers could ride their horses onto the patio in a sort of equine drive-through, or they could spend in a more considered way listening to and discussing the radio, which made it "the village social center."[26]

Wartime technical support from the U.S. embassy, NBC, and CBS subsequently led to an order of magnitude increase in transmission: Emilio Azcárraga's conglomerate, Radio Programas de México, grew tenfold between 1941 and 1942. In 1949 ten factories assembled U.S.-manufactured components into 116,000 radios (with suitably nationalist indigenous names, such as the General Electric Azteca M-578); across the Alemán sexenio ownership doubled to 2 million receivers.[27] Television, for all its eventual power—by the end of the century Mexicans watched more TV than any other people on earth—took longer to catch up. In 1958 only one in ten Mexicans got their news from a TV; only half had even seen one.[28] But film compensated. The number of cinemas rose from 863 in 1938 to 1,431 in 1948, and Mexican studios came to produce over 100 features a year between 1946 and 1952.[29] Miguel Alemán had a dream, he said, "that every Mexican could have a Cadillac, a cigar, and a ticket to the bulls."[30] That never happened; but they did get cheap transport (Mexico City bus fares were capped at predevaluation 1947 levels until 1955), cheap cigarettes, cheap cinema (tickets in Puebla's Cinema Guerrero were

Village shop, Tres Zapotes, Veracruz. "In this 'department' store the natives buy almost any commodity from clothing, harness, and canned soup to liquors and cigars. It serves as the village social center because of its radio." Richard H. Stewart, "Discovering the New World's Oldest Dated Work of Man," *National Geographic Magazine* 76, no. 2 (August 1939). National Geographic Image Collection.

25 centavos) and in the long run, cheap (in more than one sense of the term) TV.[31]

The cumulative effect of these media was to saturate Mexican public space with nationalist stories and the claims of politicians, bureaucrats, businessmen, and popular leaders to their legacies. Literacy grew quickly across the midcentury, and by 1950 more than half the population could read and write. Neither veracruzanos nor guerrerenses were all that well schooled—Guerrero was the least literate state in the Republic—but they shared in the gains, with literacy in Guerrero rising from 18 percent to 22 percent and in Veracruz from 33 percent to 40 percent across the 1940s.[32] They shared, consequently, in the barrage of progovernment messages on parade everywhere from the margins of comic books to the coverage and commentary of the great newspaper chain of José García Valseca, whose empire by the midfifties ran to twenty-seven large dailies in twelve states, some running to over one hundred thousand copies a day.[33] The rhetoric of government probity and nationalism was excellent business, influencing public opinion in four ways. There was the daily editorial choice of what to report and what not to report. There was the nationalist commentary, which it was difficult to lay on too thick. The *Diario de Xalapa* warmly welcomed the government's "patriotic-educational labor" to "bring back civic sentiment and patriotic fervor to the people's soul" through "profiting from all the commemorative dates of our History"; the editor had recently visited Mexico City for the commemoration of the Niños Héroes, about which "it might be said that this event constituted a truly international achievement, one which had the qualities of an apotheosis."[34] Younger readers delving into *Revista Pinocho* could find inspirational recruiting slogans linking the military to the patria—"No one should forget that the peace of the country is based on the pueblo's trust in its Army," "To be a firm crusader in National Military Service is to be a good patriot"—at the foot of *Los Tarzanes* on three consecutive pages.[35] There was the commercial advertising that adopted nationalist tropes: thus Ferrocarriles Nacionales de México promoted railways as vehicles for the state's "civilizing plans" that would integrate far-flung Indians such as the Seri, "outside all civilization," into the nation, while Belmont cigarettes proclaimed themselves "as genuinely ours as the dress of a Tzotzil from Tenejapa, Chiapas."[36] Finally, there was the consumption such advertising drove, a literal buying in to the national project of capitalist development that stretched from First Ladies doling out plastic Christmas toys to poor children to adults achieving "a better life in the Mexican home" through fridge ownership.[37]

Officialist printed material, even if less engaging than scandal or Santa Claus, grew likewise. The state gazettes, venerable tools that coordinated civic ritual by listing key dates, detailing ceremonies, and providing models of rhetoric and affective response, were supplemented by multiple official and semiofficial periodicals. These aimed, in the classic term of the period's political lexicon, to *orientar* Mexicans, and toward that end there emerged at least sixteen publications called *Orientaciones* between 1940 and 1952.[38] In 1947 the Veracruz government printworks published three cultural magazines and the state gazette, while in Guerrero the government bought a modern press and began producing the *Diario de Guerrero*.[39] Unions such as the Alianza de Camioneros

The party biography of Benito Juárez, cover, 1949.

had their own magazines; even some ayuntamientos felt the need for an official paper.[40] In 1949 that of Acapulco began publishing *El guerrerense* ("get ready," the port's independent paper warned, "to believe the incredible, and to find out that 'all is very well' into the bargain").[41] Further scripts came from the center, and in the first three years of the Alemán sexenio the party handed out nearly a million free biographies of Mexico's national heroes, while sending photographs and oil paintings of their heir, the president, free to all town halls.[42] The two could be combined, as when the party biography of Juárez had as its second page a photograph of Alemán: buy one, get one free.[43]

Not everything was free, though, and Mexican villagers were pushed to buy copious nationalist material, some as expensive as Casasola's six-volume *Historia Gráfica de la Revolución Mexicana*.[44] Between 1945 and 1952 the Ixcateo-

The party biography of Benito Juárez, frontispiece, 1949.

pan ayuntamiento received annual entreaties to subscribe to *El Nacional* and offers of books such as *Apología de los niños héroes* and *El Padre Hidalgo y los suyos*. The marketing of such publications was highly aggressive: copies were sent in advance and it was unsubtly intimated that sales were required by the highest levels of the state.[45] (As had been the case under Cárdenas, when the president ordered state governors to invest in works ranging from Gildardo Magaña's history of Zapatismo to the revolutionary comic book *El Periquillo Estudiantil*.)[46] *El Nacional* was essential to the teachers, shopkeepers, smallholders, and cantina owners who formed the Ixcateopan ayuntamiento, the blurb argued, as "we publicize through articles by recognized revolutionary writers the orientaciones that the reading public needs concerning the most important matters in national life."[47] Ixcateopan was both impoverished and somewhat serrano in these matters, and the salesmen got short shrift. That they did well elsewhere, though, is clear in the ubiquity of the canonical *México a través de los siglos* and the Casasola oeuvre on the bookshelves and coffee tables of the urban middle and upper-middle classes.

Coffee-table books tend to stay on coffee tables—though even there they have a fetishistic clout—and the most important mass medium for nation building was the radio, in Cárdenas's words "a factor of invaluable effectiveness for the integration of a national mentality."[48] Radio programs were immensely popular. Networks were commercial, but their owners were close allies of the party elites who ceded monopoly power for political support: XEX was run by Alemán's close ally and *prestanombre*—front man—Rómulo O'Farrill, while XEW was run by the budding magnate Emilio Azcárraga, in later times the owner of all Mexican television programming.[49] Broadcasting was from the outset a propaganda tool, mixing the commercial appeal of mariachis and radio dramas with party speeches, reports of nationalist ritual, "programs of a cultural nature, on the occasions of historical commemorations, to fortify the civic spirit," a "military cultural hour," and even *mañanitas* for the Virgen de Guadalupe.[50] For the critical ceremonies of presidential informes and transfers of power, broadcast live since 1924, Gobernación's Dirección General de Información went beyond faith in radio's intrinsic popularity—presidential speeches could be "electronic sedatives"—and ordered ayuntamientos to install loudspeakers in markets, public squares, and buildings, and to encourage businesses to place speakers outside their premises and private vehicles equipped with speakers to tune into the transmission that all stations would carry.[51] Even as competition from other media grew in the 1960s the government continued to pump out nationalist messages over the airways. *La hora nacional,* broadcast in a peak slot on Sunday evening, for decades gave detailed instruction in *historia patria:* the July 10, 1966, program began with the rhetorical questions, "*What is the Nation? What is the Fatherland?*" and in following weeks answered that it was, among many other things, the country of "the Constitutionalist ideas, Hidalgo's decrees, the indigenous rebellions" (July 24), not to mention "the Plan of the Partido Liberal, the Plan of San Luis, the Plan of Ayala, the Plan of Guadalupe, and the Law of 6 January" (September 18, presumably with the faith that hangovers from the fiestas patrias had subsided). What listeners thought in the times of the counterculture is unclear, but whatever the feelings of the *jípis* some high-up politicians still cared: when the *hora nacional*'s transmission was once delayed they asked the DFS to investigate why.[52]

Jedan dan života. Dir. Emilio Fernández, Meksiko, 1951. Courtesy of Jugoslovenska Kinoteka.

Cinema offered a similar blend of commercial attraction, distraction, and political indoctrination. It was founded on a similar ownership structure, trading off the effective subsidies of monopoly control for reliable political backing, and by the 1950s William Jenkins enjoyed overwhelming dominance, controlling the vast majority of theaters.[53] Cinemas sprang up across small-town Mexico: Paso del Macho, San Andrés Tuxtla, and Soledad de Doblado had one each, Villa Cardel had two.[54] Trucks took mobile projectors yet farther afield. Mexican films were generally loss-making, subsidized by cheap government loans and protectionism, and in return pushing, in Andrew Paxman's words, "a heady mix of escapism, contentment with one's lot, national pride, and imagined community."[55] (As he notes, there was also an element of opium-of-the-people benefits to cheap cinema.)[56] Some productions, like *Escuadrón 201* (1945), were trite and forgettable; others promoted useful core values of mexicanidad, such as stoicism and self-sacrifice, while also being good films. They were many, and by 1946 only the United States and India were making more films.[57] Some prospered abroad, and not just in the Americas: one extremely popular film in communist Yugoslavia was the otherwise forgotten *Un Día de Vida* (1950) dubbed, retitled *Jedan dan života,* and shown year after year to packed theaters.[58]

They did not always do so well at home—*Jedan dan života* apparently sank without much trace in Mexico—and while legislation specified that a majority of films be domestic products, in reality only some 15 percent of showings across the 1940s were Mexican. These were concentrated, however, in the provincial small towns about whose control the government was least secure.[59] They might come accompanied by didactic developmentalist shorts, such as *Guerra al Paludismo,* which intoned to its viewers that "Malaria kills. War on malaria. Because the *patria mexicana* of shining lights that seek for highways in the reddening skies of dawn and seek in the nights with powerful searchlights for the roads that lead to well-being knows that triumph is effort and effort is Patria!"[60] Each feature without fail came accompanied by a newsreel and these, whether produced at home by Clasa Films Mundiales SA or abroad by MGM, were reliable in their conservative, progovernment, and anticommunist coverage.

Censorship

When newsreels were on rare occasion unreliable they met with censorship and a governmental aspiration—not wholly fulfilled—to control what Mexicans heard, saw, and read. Commercial monopolies more or less guaranteed the first two: there were no independent domestic stations on the airwaves, and NAFINSA held the majority of shares in Clasa Films Mundiales SA.[61] There was, consequently, a high proportion of positive news about national development and the president in turn—frequently linked—as well as systematic coverage of such ceremonies as the anniversary of the oil expropriation.[62] If newsreels failed the test—generally unintentionally, as when audiences in dark cinemas serenaded the flickering images with catcalls, obscene double entendres, and whistles—the government wielded the scissors. When footage of Alemán giving out diplomas to teachers drew storms of whistles, the Dirección de Supervisión Cinematográfica de la Secretaría de Gobernación sent an agent around Mexico City's cinemas who snipped out the relevant sections.[63] The censors were not always all that dynamic—it took Gobernación four days to cut the above segment, and this during the national crisis of 1948—but the state behind them took the job seriously enough to defy the United States. In 1949 the censors excised scenes of the pope denouncing the enemies of religion from an MGM newsreel; the U.S. embassy spoke to the foreign ministry to request that such cuts not recur, and was told that Mexico had no international obligation to the Geneva Convention on Freedom of Information, that the ministry would not even broach the subject with Gobernación and that Mexico would proceed as it saw fit in the future.[64]

Censorship of commercial films was likewise ambitious, encompassing not just domestic but also foreign films, which needed permits for both display and (were they shot in Mexico) filming. The process was revealed in detail when Gobernación defended itself against a lack of rigor in allowing scenes that denigrated Tampico into *The Treasure of the Sierra Madre.* The film had, they replied, "been duly approved by the technical personnel who are in charge of such matters, subject to certain cuts and modifications; that all of the negatives shot in Tampico . . . had been developed in this capital under the control of the relevant agency and that besides the fact that the company in question had faithfully followed all of the instructions that it was given, the film limited itself to presenting certain barrios of Tampico that might give an idea of what the city was like in the year of 1925, the date in which the story or script took place." And besides, the relevant bureaucrat pointed out, it wasn't Mexicans who were behaving badly: "The protagonists [were] north American adventurers."[65] Such careful control of visual media carried over into the age of television, which began, in Mexico, with the transmission of Alemán's fourth informe.[66]

For all the myths of the *prensa vendida,* the sellout press, newspapers were less than reliably progovernment. Attempts at control began with the owners and editors, some overtly in hock to the government; *El Nacional* billed itself as "the official organ of the government," *Novedades* was owned by Alemán's jarocho crony Jorge Pasquel, and one of the triumvirate who ran *La Prensa* worked in the press office of Los Pinos.[67] Other press organs were more covertly controlled: the editor of the magazine *Todo* was a secret agent.[68] Censorship agencies, introduced in wartime, endured. Gobernación housed not just the Dirección de Supervisión Cinematográfica but also the Comisión Calificadora, which began with comic books and extended its reach over all illustrated periodicals. Formal print censorship—unlike newsreel or film—was serious in law but not all that serious in practice. The Comisión Calificadora was staffed by dedicated minor civil servants, who initially went unpaid, who were closed down for most of the Alemán sexenio, and whose enforcement was toothless anyway; when they brought charges against two soft-porn magazines only one editor showed up to the meeting, and the other never paid his fine.[69] But the political coverage and commentary of mainstream newspapers was a different matter, and there the censors' work was supplemented by an impressive array of informal censorship strategies. The government systematically deployed advertising contracts, soft loans, and monopoly control of newsprint to induce the compliance of the national press. When all else failed they turned to violence, and murder was enough of a possibility for even *capitalino* journalists as to form the subject of dark jokes: the cartoonist Abel Quezada drew his editor surreptitiously measuring him up for a coffin, while the editor of the satirical mayfly *Presente,* Jorge Piño Sandoval, dubbed his reporters the Suicide Squad. It wasn't all self-dramatization: Piño Sandoval reportedly fell off his balcony, while the editor of *Impacto,* Natalio Burstein, an extortion-prone, optimistic bon vivant, supposedly blew his brains out in the back of a police car in Puebla.[70] In general the unwritten rules of the PRI prohibited overly visible murders, yet the cumulative effect of all of the informal tools of censorship was enough to shut down *Presente,* the last all-out opposition publication, in 1949, and for the next decade or so national political criticism was muted, tucked into the sports pages, cultural magazines like *Cine Mundial,* and the bloody criminal pages of the *nota roja.*[71]

Such tools were also used against the provincial press. *El Trópico de Acapulco* was supposed to have supported Gómez Maganda in 1950 because he had bought them a new printing press, while the *Diario de Xalapa* became notably less confrontational once its editor was a priista deputy with the funds to acquire wire service reports, which displaced local scandal in favor of stories of Tito's rift with Stalin or the latest inventions of British engineering.[72] And violence was far more frequent outside the capital, where incorrigible dissidents, such as Ignacio de la Hoya of *La Verdad,* were threatened with not just closure but death.[73] Not all threats were in vain; life for provincial journalists was dangerous, beatings and arrests were relatively frequent, and in extremis there was murder.[74] In 1944 mysterious gunmen killed the editor of *La Opinión de Torreón;* public opinion saw through the mystery and held the president of the party's regional committee, a relative of the governor, responsible.[75] The same year the military zone commander denounced Tampico's influential panista newspaper, *El Mundo;* in March 1947 the governor sent a mob of union stooges to stone the paper's offices and the editor's house, and on the thirty-first the chief of police broke into the editor's hotel room and shot him dead (and then checked in with the hospital to make sure he really was dead).[76] The latter victim, Vicente Villasana, was not just a newspaperman but also the owner of a regional cinema chain and a prominent Panista, and his killing brought down the governor. Not all deaths were as mourned, though, and protests were not vigorous enough to rule out the killing of less visible journalists.

Yet despite these potential costs provincial reporters were more aggressive and ambitious in their coverage than their national colleagues. Reporters in Acapulco or Xalapa had better local knowledge and fewer opportunities for profitable co-option; their articles were, moreover, of much greater immediate import than that of the nationals because the reporters lived in places where some elections, at least, were of immediate relevance. Coverage of a candidate for mayor might change an election's outcome; coverage of a candidate for president could not. This is not to say that provincial papers did not cover national events; they did, and with a critical level above that of their *chilango* counterparts. The Mexico City coverage of the Balsas rebellion, for example, tended to the minimal and the misleading, while one of the biggest stories of the sexenio, the nationwide rumors regarding a near-miss assassination attempt on Alemán in August 1948, went almost wholly unreported by the nationals. In the first case Iguala's *El Suriano* gave the nearby rebellion detailed if speculative coverage, while in the second the *Diario de Xalapa* broke the press silence surrounding the alleged attack.[77] A compromised sort of independence endured across the period: in 1960 a Gobernación survey classified 50 percent of a sample of twenty-four provincial papers as independent / opportunist.[78] Between the extremes of *La Verdad* and *Diario de Guerrero* lay large swathes of newspapers of all levels of funding and political commitment, their newsmen engaged in a constant balancing act of submission and subversion. *El Periquillo* of Teloloapan was eloquent in its title alone, a reference to *El Periquillo Sarniento,* a classic (and in its turn censored) nineteenth-century novel replete with social commentary and lightly coded political criticism. The editor's inaugural declaration made the point more explicitly: "We don't deal with political matters or religious questions in our articles, but instead we will report on events of public interest, we will point out the errors of the authorities, and we will look for remedies for our ills, ever with the greatest moral probity and without impairing public servants' private lives, which as is right we will respect."[79] History does not relate whether they did or not; to their south, though, *La Verdad de Acapulco* had few scruples about unveiling the private or public lives of port and state authorities. Readers of a single, fairly typical front page could find out that "More than Half of the Cetemista Unions Are Pure Fronts,"

"The Secret Police Raid Defenseless Homes in the City," "There Are Troglodytes Opposed to the Red Cross" but that, on the upside, they had "Finally Found a Mayor Who Works" (not, regrettably, that of Acapulco).[80] Articles like these provided what Marx called "the sheet lightning of the daily press."[81] By the later 1940s the government's control was impressive in Mexico City; in the provinces, on the other hand, it was as uneven as the state itself.

Credibility, Gullibility, and the Puzzle of Reception

The upshot of these vigorous efforts by successive governments to mold minds, together with enduring popular skepticism and regional journalism, was a fragmented public sphere, in which the consumers of ideology and state truth clearly took a pick-and-mix approach. There was, contemporary sociologists concluded, an "interesting ambivalence in Mexican political culture: many Mexicans lack[ed] political experience and skill, yet their hope and confidence [were] high; combined with these widespread participant aspirational tendencies, however, [were] cynicism about and alienation from the political infrastructure and bureaucracy."[82] The balance of cynicism and belief evidently varied according to class and geography—those sociologists were talking to the winners of the midcentury economy, the urbanites—and reception is as difficult to gauge for historians as it was for the PRI.[83] One of the most visible, if less than wholly reliable, indicators was grassroots investment in the rituals of nationalism. While some ayuntamientos were mean, others invested heavily: for the 1948 fiestas patrias the San Andrés Tuxtla ayuntamiento bought fifty meters of tricolor drapes, one hundred national flags, and one thousand each of the *¡Viva México!* and *Loor Eterno a los Héroes de la Independencia* banners.[84] But it was time, more than money, that nationalist projects demanded of provincial Mexicans. Celebrations of the key patriotic festivals began months in advance with the *junta patriótica* (Guerrero) or *junta de mejoramiento moral, cívico y material* (Veracruz), boards of community leaders who organized fundraising dances and divided the other labor between various subcommittees. Nationalist ceremonies were hard work; in Ixcateopan the Independence celebrations lasted three days. They began at six o'clock in the morning on September 15 with the raising of the flag in front of schoolchildren singing the anthem, and continued with an allegorical three-act play in which Independence, La América, Hidalgo, and *la corregidora* performed a locally scripted version of the Querétaro conspiracy and the Grito de Dolores (which was given twice) before parading through the center to the noise of cannon fire, church bells, pistols, fireworks, and the village band. Two days of symbolically charged mock fighting, parades, carnivalesque social satire, speeches, and banquets ensued, ending in a late-night, pulque-fueled dance on the seventeenth.[85] The 5 de Mayo festivities, although shorter, were of similar intensity; in 1944 the villagers were woken at dawn by pealing bells, music, and fireworks before a flag ceremony in the square at seven in the morning, which was followed in the afternoon by a twenty-eight-act ceremony involving thirteen pieces of music, ten speeches, a parade, the national anthem, and two dances.[86]

Such rituals drew heavily on local traditions and could be fun. They were also sites for astute political practice, allowing rural populations to demonstrate their fundamental obedience and internalization of the state's narratives and grassroots instrumentalists, those individual entrepreneurs who realized the commercial or political possibilities of nationalism, to get ahead in life. In extreme cases they could cover for beliefs and practices far distant from the revolutionary mainstream: the Mormons of Estado de México, for example, founded their polygamous colony of church-held lands on September 15, 1947, with a prayer to God and a parade for Independence Day.[87] Nationalist ceremonies could also have genuine affective content, constructing psychological props for the state even where its physical structures were few. But participation was also enforced by routine coercion, and faenas were employed to build national identity as well as roads. In Acapulco municipal regulations obliged all householders to decorate their houses in the national colors for all the main festivals.[88] In Ixcateopan the mayor instructed totalitarian-sounding "block inspectors" to make sure that all of the people in their street turned up at the ceremonies. Members of the junta patriótica who missed meetings were threatened with ten-peso fines—equivalent to a field hand's weekly wage—and schoolchildren who cut the dawn raising of the flag had their marks lowered.[89] The result of such enforced mobilization was a display of the noble heritage, and hence legitimacy, of the state that was cheap; the 1946 Día de la Revolución in Ixcateopan cost the municipio ten pesos.[90] Yet, while cheap, nationalist ritual was also profoundly serious, seized upon at the bottom of the political ladder as a low-cost means of demonstrating efficient control, and closely monitored from above by specialized provincial government departments such as Guerrero's Dirección de Actividades Cívicas, Sociales y Culturales, founded in 1947, or Veracruz's Sección de Publicidad.[91]

The education system was supposed to produce the new Mexicans who would constitute receptive audiences to all of these efforts, indoctrinated by textbooks, rituals, radios, and even gramophones; in 1951 the SEP distributed twenty-five thousand records of the national anthem.[92] It was a time of recovery from the disastrous experiences of socialist education, which—above all in the indigenous and Catholic communities of the highlands, such as la Montaña, or northern and western Veracruz—had emptied schools and thinned out the ranks of federal teachers. The recovery was weak to nonexistent in the first half of the 1940s: in Guerrero, in fact, the decline continued, as inscriptions continued to fall and the shortage of rural teachers worsened. In mid-1941 at least 157 schools in Guerrero had no maestro at all. Where there were maestros they were often unqualified, as in Chicontepec, where in 1941 not a single maestro rural federal had graduated from an Escuela Rural Normal, or Tierra Colorada, where there were *normalistas* who lacked "the most elementary pedagogic preparation."[93] In Atliaca in 1944 only ten or fifteen out of five hundred school-age children were in school; farther north in the same mountains, fewer than one in ten were going to school in Totimehuacán, Puebla.[94] Between 1945 and 1948, on the other hand, the education system recovered and resumed growth. Union conflict declined, as the promotion of communist teachers into positions of regional influence—Rafael Jaimes, ex–Communist Youth leader from Ayotzinapa, became secretary-general of the Liga, and Leopoldo Castro became head of the PRI—gave them an interest in promoting stability over dissent.[95] The Acapulco-centered economic boom combined with a slight improvement in tax collection to radically expand the traditionally paltry state finances. Both federal and state governments dramatically increased education budgets: in Guerrero somewhat more technocratic administrations spent half a million pesos on education in 1943, and over a million pesos in 1947. This was only marginally less than the entire state budget for 1940.[96] The schoolhouse was, and would remain for decades, the main site of political discussion and socialization in the countryside; by the 1950s they had recovered, profiting from not just funding but also the church / state modus vivendi, and were teaching more Mexicans than ever before.[97]

What did they learn? First of all, the increase in school attendance should not be overstated. Existing schools filled up again, and new ones were built: in 1945 there were 20,966 primary schools in the country, in 1955, 27,250. When demography is factored in, however, the increase was less impressive, and in the school year 1957–58 less than 60 percent of school-age children were actually going to school.[98] Education remained a long way from universal. Second, children had a lot more choice of reading matter by the 1940s, and as Elena Jackson points out, "Ideologically oriented, government-produced children's culture could not often withstand the stiff competition offered by Donald Duck."[99] Third, the SEP had realized the power of parents' associations, the Church, and the right in disputes over what was taught, and to some extent cut their cloth accordingly.[100] By the late 1940s this was paying off in newly constructive relationships between educators and communities. Such improved relationships would prove polyvalent. In some cases they encouraged state formation via co-option, as a trusted maestro mediated between village and expanding state. In others inspectors and politicians turned a blind eye to state schools that were effectively Catholic schools. And in yet others the alliance between mobilized communities and embedded maestros would underpin an enduring and genuinely popular radicalism, one capable of resisting an increasingly dominant party and bureaucracy, and deforming local experiences of the state. Education, in short, was a wholly efficient tool of hegemony in terms neither of reach nor content.

The impact of the state's drive for cultural and political control was closely monitored, as elites watched the ruled watching them. Both the organization of nationalist rituals and the popular responses they evoked were documented by an array of agencies that included teachers, patriotic or civic juntas, mayors, and, in the larger cities, Gobernación agents. Two agents filed a ten-page report on the 1949 commemorations of the oil expropriation in Poza Rica which detailed the events organized, the numbers and origins of the participants, the slogans on the banners and placards, the speeches delivered, and the responses of the crowd.[101] How routine such monitoring was is not wholly clear; it is clear, however, that it became extremely intensive at the peaks of the political cycle. The Poza Rica agents were evidently under instructions to observe the dissident union leaders' use of the expropriation ceremony as a medium to attack the government, and presidential informes, election seasons and times of crisis all generated numerous and lengthy reports. The catastrophe of the 1948 devaluation and the ensuing political crisis kept them busy, touring the city to send back daily reports on the gossip, criticism, and real prices in those crucial centers for radicalization, the city markets, and anywhere else people gathered and talked to acquaintances and strangers: cafés, cantinas, bus stations, Sanborns, the Hotel Regis, and even street corners, where newspaper vendors traditionally sparked public comment.[102] Agents toured the main cinemas to see which newsreel segments had unintended consequences and report them for cutting. They were needed in more than just the poorer barrios, where dramatic inflation and price gouging hit hardest: the uproar that greeted footage praising the city's response to floods drove the city's executive, *regente*

Fernando Casas Alemán—together with, fittingly enough, the Jefe del Departamento de Espectáculos—from the posh Cine Alameda.[103]

Such unambiguous feedback caused further censorship, and the posting of unattributed posters blaming the discontent on communists.[104] It could also cause real political change. The ferocious protests of women who faced soaring prices in the city markets must have contributed to the government's quick provision of new markets whose traders sold subsidized basic foods (whose acceptance was then, in turn, investigated).[105] In Oaxaca organized and militant women market vendors made similar calculations of the bottom lines of livelihoods and toppled two tax-raising governors.[106] And the intense hostility displayed toward Casas Alemán may well have derailed his hopes of succeeding Alemán, who reportedly favored him.[107] It certainly turned Cárdenas against the regente; the ex-president told a close friend that "Casas Alemán must go at once. When thousands of people get up at a football game and roar in unison, 'La——drón, la——drón' with each step the Governor of the Federal District makes, he must go."[108] He was neither the first, the most prominent, nor the most dangerous politician to have his career truncated by a sporting crowd: five years earlier rioters in the Mexico City bullring had targeted the unlovable Maximino Avila Camacho and convincingly ended his presidential hopes.[109]

While riotous behavior was necessary to kill off careers, it took less to kill off ritual; studied, serial indifference could do the trick. Nationalist rituals were less propitious sites for acts of public subversion than darkened cinemas, rowdy bullrings, or massive stadia, their architecture—and audiences—conducive to confrontation. Yet while such rituals made for more crowd-proof shows of power, they ran the risk of any other shows; they could fail.[110] Mexicans found some nationalist stories distinctly unconvincing, and over time managed to kill them off. Alvaro Obregón, despite his followers' attempts to present him in the same paternal light as Cárdenas, was judged insufficiently popular—the 1945 anniversary of his death attracted only a few hundred of the "common people"—and his cult slowly withered on the vine. (Much as his hand withered in its jar of preserving fluid, in one of Mexico City's more unloved monuments.)[111] The cult to Cuauhtémoc attracted sustained governmental support from the Porfiriato through to the early 1950s; despite a genuine primordial appeal, however, a combination of semiotic overloading and widespread embarrassment surrounding the 1949 discovery of his forged tomb made the last emperor an underwhelming national symbol.[112] In San José de Gracia, Michoacán, the parish priest hijacked the 1947 Día de la Raza

"Portrait of a Man (Possibly Miguel Alemán)." Miguel Covarrubias. Image courtesy of Skinner, Inc., www.skinnerinc.com.

to parade three hundred of the faithful around town by torchlight, periodically singing the Himno Guadalupano, interspersing acceptable *vivas* to Hidalgo with less acceptable *vivas* to Cristobal Colón and the Virgen de Guadalupe.[113] In San Andrés Tuxtla only schoolchildren and a handful of local worthies observed the 1946 anniversary of Juárez's death, leading the school inspector to lament that "the civic spirit is dead."[114] Most cinemas in Mexico City failed to show the newsreel covering the tenth anniversary of the oil expropriation; in those that did some audience members hushed attempts to start applause for Cárdenas, while others laughed, whistled, or booed. Government expectations were eloquent; one agent reported that "despite the film being sold out, the audience made no signs of discontentment with the [expropriation footage.]"[115] By the late 1960s more than a third of a sample of thirty-five hundred schoolchildren didn't know who Lázaro Cárdenas was.[116] At times even the most reliable of cults failed.

Other would-be cults were stopped not so much by indifference as by positive antipathy. The Alemán sexenio ended in a hubristic spate of namings of roads, markets, towns, and even an oil tanker for the outgoing president; his symbolic promotion was stopped by the convincing image of personal corruption that subsequently enveloped Alemán, and in 1968 his statue in Ciudad

Universitaria—which he had unveiled as president—was destroyed by protesters.[117] "The revolutionary state," complained an editorialist in 1949, "has invented a crowd of heroes who aren't heroes."[118] As a nationalist cult met with popular rejection, however, it was slowly withdrawn from the front line of the state's efforts at cultural control. This winnowing left behind a core of master symbols of genuine affective power: at a national level, the Virgen de Guadalupe, the anthem, Hidalgo, Juárez, and parts of la Revolución. Their acceptance was clearly à la carte—committed Catholics had a different canon—and often contradictory. Cinema audiences in the capital booed revolutionary politicians, cheered a Cristero leading his troops with a banner of the Virgen, and stood in silence for the national anthem; striking northern miners visited the Monumento a la Revolución and the Basílica de Guadalupe on their way to protest; in Tecpan an effigy of Hidalgo was afforded the ultimate compliment of replacing the village's patron saint at the head of a traditional rainmaking procession.[119] The active promotion of such symbols was undertaken by federal politicians, bureaucratic entrepreneurs, and grassroots instrumentalists; the people of Ixcateopan were just as quick to appreciate the material gains that could be wrested from owning a piece of Cuauhtémoc as any power-hungry congressman.[120] Above all, successful nationalist ceremonies afforded local politicians a cheap way to communicate an image of broadly consensual dominance, the basic qualification for remaining in government. For the ruled, meanwhile, enthusiastic participation bought them space to resist in other areas, covering up the solid evidence of unpaid taxes, unheeded literacy campaigns, and unanswered call-up papers with a veneer of obedience. For all concerned, acting out the state was less complicated than acting for the state.

Yet for elites even the most affectively powerful tools of cultural nationalism carried a price; they had, at least occasionally, to be seen to live up to the national narrative. Mexicans read about the revolution in everything from primary school textbooks to the numerous publications of the Instituto Nacional de Investigaciones Históricas de la Revolución (founded in 1953), and then wrote to Gobernación and the Presidency to hold the most powerful politicians to account, contrasting their actions to their representations of the revolutionary past and their promises of a revolutionary future. The consequences of too great a distance between rhetoric and reality were serious; thus the 1947 massacre of a foot-and-mouth control squad in Senguio, Michoacán, was preceded in 1942 by a letter from the mothers of the village to the president that protested against military service and warned him that "the pueblo has been deceived a thousand and one times in the most base and shameless way, so we no longer believe nor trust you."[121] Such grassroots monitoring drove the political classes to attempt to edit reality, repressing negative or provocative information and promoting flattering versions of political and everyday life. Their far-reaching ambitions were captured in a 1949 DGIPS working paper entitled "Plan to counteract the tendentious propaganda of the opponents of the regime," which suggested the formation of a special section to distribute crib sheets defending government policy to the "managerial strata of society": teachers, mayors, police chiefs, military commanders, union, peasant and student leaders, and the chambers of commerce. In times of crisis specially trained "verbal propagandists" would be introduced in factories and meeting places, while radio broadcasts would be restricted to a government network with loudspeakers in all major public spaces.[122] By then, however, such a project was in some ways redundant, as many of its functions were already fulfilled by the party apparatus, the SEP, and the multiple instruments developed by politicians to control the mass media.

Their overall success is difficult to gauge. Although the period did see the first polling of political attitudes in Gabriel Almond's and Sidney Verba's 1959 interviews, these were limited in that their informants all came from cities of more than ten thousand people, and moreover from the comparatively well off within that group who owned telephones.[123] What is clear is that technology cut both ways, and that cheap printworks, radio sets, and even cinema trucks were used not just to support but also to subvert the one-party state. Radio may, as Justin Castro observes, have been "a pillar of the single-party state," but it was more than that alone. It was also from start to finish a vehicle for passive resistance, as when the first listeners took free radio sets, pretuned to the SEP station XFX, and hacked them so they could skip the education and listen to music instead, or for the more active resistance of listening to communist propaganda, as when later normalistas clandestinely tuned in to Radio Habana Libre.[124] Cinema trucks were vehicles to get developmentalist, nationalist, and generally progovernment film far into the countryside, but they were sometimes metaphorically hijacked; one funded by CARE drove around the hinterlands of the Southeast showing films about Castro. Radical papers outside Mexico City faced steep obstacles of funding and violence, but publications such as *La Verdad,* Oaxaca's *El Chapulín,* Ciudad Juárez's *El Alacrán,* or Tepic's *La Escoba,* their names announcing their aims, endured.[125] Blanket suppression of the national press effectively ended in 1960, when the popular magazine *Política* began a seven-year run of bitter attacks on the government; in 1962 it was joined by *El Día,* a small but influential leftist daily.[126] Even

Cover of *Política* for November 1, 1963, depicting Secretario de Gobernación Gustavo Díaz Ordaz. Courtesy of the Biblioteca Miguel Lerdo de Tejada.

middle-of-the-road or supportive publications fed cynicism to their more knowing readers through what might be called structural slyness: the provocative juxtapositions of apparently bland, mutually contradictory officialist stories, or deadpan, mock-innocent irony, implicit criticisms wrapped in apparent gullibility. That this gullibility was more apparent than real was clear in Almond's and Verba's attitudinal data, in which more than half the city dwellers surveyed with a "high level of exposure to communication" "attribute[d] no significance to their government."[127]

Moreover, some of these technologies also served the clearest of ideological alternatives to the broad church of the PRI, namely, the literal church. Radio and film might be largely closed worlds to Catholic cultural managers; more intimate broadcasting was possible, though, and the parish priest of Cosautlán used the town's only generator to power a public address system and thunder out tirades against the mayor.[128] Catholics were not excluded from the public sphere by practice or technology; above all, the cheap printing presses of the sort that ran off progovernment publications of all shapes and sizes could also run off Catholic publications ranging from the center-right news magazine *La Nación* to the radical sinarquista newspapers *El Sinarquista* and *Omega*. They were not minority tastes: before the regional press boom even began *El Sinarquista* claimed a circulation of 97,500 copies a day, and—despite the faux pas of the June 22, 1944, edition, which called on the army to rebel—it reached far into the countryside.[129] Municipios in the north of Veracruz received their sinarquista newspapers reliably, driving comisariados ejidales to ask the state government for copies of "the periódico de orientación *La Voz del Campesino*" to try and compete.[130] Moreover, the Catholic press was about more than either the bourgeois centrism of *La Nación* or the red-blooded extremism of the Sinarquistas, and cheap printing allowed cheap religious publications such as, in deeply pious San Luis Potosí, the bimonthly *Boletín de información particular del colegio "Alfonso de Ligorio"* or the *Voz franciscana: Organo de la V. Orden Tercera*. In short, print culture in midcentury Mexico was no monoculture.

Across the course of the Alemán sexenio the government clearly aspired to control rather than fundamentally to change Mexicans. Earlier, ambitious attempts to change cultural templates and social relationships—the top-down anticlericalism of the 1920s, the revolutionary education and social programs of the 1930s—had no 1940s equivalent. Even Avila Camacho's more ambitious policies—conscription and literacy programs—provoked severe resistance and were quietly wound down under Alemán. Above all, anticlericalism, that great ideological failure of the 1920s and 1930s, was abandoned and in some cases even reversed into a positive support. Avila Camacho famously said he was a believer; less famously, the Sinarquistas called Alemán a neo-Sinarquista.[131] The PRI's leaders went out of their way to demonstrate the U-turn; during a 1951 tour of the Southeast Secretary-General Rodolfo Sánchez Taboada stage-managed several church visits and told the press that the party was "profoundly respectful of the religious beliefs of the pueblo."[132] And so they were: in Jalisco ayuntamientos received a flyer urging them to enforce the rule of law, but with the exception of the anticlerical bits.[133] Such concessions were combined with an intensive project of cultural nationalism and a constant editing of reality to fit current leaders into its narratives; they were designed to win a substantial amount of grassroots consent.

Yet the language of ordinary Mexicans revealed a systematic dislike of their politicians, who were damned in terms that ranged from the pejorative "professional politician" through the high rhetorical insult of "vampire" to the streams of obscenity of hidden transcripts that were sometimes written down and sent up the political ladder.[134] "You can talk to Lic. Alemán," one small businessman told a Gobernación agent, "tell him not to fuck it up."[135] Comisarios municipales regularly reported the low opinions villagers expressed of their local authorities; even governors could get written earfuls of abuse.[136] "I don't know why," one letter lectured Governor Ruiz Cortines, "you have kept him on [as mayor of Chicontepec]. . . . [H]e's a real bastard, a thief, a son of a bitch who does not deserve anything more than to be serving his time for the many acts of evil he has committed. The tax collector Aurelio Solares Ramírez . . . mutters that the Governor of the State can suck his dick, because he says he has a brother named Marcos and that this Marcos says he has you, señor Gobernador, by the ears."[137] Numerous Mexicans were clearly not taken in by the state's intensive attempts at managing information, transmitted through monopolies in film, radio, and television, a strong concentration of newspaper control in the capital and the García Valseca chain, and through schools. Even schoolchildren got the point that all of these were unreliable: one little boy in Culiacán, Sinaloa, observed to a teacher on election day, "How different what they teach us in School to what we're seeing now!"[138] Mexicans were also, on the other hand, selectively enthusiastic about parts of the state's nationalist project, its claims to inclusive capitalist development and to genuine democracy. This strange blend of failure and success, of cynicism and belief, may help to explain the apparently schizoid attitudes surveyed in the late 1950s, which combined fundamental faith in the political system with minimal trust in its operatives. Mexicans thought quite a lot of the revolution, it turned out, but not all that much of its avatars.[139]

9 • Why Mexico Did Not Become a Military Dictatorship

The Army's Political Neutrality and Its Costs

The history of the Mexican military's discreet self-effacement after the revolution is a well-known and peculiar story, a central pillar of Mexican exceptionalism.[1] The young, predatory generals of the revolutionary army, that strange hybrid of diverse citizens in arms, ended the bloody decade of the 1910s taking a substantial majority of the federal budget and anointing themselves with national and regional powers.[2] Three rebellions in the 1920s, however, allowed the Sonoran presidents—accidental but effective soldiers—to make culls on a grand scale. Álvaro Obregón, facing down the rebellion of a majority of his troops, halved the army at a stroke. Plutarco Elías Calles pushed through critical reforms, applied the ley fuga to his main military rivals, and easily suppressed the Escobar rebellion. Both military budgets and political representation declined steeply across the 1930s, and the army stayed loyal during the last big rebellion, that of Saturnino Cedillo, in 1938. In 1940 the army's (substantially overrepresented) corporate sector of the PRM was suppressed; in 1945 soldiers were banned from participating in "political affairs or tasks, whether directly or indirectly"; that same year 550 revolutionary generals were declared retired.[3] In 1946 the last military president stepped down.[4] Among the great advances of the 1940s, *Excélsior* editorialized, was the army's realization of "its noble guidelines as a fundamental institution of the patria through stopping soldiers . . . from sticking their oar into politics."[5] By then, Edwin Lieuwen's pathfinding work concluded, the military had become "a pliable and disciplined tool of the civilian leaders of the Mexican nation."[6] Budgets supported the master narrative of cost-free demilitarization. In 1949 Mexico spent 14 percent of the national budget on the military, less than half that of

Brazil and a third that of Spain; in absolute terms one-seventieth that of Great Britain. By the early 1950s Mexico had two soldiers per thousand population; a comparatively small regular army with old equipment and a new reputation for political neutrality.[7]

That reputation could be justified merely by reference to the none-too-distant past, when the officer class posed a serious threat to civilian rule. Cárdenas, popular across the army, saw managing its general officers as his main political job, telling his private secretary, "You take care of the civilians. You take care of the governors; I'll take care of the zone commanders, the Army."[8] He was in the main successful, but a certain buccaneering approach to party rule and civilian administration survived his term; at the very end of his lame-duck period, on November 29, 1940, officers raided communist party headquarters against both his and his successor's will.[9] While the military did subsequently beat a retreat from the highest levels of national politics, they did so both later and significantly more reluctantly than hitherto believed. Their withdrawal was, consequently, significantly less complete than hitherto believed. Unconditional loyalty to civilian presidential rule became central to the armed forces' ideology and practice, differing sharply from the ideological militarism—or will to power—of the rest of Latin America's officer corps during the Cold War. Yet it came at the cost of a certain continuity in the independence, rent seeking, and petty politicking of generals and other military actors across the Mexican countryside.

This profitable autonomy was masked by the military's subtle but enduring cultural control: a long-lasting control revealed in their successful censorship of *Rojo amanecer*, a 1989 film on the Tlatelolco massacre, or in the nine years General José Francisco Gallardo spent in jail in the nineties for proposing increased transparency in the armed forces, or in the ban on political speech by individual officers and political criticism by journalists that lasted, with rare exceptions, across most of the period, or in the ongoing refusal to release any historical military records beyond personnel files; the denial, in fact, that these even existed.[10] Yet the files of officers like Alejandro Mange in Veracruz or Adrián Castrejón in Guerrero and the reports of Gobernación spies in the provinces chart in detail a rather different exchange of national influence for institutional autonomy and independent cacicazgos, an exchange that implied clear continuities with an earlier age of military politics. Not all those continuities were detrimental to the Weberian ideal. The army continued to play a critical state-building role, ensuring rural control and softening up local societies for civilian, bureaucratic domination. They also built quite literally, providing roads, water pipelines, and sewage systems, and they were increasingly competent in the disaster relief that was the subject of DN-III, one of Mexico's three military doctrines. Yet the hidden costs, the soldiers' "residual political roles," added up to a quasi-independent, parallel government structure, or "a world," as a U.S. embassy assessment had it at the end of the twentieth century, "largely separate from the rest of Mexico."[11] In other words, Mexican demilitarization was both partial and in part public relations, a conclusion borne out in Guerrero, perhaps predictably in light of that state's perennial counterinsurgencies, and in Veracruz less predictably, but with particular force.

Structure and Function

In the late 1940s the regular army, part professional, part conscript, numbered some fifty-five thousand men organized in four divisions, forty-seven infantry battalions, and twenty-one cavalry regiments. The army had three official functions, summed up as DN-I (external defense), DN-II (domestic order) and DN-III (disaster relief). Only the latter two were really germane: unthreatened by Guatemala, outgunned by the United States, the military's strategic logic was to maintain internal order without concentrating enough capability in any one place to foster rebellion or coup. Troop deployment patterns from 1948 reveal that focus with great clarity. The best-equipped and best-trained troops were those of the motorized brigade, the elite Presidential Guard—not a security detail but rather some four thousand men—and the 1st and 3rd Infantry Divisions. All of them were based in Mexico City under commanders personally trusted by Alemán.[12] The Presidential Guard, its loyalty fostered with considerably higher salaries, was commanded by his maternal uncle and consigliere, General Juan Valdés.[13] The only other division, Guadalajara's 2nd, was drawn from conscripts, unpromising material for any serious rebellion. (When sent out on maneuvers a high percentage called in sick.)[14] The provinces were divided into thirty-three Military Zones, garrisoned by understrength and top-heavy battalions, adequate for limited rural policing but insufficiently powerful to contemplate tackling the forces of the center. Guerrero, the 27th Military Zone, housed the 3rd and 20th Infantry Battalions, with barracks in Iguala and Chilpancingo. Veracruz, divided between the 19th Military Zone (Tuxpan, the northern oil fields, and the Huasteca) and the 26th Military Zone (central and southern Veracruz), revealed its greater strategic importance with a total of six infantry battalions.[15] The provincial military was widely deployed, with one in five municipios housing some soldiers, but also thinly spread across each zone, divided up into regimental garrisons in the main towns, company- or platoon-sized detachments in important or conflictual cabeceras, and flying columns patrolling the unstable frontiers of the state in places such as the Huasteca, the agrarian flashpoints of Guerrero's coasts or central Veracruz. In 1950, trying to reassert military control over the Costa Grande, General Miguel Z. Martínez posted soldiers in every ejido and settlement.[16] This was largely a reaction against his predecessor, General Castrejón, who had armed his clients, those same rural militiamen whom Martínez held responsible for his coastal problems. The ideological construction of the army as a professional, loyal, and subordinate institution dated back to General Joaquín Amaro's modernizing reforms of the 1920s; the reality—demonstrated by the substantial shifts in regional politics occasioned when zone commanders changed—remained one of a highly personalist, factional organization, whose local alliances, conduct, and reputation varied greatly according to the politics and character of individual commanders.

Less powerful but more ubiquitous than the regular army were the reserves, some 70,000 men divided among 132 infantry and cavalry corps of defensas rurales. In 1948 half the reserve formations were deployed in five states: Chihuahua, Michoacán, Jalisco, Guanajuato, and Durango.[17] Their heavy concentration in the former Cristero and villista heartlands was eloquent of their primary function as instruments of provincial state control, or, perhaps, as vehicles for the diplomatic demobilization of popular militias. (Our near-total ignorance concerning the reserves is one of the wider gaps in our understanding of the midcentury state.) The defensas rurales were both more numerous and more locally knowledgeable than the regulars; while commanders were drawn from the regular army, they tended to go native on long-term postings, while the junior and noncommissioned officers were local recruits. These units originated in the popular movements of the revolution and were formally defined as agrarista militias by Cárdenas; frequently, however, they were made up of the violently capable or politically ambitious irrespective of class.[18] In some areas the defensas rurales were legalized guardias blancas, gunmen for local conservatives. Gonzalo Lagunes spent the 1930s killing and driving away the ejidatarios who threatened his central Veracruz landholdings; in 1942 he became jefe of the Cuitláhuac reserves.[19] Marcelino Andaya, second-in-command of the Zirándaro reserves, was the local hacendado.[20] By the 1940s the state's preference for nonagrarista forces was becoming formalized through the creation of forces like the cattlemen's militias of the Costa Chica and southern Veracruz.[21] To be recognized as the local militia was a critical resource in rural politics, bringing superior weaponry—army Mausers against shotguns and pistols—and a substantial degree of political cover for its use against local rivals. When local society broke down to the extent that the army intervened, regulars tended to favor reservists. In low-conflict zones the reserves could fulfill legitimate policing functions: in Ixcateopan Manuel Rodríguez Juárez's platoon stopped drinkers from swearing in front of schoolchildren, tried to prevent the illegal logging of communal forests, and chased bandits.[22] (There may also have been a correlation between size of the detachment and behavior: larger units, under a senior regular officer, were probably less prone to the extremes of factional violence.) In other villages, especially in conflict zones, voluminous denunciations of homicide, cattle rustling, extortion, theft, and rape against the reserves evince strongly cacical tendencies. In the 1920s and 1930s the militias had been uncomfortable but essential, last-ditch state allies in suppressing provincial rebellion; by the mid-1940s, with rebellions evolving into the damp squibs of the Balsas or padillista movements, they were inconvenient artifacts of the revolution.

For all its variable quality, though, the military was for a long time the only effective violent agency in a Machiavellian environment of highly aggressive geographical and organizational fiefdoms. In exerting some form of tenuous control there—for both their superiors' and their own benefit—its officers oversaw four main types of state violence: the informal tasks of collective repression, decapitation and decimation of popular movements, and the more formally acknowledged—albeit unconstitutional—duty of maintaining everyday social control.

Collective repression was the army's main job. Soldiers broke strikes, disrupted union dissidents' activities, raided ejidos, and toppled agrarista or opposition ayuntamientos in localized coups. Threats alone sometimes sufficed. General Alejandro Mange attempted to end a strike in Boca del Río by touring the pickets "recommending" that the strikers disperse (which misfired when one striker failed to recognize his car, and shot him).[23] He was usually more successful. By the mid-1940s the military regularly intervened in the frequent stoppages that hampered port operations in Veracruz; in 1948 Mange prevented cross-class demonstrations in Orizaba against the cost of living by warning organizers that he would forcibly dissolve any march.[24] The regularity with which the army historically used collective repressive violence gave weight to such threats. During a petty counterinsurgency in Oaxaca, for example, Mange indiscriminately shot thirty-three civilians, including eleven children.[25] Soldiers beat dissidents and raided houses in repressing the oil workers' union, in a struggle for control with grassroots militant leaders which ended in the 1949 takeover of the Poza Rica oil fields and the Minatitlán refinery.[26] In extremis the military was deployed even against students, normally subject to a sort of *fuero*, the colonial exemption from the justice of the many, and in the cities into the bargain: soldiers ended the 1956 Politécnico strike by occupying the campus.[27] Across the midcentury and beyond political dissidents faced everything from mass arrest to massacre at the hands of the army.

Abuses like these occurred predominantly in rural frontier zones, where, as Arturo Warman observed, "repression [was] not the exception. It [was] a constant, surrounded by a wall of silence and indifference, concealed under the ambiguous and degrading term 'common crime.' "[28] In 1945 federal and reserve soldiers dissolved the agrarista ayuntamiento of Tlacoachistlahuaca, raiding houses and driving the councilors into exile; in 1953 a platoon of regulars removed the panista ayuntamiento of neighboring Xochihuehuetlán.[29] Such operations came close to the undeclared counterinsurgencies the army waged along the coasts of Guerrero and in parts of central Veracruz. (And other troubled zones: in Chacalito, Jalisco, soldiers arrested everybody on the ejido in 1951 and threatened to hang them if they continued resisting the local hacendado; in Morelos the army fought sporadically with Rubén Jaramillo's on-again, off-again guerrillas for two decades.)[30] In March 1945 federal forces killed five peasants who had armed themselves against the sugar mill's pistoleros in their fields near Zempoala, Veracruz.[31] In November of the same year a column occupied the hamlet of Tetitlán, Guerrero, hoping to arrest leading agraristas. The men were taken to the village school; hearing rifle fire from neighboring Tenexpa, however, the women helped them escape to the sierra. When the soldiers found out they burned the village.[32] Throughout the early 1940s the army launched seasonal campaigns along Guerrero's coasts, generating intense protests against arbitrary arrests, house raids, looting, house burning, torture, and killings.[33] Some operations were criticized as the work of rogue commanders. But generals such as Mange, Martínez, or Ramos were no loose cannons; the first ran the military on much of the Gulf Coast for over twenty years, the second was promoted from Guerrero to command of the 10th Military Region, and the third ended a distinguished career as Ruiz Cortines's secretary of defense.[34] What their victims called *atropellos* (and we would call large-scale human rights abuses) drew intense protests, but they never led to public reprimands or legal consequences—the army, after all, had its own, independent legal system—but instead transfers. Collective repression was a delicate task on the borderline of the state's accepted practice. If it misfired or was disowned by elites it sometimes damaged careers: some of the *familia revolucionaria* ruled out General Bonifacio Salinas Leal as presidential material due to his responsibility for the León massacre.[35] Yet elites saw much collective repression as justified by raison d'état, and some officers and units became specialists: Colonel Salvador Rangel's 49th Infantry Battalion, for example, was deployed against oil workers in the Azcapotzalco refinery in 1958 and rail workers at Pantaco in 1959.[36] Such successful practitioners—and Martínez and Mange were prominent among them—were rewarded rather than rebuked.

Decapitation, the assassination of dissident leaders, was less costly, more deniable, and less provocative than collective repression, and it was widely employed across the period. In 1947, for example, Lieutenant Abel, a corporal, and three hitmen accompanied the manager of La Gloria sugar mill to the Cempoala baseball ground to invite a shop steward for a beer; the lieutenant shot the union leader as he drank it.[37] In 1948 Lieutenant Villanueva shot a comisariado ejidal and two ejidatarios in Atoyac.[38] In 1951 Lieutenant Luis Hernández Rocha took four peasants out of the Teloloapan barracks and threw them to their deaths down the Pozo Meléndez, a deep vertical cave notorious for its use in disappearances.[39] Reports of killings by soldiers dressed as peasants or peasants dressed as soldiers—a reporting formula which insinuated without risking actual accusation—were frequent enough.[40] Union leaders were more prone to imprisonment than assassination, and the most notable attempt of the period, the 1949 attack on CTM Senator Alfonso Palacios, failed.[41] Their members were subject, however, to the complementary mechanism of decimation, the attritional killings of workers and agraristas *pour encourager les autres*. The numerous, historically unknown ejidatarios (and the less numerous workers) whose deaths fill the pages of Gobernación files were probably in many cases the noncommissioned officers of dissidence; in others, they may have been random, rank-and-file victims, merely in the wrong place at the wrong time. Across both states commanders were accused of maintaining black lists of ejidatarios who were to be shot, or of thinning out the ranks of ejidatarios on a commission basis for local economic elites.[42] In the conflict-ridden timber zone of Yextla, Guerrero, General Martínez was reported to have ordered his men "to cleanse the region of all persons who opposed the development of the Puentecillas sawmill."[43] Generals were also influential in decapitation and decimation through sins of omission, turning a blind eye (wherever possible) to the violence of their allies and affines, or contracting out such killings to either reserves or pistoleros. General Ramos Santos reportedly had the Ometepec reserves kill Francisco Cisneros López, Ometepec's amateur, bilingual lawyer and budding cacique of the Amuzgo whom he represented.[44] Many of the motives for decimation were economic: to prevent ejidatarios from taking up grants, to move them off already existing plots, to control their land use, or to discourage them from applying for extensions. In extreme cases decimation drove whole groups into exile: in Tierra Caliente Castrejón's clients and regulars pushed three hundred families across the Balsas River into Michoacán.[45] More commonly the attrition of regular violence softened up local societies for domination, obliging recalcitrant peasants to accept what offers of increased security they could, whether proffered by pistoleros or by the nearest arm of the state.

Recovering the central meaning of military violence is often difficult. Victims tended to present all provincial violence as factional and hence wholly illegitimate. Dissident politicians encouraged them to do so for tactical advantage.[46] Victims and perpetrators were consequently locked in a perpetual struggle to control the accepted meaning of violent acts. The country people arrested, beaten, and sometimes shot or hanged in army, reserves, or police operations were deemed ejidatarios or campesinos by their political allies, and *bandidos* or abigeos by the violent agency in question. For a historian to distinguish between factional and more legitimate violence on a case-by-case level is sometimes guesswork, and inevitably constitutes a political decision in itself. Neither were factional violence and more neutral, order-serving violence mutually exclusive categories. There was, rather, frequent overlap between the two. Yet while such distinctions are intrinsically dubious, it is clear that at least some acts of provincial violence aimed more at the maintenance of basic stability than at the explicit promotion of factional interest, and constituted—by a very crude, normative definition at least—legitimate policing operations.

Formally, these should never have happened. Article 129 of the Constitution of 1917 specified, "In time of peace, no military authority may perform any functions other than those that are directly connected with military affairs"; a 1946 circular specified that "given that various groups and civil authorities of the Republic continually come requesting detachments of Federal Forces in order to obtain constitutional guarantees, it has been ordered that the said troops should not undertake police functions."[47] Both were dead letters. State elites depended overwhelmingly on the army for policing from the armed revolution onward. In 1949 the Veracruz state government requested that the army supply prison guards; a year later Guerrero's state attorney sent seven hundred unsolved cases, most of them homicides, to General Martínez requesting his assistance.[48] It was customary for governors to include a catch-all acknowledgment of the military's role in "maintaining public order" in their annual reports, which greatly underrepresented the omnipresence of soldiers in carrying out a broad range of police tasks.[49] In towns and cities the army controlled crowds, unions, the press, gamblers, prostitutes, and even politicians.[50] On the eve of Orizaba's 1949 municipal elections Mange's chief of staff called the bitterly opposed candidates together and "instructed them in an appropriate and educated way to go into the political contest with the utmost order and that both precandidates should refrain from bringing in outside contingents and should make the said primary elections a civic function that burnished the reputation of the PRI as well as the Civil and Military Authorities."[51] Election days across the 1940s were usually policed by the army, as the civilian police were seen as inevitably politicized.[52] During contested elections local societies frequently asked garrison commanders to act as referees: when in 1946 an angry crowd stopped the PRI in Ciudad Altamirano from stealing ballot boxes, the impasse was resolved by asking the local garrison to take charge of the boxes until the vote count.[53] The transfer of power to imposed ayuntamientos similarly pulled the army into the morass of local politics: the heavily resisted Iguala ayuntamiento for 1949–50 was defended on the day it took power by soldiers who fixed bayonets and mounted machine guns on the town hall's roof.[54]

There was more than just violence to soldiers' roles in state politics, and at times the sheer range of officers' functions made local polities all but military regimes. In the aftermath of the chaotic Cerdán governorship, for example, the incoming governor dispatched soldiers across Veracruz to report on local conditions and to help deal with failed municipal governments. In the center it was Brigadier General Francisco Díaz García who toured the eleven municipios of the Coatepec district, reporting on their political classes, hearing cases for the overthrow of mayors, and assessing their achievements down to the quantity of water pipes they had bought. The power he wielded was self-evident in the subordinate he brought along, a lieutenant licensed by the state treasury to act as an Extraordinary Tax Collector (and who did indeed charge them, summoning Perote's shopkeepers to ask exactly how they intended to pay their arrears).[55] In the south General Marcelino Absalón Pérez visited eighteen municipios on the eve of the elections, not just reporting on local politics but at times sorting them out, summoning rival candidates to the town halls of Catemaco, Oluta, and Sayula "with the intention of unifying them."[56] In the north Colonel Leopoldo Bernal Martínez toured four crime-ridden municipios, gathering intelligence and meeting with the local great and good to "let them know that they were entirely at liberty to explain their respective problems so that if it were in my power I could resolve them." (Among the discoveries he made were that one mayor had used wood destined for school benches to build a ring for cockfights, while another was at liberty only because the town judge knew his arrest would spark a gunfight.) Bernal Martínez's commanding officer passed on the observations to the governor, requesting his action; he in turn passed them on to the attorney general, who instructed Chicontepec's public prosecutor to pursue "vigorous punishment" of the named malefactors. The action that counted, however, was clearly military, as the relevant general without waiting for instructions sent out infantry and cavalry to pacify the zone.[57] The army's principal role remained rural policing, and a substantial proportion of their business was to manage collective violence in the countryside.

Central to this was despistolización, gun control. Under the terms of the 1943 Ley de portación de armas de fuego firearms could be carried by the army, reserves, police, teachers, and bureaucrats; everyone else needed permits from the Secretaría de la Defensa Nacional or became liable to on-the-spot confiscation and arrest.[58] The law was observed in the breach, and more than the usual suspects went around armed; the first priest back to Tiríndaro in the 1940s packed a pistol under his cassock.[59] The decision to tighten the regulation of arms was an extremely notable decision in a country where "political life was lived with a gun at hand."[60] Gun control was difficult to enforce, though, and the army's efforts tended to be local, equivocal, and reversible. In Veracruz Mange's efforts in the middle of the 1945 crime wave reportedly disarmed all of eleven people, while corporals in remote villages came up with a desultory flintlock or two.[61] In 1952 an estimated 95 percent of guns remained unlicensed.[62] A decade after the campaign began a traveler to the sugar town of San Juan Covarrubias found "a complete and perfect realization of a town in a western, with no shortage of horses tied to hitching posts outside stores nor bandits with check shirts, big hats, and Colts on their right hips."[63] The army did more than decide whom to disarm: the zone commander simultaneously, through his powers of appointment to the reserves, decided whom to arm. As the hard men of different local factions struggled physically in the streets, milpas, and plantations they simultaneously struggled with words to convince the zone commander and the federal government of their claims to defend law, order, and the common good. The makeup of the reserves was fluid, and they sometimes changed dramatically when the zone commander changed. In Veracruz Mange disarmed many of the groups constituted by his predecessor, General Jara, and by the regional cacique General Cándido Aguilar, transferring the guns to their opponents. In Guerrero Castrejón disarmed defensas rurales inherited from his predecessor General Ramos, and launched an intense recruitment drive of his own, arming large groups of his supporters in his northern patria chica, only to find many of his clients in turn disarmed after 1948 by General Martínez.[64] Such radical shifts in local balances (or imbalances) of power generated intense correspondence between local power brokers and the center, as the beneficiaries of the new order defended it as meritocratic and the losers complained of political bias, criminal pasts, corruption, and clientelism.[65] Vital competition for arms and recognition demonstrated how, beneath a surface of multiple competing violent agencies, the federal army enjoyed considerable potential to rig the market of violence.

When the army committed acts of violence it was frequently operating in a confused world of half-formal policing missions and half-informal political maneuvering. Formally, routine rural work meant garrison duty, patrols, and escorts, the mere presence of troops fulfilling a deterrent role. When deterrence failed, small detachments were sent to suppress gunfights and clear up after village vendettas, frequently under the command of (one of the army's numerous) senior officers. In 1947, for example, a gunfight in Copalillo was dealt with by some twenty men and a brigadier general.[66] Larger conflicts—the appearance of bandits, a wave of cattle rustling, intervillage feuding or the intensifying of local agrarian disputes that all three phenomena reflected—drew larger responses: formations of several companies, sometimes reinforced with reservists, who embarked on regional sweeps that were often counterinsurgencies in all but name. Such operations were frequently phrased in a colonial frontier language of expeditionary forces or flying columns. As in similar operations in genuinely colonial territories such as the North-West Frontier of British India, the disparity of forces did not guarantee the safety of the units involved; in Guerrero, in particular, army casualties were commonplace. In 1944 a detachment escorting a federal treasury inspector was ambushed on the Costa Chica, losing four soldiers and the taxman; in the same year another two soldiers were killed while escorting an alcohol inspector on the Costa Grande; in September 1948 soldiers pursuing the killers of the Eureka Corporation's accountant lost three men in a firefight in the hills outside Acapulco.[67] (Many such clashes had a distinctly serrano logic, as locals violently resisted state agents or, in the case of the accountant, agents of the crony capitalists developing Acapulco.) Officers who faced a dangerous countryside and failing courts frequently made their own rough justice, and the informal death penalty of the Porfiriato, the ley fuga, remained relatively commonplace.[68] The protests which extrajudicial executions sparked make it clear, however, that some of the criminals whom the army saw were seen by local societies as popular leaders. Even the conservatives of the Costa Grande qualified their strong support for General Martínez's operations by calling his tactics drastic.[69] And while extrajudicial killings could temporarily shore up the state's drive for public order, they could equally well undermine the claims of both army and state to neutrality and legitimacy.

The Failures of Provincial Demilitarization

Three phenomena in particular militated against the army's depoliticization in the states. Provincial commands were frequently overstretched in trying to cover extensive, ill-communicated, and unstable territories, an overstretch revealed in large operations such as the foot-and-mouth campaign, which left troops in the rainy season in Veracruz without tents or rations.[70] In April 1949 Leyva Mancilla requested that an additional infantry company be deployed to the Costa Chica; seven months later he still had no answer.[71] This overstretch left commanders with profoundly imperfect information regarding their zones of influence, allowing crooked or incompetent subordinates to flourish and political targets to be sold to them as straightforward criminals. It also pushed them inevitably into ad hoc local alliances which, in turn, drew them further inside the faction-ridden politics of local societies. There were, moreover, debilitating contradictions at the highest level of the state, exemplified in the regular flouting of the policy on rotating commanders. Commanding officers continued to be posted to their home states, where they arrived with ready-made cacical networks: Adrián Castrejón was an ex-governor when he took over Guerrero (where he had also fought in the revolution) in 1945, while General Othón León Lobato, who took over the 26th Military Zone in 1952, was a xalapeño who had previously run for governor.[72] When commanders went native the results were generally grim for local societies; as a letter from several high-ranking officers to Alemán explained, "The jefes of the Military Zones should, in our view, be transferred [regularly], as when they settle in they make themselves Dictators, they monopolize the state's Business. . . . [A]s a concrete case you have General [Pablo] Díaz Avila, in Cuernavaca, Mor., jefe of the 24th Zone, who has great landholdings, some of which he has bought, and others of which he has taken by force."[73] Finally, many officers did not disdain the numerous opportunities for self-enrichment that provincial military command afforded. The army was an institution without the power to achieve lasting neutrality, but with more than enough power to reward extensive rent-seeking behavior.

Army officers turned their commands into successful businesses in four ways, namely, licensing other, more junior violent entrepreneurs; renting out their troops' violent capabilities; grafting from the army budget; and using their cacical power to foster their own, private enterprises. Sometimes they licensed provincial violence in quite literal terms, selling reserve commissions and gun permits; at other times they merely raked off surpluses in systematic bribes from pistoleros. In 1945 the bandit Bartolo Lara gave General Mange 3,000 pesos and a horse in exchange for a commission as a commander of reserves in the Soledad de Doblado area.[74] There may have been—as in the unreformed British army of the early nineteenth century—a going national rate for such appointments: in Tecpan, Guerrero, three years later General Pedro Pizá Martínez demanded about the same price for the same service. (Pizá Martínez, a busy man, also demanded money for gun licenses, and for permits to celebrate saints' days.)[75] Officers also rented out their violent capabilities in diverse ways that ranged from taxing public space through protection to extortion. A detachment on the Poza Rica road was paid off by the local ferry owner to block the bridge, forcing drivers to pay four pesos a crossing.[76] Across Guerrero soldiers charged ejidatarios protection money to allow them to work the fields in safety; in Copala the garrison commander asked Adulfo Gonzalez's family for money to spare his life.[77]

Not all profiteering was violent. Straightforward graft was also good business, as the army's institutional autonomy allowed generals to put down whistleblowers with trumped-up charges.[78] Charges of systematic graft reached the very top of the army: in 1948 spies reported that the secretario himself, General Gilberto Limón, had sold personal landholdings in Mexico City to the army at a 1,000 percent mark up.[79] Officers could, finally, use political alliances, free army labor, and violence to build extensive and highly competitive businesses. (They were helped in this by vague army regulations that permitted "the use of military resources in the construction of communications networks and public works that had some correlation with the overall needs of the military.")[80] In Monte Alto General Espiridión Rodríguez took over ejidal land.[81] In Alto Lucero Lieutenant Colonel Contreras ordered his local operatives to steal cattle.[82] In Chiapas General Antonio Ríos Zertuche used soldiers as agricultural workers on his estates and charged the local government 4,000 pesos a month for public works; in Mexico City he obtained a large share of the Lomas de Chapultepec at the knockdown price of sixty centavos a square meter when they were subdivided; in Veracruz he obtained the lucrative contract to clear the site of the Palma Sola military colony, keeping the timber cut as a bonus.[83] And in Veracruz the charges against

General Mange reached epic proportions, his property empire supposedly stretching into Oaxaca, connected by roads built by soldiers and funded by protection money from traders, gamblers, and gunmen.[84]

The military's reputation for professionalism and neutrality was consequently a fragile plant. A colonel inspected the Chicontepec garrison in 1946, registered the townsmen's preference for military over corrupt civilian policing, and concluded that "the federal troops who cover the region enjoy the trust and esteem of the inhabitants for their clean and honorable record."[85] Two years later the same townsmen denounced the garrison to the presidency for assaults, extortion, cattle rustling, and threatening to burn hamlets that complained.[86] Such violence—driven by economic incentives, political competition, or more frequently a Gordian combination of both rationales—did not support so much as subvert the state. In the 1940s the sum of the army's multiple roles in provincial life added up to a lot more than a military that had, in Lieuwen's misleading conclusion, "had it politically."[87] The military remained deeply inserted in the everyday life of local societies across Mexico: in the early 1950s there were detachments in some 650 of Mexico's municipios, c. 20 percent of the total.[88] These garrisons were closely intertwined with local elites and other violent actors.[89] The resulting overlap between public and private agencies of violence hampered attempts to reduce provincial violence and slowed, in cases blocked, the expansion of an effective, centralized state.

Veracruz: The Military Regime of General Alejandro Mange, 1937–1959

Veracruz may have been the cradle of civilian rule after the revolution, but it was simultaneously home to a major military cacicazgo, that of General Alejandro Mange, and as such epitomizes the enduring autonomy and personalism of the military. Mange was a staunch Callista, close enough to the *jefe máximo* to rally round him (together with Joaquín Amaro and a few others) when he returned from Los Angeles exile in December 1935.[90] The other generals were demoted, and Amaro, the architect of the postrevolutionary military, went on to resign his commission. Mange, on the other hand, was soon thereafter given command of the 26th Military Zone in Veracruz.[91] This was a prize job: the 26th was the most powerful provincial zone command, grouping three regular infantry battalions, two cavalry regiments, artillery—extremely rare—and three reserve battalions. The posting presupposed trustworthiness: Veracruz was a good place to run a rebel government, and the Ferrocarril Interoceánico gave rebels ready access to the capital.[92] Veracruz was also one of the wealthiest states, affording its commanders rich business opportunities. Finally, Mange's command endured when Miguel Alemán rose to national power as first secretario de Gobernación and then president; a distinct surprise, given that it was Mange's troops who had executed Alemán senior in 1929.[93] Alemán was quick to purge assorted provincial strongmen, including the governors of Chiapas, Oaxaca, and Tamaulipas, but he left Mange well alone. General Mange went on, in fact, to command Veracruz until his reluctant retirement in 1959.[94] His was a long-lived military cacicazgo—across several presidential terms, the formative and mature phases of the PRI, in the face of both presidential and popular enmity, and in defiance of long-standing policy requiring rotation in command—which left him extensive and diverse business interests across the state, and which exemplified the parallel state of the army.

Alejandro Mange was well placed to advance himself in that parallel state by birth if nothing else. He was born in Hermosillo, Sonora, in 1885, and so although he went to the revolution a corporal, he was a corporal who knew the Sonoran revolutionary leaders and came up through the ranks with them: Calles made him an officer, Obregón made him a major, and by 1920, when he was one of a handful present to sign the Plan of Agua Prieta, he had made general. There was more to his rapid promotion than northern cronyism though, and the breadth of experience he garnered in his first two decades as a general make it clear that Mange was a useful fighting soldier.[95] He campaigned against the Yaquis in the 1910s, Delahuertistas and Cristeros in the 1920s, and—at a lower, less visible, less admissible level—peasant and worker activists across the entire period. (He enjoyed, the U.S. military attaché noted, a "reputation as a terrorist.")[96] His exemplary service during the 1929 Escobar rebellion made him one of the key political generals of the time. He served clear across Mexico, from Aguascalientes to Zacatecas; or, in less rhetorical and more geographical terms, from Yucatán to Sinaloa. At one time or another he commanded most of the major states, whether in terms of wealth, such as Puebla or Veracruz, or in terms of instability, such as Morelos, Michoacán, or Chihuahua.[97] He must also have been an able administrator: head of the department of infantry of Defensa Nacional under Amaro, he believed himself on the point of getting the secretaría itself in 1943.[98] Denied that, he did however end his career with one of the top regional postings, overseeing the Gulf Command that centered on Veracruz.[99]

Arriving in 1937 Mange quickly tapped into the system of pistolero domination, establishing an effective dyarchy with Manuel Parra. By the early 1940s he was at the peak of his power; faced with a weak presidency, a moribund agrarian movement, and a weak governor, his alliance with the pistoleros furnished the most reliable source of some degree of stateness for large areas of central and southern Veracruz.[100] He was formally in command of not just the 26th, but the entire Gulf Coast, his control extending to the venerable and influential bourgeois press, where he posted Captain Arias Barraza to represent his interests inside *El Dictamen,* giving him constant favorable press coverage, "defending his killings and cock-ups with enthusiasm." (Moreover a son had married into the powerful owners' family, the Malpicas.)[101] Gobernación agent Gonzalo Migoni reported how "General Mange . . . possesses a multitude of properties and is a very rich landowner in the Zone he commands, and even beyond it: in Oaxaca, bordering Veracruz, where his subalterns impose taxes and charge their own 'taxes' on gambling, which is rife across the state, without anyone doing anything about it because the municipal authorities have fixed their 'contributions'; the soldiers taking part too."[102] Vox populi called repeatedly for his removal and deemed him "the biggest thief in Veracruz"; Gobernación agents detailed his real estate and business empires, his rents from gambling—cards, roulette, dice—and his protection and his selling of reserve command appointments in recurrent critiques of military corruption.[103] None of it seemed to matter.

There was no guerrerense equivalent to Alejandro Mange's long-running one-man show. Yet lower-ranking officers in that state, above all in the reserves, dug themselves into subregional fiefdoms for considerable lengths of time. And even while rotating postings a series of generals similarly exercised considerable influence in nominally civilian administrations. All General Leyva Mancilla's elected predecessors in the governorship bar one—Rodolfo Neri—had been high-ranking officers. On at least two occasions in the 1920s senior generals were decisive in determining a governor's fate.[104] Subsequent zone commanders exercised autonomy to the point of actively working in opposition to civil authorities. Both Matías Ramos Santos (1942–45) and Adrián Castrejón (1945–48) formed and jealously defended fiefdoms that ran far beyond their mandates. Castrejón had in fact campaigned in 1944 for the conservative Leyva Mancilla against the agrarista Ojeda.[105] Unlike Veracruz, however, Guerrero saw a change at the highest level of the regional military in the late 1940s. Castrejón's successor, Miguel Z. Martínez, was highly controversial, a squeaky-voiced thug whose reputation for violence followed him from post to post.[106] Yet while he was accused of numerous extrajudicial killings and corruption there is no evidence he ever operated against Leyva Mancilla. They seem, rather, to have had a close alliance. Neither do his immediate successors seem to have held themselves above their respective governors; no soldiers in 1950s Guerrero had the autonomy or the political ambitions of a Fox, a Ramos, or a Castrejón. The input of generals into state politics by no means ended, but it did wane until the outbreak of the guerra sucia in the mid-1960s.

At a lower, municipal level, on the other hand, officers of all ranks exercised long-lived and often decisive sway over local life across the period, at times with flamboyant disregard for their civilian counterparts. On the Costa Chica, for example, Colonel Monroy—commander of the 60th Reserve Battalion, known as the hanging general—did more than summarily hang alleged bandits; he also decided whether Protestant missionaries should be allowed into Ometepec, and he once led an army column to forcibly change the ayuntamiento of Tlacoachistlahuaca.[107] Tagged as Major Disaster by a Gobernación agent, he was the only officer who left traces of a court martial in the civilian archives; he was acquitted, reinstated, and promoted.[108] The attitudes of men like Monroy to civilians were summed up by his colleague Major Matías Castillo of Teloloapan's 72nd Reserve Battalion, who boasted that "he used amparos to wipe his arse."[109] Even when complaints about overly energetic repression reached critical mass, the offending officers were rarely if ever punished beyond a transfer.[110] Such enforced mobility, countering soldiers' political sway, social capital, and business interests, reflected weakness; long service in one post, on the other hand, reflected enduring strength.

The End of the Affair: Miguel Alemán and the Also-rans of 1948

Yet while agents railed, seemingly without effect, from the port of Veracruz about Mange as a genuine disgrace, "incapable of offering constitutional guarantees through the federal forces at his command which are distracted in other engagements and serve as tools for personal vendettas," three key developments in civil / military relations were about to reduce the military's autonomy on the national stage.[111] The first of these ruptures was superficially apolitical, an administrative rather than partisan question of changing the division of labor in provincial policing to increase civilian responsibilities. Yet as any Weberian would note, the implications of that change were profoundly political. Alemán's sexenio coincided with the emergence of a newly technocratic breed of governor who invested heavily in expanding civilian policing and court systems. Initially impotent, Governor Adolfo Ruiz Cortines had by the late 1940s something of his own violent autonomy vis-à-vis the army and used it convincingly to crush Mange's former pistolero allies. Armed with jeeps, generals, and Mausers, the state police of Veracruz ceased to rely completely on the army for force. This was the real beginning of what demilitarization did occur in the countryside. The professionalization of police, the suppression of pistoleros, and the attendant attempts to reduce the numbers and scale of everyday military operations were central to curbing rural violence after 1945. The impact varied greatly from state to state; the police were often run by ex-military; and the process was eminently reversible and was in fact reversed in many states in the 1960s.[112] Yet it was nevertheless salient: the generals, no longer wholly indispensable, lost appreciable leverage over local societies and both local and national politicians.

The second rupture was, by contrast, overtly political, a confrontation between generals and civilians that teetered on the brink of a coup d'état. The tensions preceded Alemán's election, and continued afterward with regular meetings of generals in Avila Camacho's house, but they intensified dramatically after the very great shock of the July 1948 devaluation.[113] As the peso crashed in two weeks from 4.85 to 7.50 to the dollar some generals began circling what appeared to many a fatally wounded administration.[114] (There was also a revolutionary movement in gestation by junior officers and Padillistas, among others, but they seemed wholly unserious.)[115] There were two more serious groups. One, meeting at Antonio Ríos Zertuche's house, centered around powerful, predominantly northern conservative commanders such as Rodrigo Quevedo, Bonifacio Salinas Leal, Anacleto López, Miguel Z. Martínez, and Román Yocupicio, and considered recruiting Abelardo Rodríguez or Salinas Leal as an emergency replacement for Alemán.[116] The second was led by the director of the Colegio Militar, General Luis Alamillo Flores. He was perhaps the army's leading thinker; he had studied in Germany, France, and West Point, observed the Spanish Civil War from close up as the military attaché in Paris and impressed Cárdenas in the extremely tense talks on military cooperation with the United States after Pearl Harbor, becoming military attaché in Washington for the duration. More to the point, he was a close client of Joaquín Amaro, for whom he had recently given a lavish dinner at the Colegio, and who in turn was reported to be holding conclaves at his house in Michoacán to discuss a military takeover, and he reportedly had initial interest from that key branch, the artillery. The Amaro group would, the DFS was told, use the classic stratagem of launching their coup during the rowdy celebrations of the fiestas patrias.[117]

It is difficult to judge just how realistic these groups' plans ever became, or to know precisely how their would-be coups were defused. Their key figures were far from the front rank of the army. Amaro was old, embittered, sidelined to Oaxaca, feared and hated across the army; after failing to gain power in a push for the presidency in 1940 he had apparently been muttering about coups for years to no effect.[118] Alamillo Flores was young but likewise disliked, even inside the Colegio Militar, for his careerism, lack of military experience, and rapid ascent; he had been on the verge of a dismissive appointment as director of physical education earlier that year.[119] Ríos Zertuche was notoriously corrupt and opportunistic, and though formerly important—he had taken charge of the Mexico City police immediately after the Obregón assassination, and gone on to command eight military zones—he had been suspected by Cárdenas of plotting almazanista rebellion in 1940, hastily shifted from Chiapas to Sonora and subsequently sidelined.[120] Salinas Leal was young and dynamic, but also held responsible for the main military embarrassment of the recent past, the León massacre, and reportedly a bit of an oaf.[121] If they were political outs, though, so were the large majority of generals who, thanks to overproduction of the top ranks in earlier years, spent life, some in dingy hotel rooms, waiting for commands which never came. (The math was simple: in 1942 there were four army divisions for fifty-four divisional generals.)[122] There was, moreover, something of a hangover from the army's exclusion from the 1946 presidential campaign, and Alemán's misrule only seemed to confirm that that exclusion had been a mistake. Some citizens agreed: the journalist Renato Leduc told the president's secretary that "as soon as you university people got to power, people started to want the military back because they stole less."[123]

Whatever the qualifications of the generals waiting in the wings, intelligence and diplomatic reports make it clear that for six weeks Alemán's survival hung in the balance. Gobernación flooded Mexico City with agents who eavesdropped in unions, cafés, markets, and the street and smelled revolution in the air. As early as July 24 there were rumors of a popular rising; flyers, corridos, and gossip all predicted the same, and the assassination or lynching of Alemán.[124] It may have been tried. On August 3, 1948, the U.S. ambassador was told that the Alamillo Flores group were planning to assassinate the president; elite airmen from Squadron 201, Mexico's only veterans of World War II, joked very publicly about just that; on August 11 strong, widespread rumors ran from Mexico City to Veracruz reporting that his car had been machine-gunned and his driver killed.[125] It is once more impossible to know. On one hand, Alemán was lying low, and was observed to have a bandaged hand two days later; on the other, his allegedly dead driver—Captain Miguel Portilla, aka El Asesino—was alive and kicking a year later.[126] But even the military yearbook, professionally noncommittal, let out an unmistakable smoke signal by demoting Alemán from the 1949 edition's frontispiece, replacing him with a soldier, a flag, and the suggestive "la patria es primero."[127] Gossip was pithier. "Thanks to Miguel's bloody idiocy," a spy heard one man say, "militarism is back all over us."[128]

Yet the Alemán faction, and with them the PRI, held on to power through duplicity, co-option, and force, and with the critical, grudging neutrality of ex-presidents Cárdenas and Avila Camacho. Lacking their support, the dissident generals backed away from a quick strike in favor of turning Alemán into a puppet ruler. On August 13 a large party of generals called on Alemán, officially to assure him of their support, in reality to exert pressure for changes in the cabinet and the general staff.[129] The atmosphere as they left was one of swaggering authority; Generals Ríos Zertuche and Maurilio Rodríguez had broken all protocol in calling the president "tú" rather than the formal "Usted," reveled in his panic, and believed they would get all they wanted from Alemán, including five generals in the cabinet. (The president had greeted them in the belief—or with true words spoken in jest—that they had come to topple him.)[130] Various sources suggested that a deal had been struck, and that the informe would deliver a drastic reshuffle to purge both Alemanista civilians and Defense Secretary Limón. This would probably have been the first of an open-ended series of capitulations: Alemán's fate was, according to both the U.S. embassy and some Mexican intelligence briefs, in the hands of the army, and reliable informants keen on a flutter put the odds of violence at 6 to 4.[131]

By the time of the informe the president had counterattacked by winning the public support of the unions and by increasing the supply of affordable food in Mexico City and provincial capitals. Two of Alemán's loathed cronies, Enrique Parra and Jorge Pasquel, had left the city and received some sort of comeuppance: Parra abandoned his pursuit of the governorship of San Luis Potosí, Pasquel his directorship of *Novedades*.[132] The others prepared for the worst in their own ways: Ramón Beteta was supposed to have put his mansion up for sale; Carlos Serrano drew equipment for forty men from the defense ministry and had a military plane placed at his disposition, ready and fueled.[133] Uncertainty remained the dominant key. Cárdenas had allegedly given the president until the middle of September to improve his administration; diplomats noted that neither Cárdenas nor Avila Camacho turned up to the much-publicized "Unity dinner" that the military offered Alemán on September 3 and wondered what it meant; but state governors followed suit with their own dinner on the sixth. Cárdenas, believed to be under constant surveillance by Gobernación's spies,[134] had supposedly been placated by Alemán's promise of wholesale cabinet firings later in the year, delayed only to preserve the image of civilian power.[135]

Alemán may have delivered part of a deal in November, when he fired the Secretario de Economía Nacional Antonio Ruiz Galindo, another veracruzano intimate with a prominent reputation for graft. That aside, though, the president gambled that the moment for a coup had passed and kept his cabinet unchanged, facing the plotters down.[136] The government used *La Prensa* to undermine both dissident groups (and critical journalists and gossipers in general) and the secret services to investigate leading generals, finding out, among other things, that Ríos Zertuche had swindled a group of generals out of half a million pesos at Palma Sola.[137] On October 21 the president called in Ríos Zertuche, extracting a public statement that he was disinterested in politics, and broke up the Alamillo Flores group by firing Alamillo Flores (replacing him with the ex-president's brother Rafael Avila Camacho) and threatening Amaro with losing his command in Oaxaca.[138] The final insult, perhaps, was a newspaper report from early November that reported the plotters' disappointment with the U.S. presidential election results, alleging that they had secured a promise of backing from the losing Thomas Dewey.[139] Not only were the dissident generals power hungry, corrupt, and in it for themselves; they were tools of the gringos into the bargain.

There was another side to the coin in Alemán's survival, which was the broad and systematic co-option of both key generals and the wider officer class. A territorial reorganization of the army created ten new regiones militares, each one grouping several zonas militares. The new commands were apportioned between some of the most political generals, to obvious effect; the most obvious correlation came with Bonifacio Salinas Leal, who, appointed to the 5th Military Region in Guadalajara, ended up leading the campaign for Alemán's reelection in the north.[140] Lower down the ranks, muttering among retired veterans and the underemployed was dealt with by a presidential decree creating the Legión de Honor Mexicana, which returned all recognized revolutionaries to a token active service—without asking anything in return—promoted them one rank, and renewed their payments of full pay and benefits.[141] The president killed two birds with one stone by dissolving the general staff, mollifying a jealous older generation while disbanding Alamillo Flores's remaining allies. The practice of systematically bribing zone commanders with money from the unaudited president's discretionary fund continued. Other ranks received land grants, houses, servants' allowances, life insurance, and soft loans; all ranks got a 44 percent mean wage increase, more than twice the pay raise given industrial workers in Mexico City.[142] Such individual and collective payoffs helped soldiers to overlook a certain institutional impoverishment, as the army budget shrank in real terms and updates to equipment ended.[143]

While some dissidents turned coats completely, others subsequently passed into the ranks of Henriquismo, where their failure to mount a serious military challenge to the election of Adolfo Ruiz Cortines confirmed the extent to which the prospect of presidential power had faded. Alemán was in part lucky, and in large part indebted to Cárdenas and other calm voices in the army. But his eventual defiance of the generals in 1948 was also critical in consolidating the new civilian age in Mexican politics. Subsequent explicitly military parties—1949's quasi-fascist Partido Nacionalista, which explicitly set out to destroy (among other servants of "Stalin's Russian Imperialism") the "totalitarian PRI," 1961's Celestino Gasca rebellion—never approached national power. Rumors circulated across the rest of the century: that the army was planning a takeover in 1976, that a faction of officers was on the brink in 1984, that the secretary of defense was trying to veto the presidential candidacy of Ernesto Zedillo in 1994. But nothing ever came of them.[144] Reflecting on the 1948 crisis, one diplomat realized that he had seen a turning point. "Mexico," he reported, "has apparently outgrown the more romantic aspects of revolutionary activity as carried on in the second decade of this century. Modern communications and modern arms and equipment have outmoded the horse, the 30–30 rifle, and the *pronunciamiento*."[145]

That shift was tested in the presidential elections that bracketed it, those of 1946 and 1952. General Henríquez Guzmán was a tentative early candidate in 1945, backed by Mange and other officers; he never became a declared rival because of Cárdenas's swaying of the army and Avila Camacho's purge and reshuffle. (Cárdenas and Avila Camacho broadly represented the left and the right of the army, respectively.) The first election of a civilian candidate was not, however, completely smooth, and supporters of Alemán's defeated priista rival, Ezequiel Padilla, launched an abortive rebellion in the highlands of Guerrero.[146] In 1951 Henríquez Guzmán left the PRI and became the candidate of the FPPM, a vehicle for three diverse groups: political outcasts of all stripes, Cardenistas, and militarists. Ex-governor Berber of Guerrero, a political untouchable, was a regional leader; Francisco Múgica, Genovevo de la O, and Rubén Jaramillo were all prominent; 1948 militarist leaders Generals Antonio Ríos Zertuche and Luis Alamillo Flores were too.[147] The henriquista campaign was never genuinely national, and Cárdenas refused to commit himself publicly to its support.[148] For all its glaring contradictions the FPPM was, however, a power to be reckoned with in Mexico City, where it denied the PRI a majority even in the official vote count. The party was also a player in several states, and the combination caused the government to fear risings on election day and in the run-up to the inauguration. Such success met with intense repression, peaking in the murderous attack by soldiers and riot police on henriquista demonstrators in Mexico City the day after the election.[149] The army backed the government as it continued to face down large crowds: on November 16, for example, spies estimated twenty-five thousand Henriquistas in a single protest march.[150] Henriquismo ended up an anticlimax, but a landmark in military–civil relations. Conceptualized in part as a classic Latin American militarist movement, patriotically correcting the corruption of civilian rule, it ended up underlining the domination of the early PRI and affording another opportunity to purge some of the most threatening or geriatric officers. In its aftermath Alemán created seventy-six new generals and sixty-six colonels.[151] The Secretaría de Defensa gave the less threatening more incentives to stay away from politics by changing the rules regarding electoral involvement; officers were supposed to retire permanently, not temporarily, from the army if they wanted to run for office.[152] The new modus vivendi was confirmed by the midterm elections of 1955, during which "there was little of interest to be noted as regards the armed forces. . . . [While] rumor-mongers whispered of secret conclaves of generals in remote villas, the army carefully avoided all political activity and on more than one occasion made it clear that it remained loyal to the Ruiz Cortines regime."[153]

By then Mexico's peculiar brand of civilian authoritarianism was quite well established; peculiar, on one hand, for an army far smaller than those of Latin America's later bureaucratic–authoritarian regimes, and on the other for its reliance on an informal senate that was itself military.[154] This was the third, and absolutely key, development: the masterly inactivity of Generals Cárdenas, Avila Camacho, and Rodríguez, who repeatedly meddled with politics across the midcentury by not meddling in politics and by stopping their colleagues from doing so either.[155] It was not Cárdenas alone, for all the hysteria of elements of the right or British diplomats, who waxed hysterical about "the Cárdenas incubus, the bane of Mexican public life for the last ten years."[156] Yet the U.S. embassy was rightly convinced that no major decisions were made without considering the probable reaction of ex-presidential generals, and Cárdenas in particular.[157] His "sphinx-like figure," the British concluded in 1948, "was still the most important personality in Mexico's political life."[158] The president or key members of his retinue met with Cárdenas regularly. Sometimes Cárdenas initiated the meetings; in March 1949 Alemán spent a week in his company in Michoacán, where it was believed he was being "called to account."[159] On other occasions Alemán tested the waters, explicitly asking Cárdenas for his prior opinion on political decisions. The most significant of these concerned presidential reelection. From late 1949 onward Alemán began preparing Mexicans for a reelection bid: the press ran frequent articles suggesting the wisdom of six more years of Alemán, leaders of the bureaucrats' union were instructed to promote his candidacy, and in April 1950 Rafael Ortega, a veracruzano deputy and leader of the COCM, announced that it would be favored by large numbers of congressmen.[160] By June 1950 the U.S. embassy believed that reelection was the most likely prospect, and toward the end of 1950 the CROM suggested an extension of three years to the current presidential term.[161] The proposal, for all the controversy it awakened, was not completely buried even at the end of his regime; *El Universal* ran an editorial in September 1952 calling for Alemán's return.[162]

But it was stopped by opposition that began with Cárdenas. The president's secretary Rogelio de la Selva, Ramón Beteta, and Adalberto Tejeda were all sent to Michoacán to try to secure Cárdenas's blessing for one of two ideas: either a straightforward change to the constitution to permit reelection or an extension of the term.[163] It was a heretical proposal, but one which the DGIPS—ordered to investigate its possible reception—considered easy to get through the checks and balances of congress and organized labor.[164] On April 8, 1950, Alemán met with Cárdenas and Avila Camacho, seemingly to discuss the possibility; in the immediate aftermath a manifesto was issued, "In Defense of the Cardenista Regime," which prominently repudiated reelection.[165] Cárdenas and Avila Camacho were simultaneously engaged in vigorous backstage maneuvering, marshaling power brokers ranging from the gunman Gonzalo N. Santos to the Marxist eminence Vicente Lombardo Toledano in their campaign to block the attempt. (Santos characteristically suggested deploying pistoleros against Alemán's followers in congress.)[166] Once out of office Alemán vigorously denied even considering the proposal, and the presidential archives contain nothing more than a revealingly emptied file entitled "el presidente—extensión período."[167] Reelection was a hubristic suggestion which, if implemented, would probably have caused a rebellion or a coup. Yet copious evidence points to the seriousness of Alemán's drive to obtain a further term in office, trying once more in 1958; and that, despite what the DGIPS called his "massive political power," it was the informal senate that managed to derail him.[168] Their power survived the presidential transition of 1952, when Ruiz Cortines relied heavily on the support of Avila Camacho and Cárdenas in breaking sharply with his predecessor and former patron. In a striking, and somewhat ironic, subsequent instance of this military demilitarization, Cárdenas met Alemán in Paris in 1955 to discuss the presidential succession; the civilian Alemán suggested a general, and General Cárdenas vetoed the idea.[169] Deploying veto power against would-be caudillos, whether military or civilian, the presidential generals were critical bulwarks of the institutional state.

The Curiosities of Civilian Rule

Yet this demilitarization carried both hidden costs and striking ambiguities. Across the 1940s and early 1950s the first Priistas and key ex-presidents reached a clearly defined modus vivendi with the armed forces, a (not wholly) tacit pact that ceded considerable regional and institutional autonomy to the generals in part exchange for increased (but not wholesale) national submissiveness and brutally effective counterinsurgency work. This pact was not merely implied: formal, institutional arrangements—the foundations of earlier, "cost-free demilitarization" arguments—reflected its terms. After 1946 there would be no more military presidents; a direct line from the armed forces to the highest level of power was preserved, on the other hand, in the four generals who headed the PRI over the next two decades.[170] On that basis José Manuel Villalpando has argued that the PRI was a military party; it was not.[171] A military party did emerge in 1954 with the Partido Auténtico de la Revolución Mexicana, but it was a shell party made by the PRI itself, set up to provide both token opposition and sinecures—*chambas*—for some of the more obsolete generals who backed Ruiz Cortines.[172] Neither were they, as Aaron Navarro argues, seduced away from militarism with jobs in the DFS; there were very few of those jobs and they were not (yet) highly lucrative.[173] Yet officers did well across the governments of the midcentury. Miguel Alemán made generals at a rapid rate, promoting more in one year than López Mateos did in his entire sexenio, and relied on no fewer than fifteen generals as governors over his term; the first Ruiz Cortines senate housed twelve military bigwigs; by the end of the López Mateos sexenio most of the borderland states—Sinaloa, Chihuahua, Tamaulipas, Coahuila—were run by military governors.[174] There was no obvious cuota de poder for governorships—unlike for seats in the senate, where a rough 20 percent was the rule—but it was not always necessary to be governor to dominate a state, and in Frank Brandenburg's analysis the zone commanders of the 1950s and 1960s enjoyed more regional power than all bar a handful of the most important governors, civilian caciques, and bureaucrats.[175] In at least one case, Campeche, a mere captain was more powerful than, governor excepted, an entire state administration.[176] In 1960s Puebla the army policed just as many municipios as the formal, civilian police did.[177] And in the capital it was invariably a general who headed the city police force all the way to 1988.[178]

Above all, though, the regime gave those divisional generals too powerful to ignore a whole new level of formal power. The list of the new regional commanders constituted a who's who of deeply political soldiers—several ex-governors, a future defense secretary, at least one possible president—several of whom had built cacicazgos in real or adopted patrias chicas.[179] Rodrigo Quevedo and his family had controlled the critical posts in the Chihuahua state administration across the 1930s, pledging, gossip had it, "to develop the state of Chihuahua with gambling, whores, and vice"; Bonifacio Salinas Leal had been the strongman of Nuevo León.[180] These two, at least, had been at the center of the military's recent steps toward retaking national power: Gobernación spies had watched closely as they organized a would-be secret junta in autumn 1948.[181] They may have been being paid off, in various ways (Quevedo and Salinas Leal were both linked to the drug trade); they may have been making comebacks; they were quite evidently participants in a quid pro quo, and they did not retire from politics.[182] Bonifacio Salinas Leal, for example, interfered in both the 1958 presidential succession and the 1960 naming of a new chief of staff.[183] A 1973 report had him plotting to topple the incumbent chief of staff, running a private intelligence service using taxi drivers and allegedly preparing a group of agents provocateurs to destabilize President Echeverría with a further student massacre. Despite this he stayed on active service until his death at the age of eighty-two.[184] Yet nobody, perhaps, did as well as Alejandro Mange, for he kept hold of Veracruz.

Everyday demilitarization in the Mexican provinces was thus partial. Top commanders lost national power, but gained new territories; they exercised less violence, but maintained extensive businesses, businesses backed, in the last analysis, by force or the threat of force. Bosques de Chihuahua, the huge lumber company in Ciudad Madera, locked from its formation in conflict with peasant communities, was formed by a conglomerate that included not just Miguel Alemán but also General Antonio Guerrero, a Chihuahua zone commander.[185] Their remaining regional power made the transaction much more than a straightforward Tocquevillian exchange of political for economic rewards. Indicators of continuing political independence are easily found across the entire army. The average length of zone command, that key metric of the balance of power between soldiers and civilians, actually increased markedly from the thirteen months of the Cárdenas sexenio to the twenty-nine months of the Alemán years.[186] A handful—Felix Ireta in Michoacán, Anacleto López in Zacatecas, Pablo Díaz Dávila in Morelos—spent well over a decade in the same post.[187] This was a glaring contravention of the shrewd policy (dating to the nineteenth century) of what the army yearbook described as "rotation in command . . . to give new elements a chance and to avoid prejudicial settling down."[188] Reserve battalion officers likewise continued to enjoy the lengthy postings that endowed them with networks and interests similar to those of any other local political actor. After spending much of the 1940s in Ometepec, Colonel Monroy—after a brief suspension while under investigation by the military procurador—returned there for much of the 1950s. In Ixcateopan Manuel Rodríguez Juárez commanded the municipal reserves from the revolution until at least 1969.[189] Fifty years with such power—even in the hands of an apparently decent man, perhaps in part because of his decency—was hardly the institutionalization that the party proclaimed.

Once more, though, it is General Mange who is the ultimate example. Divisional generals were supposed to retire at sixty-five, an age Mange reached in 1950.[190] In May Defense Secretary Limón ordered his retirement; Mange, however, refused to turn over to the army proofs of his age and subsequently had his retirement suspended by presidential decree.[191] Far from collecting a pension, in August 1950 he collected a medal for his long, distinguished service.[192] In January 1951 General Limón tried to pension Mange off once more, ordering forcible retirement; he was instead promoted to head the new 2nd Military Region, headquartered in Veracruz.[193] During the 1952 presidential election Mange summarily arrested his old enemy, General Cándido Aguilar, and reportedly had to be prevented from summarily killing him.[194] The new president—Adolfo Ruiz Cortines, another veracruzano—nevertheless continued backing Mange, who was not retired until Adolfo López Mateos began his term in 1959.[195] Even that was pacted: during retirement negotiations (called extremely urgent by the Secretaría de la Defensa Nacional) he asked that his 100 percent salary and 68,000-peso retirement bonus be supplemented with the grant of two aides, one of them César Mange. He was, according to one report, disenchanted enough with the final settlement to discuss rebellion with the Colonna brothers, old gunmen friends from the south.[196] When it came to the imperatives of old age, Alejandro Mange did not go gentle anywhere at all, raging instead over how "le quitaron la chichi."[197]

Other generals rose further at the national level: Mange was never going to join the informal senate. Others in Mexico City would make much more money: in 1955 the officer who ran the communications department of the Secretaría de la Defensa was "eased out of his job after having made a modest fortune of 8 million pesos" (and keeping some one hundred relations and friends in sinecures), the officer in charge of the city police in the early 1960s formalized a system of extortionate monthly charges across the city, while the commander of the Presidential Guard went one better, selling a governorship (Coahuila) for the best part of 6 million pesos.[198] Yet the longevity, and the bare-faced nature, of General Mange's Veracruz cacicazgo offers an exemplar of just how well military autonomy weathered civilianization. The general powerfully influenced life in Veracruz, first as zone and later as regional commander, for twenty-two years.[199] Whether this was due to (perhaps literally) knowing where the bodies were buried during two veracruzano presidencies, or whether it reflected his ability to maintain some control at any cost remains an open question.[200] It baffled contemporary observers, who stressed his personal empire building, corruption, and subversion of local government.[201] His power in the late 1930s and early 1940s, when he and a network of violent agrocapitalists ruled much of Veracruz and tried to veto the party's pick for the presidency, was admittedly extraordinary. Yet the intense focus on national rebellion, formal budgets, and the power to select presidents which underpinned earlier analyses should not conceal the partial, pacted, Faustian quality of Mexican demilitarization. Mange did preserve his command and the wealth it brought him. He preserved, according to one (scandalous but signed) denunciation, his business relationship with criminals such as the abigeos of southern Veracruz.[202] He was straightforwardly unfirable: when the defense secretary tried to forcibly retire the aging general, the president overrode the decision and promoted him instead.[203]

One of the last entries in the general's personnel file is a complaint from the Ferrocarriles Nacionales de México, dated March 31, 1959. Railway engineers investigating a train crash between Chacaltianguis and Cocuite traced it to gravel on the line. The gravel came from a road that Mange's troops were busily constructing, "to the benefit of the aforementioned soldier's personal properties"; it caused 3,110 pesos worth of damage.[204] We still know more about the costs of this literal crossroads than we do about the cost of the metaphorical crossroads where military and civilian power intersected in Mexican state formation. Yet it is increasingly clear that the army's subordination to civilian rule was in reality only to the president.[205] It was telling that one of the three categories of assessment of officers should be civil conduct and that some of the most abusive should get high marks in that category.[206] They were in constitutional terms pretty untouchable, the military fuero giving the army "a completely parallel system of justice in a wide array of areas."[207] General Mange was not alone in preserving much of his autonomy, business interests, and regional power, and he and his peers, filing reluctantly out of the palace, clung to their power to derail local societies across the supposed heyday of priista Mexico.[208] Yet that regional power, those many transactions, and, paradoxically, the veto of an informal senate itself made up of soldiers kept Mexico from following the rest of Latin America into military dictatorship.

Conclusion

In 1945 there was a stark divorce between the political, social, and economic status quo in Mexico City and the rest of the country. The Valley of Mexico, not for the first time in its history, was the comparatively settled center of a loose federation of turbulent provinces and distant frontier lands. Its political stabilization overlapped with, and was partly driven by, a settling of political scores at the highest level. The emerging single party had only taken the 1940 election through half-baked fraud and bloodshed, its practitioners of the dark arts turning tommy guns on voters in Las Lomas to impose a conservative general as president, even as he privately acknowledged defeat.[1] In 1946, on the other hand, a popular, ideologically bland civilian, Miguel Alemán, had declared resoundingly for democratic reform and been handily elected, even by skeptical counts. The national economy was picking up speed; the city was booming, as hundreds of thousands of country people, cheap labor, arrived; the first skyscraper in Latin America, the Torre Latinoamericana, had just won planning permission.[2] World War II had given a conservative faction of the ruling class a justification for suppressing competition among the elites and they had known how to use it: purging the left, dominating unions, consolidating the single party, strengthening the critical interior ministry, making peace with the ecclesiastical hierarchy and the secular right, and dealing competently with the war's winners, allowing Mexico to reap the fruits of victory at the cost of deploying a single, wholly token squadron of fighter planes.[3] When Alemán declared that he would lead Mexico into "the constructive phase of the revolution" even some cynics bought it; the British ambassador wrote with unseemly optimism of a march to democracy.[4] Other cynics, though, saw matters differently. In Daniel Cosío Villegas's eyes Mexico was in a crisis that was deepening day by day, but, "as in cases of terminal illness, no one in the family [was] talking about it."[5] And he was right because outside Mexico City the perennial crises of the revolutionary period rolled on regardless.

It was in fact difficult to phrase places like Guerrero in terms other than those of crisis in 1945. One of the most murderous states, there was an 85 percent rate of impunity for even those homicides that got to court, themselves less than half the number of actual killings; roughly one in twenty murders went (legally, at least) punished.[6] Substantial majorities of guerrerenses voted for the opposition in the presidential elections of 1940 and 1946, while the elections that really mattered to most of them, the municipal ones, met with annulments, riots, and soldiers across the state. Party and government were not at all synonymous, and governors in both 1940 and 1944 backed the PRM's opponents. Catholics outside the main towns kept up their cold war with the revolution, revealed in the school enrollments that continued to fall after 1940; in Chilapa the seminary held twice as many adolescents as the state school.[7] The economy was stagnant, the regional administration deeply impoverished, and at odds with the military. The well-connected zone commander, Matías Ramos, was more powerful than the governor, whom he ignored and even opposed; it was unsurprising that the incoming governor should be another general.[8] Even soldiers, though, were unsafe, their flying columns regularly ambushed by assailants including abigeos, "primitive rebels," ejidatarios, and municipal policemen.[9] Landowner dynasties that ran back to the Porfiriato—like that of the incoming governor, whose family's power eventually spanned a century—held out across the arable lands of Tierra Caliente and the Costa Chica, in bloody resource and political conflicts with peasant communities.[10] Agraristas were more successful along the Costa Grande, but at a similarly high cost in the face of alliances between soldiers, ranchers, pistoleros, and bureaucrats, their victories in some cases—the ejidatarios exiled en masse, the Acapulco ejidos returned to private hands—eminently reversible, their stabilizing effects hard to see. In la Montaña the legacy of even a low-intensity Segunda Cristiada was manifest in empty schoolhouses and Catholic town councils. Guerrero remained, in short, riven by mountains, poverty, and conflicts, pitting landowners against agraristas, Sinarquistas against secularists, caciques against dissidents, civilians against soldiers, and ejidatarios against ejidatarios, petty Montagues against village Capulets.

A similar range of conflicts, subject to similar strong topographical and ecological determinants, dogged Veracruz, a state almost as dangerous as Guerrero and one that people likewise began leaving; some seventy-nine thousand moved out across the 1940s, a drastic increase in outmigration.[11] The agrarian violence of the 1930s had not ended, even though so many first-generation peasant leaders were dead, and the fragmentation of the tejedista coalition and cardenista land reform had opened new opportunities for caciques to expand across the cities and countryside. Assassinations of agraristas continued, as increasingly powerful pistoleros targeted a new generation of local cadres. Regional and municipal finances were in chaos, their poverty translating into falling salaries for those key agents of the state, teachers, who left the profession or took second jobs. It was impossible to field an adequate police force.[12] The generals, far from ceding power, acquired more as their civilian counterparts floundered, and the mid-1940s was the peak of their postrevolutionary control, autonomous and essential to any exercise of rule. In the lowlands of the south Porfirian elites and their large estates endured. Few peasants, and little revolutionary mobilization, meant that many land grants were paper alone; reform came from outside, a common recipe for intercommunity violence, and the south in the first half of the 1940s was the scene of extraordinarily intense warfare between rival coalitions of ejidos.[13] On the rich lowlands of the center the contenders were ejidatarios and the mafia families of pistoleros, the bloodshed increasing after 1943 as those families abandoned a successful cartel and went to war among themselves. Meanwhile, in the mountains of the north and center, the Huasteca and the tierra fría, serrano communities ran true to historical and sociological form in rejecting the state through cattle rustling, sinarquismo, tax evasion, electoral abstention, and generalized civil disobedience. In the factories, rail yards, oil fields, port warehouses, and sugar refineries workers, far from coming together in newfound corporatist unity, divided their allegiances between three mutually hostile unions. Anyone talking of stabilization in the Veracruz of 1945 would have been written off as delusional; the dominant note of the time was not centralization but fragmentation.

To what extent is this pattern generalizable? As noted earlier, Guerrero and Veracruz were exceptional among Mexican states in economic terms; the latter rich, the former very poor. They were also outliers in terms of violence: at the midcentury only Morelos was more homicidal. If we take murder rates as crude metrics of political instability, then a clear national division emerges between the more pacific North (only one state in the top ten of homicide rates) and Southeast–East (all in the bottom ten) on one hand, and the bloody Center, Center West, and South on the other.[14] A competent statistician could doubtless draw complex, multivariate conclusions; at the broad-brushstroke level, the correlation at both municipal and regional levels with natural resources, population density, factor endowment, and endogenous, stay-at-home rebellion, whether agrarian or religious, is obvious. Places of potential wealth, available labor, and unsettled business from the revolution were prone to conflict. Places that enjoyed relative tranquility in the revolution, such as the south of Veracruz, were not necessarily tranquil in the 1940s; neither state had been all that violent in the 1910s. Other studies offer similar stories of bloodshed and confusion, military rule and hard-fought elections, inequality and growth, institutional pluralism and landowner revanchism. In Pisaflores, Hidalgo, factional violence increased across the first half of the 1940s, until the Porfirian founder's family regained control. In Naranja, Michoacán, the federal bureaucrat sent to broker peace between ejidal factions in 1945 was run out of town at pistol point.[15] Across Oaxaca the early 1940s was a time of growing urban discontent, decentralization, local democracy, and violent competition between the general in the governorship, Vicente González Fernández, and the general in the zone command, Joaquín Amaro; things only got worse in 1945, when a new governor arrived and relations between caciques and government broke down completely. By late 1946, one bureaucrat reported, "all the Sierra [was] at war."[16] Morelos, meanwhile, was swept by local revolts of ex-Zapatistas in 1943, of which the most significant was that of Rubén Jaramillo; his brief truce with the government ended in 1946, when he took to the sierra again for five more years of "armed hiding."[17] In Puebla, as on the Guerrero coasts, flying columns were essential to keep a tenuous peace across the president's home turf, lynchings continued unabated, and major towns like Atlixco were ruled by army officers; affairs only worsened after the death of Maximino Avila Camacho in 1945, as the new governor struggled to impose himself on local Avilacamachistas and the zone commander.[18] Even basic public health was unreliable. A smallpox epidemic killed eight thousand in the central states between 1942 and 1943.[19] Dysentery was endemic, as fewer than one in four Mexicans had access to piped drinking water.[20] Peasants had few tools to remedy either political or social ills; they were in precipitous political decline, with no agrarista representatives in the 1945 congresses of either Guerrero or Veracruz.[21] "The revolution never made it this far" was a common formula in the protest letters of the time, and it was often accurate, with strong Porfirian continuities in personnel—as in northern Guerrero and the Costa Chica, or southern Veracruz, or Chihuahua, or Chiapas—and structures, the ejidal boss or bank replacing the village cacique, the zone commander the jefe político.[22]

Notable continuities also characterized the period 1945–55. Yet fundamental shifts in the exercise of violence, the conduct and results of elections, prevailing economic models, the practices of corruption, and the ambitions and actions of the military made the long Alemán years a pivotal point in Mexico's twentieth-century history, one beyond compare until the second half of the 1980s. Those shifts were apparent, to different degrees, in both states.

Central to that pivot was a change in the quantity and quality of violence. Between 1941 and 1945 the official national murder rate was 31 per 100,000; between 1956 and 1960, 18. The decrease varied notably across regions; in Ometepec murders actually increased between 1950 and 1952, and in Guerrero as a whole the slight decline of the 1950s was reversed in the 1960s.[23] Furthermore, the relative numbers are misleading in terms of peoples' experiences, their chances of a peaceful life or a violent death: the ratio of killings to population was markedly reduced by the concurrent demographic boom, the appearance of large numbers of children partly masking the unabated murderousness of some of their parents. Nevertheless the unofficial (and more accurate) absolute murder rate compiled from the civil registries reveals a lesser but real decrease, recording a 12 percent drop in the national total of murders between 1950 and 1954 alone. That translated into people surviving who in an earlier (or later, for that matter) period would probably not have, political actors such as Acapulco's squatter leader Alfredo López Cisneros or dissident editor Ignacio de la Hoya. Part of the explanation for the change lay in the sheer paucity of survivors from the first generation of leaders in conflict zones; in places like central Veracruz or coastal Guerrero most of the leading radical agraristas had met violent ends by 1940, and landowner revanchism after 1940 decimated their successors. But their opponents had suffered casualties too: the ranchers of Ometepec and Tlacoachistlahuaca, the Añorve and Salmerón clans, killed numerous agraristas but also lost family members to murder or exile.[24] The logic of the Soledad de Doblado landowners, who reached out to their erstwhile agrarista enemies in 1955 to propose sharing municipal power, the sort of *turno pacífico* that followed civil war in Colombia or Cuba, was founded on both sides' losses.[25] Above all, those pistoleros whose empire-building activities went beyond individual municipios were taken out in large numbers, occasionally by jail sentences, more often by murder. At times their deaths were private initiatives; quite often, however, the state either colluded or performed extrajudicial executions. Crispín Aguilar was killed by rivals only after the local garrison had disarmed him and soldiers had swept the street where he died. It may have been a civilian who killed Rafael Cornejo Armenta, but it was secret service agents who took the ley fuga to his brothers and DFS agents who executed other inconvenient pistoleros.[26] There was consequently more to decreasing violence than war weariness, generational shifts, the settling of conflicts or the cumulative impact of years of violent competition. There was also a professionalization and an embryonic centralization of law enforcement in the later 1940s as state governments devoted more funds to the business of civilian order, and—for all the caveats of structural corruption, military staffing, and marked regional diversity—there was a quantifiable impact: police numbers, arrest rates, and conviction rates rose sharply across the country, and crime rates began to fall, in a trend that lasted the rest of the century.

In qualitative terms there were three major shifts in the practices of violence. First of all, the most anarchic and mass violence decreased. The forced migrations of the 1930s and early 1940s—the three hundred ejidatarios driven out of Tierra Caliente into Michoacán, the three hundred agraristas driven into Oaxaca by the Tlacoachistlahuaca ganaderos—declined, as did the village burnings, such as Jicayán de Tovar and Tetitlán in Guerrero, Abrevadero in Veracruz, that encouraged them.[27] Mass violence did not end—in 1957 Acapulco developers burned hamlets that were occupying prime real estate—but it became more the province of state agents, specifically the army, and it moved farther toward the peripheries.[28] Second, a monopoly of violence was an unrealistic goal, but a more regulated market of violence, with fewer players bound by tighter rules, was not; and that is what emerged. Civilian governments tried to use soldiers and pistoleros less and newly numerous police more, even if the difference was just a change of uniform, and to control more tightly the outcomes of their deployment. State policemen were perforce cheap, which only added to the allure of corruption, but they also did some police work and had some overall legitimacy. Third, there were the *reglas no escritas,* an unwritten corpus of informal political law and precedent. The reglas no escritas—a term and set of rules that almost everyone linked to the state understood—unambiguously dictated what should and should not be done, and they increasingly proscribed visible violence, especially in towns and cities, and privileged deniability. Raison d'état occasionally still called for the draconian repression of crowds—Raúl Caballero Aburto's 1952 attack on the Henriquistas in the Alameda is the obvious example—but provincial politicians who opened fire on their own were risking their careers. The idea that the Chilpancingo massacre of 1960 presented Priistas with a model to follow is absurd; the perpetrator—Caballero Aburto once more—lost his job, as did the governors who had earlier overseen shootings of demonstrators in Tapachula, Chiapas, León, Guanajuato, Etla, Oaxaca, Oaxaca City, and Morelia.[29]

Politicians no longer packed guns. They still resorted to violence, but the successful now did so at one remove. As the pistolero García put it, "They want deaths, but they also want to keep their hands nice and clean. Because the whole death thing ended with the *bola* and now everything's done according to the law. But at times the law sort of can't do the job, and then they call me."[30]

The same strategic hypocrisy applied to elections. The declarations of the newborn PRI in favor of democracy were substantiated in the vigorous competition of the party's primary elections and the sheer range of winners, from a communist in Tierra Blanca to a Mormon in San Buenaventura Nealtican.[31] The elimination of primaries in 1950 was wrapped in the same language of democracy, but with the unequivocal meaning of authoritarian centralization. Women's suffrage gave ballot papers to greater numbers of dissidents, like the Panistas of Iguala or the stalwart communist Maria de la O on the Costa Grande, but even without the vote, however, such women had already been influential inside parties—even the Sinarquistas had secretaries of women's action—and in electoral politics.[32] Moreover, women's suffrage served to provide greater head counts in favor of the ruling party.[33] So even as Priistas in places like Jalisco refused to register women voters the feared electoral lurch toward the opposition never happened.[34] The PRI leadership listened to cacicas, such as the Córdoba coffee sorters Inés Reyes and Sofía Castro, who pushed the "women's issues" of maternity benefits, schools, health, and childcare; they did not become more attentive to women's political representation, and while female turnout could be high—more women than men voted in the 1955 elections in the port of Veracruz—the numbers of priista women elected continued to be extremely low.[35] Even for those who were there was a glass ceiling. Guadalupe Urzúa Flores made it as far as federal congresswoman, with power over multiple municipios in Jalisco, but no further.[36] Elections remained important for their noncompetitive functions: the circulation of elites, the legitimacy or at least tolerance won by bargaining with voters, the intelligence on voters and local worthies that campaigns gave, the psychological centralization of normalized party wins. With a certain irony it was the cosmopolitan Mexico City that became the least conducive to representative government. Votes there for opposition presidential candidates were riskily meaningless. The equivalent to a governor, the regente, was appointed; ayuntamientos, local elections, and local newspapers were all nonexistent; intelligence and repressive systems were capacious. Outside Mexico City, on the other hand, it was too much like hard work for the center to impose a party line on all of the recalcitrant; and so some voters, particularly those who engaged in collective bargaining by riot, continued to enjoy veto powers and even some rough-and-ready democracies, places where the popular choice, irrespective of past, ideology, or identity, could by hook or by crook triumph.

That grassroots power was historically underestimated because opposition wins in the midcentury were rare and hard to see from Mexico City, concentrated as they were in smaller municipios, either unreported in the national newspapers or tucked away in the telegraphic notes of provincial correspondents. Yet victories did come to the dogged and the unimportant: in 1952 the PP was recognized as victorious in Cuetzala del Progreso, Guerrero, the state police evicting local Priistas from town hall, while in Veracruz independent slates won Atoyac, Manlio Fabio Altamirano, and Ixhuatlán de Córdoba, and a PAN-dominated junta was denounced as engineering victory in Citlaltepec with machetes.[37] The main opposition of the future, the PAN, initially won only a handful of serrano villages, such as Xochihuehuetlán, but members and sympathizers were influential at the municipal level across the indigenous highlands of la Montaña, the Sierra de Zongólica, and the Huasteca. Such opposition groups, who proclaimed themselves Priistas and then went their own way, were more widespread, and at times entire slates were Panistas in disguise, as when the powers that be in Igualapa held an election at dead of night to install a panista ayuntamiento.[38] Voter power should not be romanticized: the Xochihuehuetlán ayuntamiento was promptly removed by soldiers, and many dissidents were not liberal democrats. Yet Mexicans' veto power, and in places localized polyarchy, helped keep a broader democratic political culture alive, and with that came some surprisingly democratic results. The PRI has traditionally been seen as a bandwagon onto which the upwardly mobile clambered, and so it could be; but it was also quite frequently booty, a resource captured by those who were probably going to make it anyway, whether competent bureaucrats, clean-living kulak types, old-school caciques, or crypto-panistas.

The provincial realities of repression or representative rule could be hidden from capital dwellers, quarrels in faraway countries between people of whom they knew nothing. The cultural efforts to disguise the authoritarianism and rent seeking of the emerging regime, on the other hand, were more visible, and so were their failures. The rulers of the midcentury enjoyed a whole new technological reach—via radios, newspapers, cinemas, schoolrooms—to disseminate the messages of nationalist revolution and democracy, and those rulers' success in living up to them. They had, at the same time, a different set of tools to censor the entirety of the ether, with staunch allies in monopoly control of radio, cinema, newsreel, and later television. Print journalism was a different matter, controlled in the capital—on the front page and opinion columns, at least—but open to dissenting voices elsewhere. The results were mixed. Many Mexicans believed in the revolution "as an instrument of ultimate democratization and economic and social modernization"; in 1959 thousands of town dwellers told sociologists so. They did not believe in its inevitable incarnation in their rulers at any given moment, though: the same survey found "widespread . . . cynicism about and alienation from the political infrastructure and bureaucracy."[39] Some Priistas, like Cárdenas or Ruiz Cortines, could be put across as honest seekers of social justice; others, such as Alemán, could not. The same survey data—and from rural areas the protest letters, municipal paperwork, and work of dissident journalists—make it abundantly clear that officialist culture did not result in much particularly useful brainwashing. But officialist culture did have two stabilizing effects. It helped generate boom and bust cycles of hope, with each incoming president presented as a more promising and genuine representative of the revolution (which after the fatigue and last-minute plundering of a sexenio's end was not that hard). It also, as Gil Joseph among others has argued, maintained a common set of assumptions and words for what politicians and the ruled generally agreed should be a reality of social justice, even as they disagreed on how to get there.[40] Such a shared, normative language could be subversive, but it also helped sustain what consent and tolerance the PRI actually enjoyed.

It also had a shelf life, and it was not belief in the discourse of the revolution that kept the regime afloat for so long.[41] Presidents during the long goodbye of priista Mexico may have talked about revolution, but they talked about quite a lot of other things too, and their listeners favored precisely those politicians who said least about revolution, that is, Panistas. Even in the forties and fifties the language of revolutionary nationalism was not the only one spoken; it coexisted alongside a language of political Catholicism (firmly nationalist rather than ultramontane), a language of feminism, a language of democracy, and another of development. The last contributed notably to acceptance of the single party. Claims to democracy were hard to sustain; claims to successful development, on the other hand, had material foundations. The roads, the *camiones de redilas* that traveled them, ubiquitous cattle trucks that transported everything from actual cows to people, the clinics, hospitals, water pipes, electricity cables, and phone lines that stretched into México profundo were the most powerful tools of government, popular both in the abstract, progress publicized but out of sight, and in the immediately evident local. And while they were public goods, development projects were also opportunities for the entrepreneurial to benefit from the global economic boom. Administrations at all levels acted as gatekeepers to that boom, issuing public contracts and private permits that gave access to regional, national, and international markets. The power of those permits stretched across classes, ranging from street vendors through truckers to industrialists and drug dealers. The ultimate example of a permit was the permit for long-term usufruct of public land that was the ejidal grant, or the murkier grant of a colony. The former dried up, but the latter expanded dramatically, often as payoffs for dissidents and petitioners ranging from General Ríos Zertuche through Nabor Ojeda to a group of forlorn veterans who requested public lands near San Andrés Tuxtla.[42] The ever-present handmaiden of development, corruption, could also be a source of political stabilization. Funneling public assets and private opportunities into politically useful (or threatening) hands could buy acquiescence or support. It then gave rulers a second element of control in that such corruption could always be revealed and its benefits taken away, which helped ensure enduring obedience. Finally, a public and convincing rejection of corruption—as performed by Ruiz Cortines in both Xalapa and Los Pinos—increased the rejecter's popularity. Corruption was economically undermining, but—in the short term, anyway—a potent tool of political stabilization, whether privately deployed or publicly rejected. Abel Quezada summed its power up neatly in a 1953 cartoon caption: "Why would we pick fights with politicians if they're going to come over all honest?"[43]

In Guerrero reasons to pick fights with politicians endured beyond the midcentury, and the 1957 civic insurgency, the 1960 Chilpancingo student massacre, and the guerra sucia all argue convincingly for a lack of lasting political stabilization between 1945 and 1955. Yet it would be overuse of hindsight to ignore appreciable changes in three metrics of state power and stabilization: violence, electoral politics, and economic growth. The businesses of tourism, forestry, bracero remittances, and consumer goods for the cities brought some guerrerenses some of the profits of the postwar boom. (While the guerrerenses, in turn, provided the cheap labor, cheap food, and expanding domestic markets that helped feed that boom.)[44] Roads helped the carpenters of Ixcateopan or the craftsmen of Olinalá to get their furniture or lacquerware to Mexico City markets. The number of teachers trebled. Hospitals and clinics opened. Mortality halved between 1930 and 1952 in Ixcateopan, and the leading causes of death across Guerrero—malaria, dysentery, outright malnutrition among infants and children—waned.[45] Smallpox, a secular scourge, was effectively

Abel Quezada in *Ovaciones*, January 26, 1953. Familia Quezada Rueda.

eradicated between 1946 and 1951.[46] While absolute numbers of homicides grew across the midcentury, ratios of homicides relative to population had fallen steeply by 1960; while the rate rebounded in the sixties and seventies it never returned to the peak of the 1940s.[47] Election protests in the 1950s were far less numerous than during the 1940s. Guerrero's ruling class would never be an exemplar of political competence, but the new central power meant that the years of out-of-control governors and wholly unrepresentative ayuntamientos were over. Alejandro Gómez Maganda was a client of one governor and two presidents—Cárdenas and Alemán—but was nevertheless rapidly dispatched once his disastrousness became clear. Agraristas meanwhile made a cautious return to municipal government. There was a generational and political shift toward central and technocratic rule in Guerrero as elsewhere: the secretary-general of the Liga Agraria, the head of the state PRI, and nearly half the state congressmen elected between 1945 and 1951 were teachers.[48] One of the federal senators elected in 1952 was a top Mexico City bureaucrat and a member of the PRI's national executive committee; he was also an economist with communist sympathies, postgraduate studies at the London School of Economics and in Paris, and a seat on the Fondo de Cultura Económica's board.[49] There may not have been much gain in social stability in 1950s Guerrero, but there was by 1955 a bigger economy, better public health, and a more stable, centrally controlled government.

Change in Veracruz, whether social, economic, or political, was more dramatic. By the same metrics—development, violence, and elections—the Veracruz of 1955 bore little relation to that of ten years earlier. The greatest continuity lay in the power of the military: one of the state's two senators for 1952–58 was a general,[50] and more significantly, General Mange, one of the country's great soldier-caciques, remained a busy and unfirable rent seeker. Yet like the rest of his cohort of caciques, whether civilian or military, he was an unwilling participant in the authoritarian centralization of the time, his political autonomy under siege. Elsewhere there was a wholesale redistribution of power. Alemán's cohorts removed peasants from political office, permanently at state and federal levels, temporarily at the municipal level. By 1961 there were only two CNC representatives among the fifteen state congressmen, but a plurality of mayors came from the peasant sector, bearing out Ruiz Cortines's description of the priista settlement as legislatures for the governor, mayors for the pueblo. Union power, on the other hand, was close to extinct at the local level: more mayors were classified as ganaderos, stockbreeders, than workers.[51] The new mayors generally came from a small-town bourgeoisie: Chicontepec was run by a school inspector, Soledad de Doblado by Porfirio Pérez Olivares, now a successful exporter of foodstuffs to Mexico City, and San Andrés Tuxtla by a UNAM-educated public notary.[52] Their superiors the governors looked the same only more so. Marco Antonio Muñoz (1950–56) came from the state supreme court, Angel Carvajal (1948–50) and Antonio Modesto Quirasco (1956–62) from the federal supreme court.[53] In the second major continuity with earlier years these governors remained incapable of raising taxes. Yet they oversaw nevertheless marked development thanks to intrinsic wealth, economic growth, forced labor, and federal subsidies. The state in Veracruz grew because its leaders ran Mexico from the mid-1940s to the late 1950s, and the veracruzanos in Mexico City killed pistoleros, quadrupled police forces, crushed unions, and provided a disproportionate share of the benefits of alliance or acquiescence to those who remained, ranging from a far more peaceful and ordered society to roads, schools, and hospitals. It was appropriate, and wholly uncoincidental, that Veracruz should exemplify the more effective side of the dictablanda.

The histories of Guerrero and Veracruz diverge starkly across the midcentury, departing from many shared characteristics in the mid-1940s to end up marking opposite boundaries of the dictablanda by the 1950s. Military caciquismo was more evident in 1955 in Veracruz than in Guerrero, and the latter had made more progress in expanding its tax base. Yet the balance of the new order, in blunt terms, was skewed toward consent in Veracruz and force in Guerrero. The final question is how much the two have in common with the rest of Mexico.

The critical base for all other developments, the decline of violence, was universal. Long-standing conflicts were settled, whether by generational erosion, a clear decision for one of the contenders or a truce. The steep fall in national homicide rates was evident in even the most Hobbesian places: in dystopian Naranja the numbers of murders halved.[54] State governments formed police forces, deeply flawed, but generally better than nothing, and there were strange pockets of quality: the Mexico City traffic police became, the British ambassador thought, "an excellent body of men."[55] In the provinces the police were tools for governors to use against local strongmen and they also permitted a reduction in the numbers of those loose cannons the militias. In Chihuahua seventeen irregular cavalry regiments—unemployed Villistas?—were disbanded. The apertura democrática promised by the PRI actually arrived with primaries in 1946 and was closed when these were banned in 1950; but the consent-seeking side of the dictablanda endured in the common veto power of municipal voters and in the positive representation that some achieved. Across the 1950s state governments in Oaxaca faced the stark choice of sending in troops or acknowledging PAN victories across much of the Mixteca.[56] In the 1958 Zacatecas local elections an independent party beat the PRI convincingly, leading to compromise ayuntamientos and the exile of the regional cacique.[57] Overt opposition wins that stood were scarce—the PAN won only sixty-four between 1946 and 1980—but paper-only Priistas were common enough: the 1947 ayuntamiento in Senguio, Michoacán, contained two sinarquista regidores, while in Puebla the former Panista Nicolás Vázquez won the 1951 elections with a token PRI membership.[58] At the state level the new men formed a licenciadocracia; at the municipal level the cadres of the new order came from the peasant and small-town bourgeoisie. (Workers were conspicuous by their near-total absence from local office.) The winners rubbed shoulders with survivors of the older order, such as the caciques in Jalisco who ruled their ayuntamientos without recourse to party selection. An early 1960s sample of mayors found nearly half to have no party background, while 60 percent of the governors between 1946 and 1982 came from the federal public sector rather than the PRI.[59] To hefty numbers of all groups in provincial politics the party was, in short, of surprisingly low relevance. The new men—and the women who found different routes to political power, such as Urzúa Flores in Jalisco or "Chata la Ferrera" in Oaxaca City—purchased consent by channeling the benefits of development to their communities.[60]

But the new order also rested heavily on violence. Part of it was the popular violence of urban rioters like those who drove Manuel Bartlett Bautista out of the Tabasco governorship in 1955, which encouraged a certain central tactfulness in personnel selection.[61] A larger part was the straightforward and enduring violence of the state. Law and order remained fragile across large swathes of the countryside. In 1955 bandits took over and sacked Frontera, Tabasco; in the early 1970s Catholic crowds drove Protestants out of Chamula, Chiapas, in a major forced migration.[62] The Chamulas, staunch Priistas, were left alone; elsewhere, the petty massacres of which we know—and there will be plenty more of which we remain ignorant—continued in the more remote parts of the country, directed increasingly at other indigenous peoples such as the Huichols of western Jalisco, the Triquis of Oaxaca, or the luckless villagers of La Trinitaria in Chiapas.[63] These were the jobs of the army, "a glorified police force" who left politics at the national level but remained omnipresent outside Mexico City.[64] The military continued to perform a multiplicity of political roles, and whenever the civilian regime faced a serious threat they turned to soldiers: strike breakers and union heavies in the mines, oil refineries, and railway yards, scabs in khaki when doctors struck, classroom monitors with guns when students rebelled. Officers served as substitutes for imploding politicians (in Tabasco Bartlett was replaced by General Miguel Orrico de Llanos), outright assassins (shooting Rubén Jaramillo and his family), and mafiaesque enforcers (the dissident Alfonso Garzón abandoned campaigning in Baja California when a general told him he could become a household name too, just like Jaramillo).[65] Their violence was more centrally directed—the latter general was dispatched from the capital for this specific mission, and reinforcements were ordered to the Mexicali Valley—and the political autonomy of the generals was correspondingly lesser. A Turkish deep state this was not. The Faustian pact that underlay their services, however, and the critical need for soldier-policemen continued to favor military empire building; quite literally in the case of one southern colonel, who took fifteen men and set up an illegal mahogany camp across the border in Guatemala.[66]

There is not much exceptionalism in such local regimes, and at a local level parts of Mexico looked much like other parts of Latin America. There were Salvadorian levels of oligarchy in some of the coffee, forestry, and stockbreeding zones, such as the Quevedo family's homelands in Chihuahua; favela-like levels of inequality in some of the colonias populares of Acapulco, or Mexico City, or the fiber-making *ixtlero* ejidos of the arid north; a Guatemalan degree of indigenous political marginalization in the foothills of the Costa Chica; Argentine methods and degrees of mass murder in other parts of Guerrero.[67] Officers like Pablo Díaz in Morelos or Bonifacio Salinas Leal were aspiring personalist dictators, mainland Batistas; others, like Luis Alamillo Flores, perhaps more akin to the ideological militarists of the southern cone, convinced of the intrinsic superiority of military rule in dangerous times.[68] The spies who drew up documents like "the Invisible Tyranny," with its program for "a world dominated by an Invisible Tyranny that adopts the outward form of a democratic government" or the guerrerense congressmen who passed Decreto 29—which prescribed up to twelve years in prison for "diffusion of ideas, programs or plans tending to disturb public order"—shared the more Orwellian ambitions for thought control of the Argentine junta.[69] Miguel Alemán's extraordinarily overt corruption and ambitions for an extraconstitutional stay in power make him look more like a caudillo in civvies than any follower of the reglas no escritas.

But Mexico as a whole remained exceptional in critical aspects of its social and political development. Despite the common patterns of the postwar economies—an overvalued currency, inflationary pressures, import substitution industrialization, the shifts rightward, the transplanting of the American language of the Cold War—Mexico's midcentury rupture led the country in rather different directions. The most evident exception was the avoidance of military dictatorship, a deviant path that only Costa Rica shared, and one that continued on past the time of the dictablanda. In Chile Agustín Pinochet closed down the remaining parties, including his natural allies the Christian Democrats, in 1977; simultaneously in Mexico the Christian democrats of the PAN were winning more and more elections. In Argentina in the midseventies the military was kidnapping Leftists and sending them to La Perla, a death camp; in Mexico the government was funding a workers' university, the Universidad Obrera de México, and welcoming Leftist dissidents from across the hemisphere.[70] Behind this foundational divergence lay a cross-class suspicion of political generals, a legacy of the revolution, and its operationalization by an informal senate of military ex-presidents. The influence of Lázaro Cárdenas as a revolutionary force in office has long been revised downward: not very revolutionary according to the revisionists of the 1960s, and not much of a force either according to the postrevisionists of the nineties and aughts.[71] His influence as a revolutionary force out of office should be revised upward, however, because Cárdenas was the most influential member of the informal senate, exercising a veto on a harder-line or personalist dictatorship at least twice during his postpresidential career: in 1948 against the generals and in 1950 against Alemán.[72] The military paradoxically kept the military out of power, through an arrangement much like that between the government and Mexico's other social groups: collective bargaining, targeted distribution of wealth (or its removal), and a bounded laissez-faire.

In the new order that emerged out of the revolution's end there were strokes of institutional ingenuity, key among them no reelection and a party that was very broad and very shallow. Yet intelligent design by elites should not be overrated. The strange compacts of modern Mexican politics and society were more the products of evolution, the selective pressures of force and consent exerted by both rulers and ruled. The stabilization of the new regime should not be overrated either. The exercise of power remained a juggling act of fragile objects; neither a self-respecting authoritarian nor an imperial president would define politics, as Ruiz Cortines did, as "the art of toadying."[73] But the complex and malleable relations between Mexicans and their unrevolutionary governments allowed a crude and institutional stability to last rather a long time; longer than any other governing arrangement in Mexican history. The French revolution, Tocqueville wrote, ended up as a surrender of *liberté* in exchange for *égalité*.[74] The Mexican revolution ended in a more complicated transaction: the exchange of possibility for stability, with precious little equality and an ambiguously limited liberty. The benefits of a nebulous fraternity were supposed to—and to some extent did—compensate for those shortcomings. The sum was an unrevolutionary Mexico, a strange dictatorship in which rulers, and at times ruled, claimed to follow pragmatic paths to a higher ground.

Glossary

abigeo—cattle rustler
acarreados—members of a rent-a-crowd
afromestizo—a mestizo with some African ancestry
agraristas—peasant militants
alcabala—local taxes on goods, generally collected on roads or at market entrances
amparo—a wide-ranging writ of habeas corpus
apertura democrática—democratic spring
auscultación—taking the pulse of a potential party candidate's constituency
autodefensas—twenty-first-century community militia
ayuntamiento—town council
bola—the scrap, synonym for the armed revolution
braceros—Mexicans with government permits for seasonal labor in the United States
bronco—wild, untamed
cabecera municipal—the seat of government of a municipality
cacicazgo—the territory run by a cacique
cacique/cacica—local or regional boss
camarilla—high-level, narrow, and tight-knit faction; cross between kitchen cabinet and old boys club
camiones de redilas—cattle trucks or pickups, doubling as local buses
Cardenista—a follower of President Lázaro Cárdenas, 1943–40
cargada—the stampede of politicians to join forces with a candidate once they are known to be the preferred of the higher-ups
carro completo—an election decided uncompromisingly in favor of one faction's candidates, a whitewash/full house
chambas—cushy job with minimal demands, usually the fruit of patronage
colonias agrícolas/militares—government land grants that are not subject to control by the Ministry of Agrarian Reform

colonias populares—peripheral housing areas, often illegal, for the poor; sometimes, but not universally, slums
comisariado ejidal—the ejido's three-person board of directors
comisario municipal—the town council's representative in subject villages
condueñazgos—legally recognized, generally indigenous, collective landholding
consejo municipal—a town council appointed by a governor as opposed to elected by the public
constitucionales—general elections for public office, as opposed to party primaries
convocatoria—a party's call for candidates to register for a primary election
corrido—folk song, often political
costeños—people from the coast
cuota de poder—a group's acknowledged share of political positions in a given political institution
defensa social/rural—popular militia, usually institutionalized as army reservists
desamortización—disentailment; compulsory privatization and division of communal lands
dictablanda—a soft dictatorship
ejidatario—member of an ejido
ejido—farming community and the land it holds in usufruct from the state
faena—unpaid community labor, sometimes voluntary, sometimes a corvée tax
fiebra aftosa—foot-and-mouth disease
fiestas patrias—the September celebrations of Independence
foco guerrillero—small rebel enclave from which, in Régis Debray's theory, a state can be captured through guerrilla warfare
ganaderos—stockbreeders
Gobernación—the Interior Ministry, the center of day-to-day government
guardias blancas—conservative militias
guerra sucia—the dirty war conducted against guerrillas in the 1960s and 1970s, with particular reference to the state of Guerrero
guerrerenses—people from the state of Guerrero
hacendado—owner of an hacienda, a large agricultural estate
historia patria—nationalist history
indígenas—blanket term for indigenous people or peoples
indigenista—a proponent of policy (or rhetoric) intended to favor indigenous people
informe—the annual presidential address to the nation
ixtleros—producers of fiber/twine from a species of agave, the *ixtle*
jarochos—people from Veracruz
jefe militar—local commander-in-chief
jefe político—a nineteenth- / early-twentieth-century political boss, answerable directly to the president
junta computadora—organization in charge of the vote count

La Liga—shorthand for the Liga de Comunidades Agrarias, a powerful peasants' union

ley fuga—the justice of "shot while trying to escape," i.e., extrajudicial execution

licenciado—one who has a degree; more generally a term of deference for a bureaucrat

maestro—a teacher; also a term of respect for an intellectual of any level

México profundo—the world of hidden continuities of indigenous cultures, a concept developed by the anthropologist Guillermo Bonfil Batalla

municipio—basic unit of government, broadly equivalent to a county

orientación—political guidance toward support for a candidate favored by the hierarchy

Panista—member of the Partido Acción Nacional, the Christian democrat opposition

Patria—the Fatherland

patria chica—"the small fatherland," i.e., village or small region that draws a person's affective allegiance

pistoleros—gunmen great and small

presidente municipal—mayor

Priista—member of the Partido Revolucionario Institucional, the state party

primarias—primary elections inside a party, also known as *internas*

principales—village elders

problema electoral—the "electoral problem," i.e., how to get the elites' favored candidates decorously elected

pueblo—a village or, in the abstract, the people

regente—the equivalent of a governor or mayor of Mexico City, a presidential appointee

regidor—town councilor

registro civil—the civil registry where local governments record births, marriages, and deaths

reglas no escritas—the universally understood unwritten rules of political life

rifle sanitario—the slaughter of livestock in the campaign against foot-and-mouth disease

rurales—nineteenth-century paramilitary rural police

serrano—n.: a man of the mountains; adj.: of the mountains

sexenio—the six-year presidential term

Sinarquista—member of the far-right Unión Nacional Sinarquista

temporal—seasonal rainland

tierra de riego—irrigated land

tierra fría—highlands above two thousand meters

tierra templada—temperate hill country

tinterillo—(pejorative) a pen pusher, low-level office worker

tlacolol—hillside swidden land

veracruzanos—people from the state of Veracruz

vicios tradicionales—(pejorative) generally elite term for plebeian pursuits (which they share) of drinking, gambling, brawling, cockfighting, and whoring

la Violencia—Colombia's bloody midcentury civil war (1948–1958)

Notes

Introduction

1. And the title of a putrid Vicente Fernández film from 1979. For an overview emphasizing the *idiosincrasia,* see Alan Knight, "The Peculiarities of Mexican History: Mexico Compared to Latin America, 1821–1992," *Journal of Latin American Studies* 24: Quincentenary Supplement (1992): 99–144.

2. Extensive land reform in Bolivia and Peru was nowhere near as extensive as in Mexico, and neither was the dramatic social mobility—initially, at least—in the ruling class.

3. As Frank Tannenbaum first put it, there was no Lenin in Mexico. Sarah Osten has shown how the socialist parties of the south fulfilled something of that role in the first half of the twenties, exercising a lasting organizational influence over the later single party; their socialism, however, proved dispensable. Emilio Kourí, ed., *En busca de Molina Enríquez: Cien años de los grandes problemas nacionales* (Mexico City: Colegio de México, 2009), 14; Sarah Osten, *The Mexican Revolution's Wake: The Making of a Political System, 1920–1929* (Cambridge: Cambridge University Press, 2018), 345–56.

4. Dangerous, E. H. Carr argued, for their utopianism in the 1920s and dystopianism in the 1930s, the "abrupt descent . . . from a utopia which took little account of the reality to a reality from which every element of utopia was rigorously excluded." E. H. Carr, *The Twenty Years' Crisis, 1919–1939: An Introduction to the Study of International Relations* (London: Palgrave Macmillan, 2016 [1939]), 207. On the crowd-sourced nature of the constitution and its relative unimportance to the government that drafted it, see Alan Knight, *The Mexican Revolution*, 2 vols. (Lincoln: University of Nebraska Press, 1990), 2:469–71, and the essays by Felipe Arturo Ávila Espinosa, Miles Rodríguez, and Israel Arroyo García in Catherine Andrews, ed., *La tradición constitucional en México (1808–1940)* (Mexico City: Librería CIDE, 2018), 215–60, 303–24.

5. Genaro Vázquez was similarly heterodox. Alexander Aviña, *Specters of Revolution: Peasant Guerrillas in the Mexican Cold War Countryside* (Oxford: Oxford University

Press, 2014), 43–44, 163–64, 169, 211; Tanalís Padilla, *Rural Resistance in the Land of Zapata: The Jaramillista Movement and the Myth of the Pax Priista, 1940–1962* (Durham: Duke University Press, 2008), 44, 49.

6. Jason H. Dormady, *Primitive Revolution: Restorationist Religion and the Idea of the Mexican Revolution, 1940–1968* (Albuquerque: University of New Mexico Press, 2011), 33.

7. François Furet, *Marx and the French Revolution* (Chicago: University of Chicago Press, 1966), 66.

8. Or, in the case of neozapatismo, kabuki theater. This is not to downplay the human cost of the brutal counterinsurgency of the Dirty Wars, but rather the guerillas' chances of—and questionable aspirations for—revolutionary takeover. In terms of farce, the 1929 Escobar Rebellion (dubbed the "railroad and bank" rebellion because Escobar and co. robbed only the banks and took the train to the border), the 1938 Cedillo Rebellion (in which a reluctant leader was hounded into revolt), the 1946 Jaramillista Rebellion (an "armed hiding" that at one point had rebels surrounding Zacatepec, waiting for a signal to attack that never came), the 1947 Balsas Rebellion (where the rebels were stood up by half their group), and the 1961 rising of Celestino Gasca (described by the government as "delirios más propios de un 'alienista' que de las autoridades") all had elements of the form. John Foster Dulles, *Yesterday in Mexico: A Chronicle of the Revolution, 1919–1936* (Austin: University of Texas Press, 1961); Dudley Ankerson, *Agrarian Warlord: Saturnino Cedillo and the Mexican Revolution in San Luis Potosí* (DeKalb: Northern Illinois University Press, 1984), 186–88; Padilla, *Rural Resistance,* 145, 147; Elisa Servín, "Hacia el levantamiento armado: Del henriquismo a los federacionistas leales en los años cincuenta," in Verónica Oikión Solano and Marta Eugenia García Ugarte, eds., *Movimientos armados en México, siglo XX,* 3 vols. (Mexico City: Colegio de Michoacán/CIESAS, 2008), 2:313. The revolution also produced one excellent literal farce, Jorge Ibargüengoitia's *Los relámpagos de agosto* (Mexico City: Joaquín Mortiz, 2003 [1964]).

9. Paul Gillingham and Benjamin T. Smith, "Introduction: The Paradoxes of Revolution," in Paul Gillingham and Benjamin T. Smith, eds., *Dictablanda: Politics, Work, and Culture in Mexico, 1938–1968* (Durham: Duke University Press, 2014), 6.

10. For Jaime Pensado and Enrique Ochoa the concept is misleadingly pacific, "abating the magnitude of state repression that characterized the 1960s and '70s." The latter decade is not one to which the label was applied. To Louise Walker it is insufficiently violent and insufficiently hegemonic all at once. Jaime M. Pensado and Enrique C. Ochoa, *México beyond 1968: Revolutionaries, Radicals, and Repression during the Global Sixties and Subversive Seventies* (Tucson: University of Arizona Press, 2018), introduction. Louise E. Walker, review of Gillingham and Smith, "Dictablanda," *Hispanic American Historical Review* 95, no. 4 (2015): 692–94.

11. Soledad Loaeza, "Sobre Paul Gillingham y Benjamin T. Smith (eds.), Dictablanda: Politics, Work, and Culture in Mexico 1938–1968," *Historia Mexicana* 65, no. 3 (2013):

1512; Guillermo O'Donnell and Philippe C. Schmitter, *Transitions from Authoritarian Rule: Tentative Conclusions about Uncertain Democracies* (Baltimore: Johns Hopkins University Press, 2013), 8–14; Daniel Cosío Villegas quoted in Enrique Krauze, *Místico de la autoridad: Porfirio Díaz* (Mexico City: Fondo de Cultura Económica, 1987), 34.

12. Walker, "Dictablanda," 694.

13. Rogelio Hernández Rodríguez, *El centro dividido: La nueva autonomía de los gobernadores* (Mexico City: Colegio de México, 2009), 39, 71.

14. Joy K. Langston, *Democratization and Authoritarian Party Survival: Mexico's PRI* (Oxford: Oxford University Press, 2017), chap. 3; pers. com., John Womack Jr., July 3, 2012.

15. Benjamin T. Smith, "Who Governed? Grassroots Politics in Mexico under the Partido Revolucionario Institucional, 1958–1970," *Past and Present* 225, no. 4 (2014): 258.

16. I.e., a Swiss cheese, a puffer fish, or a philanthropic ogre. Alan Knight, "Historical Continuities in Social Movements," in Joe Foweraker and Ann L. Craig, eds., *Popular Movements and Political Change in Mexico* (Boulder: Lynne Rienner Publications, 1990), 100; Paul Gillingham, "Maximino's Bulls: Popular Protest after the Mexican Revolution," *Past and Present* 206, no. 1 (2010): 145–81; Octavio Paz, *The Labyrinth of Solitude* (London: Penguin, 1990), 377.

17. Gilbert Joseph, Anne Rubenstein, and Eric Zolov, "Assembling the Fragments: Writing a Cultural History of Mexico since 1940," in Gilbert Joseph, Anne Rubenstein, and Eric Zolov, eds., *Fragments of a Golden Age: The Politics of Culture in Mexico since 1940* (Durham: Duke University Press, 2001), 15.

18. Sergio Aguayo, *El 68: Los estudiantes, el presidente y la CIA* (Mexico City: Ideas y Palabras, 2018); Susana Draper, *1968 Mexico: Constellations of Freedom and Democracy* (Durham: Duke University Press, 2018); Patrick Iber, *Neither Peace nor Freedom: The Cultural Cold War in Latin America* (Cambridge: Harvard University Press, 2015); Renata Keller, *Mexico's Cold War: Cuba, the United States, and the Legacy of the Mexican Revolution* (Cambridge: Cambridge University Press, 2015); Jaime M. Pensado, *Rebel Mexico: Student Unrest and Authoritarian Political Culture during the Long Sixties* (Stanford: Stanford University Press, 2013); Pensado and Ochoa, *México Beyond 1968*.

19. Aviña, *Specters of Revolution;* Padilla, *Rural Resistance;* Benjamin T. Smith, *The Mexican Press and Civil Society, 1940–1976: Stories from the Newsroom, Stories from the Street* (Chapel Hill: University of North Carolina Press, 2018); Roberto Alegre, *Railroad Radicals: Gender, Class, and Memory in Cold War Mexico* (Lincoln: University of Nebraska Press, 2013); Aaron W. Navarro, *Political Intelligence and the Creation of Modern Mexico, 1938–1954* (University Park: Pennsylvania State Press, 2010); the assorted essays in Tanalís Padilla and Louise E. Walker, guest editors, "Dossier: Spy Reports: Content, Methodology, and Historiography in Mexico's Secret Police Archive," *Journal of Iberian and Latin American Research* 19, no. 1 (2013); Fernando Herrera Calderón and Adela Cedillo, eds., *Challenging Authoritarianism in Mexico: Revolutionary Struggles and the Dirty War, 1964–1982* (New York: Routledge, 2012).

20. Blanca Torres, *Hacia la utopía industrial* (Mexico City: Colegio de México, 1984); Luis Medina, *Historia de la Revolución Mexicana, 1940–1952: Civilismo y modernización del autoritarismo* (Mexico City: Colegio de México, 1979).

21. Luis Aboites Aguilar, *Excepciones y privilegios: Modernización tributaria y centralización en México, 1922–1972* (Mexico City: Colegio de México, 2003); Jorge Alonso, *El rito electoral en Jalisco, 1940–1992* (Mexico City: CIESAS, 1993); Tiziana Bertaccini, *El régimen priista frente a las clases medias, 1943–1964* (Mexico City: Consejo Nacional para la Cultura y las Artes, 2009); Heather Fowler-Salamini, *Working Women, Entrepreneurs and the Mexican Revolution: The Coffee Culture of Córdoba, Veracruz* (Lincoln: University of Nebraska Press, 2013); Rogelio Hernández Rodríguez, *Historia mínima del PRI* (Mexico City: Colegio de México, 2016); Rogelio Hernández Rodríguez, *La formación del político mexicano: el caso de Carlos A. Madrazo* (Mexico City: Colegio de México, 1991); Soledad Loaeza, *El Partido de Acción Nacional: La larga marcha, 1939–1994* (Mexico City: Fondo de Cultura Económica, 2000); Stephen R. Niblo, *Mexico in the 1940s: Modernity, Politics and Corruption* (Wilmington, DE: Scholarly Resources, 1999); Thomas Rath, *Myths of Demilitarization in Postrevolutionary Mexico, 1920–1960* (Chapel Hill: University of North Carolina Press, 2013); Ariel Rodríguez Kurí, “Los años maravillosos: Adolfo Ruiz Cortines,” in Will Fowler, ed., *Gobernantes mexicanos* (Mexico City: Fondo de Cultura Económica, 2008), 2:263–86; Elisa Servín, *La oposición política: la otra cara del siglo XX mexicano* (Mexico City: Fondo de Cultura Económica, 2006); Benjamin T. Smith, *Pistoleros and Popular Movements: The Politics of State Formation in Postrevolutionary Oaxaca* (Lincoln: University of Nebraska Press, 2009).

22. Beatriz Magaloni, *Voting for Autocracy: Hegemonic Party Survival and Its Demise in Mexico* (Cambridge: Cambridge University Press, 2006), 82–85. An exception is the neat symmetry of the case of Antonio Jaramillo, the agrarista who—unlike his dissident and guerrilla brothers, both murdered—came to a mutually rewarding accommodation with the state. Gladys McCormick, *The Logic of Compromise in Mexico: How the Countryside Was Key to the Emergence of Authoritarianism* (Chapel Hill: University of North Carolina Press, 2016), 102–5.

23. Presented as wartime exigency but never revoked, rather like Britain’s Defense of the Realm Act (DORA), which placed authoritarian limits on bars—forced to close at 11:00—that lasted until the end of the twentieth century.

24. Alan Knight, “The End of the Mexican Revolution? From Cárdenas to Avila Camacho, 1937–1941,” in Gillingham and Smith, *Dictablanda*, 47–63, 50. José Itturiaga dates the end of the revolution to 1943. Torres, *Hacia la utopía industrial*, 19.

25. Halbert Jones, *The War Has Brought Peace to Mexico: World War II and the Consolidation of the Post-Revolutionary State* (Albuquerque: University of New Mexico Press, 2014), 9; Rath, *Myths of Demilitarization*, 75–77; Roberto Blancarte, “Intransigence, Anticommunism, and Reconciliation: Church/State Relations in Transition,” in Gillingham and Smith, *Dictablanda*, 78.

26. See below, chapter 9.

27. Jordi Díez, "Civil–Military Relations in Mexico: The Unfinished Transition," in Roderic Ai Camp, ed., *The Oxford Handbook of Mexican Politics* (Oxford: Oxford University Press, 2012), 266.

28. Tzvi Medin, *El minimato presidencial: historia política del maximato* (Mexico City: Colegio de México, 1982), 106.

29. Some 734, many by textile and mining workers. Kevin J. Middlebrook, *The Paradox of Revolution: Labor, the State, and Authoritarianism in Mexico* (Baltimore: Johns Hopkins University Press, 1995), 171.

30. Nathan L. Whetten, *Rural Mexico* (Chicago: University of Chicago Press, 1948), 501–9.

31. Edgar J. Hoover to Assistant Secretary of State Borle, 09/14/1943, NARG-812.00/32203. (This and all subsequent primary source dates follow the month/day/year format.)

32. Frederik Logevall, "Bernard Fall: The Man Who Knew the War," *New York Times*, 02/17/2017.

33. *Novedades*, 03/06/1984.

34. The idea that Avila Camacho's dullness masked political shrewdness is appealing but questionable. Jones, *The War Has Brought Peace*, 28, 216–17.

35. Estimates of the casualties of the guerra sucia (1964–82) suggest between four hundred and three thousand disappearances, the latter significantly more than the c. two thousand disappeared in Pinochet's Chile, with similar stories of kidnappings, torture, sexual violence, and death flights. "Concentrado General Desaparecidos" Fiscal Especial para Movimientos Sociales y Políticos del Pasado (FEMOSPP), draft report, 2006, https://nsarchive2.gwu.edu//NSAEBB/NSAEBB180/index2.htm; Herrera Calderón and Cedillo, eds., *Challenging Authoritarianism*, 8. For general treatments of state violence in the period, see, among others, Laura Castellano, *México armado, 1943–1981* (Mexico City: Ediciones Era, 2007); Carlos Montemayor, *La Violencia del estado en Mexico: Antes y después del 1968* (Mexico City: Random House Debate, 2010); Jorge Luis Sierra Guzmán, *El enemigo interno: contrainsurgencia y fuerzas armadas en México* (Mexico City: Plaza y Valdés, 2003). For soldiers in politics, see Raúl Benítez Manaut, "México: Avances y límites de las relaciones civiles–militares ante la democratización Los retos de 2013," in Javier Garciadiego, coord., *El Ejército Mexicano: 100 años de historia* (Mexico City: Colegio de México, 2014), 411–54; Rath, *Myths of Demilitarization*. For the *Brave New World* fantasies of some bureaucrats, see Jacinto Rodríguez Munguía, "'The Invisible Tyranny'; or, the Origin of the 'Perfect Dictatorship,' " in Paul Gillingham, Michael Lettieri, and Benjamin T. Smith, eds., *Journalism, Satire, and Censorship in Mexico* (Albuquerque: University of New Mexico Press, 2018), 183–202.

36. When manifesting its independence the Secretaría de Relaciones Exteriores tended to throw the US a bone, getting the US's anti-Soviet resolution onto the agenda at the 1954 Caracas Conference so that it might pass and then abstaining during voting, or likewise abstaining from the vote to expel Cuba at the 1962 meeting of the OAS while inveighing

against Marxist–Leninism. Ashley Black, "The Politics of Asylum: Caribbean Revolutionaries, Humanitarianism, and Foreign Policy in Mexico, 1944–1961" (Ph.D. diss., Stony Brook University, 2018), 18. The relationship with the CIA began in 1958, when incoming president Adolfo López Mateos had breakfast with the CIA station chief, Winston Scott, and continued through the presidency of Gustavo Díaz Ordaz. The two presidents witnessed Scott's civil marriage. Scott was an unreliable witness who was brought home in the end for going native, so one might wonder who was playing whom in these relationships; but CIA documents attest to the program he set up, LITEMPO, that claimed these two presidents and other key figures—including Luis Echeverría and the head of the Dirección Federal de Seguridad—as salaried agents; Díaz Ordaz was LITEMPO-1. Unconfessably close relations had begun at least a decade earlier, with Alemán's secretary and éminence grise Rogelio de la Selva promising the US embassy to help them in any way he could if he managed to get Alemán reelected. According to Steve Niblo, the embassy held veto power over foreign loans to Mexico from the start of the sexenio. Aguayo, *El 68*, 16–19; Burrows to State, 01/31/1951, NARG-71200/1-3151; Niblo, *Mexico in the 1940s*, 174.

37. Castro reciprocated, publicly praising the Mexican Revolution while privately despising its heirs and using—against the two governments' tacit agreement—Mexican territory for transshipping guns and revolutionaries. Keller, *Mexico's Cold War*, 73–74, 156-65, 192–95.

38. Historical GDP per capita rankings 1950 and 1973, after Angus Maddison, at www.nationmaster.com; Klaus Deininger and Lyn Squire, "A New Data Set Measuring Income Inequality," *World Bank Economic Review* 10 (1996): 565–91.

39. Vazquéz, US embassy to State, 08/11/1960, NARG-712.00/8-1160; Sullivan to Foreign Office, 07/16/1956, FO371/AM1015/13.

40. For a lengthier review of the exceptional aspects of Mexican history which argues that Mexico "jumped the rails" of Latin American comparatives in 1910, see Alan Knight, "The Peculiarities of Mexican History: Mexico Compared to Latin America, 1821–1992," *Journal of Latin American Studies* 24: Quincentenary Supplement (1992): 99–144, 103. For critiques, see Peter H. Smith, "Mexican Democracy in Comparative Perspective," in Camp, ed., *The Oxford Handbook of Mexican Politics*, 77–100, and—in its commentary on the "Revolution to Evolution" and "Revolution to Demolition" versions, different and normative stories from the one here—Arthur Schmidt, "Making It Real Compared to What? Reconceptualizing Mexican History since 1940," in Joseph, Rubenstein, and Zolov, *Fragments of a Golden Age*, 23–70. For Mexico as a precocious and distinctive example of a hybrid regime, see Gillingham and Smith, *Dictablanda*, vii–44.

41. Avila Camacho owned property in Veracruz and relied increasingly on a group of veracruzano politicians headed by Miguel Alemán in the Secretaría de Gobernación.

42. Gonzalo N. Santos, *Memorias* (Mexico City: Grijalbo, 1984), 650.

43. On 20 May 1952, for example, Alemán, Cárdenas, and Henríquez Guzmán were all in Acapulco. Cárdenas to De la Fuente, 05/20/1952, AGN/DFS-Guerrero-100-10-14-52H313L4.

44. On the enduring autonomy of governors, see Hernández Rodríguez, *El centro dividido*, 11–17.

45. And is not wholly original; Eduardo Blanquel has suggested 1943–52 as a coherent period in Mexico's political history. In spanning Alemán's securing of the presidential candidacy and life after the break with his successor, it also offers a more complete account of the Alemán years than that afforded by a classic sexenio chronology. Eduardo Blanquel, "Esquema de una Periodización de la Historia Política del México Contemporáneo," in James W. Wilkie et al., eds., *Contemporary Mexico: Papers of the IV International Congress of Mexican History* (Berkeley: University of California Press, 1973), 728–29.

46. For the metaphor of Hapsburg facets to the modern Mexican state, see Alan Knight, "The Mexican State, Porfirian and Revolutionary, 1876–1930," in Miguel A. Centeno and Agustín E. Ferraro, eds., *State and Nation Making in Latin America: Republics of the Possible* (Princeton: Princeton University Press, 2013), 116–38.

47. Sullivan to Morgan Man, Foreign & Commonwealth Office, 02/22/1956, FCO37/AM1015/4.

48. A further criterion was the existence, for all bar San Jerónimo, of a corpus of memoirs and histories. These local studies constitute a small sample and are nothing like as detailed as ethnographies or microhistories. They are, on the other hand, indispensable entry points to grassroots politics, sites for studying the activities of regional governments (particularly useful in Guerrero, whose state archive is distinctly poor), and controls on the generalizations advanced.

49. The reports on 1940s Veracruz, for example, demand particular sensitivity as agents were reporting to Miguel Alemán, who, while secretario de Gobernación and president, was simultaneously the main cacique of that state. PS-10 to Gobernación, 10/3/1939, AGN/DGIPS-140/9. For considerations on the use of the archives, see Tanalís Padilla and Louise E. Walker, "In the Archives: History and Politics," *Journal of Iberian and Latin American Research* 19, no.1 (2013): 1–10.

50. Navarro, *Political Intelligence*, 186, and "El ejército mexicano en la época de la posguerra: el argumento égida," in Javier Garciadiego, coord., *El Ejército Mexicano: 100 años de historia* (Mexico City: Colegio de México, 2014). For a more skeptical history, see Sergio Aguayo Quezada, *La Charola: una historia de los servicios de inteligencia en México* (Mexico City: Grijalbo, 2001).

51. Excluding Mexico City, where their presence was reinforced by other actors such as the Servicio Secreto and was significantly heavier. Rath, *Myths of Demilitarization*, 99; "Relación de los inspectores de la DGIPS comisionados en diversos estados de la República para observar el desarrollo de las elecciones de poderes federales," June 1952, AGN/DGIPS-814/2-1/52/70; Hernández Rodríguez, *El centro dividido*, 65. Compare such low numbers of agents with the strength of East Germany's Ministerium für Staatssicherheit (Stasi), which employed 2,700 agents in 1950 and 22,843 by 1960. Mike Dennis, *The Stasi: Myth and Reality* (London: Routledge, 2003), 78.

52. At its 1943 peak the FBI had twenty-one agents in Ecuador. Marc Becker, *The FBI in Latin America: The Ecuador Files* (Durham: Duke University Press, 2017), 43.

53. "Relación del personal" and "Projecto de cambio de personal," AGN/DGIPS-1980/1950–61A.

54. James C. Scott, *Domination and the Arts of Resistance* (New Haven: Yale University Press, 1990), 210.

55. I-33 to Manuel Antonio Ortilla, 07/25/1945, AGN/DGIPS-788/2-1/45/347; J. M. Martínez to Alemán, July 1952, AGN/DGG-110B/2/311P(29)2.

56. The classic works focus on the revolutionary period and are led by Mary Kay Vaughan, *Cultural Politics in Revolution: Teachers, Peasants, and Schools in Mexico, 1930–1940* (Tucson: University of Arizona Press, 1997); Jeffrey W. Rubin, *Decentering the Regime: Ethnicity, Radicalism, and Democracy in Juchitán, Mexico* (Durham: Duke University Press, 1997); and Gilbert M. Joseph and Daniel Nugent, eds., *Everyday Forms of State Formation: Revolution and the Negotiation of Rule in Modern Mexico* (Durham: Duke University Press, 1994). In their influential deployment of the framework for the period after 1940 Joseph, Rubenstein, and Zolov propose that there was a "relative continuity of political practice and . . . relative stability of social hierarchies" and that this demanded a cultural project without which "the PRI's economic and political project would surely have failed." Joseph, Rubenstein, and Zolov, "Assembling the Fragments," 15.

57. Gramsci acknowledged that hegemony involved give and take but specified strict limits to the giving of the governing class: "The fact of hegemony presupposes that account be taken of the interests and the tendencies of the groups over which hegemony is to be exercised, and that a certain compromise equilibrium should be formed—in other words, that the leading group should make sacrifices of an economic–corporate kind. But there is also no doubt that such sacrifices and such a compromise cannot touch the essential." When, where, or even whether the compromises between rulers and ruled in Mexico touched the essential are central questions for understanding the country after 1940. Antonio Gramsci, *Selections from the Prison Notebooks* (London: Lawrence and Wishart, 1996), 161.

1. Archipelagos of Power: Guerrero

1. While Paucić is sometimes remembered as an Austrian his surname is either Bosnian or Croatian, and he is held to have come originally from Trieste. He was probably one of the regional elites who were customarily educated in Vienna during the late Austro-Hungarian Empire. Author's interview, Hermilo Castorena, Chilpancingo, 11/26/1997; Alvaro López Miramontes, "Panorama historiográfica del estado de Guerrero," in Alvaro López Miramontes et al., *Ensayos para la historia del estado de Guerrero* (Chilpancingo: Instituto Guerrerense de la Cultura, 1985), 23; Jaime Salazar Adame, "Alejandro Wladimir Paucic Smerdau: Un investigador anónimo del Estado de Guer-

rero." Paper given at the Seminario de estudios sobre Guerrero, Universidad Autónoma de Guerrero, Mexico City, 08/4/2009.

2. AP108/320.32PER.

3. John W. Webber, "Down Mexico's Río Balsas," *National Geographic Magazine* 90, no. 2 (1946): 253.

4. Author's interviews, Edgar Pavía Guzmán, Chilpancingo, 04/04–05/2002.

5. Count Klemens von Metternich's description of Italy: "A geographical expression, a useful shorthand description but without political significance." Walter Laquer, *After the Fall: The End of the European Dream and the Decline of a Continent* (London: Macmillan, 2012), 295.

6. Dirección General de Estadística, *Censo y división territorial de población del estado de Guerrero verificados el 28 de octubre de 1900* (Mexico City: Dirección General de Estadística, 1905), 4.

7. Eduardo Miranda Arrieta, *Economía y comunicaciones en el Estado de Guerrero, 1877–1910* (Michoacán: Universidad Michoacana de San Nicolás de Hidalgo, 1994), 137–68; V. de Paúl Andrade, "Un viaje a Chilapa leído en la sesión del 22 de abril de 1911," in Carlos Illades and Martha Ortega, eds., *Guerrero: textos de su historia* (Mexico City: Instituto de Investigaciones Dr. José Maria Luis Mora, 1989), 2:163–66; Ian Jacobs, *Ranchero Revolt: The Mexican Revolution in Guerrero* (Austin: University of Texas Press, 1982), xiii, 36.

8. Robert S. Wicks and Roland H. Harrison, *Buried Cities, Forgotten Gods: William Niven's Life of Discovery and Revolution in Mexico and the American Southwest* (Lubbock: Texas Tech University Press, 1999), 135–40.

9. An isolationist strategy also followed by the coffee and sugar planters of north-central Chiapas. Aaron Bobrow-Strain, *Intimate Enemies: Landowners, Power, and Violence in Chiapas* (Durham: Duke University Press, 2007), 65–66.

10. Mario Gill, "Los Escudero, de Acapulco," *Historia Mexicana* 3, no. 4 (1953): 292.

11. Alexander von Humboldt, *Political Essay on the Kingdom of New Spain,* 3 vols., trans. John Black (London, 1814), 1:xxvi.

12. INAH/AS-PHO/CUAUH/5/15, 72.

13. *Censo 1900,* 16; Sansalvador to DEF Chilpancingo, 04/29/1927, SEP/DGEP-1668/iv-4(727.1)5.

14. Edward William Nelson, "A Winter Expedition in Southwestern Mexico," *National Geographic Magazine* 15, no. 9 (1904): 354.

15. Instructions to agents for travel in Guerrero, 1932, AGN/DGIPS-173/311(7.1)"32."

16. The governor who levied it, Hector F. López, was deposed shortly thereafter, thanks in part to this fiscal fiasco. Report, political situation Guerrero, 05/28/1926, AGN/DGIPS-136/310(7.1)1; Vicente Carreto Leyva to Baltazar Leyva Mancilla, 01/24/1947, AHEG-ramo ejecutivo/53/13.

17. Rand McNally, *1938 Auto Road Atlas of the United States, Canada, and Mexico* (Chicago: Rand McNally, 1938), 94.

18. Webber, "Down Mexico's Río Balsas," 254.

19. Ministerio de Fomento, *Censo del Estado de Guerrero (1895)* (Mexico City, 1899), 50.

20. In September 1891 two traveling merchants were killed in Alahuitzlán, Aldama, by bandits. *Periódico Oficial del Gobierno del Estado de Guerrero,* 04/11/1891.

21. Moisés T. de la Peña, *Guerrero Económico,* 2 vols. (Chilpancingo: Gobierno del Estado de Guerrero, 1949), 2:599–601.

22. The noun "Indian" is used throughout to refer to indigenous peoples either when specific ethnic identities are unavailable in the sources or when the term refers to multiple ethnicities. While the term can be pejorative it is also one that has extensive emic usage across both mestizo and indigenous societies in Mexico and one that has no other simple equivalent in English.

23. Marie Robinson Wright, *Picturesque Mexico* (Philadelphia: J. B. Lippincott, 1897), 330–32; Louis Lejeune, *Tierras mexicanas* (Mexico City: Consejo Nacional para la Cultura y las Artes, 1995), 186–89; Alfonso Luis Velasco, "Los recursos materiales," reproduced in Illades and Ortega, *Guerrero,* 2:88–99; Wicks and Harrison, *Buried Cities, Forgotten Gods,* 127–28; *Periódico Oficial,* no. 41, 1891; Jaime Salazar Adame, "Periodo 1867–1910," in Jaime Salazar Adame, ed., *Historia de la cuestión agraria mexicana: estado de Guerrero, 1867–1940* (Mexico: Gobierno del Estado de Guerrero, 1987), 62.

24. Such revisionism is not confined to Guerrero. Margaret Chowning, "Reassessing the Prospects for Profit in Nineteenth-Century Mexican Agriculture from a Regional Perspective: Michoacán, 1810–1860," in Stephen H. Haber, ed., *How Latin America Fell Behind: Essays on the Economic Histories of Brazil and Mexico, 1800–1914* (Stanford: Stanford University Press, 1997), 179–215; Richard J. Salvucci, "Mexican National Income in the Era of Independence, 1800–40," in Haber, ed., *How Latin America Fell Behind,* 216–42.

25. María Teresa Pavía Guzmán, "Hacía una nueva historia de la economía suriana del siglo XIX," in Tomás Bustamante Alvarez and Sergio Sarmiento Silva, eds., *El Sur en movimiento: la reinvención de Guerrero del siglo XXI* (Chilpancingo: Consejo de Ciencia y Tecnología del Estado de Guerrero, 2001), 111–26.

26. Peter Guardino, *Peasants, Politics and the Formation of Mexico's National State: Guerrero, 1800–1857* (Stanford: Stanford University Press, 1996), 110–23; Antonio Peñafiel, *Anuario estadístico de la República Mexicana 1907* (Mexico City: Dirección General de Estadística, 1912), 547; Jacobs, *Ranchero Revolt,* 37; *Periódico Oficial,* no. 74, 1890; Velasco, "Los recursos materiales," 93; Pavía Guzmán, "Hacía una nueva historia de la economía suriana," 111–26; Danièle Dehouve, *Cuando los banqueros eran santos: historia económica y social de la provincia de Tlapa, Guerrero* (Chilpancingo: Universidad Autónoma del Estado de Guerrero, 2002), 67–69, 73, 216.

27. Renato Ravelo Lecuona, "Período 1910–1920," in Salazar Adame, *La Cuestión Agraria Mexicana,* 96–97; INAH/AS-PHO/CUAUH/5, 14.

28. Moisés González Navarro, *Estadísticas sociales del Porfiriato, 1877–1910* (Mexico City: Dirección General de Estadística, 1956), 9.

29. INEGI, *Estadísticas históricas de México* CD-ROM (Mexico City: Instituto Nacional de Estadística y Geografía, 2000).

30. The Ometepec elite maintained small plots in the town's *fundo legal;* in Ixcateopan, Salvador Rodríguez Juárez, the village doctor, kept six hectares in nearby Los Huayabos. Assorted correspondence, 12/15/1937 to 03/27/1940, AGN/LCR/404.1/6292; padrón de predios agrícolas, AMI-1939/1.

31. Jacobs, *Ranchero Revolt,* 34.

32. Mario Appelius, *El Aguila de Chapultepec: México bajo los aspectos geográfico, histórico, étnico, político, natural, social y económico* (Barcelona: Maucci, 1931), 356.

33. Frank Sinatra, "Come Fly With Me" (Capitol Records, 1958); Codoner to State Department, July 1945, NARG-812.00/7-3145.

34. Ben Fallaw, *Religion and State Formation in Postrevolutionary Mexico* (Durham: Duke University Press, 2013), 112.

35. Monthly report, Ixcateopan to *jefe político,* October 1889, AMI-1889.

36. To Ben Fallaw the metaphor also applies to the institutional presence of the church, dispersed across a "levitical archipelago" of urban islands such as Chilapa, Iguala, Olinalá, Azoyú, and Ometepec. Fallaw, *Religion and State Formation,* 108, 133.

37. De la Peña, *Guerrero Económico,* 2:159.

38. Tomás Bustamante Alvarez, *Las transformaciones de la agricultura o las paradojas del desarrollo regional: Tierra Caliente, Guerrero* (Mexico City: Procuradoría Agraria, 1996), 64–66.

39. Lejeune, *Tierras mexicanas,* 181–89; Adolfo Dollero, *México al día (impresiones y notas de viaje)* (Paris: Vda. de C. Bouret, 1911), 587.

40. De la Peña, *Guerrero Económico,* 2:608–939; Lejeune, *Tierras mexicanas,* 181–89; Adolfo Dollero, *México al día (impresiones y notas de viaje)* (Paris: Vda. de C. Bouret, 1911), 587.

41. Pavía Guzmán, "La economía suriana," 113; Bustamante, *Tierra Caliente,* 88.

42. Bustamante, *Tierra Caliente,* 89, 148, 161; Peñafiel, *Anuario estadístico 1907,* 434, 546.

43. Christine A. Hastorf, "Rio Balsas most likely region for maize cultivation," *Proceedings of the National Academy of Sciences of the United States of America* 106, no. 13 (2009): 4957–58.

44. Velasco, "Los recursos materiales," 88, 97.

45. Namely, forty-three servants, forty-two seamstresses, eight silversmiths, and four tailors. Report, political situation Guerrero, 05/28/1926, AGN/DG-IPS-136/310(7.1)1, 4; Ministerio de Fomento, *Censo y división territorial del estado de guerrero, verificados en 1900* (Mexico City: Ministerio de Fomento, 1905), 40–73.

46. Guardino, *Peasants,* 119.

47. *Censo 1900,* 40–73; Salazar Adame, "1867–1910," in Salazar Adame, *La Cuestión Agraria Mexicana,* 65–66; Bustamante, *Tierra Caliente,* 84–87.

48. Francisco Vázquez Añorve, *Un recorrido interesante, o El ayer de mi costa* (Puebla: Epipsa, 1974), 19, 106.

49. Jacobs, *Ranchero Revolt*, 70.

50. Bustamante, *Tierra Caliente*, 90, 104–9.

51. Report, political situation Guerrero, 05/28/1926, AGN/DGIPS-136/310(7.1)1.

52. Bustamante, *Tierra Caliente*, 104–8, 119–20, 133–34.

53. *Periódico Oficial*, 06/10/1922.

54. Bustamante, *Tierra Caliente*, 124, 129–30; Daniel Molina Álvarez, "Período 1920–1934," in Salazar Adame, *La Cuestión Agraria Mexicana*, 304; De la Peña, *Guerrero Económico*, 1:431.

55. De la Peña, *Guerrero Económico*, 1:434, 195–97; Tomás Bustamante, "La reforma agraria en Guerrero durante el gobierno de Lázaro Cárdenas," in Salazar Adame, *La Cuestión Agraria Mexicana*, 470.

56. Dirección General de Estadística, *Tercer censo de población de los Estados Unidos Mexicanos verificado el 27 de octubre de 1910* (Mexico City: Dirección General de Estadística, 1918–1920), 1:17.

57. In 1872 only 16 of Taxco's listed 144 mines were still being worked; by 1887 the state's silver production, in the hands of *buscones*, prospectors, was worth only twice as much as its cheese production. Laura Espejel López and Salvador Rueda Smithers, *Reconstrucción histórica de una comunidad del norte de Guerrero: Ichcateopan* (Mexico City: Dirección de Estudios Históricos, Instituto Nacional de Antropología e Historia, Seminario de Movimientos Campesinos del Siglo XX, 1979), 21–26, 72–87; Francisco Arce, *Memoria presentada al X Congreso Constitucional del Estado* (Chilpancingo: Gobierno del Estado de Guerrero, 1888), xxiv–xxv.

58. De la Peña, *Guerrero Económico*, 2:607–9.

59. Jacobs, *Ranchero Revolt*, 36–37; Jesús Guzmán Urióstegui, *Evila Franco Nájera, a pesar del olvido* (Mexico City: Instituto Nacional de Estudios Históricos de la Revolución Mexicana 1995), 29–30.

60. About one-third of all Guerrero's ranches were in these two districts. Salazar Adame, "1867–1910," in Salazar Adame, *La Cuestión Agraria Mexicana*, 16; González Navarro, *Estadísticas sociales del Porfiriato*, 41.

61. Luis Reyes García, *Documentos manuscritos y pictóricos de Ichcateopan, Guerrero* (Mexico City: Universidad Nacional Autónoma de México, 1979), 139; "Manifestación de predios rústicos," Ixcateopan 1929, AMI-1929; "Padrón de predios agrícolas, Ixcateopan 1939," AMI-1939/1; INAH/AS-PHO/CUAUH/5/12, 1–5.

62. Jacobs, *Ranchero Revolt*, 64.

63. Ibid., 41–59.

64. Vecinos Tenanguillo to Chilpancingo, 11/24/1885, AGN/BN-218-101/152, 212-101/95.

65. *Censo 1900*, 48–69; "Padrón de predios agrícolas, Ixcateopan 1939," AMI-1939/1; "Manifestación de predios rústicos, Ixcateopan 1929," AMI-1929.

66. Jacobs, *Ranchero Revolt*, 140–41.

67. "Circular del 9 del octubre de 1856," Francisco González de Cossío et al., *Legislación indigenista de México* (Mexico City: Instituto Indigenista Interamericano, 1958), 51.

68. Jacobs, *Ranchero Revolt,* 35–37, 64–67, 71, 74, 150; Dollero, *México al día,* 586, 907.

69. *Periódico Oficial,* 11/04/1891, 01/26/1907; Bertha Beatriz Martínez Garza et al., eds., *Historia de las Ligas de Comunidades Agrarias y Sindicatos Campesinos* (Mexico City: Confederación Nacional Campesina, Centro de Estudios Históricos del Agrarismo en México: 1988), 3:367.

70. Hacienda Chilpancingo to Hacienda Federal, 03/03/1884, AGN/BN-218-101/152; *Periódico Oficial,* 04/04/1902.

71. "Manifestación de predios rústicos, Ixcateopan 1929," AMI-1929; "Padrón de predios agrícolas, Ixcateopan 1939," AMI-1939/1; Román Parra Terán, "Ixcateopan en el Siglo XIX" (MA diss., Universidad Autónoma de Guerrero, 1997), 47; Josefina García Quintana, *Cuauhtémoc en el Siglo XIX* (Mexico City: Universidad Autónoma de México, 1977), 80–81.

72. Parra Terán, "Ixcateopan en el Siglo XIX," 99.

73. Jacobs, *Ranchero Revolt,* 12–28, 79–80.

74. In 1923 Neri's grants in Hidalgo alone totaled nearly twenty-five thousand hectares. Jacobs, *Ranchero Revolt,* 117, 156.

75. *Periódico Oficial,* 09/06/1933.

76. Jacobs, *Ranchero Revolt,* 131–32.

77. PS-10 to Gobernación, 07/18/1940, AGN/DGIPS-173/311(7.2)1.

78. For the evolution of Chilapa's nineteenth-century economy, with its muleteers, maize merchants, textile producers, and rebels, see Chris Kyle, *Feeding Chilapa: The Birth, Life, and Death of a Mexican Region* (Norman: University of Oklahoma Press, 2008), 42–110.

79. Dehouve, *Cuando los banqueros eran santos,* 31, 69–73, 216–17, 241, 270; M. Muñoz, "Mixteca-Nahua-Tlapaneca," in *Memorias del Instituto Nacional Indigenista* (Mexico City: Instituto Nacional Indigenista, 1963), 9:29–31, 50–51; De la Peña, *Guerrero Económico,* 2:42.

80. While tax receipts in Guerrero increased by nearly 2,000 percent between 1882 and 1943, those of the district of Morelos, for example, grew by a mere 250 percent. De la Peña, *Guerrero Económico,* 2:607–9.

81. Martínez et al., *Historia de las Ligas,* 366–72.

82. Rick A. López, *Crafting Mexico: Intellectuals, Artisans, and the State after the Revolution* (Durham: Duke University Press, 2010), 211–15.

83. Liga to Alemán, 01/16/1951, AGN/MAV-123(11)3643; Dehouve, *Cuando los banqueros eran santos,* 67–73; Jaime García Leyva, "Revoltosos, Bandidos y Rebeldes en la Montaña de Guerrero: 1850–1900," in Tomás Bustamante Alvarez, Gil Arturo Ferrer Vicario, and Joel Iturio Nava, eds., *Guerrero en el contexto de las revoluciones en México* (Mexico City: Editorial Fontamara, 2010), 96–97; Muñoz, "Mixteca-Nahua-Tlapaneca," 55–57.

84. Dehouve, *Cuando los banqueros eran santos,* 74, 215, 218, 239; López, *Crafting Mexico,* 215–17.

85. *Censo 1900;* Dirección General de Estadística, *Séptimo censo general de población 6 de junio de 1950 edo de gro* (Mexico City: Dirección General de Estadística, 1953); Muñoz, "Mixteca-Nahua-Tlapaneca," 57–59.

86. Dehouve, *Cuando los banqueros eran santos,* 74, 239–45, 253, 293–94, 299; Muñoz, "Mixteca-Nahua-Tlapaneca," 87–91.

87. Presidente municipal Malinaltepec to Avila Camacho, 02/17/1943, AGN/MAC-135.2/157.

88. Muñoz, "Mixteca-Nahua-Tlapaneca," 55–59; Martínez et al., *Historia de las Ligas,* 366–37; Bustamante, "1934–1940," in Salazar Adame, *La Cuestión Agraria Mexicana,* 475–530.

89. Dehouve, *Cuando los banqueros eran santos,* 302.

90. "Relación de los Maestros Federales . . . en la 5a zona escolar," 09/21/1927, SEP/DGEP-1668/iv-4 (727.1).

91. Dehouve, *Cuando los banqueros eran santos,* 285–89.

92. Fallaw, *Religion and State Formation,* 108.

93. Report, Sinarquismo Guerrero, 11/04/1941, AGN/DGIPS-133/24/310/24; Fallaw, *Religion and State Formation,* 117.

94. Reyes to SEP, 07/16/1927, SEP/DGEP-1668/12-6-8-10; Catalán Calvo to SEP, 10/05/1943, SEP/DGEP-488/76 "instrucción militar"; report, federal elections Guerrero, 07/08/1940, AGN/DGIPS-173/311(7.2)1.

95. AGN/DGIPS-799/2-1/48/431.

96. Córdoba Lara to Avila Camacho, 04/17/1942; Andraca to Gobernación, 05/27/1942, AGN/DGG-2/012.2(9)/12/2/380(9)/30.

97. *El Sinarquista,* July 1938, cited in Whetten, *Rural Mexico,* 489–91; reports, federal elections Guerrero, 07/08/1940, 07/18/1940, AGN/DGIPS-173/311(7.2)1.

98. Dollero, *México al día,* 906.

99. Nelson, "A Winter Expedition," 355.

100. The Millers' and the Uruñuelas' cotton gins were burned down in the 1910s, while the 1925–26 strike at El Ticuí deprived cultivators of cotton seed to replant. Vázquez Añorve, *El ayer de mi costa,* 24; De la Peña, *Guerrero Económico,* 1:39, 46–47; Miguel Angel Gutiérrez Avila, *Derecho consuetudinario y derecho positivo entre los mixtecos, amuzgos y afromestizos de la costa chica de Guerrero* (Mexico City: Comisión Nacional de Derechos Humanos, 1997), 92; Knight, *The Mexican Revolution,* 2:199; report, political situation Guerrero, 05/28/1926, AGN/DGIPS-136/310(7.1)1 11.

101. On the admittedly shaky evidence of undeflated tax receipts. De la Peña, *Guerrero Económico,* 1:39–40, 55–56, 558–60, 609; Elizabeth Jiménez García et al., *Historia General de Guerrero: Revolución y Reconstrucción* (Mexico City: Instituto Nacional de Antropología e Historia, 1998), 4:206–8; Lorena Paz Paredes and Rosario Cobo, "Café Caliente," in Armando Bartra, ed., *Crónicas del Sur: utopías campesinas en Guerrero* (Mexico City: Ediciones Era, 2000), 133–34; report, political situation Guerrero, 05/28/1926, AGN/DGIPS-136/310(7.1)1.

102. Gill, "Los Escudero, de Acapulco"; Rogelio Vizcaíno and Paco Ignacio Taibo II, "Acapulco en los tiempos de Juan Escudero," in Illades and Ortega, *Guerrero,* 2:279–84.

103. Guardino, *Peasants,* 95, 116–23, 144.

104. Report, political situation Guerrero, 05/28/1926, AGN/DGIPS-136/310(7.1)1.

105. Salazar Adame, *La Cuestión Agraria Mexicana,* 315–25.

106. Cited in Molina, "1920–1934," in Salazar Adame, *La Cuestión Agraria Mexicana,* 231.

107. *Censo (1895),* 35; *Censo 1900,* 42, 106–39, 172–205; *Periódico Oficial,* no. 57, 1890.

108. Report, political situation Guerrero, 05/28/1926, AGN/DGIPS-136/310(7.1)1.

109. De la Peña, *Guerrero Económico,* 1:47; *Censo 1900,* 106–39, 172–205.

110. Renato Ravelo Lecuona and Tomás Bustamante, *Historia General de Guerrero,* 4 vols. (Mexico City: INAH, Gobierno del Estado de Guerrero, 1998), 4:208, 237–38, 255; Bustamante, "1934–1940," in Salazar Adame, *La Cuestión Agraria Mexicana,* 377, 472; Armando Bartra, *Guerrero bronco: campesinos, ciudadanos y guerrilleros en la Costa Grande* (Mexico City: Ediciones Era, 2000), 77; "List of . . . British Vice Consuls, January 1st 1905," FO50/544.

111. Aviña, *Specters of Revolution,* 33.

112. Bartra holds that "for the first time the politico-social leadership of the majorities came, in almost all cases, from their own ranks"; overlooking the backgrounds of Juan Escudero (Acapulco merchant family), the Vidales brothers (Acapulco merchant family), and María de la O (a lawyer's wife). Molina, "1920–1934," in Salazar Adame, *La Cuestión Agraria Mexicana,* 240–43, 282–85; Bartra, *Guerrero bronco,* 54–64.

113. Report, political situation Guerrero, 05/28/1926, AGN/DGIPS-136/310(7.1)1; Molina, "1920–1934," in Salazar Adame, ed., *La Cuestión Agraria Mexicana,* 258.

114. Report, political situation Guerrero, 05/28/1926, AGN/DGIPS-136/310(7.1)1.

115. AGN/DGIPS-136/310(7.1)"36," Knight, *The Mexican Revolution,* 2:199.

116. Fallaw, *Religion and State Formation,* 140–41.

117. Report, federal elections in Guerrero, 07/18/1940, AGN/DGIPS-173/311(7.2)1; ORC libro de nacimientos 1939.

118. Ernest Gruening, *Mexico and Its Heritage* (New York: D. Appleton, 1940), 432; Vicente Fuentes Díaz, *Guerrero: un pasado aciago, un porvenir promisorio* (Mexico City: Cámara de Diputados, 2000), 36; federal deputies' open letter in defense of governor, 1948, AP108/320.32 PER; Leyva Mancilla reports 1947, 1948, 1951, AP-175/352.072.073ETN.

119. Commemorative plaque, Ixcateopan village museum, 1979; *Excélsior,* 02/20/1949, AP-51/133.55 FIC.

120. Miguel Angel Gutiérrez Avila, *Corrido y violencia entre los Afromestizos de la Costa Chica de Guerrero y Oaxaca* (Chilpancingo: Universidad Autónoma de Guerrero, 1988), 15–19; T. Philip Terry, *Terry's Guide to Mexico* (Hingham, MA: Rapid Service Press, 1947), 259–60.

121. Report, political situation Guerrero, 05/28/1926, AGN/DGIPS-136/310(7.1)1; De la Peña, *Guerrero Económico,* 1:565; Jorge Alberto Sánchez Ortega, "Los escenarios y los actores sociales actuales: De la metáfora a la cultura: la invención política del Guerrero bronco," in Bustamante and Sarmiento, *La reinvención de Guerrero,* 223–43; Jiménez García et al., *Historia General de Guerrero,* 4:306.

122. "Corrido a David Flores Reynada," AGN/DGIPS-136/310(7.1)"34"; Gutiérrez Avila, *Corrido y violencia,* 15–17; author's interview, Edgar Pavía Guzmán, Chilpancingo 4–5/04/2002.

123. Author's interview, Vicente Ramírez Sandoval, Ometepec 9/04/2002.

124. The metaphor is Alan Knight's. For more, see Alan Knight, "México bronco, México manso: una reflexión sobre la cultura cívica mexicana," *Política y Gobierno* 3, no. 1 (1996): 12–15.

125. Bateman to Bevin, 01/21/1947, FO371/60940/AN602.

126. Peter H. Smith, *Labyrinths of Power: Political Recruitment in Twentieth-Century Mexico* (Princeton: Princeton University Press, 1979), 268.

127. PS-12 to Gobernación, 02/16/1945, AGN/DGIPS-788/2–1/45/374.

128. García Leyva, "Revoltosos, Bandidos y Rebeldes", 95; Gil Arturo Ferrer Vicario, "Guerrero, un trozo de su historia Porfiriato y Revolución," in Bustamante Alvarez et al., *Guerrero en el contexto de las revoluciones,* 170.

129. Ojeda to Alemán, 11/16/1944, AGN/DGG-2/311G(9)2/239/II, Sánchez de Tagle to Gobernación, 11/28/1944, AGN/DGIPS-87/2-1/131-691. Concerning bride capture, see Gonzalo Aguirre Beltrán, *Cuijla: esbozo etnográfico de un pueblo negro* (Mexico City: Fondo de Cultura Económica, 1995), 148–63.

130. Author's interview, Felicísima Reyes Jiménez, Ometepec 06/26/2002.

131. PS-4 to Gobernación, 05/17/1945, AGN/DGIPS-788/2-1/45/347.

132. Report, political situation Guerrero, 05/28/1926, AGN/DGIPS-136/310(7.1)1, Liga Ometepec to Cárdenas, 05/12/1938, reproduced in Bustamante, "1934–1940," in Salazar Adame, *La Cuestión Agraria Mexicana,* 418–20.

133. Almazán's brother had married into the powerful Reguera family. Vázquez Añorve, *El ayer de mi costa,* 405.

134. Dudley Ankerson, *Agrarian Warlord: Saturnino Cedillo and the Mexican Revolution in San Luis Potosí* (DeKalb: Northern Illinois University Press, 1984), 188–90.

135. PS-10 to Gobernación, 07/18/1940, AGN/DGIPS-173/311(7.2)1.

136. Reports on arms smuggling, 05/08/1939, 05/06/1940, AGN/DGIPS-127/2–1/266.7(727.1)1 & 2.

137. *La Verdad,* 03/09/1949.

138. Leyva Mancilla report 1950, AP-175/352.072.073ETN.

139. The criminology statistics for each state compiled for Pablo Piccato only begin to detail distinct categories of crime from 1937 onward. Pablo Piccato, "Estadísticas del crimen en México: Series históricas, 1901–2001," http://www.columbia.edu/estadisticascrimen/EstadisticasSigloXX.htm.

140. Appelius, *El Aguila de Chapultepec,* 257; report, political situation Guerrero, 03/08/1926, AGN/DGIPS-136/310(7.1)1.

141. CROM Arcelia to Secretary-General CROM, 04/20/1934, AGN/DG-IPS-136/310(7.1)"34"; Fallaw, *Religion and State Formation,* 130; Partido Agrarista de Guerrero to Gobernación, 07/18/1940; PS-10 to Gobernación, 07/18/1940, AGN/DG-IPS-173/311(7.2)1.

142. Bartra, *Guerrero bronco,* 88.

143. Liga Acapulco to Cárdenas, 02/21/1940, AGN/DGG-2.012.2(9)/19/31.

144. Guardino, *Peasants,* 136–59; Jacobs, *Ranchero Revolt,* 3–28.

145. Salazar Adame, "1867–1910," in Salazar Adame, *La Cuestión Agraria Mexicana,* 67.

146. Ravelo and Bustamante, *Historia General de Guerrero,* 4:235–37; Bustamante, *Tierra Caliente,* 85; Vázquez Añorve, *El ayer de mi costa,* 111.

147. Manifestación de predios rústicos, Ixcateopan, AMI-1929; Padrón de predios agrícolas, Ixcateopan, AMI-1939/1; Parra Terán, "Ixcateopan en el Siglo XIX," 47.

148. For the concept of cognitive capacity, see Laurence Whitehead, "State Organization in Latin America since 1930," in Leslie Bethell, *The Cambridge History of Latin America, vol. 6: Latin America since 1930: Economy, Society, and Politics* (Cambridge: Cambridge University Press, 1994), 46–48.

149. Jacobs, *Ranchero Revolt,* 107.

150. Norberto Valdéz, *Ethnicity, Class and the Indigenous Struggle for Land in Guerrero, Mexico* (New York: Routledge, 1998), 71; B. Leyva Mancilla, "Datos Biográficos," PPBLV, 1; Knight, *The Mexican Revolution,* 2:190, 199; Bustamante, *Tierra Caliente,* 111; Bartra, *Guerrero bronco,* 35.

151. Dehouve, *Cuando los banqueros eran santos,* 73; Bustamante, "1934–1940," in Salazar Adame, *La Cuestión Agraria Mexicana,* 345; De la Peña, *Guerrero Económico,* 2:17.

152. By Castrejón's Zapatistas, quartered in Ixcateopan. *Así Somos* . . . 02/15/1996.

153. John Womack Jr., *Zapata and the Mexican Revolution* (London: Thames and Hudson, 1969), 138–40, 310–11, 370.

154. Epigmenio López Barroso, *Diccionario Geográfico, Histórico y Estadístico del Distrito de Abasolo, del Estado de Guerrero* (Mexico City: Ediciones Botas, 1967), 27–28; Gela Manzano and Isaías Alanís, *Ometepec: historia y cultura* (Mexico City: Grupo Editorial Eón, 1996), 52–53.

155. Martínez et al., *Historia de las Ligas,* 364–65.

156. Miguel Angel Gutiérrez Avila, *Nabor Ojeda Caballero, el Batallador del Sur* (Mexico City: Centro de Estudios Históricos del Agrarismo en México, Confederación Nacional Campesina, 1991), 26–28; Bustamante, "La reforma agraria," 392–93.

157. Liga to Cárdenas, 11/07/1937, AGN/LCR-543.1/37.

158. PS-45 to Gobernación, 10/14/1936, AGN/DGIPS-173/311(7.1)"36"; Martínez to Gobernación, 10/09/1936, AGN/DGIPS-173/311(7.1)"36."

159. Ojeda campaign speech, Taxco, 06/24/1944, AGN/DGIPS-782/2–1/44/274.

160. Report, federal elections in Guerrero, 07/18/1940, AGN/DGIPS-173/311(7.2)1.

161. She should have known; her brothers, local worthies in Teloloapan, were accused of multiple killings. *Trópico,* 04/08/1945; Palacios to Procurador General de Justicia, Mexico City, 05/01/1945, AGN/DGG-2/012.2(9)/19/18.

162. Jacobs, *Ranchero Revolt,* 133–34.

163. A conclusion that holds on a national level: the rate of gubernatorial dismissal decreased steadily between 1929 and 1970 as presidential power increased. Carlos Moncada, *¡Cayeron! 67 Gobernadores derrocados (1929–1979)* (Mexico City: C. Moncada, 1979), 389–92.

164. Namely, Alejandro Gómez Maganda and Raúl Caballero Aburto. The ranks of deposed governors were further swollen by Israel Nogueda Otero (1975) and Rubén Figueroa Alcocer (1996).

165. Author's analysis, election reports, AGN/DGG-2.311M(9)/5B, 6B; *Excélsior,* 01/08/1939.

166. Friedeberg to Gobernación, 07/07/1940, AGN/DGIPS-173/311(7.2)1, undated report, AGN/DGIPS-809/2-1/51/524, Liga Acapulco to Cárdenas, 02/21/1940, AGN/DGG-2.012.2(9)/19/31.

167. Alba Teresa Estrada Castañon, *Guerrero: sociedad, economía, política, cultura* (Mexico City: UNAM, 1994), 108.

168. As one retired general from Cocula put it to the secretary of defense, "My whole state was Padillista, as no one knows better than you." PS-10 to Gobernación, 07/15, 18/1940, AGN/DGIPS-173/311(7.2)1, AGN/MAC-544.1/11-4; Godínez to SEDENA, 12/01/1946, SDN-1-374/vi.

169. *Trópico,* 01/07/1945; author's analysis, election reports, AGN/DGG-2.311M(9) series.

170. PS-37 to Gobernación, 12/03/1946, AGN/DGIPS-793/2-1/46/428; PS-31 to Gobernación, 09/26/1947, AGN/DGIPS-84/MRT. For an instance of collective bargaining by riot ending political careers at the highest level, see Gillingham, "Maximino's Bulls," 186–200.

171. According to the Liga, Berber was a "protector of killers with respect to whom, in some cases, the same Secretaría de Gobernación has intervened that they be punished without any result whatsoever." Liga to Cárdenas, 02/21/1940, AGN/DGG-2.012.2(9)/19/31.

172. Jacobs, *Ranchero Revolt,* 157, 165.

173. Torres to SEP, 04/03/1935, SEP/DGEP-1336/8.

174. Fernando Saúl Alanís Enciso, trans. Russ Davidson, foreword Mark Overmyer-Velázquez, *They Should Stay There: The Story of Mexican Migration and Repatriation during the Great Depression* (Chapel Hill: University of North Carolina Press, 2017), 26, 169–70.

175. De la Peña, *Guerrero económico,* 2:611.

176. Guardino, *Peasants,* 136–39; Parra to SEP, 06/12/1941, SEP/DGEP-5470/14-55-8-11.

177. Subdirector literacy campaign Chilpancingo to presidentes municipales, 11/22/1945, AMI-1945.

178. SEP to DEF Guerrero, 09/21/1943, SEP/DGEP-5839 ant. 4750 exp 6-24-8-202.

179. Gutiérrez Avila, *Ojeda,* 60.

2. A Rich Place, a Poor State: Veracruz

1. "Register of directors," Interoceanic Railway of Mexico, BT-31/31101/26575.

2. "Summary of capital and shares, 11/28/1898," BT-31/31101/26575; "Register of directors," Interoceanic Railway of Mexico, BT-31/31101/26575.

3. Pearson's Veracruz interests in 1910 included Mexican Eagle Oil, the Eagle Oil Transport Co., the Tehuantepec Railway, the Santa Gertrudis jute mill, the Veracruz Land and Cattle Co., and the electricity and tram companies of Córdoba, Orizaba, and Veracruz. Braniff was among the founders of the largest textile company, CIDOSA, Monterrey's principal steel works, director of the San Rafael paper mill and president of the Banco de Londres y México. Alfred P. Tischendorf, *Great Britain and Mexico in the Era of Porfirio Díaz* (Durham: Duke University Press, 1961), 142; Arthur P. Schmidt, *The Social and Economic Effects of the Railroad in Puebla and Veracruz, Mexico, 1867–1911* (New York: Garland, 1987), 133–35, Desmond Young, *Member for Mexico: A Biography of Weetman Pearson, First Viscount Cowdray* (London: Cassell, 1966), 102; Rodney D. Anderson, *Outcasts in Their Own Land: Mexican Industrial Workers, 1906–1911* (DeKalb: Northern Illinois University Press, 1976), 103.

4. Moisés T. de la Peña, *Veracruz económico,* 2 vols. (Veracruz-Llave: Gobierno del Estado de Veracruz, 1946), 2:49.

5. The "commodity lottery" is defined by Carlos Díaz-Alejandro as "what nature has blessed or cursed you with, plus what nature permitted man to introduce." Cited in Rosemary Thorp, *Progress, Poverty and Exclusion: An Economic History of Latin America in the 20th Century* (Baltimore: Johns Hopkins University Press, 1998), 48.

6. The gross value of foreign capital stock in developing countries, adjusted for inflation, reached 12.5 percent of world GDP in 1914; in 1985 it was only 7 percent. Stefano Manzocchi, *Foreign Capital in Developing Economies: Perspectives from the Theory of Economic Growth* (London: Macmillan, 1999), 16.

7. Erika Pani, *Para pertenecer a la gran familia mexicana: procesos de naturalización en el siglo XIX* (Mexico City: Colegio de México, 2015), 149.

8. Paul J. Vanderwood, *Disorder and Progress: Bandits, Police, and Mexican Development* (Lincoln: University of Nebraska Press, 1981).

9. Juana Martínez Alarcón, *San Cristóbal: un ingenio y sus trabajadores, 1896–1934* (Xalapa: Universidad Veracruzana, 1986), 40–51.

10. Enrique Cárdenas, "A Macroeconomic Interpretation of Nineteenth-Century Mexico," in Haber, *How Latin America Fell Behind,* 79.

11. Porfirio Pérez Olivares, *Memorias de un dirigente agrario de Soledad de Doblado* (Xalapa: Universidad Veracruzana, 1992), 32–38.

12. Leonardo Chagoya, "Memoria . . . de Chicontepec . . . 18 de Agosto de 1898," in Soledad García Morales and José Velasco Toro, eds., *Memorias e informes de jefes políticos y autoridades del régimen porfirista, 1883–1911, Estado de Veracruz* (Xalapa: Universidad Veracruzana, 1997), 1:285; Schmidt, *The Railroad,* 248.

13. Haber, *Industry and Underdevelopment,* 27–38, 56–57; Martín Gerardo Aguilar Sánchez, *Los conflictos ferrocarrileros en Veracruz: 1910–1927* (Mexico City: Colofón Ediciones Académicas Sociología 2017), 60. The differential was not enough to stop a dramatic increase in net sales in the first years of the twentieth century, though, when those of the Orizaba Valley's Santa Rosa mill roughly doubled, as did their competitors' share prices. Aurora Gómez-Galvarriato, *Industry and Revolution: Social and Economic Change in the Orizaba Valley, Mexico* (Cambridge: Harvard University Press, 2013), 249, 251.

14. Cárdenas, "Nineteenth-Century Mexico," 78–79.

15. Consul Baker, "Report on the Mines and Minerals of the State of Vera Cruz," 1887, FO204/206.

16. An annual output that went unsurpassed until the mid-1970s. Young, *Member for Mexico,* 133–35; De la Peña, *Veracruz económico,* 2:437–38; INEGI, *Estadísticas históricas* CD-ROM.

17. De la Peña, *Veracruz económico,* 2:484–87.

18. Foreign employers generally claimed that they paid well above going Mexican rates. Heather Fowler, *Agrarian Radicalism in Veracruz, 1920–1938* (Lincoln: University of Nebraska Press, 1978), 7.

19. Tischendorf, *Great Britain and Mexico,* 122–25.

20. Myrna I. Santiago, *The Ecology of Oil: Environment, Labor, and the Mexican Revolution, 1900–1938* (Cambridge: Cambridge University Press, 2009), 86–90, 154–63.

21. De la Peña, *Veracruz económico,* 2:445; INEGI, *Estadísticas históricas* CD-ROM.

22. Salvador Novo, "Este y otros viajes," in Martha Poblett Miranda, ed., *Cien viajeros en Veracruz: crónicas y relatos,* 11 vols. (Xalapa: Gobierno del Estado de Veracruz, 1992), 11:196–97; De la Peña, *Veracruz económico,* 2:445.

23. Pulford, Tampico, to British Embassy 10/02/1916, FO115/2004/2099.

24. Peñafiel, *Anuario estadístico 1907;* Departamento de la Estadística Nacional, *Anuario estadístico, 1923–1924* (Mexico City: Departamento de la Estadística Nacional, 1925); Livia García Quinto, "Breve Historia del Ingenio 'El Modelo,' 1900–1974" (MA diss., Universidad Veracruzana, 1975), 36; Martínez Alarcón, *San Cristóbal,* 51–56.

25. Aurora Gómez-Galvarriato, "Measuring the Impact of Institutional Change in Capital—Labor Relations in the Mexican Textile Industry," in Jeffrey L. Bortz and Stephen H. Haber, eds., *The Mexican Economy, 1870–1930: Essays on the Economic History of Institutions, Revolution and Growth* (Stanford: Stanford University Press, 2002), 305; Haber, *Industry and Underdevelopment,* 137.

26. From 1,132,859 people in 1910 to 1,159,935 in 1921. Tax receipts deflated using wholesale price index Mexico City 1886–1978. INEGI, *Estadísticas históricas* CD-ROM; De la Peña, *Veracruz económico,* 2:484.

27. Gómez-Galvarriato, *Industry and Revolution,* 181.

28. *Oxford Latin American Economic History Database,* http://moxlad.cienciassociales.edu.uy/en.

29. Martínez Alarcón, *San Cristóbal,* 56; Haber, *Industry and Underdevelopment,* 140–41.

30. Examples include Manuel Parra of the Hacienda de Almolonga and Antonio Domínguez of San Juan Bautista-Tuzamapan. Antonio Santoyo, *La Mano Negra: Poder regional y Estado en México (Veracruz, 1928–1943)* (Mexico City: Consejo Nacional para la Cultura y las Artes, 1995); María Cristina Núñez Madrazo, "Entre patrones, caciques y líderes: Procesos políticos locales en una comunidad cañera del centro del estado de Veracruz," *Sotavento* 5 (2000).

31. José González Sierra, *Monopolio del huo (elementos para la historia del tabaco en México y algunos conflictos de tabaqueros veracruzanos: 1915–1930)* (Xalapa: Universidad Veracruzana, 1987), 115; Alberto J. Olvera, "La estructura económica y social de Veracruz hacia 1930: Un análisis inicial," in *Anuario del Centro de Estudios Históricos de la Universidad Veracruzana* (Xalapa: Universidad Veracruzana, 1983), 3:44.

32. The 1929 Censo Industrial valued industrial production at 102,113,300 pesos; the 1944 Padrón Industrial at 202,859,819 pesos, which once deflated to 1930 levels are equivalent to just over 91 million pesos. Olvera, "La Estructura Ecónomica de Veracruz," 36; Secretaría de la Economía Nacional, *Censo de Población 1950 Estado de Veracruz* (Mexico City: Secretaría de la Economía Nacional, 1953), 9.

33. Romana Falcón and Soledad García Morales, *La semilla en el surco: Adalberto Tejeda y el radicalismo en Veracruz (1883–1960)* (Mexico City: Colegio de México, 1986), 237.

34. E. H. Carr, *The Twenty Years' Crisis, 1919–1939: An Introduction to the Study of International Relations* (London: Palgrave Macmillan, 2016 [1939]).

35. INEGI, *Estadísticas históricas* CD-ROM.

36. De la Peña, *Veracruz económico,* 1:209–10.

37. Gómez-Galvarriato, *Industry and Revolution,* 200–232.

38. INEGI, *Estadísticas históricas* CD-ROM; De la Peña, *Veracruz económico,* 2:484–86, 507.

39. Ruiz Cortines report 1946, BD-XIII/7377; Migoni to Gobernación, 02/23/1946, AGN/DGIPS-791/2-1/46/405.

40. Consular reports, 01/30/1942, 04/29/1942, 07/25/1942, 10/23/1942, FO371/30586; De la Peña, *Veracruz económico,* 2:249.

41. Inspector XII[a] zona Veracruz to SEP, 07/31/1942, SEP/DGEP-5543/16-19-2-25.

42. Leignadier to Foreign Office, 01/30/1942, FO371/30586; Forzán to Gobernación, 01/26/1944, AGN/DGIPS-98/6; Migoni to Gobernación, 04/20/1945, AGN/DGIPS-787/2-1/45/282.

43. When adjusted for inflation. De la Peña blamed this in part on fiscal incompetence by the state government. INEGI, *Estadísticas históricas* CD-ROM; De la Peña, *Veracruz económico,* 2:484–89, 507.

44. Ruiz Cortines report 1946, BD-XIII/7380; Ruiz Cortines report, 1947, BD-XIV/7507; Migoni to Gobernación, 10/05/1945, AGN/DGIPS-787/2-1/45/282.

45. *Diario de Xalapa,* 08/08/1947.

46. INEGI, *Estadísticas históricas* CD-ROM.

47. *El Cosmopolita,* 1891–1911. Claudia del Palacio Montiel, *Indice del fondo hemerográfico veracruzano del IEHS* (Xalapa: Universidad Veracruzana, 1999), 65.

48. In 1910, for example, 31,000 veracruzanos lived outside of the state, while 10,947 foreigners lived in the state. Secretaría de Agricultura y Fomento, *División Territorial de los EUM correspondiente al censo de 1910* (Mexico City: Secretaría de Agricultura y Fomento, 1918), 11–12.

49. Eulalia Ribera Carbó, "Traza, ocupación del espacio y segregación: La morfología urbana de Orizaba en el siglo XIX," in Carlos Contreras Cruz and Claudia Patricia Pardo Hernández, eds., *De Veracruz a Puebla: un itinerario entre la colonia y el porfiriato* (Mexico City: Instituto de Investigaciones Dr. José Maria Luis Mora, 1999), 34–39; M. González Fernández, "Memoria . . . de Los Tuxtlas . . . 28 de Junio de 1890," in García and Velasco, eds., *Memorias e informes,* 6:40; León Medel y Alvarado, *Historia de San Andrés Tuxtla (1525–1975)* (Xalapa: Gobierno del Estado de Veracruz, 1993), 1:269; *Enciclopedia Municipal de Veracruz: Chicontepec* (Mexico City: Secretaría de Gobernación y Gobierno del Estado de Veracruz-Llave, 1998), 77.

50. INEGI, *Estadísticas históricas* CD-ROM.

51. Dehesa reports 1908, 1909, BD-IX/5047, 5063; Pérez Olivares, *Memorias,* 12, 25; Ministerio de Fomento, *Censo y división territorial del Estado de Veracruz, verificados en 1900* (Mexico City: Ministerio de Fomento, 1904), 114–85.

52. S. Santaella, "Memoria . . . de Zongólica . . . 16 de Septiembre de 1896," in García and Velasco, *Memorias e informes,* 5:112.

53. David A. Skerritt, "Peasant Organisation in Veracruz, Mexico: 1920 to the Present" (D.Phil. diss., Oxford University, 1996), 2–3; Romana Falcón, *El agrarismo en Veracruz: la etapa radical (1928–1935)* (Mexico City: Colegio de México, 1977), 7–10; Michael Bess, *Routes of Compromise: Building Roads and Shaping the Nation in Mexico, 1917–1952* (Lincoln: University of Nebraska Press, 2017), 13, 130–31.

54. Rand McNally, *1938 Auto Road Atlas,* 94.

55. A breakdown criticized by José González Sierra as both arbitrary and vague. One politician in 1940 suggested thinking about Veracruz in terms of five distinct regions, namely, the Huasteca; Papantla to Xalapa; a central region stretching from Veracruz to Jalacingo; the coast of Sotavento, from Alvarado to los Tuxtlas; and the deep south. This was not a bad idea, but the old tripartite division has the momentum of long usage behind it. Arriola to Pérez Aldama, 03/16/1940, AGN/DGIPS-78/6. "Génesis y consolidación de un proyecto de historia regional," *Anuario del Centro de Estu-*

dios Históricos de la Universidad Veracruzana (Xalapa: Universidad Veracruzana, s.f.), 9:195.

56. Alfred H. Siemens, *Between the Summit and the Sea: Central Veracruz in the Nineteenth Century* (Vancouver: University of British Columbia Press, 1990), 32–33.

57. Alexander von Humboldt, *Political Essay on the Kingdom of New Spain,* 3 vols., trans. John Black (London, 1814), 1:xcix.

58. Fanny Calderón de la Barca, *Life in Mexico* (Berkeley: University of California Press, 1982), 47; Karl Bartolomeus Heller, translated and edited by Terry Rugeley, *Alone in Mexico: The Astonishing Travels of Karl Heller, 1845–1848* (Tuscaloosa: University of Alabama Press, 2007), 39.

59. Siemens, *Between the Summit and the Sea,* 114–16.

60. Heller, *Alone in Mexico,* 35.

61. Although a majority of infants were vaccinated, adult vaccination was almost certainly focused on the elites; in 1897 only 5 percent of adults in Veracruz had received the "pus." Moisés González Navarro, *El Porfiriato: la vida social* (Mexico City: Ed. Hermes, 1957), 69–70.

62. Dehesa report 1894, BD-VIII/4268, G. M. Velez, "Informe . . . de Veracruz . . . de Agosto de 1886," in García and Velasco, *Memorias e informes,* 5:183–87.

63. Dehesa report 1908, BD-IX/5039.

64. Charles M. Flandrau, *¡Viva México!* (London: Eland Books, 1985), 215.

65. Dehesa report 1894, BD-VIII/4440; Schmidt, *The Railroad,* 78, 251.

66. Petition for ejido in *Gaceta Oficial del Estado de Veracruz,* 02/09/1918; Pérez Olivares, *Memorias,* 41.

67. In the canton of Huatusco ranches could be formed from a handful of hectares. David Skerritt, *Rancheros sobre tierra fértil* (Xalapa: Universidad Veracruzana, 1993), 99–115; Dehesa report 1894, BD-VIII/4279–4284; González Navarro, *El Porfiriato,* 210.

68. Secretaría de Agricultura y Fomento, *Censo de 1910,* 11–12; *Enciclopedia Municipal de Veracruz: Perote* (Mexico City: Secretaría de Gobernación y Gobierno del Estado de Veracruz-Llave, 1998), 85; Ministerio de Fomento, *Censo de 1900,* 114–88.

69. In 1909 alone the ayuntamiento of Soledad de Doblado paved the village's streets and main square, installed telephones in some of the outlying hamlets, and ordered the construction of six schools. Dehesa report 1909, BD-IX/5054, 5061–5062, 5066.

70. Abel Juárez Martínez, "Reacomodo de las fuerzas sociales en el Valle de Perote, 1910–1920," in *Anuario del Centro de Estudios Históricos de la Universidad Veracruzana* (Xalapa: Universidad Veracruzana, n.d.), 8:105–6.

71. Karl B. Koth, "Teodoro A. Dehesa and Veracruz in the Porfiriato, 1892–1913: A Case Study of Mexican Federal–State Relations" (Ph.D. diss., University of Manitoba, 1987), i–vii.

72. Dehesa, "Discursos Oficiales [del] 5 de mayo de 1911," BD-IX/5097; *El Correo de Sotavento,* 06/16/1910, cited in Ricardo Corzo Ramírez, José González Sierra, and David

Skerritt, . . . *nunca un desleal: Cándido Aguilar (1889–1960)* (Mexico City: Colegio de México, 1986), 18.

73. Paulino Martínez, *La Hecatombe de Veracruz: Corona fúnebre en memoria de las víctimas sacrificadas la noche del 24 al 25 de Junio de 1879* (Mexico City: Fiat Lux, 1910), 15–19, 61–62; Daniel Cosío Villegas, *El Porfiriato: la vida política interior primera parte* (Mexico City: Ed. Hermes, 1960), 599–600.

74. Bernardo García Díaz, *Un pueblo fabril del Porfiriato: Santa Rosa, Veracruz* (Mexico City: Fondo de Cultura Económica, 1981), 44–48.

75. Between 1893 and 1908 salaries in the Gulf were the highest of any region in Mexico. The Orizaba dispute of 1902 was readily resolved in the workers' favor, and the major railway strike of the 1900s (in the north on the Ferrocarril Central Mexicano) spread across four states but not to Veracruz. INEGI, *Estadísticas históricas* CD-ROM; Anderson, *Outcasts in Their Own Land,* 137–42; Aguilar Sánchez, *Los conflictos ferrocarrileros,* 58–68.

76. In Actopan, for example, only 26 percent of the population was Indian in 1820; in Zongólica the jefe político could report few Indians in the cabecera by 1896. Skerritt, *Rancheros,* 34; Santaella, "Memoria de 1896," in García and Velasco, *Memorias e informes,* 5:109.

77. Corzo Ramírez et al., *Cándido Aguilar,* 14–21.

78. Juárez Martínez, "El Valle de Perote," 107; Heather Fowler, "The Agrarian Revolution in the State of Veracruz, 1920–1940: The Role of Peasant Organizations" (Ph.D. diss., University of Washington, 1970), 24. For Félix Díaz's undistinguished military and diplomatic career during the Porfiriato, the disdain harbored for him by the *científicos,* and the staggering incompetence of his 1912 rebellion, see "Félix Díaz y la rebelión de 1912 en Veracruz," in *Crónica de un cuartelazo anunciado* (Mexico City: Colegio de México, forthcoming).

79. George A. Genz, "Entrepreneurship and Caciquismo: A Study of Community Power in a Mexican Gulf Coast Village" (Ph.D. diss., Michigan State University, 1975), 121–26.

80. Andrew Grant Wood, *Revolution in the Street: Women, Workers, and Urban Protest in Veracruz, 1870–1927* (Wilmington, DE: Scholarly Resources, 2001), 26–27, 68–69.

81. Fowler-Salamini, *Working Women,* 150–51.

82. Pérez Olivares, *Memorias,* 13–14; Juárez Martínez, "El Valle de Perote," 109–11; Fowler, *Agrarian Radicalism,* 27–29.

83. García Quinto, "El Modelo," 57.

84. Wood, *Revolution in the Street,* 76–78, 148–50, 208–9.

85. Andrew Grant Wood, " 'The Proletarian Women Will Make the Social Revolution': Female Participation in the Veracruz Rent Strike, 1922–1927," in Stephanie Mitchell and Patience A. Schell, eds., *The Women's Revolution in Mexico, 1910–1953* (Lanham, MD: Rowman and Littlefield, 2007), 160–61.

86. Fowler, *Agrarian Radicalism,* 138; De la Peña, *Veracruz económico,* 1:155–66.

87. Fowler, "The Agrarian Revolution," 480.

88. PS-30 to Jara, 09/26/1925, AGN/DGIPS-170/8; Fowler, "The Agrarian Revolution," 488.

89. PS-13 to Gobernación, 10/25/1925, and assorted undated reports, AGN/DGIPS-170/8.

90. Fowler, *Agrarian Radicalism*, 117–20.

91. Assorted undated reports, AGN/DGIPS-171/6.

92. "Actividades reaccionarias en el estado de Veracruz," 10/04/1939, AGN/DGIPS-140/9.

93. Ryan M. Alexander, "Alemán before Alemán," in Andrew Paxman, *Los Gobernadores: Caciques del pasado y del presente* (Mexico City: Grijalbo, 2018), 243–70; PS-85 to Gobernación, 03/27/1936, AGN/DGIPS-171/7; PS-2 to Gobernación, 02/22/1940, AGN/DGIPS-78/5.

94. PS-2 to Gobernación, 03/03/1940, AGN/DGIPS-78/5; PS-50 Orizaba to Gobernación, 10/03/1940, AGN/DGIPS-140/9.

95. As Sarah Osten notes, it is interesting in itself that the phrase was not applied in Veracruz but rather reserved for the four states of the Southeast. Osten, *The Mexican Revolution's Wake*, 6.

96. Carleton Beals's description, cited in Thomas Benjamin, "Laboratories of the New State, 1920–1929: Regional Social Reform and Experiments in Mass Politics," in Thomas Benjamin and Mark Wasserman, eds., *Provinces of the Revolution: Essays on Regional Mexican History, 1910–1929* (Albuquerque: University of New Mexico Press, 1990), 71.

97. De la Peña, *Veracruz económico*, 1:64–65, 79.

98. Skerritt, "Peasant Organisation," 5; INEGI, *Estadísticas históricas* CD-ROM.

99. All of whom perforce spoke at least some Popoloca. Miguel Alemán Valdés, *Remembranzas y testimonios* (Mexico City: Grijalbo, 1987), 16.

100. Medel, *San Andrés Tuxtla*, 1:190–91.

101. Martínez Alarcón, *San Cristóbal*, 29–34; De la Peña, *Veracruz económico*, 2:253.

102. Schmidt, *The Railroad*, 71–73; De la Peña, *Veracruz económico*, 2:277.

103. Tischendorf, *Great Britain and Mexico*, 66–67, 123–25.

104. Patricia Romero Lankao, "Coatzacoalcos–Minatitlán: el proceso histórico de transformación de la región y sus consecuencias socio-ambientales" (B.A. thesis, UNAM, 1986), 22.

105. José González Sierra, *Los Tuxtlas* (Xalapa: Universidad Veracruzana, 1991), 36–37.

106. Romero Lankao, "Coatzacoalcos–Minatitlán," 17–28.

107. Martínez Alarcón, *San Cristóbal*, 38–40.

108. Dehesa report 1894, BD-VIII/4554.

109. Hernández Pérez, "Memoria . . . de Los Tuxtlas . . . 7 de Junio de 1897," in García Velasco, *Memorias e informes*, 6:64.

110. "Plano topográfico y mercantil de la ciudad de San Andrés Tuxtla, 1906," PPMT; John R. Southworth, *El Estado de Veracruz-Llave: su historia, comercio, agricultura e industrias, en inglés y español* (Liverpool: Blake and Mackenzie, 1900), 146–51.

111. Ministerio de Fomento, *Censo de 1900*, 16, 294–171.

112. "Plano topográfico y mercantil de la ciudad de San Andrés Tuxtla, 1906," PPMT.

113. Cándido Donato Padua, *Movimiento Revolucionario—1906 en Veracruz: relación cronológica de las actividades del PLM en los ex cantones de Acayucpan, Minatitlán, San Andrés Tuxtla y centro del país* (Mexico City: n.p., 1936), 5–12.

114. Dehesa report 1894, BD-VIII/4279–4294; Rodríguez, "Memoria . . . de Minatitlán . . . 17 de Abril de 1891," in García and Velasco, *Memorias e informes*, 6:178.

115. Fowler, "The Agrarian Revolution," 515–17; Fowler, *Agrarian Radicalism*, 10–11.

116. Raymond B. Craib, *Cartographic Mexico: A History of State Fixations and Fugitive Landscapes* (Durham: Duke University Press, 2004), 55–90; Emilio Kourí, *A Pueblo Divided: Business, Property and Community in Papantla, Mexico* (Stanford: Stanford University Press, 2004).

117. Skerritt, "Peasant Organisation," 11, 13.

118. Hernández Pérez, "Memoria de 1897," in García and Velasco, *Memorias e informes*, 6:63.

119. Craib, *Cartographic Mexico*, 124.

120. Falcón, *El agrarismo en Veracruz*, 28–29; De la Peña, *Veracruz económico*, 1:139.

121. Medel, *San Andrés Tuxtla*, 1:399–404; Hernández Pérez, "Memoria de 1897," in García and Velasco, *Memorias e informes*, 6:57–58.

122. In Acayucán the jefe político ordered forcible vaccinations. González Fernández, "Memoria . . . de Los Tuxtlas . . . 28 de Junio de 1890"; Rosas Landa, "Memoria . . . de Acayucán . . . 15 de Abril de 1891"; Gómez, "Memoria . . . de Cosamaloapan . . . 10 Mayo de 1907," in García and Velasco, *Memorias e informes*, 6:44–45, 110, 119.

123. Medel, *San Andrés Tuxtla*, 3:86, 1:528; Padua, *Movimiento Revolucionario*, 14.

124. Alemán, *Remembranzas*, 17–18.

125. Padua, *Movimiento Revolucionario*, 11.

126. Ibid., 64–65; Fowler, "The Agrarian Revolution," 520; Medel, *San Andrés Tuxtla*, 1:509–26.

127. Martínez Alarcón, *San Cristóbal*, 51–56; Medel, *San Andrés Tuxtla*, 1:528, 546–55; Santiago Martínez Hernández, *Tiempos de Revolución: la Revolución en el Sur de Veracruz vista por un campesino zoque-popoluca* (Mexico City: Premiá Editora, 1982), 44–46.

128. González Sierra, *Los Tuxtlas*, 75; Padua, *Movimiento Revolucionario*, 111–16.

129. Stabilization is a relative term; self-proclaimed Villistas seized Santiago Tuxtla in 1916 and raided San Andrés in 1919. Medel, *San Andrés Tuxtla*, 2:83–90, 174–76.

130. Falcón and García, *La semilla en el surco*, 147–48.

131. Martínez Alarcón, *San Cristóbal*, 80; Fowler, "The Agrarian Revolution," 517–23.

132. Falcón, *El agrarismo en Veracruz,* 36.

133. Fowler, "The Agrarian Revolution," 528–29.

134. Carlos Carrión was a key powerbroker in the 1940 federal election; Francisco Turrent was federal deputy for San Andrés in 1949. I-26 to Gobernación, 10/13/1925, AGN/DGIPS-170/8; Elías to Cerdán, 09/10/1940, AHEV-766/547/178; "List of federal deputies for 1949," AGN/DGIPS-109/2-1/236/1.

135. De la Peña, *Veracruz estadístico,* 1:133–34.

136. I-21 to Gobernación, 09/30/1931, AGN/DGIPS-171/1.

137. Vecinos Tierra Blanca to Rodríguez, 01/16/1933, SEP/DGEP-5349/12-5-2-154; López Huitrón to Cárdenas, 10/08/1937, AGN/LCR-404.4/35.

138. Olvera, "La estructura económica de Veracruz," 33.

139. I-11 to Gobernación, 03/17/1932, AGN/DGIPS-171/2; assorted reports June–July 1936, AGN/DGIPS-171/7.

140. Martínez Alarcón, *San Cristóbal,* 113–41.

141. López Huitrón to Cárdenas, 09/23/1938, AGN/LCR-404.4/35; Elías to Cerdán, 09/10/1940, AHEV-766/547/178.

142. I-14 to Gobernación, 01/24/1925, I-2 to Gobernación, 05/18/1925, AGN/DGIPS170/7; John Lear, *Workers, Neighbors, and Citizens: The Revolution in Mexico City* (Lincoln: University of Nebraska Press, 2001), 160; Iber, *Neither Peace nor Freedom,* 150–51.

143. Fowler, "The Agrarian Revolution," 527–33.

144. De la Peña, *Veracruz estadístico,* 1:276; PS-2 to Gobernación, 08/25/1938, AGN/DGIPS-135/310(6.1)"38."

145. Moreno to Cárdenas, 01/20/1940, AGN/DGG-2/012.2(26)/1/65; assorted protests, AGN/LCR-555.1/149.

146. Rascón to Cárdenas, 08/22/1938, AGN/LCR-404.1/4091; comisariado ejidal Caleria to Cárdenas, 02/23/1940, AGN/LCR-542.1/211; assorted papers, AGA25/28320.

147. De la Peña, *Veracruz Económico,* 1:336–41.

148. Ibid., 1:28.

149. Dehesa report 1894, BD-VIII/4440.

150. In Chicontepec, for example, Southworth found three leather tanneries, twenty bakers, and sixty small distilleries. Southworth, *Veracruz-Llave,* 153.

151. De la Peña, *Veracruz Económico,* 1:139; Falcón and García, *La semilla en el surco,* 28.

152. De la Peña, *Veracruz Económico,* 2:494, 607; Ministerio de Fomento, *Censo del Estado de Guerrero 1900,* 50; Ministerio de Fomento, *Censo de 1900,* 8, 204, 252–77; Falcón and García, *La semilla en el surco,* 19–22.

153. Chagoya, "Memoria . . . de Chicontepec . . . 5 de Julio de 1890," in García and Velasco, *Memorias e informes,* 1:194–95.

154. Chagoya, "Memoria . . . de Chicontepec . . . 29 de Abril de 1891," in García and Velasco, *Memorias e informes,* 1:246–47.

155. López report 1923, AGA24/5376; Chagoya, "Memoria . . . de Chicontepec . . . 1891," in García and Velasco, *Memorias e informes,* 1:228; *Enciclopedia Municipal de Veracruz: Chicontepec,* 78–79, 102–5.

156. Kourí, *A Pueblo Divided,* 199–204, 276–80.

157. In De la Peña's opinion *desamortización* "barely passed Papantla." De la Peña, *Veracruz Económico,* 1:138–39.

158. Although the emic definition of a small ranch in the Huasteca is generous; the properties of Manuel Peláez, generally classed as a rancher, amounted to over thirty thousand hectares. Myrna I. Santiago, "Huasteca Crude: Indians, Ecology, and Labor in the Mexican Oil Industry, Northern Veracruz, 1900–1938" (Ph.D. diss., University of California Berkeley, 1997), 33–34.

159. Dehesa report 1910, BD-IX/5069.

160. See, for example, the 1836 Totonac document that deems cattle "against the order of nature" or the 1856 Plan de Tantoyuca that declared "war to the death against private property" and "the capitalists." Cited, respectively, in Santiago, "Huasteca Crude," 37; Falcón and García, *La semilla en el surco,* 29.

161. Santiago, "Huasteca Crude," 31–36; Falcón and García, *La semilla en el surco,* 28–29; De la Peña, *Veracruz Económico,* 1:138; Kourí, *A Pueblo Divided,* 205–35.

162. Skerritt, "Peasant Organisation," 24–25.

163. De la Peña, *Veracruz Económico,* 1:225; Reyna, "Memoria de 1890," "Memoria de 1891," in García and Velasco, *Memorias e informes,* 1:79–105.

164. Texcatepec lost its municipal status on December 8, 1891. Dehesa report 1894, BD-VIII/4282.

165. Dehesa report 1894, BD-VIII/4290, 4352.

166. Santiago, "Huasteca Crude," 33, 60–61; López report, AGA24/5376; *Enciclopedia Municipal de Veracruz: Chicontepec,* 84.

167. Of which perhaps half a million hectares were actually occupied by oil camps. Santiago, "Huasteca Crude," 54–55, 120–22; Ivonne Carillo Dewar, *Industria petrolera y desarrollo capitalista en el norte de Veracruz, 1900–1990* (Xalapa: Universidad Veracruzana, 1993), 49.

168. Young, *Member for Mexico,* 73; Santiago, "Huasteca Crude," 51–113.

169. Falcón and García, *La semilla en el surco,* 67–71.

170. For an overview of the relationship between the oil industry, the revolution, and the peasantry, see Ana María Serna, *Manuel Peláez y la vida rural en la Faja de Oro: Petróleo, revolución y sociedad en el norte de Veracruz, 1910–1928* (Mexico City: Instituto de Investigaciones Dr. José Maria Luis Mora, 2008).

171. Santiago, "Huasteca Crude," 51–53.

172. De la Peña, *Veracruz Económico,* 1:216.

173. In Womack's pithy description, "country people who did not want to move and therefore got into a revolution." Womack, *Zapata,* ix.

174. Santiago, "Huasteca Crude," 85.

175. Fowler, *Agrarian Radicalism*, 27.

176. *Enciclopedia Municipal de Veracruz: Chicontepec*, 107–9.

177. Banco Ganadero SA de Tampico to Avila Camacho, 10/22/1943, AGN/MAC-540.1/2.

178. López to SEP, 04/30/1936, SEP/DGEP-1347/16.

179. Assorted correspondence 1937–38, AGN/LCR-559.1/6; Cerdán to Alemán, 04/16/1943, AGN/DGIPS-773/1.

180. I-75 to Gobernación, 09/09/1935, 10/03/1935, AGN/DGIPS-171/6.

181. Banco Ganadero SA de Tampico to Avila Camacho, 08/12/1942, AGN/MAC-540.1/2.

182. Muñoz report 1951, BD-XV/8241.

183. Governor's report 1951, BD-XV/8214; 1950, BD-XIV/788; 1946, BD-XIII/7378, 7388.

184. *Diario de Xalapa*, 04/23/1949, 03/24/1948; Siemens, *Between the Summit and the Sea*, 70; *Adelante*, 09/17/1949; Ortiz to Román Lugo, 1945, AHEV-1324/548/0; Muñoz report 1951, BD-XV/8214.

185. Octavio Aguilar de la Parra, *Mi tío, el cacique . . . ensayo político anecdótico* (Mexico City: Corporación Editorial, 1985), 169–70.

186. T. Philip Terry, *Terry's Guide to Mexico* (Boston: Houghton Mifflin, 1911), 462.

187. Alfonso Valencia Ríos, *Historia de El Dictamen* (Xalapa: Editorial del Gobierno del Estado, 1979), 11; Del Palacio Montiel, *Indice del fondo hemerográfico*, 38–53.

188. Fowler, *Agrarian Radicalism*, 100; Medin, *El minimato presidencial*, 96.

189. Corzo Ramírez et al., *Cándido Aguilar*, 285.

190. Roderic A. Camp, *Mexican Political Biographies* (Austin: University of Texas Press, 1995), 924–25; "Relación de las comandancias de las zonas militares," 09/01/1948, AGN/MAV-550/19.

191. Inside Veracruz Alemán's governorship had been distinguished by a heavy initial reliance on schoolmates from the D.F., dubbed the *polacos*. Author's interview, Francisco Villalón, México, D.F. 05/13/1998.

192. Corzo Ramírez et al., *Cándido Aguilar*, 272; Falcón and García, *La semilla en el surco*, 362.

193. PS-10 to Gobernación, 10/03/1939, AGN/DGIPS-140/9; F. Martínez to Gobernación, 12/29/1939, AGN/DGIPS-77/5-130-625; Fowler, *Agrarian Radicalism*, 132–33.

194. Paul Gillingham, "Military Caciquismo in the Priista State," in Ben Fallaw and Terry Rugeley, eds., *Forced Marches: Militaries, Cacicazgos, and the Uneven Development of Mexican Politics* (Tucson: University of Arizona Press, 2012), 210–37.

195. Falcón and García, *La semilla en el surco*, 194, 391; Fowler, *Agrarian Radicalism*, 121–29; PS-2 to Gobernación, 02/27/1940, AGN/DGIPS-78/5.

196. Informes de tesorería, AHEV-1229/024/0.

197. *Diario de Xalapa*, 05/09/1945.

198. Consular reports, 01/30/1941 to 10/23/1942, FO371/30586.

199. Paul Gillingham, "Who Killed Crispín Aguilar? Violence and Order in the Post-revolutionary Countryside," in Wil Pansters, ed., *Violence, Coercion and State-Making in Twentieth-Century Mexico: The Other Half of the Centaur* (Stanford: Stanford University Press, 2012), 91–111.

200. PS-2 to Gobernación, 26 February, 03/03/1940, AGN/DGIPS-78/5 & 6; Gillingham, "Military Caciquismo," 223.

201. Forzán to Gobernación, 01/26/1944, AGN/DGIPS-98/6.

3. Peasants, Presidents, and Carpetbaggers

1. Santos, *Memorias*, 871.

2. *El Universal*, 07/12/1948.

3. PS-42 to Gobernación, 05/16/1944, AGN/DGIPS-782/2-1/44/274; Comisariado ejidal Las Cruces to Catalán Calvo, 09/01/1944, AGN/DGG-2/311G(9)2/241; Díaz Cerda to Gobernación, 01/19/1945, AGN/DGG-2.311M(9)/4B; Alvarez to SEP, 10/15/1942, SEP/DGEP-5611/16-9-4-74.

4. Catalán Calvo to PRM, December 1944, AGN/DGG-2.311M(9)/5B/75.

5. PS-12 to Gobernación, 12/16/1945, AGN/DGIPS-788/2-1/45/374.

6. See Donato Miranda's speech in Chilapa, 09/23/1944, AGN/DGG-2/311G(9)2/241, or Ojeda's claim that the governor "lived getting drunk in Chilpancingo and living in palaces in Acapulco," PS-12 to Gobernación, 08/28/1944, AGN/DGIPS-782/2-1/44/274.

7. Manuel Avila Camacho himself complained that he was perceived as a weak president. "Annual Report on Mexico, 1946," FO371/60940/AN397.

8. The numbers of federal *maestros rurales* in Guerrero jumped from 291 in 1928 to 820 in 1936. Secretaría de Educación Pública, *Memoria que indica el estado que guarda el ramo de educación pública el 31 de agosto de 1930* (Mexico City: Secretaría de Educación Pública, 1930); Secretaría de Educación Pública, *Memoria de la SEP de septiembre de 1936 a agosto de 1937* (Mexico City: Secretaría de Educación Pública, 1937).

9. PS-10 to Gobernación, 07/18/1940, AGN/DGIPS-173/311(7.2)1.

10. Cadena to Avila Camacho, 10/15/1942, AGN/DGG-2.311M(9)/5B/53; ORC assorted libros.

11. Ojeda to Avila Camacho, 04/05/1943, AGN/MAC-542.1/9; Gutiérrez Avila, *Ojeda*, 64–65.

12. Costa Chica refugees to Padilla, 06/01/1943, AGN/MAC-542.1/579.

13. Rueda Flores to 27a zona, 05/30/1942, AGN/MAC-405.1/3; PS-12 to Gobernación, 02/16/1945, AGN/DGIPS-788/2-1/45/374.

14. Comisariados ejidales Acapulco to Avila Camacho, 07/14/1943, AGN/MAC-542.1/579.

15. *Trópico*, 01/07/1945.

16. Liga to Cárdenas, 11/07/1937, AGN/LCR-543.1/37; Ojeda to Alemán, 11/11/1944, AGN/DGG-2/311G(9)/239/2/II.

17. Assorted telegrams to Avila Camacho, December 1940, AGN/MAC-544.2/11-3; *Ultimas Noticias,* 12/06/1940; Ortíz to presidency, 01/19/1945, AGN/MAC-544.2/11-1; Marcial Rodríguez Saldaña, *La desaparición de poderes en el estado de Guerrero* (Chilpancingo: Universidad Autónoma de Guerrero, 1992), 116.

18. Gutiérrez Avila, *Ojeda,* 27–56; CCM to Cárdenas, 09/07/1937, AGN/LCR-404.1/6292; Ojeda to Avila Camacho, 11/12/1942, Nogueda Radilla to Avila Camacho, 06/16/1943, AGN/MAC-542.1/9.

19. PS-87 to Gobernación, 06/19/1944, PS-42 to Gobernación, 04/28, 30/1944, AGN/DGIPS-782/2–1/44/274.

20. Pérez Aldama to Gobernación, 08/28/1944, AGN/DGIPS-88; Loreto Orozco to Gobernación, 06/01/1944, AGN/DGIPS-782/2-1/131/779; PS-42 to Gobernación, 05/16/1944, AGN/DGIPS-782/2-1/44/274.

21. PS-42 to Gobernación, 04/28/1944, AGN/DGIPS-782/2-1/44/274.

22. I am grateful to Baltasar Leyva Ventura for generously providing me with a collection of family papers. B. Leyva Mancilla, "Datos biográficos" (undated MS), 1–2, "Hoja de servicio militar."

23. *Así somos,* 09/30/1993; report, political situation in Guerrero, 03/08/1926, AGN/DGIPS-136/310(7.1)1; Profile of Francisco Carreto, undated, AGN/DGIPS-809/2-1/51/524; Bustamante, "1934–1940," Salazar Adame, *La Cuestión Agraria Mexicana,* 445; author's interview, Juan Pablo Leyva, Chilpancingo, 06/21/2002; Alba Calderón to Gobernación, 01/04/1949, AGN/DGIPS-103/EAC; Vázquez, *Excélsior,* to Leyva Mancilla, 07/07/1945, AHEG-ramo ejecutivo/52/17; Comisariados ejidales Coyuca de Catalán to Alemán, 02/20/1948, AGN/DGIPS-799/2-1/48/431; Caccia Bernal to Gobernación, 02/02/1949, AGN/DGIPS-800/2-1/49/444.

24. Ruffo Figueroa, who became senator for Guerrero in 1946, likewise made his name outside the state, rising in Mexico City from librarian through the Treasury to end up as secretary-general of the Federación de Sindicatos de Trabajadores al Servicio del Estado. By 1962 over half of the nine precandidates for the governorship were from out of state. *El Universal* 07/12/1948; Michael Lettieri, "A Model Dinosaur: Power, Personal Networks and the Career of Rubén Figueroa," in *Mexican Studies/Estudios Mexicanos* 31 no. 2 (Summer 2015): 305–42.

25. Author's interview, Juan Pablo Leyva, Chilpancingo, 06/21/2002; Ojeda to Avila Camacho, 10/23/1944, AGN/DGG-2/311G(9)2/239/II.

26. PS-87 to Gobernación, 06/19/1944, AGN/DGIPS-782/2-1/44/274.

27. F. J. López Romero, "Adios señor general Leyva Mancilla" (undated clipping, Leyva Mancilla papers).

28. Author's interview, Juan Pablo Leyva, Chilpancingo, 06/21/2002.

29. Ojeda speech, Taxco, 06/25/1944, AGN/DGIPS-782/2-1/44/274; Leyva Mancilla, "Datos Biográficos," 1.

30. PS-42 to Gobernación, 05/16/1944, AGN/DGIPS-782/2-1/44/274; PS-6 to Gobernación, 11/21/1944, AGN/DGIPS-782/2-1/44/274; Ojeda to Alemán, 08/04/1948, AGN/MAV-544.2/11.

31. Liga to Avila Camacho, 06/12/1944, Liga Femenil "Mártires Hermanos Escudero" San Jerónimo to Gobernación, 06/28/1944, AGN/DGG-2/311G(9)2/239.

32. PS-42 to Gobernación, 04/30/1944, AGN/DGIPS-782/2-1/44/274; Saavedra to Gobernación, 11/22/1944, AGN/DGIPS-88.

33. Ojeda to Cárdenas, 06/15/1944, SDN-1-374/VII.

34. Ojeda to Alemán, 06/05/1944, Moises Reyes Parra to Alemán, 06/05/1944, Comisariado ejidal Los Arenales to Alemán, 06/10/1944, AGN/DGG-2/311G(9)/241/2/IV; Liga to Avila Camacho, 02/21/1941, AGN/DGG-2/012.2(9)/19/31; PS-12 to Gobernación, 07/10/1944, AGN/DGIPS-782/2-1/44/274; Ojeda to Avila Camacho, 08/31/1944, AGN/DGG-2/311G(9)/241/2/IV; Ojeda to Avila Camacho, 11/22/1944, AGN/DGG-2/311G(9)/239/2.

35. Comité Regional Campesino Chilapa to SEP, 10/15/1944, AGN/DGG-2/311G(9)/239/2.

36. Sindicato Minero Nacional to Avila Camacho, 11/08/1944, Ojeda to Avila Camacho, 11/11/1944, AGN/DGG-2/311G(9)/241/2/VI.

37. Orozco Aldaco to Avila Camacho, 11/09/1944, AGN/DGG-2/311G(9)/239/2/II; Comisariado ejidal Las Cruces to Alemán, 09/01/1944, AGN/DGG-2/311G(9)/241/2/IV.

38. Ojeda to Avila Camacho, 11/22/1944, AGN/DGG-2/311G(9)/239/2; Ojeda to Alemán, 11/27/1944, AGN/DGG-2/311G(9)/241/2/VI; Ojeda to Avila Camacho, 01/03/1945, AGN/DGG-2/311G(9)/239/2/I.

39. Caracas Cruz to Gobernación, 01/15/1945, AGN/DGIPS-788/2-1/45/347; Inspector Acapulco to Gobernación, 01/21/1945, Córdoba Lara to Avila Camacho, 01/15/1945, AGN/DGG-2/311G(9)/241/2/VI.

40. PS-6 to Gobernación, 11/21/1944, AGN/DGIPS-782/2-1/44/274; Liga to Avila Camacho, 12/20/1944, AGN/DGG-2/311M(9)/80; Catalán Calvo to Gobernación, 01/02/1945, AGN/DGG-2.311M(9)/5B/75.

41. The governor who had to install them agreed. President comité municipal PRM to Chilpancingo, 12/06/1944, AGN/DGG-2.311M(9)/4B/12; Catalán Calvo to PRM, AGN/DGG-2.311M(9)/5B/75.

42. Catalán Calvo to Gobernación, 01/02/1945, AGN/DGG-2.311M(9)/5B/75; Palacios to Procurador General de Justicia, DF, 05/01/1945, AGN/DGG-2/012.2(9)/19/18; PS-33 to Gobernación, 07/23/1945, AGN/DGIPS-788/2-1/45/347; press clipping, 12/08/1952, AP189/394.2DEL.

43. Martínez to Gobernación, 01/02/1945, AGN/DGG-2.311M(9)/4B/24; Ojedistas Cd Altamirano to Gobernación, 01/02/1945, AGN/DGG-2.311M(9)/4B/40.

44. Author's analysis, electoral reports from seventy-two municipios Guerrero, AGN/DGG-2.311M(9) series.

45. Ojeda to Alemán, 01/27/1945, AGN/DGIPS-788/2-1/45/347; vecinos Petaquillas to Avila Camacho, 02/24/1945, AGN/DGG-2.311M(9)80/5B/75; Prudente to Chilpancingo, 07/19/1945, AGN/DGG-2/311P(9)/1/97B; PS-1 & PS-2 to Gobernación,

08/07/1945, AGN/DGIPS-89/2-1/131/726; Ojeda to Gobernación, 10/06/1945, AGN/DGG-2/311P(29)1/97B.

46. The Gobernación report argued unconvincingly that the carefully arranged ambush of Francisco Hernández Solís was the work of a lone embittered peon trying to avoid a minor debt. In this case the details provided by agraristas, including multiple reports of the killers hiding out in the presidente municipal's house, are more convincing. PS-4 to Gobernación, 05/17/1945, AGN/DGIPS-788/2-1/45/347; Ojeda to Avila Camacho, 05/14/1945, AGN/MAC-544.2/11–4; Gutiérrez Avila, *Ojeda*, 66.

47. *El Universal*, 05/27/1945; *La Verdad*, 02/24/1949; Migoni to Gobernación, 10/09/1945, AGN/DGIPS-2034/2-1/AGD/818.

48. PS-20 to Gobernación, 09/07/1945, AGN/DGIPS-92/2-1/131/774GM.

49. *Diario de Xalapa*, 06/11/1945.

50. Assorted election reports, AGN/DGG-2.311M(9)/4B.

51. Gurrola to Gobernación, 11/16/1946, AGN/DGIPS-792/2-1/46/425; Gobernación to SEDENA, 11/27/1946, AGN/DGIPS-793/2-1/46/428; Baig Serra to Gobernación, 11/27/1946, AGN/DGIPS-792/2-1/46/425.

52. For Luis Medina, the padillistas had begun to disperse in September, and the process was "so rapid and profound that they very quickly ceased to be a political concern." Medina, *Civilismo y modernización*, 91.

53. These included "some prominent members" of the company, which—given Alemán's subsequent military takeover of the oil fields—might indicate orchestration by the government. Baig Serra to Gobernación, 11/26/1946, Baig Serra to Gobernación, 11/27/1946, AGN/DGIPS-792/2-1/46/425.

54. IPS 37 to Lamberto Ortega, 12/03/1946, AGN/DGIPS-793/2-1/46/428.

55. Another ex-governor, Héctor F. López, had been one of the national leaders of Padilla's Partido Democrático Mexicano. Medina, *Civilismo y modernización*, 61.

56. Leyva Mancilla to Gobernación, 11/27/1946, AGN/DGIPS-793/2-1/46/428.

57. PS-7 to Gobernación, 12/03/1946, AGN/DGIPS-793/2-1/46/428.

58. The earliest warning in his correspondence was a letter from a personal agent of his in Jalisco, dated 26 November. García Mercado to Leyva Mancilla, 11/26/1946, AHEG-ramo ejecutivo/523/8.

59. Gobernación to SEDENA, 11/27/1946, AGN/DGIPS-793/2-1/46/428; SNTE Teloloapan to Alemán, 11/29/1946, AGN/MAV-559.1/1; Ojeda to Alemán, 12/19/1946, AGN/MAV-559.1/1.

60. Ojeda to Alemán, 12/19/1946, AGN/MAV-559.1/1.

61. PS-7 to Gobernación, 12/03/1946, AGN/DGIPS-793/2-1/46/428.

62. Ojeda to Alemán, 12/19/1946, 09/21/1947, AGN/MAV-559.1/1.

63. Departamento de Agricultura y Ganadería memorandum on foot-and-mouth Veracruz, 02/25/1947, AGN/MAV-425.5/2–29.

64. Bateman to Bevin, 02/24/1947, FO371/60940/AN958, memorandum, instructions re foot-and-mouth, Chilpancingo, 12/1947, AMI-1947.

65. Leyva Mancilla reports, 1947, 1948, AP-175/352.072.073ETN; author's interviews, Edgar Pavía Guzmán, Chilpancingo 04/04, 5/2002; Morales Camacho and Ríos Thivol to Gobernación, 09/04/1947, AGN/DGIPS-84/2-1/131/655.

66. Orden 137 del Director Federal de Seguridad de destacar un agente en Guerrero, date unknown, AGN/DFS-1-93 exp 100-10-1 L.1A.

67. Ruffo Figueroa to Alemán, 10/07/1947, AGN/MAV-559.1/1; author's interviews, Edgar Pavía Guzmán, Chilpancingo 04/04, 5/2002.

68. Edgar Pavía Guzmán, *Acciones Políticas Ganaderas en Guerrero* (Chilpancingo: Asociación de historiadores de Guerrero, 1997), 34.

69. Comisión Mexico–Americana para la Eradicación de la Fiebre Aftosa pamphlet, "Comités de Orientación para la Lucha Contra la Fiebre Aftosa" (Mexico City, 1947), 1; Delgado to Ojeda, 09/23/1947, Marín to Hernández, 11/17/1947, AGN/MAV-559.1/1.

70. Orden 137 del Director Federal de Seguridad de destacar un agente en Guerrero, date unknown, AGN/DFS-1-93-100-10-1.L.1A.

71. Pavía Guzmán, *Acciones Políticas Ganaderas*, 31.

72. PS-45 to Gobernación, 08/06/1947, AGN/DGIPS-796/2-1/47/430; Delgado to Ojeda, 09/23/1947, Urióstegui to Ojeda, 09/20/1947, AGN/MAV-559.1/1.

73. Ríos Thivol to Gobernación, 09/26/1947, AGN/DGIPS-84/MRT; Ruffo Figueroa to Alemán, 10/07/1947, AGN/MAV-559.1/1; *La Prensa*, 09/23/1947; *El Suriano*, 09/23/1947; *El Universal*, 09/25/1947; author's interviews, Edgar Pavía Guzmán, Chilpancingo 04/04, 5/2002.

74. Webber, "Down Mexico's Río Balsas," 254.

75. Bateman to Bevin, 09/30/1947, FO371/AN3527/395/26.

76. Ruffo Figueroa to Alemán, 10/07/1947, AGN/MAV-559.1/1.

77. Ríos Thivol to Gobernación, 09/16/1947, AGN/DGIPS-84/MRT/III.

78. Ríos Thivol to Gobernación, 09/26/1947, AGN/DGIPS-84/MRT; Urióstegui to Ojeda, 09/20/1947, AGN/MAV-559.1/1; PS-34 & PS-8 to Gobernación, 09/24/1947, AGN/DGIPS-796/2-1/47/430.

79. Ojeda to Alemán, 09/21, 22/1947, AGN/MAV-559.1/1; Coquet to Gobernación, 06/29/1948, AGN/DGIPS-799/2-1/48/431.

80. Ríos Thivol to Gobernación, 09/26/1947, AGN/DGIPS-84/MRT; Jaimes to Leyva Mancilla, 11/29/1947, PS-23 to Gobernación, 12/05/1947, AGN/DGIPS-796/1–2/47/430; Agents 8 and 13 to DFS, 10/23/1947, AGN/DFS-Castrejón Adrián "General" Legajo, 1 12–13.

81. Leyva Mancilla to Gobernación, 11/26/1947, AGN/DGIPS-796/1–2/47/430.

82. Bateman to Bevin, 02/24/1947, FO371/60940/AN958.

83. Moncada, *¡Cayeron!*, 157–227.

84. The Ometepec landowner Higinio Morga. Gobernación to Leyva Mancilla, 12/04/1947, AGN/DGIPS-796/1–2/47/430.2.

85. Comisariados ejidales Mina to Alemán, 02/20/1948, AGN/DGIPS-799/2-1/48/431.

86. Liga to Alemán, 03/01/1948, AGN/MAV-404.1/1990; Ojeda to Gobernación, 11/05/1948, AGN/DGG-2.311M(9)/4B/74.

87. Gómez Galeana to Alemán, 04/25/1947, Aburto Gómez to Alemán, 02/03/1948, AGN/DGIPS-12/2/380(9)38; PS-50 and PS-58 to Gobernación, 08/06/1948, AGN/DGIPS-799/2-1/48/431.

88. *Excélsior,* 09/28/1948; SEDENA to Ojeda, 09/13/1948, AGN/MAV-559.1/1.

89. Comisariado ejidal Pilcaya to Alemán, 11/01/1947, AGN/MAV-425.5/11.

90. Coyuca de Catalán, Acapulco, Coahuayutla, Cuajinicuilapa, Cuautepec, San Jerónimo, San Marcos, Olinalá, Tepetlalcingo, Zirándaro, and Tlacotepec. Liga to Alemán, 05/01/1948, AGN/DGIPS-799/2-1/48/431.

91. Assorted correspondence, 1948, SDN-1-374/VI.

92. *Hoja de servicios* General Miguel Z. Martínez, SDN-398/XVI.

93. Report, political situation Guerrero, 03/08/1926, AGN/DGIPS-136/310 (7.1)1; Rodríguez Saldaña, *La desaparición de poderes,* 107, 117.

94. Barajas to Gobernación, 06/28/1948, PS-31 to Gobernación, 06/28/1948, Coquet to Gobernación, 06/29/1948, AGN/DGIPS-799/2-1/48/431; Prado Macías to Ojeda, 01/24/1949, AGN/MAV-544.5/340.

95. PS-34 to Gobernación, 12/07/1948, AGN/DGIPS-91/2-1/131/748.

96. Ojeda to Alemán, 08/04/1948, AGN/MAV-544.2/11.

97. Assorted protests, AGN/DGG-2.311M(9)/4B/76, 78, AGN/DGG-2.311M(9)/3B/6.

98. Sectores popular y obrero Acapulco to Gobernación, 10/30/1948, AGN/DGG-2.311M(9)/4B; Zamora to Gobernación, 10/26/1948, AGN/MAV-544.2/11/28.

99. Román Castro to Sánchez Taboada, 10/19/1948, AGN/DGG-2.311M(9)/3B; Ojeda to Gobernación, 11/05/1948, 01/12/1948, 12/17/1948, AGN/DGG-2.311M(9)/4B/74, 80; Ojeda to Gobernación, 12/09/1948, AGN/DGG-2.311M(9)/3B/11; Reivindicación Social Arcelia to Gobernación, 10/26/1948, AGN/DGG-2.311M(9)/3B/8, 27.

100. Assorted telegrams, AGN/DGG-2.311M(9)/3B/6.

101. PS-58 to Gobernación, 12/07/1948, AGN/DGIPS-799/2-1/40/431, *La Verdad,* 01/04/1949.

102. Iguala, Ometepec, Taxco, Teloloapan, and Tixtla. Ojeda to Gobernación, 12/28/1948, AGN/DGG-2.311M(9)/3B/6.

103. *La Verdad*'s incomplete list counted sixteen parallel ayuntamientos. *La Verdad,* 01/04/1949.

104. Comité Democrático Independiente Ajuchitlán to Gobernación, 01/01/1949, AGN/DGG-2.311M(9)/3B/6.

105. Gobernación to Leyva Mancilla, 12/28/1948, AGN/DGG-2.311M(9)/3B/6.

106. Leyva Mancilla to Gobernación, 01/05/1949, AGN/DGIPS-800/2-1/49/444.

107. Assorted reports, AGN/DGIPS-800/2-1/49/444, AGN/DGIPS-91/2-1/131/748, AGN/DGIPS-94/2-1/131/802 and 2.1/131/805.

108. Florentino Figueroa and Job Gutiérrez Ramos. JNM to Gobernación, 10/11/1948, AGN/DGIPS-103/EAC; PS-34 to Gobernación, 12/07/1948, AGN/DGIPS-91/2-1/131/748/CMC.

109. Ojeda to Gobernación, 12/31/1948, 6/01/1948, AGN/DGG/2.311M(9)/3B/6.

110. Alba Calderón to Gobernación, 01/04/1949, AGN/DGIPS-103/EAC.

111. Caccia Bernal to Gobernación, 02/02/1949, AGN/DGIPS-800/2-1/49/444.

112. Carreto Rodríguez to DFS, 03/22/1949, AGN/DFS-Guerrero/48-8H69L1; Ojeda to Ruiz Cortines, 03/07/1949, AGN/DGG/2.311M(9)/3B/6.

113. *La Verdad,* 02/23, 24, 26/1949, 03/02, 08, 20/1949; Rosales to De la Selva, 05/03/1949, AGN/MAV-132.1/198.

114. Carreto Rodríguez to DFS, 03/22/1949, AGN/DFS-Guerrero/48-8H69L1.

115. *La Verdad,* 03/05, 09/1949; *Excélsior,* 03/20/1949.

116. Through the formulaic request for indefinite leave. *La Verdad,* 03/30/1949, 04/06/1949.

117. Leyva Mancilla report 1946, AP-175/352.072.073ETN.

118. *El Popular,* 10/08/1952; Leyva Mancilla report 1951, AP-175/352.072.073ETN; circular to subrecaudadores de rentas, 08/20/1947, AHEG-ramo ejecutivo-53/"gobernación y justicia 1947."

119. Governors' informes, De la Peña, *Guerrero estadístico,* 2:599–622, INEGI *Estadísticas históricas* CD-ROM; this volume chap. 4.

120. INEGI, *Estadísticas históricas* CD-ROM; Gómez Maganda report 1952, AP-173/352.072.073ETN.

121. De la Peña, *Guerrero estadístico,* 2:622; Leyva Mancilla reports 1949, 1950, 1951, AP-175/352.072.073ETN; author's interviews, Edgar Pavía Guzmán, Chilpancingo 05/04, 05/2002, Hermilo Castorena, Chilpancingo, 11/26/1997. Leyva Mancilla took great interest in the malaria campaign; he had contracted a severe case himself during the revolution. Leyva Mancilla, "Datos biográficos," 1.

122. Leyva Mancilla report 1951, AP-175/352.072.073ETN; *Periódico Oficial,* 09/25/1946.

123. Córdoba Lara was never prosecuted; Francisco Leyva was allowed to leave unhampered for the US. *La Prensa,* 06/21/1950; Natalia Guadarrama de Sámano to Ruiz Cortines, 02/27, 28/1950, AGN/DGG-2/012.2(9)/20/42.

124. Alba Calderón to Gobernación, 01/04/1949, AGN/DGIPS-103/EAC; *La Verdad,* 03/31/1949; Caccia Bernal to Gobernación, 02/02/1949, AGN/DGIPS-800/2-1/49/444.

125. Lettieri, "A Model Dinosaur," 317; Leyva Mancilla report 1951, AP-175/352.072.073ETN; *La Verdad,* 05/04/1949; Agent 65 to DFS, 01/26/1951, AGN/DFS-Castrejón Adrián General Legajo 1 27.

126. De la Peña, *Guerrero estadístico,* 2:559–78.

127. James W. Wilkie, "El complejo militar–industrial en México durante la década de 1930; diálogo con el General Juan Andreu Almazán," *Revista Mexicana de Ciencia Política* 20, no. 77 (1974): 59–65.

128. Stephen R. Niblo and Diane M. Niblo, "Acapulco in Dreams and Reality," *Mexican Studies/Estudios Mexicanos* 24, no. 1 (2008): 40.

129. Niblo, *Mexico in the 1940s*, 275; *Trópico*, 03/18/1945.

130. Acosta to Sánchez Taboada, 08/27/1948, AGN/DGG-2.311M(9)/4B/74; Roger J. Bergeret Muñoz et al., "Evolución y mutación del modelo turístico de Guerrero: Caso Acapulco 1945–2000," in Bustamante and Sarmiento, *La reinvención de Guerrero*, 495.

131. Valdés, for example, took over the Cooperativa de Cacalutla's lands. Antonio Balderas Cañas, "El sector privado," in Max Arturo López Hernández et al., eds., *La formación del poder en el estado de Guerrero* (Chilpancingo: Universidad Autónoma de Guerrero, 1997), 83–97; Impulsora de Acapulco, SA and El Papagayo, SA to Alemán, 01/23/1951, AGN/DGIPS-809/2-1/51/524; Gill, "Los Escudero, de Acapulco," 308.

132. Niblo and Niblo, "Acapulco in Dreams and Reality," 42.

133. INAH/AS-PHO/CUAUH/5/34, 42; INAH/AS-PHO/CUAUH/5/2, 5; Ignacio Marquina, *Memorias* (Mexico City: Instituto Nacional de Antropología e Historia, 1994), 168.

134. See, for example, *La Prensa*, 10/28/1949, where Leyva Mancilla calls the hostile INAH report "a crime against the patria."

135. RVS to Gobernación, 03/21/1950, AGN/DGIPS-102/RVS.

136. RVS to Gobernación, 06/01, 10, 13/1950, AGN/DGIPS-102/RVS; Leyva Mancilla military records, PPBLV.

137. Ariza Cardona to Ruiz Cortines, 09/18/1954, AGN/DGG-2.311M(9)/2B/155.

138. Leyva Mancilla, "Datos biográficos," 3; José Francisco Ruiz Massieu, funeral eulogy to Baltasar R. Leyva Mancilla, PPBLV, 5.

139. LOP to Gobernación, 10/20/1949, AGN/DGIPS-800/2-1/49/444.

140. The ritual pro-Ojeda telegrams from January 1950 were notably thin and originated from a handful of municipios. Assorted telegrams, AGN/DGG-2.311G(9)3/242; RVS to Gobernación, 06/14/1950, AGN/DGIPS-102/RVS.

141. López Salgado to Ojeda, 10/01/1948, AGN/DGG-2.311G(9)3/242; RVS to Gobernación, 03/21/1950, AGN/DGIPS-102/RVS.

142. Assorted telegrams to Alemán, 01/16–21/1950, AGN/DGG-2.311G(9)3/242; RVS to Gobernación, 04/26/1950, AGN/DGIPS-102/RVS; Burrows to State Department, 04/21/1950, NARG-712.00/4–2150.

143. RVS to Gobernación, 03/21/1950, 04/24/1950, 06/01/1950, AGN/DGIPS-102/RVS.

144. Only Caballero Aburto distributed posters and flyers before the presidential decision; Gómez Maganda began to do so the day he was informed of his candidacy. Assorted reports, RVS to Gobernación, 04/12/1950 to 06/28/1950, AGN/DGIPS-102/RVS.

145. RVS to Gobernación, 06/28/1950, AGN/DGIPS-102/RVS.

146. JCB to Gobernación, 10/05/1949, AGN/DGIPS-119/32.

147. RVS to Gobernación, 04/12/1950, AGN/DGIPS-102/RVS.

148. Catalán Calvo to de la Selva, 03/02/1950, AGN/MAV-544.2/11; Sociedad guerrerense to Alemán, 06/29/1950, AGN/DGG-2.311G(9)3/242.

149. RVS to Gobernación, 06/28/1950, AGN/DGIPS-102/RVS.

150. RVS to Gobernación, 06/28/1950 to 07/10/1950, AGN/DGIPS-102/RVS.

151. Ojeda to Sánchez Taboada, 07/05/1950, Ojeda to Alemán, 07/11/1950, Ojeda to Ruiz Cortines, 08/15/1950, AGN/DGG-2.311 G(9)3/242.

152. Assorted reports, January–June 1952, AGN/DFS-Guerrero-100–10–14–51H194L4, H203L4, H219L4, AGN/DFS-Guerrero-100–10–14–52H247L4, H264L4, H302L4, H313L4, H319L4, H2L5.

153. Santos, *Memorias,* 895; press clippings, August to October 1952, AGN/DGIPS-809/2-1/51/254.

154. Rodríguez Saldaña, *La desaparición de poderes,* 126, 130–33; *El Popular,* 10/08/1952; *Periódico Oficial,* 04/22/1953.

155. AP51/133.55 FIC.

156. AP189/394.2DEL; Torres to de la Selva, 09/22/1952, AGN/MAV-742/39535; Lanche Guillen to Gobernación, 05/04/1953, Lanche Guillén to Ruiz Cortines, 07/06/1953, AGN/DGG-2/012.2(9)/20/60 and 72; *La Prensa,* 10/13/1952; *El Popular,* 10/08/1952.

157. Rodríguez Saldaña, *La desaparición de poderes,* 126–33.

158. RVS to Gobernación, 10/20/1949, AGN/DGIPS-102/RVS.

159. Assorted letters, PAN to Gobernación, January 1952, AGN/DGG-2/311P(29)2/110B.

160. Rodríguez Saldaña, *La desaparición de poderes,* 125.

161. Laidlaw to State Department, 02/17/1950, NARG-712.00/2-1750.

162. Ojeda to Alemán, 10/18/1944, AGN/DGG-2/311G(9)2/239/II.

163. López Salgado to Avila Camacho, 05/07/1942, AGN/MAC-405.1/3.

164. Campesinos Ajuchitlán to Alemán, 12/08/1948, AGN/DGG-2.311M(9)/3B/6; *Excélsior,* assorted clippings October 1947, AGN/DGIPS-796/1–2/47/430.2.

165. Torreblanca to Alemán, 12/04/1946, AGN/MAV-542.1/2.

166. RVS to Gobernación, 03/21/1950, AGN/DGIPS-102/RVS.

167. Suarez Ruano to DFS, 03/09/1962, AGN/DFS-Guerrero-100-10-1-1962H229L10.

168. Gómez Maganda to Ruiz Cortines, 10/02/1950, AGN/DGG-2.311G(9)/242.

169. De la Peña, *Guerrero estadístico,* 2:599; Muñoz report 1950–53, BD-XV/8134.

170. Jiménez Garcia et al., *Historia General de Guerrero,* 4:208, 237–38, 255; Florencio Encarnación Ursúa, *Las Luchas de los Copreros guerrerenses* (Mexico City: Editora y Distribuidora Nacional, 1977), 74–78.

171. Of the four Aguirre brothers, three became bureaucrats; in 1996 Delfino's son Angel became governor. López Barroso, *Diccionario,* 14–20.

172. DFS report to De la Fuente, 02/22/1952, AGN/DFS-Guerrero-100-10-14-52H264L4; memorandum, election monitoring, June 1952, AGN/DGIPS-814/2-1/52/70.

173. Martínez to De la Fuente, 12/6/1950, AGN/DFS-Castrejón Adrían General VP Legajo 1 26.

174. FFM to Gobernación, 03/16/1950, AGN/DGIPS-129/26; Camp, *Mexican Political Biographies*, 594.

175. PS-34 and PS-8 to Gobernación, 09/24/1947, AGN/DGIPS-796/2-1/47/430.

176. Leyva Mancilla report 1951, AP-175/352.072.073ETN.

177. Over the border in Oaxaca the Colonia Militar Alvaro Obregón, with its four hundred troops, part-time pistoleros, and mobile voters, was the foundation of Heliodoro Charis's cacicazgo. Smith, *Pistoleros and Popular Movements*, 140–42.

4. Party, Peace, and Caciquismo

1. Ríos Thivol to Gobernación, 08/26/1949, AGN/DGIPS-802/2-1/49/546; PS-12 to Gobernación, 08/28/1949, AGN/DGIPS-782/2-1/44/274.

2. Pablo Piccato, *A History of Infamy: Crime, Truth and Justice in Mexico* (Oakland: University of California Press, 2017), 179; *Diario de Xalapa*, 07/01/1952.

3. Treasury report, AHEV-1229/024/1; *Adelante*, 12/15/1946, Leyva Mancilla report 1948, AP-175/352.072.073ETN.

4. LNCUG to Ruiz Cortines, 10/26/1945, AHEV-1324/548/0.

5. *Diario de Xalapa*, 05/25/1945.

6. "Lista incompleta de crímenes cometidos . . . por Crispín Aguilar," AGN/DGIPS-787/2-1/45/282.

7. González was a deputy at the time; Anaya had been a deputy in the early 1930s. Liga Altotonga to Avila Camacho, 09/17/1942, AGN/DGG-2/012.2(26)62/66/54; Fowler, *Agrarian Radicalism*, 137.

8. Fowler, *Agrarian Radicalism*, 100.

9. PS-7 to Gobernación, 01/15/1943, AGN/DGIPS-776/1; comisariado ejidal Ignacio de la Llave to Ruiz Cortines, 09/10/1946, AHEV-1399/417/24.

10. Migoni to Gobernación, 06/14/1945, AGN/DGIPS-787/2-1/45/282.

11. Assorted correspondence, AHEV-1234/544/0.

12. David Skerritt's chronology of peasant mobilization identifies 1945 as the peak of peasant submission. Skerritt, "Peasant Organisation," 114–65.

13. Urrutia to Gobernación, 05/13/1940, PS-10 to Gobernación, 10/03/1939, AGN/DGIPS-140/9.

14. Paxtián to Cárdenas, 10/23/1940, AGN/LCR-542.1/211.

15. PS-10 to Gobernación, 10/03/1939, AGN/DGIPS-140/9; Migoni to Gobernación, 02/14/1946, AGN/DGIPS-791/2-1/46/405.

16. Alberto J. Olvera, "The Rise and Fall of Union Democracy at Poza Rica," in Jonathan C. Brown and Alan Knight, *The Mexican Petroleum Industry in the Twentieth Century* (Austin: University of Texas Press, 1992), 84; Rafael Loyola Díaz, *El ocaso del radicalismo revolucionario: ferrocarrileros y petroleros: 1938–1947* (Mexico City: UNAM,

1991), 111–16, 192 ; PS-2 to Gobernación, 01/13/1940, AGN/DGIPS-78/5 ; Migoni to Gobernación, 02/23/1946, AGN/DGIPS-791/2-1/46/405.

17. Santoyo, *La mano negra*, 153–54.

18. Consular reports, 01/30/1942, 04/29/1942, 07/25/1942, FO371/30586.

19. Skerritt, "Peasant Organisation," 141.

20. PS-42 to Gobernación, 04/26/1945, AGN/DGIPS-787/2-1/45/282.

21. PS-2 to Gobernación, 01/10/1940, AGN/DGIPS-78/5; PS-5 to Gobernación, 05/06/1947, AGN/DGIPS-796/2-1/47/424.

22. Olvera, "Union Democracy at Poza Rica," 70–85; Santiago, "Huasteca Crude."

23. Forzán to Gobernación, 01/20, 26/1944, AGN/DGIPS-98/6.

24. Arriola to Pérez Aldama, 03/20/1940, AGN/DGIPS-78/6; Migoni to Gobernación, 06/20/1946, AGN/DGIPS-791/2-1/46/405.

25. Assorted correspondence, AHEV-1412/549/0.

26. *Diario de Xalapa*, 05/25/1945.

27. "Lista incompleta de crímenes cometidos . . . por Crispín Aguilar," AGN/DGIPS-787/2-1/45/282; *Diario de Xalapa*, 04/14/1950.

28. David Skerritt, "¿Qué es la *mano negra*?" in *Anuario del Centro de Estudios Históricos de la Universidad Veracruzana* (Xalapa: Universidad Veracruzana, 1980), 3:129–38.

29. *Diario de Xalapa*, 03/09/1950, 04/12/1950; corridos a Manuel Viveros, Manuel Parra, in G. Trigos, *El corrido veracruzano (una antología)* (Xalapa: Universidad Veracruzana, Instituto veracruzano de Cultura 1990), 64–67.

30. "Lista incompleta de crímenes cometidos . . . por Crispín Aguilar," AGN/DGIPS-787/2-1/45/282, Migoni to Gobernación, 10/10/1945, AGN/DGIPS-787/2-1/45/282.

31. Maldonado to Cárdenas, 12/04/1934, AGN/DGG-2/012.2(26)143/68/41; Santoyo, *La mano negra*, 152.

32. *El Dictamen*, 11/04/1947.

33. Aguilar to Avila Camacho, 08/23/1942, AGN/DGG-2/317.4(26)24/64.

34. PS-10 to Gobernación, 10/03/1939, AGN/DGIPS-140/9; Erasmo Hernández García, "Redes políticas y sociales: consolidación y permanencia del régimen posrevolucionario en Veracruz, 1920–1970" (Ph.D. diss., Universidad Veracruzana, 2010), 150.

35. Santos, *Memorias*, 650; Hernández García, "Redes políticas y sociales," 151.

36. Fowler, *Agrarian Radicalism*, 137; Corzo Ramírez et al., *Cándido Aguilar*, 291; Pérez Olivares, *Memorias*, 63; PS.10 to Gobernación, 10/03/1939, AGN/DGIPS-140/9; PS-2 to Gobernación, 01/19/1940, 02/19/1940, AGN/DGIPS-78/5.

37. Luis Medina, *Historia de la Revolución Mexicana, 1940–1952: Del cardenismo al avilacamachismo* (Mexico City: Colegio de México, 1978), 203; Corzo Ramírez et al., *Cándido Aguilar*, 14; Guzmán Carriles to Avila Camacho, 12/12/1942, AGN/DGG-2/311P(26)2/107.

38. Camp, *Mexican Political Biographies*, 924–25.

39. And the optimistic Jorge Cerdán. I-62 to Gobernación, 12/06/1943, AGN/DGIPS-776/1; Migoni to Gobernación, 07/18/1945, AGN/DGIPS-787/2-1/45/282.

40. López Vda. de Pampín to Alemán, 07/11/1951, AGN/MAV-001/4232.

41. *Diario de Xalapa*, 05/07/1945; Migoni to Gobernación, 04/05/1945, AGN/DGIPS-787/2-1/45/282; various authors, *Historia documental del Partido de la Revolución, tomo V: PRM–PRI, 1945–1950* (Mexico City: Partido Revolucionario Institucional, 1982), 398–402.

42. Migoni to Gobernación, 02/23/1946, 06/07/1946, AGN/DGIPS-791/2-1/46/405.

43. *Diario de Xalapa*, 06/11, 21/1945; Rodríguez to Alemán, 06/15/1945, Rueda to Avila Camacho, 06/28/1945, AGN/DGG-2/311P(26)/1/107.

44. *Diario de Xalapa*, 05/28/1945.

45. PS-2 to Gobernación, 03/05/1940, AGN/DGIPS-78/5.

46. This outline of Aguilar's geographical base comes from my analysis of the 1946 municipal election documentation in AHEV-1412/549/0 and the AGN/DGG-2.311M(26) series, supplemented by DGIPS reports such as PS-7 to Gobernación, 05/07/1940, AGN/DGIPS-127/2-1/266.7(726.1)/1.

47. "Un hijo de la chingada pelele." Migoni to Gobernación, 06/18, 21/1945, 09/26, 29/1945, 10/7, 10, 13/1945, AGN/DGIPS-787/2-1/45/282.

48. Codoner to State Department, July 1945, NARG-812.00/Guerrero/7-3145; Third Secretary Massey to State Department, 09/28/1948, NARG-812.00/9-2848; PS-19 to Gobernación, 08/03/1945, AGN/DGIPS-132/2-1/302.4(0.11)/2.

49. *Diario de Xalapa*, 06/23/1945.

50. Migoni to Gobernación, 06/14/1945, AGN/DGIPS-787/2-1/45/282.

51. Mange to Avila Camacho, 07/05/1945, SDN-1-356/X.

52. *Diario de Xalapa*, 07/04/1945.

53. Migoni to Gobernación, 06/14/1945, 10/17/1945, AGN/DGIPS-787/2-1/45/282.

54. Ejidatarios Ignacio de la Llave to Alemán, 06/26/1946, AGN/DGIPS-791/2-1/46/405; Cristiani to Gobernación Veracruz, 02/10/1947, AHEV-1506/544/0; González León to Coatzacoalcos garrison commander, 02/24/1946, Hernández Ayala to Gobernación, undated, Padillistas Córdoba to Gobernación, 03/13/1946, AGN/DGG-2/311P(26)/1/107.

55. For numerous protests, see AGN/DGG-2/311P(26)/1/107.

56. And these by Aguilaristas controlling their own clients. Migoni to Gobernación, 06/14/1945, AGN/DGIPS-787/2-1/45/282.

57. Migoni to Gobernación, 09/28/1945, 10/05/1945, AGN/DGIPS-787/2-1/45/282.

58. *Diario de Xalapa*, 07/01/1945.

59. Electoral Roll Commission to Ruiz Cortines, 03/02/1946, AHEV-1408/548.1/0.

60. Beteta to Ruiz Cortines, 04/11/1946, AHEV-1408/548.1/0.

61. Electoral Roll Commission to Ruiz Cortines, 02/27/1946, AHEV-1408/548.1/0.

62. *Excélsior,* 05/05/1946; Xalapa Electoral Commission to Federal Commission for Election Monitoring, 06/22/1946, "Relación de los municipios donde han sido defectuosos los trabajos de empadronamiento," AHEV-1408/548.1/0.

63. In Acayucán, Chinameca, Hueyapan, Jáltipan, Jesús Carranza, San Andrés Tuxtla, and San Juan Evangelista, whose combined votes summed 5,987. "Padrón de votantes," "Informes numéricos de votación," AHEV-1408/548.1/0.

64. Ruiz Cortines report 1945, BD-XIII/7326.

65. Assorted correspondence, SDN-1-356/VI; Santoyo, *La mano negra,* 131.

66. Tejeda to Amaro, 12/17/1926, AGN/DGIPS-106/135(S5)6; Arriola to Campos Gómez, 06/11/1940, AGN/DGIPS-87/2; Parra to Cárdenas, 08/09/1940, AGN/LCR-542.1/211; "Actividades reaccionarias en el estado de Veracruz," 10/04/1939, AGN/DGIPS-140/9.

67. PS-50 to Gobernación, 06/26/1940, AGN/DGIPS-87/2.

68. *Diario de Xalapa,* 07/01/1945, 07/02/1945, 07/03/1945.

69. PS-1 and PS-18 to Gobernación, 05/02/1945, AGN/DGIPS-88/Carlos Saavedra.

70. PS-1 and PS-18 to Gobernación, 05/02/1945, AGN/DGIPS-88/Carlos Saavedra.

71. Informes de gobernación, AHEV-1229/024/1.

72. Ruiz Cortines 1945 report, BD-XIII/7330, 7334.

73. And 166 confiscations, most of them shotguns. *Diario de Xalapa,* 05/05/1945, 05/23/1945; Lara Salazar to Gobernación Veracruz, 08/20/1948, AHEV-1519/024/1.

74. The *Diario de Xalapa* from March through July 1945 is rich in details, as are Gonzalo Migoni's reports to Gobernación in AGN/DGIPS-787/2-1/45/282.

75. *Diario de Xalapa,* 07/23/1945, 9/01/1948.

76. *Diario de Xalapa,* 05/11/1947, 05/14/1947, 08/13/1947; Ruiz Cortines report 1947, BD-XIII/7529.

77. *Diario de Xalapa,* 12/24/1947, 03/09/1950; *Excélsior,* 11/02/1947; Mange to de Llano, *Excélsior,* 11/03/1947, SDN-1-356/X.

78. Gillingham, "Who Killed Crispín Aguilar?" 91–111.

79. *Diario de Xalapa,* 05/03/1950; Piccato, *A History of Infamy,* 231–60.

80. Speaks to ambassador, 08/03/1948, NARG-812.00/8–548; *Diario de Xalapa,* 07/01/1952.

81. Namely, Manuel, Armando, Alfonso, and Carlos. The killer, Marcelino Blanco, was reported to be acting for an unnamed third party; before any light could be shed on the *autor intelectual*—the mastermind behind the murder—Blanco was caught by friends of the Armentas in the sierra and beaten to death. *Diario de Xalapa* 07/11/952, 07/02/1952, 07/03/1952, 07/04/1952.

82. AGN/DGG-2-317.4(26) series; treasury reports, AHEV-1229/024/0; *Diario de Xalapa,* 03/30/1945, 07/16/1948.

83. Ruiz Cortines report 1945, BD-XIII/7325.

84. Governors' reports 1945–48, BD-XIII/7333, 7469, BD-XIV/7699.

85. Ruiz Cortines 1945, 1946, 1947 reports, BD-XIII/7325–7329, 7341, 7387–7388, 7437, 7439, BD-XIV/7508, 7536.

86. De la Peña, *Veracruz Económico,* 1:302.

87. *Diario de Xalapa,* 12/25/1947.

88. Governors' reports 1944, 1946, BD-XIII/7215–7218, 7408; *Adelante,* 12/02/1945; De la Peña, *Veracruz Económico,* 2:479–83; *Diario de Xalapa,* 08/27/1948.

89. Before the two intervening devaluations are taken into account. De la Peña, *Veracruz Económico,* 2:489.

90. Ruiz Cortines report 1947, BD-XIV/7508, 7567.

91. Luis Aboites Aguilar, "The Illusion of National Power: Water Infrastructure in Mexican Cities, 1930–1990," in Christopher R. Boyer, ed., *A Land between Waters: Environmental Histories of Modern Mexico* (Tucson: University of Arizona Press, 2012), 229.

92. Ruiz Cortines report 1945, BD-XIII/7352.

93. Egon Kisch, "Los indios de la vainilla," in Poblett Miranda, *Cien viajeros,* 9:251.

94. Ruiz Cortines reports 1945, 1947, BD-XIII/7352, BD-XIV/7554.

95. Ruiz Cortines reports 1947, 1948, BD-XIV/7567, 7671; General Garate to Avila Camacho, 03/31/1946, AHEV-1360/166/1(179).

96. Governors' reports 1945–1952, BD-XIII/7352–7358, 7455–7456, BD-XIV/7553, 7654, 7909, BD-XV/8081, 8216, 8283.

97. INEGI, *Estadísticas históricas* CD-ROM.

98. De la Peña, *Veracuz Económico,* 2:293–302; author's interview, Adalberto Toto Linares, San Andrés Tuxtla, 12/18/2002; Ruiz Cortines report 1945, BD-XIII/7346.

99. Salvador Novo, "Poza Rica," in Poblett Miranda, *Cien viajeros,* 11:194; Marcela Mijares Lara, "Juan Andreu Almazán y la compañía Constructora Anahuác: Negocios y política durante la posrevolución (1927–1932)," in Marco Palacios, ed., *Negocios, empresarios y entornos políticos en México, 1827–1958* (Mexico City: Colegio de México, 2015), 249. Henríquez Guzmán also won the contract to build the oil pipeline from Poza Rica to Mexico City.

100. De la Peña, *Veracruz Económico,* 2:302–4.

101. Pérez Olivares, *Memorias,* 63–69.

102. Ruiz Cortines report 1945, BD-XIII/7336.

103. PS-2 to Gobernación, 01/12/1940, AGN/DGIPS-78/5.

104. URGS Coatzacoalcos to Alemán, 10/09/1948, AGN/MAV-425.5/2–29.

105. PS-1, PS-18 to Gobernación, 05/02/1945, AGN/DGIPS-88/Carlos Saavedra.

106. Governors' reports 1945–53, BD-XIII/7397–7399, BD-XIV/7750, 7867–7868, BD-XV/8017, 8199.

107. Lara Salazar to Gobernación Veracruz, 08/20/1948, AHEV-1519/024/1.

108. *Diario de Xalapa,* 05/11/1947–05/15/1947, 08/13/1947, 12/24/1947; Muñoz report 1950–1953, BD-XV/8018.

109. *La Prensa,* 02/03/1951.

110. Compared to 80 percent of town children. De la Peña, *Veracruz Económico,* 1:297–311.

111. Governors' reports 1945–53, BD-XIII/7354, BD-XIV/7573–7576, 7579, 7685, 7691, BD-XV/8037; De la Peña, *Veracruz Económico,* 1:302.

112. Migoni to Gobernación, 10/05/1945, AGN/DGIPS-787/2-1/45/282; *Diario de Xalapa,* 06/26/1952.

113. As occurred after the 1947 Tuxpan hurricane. AGN/MAV-561.3/34.

114. Departamento de Agricultura y Ganadería memorandum, foot-and-mouth Veracruz, 02/25/1947; Comité Reconstructivo Mexicano to Alemán, 01/02/1947; Palacios to Alemán, 01/04/1947, AGN/MAV-425.5/2–29.

115. Ruiz Cortines to SEDENA, 01/07/1947, AGN/MAV-425.5/2-29.

116. López to Alemán, 03/01/1947, AGN/MAV-425.5/2-29.

117. Unión Municipal de Ejidatarios y Ganaderos Ixtaczoquitlan to Alemán, 04/26/1947, AGN/MAV-425.5/2-29.

118. "Nuevas modalidades e instrucciones dictadas para proseguir la campaña de erradicación de la fiebre aftosa," 10/21/1947, AMI-1947; assorted correspondence regional ganadero unions to Alemán, June–September 1947, AGN/MAV-425.5/2-29.

119. Governors' reports 1947, 1948, BD-XIII/7545–7547, 7648, BD-XIV/7885; Sánchez Salazar, 19a zona Tuxpan, to Alemán, 06/27/1947; Foot-and-mouth Commission to Dr. Mortera, Villa Azueta, 12/17/1947, AGN/MAV-425.5/2-29.

120. Carvajal Bernal reports 1949, 1950, BD-XIV/7739, 7762, 7886.

121. *Diario de Xalapa,* 08/10/1949, 09/15/1949; Ruiz Cortines report 1947, BD-XIV/7507.

122. Ugalde to Gobernación, 08/11/1947, AGN/DGIPS-90/F. Ugalde; PCM Veracruz to Ruiz Cortines, 09/18/1946, AHEV-1412/549/0.

123. Municipal elections report, 12/02/1946, AHEV-1412/549/0; *Adelante,* 06/02/1949; Samudio to Ruiz Cortines, 12/12/1952, AGN/DGG-2.311M(26)/76/10.

124. "Information service" to Ruiz Cortines, 12/15/1944, AHEV-1235/051/137.

125. Garate to Avila Camacho, 03/31/1946, AHEV-1360/166/1(179).

126. *La Tribuna de Tuxpan,* 11/17/1946.

127. Pérez Olivares, *Memorias,* 71.

128. General Absalón Pérez to Ruiz Cortines, 08/22/1946, Contreras to Ruiz Cortines, 10/07/1946, Municipal elections reports, 12/02/1946, AHEV-1412/549/0, undated, AHEV-1411/548-3/0.

129. Inspectors 2 and 52 to Gobernación, 4/01/1947, AGN/DGIPS-791/2-1/46/405; Rodríguez to Liga, 11/15/1946, AHEV-1412/549/0.

130. Moreno to Carvajal, 08/13/1949, AHEV-1696/549/01.

131. Corzo Ramírez et al., *Cándido Aguilar,* 303–4.

132. In the cases that have been traced—namely, the border municipios of Otatitlán and Jesús Carranza—their victories were duly recognized by congress; the regidores of San Andrés Tuxtla may have been "crypto-Aguilaristas." Municipal elections report,

12/02/1946, AHEV-1412/549/0; organizaciones campesinas to Gobernación, 01/21/1947, AGN/DGG-2.311M(26)/75/40; Inspectors 2 and 58 to Gobernación, 09/09/1947, AGN/DGIPS-101/2-1/131/1013.

133. Galaviz to Ruiz Cortines, 11/29/1946, AHEV-1412/549/0.

134. In Córdoba the "official" candidate, José Zúñiga Acevedo, was a former Aguilarista whose subsequent ascent in the PRI presumably indicates his abandonment of the declining general. Assorted reports, AGN/DGIPS-796/2-1/47/424; *Diario de Xalapa*, 08/03/1949.

135. *Diario de Xalapa*, 07/7/1947, 07/08/1947, 09/13/1947.

136. Díaz García to Ruiz Cortines, 11/25/1947, AHEV-1506/542/1; Corzo Ramírez et al, *Cándido Aguilar*, 306–8.

137. *Diario de Xalapa*, 08/23/1948; *Excélsior*, 08/23/1948.

138. *Todo*, 06/12/1949; *Diario de Xalapa*, 07/04/1949, 07/24/1949.

139. Ibáñez to Gobernación, 01/24/1949, AGN/DGIPS-94/2.1/131/805; *Diario de Xalapa*, 08/04/1949, 08/09/1949, 08/14/1949.

140. *Diario de Xalapa*, 01/03/1948.

141. Assorted telegrams, Tierra Blanca to Ruiz Cortines, 08/06, 07, 08/1949, AGN/DGG-2.311M(26)/77/2; election memo, 09/10/1949, AHEV-1696/549/01; Arroyo Telles to PRI, 10/12/1949, AGN/DGG-2.311M(26)/77/4; Pérez Olivares, *Memorias*, 74.

142. López to Liga, 08/21/1949, AHEV-1700/549/65; *Diario de Xalapa*, 09/22/1949.

143. *Diario de Xalapa*, 11/11/1949.

144. Baig Sierra to Gobernación, 11/26/1946, AGN/DGIPS-792/2-1/46/425; Betancourt to Alemán, 12/30/1946, AGN/MAV-609/4.

145. Report on Coatzacoalcos political situation, 04/07/1949, AGN/DGIPS-802/2-1/49/545; assorted correspondence, July to October 1949, AGN/MAV-437.3/195; Aguilar de la Parra, *Mi tío, el cacique*, 91–92.

146. Moreno to Carvajal, 08/16/1949, AHEV-1696/549/01; Migoni to Gobernación, 06/20/1946, AGN/DGIPS-791/2-1/46/405; Arriola to Pérez Aldama, 03/20/1940, AGN/DGIPS-78/6.

147. Orizaba railworkers to Alemán, 03/24/1952, AGN/DGG-2.311P(26)/2/107.

148. Governors' reports 1949, 1952, BD-XIV/7659, BD-XV/8280–8281.

149. "Principal Henriquista Leaders, Veracruz," AGN/DGIPS-810/2-1/51/538.

150. *El Universal*, 09/06/1952, 11/01/1952.

151. *Diario de Xalapa*, 05/19/1950, 09/13/1950.

152. *Diario de Xalapa*, 07/03/1949.

153. Comité Regional Campesino Minatitlán to Alemán, 10/22/1949, 02/09/1950, AGN/DGG-2/311G(26)/3/333.

154. Assorted clippings and correspondence, AGN/DGIPS-804/5.

155. Aguilar speeches to PR convention, Fortín, 10/17/1951, tramworkers, 06/27/1952, transcripts in AGN/DGIPS-19/13.

156. *Ultimas Noticias,* 11/22/1950; *Novedades,* 08/28/1952.

157. *Diario de Xalapa,* 07/13/1952; Corzo Ramírez et al., *Cándido Aguilar,* 328.

158. Aguilar, *Mi tío, el cacique,* 115–18, 146–52.

159. Juan Matías Valdés to Alemán, 10/10/1949, AGN/DGG-2.311M(26)/78/6.

160. *Diario de Xalapa,* 07/01, 04/1952, 07/16/1952.

161. *Novedades,* 08/03/1949; *Diario de Xalapa,* 07/30/1949, 09/28/1949.

162. *Excélsior*'s reporting of the women's turnout as apathetic and insignificant is contradicted by both military and the governor's reports. *Excélsior,* 12/08/1949; Rosado Morales to Carvajal, 08/29/1949, AHEV-1696/549/01; Carvajal to Gobernación, 08/29/1949, AGN/DGG-2.311M(26)/77/4; assorted correspondence, AGN/DGG-2.311M(26)/78/16 & 70.

163. Pérez Olivares, *Memorias,* 74.

164. Ibid., 74–75.

165. The military grant was reportedly of 90,000 hectares; the ejidal grants in Veracruz 1946–52 totaled 124,000 hectares. *Diario de Xalapa,* 07/07/1949; INEGI, *Estadísticas históricas* CD-ROM.

166. Carvajal report 1948, BD-XIV/7703.

167. Migoni to Gobernación, 06/14/1945, AGN/DGIPS-787/2-1/45/282; Lobato to Ferrer Galván, 03/31/1949, AHEV-1694/548/114; Pérez Olivares, *Memorias,* 49.

168. Galaviz to Ruiz Cortines, 04/11/1947, AHEV-1506/548/0.

169. In 1961 only two of Veracruz's fifteen state congressional seats went to the CNC; agraristas did, however, control a plurality of presidentes municipales. "Filiación política de los actuales diputados locales," 1961, AGN/DGIPS-1450A/6/10; list of presidentes municipales, 1961, AGN/DGIPS-1980A.

170. Falcón, *El agrarismo en Veracruz,* 41; Fowler, *Agrarian Radicalism,* 138.

171. IPS-5 to Gobernación, 05/06/1947, AGN/DGIPS-796/2-1/47/424; AOR and NAO to Gobernación, 07/19/1948, AGN/DGIPS-798/2-1/48/400; CROM to Alemán, 03/30/1951, AGN/MAV-123/1746; PS-31, 34, 43 to Gobernación, 04/28/1949, AGN/DGIPS-84/MRT.

172. *La Prensa,* 08/19/1948; *El Popular,* 10/02/1948; DFS report 05/03/1954, AGN/DFS-VP/Eucario León.

173. De la Peña, *Veracruz Económico,* 1:317–18.

174. Vice-Consul Eastham, Coatzacoalcos, despatch 06/30/1950, NARG-712.00/7-1950.

175. Aguilar Aceves to de la Selva, 03/10/1950, AGN/MAV-243.2/11121, Pérez to SEDENA, 01/07/1959, SDN-1-356/XII.

176. *Diario de Xalapa,* 12/24/1947, 07/23/1952.

177. Gillingham, "Military Caciquismo," 210–37.

178. *Diario de Xalapa,* 05/25/1945.

179. Assorted correspondence, AHEV-1700/549/57.

180. Ultimately successful in 1995. *Diario de Xalapa,* 06/15/1950, 06/28/1952.

181. De la Cruz to Carvajal, 12/06/1948, AHEV-1694/548/0.

182. PAN to Gobernación, 03/09/1950, AGN/DGIPS-805/2-1/50/370; undated clipping, AHEV-1694/548/114.

183. Where Antonio Salga, the second *agente municipal* in the place's history, opened the first store, cantina, and fish restaurant and ran local politics for the next thirty years. Genz, "Entrepreneurship and caciquismo," 121–29, 287–90.

184. Skerritt, "Peasant Organisation," 4.

185. For Mexico as a gatekeeper state, see Gillingham and Smith, "Introduction," Gillingham and Smith, *Dictablanda*, 32.

186. Diaz Muñoz was expelled from the southern branch of his union in 1951 after his fellow members were barred from the national convention for associating with him. *La Verdad de Minatitlán*, 12/09/1951.

187. Muñoz report 1951, BD-XV/8237.

188. Seconded by dissidents in Xalapa, Veracruz, and Tierra Blanca. Alegre, *Railroad Radicals*, 108–20.

5. Elections, Fraud, and Democracy

1. Literally, pistoleros: Mexican gunmen for hire. Robert Caro, *Means of Ascent: The Years of Lyndon Johnson* (New York: Vintage, 1990), 182. For a detailed account of the entire election, see chapters 9, 13, and 14.

2. Ibid., 10.

3. Pablo González Casanova, *Democracy in Mexico* (New York: Oxford University Press, 1970), 12–13.

4. *Diario de Xalapa*, 07/07/1952.

5. *Excélsior*, 12/22/1949, 02/03/1951; *La Prensa*, 12/21/1950, 02/01/1951.

6. On the tradition of underestimating the critical press in Mexico, see Paul Gillingham, Michael Lettieri, and Benjamin T. Smith, "Journalism, Satire, and Censorship in Mexico," in Gillingham, Lettieri, and Smith, *Journalism, Satire, and Censorship*, 1–32.

7. *Diario del Hogar*, 08/15/1893.

8. "That the right to elect should be meaningless in Mexico is by no means the government's responsibility, but rather the present effect of the apathy that typifies the Mexican people." *Diario del Hogar*, 8/15/1893. For Bulnes's opinions, see Daniel Cosío Villegas, "El Porfiriato, era de consolidación," *Historia Mexicana* 13 (1963): 76–87.

9. José Yves Limantour, *Apuntes sobre mi vida política* (Mexico City: Editorial Porrúa, 1965), 155.

10. Emilio Rabasa, *La Organización Política de México: la Constitución y la Dictadura* (Madrid: Editorial América, 1917), 171; Limantour, *Apuntes*, 174.

11. James Creelman, "President Díaz: Hero of the Americas," *Pearson's Magazine* 19, no. 3 (1908): 236. Such arguments were replicated by modernization theorists of

the Cold War such as Maxwell Taylor, the US ambassador to South Vietnam, who observed with regret that "there seems to be a national [Vietnamese] attribute which makes for factionalism and limits the development of a truly national spirit. Whether this tendency is innate or a development growing out of the conditions of political suppression under which successive generations have lived is hard to determine. . . . Given time, many of these [words illegible] undoubtedly change for the better, but we are unfortunately pressed for time and unhappily perceive no short-term solution for the establishment of stable and sound government." Cited in David Halberstam, *The Best and the Brightest* (New York: Modern Library, 2001), 525.

12. Alvaro Matute, *Historia de la Revolución Mexicana, 1917–1924: la carrera del caudillo* (Mexico City: Colegio de México, 1980), 17, 51.

13. Cited in Lorenzo Meyer, Rafael Segovia, and Alejandra Lajous, *Historia de la Revolución Mexicana, 1928–1934: los inicios de la institucionalización* (Mexico City: Colegio de México, 1978), 36.

14. Smith, *Labyrinths of Power,* 144–58.

15. An assumption still current among North American political scientists, more *matizado* by Mexican scholars such as González Casanova and Rogelio Hernández Rodríguez. Caroline C. Beer, *Electoral Competition and Institutional Change in Mexico* (Notre Dame: University of Notre Dame Press, 2003), 11; Todd A. Eisenstadt, *Courting Democracy in Mexico: Party Strategies and Electoral Institutions* (Cambridge: Cambridge University Press, 2004), 94. Pablo González Casanova's later work stressed the long-term "democratic meaning" of elections. Pablo González Casanova, "Democracia en tiempos de crisis," in Pablo González Casanova, ed., *Las elecciones en México: evolución y perspectiva* (Mexico City: Siglo XXI, 1985), 17–18; Hernández Rodríguez, *El centro dividido,* 38–47.

16. Guardino, *Peasants,* 86–100; Peter Guardino, *The Time of Liberty: Popular Political Culture in Oaxaca, 1750–1850* (Durham: Duke University Press, 2005); Michael Costeloe, "Generals versus Politicians: Santa Anna and the 1842 Congressional Elections in Mexico," *Bulletin of Latin American Research* 8, no. 2 (1989): 257–58.

17. Florencia Mallon, *Peasant and Nation* (Berkeley: University of California Press, 1995), 248–56; Guy P. C. Thomson and David G. LaFrance, *Patriotism, Politics, and Popular Liberalism in Nineteenth-Century Mexico: Juan Francisco Lucas and the Puebla Sierra* (Wilmington, DE: Scholarly Resources, 1998), 202–4.

18. Daniel Cosío Villegas, *La Constitución de 1857 y sus críticos* (Mexico City: Secretaría de Educación Pública, 1973), 130–35.

19. Knight, *The Mexican Revolution,* 1:53–57; Bartra, *Guerrero bronco,* 52–54; Timothy J. Henderson, *The Worm in the Wheat: Rosalie Evans and Agrarian Struggle in the Puebla–Tlaxcala Valley of Mexico, 1906–1927* (Durham: Duke University Press, 1998), 104–7; Osten, *The Mexican Revolution's Wake,* 161–94.

20. Meyer et al., *Historia de la Revolución Mexicana, 1928–1934,* 58, 88.

21. Santos, *Memorias,* 255–56.

22. Assorted election reports, AGN/DGG-2.311M(9)/5B, 6B; *Excélsior,* 01/8/1939; Mark Wasserman, *Persistent Oligarchs: Elites and Politics in Chihuahua, Mexico, 1910–1940* (Durham: Duke University Press, 1993), 56; Ben Fallaw, *Cárdenas Compromised: The Failure of Reform in Post-revolutionary Yucatán* (Durham: Duke University Press, 2001), 132; Adrian Bantjes, *As If Jesus Walked on Earth: Cardenismo, Sonora, and the Mexican Revolution* (Wilmington, DE: Scholarly Resources, 1998), 66; Rogelio Hernández Rodríguez, *La formación del político mexicano: el caso de Carlos A. Madrazo* (Mexico City: Colegio de México, 1991), 48; Smith, *Pistoleros and Popular Movements,* 125–31.

23. Ugalde to Gobernación, 08/11/1947, AGN/DGIPS-90/F. Ugalde.

24. Ojeda to Avila Camacho, 09/21/1944, AGN/DGG-2/311G(9)2/241/v.IV.

25. *Trópico,* 01/07/1945; Ojeda to Alemán, 10/18/1944, AGN/DGG-2/311G(9)/239/2 v.II; Massey to State Department, 03/30/1949, NARG-812.00/3–3049; *Excélsior,* 01/20/1946; *Diario de Xalapa,* 08/29/1949.

26. "Calendario de Elecciones Internas del PRI," San Luis Potosí 1948, AGN/DGIPS-797/2-1/48/392.

27. Laidlaw to State Department, 02/17/1950, NARG-712.00/2-175.

28. See articles 18, 24, 25 of the *Ley electoral del Municipio libre y sus reformas* (Xalapa, 1925) and article 38 of the *Ley de reforma electoral,* 03/19/1940, AGN/DGIPS-140/9; article 66 of Guerrero's 1946 state electoral law, *Periódico Oficial del Estado de Guerrero,* 09/25/1946.

29. In December 1942, December 1945, February 1949, December 1949, and May 1951.

30. Undated clipping, *Excélsior,* AP-259/537ELE.

31. Fagoaga to Gobernación, 05/6/1948, AGN/DGIPS-797/2-1/48/392.

32. *Diario de Xalapa,* 07/14/1947.

33. *Trópico,* 01/07/1945.

34. PRI statutes 1946, chapter 4, article 56, 71, 74, in various authors, *Historia documental del Partido,* 189–90, 276–79.

35. Manifesto for Jesús González Gallo, 05/26/1947, AGN/DGIPS-803/1. Backers of Ruiz Cortines similarly claimed lengthy service, one group dating their formation (possibly imaginatively) back to 1948. Open letter, Frente de Unidad Orizabeña, 10/11/1951, AGN/DGIPS-810/2-1/51/538.

36. Pavón Silva to Gobernación, 05/06/1948, AGN/DGIPS-797/2-1/48/392; Corzo Ramírez et al., *Cándido Aguilar,* 300.

37. Burrows to State Dept, 04/18/1950, NARG-712.00/4–1850; Taylor to Eden, 11/21/1952, FO371/97540; "Mexico: Annual Review for 1950," 02/06/1951, FO 371/90819.

38. A *chamba* is a job, generally obtained through some form of nepotism or clientelism or both. Martínez Gómez Alemán to Alemán, 05/16/1952, AGN/DGG-2.311M(26)/79.

39. J. M. Valdés to Alemán, 10/10/1949, Comité Político José Azueta to Gobernación, 09/07/1955, AGN/DGG-2.311M(26)/78/6; PS-8 to Gobernación, 07/12/1948, AGN/DGIPS-90/2-1/131/737.

40. As in Brazil, where the supposedly meaningless municipal elections were competitive enough for rubber tappers to walk off their jobs en masse in order to vote, leading the rubber planters to ask for their postponement. Barbara Weinstein, *The Amazon Rubber Boom, 1850–1920* (Stanford: Stanford University Press, 1983), 65.

41. Cited in Niblo, *Mexico in the 1940s*, 223–24.

42. Albert L. Michaels, "Las elecciones de 1940," *Historia Mexicana* 21, no. 1 (1971): 81; *Diario de Xalapa*, 05/07/1945; Massey to State Department, 05/11/1949, NARG-812.00/5–1149; assorted letters, PAN secretary-general to Gobernación, January 1952, AGN/DGG-2/311P(29)2/110B.

43. Pérez Aldama to Gobernación, 08/28/1944, AGN/DGIPS-88; *Trópico*, 06/25/1944; Ortíz to presidency, 01/19/1941, AGN/MAC-544.2/11-1.

44. Massey to State Department, 05/11/1949, NARG-812.00/5-1149.

45. PS-2 to Gobernación, 01/10/1940, AGN/DGIPS-78/5; ejidatarios indígenas Xochistlahuaca to Catalán Calvo, 01/10/1945, AGN/DGG-2.311M(9)/4B/44; petition of Chilachapa, Cuetzala, 12/26/1944, AGN/DGG-2.311M(9)/4B/50; Pérez, Coxquihui to Coalición Revolucionaria de Trabajadores Veracruzanos, 1943, AGN/DGG-2.311M(26)/74/30.

46. Barajas to Gobernación, 06/28/1948, AGN/DGIPS-799/2-1/48/431.

47. Ejidatarios of Mamadi, Azoyú, to Gobernación, 12/12/1948, AGN/DGG-2.311M(9)/3B/7.

48. As occurred in Ayahualulco, Veracruz, in 1945 or in Olinalá and San Marcos, Guerrero, in 1949. Election summary, AHEV-1412/549/0; Leyva Mancilla report 1949, AP-175/352.072.073ETN.

49. In Iguala disputed Carnival queen results caused a riot; in Puebla Maximino Avila Camacho went to great lengths to rig the 1938 contest in favor of his reportedly rather plain daughter. Iguala Presidente Municipal to SEP, 02/16/1942, SEP/DGEP-5611 ant. 3854 exp 16-9-4-107; Andrew Paxman, "Changing Opinions in *La Opinión*: Maximino Avila Camacho and the Puebla Press, 1936–1941," in Gillingham, Lettieri, and Smith, *Journalism, Satire, and Censorship*, 83–84.

50. Liga to Avila Camacho, 11/28/1944, AGN/DGG-2.311M(9)/5B/75; Gobernación to Ruiz Cortines, 06/19/1947, AHEV-1507/548/57; Pavón to Alemán, 09/20/1949, AGN/DGG-2.311M(26)/77/2; Bateman to Bevin, 12/06/1945, FO371/44478.

51. Ojeda to Avila Camacho, 11/22/1944, AGN/DGG-2/311G(9)/239/2.

52. "La confesión del señor Nabor Ojeda," AGN/DGIPS-782/2-1/44/274; "Carta abierta del General Victoriano Huerta al Lic. Ezequiel Padilla," AHEV-1324/548/0.

53. Agent I-85 to Gobernación, 03/30/1936, AGN/DGIPS-171/7.

54. Manufacturing popular support could also convince an unconvinced central government of a regional politician's suitability for the job; for an excellent report of a

meeting of *acarreados*, see I-10 to Gobernación, 03/17/1932, AGN/DGIPS-171/2. Such purchased support continued to be central to political campaigns through the 1940s; in 1952 Guerrero's Henriquistas found it necessary to pay dissident peasants to attend their conventions. Mizayawa to de la Fuente, 10/15/1951, AGN/DFS-Guerrero/100-10-14-51H102L 4.

55. Michael Lettieri, "In the Service of the *Gremio:* Bus Industry Magazines, PRI Corporatism, and the Politics of Trade Publications," in Gillingham, Lettieri, and Smith, *Journalism, Satire, and Censorship*, 146.

56. Report on PDM meeting 5th district, Mexico City, 07/03/1946, AGN/DGIPS-24.

57. According, admittedly, to Cándido Aguilar. Transcript Fortín speech, 10/17/1951, AGN/DGIPS-19/13.

58. Ojeda to Alemán, 07/11/1944, AGN/DGG-2.311M(9)/5B/63; Reza Sotelo to Gobernación, 10/26/1948, AGN/DGG-2.311M(9)/6.

59. Catalán Calvo to Liga Guerrero, 08/01/1944, AGN/DGG-2/311G(9)2/239/v.I.

60. PS-2 to Gobernación, 03/02/1940, AGN/DGIPS-78/5; Ojeda to Alemán, 11/11/1944, AGN/DGG-2/311G(9)2/239 v.II.

61. Ortega to Gobernación, 02/13/1946, AGN/DGG-2/311P(26)/1/107.

62. Author's analysis, AGN/DGG-2.311 M(9) and M(26) series; *Diario de Xalapa*, 07/10/1950.

63. JNM to Gobernación, 10/11/1948, AGN/DGIPS-102/JNM; CNC/CNOP Paso del Macho to Gobernación, 10/9/1952, AGN/DGG-2.311M(26)/78/8.

64. Ojeda to Gobernación, 12/17/1948, AGN/DGG-2.311M(9)/4B/80; Reivindicación Social to Gobernación, 10/26/1948, AGN/DGG-2.311M(9)/3B/8.

65. Alemán Celestino to Alemán, 08/12/1949, AGN/DGG-2.311M(26)/77/45; *Diario de Xalapa*, 09/13/1949.

66. Confederación Nacional de Ayuntamientos de la República circular no. 13, 06/07/1946, AMI-1946.

67. Cárdenas to de la Fuente, 05/25/1952, AGN/DFS-Guerrero/exp100-10-14-51H319L4; Massey to State Department, 05/04/1949, NARG-812.00/5-449; FPPM to Gobernación, December 1951, AGN/DGG-2/311P(26)2/107.

68. Forzán to Gobernación, 07/04/1944, AGN/DGIPS-98/6.

69. Friedenberg to Gobernación, 07/08/1940, AGN/DGIPS-173/311(7.2)1.

70. Pavón Silva to Gobernación, 08/22/1947, Acedo Cárdenas to state legislature, 11/11/1947, AGN/DGIPS-794/180.

71. Party statutes of 1946, chapter 4, article 61, in various authors, *Historia documental del Partido*, 277.

72. Delgado Cruz Grande, Guerrero, to Alemán, 12/05/1944, AGN/DGG-2.311M(9)/5B/71; Román, Ajuchitlán to Sánchez Taboada, 10/19/1948, AGN/DGG-2.311M(9)/3/122; ejidatarios Cuetzala del Progreso to Ruiz Cortines, 01/01/1953, AGN/DGG-2.311M(9)/3B/23.

73. Nava to Gobernación, 12/08/1944, acta, junta computadora Mochitlán, 12/07/1944, AGN/DGG-2.311M(9)/4B/14, 6.

74. PS-37 to Gobernación, 05/05/1947, AGN/DGIPS-796/2-1/47/424.

75. PS-20 to Gobernación, May 1947, AGN/DGIPS-796/2-1/47/424; Amaro Martínez to Gobernación Xalapa, 07/25/1947, AHEV-1508/548/121; PRI "Relación de candidatos," AHEV-1506/548/0.

76. FNP, CNOP Sayula to Ruiz Cortines, 12/16/1952, AGN/DGG-2.311M(26)/78/16.

77. *Diario de Xalapa,* 08/09/1947; Liga to Sánchez Taboada, 05/28/1947, AHEV-1506/548/0.

78. *Trópico,* 01/14/1945; Catalán Calvo to Gobernación, 01/02/1945, AGN/DGG-2.311M(9)/5B/75.

79. For examples, see AGN/DGIPS cajas 78, 129, 767, 797.

80. Navarro, *Political Intelligence,* 171.

81. Circular, SNTE Guerrero, 02/05/1950, AGN/DGIPS-800/2-1/49/444.

82. Turrent to Carvajal, 08/16/1949, AHEV-1696/549/01.

83. "Estado de Veracruz: Aspirantes a Presidentes Municipales" series (1964), AGN/DGIPS-1997A/2-1/010(18)"64"/52.

84. Ruíz to Carvajal, 12/19/1949, AGN/DGG-2.311M(26)/77.

85. Joy K. Langston, "Elite Ruptures: When Do Ruling Parties Split?" in Andreas Schedler, ed., *Electoral Authoritarianism: The Dynamics of Unfree Competition* (Boulder: Lynne Reiner Publishers, 2006), 62–64.

86. Robert Dahl, *Polyarchy: Participation and Opposition* (New Haven: Yale University Press, 1971), 15.

87. JNM to Gobernación, 10/11/1948, AGN/DGIPS-102/JNM.

88. PS-8 to Gobernación, 12/27/1947, AGN/DGIPS-90/2-1/131/737.

89. PS-8 to Gobernación, 12/27/1947, 12/11/1947, AGN/DGIPS-90/2-1/131/737.

90. Absalón Pérez to Ruiz Cortines, 08/22/1946, Contreras to Ruiz Cortines, 12/07/1946, AHEV-1412/549/0.

91. *Diario de Xalapa,* 08/03, 12, 28/1949.

92. Partial list of results, 1950 Veracruz municipal elections, AGN/DGG-2.311M(26)/79/8.

93. *Diario de Xalapa,* 09/12, 22/1949, 08/23/1949.

94. PS-5, PS-9 to Gobernación, 05/06/1947, AGN/DGIPS-796/2-1/47/424; list of federal deputies 1952, AGN/DGIPS-791/2-1/46/67; *Diario de Xalapa,* 08/03/1949.

95. SNTE Guerrero to Ruiz Cortines, 08/15/1950, AGN/DGG-2.311G(9)3/242/Nov 1948.

96. Nieto to Gobernación, 01/01/1945, AGN/DGG-2.311M(9)/5B/69.

97. Quirino Martínez to Gobernación, 01/06/1947, AGN/DGG-2.311M(26)/75/8.

98. CTM Coatzacoalcos to Ruiz Cortines, 12/27/1946, AGN/DGG-2.311M(26)/75/4.

99. Secretario de Gobierno Guerrero to Gobernación, 01/16/1947, AGN/DGG-2.311M(9)/4B/66; Leyva Mancilla report 1947, AP-175/352.072.073ETN; *El Universal* 01/02/1948.

100. Wil Pansters, "Tropical Passion in the Desert: Gonzalo N. Santos and Local Elections in Northern San Luis Potosí, 1943–1958," in Gillingham and Smith, *Dictablanda*, 132; *La Verdad*, 01/04/1949.

101. Comité Democrático Independiente Ajuchitlán to Gobernación, 01/01/1949, AGN/DGG-2.311 M(9)/3/122.

102. Nieto to Gobernación, 01/01/1945, AGN/DGG-5B/2.311M(9)69; Leyva Mancilla to Gobernación, 06/27/1949, AGN/DGG-2.311M(9)/3/122.

103. Alexander Aviña, "Seizing Hold of Memories in Moments of Danger: Guerrillas and Revolution in Guerrero, Mexico," in Herrera Calderón and Cedillo, *Challenging Authoritarianism*, 52.

104. Padilla, *Rural Resistance*, 139.

105. See, for example, William B. Taylor, *Drinking, Homicide, and Rebellion in Colonial Mexican Villages* (Stanford: Stanford University Press, 1979), 168–70.

106. Smith, *Pistoleros and Popular Movements*, 266.

107. Regional Committee to Central Committee PRI, 05/29/1946, AHEV-1412/549/0.

108. A reasoning shared by Magaloni, *Voting for Autocracy*, 6.

109. Servín, *La oposición política*, 16; Morales to Alemán, 09/05/1949, Ceballos to Ruiz Cortines, 01/04/1950, AGN/DGG-2.311M(26)/78/16, 70.

110. Smith, *Pistoleros and Popular Movements*, 229.

111. *El Universal*, 11/01/1952, 01/09/1953.

112. For veto players, see George Tsebelis, "Decision Making in Political Systems: Veto Players in Presidentialism, Parliamentarism, Multicameralism and Multipartyism," *British Journal of Political Science* 25 (1995): 289.

113. Galaviz to Ruiz Cortines, 11/29/1946, AHEV-1412/549/0.

114. Román to Alemán, 12/03/1947, AGN/DGG-2.311M(9)/4B/59; *Novedades*, 01/21/1948; Sedena to 26th Military Zone, 07/21/1942, AGN/DGG-2/317.4(26)/64/24.

115. Rath, *Myths of Demilitarization*, 125–26; Pansters, "Tropical Passion in the Desert," 138.

116. Pansters, "Tropical Passion in the Desert," 141–44.

117. Fagoaga to Gobernación, 05/06/1948, AGN/DGIPS-797/2-1/48/392.

118. *Excélsior*, 09/05/1952; *Novedades*, 08/06/1952, 09/09/1952, 10/04/1952.

119. PS-20 to Gobernación, 02/06/1947, AGN/DGIPS-79/2-1/130/633; Dickinson to State Department, 04/02/1948, NARG-812.00/4.248.

120. Hernández Rodríguez, *El centro dividido*, 151.

121. Rubin, *Decentering the Regime*, 52–54; Frank Cancian, *The Decline of Community in Zinacantán: Economy, Public Life, and Social Stratification, 1960–1987* (Stanford: Stanford University Press, 1992), 129–30.

122. "Estado de Veracruz: Aspirantes a presidentes municipales," AGN/DGIPS-1980/1950–1961ffi/166; Enrique Riveron Fragoso to DFS, 09/12/1958, AGN/DFS-Salvador Nava/VP/L1, 1.

123. Benjamin T. Smith, *The Roots of Conservatism in Mexico: Catholicism, Society, and Politics in the Mixteca Baja, 1750–1962* (Albuquerque: University of New Mexico Press, 2012), 271–73.

124. Memo "Actividades del Gral. Cuenca Díaz," 03/22/1965, AGN/DGIPS-1294/1.

125. Alvaro Arreola Ayala, "Elecciones municipales," in González Casanova, *Las elecciones en México,* 337.

126. Hernández Rodríguez, *El centro dividido,* 41–42.

127. Quoted in Alberto J. Pani, *El retroceso democrático del nuevo régimen* (Mexico City: A. J. Pani, 1947), 10.

128. Annual report for Mexico 1944, 01/22/1945, FO371/44478.

129. Catalán Calvo report, 1944, AP-158/350.003.73INF.

130. Bateman to Bevin, 11/21/1945, FO371/44478. It was probably no coincidence that Frank Tannenbaum, at the time the leading intellectual concerning Mexico, wrote about personalist government in Mexican politics in the October issue of *Foreign Affairs.* Frank Tannenbaum, "Personal Government in Mexico," *Foreign Affairs* 27, no. 1 (October 1948): 44–57.

131. For the massacre, see Daniel Newcomer, *Reconciling Modernity: Urban State Formation in 1940s León, Mexico* (Lincoln: University of Nebraska Press, 2004), 143–76.

132. Declaration of Principles, in various authors, *Historia documental del Partido,* 254; *El Nacional,* 01/21/1946.

133. Martínez to Gobernación, 10/22/1946, AGN/DGG-2.311M(26)/74/8.

134. Bateman to Bevin, 02/24/1947, FO371/60940; Rodolfo Usigli, "El caso de 'El Gesticulador,' " in Rodolfo Usigli, *Teatro completo,* 4 vols. (Mexico City: Fondo de Cultura Económica, 1996–97), 2:541; Aguilar speech, Fortín, 10/11/1951, AGN/DGIPS-19/13.

135. Bateman to Bevin, 01/21/1947, FO371/60940; Washington to State Department, 06/07/1948, NARG-812.00/6–748; Dickinson to State Department, 04/02/1948, NARG-812.00/4.248.

136. Leslie Bethell and Ian Roxborough, "Latin America between the Second World War and the Cold War: Some Reflections on the 1945–1948 Conjuncture," *Journal of Latin American Studies* 20, no. 1 (1988): 167–89.

137. Black, "The Politics of Asylum," 60.

138. *Trópico,* 01/14/1945; Alemanistas Maltrata to Alemán, 12/28/1946, AGN/DGG-2.311M(26)/74/48.

139. Torres to Carbajal, 11/30/1949, AHEV-1702/549/115; INEGI, *Censo del estado de Veracruz 1950* (Mexico City: Instituto Nacional de Estadística y Geografía, 1953), 28.

140. Ríos Thivol to Gobernación, 11/05/1951, AGN/DGIPS-84/2-1/131/655/v.IV.

141. "You can't make it by behaving yourself." Padilla, *Rural Resistance,* 108–38.

142. *Diario de Xalapa,* 07/24/1949; *Diario de Guerrero,* 06/27/1950.

143. Credible turnout figures are available only where honest spies were on the ground, and while certain elections were dramatically voterless, localized, near-com-

plete abstentions had always occurred. Yet the increasing concern of party managers for turnout figures in the second half of the 1940s is highly suggestive, as are their public threats to fine or jail those who failed to register. *La Verdad*, 05/06/1949.

144. Admittedly when incumbents failed to run; but this was universal in Mexico. Julius Turner, "Primary Elections as the Alternative to Party Competition in 'Safe' Districts," *Journal of Politics* 15, no. 2 (1953): 197–98, 206–7.

145. Caro, *Means of Ascent*, 175.

146. Turner, "Primary Elections," 210.

147. Foreign Office, "Annual Report on Mexico for 1948," FO371/74076; *Diario Oficial de la Federación*, 02/21/1949; "Annual Political Report for Mexico, 1949," FO371/81501; "Political and Economic Developments in Mexico, December 1949," NARG-712.00/2; Laidlaw to State Department, 02/17/1950, NARG-712.00/2-1750.

148. JNM and JGV to Gobernación, 02/02, 03/1950, AGN/DGIPS-19/12.

149. Various authors, *Historia documental del Partido*, 213.

150. "Recent Political Events in Mexico," 03/04/1950, FO371/81503/AM1015/1.

151. Various authors, *Historia documental del Partido*, 187, 279, 669–70.

152. Ortega to Gobernación, 02/13/1946, AGN/DGG-2/311P(26)/1/107.

153. Vecinos de Acapulco to state legislature, 12/01/1948, AGN/DGG-2.311M(9)/4B/74.

154. Rodríguez, *La desaparición de poderes*, 125; Gómez Maganda to presidentes municipales, 07/03/1952, AMI-1952/104.

155. Rapp to FO, 12/09/1948, FO371/67994; report on PDM meeting 5th district, Mexico City, 07/03/1946, AGN/DGIPS-24. The device of inking thumbs to mark those who had voted did (much later) become law; it relied, however, on the correct indelible ink being used.

156. *Diario de Xalapa*, 09/13/1950.

157. A method of excluding regional parties followed in Vladimir Putin's Russia, where parliamentary parties must have members in all eighty-nine regions. Steven Levitsky and Lucan A. Way, *Competitive Authoritarianism: Hybrid Regimes after the Cold War* (Cambridge: Cambridge University Press, 2010), 197.

158. Francisco José Paoli Bolio, "Legislación electoral y proceso político, 1917–1982," in González Casanova, *Las elecciones en México*, 146–52.

159. Garran to Slater, FO, 01/25/1963, FCO371/AM1015/13.

160. Gabriel A. Almond and Sidney Verba, *The Civic Culture: Political Attitude and Democracy in Five Nations* (Newbury Park, CA: Sage Publications, 1989), 181.

161. "Recent Political Events in Mexico," 03/04/1950, FO371/81503/AM1015/1.

162. Author's analysis, "Presidentes Municipales del Estado de Veracruz" series, AGN/DGIPS-1997A/2-1/010(18)"64"/52.

163. Paoli Bolio, "Legislación y proceso político, 1917–1982," and Rogelio Ramos Oranday, "Oposición y abstencionismo en las elecciones presidenciales, 1964–1982," in González Casanova, *Las elecciones en México*, 148–61, 163–94.

164. Magaloni, *Voting for Autocracy*, 8–9.

165. JNM to Gobernación, 10/11/1948, AGN/DGIPS-102/JNM.

166. Pérez Olivares, *Memorias*, 74.

167. PS-34 to Gobernación, 10/11/1948, AGN/DGIPS-102/JNM; PS-34 to Gobernación, 12/07/1948, AGN/DGIPS-91/2-1/131/748/CMC.

168. Robert Dahl sets out two distinctly different definitions of a polyarchy. The earlier defines a polyarchy as "a modern representative democracy with universal suffrage" characterized by elected officials; free, fair, and frequent elections; freedom of expression; alternative sources of information; associational autonomy; and inclusive citizenship. His later work proffers a more minimal, ambiguous, and (in Mexico at least) useful definition of polyarchy as a system permitting regularized participation and contestation. Robert Dahl, *On Democracy* (New Haven: Yale University Press, 1998), 85–90; Dahl, *Polyarchy*. Perhaps influenced by the democratic reforms of the midsixties, Dankwart Rustow considered Mexico in 1965 to be a polyarchy. Juan J. Linz, *Totalitarian and Authoritarian Regimes* (London: Lynne Rienner Publishers, 2000), 55.

169. John A. Booth and Mitchell A. Seligson, "The Political Culture of Authoritarianism in Mexico: A Reexamination," *Latin American Research Review* 19, no. 1 (1984): 106–24.

170. Rubin, *Decentering the Regime*, 61, 245.

171. Coatzacoalcos cólonos to Alemán, 09/02/1952, AGN/DGG-2.311P(26)/2/107; Centro Político Acción Cívica Acapulco to Gobernación, 11/21/1952, AGN/DGG-2.311M(9)/4B/74; Vecinos Metlatonoc to Alemán, 11/15/1952, AGN/DGG-2.311M(9)/2B/155; *El Universal*, 09/06/1952.

172. Manuel Gómez Morín interview in James W. Wilkie and Edna Monzón de Wilkie, eds., *México visto en el siglo XX: entrevistas de historia oral* (Mexico City: Instituto Mexicano de Investigaciones Económicas, 1969), 200.

173. For examples from the 1960s, see AGN/DGIPS-1320. In Ben Smith's prosopography of 1960s mayors the majority are middle-aged Catholic males, significantly wealthier than the norm, who belong to the Sector Popular; but the peasant sector is also well represented, the majority of the sample work as small farmers or ejidatarios, and the most important qualifications for selection are "administrative experience, a reasonably clean record and civic engagement." Smith, "Who Governed?" 254, 258.

174. Ortíz to Liga, 11/09/1949, AGN/DGG-2.311M(26)/78/8; Pavón Silva to Gobernación, 09/05/1948, AGN/DGIPS-800/2-1/49/444.

175. Jolie Olcott, pers. com., 11/15/2011.

176. *Trinchera de Culiacán*, 01/03/1967; *Acapulco Gráfico*, 11/30/1952.

177. Hernández Rodríguez, *La formación del político mexicano*, 132–35.

178. Namely, Aguascalientes, Baja California, Chihuahua, Durango, Guerrero, Michoacán, Oaxaca, Puebla, Sinaloa, and Tamaulipas. Ibid., 149–50; memo, DGIPS to Gobernación, 03/11/1965; Bustamante Díaz and De la Peña Hernández to DFS, 03/11/1965, AGN/DGIPS-1303/1.

179. *Excélsior,* 11/19/1965.

180. Gramsci, *The Prison Notebooks,* 149–52.

181. Levitsky and Way, *Competitive Authoritarianism,* 12, 30.

182. PS-16 to Gobernación, 01/11/1949, AGN/DGIPS-94/2-1/131/802.

183. Though not all traffic in the nineties was in the direction of democracy; the coffee ejidos of central Veracruz became less democratic under the 1992 agrarian reforms. Helga Baitenmann, "The Article 27 Reforms and the Promise of Local Democratization in Central Veracruz," in Wayne A. Cornelius and David Myhre, eds., *The Transformation of Rural Mexico: Reforming the Ejido Sector* (La Jolla: University of California San Diego, 1998), 121.

6. Law and Order in *México Profundo*

1. In terms of total deaths. Libro de defunciones, 1950, ORC; Mary Roldán, *Blood and Fire: La Violencia in Antioquia, Colombia, 1946–1953* (Durham: Duke University Press, 2002), 5, 299.

2. Gonzalo Sánchez, "The Violence: An Interpretative Synthesis," in Charles Bergquist, Ricardo Peñaranda, and Gonzalo Sánchez, eds., *Violence in Colombia: The Contemporary Crisis in Historical Perspective* (Wilmington, DE: Scholarly Resources, 1992), 76.

3. For pistoleros, see Piccato, *A History of Infamy;* Smith, *Pistoleros and Popular Movements;* Gillingham, "Who Killed Crispín Aguilar?" For guerrillas, Padilla, *Rural Resistance;* Oikión Solano and García Ugarte, eds., *Movimientos armados;* Castellanos, *México armado;* Carlos Montemayor, *La guerrilla recurrente* (Mexico City: Debate, 2007); Aviña, *Specters of Revolution;* Herrera Calderón and Cedillo, *Challenging Authoritarianism.* For soldiers, Rath, *Myths of Demilitarization;* Jorge Luis Sierra Guzmán, *El enemigo interno: contrainsurgencia y fuerzas armadas en México* (Mexico City: Plaza y Valdés and Universidad Iberoamericana, 2003); Gillingham, "Military Caciquismo." For students, Aguayo, *El 68;* Pensado, *Rebel Mexico.*

4. "Monografía de la 13a zona escolar del estado de Guerrero," in various authors, *Centenario* (Chilpancingo: Gobierno del Estado de Guerrero, 1949), 56–57; Paz, *The Labyrinth of Solitude,* 65–88.

5. "Monografía de la 13a zona escolar del estado de Guerrero," in *Centenario,* 56–57.

6. Problems of unknowability were not confined to Mexico. Colombians were unaware of the scale of the Violencia until it was almost over because "so much of the killing took place in remote rural areas that it was impossible to gain a clear picture of what was going on there." James D. Henderson, *When Colombia Bled: A History of the Violencia in Tolima* (Tuscaloosa: University of Alabama, 1985), 2.

7. Gonzalo Aguirre Beltrán, *Cuijla: esbozo etnográfico de un pueblo negro* (Mexico City: Universidad Veracruzana; Instituto Nacional Indigenista; Gobierno del Estado de Veracruz; Fondo de Cultura Económica, 1995 [1958]); Friedrich, *The Princes of Naranja,* 194; Muñoz, "Mixteca-Nahua-Tlapaneca," vol. 9.

8. Friedrich, *The Princes of Naranja*, 146, 271–75.

9. Tejeda to Cárdenas, 04/30/1940, AGN/LCR-542.1/211; "Crímenes cometidos . . . por Crispín Aguilar," AGN/DGIPS-787/2-1/45/282.

10. Liga to Avila Camacho, 08/31/1942, AGN/MAC-540.1/2; Garate to Avila Camacho, 03/31/1946, AHEV-1360/166/1(179).

11. See anonymous letter to the editor *La Verdad*, 1948, AGN/DGIPS-799/2-1/48/431; *Diario de Xalapa*, 04/15/1950; Comisariados ejidales Coyuca de Catalán to Alemán, 02/20/1948, AGN/DGIPS-799/2-1/48/431; Governor Octavio Vázquez Vela to Procurador, 06/19/1935, AGN/DGG-2.012.2(26)55/68/38.

12. Pablo Vargas González, "Estado y reivindicaciones agrarias: La guerra sofocada en la Huasteca hidalguense, 1974–1987," in Oikión Solano and García Ugarte, eds., *Movimientos armados*, 598.

13. Lara Salazar to Gobernación Veracruz, 08/20/1948, AHEV-1519/024/1.

14. Pablo Piccato, "Estadísticas del crimen en México: Series históricas, 1901–2001," http://www.columbia.edu/estadisticascrimen/EstadisticasSigloXX.htm; "Defunciones por homicidio según entidades federativas," Centro Cultural Isidro Fabela, AQC, Caja 14 (henceforth AQC-14).

15. Nineteen fifty-three on a national level, 1955 and 1957 in Veracruz. See figure showing official homicide rates later in the chapter.

16. Anonymous to editor *La Verdad*, 1948, AGN/DGIPS-799/2-1/48/431.

17. Acting presidente municipal Tepetlán to Cárdenas, 08/11/1939, AGN/LCR 541/2152.

18. As the probability of reprisal increased and trust in the police decreased. Such was the case in Jamiltepec, Oaxaca. Véronique Flanet, *Viviré si Dios quiere: un estudio de la violencia en la mixteca de la costa* (Mexico City: Consejo Nacional para la Cultura y las Artes; Dirección General de Publicaciones; Instituto Nacional Indigenista, 1990), 126–31.

19. Aguirre Beltrán, *Cuijla*, 85–87; Flanet, *Viviré si Dios quiere*, 126–31.

20. De la Peña, *Guerrero económico*, 1:358.

21. Leyva Mancilla report 1950, AP-175/352.072.073ETN.

22. John Brewer, Bill Lockhart, and Paula Rodgers, "Crime in Ireland since the Second World War," *Journal of the Statistical and Social Inquiry Society of Ireland* 27, no. 3 (1996): 136–37. For a skeptical look at contemporary Nicaraguan homicide rates, see Dennis Rodgers, "Living in the Shadow of Death: Gangs, Violence and Social Order in Urban Nicaragua, 1996–2002," *Journal of Latin American Studies* 38, no. 2 (2006): 270.

23. Twenty-nine per 100,000 compared to 61 per 100,000. Mary Roldán stresses the problems of accurate quantification of violence in Colombia, pointing out that there are motives for both under- and over-reporting. Cited in Henderson, *When Colombia Bled*, 254; Roldán, *Blood and Fire*, 299, 315.

24. Donald Campbell in E. S. Overman, ed., *Methodology and Epistemology for Social Sciences: Selected Papers* (Chicago: University of Chicago Press, 1988), 360. For a con-

temporary example, civilian casualties during the occupation of Iraq, 2003–6, were estimated to sum between 44,000 and 48,000 by the occupiers; and 655,000—an order of magnitude greater—by *The Lancet*. L. Roberts, R. Lafta, R. Garfield, J. Khudhairi, and G. Burnham, "Mortality before and after the 2003 Invasion of Iraq: Cluster Sample Survey," *The Lancet* 364, no. 9448 (2006): 1857–64.

25. Variable degrees of "stateness" is J. P. Nettl's concept, cited in Joel Migdal, *Strong Societies and Weak States: State–Society Relations and State Capabilities in the Third World* (Princeton: Princeton University Press, 1988), 18.

26. Namely, Caldas, Huila, Santander, Norte Santander, Tolima, and Valle.

27. Muñoz, "Mixteca-Nahua-Tlapaneca," 34, 146; López, *Crafting Mexico*, 264–66. As Marcelo Bergman points out, homicide rates per 100,000 are easily distorted in small communities, making single-year snapshots less informative than a long-term, "grassroots statistics" approach to multiple sites. Pers. com. Marcelo Bergman 2007.

28. Emilia Vázquez, "De la intermediación política a la construcción local del Estado: distintos abordajes teóricos en el análisis de procesos políticos en una región del Istmo veracruzano." Paper presented at the coloquio internacional CIESAS-IRD, Xalapa, November 2006, 50.

29. General Ramos Santos, "Informe sobre la situación que prevalece en esta Entidad," 09/30/1945, SDN-1-228/VIII; Martínez to SEDENA, 06/13/1950, SDN-1-398/IX; Migoni to Gobernación, 08/04/1945, AGN/DGIPS-787/2-1/45/282.

30. IRC libro de defunciones 1947, INAH/AS-PHO/CUAUH/5/33, 27. Manuel Rodríguez to presidente municipal Ixcateopan, 10/01/1946, AMI-1946. As Pablo Piccato says, "You knew a pistolero when you saw one." Piccato, *A History of Infamy*, chap. 5.

31. IRC libro de defunciones 1947; INAH/AS-PHO/CUAUH/5/33, 27.

32. A conclusion that connects with regional studies of cardenismo, which stress the absence of a stabilizing social compact between peasants and state. John Gledhill, *Casi Nada: A Study of Agrarian Reform in the Homeland of Cardenismo* (Austin: University of Texas Press, 1991), chaps. 2, 4; Fallaw, *Cárdenas Compromised*, 163–64; Bantjes, *As If Jesus Walked on Earth*, 219–24.

33. Morales Camacho and Ríos Thivol to Gobernación, 09/04/1947, AGN/DGIPS-84/2-1/131/655. That lynching was marked by performative violence and mutilation. This chapter does not propose to examine the cultural norms of violence so much as its incidence, structure and function, and evolution. However, (a) at a general level Mexican violence may in this period have been less routinely sadistic or performative than that of Colombia; (b) this does not mean that torture and mutilation were wholly absent; (c) modes of violence were clearly regionally determined; thus in Naranja, Michoacán, opponents were generally shot without fuss, whereas in central Veracruz burying alive was reported. Friedrich, *The Princes of Naranja*, 146, 271–75; Liga to Avila Camacho, 08/31/1942, AGN/MAC/540.1/2; *Diario de Xalapa*, 04/15/1950. For Colombian modes of violence, see Gerard Martin, "The 'Tradition of Violence' in Colombia,"

in Göran Aijmer and Jon Abbink, eds., *Meanings of Violence: A Cross-Cultural Perspective* (Oxford: Oxford University Press, 2000), 171.

34. Ellen Brennan-Galvin, "Crime and Violence in an Urbanizing World," *Journal of International Affairs* 56, no. 1 (2002): 123–45. For a typology along these lines that is of use because of its phenomenological detail, see Wil G. Pansters, "Zones of State-Making: Violence, Coercion and Hegemony in Twentieth-Century Mexico," in Pansters, *Violence, Coercion, and State-Making*, 20.

35. Moreover, as Piccato argues, "All were political in that they tested institutions and confirmed the irrelevance of the judiciary." Pablo Piccato, "*Pistoleros, ley fuga* and Uncertainty in Public Debates about Murder," in Gillingham and Smith, *Dictablanda*, 332.

36. Pierre Bourdieu, *Outline of a Theory of Practice* (Cambridge: Cambridge University Press, 1977), 178–81.

37. Migoni to Gobernación, 08/04/1945, AGN/DGIPS-787/2-1/45/282.

38. Kathryn A. Sloan, *Death in the City: Suicide and the Social Imaginary in Modern Mexico* (Oakland: University of California Press, 2017), 164.

39. Pablo Piccato, *City of Suspects: Crime in Mexico City, 1900–1931* (Durham: Duke University Press, 2001), 41–45; Vanderwood, *Disorder and Progress*, 107–12, 132–38.

40. Dehesa report 1894, BD-VIII/4270–4271, 4435, 4411; Vanderwood, *Disorder and Progress*, 123.

41. Piccato, *City of Suspects*, 224; Guillermo M. Vélez, "Memoria . . . de Veracruz . . . 9 de Julio de 1891," in García and Velasco, *Memorias e informes*, 5:251.

42. *Periódico Oficial*, 03/1/1887, 09/08/1887, AP171/352.0072.PRE.

43. Vanderwood, *Disorder and Progress*, 120–24; *Periódico Oficial*, 11/04/1891; AP189/394.2.DEL; Jaime Salazar Adame, "Movimientos populares durante el Porfiriato en el Estado de Guerrero (1885–1891)," in Friedrich Katz and Jane-Dale Lloyd, eds., *Porfirio Díaz frente al descontento regional (1891–1893)* (Mexico City: Universidad Iberoamericana, 1986), 97–121; Medel, *San Andrés Tuxtla*, 518.

44. Piccato, *City of Suspects*, 140–42, 185; Vanderwood, *Disorder and Progress*, 177–78.

45. Vadim Volkov, *Violent Entrepreneurs: The Use of Force in the Making of Russian Capitalism* (Ithaca: Cornell University Press, 2002), 27.

46. Report, political situation Guerrero, 03/08/1926, AGN/DGIPS-136/310(7.1)1.

47. Casas Alemán to Cárdenas, 01/31/1938, Martín Anotta to Cárdenas, 07/07/1938, Paxtián to Caneworkers' Union, 12/06/1939, Jara to Cárdenas, 12/15/1939, Cárdenas to Paxtián, 11/1/1940, AGN/LCR-542.1/211.

48. De la Peña, *Veracruz Económico*, 2:503, 507; De la Peña, *Guerrero económico*, 2:622.

49. Ruiz Cortines report 1945, BD-XIII/7336.

50. Jimenez López to Gobernación, 03/17/1947, AGN/DGIPS-794/2-1/47/398.

51. Garate to Avila Camacho, 03/31/1946, AHEV-1360/166/1(179); Logia Fenix no. 57 to Alemán, 05/05/1948, AGN/MAV-542.1/607.

52. Gema Kloppe-Santamaria, "Lynching and the Politics of State Formation in Post-Revolutionary Puebla (1930s–50s)," *Journal of Latin American Studies* 51, no. 3 (August 2019): 22.

53. Migoni to Gobernación, 10/5/1945, AGN/DGIPS-787/2-1/45/282; Migoni to Gobernación, 07/15/1946, AGN/DGIPS-791/2-1/46/405; I-33 to Gobernación, 09/07/1945, AGN/DGIPS-788/2.

54. Gutiérrez Avila, *Ojeda,* 60; Bateman to Bevin, 04/11/1947, FO371/60940/AN1478.

55. His pursuit may have been complicated by official uncertainty as to what he was actually called and what he actually looked like. IPS-7 to Gobernación, 10/31/1955, AGN/DGIPS-2014B; Benjamin T. Smith, "The Rise and Fall of Narcopopulism: Drugs, Politics, and Society in Sinaloa, 1930–1980," *Journal for the Study of Radicalism* 7, no. 2 (2013): 128.

56. Parr to presidente municipal, 08/01/1938, AMI-1938.

57. Reyes to Lara Salazar, 01/01/1949, AHEV-1615/051/137.

58. Rodríguez and López Portillo to Gobernación, 09/09/1947, AGN/DGIPS-101/2-1/131/1013; Leyva Mancilla to Gobernación, 04/12/1947, 04/21/1947, AGN/DGG-2/317.4(9)/45/33.

59. Garate to Ruiz Cortines, 07/19/1946, AHEV-1360/166/2, *Diario de Xalapa,* 05/12/1945.

60. Carvajal report 1950, BD-XIV/7867.

61. Piccato, "Estadísticas del crimen en México."

62. Friedrich, *The Princes of Naranja,* 116–17.

63. PS-1 & PS-2 to Gobernación, 08/07/1945, AGN/DGIPS-89/2-1/131/726.

64. Leyva Mancilla report 1946, AP-175/352.072.073ETN.

65. Salazar to Senate, 10/25/1942, AGN/DGG-2/012.2(9)/19/18.

66. PS-7 to Gobernación, 05/10/1940, AGN/DGIPS-140/9.

67. Author's analysis, Piccato, "Estadísticas del crimen en México."

68. Guzmán Carriles to Avila Camacho, 12/12/1942, AGN/DGG-2/311P(26)2/107.

69. Amparo of José Antonio Nogueda Radilla, 05/18/1940, AGN/DGG-2/012.2(9)/19/31; Ojeda to Avila Camacho, 06/11/1942, AGN/MAC-542.1/9.

70. Piccato, *A History of Infamy,* 263.

71. Catalán Calvo report 1945, AHEG-ramo ejecutivo/52.

72. Dehouve, *Cuando los banqueros eran santos,* 303.

73. Statement of Manuel Vázquez, 05/23/1940, AGN/DGG-2/380(9)/20/35.

74. *La Verdad,* 06/10/1949.

75. De la Peña, *Guerrero económico,* 2:621.

76. Report, political situation Guerrero, 03/08/1926, AGN/DGIPS-136/310(7.1)1.

77. Limón to Veracruz Supreme Court, 09/17/1951, AGN/MAV-134/11307.

78. Carvajal report 1949, BD-XIV/7749–7750.

79. Catalán Calvo report 1945, AHEG-ramo ejecutivo/52.

80. De la Peña, *Guerrero económico,* 1:359; *Diario de Xalapa,* 05/11/1945.

81. INAH/AS-PHO/CUAUH/5/11, 9–10.

82. Acapulco police to 27th Military Zone, 10/5/1948, AGN/DGG-2.311M(9)/3B/30.

83. Muñoz, "Mixteca-Nahua-Tlapaneca," 145–46.

84. Author's interview, Edgar Pavía Guzmán, Chilpancingo 04/4, 5/2002.

85. PPT Cuadro 34. Tasas de criminalidad por 100,000 habitantes, fuero común y federal. Estados Unidos Mexicanos, 1926–2001.

86. François Chevalier and Javier Pérez Siller, *Viajes y pasiones: imágenes y recuerdos del México rural* (Mexico City: Instituto Francés de América Latina, 1998), 96.

87. Friedrich, *The Princes of Naranja,* 37.

88. Santamaría, "Lynching and the Politics of State Formation."

89. Cited in Bettina E. Schmidt and Ingo W. Schröder, eds., *Anthropology of Violence and Conflict* (London: Routledge, 1995), 5.

90. Quiroz Cuarón report on homicide in Mexico, 1956, 8, AQC-14.

91. Rafael Bernal, *El complot mongol* (Mexico City: Grupo Planeta, 2013), 42.

92. Not that exceptional a case; as Paul Friedrich remarked, "In Naranja, as in many Mexican pueblos, the most redoubtable gunmen are often at or near the center of the political rulership." Friedrich, *The Princes of Naranja,* 4–14, 14.

93. Sector Popular Veracruz to Avila Camacho, 10/27/1942, AGN/MAC-541/633; Paxtián to Cárdenas, 10/23/1940, AGN/LCR-542.1/211.

94. Aguilar Aceves to de la Selva, 03/10/1950, AGN/MAV-243.2/11121.

95. Report, political situation Guerrero, 05/28/1926, AGN/DGIPS-136/310(7.1)1; Migoni to Gobernación, 08/04/1945, AGN/DGIPS-787/2-1/45/282.

96. Ernest Gellner, *Nations and Nationalism* (Ithaca: Cornell University Press, 2009), 4.

97. Baig Serra to Inspección General de Policía DF, 04/12/1946, AGN/DG-IPS-82/23; Agente del Ministerio Público Fresnillo, Zac., to Gobernación, 12/11/1945, AGN/DGIPS-127/2-1/266.8/6.

98. Piccato, *A History of Infamy,* 171.

99. Bernal, *El complot mongol,* 108.

100. As it was, Volkov argues, in 1990s Russia. Volkov, *Violent Entrepreneurs,* 26.

101. Pansters, "Zones of State-Making," 24.

102. Comisariado ejidal Corral Falso to Alemán, 04/23/1950, SDN-1-398/XIV.

103. *La Verdad,* 03/13/1949.

104. Report, political situation Guerrero, 03/08/1926, AGN/DGIPS-136/310(7.1)1. In some cases violence was indeed rooted in local feuds. As Chris Boehm has argued for the Montenegran highlands, however, the feud can be a systematic, brutally efficient mechanism for regulating interpeasant violence, which frequently becomes less regulated and more intensive when the state interferes to arm and protect some participants. Christopher Boehm, *Blood Revenge: The Enactment and Management of Conflict in Montenegro and Other Tribal Societies* (Philadelphia: University of Pennsylvania Press, 1987).

105. Fernand Braudel, *The Mediterranean and the Mediterranean World in the Age of Philip II*, 2 vols. (London: Collins, 1973), 2:659.

106. The other two being *The Social Contract* and *Das Kapital*. Friedrich, *The Princes of Naranja*, 34, 73, 95, 150; Aldous Huxley, *Beyond the Mexique Bay* (New York: Harper, 1934), 283–84.

107. Santoyo, *La mano negra;* Núñez Madrazo, "Entre patrones, caciques y líderes," 67–105.

108. *Diario de Xalapa*, 07/23/1945; Migoni to Gobernación, 09/28/1945, AGN/DG-IPS-787/2-1/45/282.

109. *El Dictamen*, 11/04/1947.

110. *Diario de Xalapa*, 12/29/1947, 07/1/1952.

111. Comisariados ejidales Los Tuxtlas to Cárdenas, 07/28/1938, AGN/LCR-542.1/211; Quiroga to Avila Camacho, 07/22/1944, AGN/MAC-541/633.

112. Castro to Cárdenas, 11/28/1939, AGN/LCR-542.1/211; Arriola Molina to Campos Gómez, 06/11/1940, AGN/DGIPS-87/2.

113. Corzo Ramírez et al., *Cándido Aguilar*, 293–94.

114. Arriola to Crescenciano Campos Gómez, 06/11/1940, PS-50 to Gobernación, 06/26/1940, AGN/DGIPS-87/2; Maldonado to Cárdenas, 12/04/1934, AGN/DGG/2/012.2(26)143/68/41; Santoyo, *La mano negra*, 152.

115. Roberto Blanco Moheno, *Memorias de un reportero* (Mexico City: Libro Mex, 1965), 93, 242.

116. Trigos, *El corrido veracruzano*, 65–67.

117. Interview with Estanislau Arroyo Zapata, in Skerritt, "¿Qué es la *mano negra?*" 134–35.

118. Skerritt, "Peasant Organisation," 289–90; PS-50 to Gobernación, 06/26/1940, AGN/DGIPS-87/2.

119. Blanco Moheno, *Memorias*, 89; "Actividades reaccionarias en el estado de Veracruz," 10/04/1939, AGN/DGIPS-140/9.

120. Skerritt, "¿Qué es la *mano negra?*" 134.

121. "Lista incompleta de crímenes cometidos . . . por Crispín Aguilar," AGN/DG-IPS-787/2-1/45/282; *Diario de Xalapa*, 12/29/1947.

122. Liga to CNC, 12/01/1947, AGN/MAV-541/218.

123. "Lista incompleta de crímenes cometidos . . . por Crispín Aguilar," AGN/DG-IPS-787/2-1/45/282; Aguilar to Avila Camacho, 08/23/1942, AGN/DGG-2/317.4(26)/24/64; *Excélsior*, 11/01/1947; Liga Villa Cardel to CNC, 12/01/1947, AGN/MAV-541/218.

124. Mange to Rodrigo de Llano, *Excélsior*, 11/03/1947.

125. The *Diario de Xalapa* from March through July 1945 is rich in details, as are Gonzalo Migoni's reports to Gobernación in AGN/DGIPS-787/2-1/45/282.

126. Thomas Hobbes, *Leviathan* (London: Penguin, 1987), chap. 11.

127. Trigos, *El corrido veracruzano*, 36.

128. *Diario de Xalapa,* 12/24/1947, 05/09/1950; *Excélsior,* 11/02/1947; Mange to de Llano, *Excélsior,* 11/03/1947.

129. *Diario de Xalapa,* 05/11, 14/1947, 08/13/1947; Ruiz Cortines 1947 report, BD-XIII/7529.

130. *Diario de Xalapa,* 09/23/1949, 05/09/1950.

131. *Diario de Xalapa,* 03/23, 25/1949.

132. Legal Attaché Speaks to ambassador, 08/03/1948, NARG-812.00/8–548; *Diario de Xalapa,* 09/01/1949.

133. *Diario de Xalapa,* 04/09/1950–04/15/1950.

134. Ibid., 04/09, 14/1950.

135. Ibid., 04/15/1950, 05/13, 22/1950.

136. Ibid., 07/01/1952–07/04/1952, 07/16/1952–07/23/1952.

137. Just how marked this pattern was needs further research; while Quiroz Cuarón hypothesized the same correlation, his figures at a national level showed no meaningful seasonal variation in homicide rates. This could obey the fact that homicide reporting rates tend to be low where agrarian conflict is high. "Mortalidad por homicidio según estación 1950–1954," AQC-14.

138. Catalán Calvo to Avila Camacho, 06/12/1943, AGN/MAC-405.1/3.

139. Assorted correspondence, 27th Military Zone, AGN/MAC 542.1/579.

140. A pattern suggested by the marked annual fluctuation of homicide rates in Ixcateopan and Ometepec and by Flanet's later work on the Costa Chica of Oaxaca. Flanet, *Viviré si Dios quiere,* 184.

141. Quiroz Cuarón report on homicide in Mexico, 1956, 9, AQC-14.

142. PS-31 to DGIPS, 10/07/1943, 11/01/1943, AGN/DGIPS-94/2-1/131/802.

143. Petition to ayuntamiento Ixcateopan, 12/10/1948, AMI-1948; Flanet, *Viviré si Dios quiere,* 42.

144. Gómez Maganda report 1952, AP-173/352.072.073ETN.

145. For the practices and prevalence of torture, "at the heart of police investigation, hidden from sight but widely known to occur," see Piccato, *A History of Infamy,* 117–19.

146. Governors' reports Veracruz 1945–53, BD-XIII/7529, BD-XIV/7613, BD-XIV/7744, BD-XIV/7750, BD-XV/8017–8019, BD-XV/8200.

147. De la Peña, *Veracruz Económico,* 1:252.

148. Muñoz report 1950–53, BD-XV/8018.

149. Torres to de la Selva, 10/02/1952, AGN/MAV-742/39535.

150. *Novedades,* 06/06/1964.

151. Kloppe-Santamaria, "Lynching and the Politics of State Formation," 24.

152. Finley to State, 12/21/1942, NARG-812.00/32086; *Diario de Xalapa,* 06/05/1950.

153. Torres to de la Selva, 09/24, 25/1952, AGN/MAV-742/39535.

154. *La Verdad,* 03/31/1949; Suárez Ruano to DFS, 03/09/1962, AGN/DFS-Guerrero/100-10-1-1962/H229L10.

155. A reference to the *picadores* of the bullfight. Trigos, *El corrido veracruzano*, 76.

156. Speaks to ambassador, 08/03/1948, NARG-812.00/8-548; Estado Mayor Presidencial to Gobernación, 12/24/1952, AGN/DGG-2.311M(9)155/2; *Diario de Xalapa*, 08/15/1948.

157. De la Peña, *Guerrero económico*, 2:622; Paucic notes on Leyva Mancilla, AP-108/320.32PER; Blanco Moheno, *Memorias*, 242.

158. Ojeda to Avila Camacho, 07/10/1941, AGN/MAC-541/269; *La Verdad*, 02/23/1949.

159. Such as the deaths of the Hacienda bureaucrat Iñigo Noriega and the journalist Natalio Burnstein. *Excélsior*, 12/9/1949, 04/6/1950.

160. Bateman to Bevin, 04/11/1947, FO371/60940/AN1478.

161. "Mátalos en caliente," the infamous order reportedly telegraphed from Porfirio Díaz to Veracruz to the captors of the 1879 rebels.

162. In Veracruz Registro Civil data show a lesser decrease, but absolute numbers still dropped some 10 percent across the period. "Defunciones por homicidio según entidades federativas," "Mortalidad por homicidio según medio urbano o rural," AQC-14.

163. AQC-14.

164. "Defunciones por homicidio según entidades federativas," "Mortalidad por homicidio países con datos publicados, 1953," AQC-14. Homicide rates in western Europe—Germany, France, Italy, Britain—were all below 2 per 100,000 by this date. https://ourworldindata.org/homicides.

165. Alberto Alesina, Salvatore Piccolo, and Paolo Pinotti, "Organized Crime, Violence, and Politics." Working paper, Department of Economics, Harvard University, 2016, A8. http://nrs.harvard.edu/urn-3:HUL.InstRepos:27760119.

166. Reinforcing the continuity, Arredondo was also a confidential agent of the Secret Service. Piccato, *A History of Infamy*, 185.

167. Aguilar de la Parra, *Mi tío, el cacique*, 92; Fuentes Díaz, *Guerrero*, 32–33; Sam Quinones, *True Tales from Another Mexico: The Lynch Mob, the Popsicle Kings, Chalino, and the Bronx* (Albuquerque: University of New Mexico Press, 2001), 249–67.

168. Genz, "Entrepreneurship and caciquismo," 291–94.

169. Pansters and Smith, "Writing Twentieth Century Mexico's Drug Histories"; Nathaniel Morris, "Heroin, the Herreras and the 'Chicago Connection': The Drug Trade in Durango, 1950–1985," both in Wil G. Pansters and Benjamin T. Smith, *Histories of Drug Trafficking in Twentieth Century Mexico* (Albuquerque: University of New Mexico Press, forthcoming 2021).

170. CIA report, "Mexico: The Problems of Progress," 10/2/1967, http://www.gwu.edu/~nsarchiv/NSAEBB/NSAEBB92/mexelect_1.pdf .

171. Though in both countries the criminalization of dissent rose. Luis Herrán Avila, "Rebels, Outlaws and Enemies," in Gema Kloppe-Santamaria and David Carey Jr., *Violence and Crime in Latin America: Representations and Politics* (Norman: University of Oklahoma Press, 2017).

172. Sánchez, "The Violence: An Interpretative Synthesis," 79–91; Roldán, *Blood and Fire*, 41–43.

173. Obtained through a comparison of *presuntos* vs. *sentenciados*; see table 6.3.

174. The sustained decline was also owing to demographic factors, notably the increase in literacy and the aging of the population. Piccato, *A History of Infamy*, 277.

7. Development, Corruption, and the Demands of the State

1. Miguel Alemán Valdés, *Miguel Alemán contesta* . . . (Austin: University of Texas Press, 1975), 9. The party secretary, Rodolfo Sánchez Taboada, publicly agreed.

2. Various authors, *Alemán y la comisión del maíz* (Mexico City: Editorial Ruta, 1951), 31; INEGI, *Estadísticas históricas* CD-ROM.

3. By the 1960s agraristas had ended up well represented in village government, though; 39 percent of Ben Smith's sample of presidentes municipales were ejidatarios, the single largest professional group (though collectively they were outnumbered by the broad churchgoers of the *sector popular*). Smith, "Who Governed?," 243, 247.

4. Muñoz profile, AGN/DGIPS-120/53.

5. RVS to Gobernación, 03/24/1950, 04/03/1950, AGN/DGIPS-102/RVS; Catalán Calvo to Gobernación, 02/02/1945, AGN/DGG-2.311M(9)/5B/75; Comité Ejecutivo Regional del PRI to presidente municipal Ixcateopan, undated, AMI-1948; *Diario de Xalapa*, 05/25/1945.

6. Friedrich, *The Princes of Naranja;* Paul Gillingham, "Ambiguous Missionaries: Rural Teachers and State Façades in Guerrero, 1930–1950," *Mexican Studies/Estudios Mexicanos* 22, no. 2 (2006): 331–60; Guillermo de la Peña, "The End of Revolutionary Anthropology? Notes on *Indigenismo*," in Gillingham and Smith, *Dictablanda*, 291; "Relación de candidatos a Presidente Municipales del PRI en los 202 municipios del estado de Veracruz," AGN/DGIPS-1997ffi/2-1/010(18)"64"/52.

7. Bernal, *El complot mongol*, 112.

8. María Antonia Martínez, *El despegue constructivo de la Revolución: Sociedad y política en el alemanismo* (Mexico City: CIESAS, Miguel Angel Porrua, 2004), 50–52, 57, 89.

9. *Montevideo-Oxford Latin American Economic History Database* (MOXLAD), http://moxlad.cienciassociales.edu.uy/.

10. A large majority of ejidatarios' credit came from sources other than the Banco Ejidal. Nicole Mottier, "What Agricultural Credit and Debt Can Tell Us about the State in Mid-Century Mexico." Paper presented at the meeting of the American Historical Association 2012.

11. Andrew Paxman, *Jenkins of Mexico: How a Southern Farm Boy Became a Mexican Magnate* (New York: Oxford University Press, 2017), 328–29.

12. Ruiz Cortines report 1945, BD-XIII/7350; Carvajal report 1950, BD-XIV/7884; BD-Muñoz reports 1951, 1952, BD-XV/8237, 8302.

13. *El Nacional*, 10/03/1950.

14. *La Verdad,* 09/29/1949.

15. *Novedades,* 09/02/1952.

16. Michael Snodgrass, "The Golden Age of Charrismo: Workers, Braceros, and the Political Machinery of Post-Revolutionary Mexico," in Gillingham and Smith, *Dictablanda,* 176.

17. *Excélsior,* 09/02/1952.

18. INEGI, *Estadísticas históricas* CD-ROM.

19. Leyva Mancilla reports 1950, 1951, AP-175/352.072.073ETN.

20. Muñoz report 1950–53, BD-XV/8125; *Excélsior,* 02/09/1952.

21. Assorted correspondence, AMI-1951.

22. Salubridad to presidente municipal, 04/18/1952, AMI-1952/131.

23. Ruiz Cortines report 1947, BD-XIV/7554; *La Verdad,* 08/09/1949; INEGI *Estadísticas históricas* CD-ROM. On Mexico's subsequent campaign against malaria and the mixed responses it evoked *en provincia,* see Marcos Cueto, "Appropriation and Resistance: Local Responses to Malaria Eradication in Mexico, 1955–1970," *Journal of Latin American Studies* 37, no. 3 (2005): 533–59.

24. Muñoz report 1952, BD-XV/8283.

25. Carvajal reports 1948, 1949, BD-XIV/7669, 7782.

26. Del Campo to Leyva Mancilla, 10/27/1947, AMI-1947; Carvajal report 1948, BD-XIV/7669.

27. Similarly ingenious quacks were to be found on the radio in the north, where broadcasters such as John R. Brinkley hawked the virtues of creative remedies—such as goat testicle, which, when sewn into human testicles, would naturally restore sexual potency—to credulous punters on the other side of the border. J. Justin Castro, *Radio in Revolution: Wireless Technology and State Power in Mexico, 1897–1938* (Lincoln: University of Nebraska Press, 2016), 158; *Adelante,* 05/17/1946.

28. *La Verdad,* 01/19/1949.

29. *La Verdad,* 08/31/1949.

30. Acta, 05/19/1952, AMI-1952.

31. *La Verdad,* 06/21/1949.

32. INEGI, *Estadísticas históricas* CD-ROM.

33. Secretaría de Economía, *Anuario estadístico de los Estados Unidos Mexicanos 1943–1945* (Mexico City: Secretaría de Economía, 1950), 256–59, 345–47; SEP to CNC, 08/31/1942, SEP/DGEP-5611/17–19–5–25; De la Peña, *Guerrero económico,* 1:417–18.

34. CTM Veracruz to Avila Camacho, 10/06/1941, SEP/DGEP-5476/14–55–9–80.

35. De la Peña, *Veracruz Económico,* 1:303–28.

36. Gillingham, "Ambiguous Missionaries," 332, 355–56.

37. Vaughan, *Cultural Politics in Revolution,* 195–99.

38. DEF to Federal Inspectors Guerrero, 11/27/1941, SEP/DGEP-488//76exp "sociedades de padres de familia."

39. A 1940 SEP survey found only two maestros who spoke an indigenous language in the entire state, when 13 percent of guerrerenses spoke an indigenous language. De la Peña, *Guerrero económico,* 1:402; various correspondence 1940, SEP/DGEP-488/76ex "ed indígena"; INEGI, *Estadísticas históricas* CD-ROM.

40. INEGI, *Estadísticas históricas* CD-ROM.

41. Governors' reports of Guerrero, 1945–51, AP-173–175; Carvajal report 1950, BD-XIV/7922.

42. Bustamante, *Tierra Caliente,* 39, 77.

43. Skerritt, "Peasant Organisation," 156; Gutíerrez Avila, *Ojeda,* 77–79.

44. Padilla, *Rural Resistance,* 186–92.

45. Marcel Anduiza, "Squatter Movements in Acapulco: The 'Civic Revolt' and the PRI's Corporatist Morass, 1955–1967." Paper presented at the Latin American Studies Association meeting, 2014.

46. Assorted telegrams, August–September 1950, AGN/MAV-840/5503.

47. See also the telegram campaign requesting that Brigadier-General José María Rosado Morales remain in command of the Acayucán garrison, AGN/MAV-811.1/11164, AGN/MAV-542.1/769.

48. "Annual Political Report for 1949," FO371/81501.

49. The timetable was quite precise: total, budgetable, current, and capital expenditures all systematically increased the quarter prior to and the quarter encompassing elections. Magaloni, *Voting for Autocracy,* 103, 106.

50. Alba to Gobernación, 09/09/1948, AGN/DGIPS-103/Mario Coquet/November 1947.

51. Guillermo de la Peña, "The End of Revolutionary Anthropology?" in Gillingham and Smith, *Dictablanda;* De la Peña, *Veracruz Económico,* 2:303–4.

52. Sóstenes to Alemán, 08/15/1949, AGN/MAV-542.1/978.

53. Author's interview, Joaquín Flores, Pachivia, 06/12/2002.

54. Declaration to agente del ministerio público Teloloapan, 07/25/1949, AGN/DGG-2.311M(9)/4B/80.

55. Leyva Mancilla report 1951, AP-175/352.072.073ETN; ejidatarios Taxco to Alemán, 01/27/1951, AGN/MAV-123/15064.

56. Ríos Thivol to Gobernación, 08/26/1949, AGN/DGIPS-802/2-1/49/546.

57. Lorenz to Alemán, 06/21/1947, AGN/MAV-534.6/103; Martínez to Alemán, 05/08/1949, AGN/MAV-123/2776; *El Popular,* 11/23/1948.

58. Presidente municipal's report 1947–48, AMI-1948.

59. Sóstenes to Alemán, 08/15/1949, AGN/MAV-542.1/978; ejidatarios Taxco to Alemán, 01/27/1951, AGN/MAV-123/15064.

60. Actas, 03/21, 22/1947, AMI-1947; presidente municipal's report 1947–48, AMI-1948.

61. Assorted correspondence, comisarios municipales to Ixcateopan, 1948, AMI-1948.

62. Comisario municipal El Potrero to presidente municipal, 12/26/1948, AMI-1948.

63. Silva Alvarez a quien corresponda, San Andrés Tuxtla, 12/27/1955, SATAM-presidencia/1/35–38.

64. Benjamin T. Smith, "Building a State on the Cheap: Taxation, Social Movements, and Politics," in Gillingham and Smith, *Dictablanda;* Rand McNally, *1950 Auto Road Atlas.*

65. I-33 to Gobernación, 07/23/1945, AGN/DGIPS-788/2-1/45/347; DGIPS report, 03/23/1950, AGN/DGG-M(26)78/52.

66. *Novedades,* 02/22/1951.

67. Skerritt, "Peasant Organisation," 158.

68. *La Verdad,* 09/04, 06/1949.

69. De la Peña, *Guerrero Ecomómico,* 2:56.

70. Carol Zabin, "Free Markets and Forests: Community-Based Forestry in the Age of Neoliberalism," in Cornelius and Myhre, *The Transformation of Rural Mexico,* 404.

71. Porfirio Hernández, "Cumbres y barrancas," in Poblett Miranda, *Cien viajeros,* 9:86–87.

72. Estado de México, Michoacán, and Oaxaca were the other main sites for extensive softwood logging. Christopher Boyer, "Community, Crony Capitalism, and Fortress Conservation in Mexican Forests," in Gillingham and Smith, *Dictablanda,* 219, 226–27.

73. Ixcateopan villagers to Alemán, 02/01/1949, AGN/MAV-501.2/158.

74. *La Verdad,* 08/02/1949.

75. Author's interview, Gonzalo Eguiluz, Ixcateopan 06/10/2002.

76. Leyva Mancilla report 1951, AP-175/352.072.073ETN.

77. De la Peña, *Guerrero económico,* 2:66, 71.

78. *Orientación guerrerense,* no. 46, 04/15/1944, AGN/DGIPS-782/2-1/44/274; Carvajal report 1950, BD-XIV/7883; "President Alemán's Message on the State of the Nation, Economic Aspects," 09/12/1951, NARG-712.21/9–1251.

79. Boyer, "Community, Crony Capitalism, and Fortress Conservation," 230–31.

80. *La Verdad,* 01/12/1949; De la Peña, *Guerrero económico,* 2:74.

81. Assorted documents, AHEV-1317/422/0, AHEV-1399/422/0, AHEV-1501/422/0, AHEV-1594/422/0, AHEV-1684/422/0.

82. Manuel Hinojosa Ortiz, *Los bosques de México: relato de un despilfarro y una injusticia* (Mexico City: Instituto Mexicano de Investigaciones Económicas, 1958), 12.

83. Castellanos, *México armado,* 67.

84. Cited in Martínez, *El despegue constructivo,* 44.

85. In 1930 pesos. Author's analysis, INEGI, *Estadísticas históricas* CD-ROM.

86. *Excélsior,* 09/02/1952.

87. Leyva Mancilla report 1948, AP-175/352.072.073ETN.

88. *Adelante,* 12/19/1946.

89. Muñoz report 1950–53, BD-XV/8073.

90. *Excélsior*, 09/02/1952.

91. Steven J. Bachelor, "Toiling for the 'New Invaders': Autoworkers, Transnational Corporations, and Working-Class Culture in Mexico City, 1955–1965," in Joseph, Rubenstein, and Zolov, *Fragments of a Golden Age*, 273–78.

92. Thorp, *Progress, Poverty and Exclusion*, 28, 352.

93. Discurso del Lic. Antonio Villalobos al iniciarse la Segunda Convención Nacional Ordinaria del PRM, 01/18/1946, in various authors, *Historia documental del Partido de la Revolución*, 200.

94. "Modern" defined as post-1940, as opposed to revolutionary. Medina, *Civilismo y modernización*, 93–94; Niblo, *Mexico in the 1940s*, chap. 5.

95. For an overview, see Alan Knight, "Corruption in Twentieth Century Mexico," in Walter Little and Eduardo Posada-Carbó, eds., *Political Corruption in Europe and Latin America* (London: Palgrave Macmillan, 1996), 219–36.

96. The *amigotes* were Alemán's closest circle, "the unsavory backroom Cabinet of the President," consisting of Ramón Beteta, Jorge Pasquel, Antonio Díaz Bermudez, Carlos Serrano, and Aaron Sáenz, all notorious for their self-enrichment. Foreign Office, *Further correspondence respecting Mexico Part 6, January to December 1952*, 13, 17.

97. In 1950. This dubious honor—presidential peculation outweighing national debt—is shared by Juan Perón, Rafael Trujillo, and Marcos Pérez Jiménez. It is one measure of inflation and debt crisis that the López Portillo camarilla's baroque peculation is comparable to just the interest on the national debt rather than the debt itself. Laurence Whitehead, "On Presidential Graft: The Latin American Evidence," in M. Clarke, ed., *Corruption: Causes, Consequences and Control* (London: Pinter, 1983), 150; Stephen D. Morris, *Corruption and Politics in Latin America: National and Regional Dynamics* (Boulder: Lynne Rienner Publishers, 2010), xvi.

98. Santa Anna was believed to have taken $600,000 for services rendered in negotiating the Gadsden Purchase of 1853, which transferred southern Sonora to the US Inspectors 15 and 50, delegate, to Director DGIPS, 08/21/1948, AGN/DGIPS-111; Jürgen Buchenau, *The Last Caudillo: Alvaro Obregón and the Mexican Revolution* (Somerset: Wiley-Blackwell, 2011), 15.

99. Knight, *Mexican Revolution*, 2:460.

100. For considerations on that balance in the capital, see Ingrid Bleynat, "The Business of Governing: Corruption and Informal Politics in Mexico City's Markets, 1946–1958," *Journal of Latin American Studies* 50, no. 2 (2018): 355–81.

101. Niblo, *Mexico in the 1940s*, 168–69.

102. Rath, *Myths of Demilitarization*, 39, 103.

103. Santos, *Memorias*.

104. Memorandum, "Relación de periódicos de las diferentes entidades federativas de la República," 06/11/1960, AGN/DGIPS-1279.

105. Smith, "The Rise and Fall of Narcopopulism," 137–38.

106. Memorandum, 04/11/1952, "Estado de Guerrero: Agitación con motivo de la vigencia de la ley de ingresos de 1952," AGN/DGIPS-104/2-1/131/1074.

107. Julia del Palacio Langer, "Agrarian Reform, Oil Expropriation, and the Making of National Property in Post-revolutionary Mexico" (Ph.D. diss., Columbia University, 2014), 201–2.

108. Ricardo de la Garza y Garza, Memorandum, 04/23/1953, AGN/DFS-VP Eucario León.

109. Guzmán Carriles to Avila Camacho, 12/12/1942, AGN/DGG-2/311P(26)2/107.

110. *La Verdad*, 06/10/1949.

111. Statement of Manuel Vázquez, 05/23/1940, AGN/DGG-2/380(9)/20/35; "Salario medio pagado a la semana," INEGI, *Estadísticas históricas* CD-ROM.

112. *La Verdad*, 06/10/1949.

113. *La Verdad*, 08/04/1949.

114. Carvajal report 1949, BD-XIV/7749–7750.

115. More functionally than historically: gatekeeper states are generally seen as relatively newly independent, still in many ways highly dependent, with less diverse economies, flimsier institutions, and weaker national identities. For a definition and comparative examples of gatekeeper states, see Frederick Cooper, *Africa since 1940: The Past of the Present* (Cambridge: Cambridge University Press, 2002), 5, 156–90.

116. "Protectionism . . . provided the material means for the PRI to forge the crony arrangements that underpinned its enduring authority." Susan Gauss, *Made in Mexico: Regions, Nation, and the State in the Rise of Mexican Industrialism, 1920s–1940s* (University Park: Pennsylvania State Press, 2010), 199, 204.

117. Notorious for its profitability for the bureaucrats and politicians that ran it; Maximino Avila Camacho did not take it over at gunpoint on a whim.

118. "No me den, pero pónme donde hay." Paper by Luis Barrón, Simposio "La construcción del cargo público," CIDE/University of Warwick/AHRC, November 2017.

119. Foreign Office, *Further correspondence . . . 1952*, 13. Gonzalo N. Santos enjoyed a similar arrangement. Santos, *Memorias*.

120. Magaloni, *Voting for Autocracy*, 104, 108.

121. Memorandum, "Discurso del Gral Jacinto B. Treviño," 1948, AGN/DFS-VP Jacinto B. Treviño.

122. Friedrich Katz, *The Life and Times of Pancho Villa* (Stanford: Stanford University Press, 1998), 637.

123. Memo, undated, AGN/DGIPS-1465/3.

124. Monthly accounts, libros de tesorería 1949, SATAM-tesorería/1949.

125. *Diario de Xalapa*, 07/02/1952.

126. Ibid., 10/05/1952.

127. PS-34 to Gobernación, 04/08/1946, AGN/DGIPS-91-2-1/131/748; Friedrich, *The Princes of Naranja*, 124.

128. He committed suicide en route to face charges in Mexico City. Niblo, *Mexico in the 1940s,* 234.

129. Smith, "Building a State on the Cheap," 255–75, 270.

130. An outside investigation of tax farming in Guerrero ended when the state police shot and killed the relevant bureaucrat. Salazar Adame, *La Cuestión Agraria Mexicana,* 445; Memorandum, Sector Popular to Gobernación, 08/13/1944, AGN/DGG-239–2/311 G (9) 2; Barajas to Gobernación, 06/28/1948, PS-31 to Gobernación, 06/28/1948, Coquet to Gobernación, 06/29/1948, AGN/DGIPS-799/2-1/48/431.

131. Paxman, *Jenkins of Mexico,* 320.

132. Informes de tesorería, AHEV-1229/024/0. The 1952 purge reached even Acayucán, Alemán's hometown. For suspensions, dismissals, and arrests and calls for more, see *Diario de Xalapa,* 06/20, 21/1952, 07/2/1952.

133. Paxman, *Jenkins,* 321. Enough such arrangements may have existed to form something of a fiscal deep state.

134. The Sanitary Code alone had over 250 articles and was still open to interpretation by the Supreme Court; did the prohibition on opening new premises for the sale of alcohol apply solely to cantinas, whose main function it was, or did it include *loncherías,* for whom it was a secondary concern? José Antonio Caballero, "Amparos y *abogángsters:* La justicia en México entre 1940 y 1968," in Elisa Servín, ed., *Del nacionalismo al neoliberalismo, 1940–1994* (Mexico City: Colegio de México, 2010), 179–80; Malcolm Lowry, *Under the Volcano* (New York: Harper Collins, 2007), 243.

135. Memo to Secretario de Gobernación, 08/27/1947, AGN/DGIPS-794.

136. Moisés T. de la Peña, *Chihuahua económico,* 3 vols. (Mexico City: Adrián Morales, 1948), 3:259–60.

137. Report, Castillo Venegas, 08/21/1954, AGN/DFS-VP Eucario León.

138. Samuel P. Huntington, *Political Order in Changing Societies* (New Haven: Yale University Press, 1968), 69.

139. Alan Riding, *Distant Neighbors: A Portrait of the Mexicans* (New York: Knopf, 1989).

140. Andrei Shleifer and Robert W. Vishny, *The Grabbing Hand: Government Pathologies and Their Cures* (Cambridge: Harvard University Press, 1998), 92, 103.

141. Ingrid Bleynat restates a version of the modernization thesis in a case study of Mexico City market vendors and their political masters / intermediaries, concluding that "sometimes corruption represents governance under hard constraints." Bleynat, "The Business of Governing," 381.

142. Specifically, in a clear chronological coincidence, from 1947 to 1973. Eric Hobsbawm, *Age of Extremes: The Short Twentieth Century* (London: Joseph, 1994), 6, 8.

143. Maddison, at www.nationmaster.com; Deininger and Squire, "Income Inequality."

144. Vice-Consul Eastham, Coatzacoalcos, despatch 06/30/1950, NARG-712.00/7–1950.

145. Inflation-adjusted real costs in 1929 pesos. Bess, *Routes of Compromise,* 158–59; Thurston to Secretary of State, 08/20/1948, NARG-812.00/8–2048.

146. Gillingham, "Military Caciquismo," 224–25.

147. Agent 35 to Director Federal de Seguridad, 08/26/1948, AGN/DFS-Amaro Joaquín VP L1 6.

148. Sullivan to Eden, 01/12/1955, FO-371-AM1015/2, in *Confidential Print of the Foreign Office for 1955,* 5.

149. *La Prensa,* 10/07/1948; Rath, *Myths of Demilitarization,* 97.

150. State congress decree no. 51, 04/20/1945, undated Comisión de Agricultura y Policia Rural circular, AMI-1945; presidente municipal Ixcateopan to jefe de seguridad pública, 03/09/1946, AMI-1946; presidente municipal Dos Ríos, Ver., to agentes municipales, 10/31/1947, AHEV-1463/1641/1(82); Gobernación circular, 10/17/1949, AHEG-ramo ejecutivo/54/6; Oficialia Mayor de Gobernación, Chilpancingo, to presidente municipal Ixcateopan, 08/19/1952, AMI-1952.

151. A proposal echoed, ironically enough, in Rubén Jaramillo's contemporaneous Plan de Cerro Prieto. Agricultural production forms, Soledad de Doblado, 1949, AHEV-1692/498/137; Gobernación y Justicia Chilpancingo circular, 02/09/1945, AMI-1945; Padilla, *Rural Resistance,* 97.

152. Ruiz Cortines report 1945, BD-XIII/7325.

153. See the follow-up to Regino to Alemán, 08/10/1949, AGN/MAV-542.1/975; Liga to Alemán, 11/17/1947, AGN/MAV-551.2/7.

154. Muñoz, "Mixteca-Nahua-Tlapaneca," 50–51.

155. "Manifestación de predios rústicos, 1929," AMI-1929; De la Peña, *Veracruz Económico,* 1:42–43.

156. De la Peña, *Guerrero económico,* 2:611; *El Popular,* 8/10/1952; "President Alemán's Message on the State of the Nation, Economic Aspects," 09/12/1951, NARG-712.21/9–1251.

157. *Diario de Xalapa,* 09/13/1947.

158. Extract from *El Mundo,* in I-184 to Gobernación, 05/11/1944, AGN/DGIPS-100.

159. Mottier, "What Agricultural Credit and Debt Can Tell Us"; conviction rates in homicide cases, fuero común, 1950–60, table 6.3.

160. Gobernación report, 09/02/1948, AGN/DGIPS-132/2-1/303"1948."

161. Ruiz Cortines report 1946, BD-XIV/7469; oficialía mayor to presidente municipal, 02/27/1947, AMI-1947.

162. Internal investigation, AGN/DGIPS-90/ACC.

163. Guardino, *Peasants,* 101–2; Katz and Lloyd, *Díaz frente al descontento regional,* 11–18; Jacobs, *Rancher Revolt,* 79; Carreto Leyva to Leyva Mancilla, 01/24/1947, AHEG-ramo ejecutivo/53/13.

164. Smith, *Pistoleros and Popular Movements,* 310–24, 376–401.

165. *Diario de Xalapa,* 07/13/1949.

166. Treasury report, AHEV-1229/024/0.

167. Ruiz Cortines reports 1945, 1947, BD-XIII/7328, BD-XIV/7508; Carvajal report 1948, BD-XIV/7651.

168. Coquet to Carvajal, 03/22/1949, AGN/DGIPS-802/2-1/49/545.

169. Parra to presidente municipal, 06/18/1945, AMI-1945.

170. Ruiz Cortines report 1945, BD-XIII/7328.

171. De la Peña, *Veracruz Económico,* 2:492.

172. Smith, "Building a State on the Cheap"; INEGI, *Estadísticas históricas* CD-ROM.

173. Migdal, *Strong Societies and Weak States,* 280–82.

174. Ruiz Cortines reports 1945, 1947, BD-XIII/7331, BD-XIV/7533–7536; Leyva Mancilla report 1951, AP-175/352.072.073ETN.

175. *Adelante,* 12/02/1945; acta, 01/19/1951, AMI-1951.

176. Ruiz Cortines report 1946, BD-XIV/7411.

177. Carvajal report 1950, BD-XVI/7893.

178. Acta, 01/19/1951, AMI-1951; INEGI, *Estadísticas históricas* CD-ROM.

179. INEGI, *Estadística históricas* CD-ROM.

180. Campaña Nacional Contra el Analfabetismo circular no. 4, AMI-1945; *La Prensa,* 01/01/1945.

181. Campaña Nacional Contra el Analfabetismo memo (undated, 1948?), AHEV-1509/600/13/(82).

182. Circular, Castro to presidentes municipales, 06/28/1945, AMI-1945.

183. Assorted municipal reports, AHEV-1509.

184. Lillian Guerra, *Visions of Power in Cuba: Revolution, Redemption, and Resistance, 1959–1971* (Chapel Hill: University of North Carolina Press, 2012), 158.

185. Assorted correspondence, AMI-1945, AMI-1946.

186. Olguín to presidente municipal Ixcateopan, 04/15/1946, AMI-1945/100.

187. General Rubén García, cited in Thomas Rath, " '*Que el cielo un soldado en cada hijo te dió . . .*' Conscription, Recalcitrance and Resistance in Mexico in the 1940s," *Journal of Latin American Studies* 37, no. 3 (2005): 513.

188. Ibid., 516–19.

189. Presidente municipal Alto Lucero to Ruiz Cortines, 11/11/1947, AHEV-1463/164/1(82); Jasso to Carvajal, 08/31/1948, AHEV-1552/164/1.

190. Mange to SEDENA, 12/01/1948, AHEV-1552/164/1.

191. Presidente municipal Soteapan to Ruiz Cortines, 07/04/1948, AHEV-1552/164/1.

192. Quintana to Oficinas de Reclutamiento, 03/08/1944, 08/31/1944, 09/17, 18/1944, 10/02, 10/1944, AMI-1944.

193. *Diario de Xalapa,* 09/24/1949.

194. Gobernación to Ruiz Cortines, 03/26/1946, AHEV-1360/164/1(82).

195. Presidente municipal's report, 1945–46, AMI-1946; presidente municipal to Rodríguez Juárez, 06/27/1947, AMI-1947.

196. Rath, "Conscription, Recalcitrance and Resistance," 529; *Diario de Xalapa,* 05/19/1950; secretario del gobierno Guerrero to presidentes municipales, 01/17/1952, AMI-1952.

197. Aguilar de la Parra, *Mi tío, el cacique,* 144–46.

198. Gómez Maganda report 1952, AP-173/352.072.073ETN.

8. Talking about a Revolution

1. "Dirigida," for example, was a popular choice. *Excélsior,* 11/16/1965. For a popular rejection of democracy with adjectives, see Enrique Krauze, *Por una democracia sin adjetivos* (Mexico City: Joaquín Mortiz, 1986). For taxonomies of authoritarianism, see Gabriel Almond, "The Intellectual History of the Civic Culture Concept," in Gabriel Almond and Sidney Verba, eds., *The Civic Culture Revisited: An Analytic Study* (Boston: Little, Brown, 1980), 22; Wil G. Pansters, ed., *Citizens of the Pyramid: Essays on Mexican Political Culture* (Amsterdam: Rijksuniversiteit te Utrecht, 1997), 1; Peter H. Smith, "Mexico since 1946: Dynamics of an Authoritarian Regime," in Leslie Bethell, ed. *Mexico since Independence* (Cambridge: Cambridge University Press, 1991), 332–33; González Casanova, *Democracy in Mexico,* 11–30; John J. Bailey, *Governing Mexico: The Statecraft of Crisis Management* (Hampshire: Macmillan, 1988), 12; José L. Reyna, "Redefining the Authoritarian Regime," in José Luis Reyna and Richard S. Weinert, eds., *Authoritarianism in Mexico* (Philadelphia: Institute for the Study of Human Issues, 1977), 155–71; Mario Vargas Llosa, "La dictadura perfecta," in *Desafíos a la libertad* (Madrid: El País, 1994); Paul Gillingham, "Preface," in Gillingham and Smith, *Dictablanda,* 7–12.

2. British embassy Mexico City to Slater, 01/25/1963, FO371/AM1015/13.

3. Bourdieu, *Outline of a Theory of Practice,* 190–94.

4. Alan Knight, "Peasants into Patriots: Thoughts on the Making of the Mexican Nation," *Mexican Studies/Estudios Mexicanos* 10, no. 1 (1994): 141.

5. As Anthony Pagden remarks, creole nationalism "was poised forever on the edge of absurdity." Pagden, cited in Rebecca Earle, *The Return of the Native: Indians and Myth-making in Spanish America, 1810–1930* (Durham: Duke University Press, 2007), 42; for examples of unlikely indigenistas, see also 31, 60–63, 72–75, 94; one of the most unlikely was the emperor Maximilian, who gave an Independence Day speech that called Mexico Anahuac while inveighing against colonialism. Robert H. Duncan, "Embracing a Suitable Past: Independence Celebrations under Mexico's Second Empire, 1864–1866," *Journal of Latin American Studies* 30 (1998): 263.

6. Guy P. C. Thomson, "Bulwarks of Patriotic Liberalism: The National Guard, Philharmonic Corps and Patriotic Juntas in Mexico, 1847–1888," *Journal of Latin American Studies* 22, nos. 1–2 (1990): 31–68.

7. Mateo Podan, "Admonitorios," *La Prensa,* 11/08/1950.

8. Hector Aguilar Camín, "Nociones presidenciales de cultura nacional de Alvaro Obregón a Gustavo Díaz Ordaz, 1920–1968," in José Emilio Pacheco, ed., *En torno a la cultura nacional* (Mexico City: Secretaría de Educación Pública, 1982), 110–15.

9. Ilene V. O'Malley, *The Myth of the Revolution: Hero Cults and the Institutionalization of the Mexican State, 1920–1940* (New York: Praeger, 1986), 70–87; Jones, *The War Has Brought Peace to Mexico,* 105.

10. *Excélsior,* 10/10/1949; *La Prensa,* 02/01/1951; State Congress to presidente municipal Ixcateopan, January 1952, AMI-1952/107; Muñoz report 1950–53, BD-XV/8013.

11. *El Nacional,* 02/03/1950.

12. Samuel Brunk, "Remembering Emiliano Zapata: Three Moments in the Posthumous Career of the Martyr of Chinameca," *Hispanic American Historical Review* 78, no. 3 (1998): 470–71.

13. *La Prensa,* 09/01/1950.

14. José López Bermúdez, *Canto a Cuauhtémoc* (Tuxtla Gutierrez, Chiapas: Edición del gobierno del estado de Chiapas, 1951), 72–73.

15. Katz, *Villa,* 774, 789–93.

16. And largely did under the leadership of the slippery Lombardo, who "to circumvent the apparent class contradiction in this position . . . asserted that while the proletariat *could* lead the bourgeois-democratic revolution, it was less clear whether in fact it *should.*" William Booth, "Hegemonic Nationalism, Subordinate Marxism: The Mexican Left, 1945–1947," *Journal of Latin American Studies* 50, no. 1 (2017): 47–48.

17. Alan Knight, "The Myth of the Mexican Revolution," *Past and Present* 209, no. 1 (2010): 228, 255.

18. Personal communication, Jennifer Jolly, 08/17/2019.

19. Catalogue, Hemeroteca Nacional, UNAM.

20. José Miranda Román to Municipal Treasurer, Ixcateopan, 07/14/1945, AMI-1945.

21. Anne Rubenstein, *Bad Language, Naked Ladies and Other Threats to the Nation: A Political History of Comic Books in Mexico* (Durham: Duke University Press, 1998), 18.

22. Paul Gillingham, "The Regional Press Boom, c.1945–c.1965: How Much News Was Fit to Print?" in Gillingham, Lettieri, and Smith, *Journalism, Satire, and Censorship,* 164.

23. Stanley Ross, "El historiador y el periodismo mexicano," *Historia Mexicana* 14, no. 3 (1965): 379; Pablo González Casanova, *La democracia en México* (Mexico City: Ediciones Era, 1983), 222.

24. Robert H. K. Marett, *An Eye-witness of Mexico* (London: Oxford University Press, 1939), 79, 207.

25. Castro, *Radio in Revolution,* 166.

26. Matthew W. Stirling, "Discovering the New World's Oldest Dated Work of Man," *National Geographic Magazine* 76 (1939): 189.

27. Niblo, *Mexico in the 1940s,* 316, 343–44; Paul Gillingham, *Cuauhtémoc's Bones: Forging National Identity in Modern Mexico* (Albuquerque: University of New Mexico Press, 2011), 180; Andrew Paxman, "Cooling to Cinema and Warming to Television: State Mass Media Policy, 1940–1964," in Gillingham and Smith, *Dictablanda,* 305.

28. Gillingham, Lettieri, Smith, "Journalism, Satire, and Censorship in Mexico," 20.

29. Paxman, *Jenkins of Mexico,* 272; Paxman, "Cooling to Cinema."

30. Enrique Krauze, *La Presidencia Imperial: ascenso y caída del sistema político mexicano (1940–1996)* (Mexico City: Tusquets Editores, 1997), 100.

31. Michael Lettieri, *The Motor of the PRI: Political Entrepreneurs and Authoritarian Rule, 1927–1985* (Albuquerque: University of New Mexico Press, forthcoming), chap. 3; Paxman, *Jenkins of Mexico*, 318.

32. Census data in INEGI, *Estadísticas Históricas de México* CD-ROM.

33. Rubenstein, *Bad Language, Naked Ladies and Other Threats to the Nation*, 31; Gillingham, "The Regional Press Boom," 164.

34. *Diario de Xalapa*, 01/12/1948.

35. Abel Quezada, *El mejor de los mundos imposibles* (Mexico City: Consejo Nacional para la Cultura y los Artes, 1999), 303.

36. *El Nacional*, 09/29/1949; *Excélsior*, 02/08/1949.

37. Susana Sosenski Correa, "El niño consumidor: Una construcción publicitaria de la prensa mexicana en la década de 1950," in Ariadna Acevedo Rodrigo and Paula López Caballero, eds., *Ciudadanos inesperados: espacios de formación de la cuidadanía ayer y hoy* (Mexico City: Colegio de México, 2012), 197, 199.

38. Catalogue, Hemeroteca Nacional, UNAM.

39. Ruiz Cortines report 1947, BD-XIV/7517; Leyva Mancilla report 1948, AP-175/352.072.073ETN.

40. Though, as Michael Lettieri shows, the Alianza Camionero ended up "a somewhat unintended space where criticism could flourish." Lettieri, "In the Service of the *Gremio*," in Gillingham, Lettieri, and Smith, *Journalism, Satire, and Censorship*, 139.

41. *La Verdad*, 02/06/1949.

42. *El Nacional*, 02/03/1950.

43. Partido Revolucionario Institucional, Comité Central Ejecutivo, *Juárez: Una lección de historia patria* (Mexico City: Partido Revolucionario Institucional, 1949).

44. Secretario de Gobierno Chilpancingo to presidentes municipales, 07/13/1944, AHEG-ramo ejecutivo/51/"circulares de Gobernación 1944"; Senate to presidentes municipales, 01/07/1947, AMI-1947; Casasola to Leyva Mancilla, 06/05/1947, AHEG-ramo ejecutivo/51/4.

45. Bloque de Periodistas Revolucionarios to presidente municipal, 10/22/1951, AMI-1951; Club de Leones Ameca, Jalisco, to presidente municipal, 04/14/1952, AMI-1952.

46. Brunk, "Remembering Emiliano Zapata," 471–72; Rubenstein, *Bad Language, Naked Ladies and Other Threats to the Nation*, 87.

47. *El Nacional* to presidente municipal, 02/20/1948, AMI-1948.

48. Quoted in Paxman, *Jenkins of Mexico*, 275.

49. Claudia Fernández and Andrew Paxman, *El Tigre: Emilio Azcárraga y su imperio Televisa* (Mexico City: Grijalbo, 2000), 53.

50. *Diario de Xalapa*, 05/01/1945, 06/07/1945; Carvajal report 1949, BD-XIV/7753; Fernández and Paxman, *El Tigre*, 201.

51. Gobernación to presidentes municipales, 08/23/1947, AHEG-ramo ejecutivo/51/"gobernación y justicia 1947"; Dirección General de Información to Chilpancingo, 11/22/1952, AMI-1952; Joy Elizabeth Hayes, *Radio Nation: Communication, Popular Culture, and Nationalism in Mexico, 1920–1950* (Tucson: University of Arizona Press, 2000), 82; Castro, *Radio in Revolution*, 165.

52. "Textos para transmitir el 10 de julio 1966," AGN/DGIPS-1458B, AGN/DFS-103 Legajos 10–116 L.2 a 10–120.

53. An estimated 80 percent; the only competition left was Abelardo Rodríguez's chain of cinemas in the northwest and fifteen theaters in Mexico City. Paxman, *Jenkins of* Mexico, 272, 296.

54. Assorted correspondence Barrat to Gobernación, 1947–48, AHEV-1552/159/0.

55. Paxman, *Jenkins of Mexico*, 274.

56. Paxman, "Cooling to Cinema."

57. Paxman, *Jenkins of Mexico*, 250.

58. The soundtrack too was popular, featuring subtitled versions of "Adelita" and "Las mañanitas" and released as an LP.

59. Paxman, "Cooling to Cinema," 309; Paxman, *Jenkins of Mexico*, 294.

60. María Rosa Gudiño Cejudo, "Estado benefactor y ciudadanos obedientes: Guerra al Paludismo, Cruzada Heróica y Erradicación del Paludismo en México, tres cortometrajes para una campaña, 1955–1960," in Acevedo Rodrigo and López Caballero, *Ciudadanos Inesperados*, 180.

61. Martínez, *El despegue constructivo*, 59.

62. Assorted reports, AGN/DGIPS-128/2-1/268.2/4.

63. This was at the peak of the devaluation crisis, when such agents were busy. Memo to Gobernación, 08/14/1948, AGN/DGIPS-111/2-1/260/82.

64. Merrill Gay to John G. McCarthy, Motion Picture Association of New York, 08/09/1949, NARG-812.4061 MP/5–1349.

65. *Excélsior*, 03/08/1947.

66. Fernández and Paxman, *El Tigre*, 54.

67. *El Nacional* to presidente municipal Ixcateopan, 01/02/1945, AMI-1945; Niblo, *Mexico in the 1940s*, 346–48.

68. Personnel files, AGN/DGIPS-80/1, 2.

69. Rubenstein, *Bad Language, Naked Ladies and Other Threats to the Nation*, 95–97, 110–28.

70. *Ovaciones*, 06/20/1950; Smith, *The Mexican Press*, 108, 110; *El Universal*, 04/07/1950.

71. Pablo Piccato, "Murders of Nota Roja: Truth and Justice in Mexican Crime News," *Past & Present* 223, no. 1 (2014): 195–231. For a sample of Quezada's political commentary in *Cine Mundial*, see Quezada, *El mejor de los mundos imposibles*.

72. RVS to Gobernación, 04/11/1950, AGN/DGIPS-102/RVS.

73. *La Verdad*, 01/20, 21/1949, 03/14/1949, 04/03/1949. In comparison to the twenty-first century the death count was nevertheless comparatively low, with some nineteen recorded murders of journalists between 1940 and 1960. Gillingham, "The Regional Press Boom," 163.

74. *Excélsior*, 09/14/1947; De la Hoya to Alemán, 10/02/1947, AGN/MAV-542.1/404; editor *La Crítica*, Orizaba, to Alemán, 09/09/1948, AGN/DG-IPS-802/2-1/49/546; *El Universal*, 07/02/1949; *Diario de Xalapa*, 06/19/1950.

75. IPS-80 to Gobernación, 05/14/1944, AGN/DGIPS-95/2-1/131/825.

76. Urquizo to Gobernación, 10/09/1944, AGN/DGG-110B/2/311P(29)/1 06821; *Excélsior*, 03/06/1947; Bateman to Bevin 04/11/1947, FO371/60940; *El Informador*, 04/01/1947.

77. *El Suriano*, 09/23/1947; *Diario de Xalapa*, 08/15/1948.

78. Gillingham, "The Regional Press Boom," 162.

79. José Miranda Román to Municipal Treasurer, Ixcateopan, 07/14/1945, AMI-1945.

80. *La Verdad*, 02/23/1949.

81. Karl Marx, *The 18th Brumaire of Louis Bonaparte* (New York: International Publishers, 2008), 20.

82. Almond and Verba, *The Civic Culture*, 39.

83. The division between production and reception has been criticized by Joseph, Rubenstein, and Zolov as a misleadingly "false opposition." It remains useful in terms of the analysis of nationalism and propaganda because, for all the influential impact of consumer feedback—and grassroots instrumentalism—on its themes and forms, the majority of nationalist and officialist propaganda materials and practices remained the product of government agencies (at all levels) or the private companies that followed their lead, and those agencies made sure that as many Mexicans as possible received them. What they then did with those materials is another question, treated above. Joseph, Rubenstein, and Zolov, "Assembling the Fragments," 17; Gillingham, *Cuauhtémoc's Bones*, 197–204, 220–26.

84. Assorted correspondence, July–August 1948, SATAM-presidencia/1/23S1948.

85. Author's interview, Román Parra Terán, Chilpancingo, 11/25/2002.

86. Cinco de mayo program, AMI-1944.

87. Dormady, *Primitive Revolution*, 81–86, 134.

88. *La Verdad*, 02/02/1949.

89. Quintana to block inspectors, 05/02/1944, AMI-1944; acta, 04/30/1947, AMI-1947; author's interview, Román Parra Terán, Chilpancingo, 11/25/2002.

90. Muncipal accounts for November 1946, AMI-1946.

91. Leyva Mancilla report 1947, AP-175/352.072.073ETN.

92. *El Sol de Acapulco*, 06/09/1951.

93. Secretaría de Economía, *Anuario estadístico de los Estados Unidos Mexicanos 1943–1945* (Mexico City, 1950), 256–59, 345–47; STERM Guerrero to SEP, 06/28/1941,

SEP/DGEP-5470 ant. 2768 exp 14–55–7–13; Murillo Vidal to SEP, 07/21/1941, SEP/DGEP-5476 ant 2775 exp 14–55–9–80; Inspector 10a zona to SEP, Annual report 1941–42, SEP/DGEP-5611 ant. 3854 exp 16–9–3–3.

94. Asuntos Indígenas to SEP, 03/31/1944, SEP/DGEP-5674 ant. 1870 exp 17–20–2–47; Whetten, *Rural Mexico*, 491.

95. Juan Caccia Bernal to Gobernación, 02/02/1949, AGN/DGIPS-800/2-1/49/444; Castro García to Ruiz Cortines, 09/29/1950, AGN/DGG-242/2.311 G(9).

96. Rafael Catalán Calvo, *Informe del C. gobernador constitucional del estado de Guerrero* (Chilpancingo, 1944), 33; De la Peña, *Guerrero económico*, 2:605.

97. Rafael Segovia, *La politización del niño mexicano* (Mexico City: Colegio de México, 1975), 15.

98. 4,400,000 of 7,400,000. Sosenski Correa, "El niño consumidor mexicana en la década de 1950," 195.

99. Elena Jackson Albarrán, *Seen and Heard in Mexico: Children and Revolutionary Cultural Nationalism* (Lincoln: University of Nebraska Press, 2014), 323.

100. Victoria Lerner, "Historia de la Reforma Educativa, 1933–1945," *Historia Mexicana* 29, no. 1 (1979): 91–132.

101. Rodríguez Rivero and Alba Calderón to Gobernación, 03/19/1949, AGN/DGIPS-101/2-1/131/1013.

102. Assorted reports, July–August 1948, AGN/DGIPS-94/2-1/131/802, AGN/DGIPS-101/2-1/131/1012; assorted reports, 09/02/1948, AGN/DGIPS-132/2-1/303"1948."

103. Though they may also have seen this as just an extension of the junkets that were traditional perks of the secret police and chosen the smarter cinemas for questions of taste. Memos, 08/14, 17/1948, AGN/DGIPS-111/2-1/260/82.

104. Poster, AGN/DGIPS-111/2-1/260/82.

105. Memo, 08/14/1948, AGN/DGIPS-111/2-1/260/82.

106. Smith, *Pistoleros and Popular Movements*, 302–27, 387–401.

107. Monthly political report, 10/25/1951, FO371/90820.

108. "Rob . . . ber. Rob . . . ber." Thurston to State Department, 08/12/1948, NARG-812.00/8–2148.

109. Gillingham, "Maximino's Bulls," 145–81.

110. Peter Metcalf and Richard Huntingdon, *Celebrations of Death: The Anthropology of Mortuary Ritual* (Cambridge: Cambridge University Press, 1991), 6.

111. PS-20 to Gobernación, undated, AGN/DGIPS-79/2-1/130/633; Jürgen Buchenau, "The Arm and Body of a Revolution: Remembering Mexico's Last Caudillo, Alvaro Obregón," in Lyman L. Johnson, ed., *Death, Dismemberment and Memory: Body Politics in Latin America* (Albuquerque: University of New Mexico Press, 2004), 198–99.

112. Gillingham, *Cuauhtémoc's Bones*, 194–96.

113. López Portillo and Barajas Salcedo to Gobernación, 11/05/1947, AGN/DGIPS-751/319.

114. *Adelante,* 07/21/1946.

115. Assorted reports, AGN/DGIPS-128/2-1/268.2/4.

116. It could have been worse; only one in ten fourteen-year-olds knew the name of the president of the PAN. Segovia, *La politización del niño mexicano,* 26, 35–36.

117. Muñoz report 1952, BD-XV/8292; *El Nacional,* 03/04, 06/1951; *Excélsior,* 10/13/1950, 02/25/1951.

118. *Excélsior,* 09/30/1949.

119. Assorted reports, 09/06, 07/1948, AGN/DGIPS-128/2-1/268.2/4; Ríos Thivol to Gobernación, 04/06/1948, AGN/DGIPS-84/IV; *La Verdad,* 08/31/1949; Snodgrass, "The Golden Age of Charrismo," 176–77.

120. Gillingham, *Cuauhtémoc's Bones,* 203–14.

121. Mothers of Senguio to Avila Camacho, 12/14/1942, AGN/MAC-752/545.2/14–15. I thank Thom Rath for providing me with a copy of this document.

122. Conrado Velázquez memo, 08/18/1949, AGN/DGIPS-119/38. For a similar, more explicitly Orwellian document from the 1960s, see Rodríguez Munguía, "'The Invisible Tyranny,'" 183. The Sinarquistas had much the same dream; in their blueprint for a sinarquista future, "México-1960," they would form a "new conscience" through overwhelming dominance of the mass media, tolerating "an autonomous and weak press." Great minds. Whetten, *Rural Mexico,* 518–20.

123. Almond and Verba, *The Civic Culture,* 40–41.

124. Castro, *Radio in Revolution,* 4, 169; Tanalís Padilla, "Rural Education, Political Radicalism, and Normalista Identity in post-1940 Mexico," in Gillingham and Smith, *Dictablanda,* 353–54.

125. Smith, *The Mexican Press,* 35.

126. Renata Keller, "Testing the Limits of Censorship? *Política* Magazine and the 'Perfect Dictatorship,' 1960–1967," in Gillingham, Lettieri, Smith, *Journalism, Satire, and Censorship,* 221–35; Vanessa Freije, *Scandalous Democracy: Journalists and the Politics of Corruption in Mexico* (Durham: Duke University Press, 2019), chap. 1.

127. Almond and Verba, *The Civic Culture,* 55.

128. They were so effective that the mayor had to be escorted "hasta para hacer una necesidad biológica." Francisco Díaz García to governor, 04/07/1947, AHEV-1506/548/0.

129. Jean Meyer, *Le Sinarquisme: un fascisme mexicain? 1937–1947* (Paris: Hachette, 1977), 36; Whetten, *Rural Mexico,* 489–90.

130. Letter, governor to Gobernación, 11/19/1945, AHEV-1234/544/0.

131. Whetten, *Rural Mexico,* 521–23.

132. *Excélsior,* 06/19/1951.

133. Dormady, *Primitive Revolution,* 46.

134. See, for examples of the vampire trope, *Diario de Xalapa,* 05/07/1945; Liga to Catalán Calvo, 01/02/1945, AGN/DGG-2.311M(9)14; Peñalosa Varo to Avila Camacho, 05/18/1944, AGN/DGG-2/311G(9)2/241.

135. Memo, Inspector PS-20 to Gobernación, 08/14/1948, AGN/DGIPS-111 /2-1/260/82.

136. Olguín to presidente municipal Ixcateopan, 04/15/1946, AMI-1945/100; acta, 10/14/1948, AMI-1948.

137. "A él le pela la verga." Chávez Rodríguez to Ruiz Cortines, 01/16/1946, AHEV-1335/051/57.

138. An unsurprising conclusion, given that his peers were that day being deployed as *acarreados.* Decades later one in three schoolchildren didn't know that the presidency was an elected position, and fewer than half of pupils in 3a secundaria of the public system knew that senators were elected. Jorge Guillermo Bátiz, Culiacán, to Perez Martínez, November 1947, AGN/DGIPS-794/2-1/47/396; Segovia, *La politización del niño mexicano,* 26, 28–29.

139. Almond and Verba, *The Civic Culture,* 39, 203, 310.

9. Why Mexico Did Not Become a Military Dictatorship

1. Edwin Lieuwen, *Mexican Militarism: The Political Rise and Fall of the Revolutionary Army, 1910–1940* (Albuquerque: University of New Mexico Press, 1968). See also González Casanova, *Democracy in Mexico,* 36–38; Smith, *Labyrinths of Power,* 38.

2. An estimated 66 percent of the total federal budget in 1919 went to the armed forces. Lieuwen, *Mexican Militarism,* 153.

3. Thom Rath suggests that this was spin, as many of the announced retirements seem not to have actually happened. Rath, *Myths of Demilitarization,* 95.

4. Avila Camacho decree of 12/03/1945, reproduced in various authors, *Historia documental del Partido de la Revolución,* 5:173–75; Lieuwen, *Mexican Militarism,* 144.

5. *Excélsior,* 10/01/1951.

6. Lieuwen, *Mexican Militarism,* 148–49.

7. Dirección General de Estadística, *Séptimo censo general de población 6 de junio de 1950 resumen general* (Mexico City, 1953); reports on the Mexican army, 1951, 1953, FO-371/97547 and FO371/109037.

8. Quoted in Ben Fallaw, "Praetorian Politics, Militant Jacobinism and Generalized Corruption: Francisco J. Múgica in Campeche and Yucatan (1934–35) and José Domínguez Cota in Guanajuato (1938–1940)." Paper delivered at the Southern Conference of Latin American Studies, Albuquerque, 2006.

9. Niblo, *Mexico in the 1940s,* 96–97.

10. Gallardo Rodríguez had published excerpts from his master's thesis, "The Need for a Military Ombudsman in Mexico." Salvador Velazco, "*Rojo amanecer* y *La ley de Herodes:* cine político de la transición mexicana," *Hispanic Research Journal* 6, no. 1 (2005): 67–73; Mónica Beltrán Gaos, *La Comisión Nacional de los Derechos Humanos de México* (Valencia: Editorial de la UPV, 2005), 145–47.

11. David F. Ronfeldt, "The Mexican Army and Political Order since 1940," in James Wilkie, Michael Meyer, and Edna Monzón de Wilkie, *Contemporary Mexico: Papers of the IV International Congress of Mexican History* (Berkeley: University of California Press, 1976), 317–36; Benítez Manaut, "México: Avances y límites de las relaciones civiles–militares," 411–54; US embassy cable, "The Mexican Army—Still Passive, Isolated, and Above the Fray?" 05/11/1995, http://www.gwu.edu/~nsarchiv/NSAEBB/NSAEBB120/index.htm#docs.

12. All the artillery, bar three coastal batteries and a regiment in Guadalajara, was likewise kept in Mexico City. "Relación de las Grandes Unidades del Ejército," 09/01/1948, Dirección de Artillería, "Relación," 09/02/1948, AGN/MAV-550/19.

13. Valdés's personnel file as one of Miguel Alemán's DGIPS agents has regrettably been emptied; the regularity with which he was posted to Veracruz, however, and the frequent references of other sources to his pistolero networks there clearly point to his central role in the hardball side of Alemán's control of his home state. AGN/DGIPS-88/2-1/131/708. For salary differentials—privates were apparently paid as much as sergeants in other regiments—see Rapp to Bevin, 07/22/1948, *Foreign & Commonwealth Office Confidential Print for 1948*, 40.

14. In 1943. Rath, " *'Que el cielo en cada hijo un soldado te dió . . . ,'* " 527.

15. "Relación que manifiesta los batallones de infantería," AGN/MAV-550/19.

16. Comisariado ejidal Corral Falso to Alemán, 04/23/1950, SDN-1-398/XIV.

17. "Relación de las Defensas Rurales," 09/01/1948, AGN/MAV-550/19.

18. Departamento de Asuntos Indígenas to Avila Camacho, 11/23/1942, AGN/MAC-542.1/579.

19. Liga to Cárdenas, 06/28/1939, 07/04/1939, AGN/LCR-403/313; S. González to Cárdenas, 10/30/1939, AGN/LCR-541/411; Liga Puebla to Avila Camacho, 01/09/1942, AGN/MAC-540.1/2; G. Lagunes to Avila Camacho, 04/07/1945, AGN/MAC-551.1/132.

20. Liga to Alemán, 10/17/1947, AGN/MAV-551.2/7.

21. Catalán Calvo, *Informe del C. Gobernador*, 12.

22. Rodríguez Juárez to Quintana, 05/19/1944, AMI-1944; presidente municipal to Rodríguez Juárez, 04/09/1945, AMI-1945; Rodríguez Juárez to Monroy, 07/02/1948, AMI-1948.

23. Document summary, 12/14/1938, SDN-1-356/VI.

24. Migoni to Gobernación, 08/09/1945, AGN/DGIPS-787/2-1; *Diario de Xalapa*, 08/23/1948.

25. Benjamin T. Smith, "Heliodoro Charis Castro and the Soldiers of Juchitán: Indigenous Militarism, Local Rule, and the Mexican State," in Fallaw and Rugeley, *Forced Marches*, 114.

26. Report on Coatzacoalcos political situation, 04/07/1949, AGN/DGIPS-787/2-1/49/545, assorted correspondence, July–October 1949, AGN/MAV-437.3/195.

27. Pensado, *Rebel Mexico*, 100–128.

28. Cited in Tanalís Padilla, *Rural Resistance*, 221.

29. PS-1 and PS-2 to Gobernación, 08/07/1945, AGN/DGIPS-89/2-1/131/726; assorted letters, PAN secretary-general to Gobernación, January 1952, AGN/DGG-2/311P(29)2/110B.

30. Partido Constitucionalista Mexicano to Alemán, 05/15/1951, AGN/MAV-811.5/2927; Padilla, *Rural Resistance*, 91–105, 139–60.

31. "Crímenes cometidos . . . por Crispín Aguilar," AGN/DGIPS-787/2-1/45/282.

32. Encarnación Ursúa, *Los copreros*, 44–48.

33. Assorted correspondence, AGN/MAC-542.1/579.

34. Acting Vice-Consul Barranco to Foreign Office, 10/23/1942, FO371/30586; *El Universal*, 01/30/1952; Camp, *Mexican Political Biographies*, 904–40.

35. *La Prensa*, 10/07/1948.

36. José Manuel Villalpando, "Política y ejército, 1945–1994," in Garciadiego, coord., *El Ejército Mexicano*, 327–28.

37. *Excélsior*, 11/02/1947.

38. Ojeda to Gobernación, 12/10/1948, AGN/DGG-2.311M(9))/3B/6.

39. Ortiz and Figueroa to Alemán, 12/31/1951, AGN/MAV-123/30004.

40. Borges Ortiz to Rodríguez, 10/29/1934, AGN/DGG-2/012.2(26)137/68/37; Migoni to Gobernación, 08/24/1945, AGN/DGIPS-787/2-1/45/282; *Diario de Xalapa*, 07/18/1945.

41. Rebolledo to Agente del Ministerio Público Veracruz, 02/02/1949, AGN/DGG-2/380(26)90/42.

42. Gobernación to Vázquez Vela, 03/27/1935, AGN/LCR-541/411; Encarnación Ursúa, *Los copreros*, 54; Ocampo and Zamora open letter to Alemán, *Excélsior*, 03/09/1949.

43. Mizayawa to de la Fuente, 06/15/1951, AGN/DFS-Guerrero/100–10–14–51H129L3. He may have been influenced by the gifts of lumber he had earlier received. Martínez to Lt-Col. Eusebio González Saldaña, 04/12/1949, SDN-1-398/XVI.

44. López Barroso, *Diccionario*, 62–63.

45. Gómez Galeana to Alemán, 04/25/1947, AGN/DGIPS-12/2/389(9)38.

46. See, for example, Ramos to Avila Camacho, 06/20/1944, AGN/MAC-542.1/579.

47. Mange to Ruiz Cortines, 02/25/1946, AHEV-1360/166/2.

48. Carvajal to Mange, 08/04/1949, AHEV-1640/166/1; Mario Coquet to Gobernación, 06/22/1950, AGN/DGIPS-800/2-1/49/444.

49. Carvajal report 1949, BD-XIV/7743.

50. *La Verdad*, 05/07/1949; Alvarado to Martínez, 05/15/1941, AGN/MAC-542.1/269; PS-31, 34, 43 to Gobernación, 04/28/1949, AGN/DGIPS-84/MRT; Presidente municipal Acapulco to SEDENA, 06/21/1950, SDN-1-398/XVI.

51. PS-31 to Gobernación, 08/29/1949, AGN/DGIPS-84/MRT.

52. Flores to Gobernación, 12/06/1952, AGN/DGG-2.311M(9)155/2B.

53. PDM Ciudad Altamirano to Avila Camacho, 07/08/1946, AGN/MAC-544.1/11–4.

54. *La Verdad,* 01/04/1949.

55. Díaz García to governor, 04/07/1947, AHEV-1506/548/0.

56. Absalón Pérez to Ruiz Cortines, 08/22/1946, AHEV-1412 exp 549/0.

57. Informe mensual, Brigadier Raúl Garate to the presidency, 03/31/1946, Procurador General to Agente del Ministerio Público Chicontepec, 04/22/1946, AHEV-1360/166/1 (179).

58. *Diario de Xalapa,* 04/14/1945; circular, Ramos to defensas rurales, 11/05/1943, AGN/MAC-542.1/579.

59. Paul Friedrich, *Agrarian Revolt in a Mexican Village* (Chicago: University of Chicago Press, 1970), 107.

60. Frank Tannenbaum, *Peace by Revolution: Mexico after 1910* (New York: Columbia University Press, 1966), 104.

61. *Diario de Xalapa,* 05/23/1945; Liga de Comunidades Agrarias to Ruiz Cortines, 10/15/1945, AHEV-1338 exp 052/14 (14).

62. *Diario de Xalapa,* 06/05/1952.

63. Albert t'Serstevens, "México, país de tres niveles," in Poblett Miranda, *Cien viajeros,* 9:324.

64. Federación Sindical de Obreros y Campesinos del Estado de Veracruz to Cárdenas, 06/28/1937, SDN-1-356/IX; Presidencia to SEDENA, 04/09/1948, SDN-1-374/VI; PS-11 to Gobernación, 06/26/1948, AGN/DGIPS-799/2-1/48/431; Ojeda to Gobernación, 11/12/1948, AGN/DGG-2.311M(9)/3B/6; Memo, Presidencia to SEDENA, 04/09/1948, SDN-1-374/VI.

65. Assorted correspondence, AGN/MAV-542.1/506, AGN/MAV-542.1/2.

66. Altamirano to SEDENA, 02/25/1947, SDN-1-374/VI.

67. Ramos to Avila Camacho, 09/28/1944, AGN/MAC-542.1/579; *Trópico,* 10/01/1944; *Excélsior,* 09/28/1948.

68. Author's interview, Vicente Ramírez Sandoval, Ometepec, 04/09/2002; Guzmán Carriles to Avila Camacho, 12/12/1942, AGN/DGG-2/311P(26)2/107; *La Verdad,* 03/25/1949.

69. Coquet to Gobernación, 06/22/1950, AGN/DGIPS-800/2-1/49/444.

70. Sánchez Salazar, 19a zona Tuzpam, to Alemán, 06/27/1947, AGN/MAV-425.5/2-29.

71. Leyva Mancilla to Alemán, 04/23/1949, 11/29/1949, AGN/MAV-556.4/29.

72. *Diario de Xalapa,* 06/06/1952.

73. Revolutionary veterans to Alemán, 05/29/1948, AGN/MAV-556.63/48.

74. Amorós to Ruiz Cortines, 08/06/1945, AGN/MAC-542.1/891; Migoni to Gobernación, 10/10/1945, AGN/DGIPS-787/2-1/45/282.

75. Ojeda to Gobernación, 12/10/1948, AGN/DGG-2.311M(9)/3B/6.

76. Gómez Galindo to Alemán, 01/16/1947, AGN/MAV-515.5/3.

77. Comisariados ejidales Coyuca de Catalán to Alemán, 02/20/1948, AGN/DGIPS-799/2-1/48/431; *La Verdad,* 07/29/1949; campesinas Copala to Alemán, 04/09/1949, AGN/MAV-404.1/1990.

78. Sergeants Hernández Espinosa and Bailón Segundo to Alemán, 04/07/1947, AGN/MAV-556.63/26.

79. Memorandum, 10/25/1948, AGN/DGIPS-24 "militares políticos-1948-sep."

80. Article 81 of the Ley Orgánica del Ejército, cited in Navarro, *Political Intelligence,* 23.

81. *La Verdad,* 06/15/1949.

82. *Diario de Xalapa,* 03/28/1945.

83. "Situación política estado de Chiapas," 09/23/1940, AGN/DGIPS-83/10; *La Prensa,* 10/07/1948.

84. Ferrocarriles Nacionales de México to SEDENA, 03/31/1959, SDN-1-356/XII; Migoni to Gobernación, 10/10/1945.

85. Garate to Avila Camacho, 03/31/1946, AHEV-1360/166/1(179).

86. Presidente municipal Chicontepec to Alemán, 03/08/1948, AGN/MAV-542.1/592; Bautista to Alemán, 05/15/1948, AGN/MAV-540.1/15.

87. Edwin Lieuwen, "Depoliticisation of the Mexican Revolutionary Army, 1915–1940," in David F. Ronfeldt, ed., *The Modern Mexican Military: A Reassessment* (La Jolla: Center for US–Mexican Studies, University of California San Diego, 1984), 61.

88. Rath, *Myths of Demilitarization,* 117.

89. Gillingham, "Force and Consent," 205–44.

90. Dulles, *Yesterday in Mexico,* 659–60.

91. C. H. Bateman, "Report on Leading Personalities in Mexico for the Year 1946," FO371/60955; Alejandro Mange Toyos, hoja de servicios, SDN-1-356, vol. 11.

92. SEDENA disposition of forces, 09/01/1948, AGN/MAV-550/19.

93. Dulles, *Yesterday in Mexico,* 445.

94. Alejandro Mange Toyos, hoja de servicios SDN-1-356/XI.

95. Ibid.

96. Rath, *Myths of Demilitarization,* 28.

97. Mange, hoja de servicios SDN-1-356/XI.

98. Gibson to State, 05/17/1943, NARG-812.00/32150.

99. Mange, hoja de servicios SDN-1-356/XI; Dulles, *Yesterday in Mexico,* 33.

100. For the concept of stateness, see J. P. Nettl, *Political Mobilization: A Sociological Analysis of Methods and Concepts* (London: Basic Books, 1967), 33.

101. Migoni to Gobernación, 06/14, 15, 21/1945, AGN/DGIPS-787/2-1/45/282; López vda. de Pampín to Alemán, s.f., AGN/MAV-001/4232.

102. Migoni to Gobernación, 10/10/1945, AGN/DGIPS-787/2-1/457282.

103. Pérez to SEDENA, 01/07/1959, SDN-1-356/XII; Migoni to Gobernación, 06/23/1945, 10/10, 19/1945, AGN/DGIPS-787/2-1/45/282; Migoni to Gobernación,

06/06/1946, AGN/DGIPS-791/2-1/46/405; Amorós to Ruiz Cortines, 08/06/1945, AGN/MAC-542.1/891; López vda de Pampín to Alemán, s.f., AGN/MAV-001/4232.

104. In 1926 Hector López, on the verge of overthrow by his own legislature, was sustained by General Amaro, who ordered the 13th Battalion in Chilpancingo to assist the governor "in any way possible," including the forcible removal of the dissident congressmen. A year later the new federal commander Claudio Fox was critical in removing López from office in favor of a military candidate, Castrejón. Political situation Guerrero, 05/28/1926, AGN/DGIPS-136/310(7.1)1; Jacobs, *Ranchero Revolution*, 126.

105. Ojeda to Cárdenas, 06/15/1944, SDN-1-374/VII.

106. Rath, *Myths of Demilitarization*, 121–22.

107. Author's interview, Vicente Ramírez Sandoval, Ometepec, 04/09/2002; Marguerite P. Boyce, *Yo oí a los burros rebuznar: 30 años en el campo misionero* (Mexico City: CUPSA, 1996), 36; PS-1 and PS-2 to Gobernación, 08/07/1945, AGN/DGIPS-89/2-1/131/726.

108. The army keeps the military procuradoría's files closed. PS-1 and PS-2 to Gobernación, 08/07/1945, AGN/DGIPS-89/2-1/131/726; assorted telegrams to Alemán, August–September 1950, AGN/MAV-840/5503.

109. Ortiz and Figueroa to Alemán, 12/31/1951, AGN/MAV-123/30004.

110. Departamento de Asuntos Indígenas to Avila Camacho, 11/23/1942, AGN/MAC-542.1/579; assorted correspondence, AGN/MAV-541/96.

111. Migoni to Gobernación, 10/10, 19/1945, AGN/DGIPS-787/2-1/45/282.

112. Pansters and Smith, "Writing Twentieth Century Mexico's Drug Histories."

113. "Annual Report on Mexico for 1948," FO371/74076; Walter Washington to Secretary of State, 05/19/1948, NARG-812.00/5-1948.

114. There were no dollar sellers at the official rate of 6.70. Pavón Silva to Gobernación, 08/02/1948, AGN/DGIPS-111/2-1/260/82. For popular predictions of a violent end to the regime, see DGIPS director Lamberto Ortega Peregrina's intelligence summaries in AGN/DGIPS-111/2-1/260/82.

115. Among other preparations they alerted foreign embassies well in advance of their detailed plans, summed up in an indignant five-page proclamation to the nation. Carlos Alatorre et al., "Proclamación a la nación," AGN/DGIPS-115/2-1/263.6/7; Nuevo Laredo Consulate to Secretary of State, 10/07/1948, NARG-812.00/10–748; Massey to Secretary of State, 10/15/1948, NARG-812.00/10–1548.

116. Memoranda, 08/17/1948–08/19/1948, AGN/DGIPS-24/"militares políticos"-1948-sep; Memorandum, 08/23/1948, AGN/DGIPS-24/3; *La Prensa*, 09/06/1948.

117. Memorandum, 10/25/1948, AGD/DGIPS-24/"militares políticos"-1948-sep; Memorandum, 08/27/1948, AGN/DFS-28–16–48/H-41; *La Prensa*, 10/02/1948.

118. The rumors ran back at least as far as 1931. Sharp to Secretary of State, 08/31/1948, NARG-812.00/8–3148; Agente 19 to DFS, 10/27/1948, AGN/DFS-VP Amaro, Gral Joaquín; Medin, *El minimato presidencial*, 106; Navarro, *Political Intelligence*, 35–43.

119. Agent 51 to DFS, 01/27/1948, AGN/DFS-VP Alamillo Flores, General Luis.

120. "Antecedentes del General de División Antonio Ríos Zertuche Cuellar," AGN/DFS-VP Ríos Zertuche.

121. *La Prensa,* 10/07/1948.

122. Rath, *Myths of Demilitarization,* 85.

123. Benjamin T. Smith, "The Year Mexico Stopped Laughing: The Crowd, Satire, and Censorship in Mexico City," in Gillingham, Lettieri, and Smith, *Journalism, Satire, and Censorship,* 122.

124. Assorted reports, 07/22/1948 to 08/30/1948, AGN/DGIPS-111/2-1/260/82.

125. Speaks to ambassador, 08/03/1948, NARG-812.00/8–548; PS-16 to Gobernación, 08/11/1948, memorandum, 08/13/1948, AGN/DGIPS-111/2-1/260/82; *Diario de Xalapa,* 08/15/1948.

126. Agent 35 to DFS, 08/26/1948, AGN/DFS-VP Amaro, Gral Joaquín; Gral Antonio Gómez Velasco to Rogelio de la Selva, 10/15/1949, AGN/MAV-710.1/391.

127. Speaks to ambassador, 08/03/1948, NARG-812.00/8–548; Memorandum, 08/23/1948, AGN/DGIPS-24/3; SEDENA, *Memoria de la Secretaría de la Defensa Nacional Septiembre 1948–Agosto 1949.*

128. Caccia Bernal and Alba Calderón to Gobernación, 08/30/1948, AGN/DGIPS-111/2-1/260/82.

129. Rapp to Bevin, 08/19/1948, FO371/67994.

130. Agent 35 to DFS, 08/26/1948, AGN/DFS-VP Amaro, Gral Joaquín; Memorandum, 08/31/1948, AGN/DGIPS-24/3.

131. Thurston to Secretary of State, 08/5, 20/1948, NARG-812.00/8–548, 8–2048; memorandum, 08/23/1948, AGN/DGIPS-24/3.

132. Smith, "The Year Mexico Stopped Laughing," 121.

133. Serrano seems to have had his own secret squad of men for some time, as suggested by his frequent requests for thousands of rifle cartridges from the Secretaría de la Defensa. Cuenca Díaz to Dir. de Aeronaútica Mil., 09/24/1948, Limón to Gral de Brig Jefe del Servicio de Parques, 10/24/1947, 12/26/1947, Limón to General Brig. IC Intendente General, 09/06/1948, SDN-XI/III/4-4802. I thank Sergio Aguayo for sharing Serrano's army files.

134. He was rumored to have responded by dismissing his bodyguard and moving his bed out onto the patio for better visibility. Speaks to ambassador, 08/03/1948, NARG-812.00/8-548; Turkel memorandum, 10/01/1948, NARG-812.00/10-848.

135. Massey to Secretary of State, 09/28/1948, NARG-812.00/9-2848.

136. "Leading Personalities in Mexico 1951" for 1951, *Foreign & Commonwealth Office Confidential Print for 1951,* 15; Memoranda, 02/08, 16/1949, AGN/DGIPS-24/3.

137. Arturo Torres Jr to DFS, 10/17/1949, AGN/DFS-VP Ríos Zertuche. Subsequent investigations revealed, among other things, that Pablo Díaz Dávila might have lied about being a Maderista, and that as a young officer Rafael Avila Camacho had been

jailed for failing his geometry classes. Ríos Thivol to Gobernación, 10/11/1949, 10/22/1949, AGN/DGIPS-84/2-1/131/655/IV.

138. *La Prensa*, 10/22/1948; *El Nacional*, 10/22/1948.

139. *La Prensa*, 11/10/1948.

140. Burrows to State Department, 07/19/1950, NARG-712.00/7-1950.

141. It may also have left them subject to military discipline once more and brought with it prohibition from political activity; this needs research. Among the recipients was Mexico's answer to James Bond, Manuel Ríos Thivol. Ríos Thivol to Gobernación, 11/04/1949, AGN/DGIPS-84/2-1/131/655/IV; Corzo Ramírez et al., *Cándido Aguilar*, 306–8.

142. PS-19 to Gobernación, 08/03/1945, AGN/DGIPS-132/2-1/302.4(0.11)/2; *Diario Oficial de la Federación*, 01/20/1949; *El Universal*, 06/19/1951; Niblo, *Mexico in the 1940s*, 169; *La Verdad*, 06/02/1949; *El Nacional*, 06/19/1951; *Diario de Xalapa*, 06/21/1952; SEDENA, *Memoria de la Secretaría de la Defensa Nacional Septiembre 1946–Agosto 1947;* Jeffrey Bortz and Marcos Aguila, "Earning a Living: A History of Real Wage Studies in Twentieth-Century Mexico," *Latin American Research Review* 41, no. 2 (2006): 127.

143. "Military Budgets of Assorted Countries," 08/02/1949, CIA-SC-1999-00005. Industria Militar stopped producing Mexico's only automatic small arm, the Mendoza 7mm, after a short run in the early 1950s. Frederick Gollaher to Chief of CIA Mission, Guatemala, 12/28/1953, CIA-SS-2003-00002.

144. Although the Gasca call to arms to the remnants of the Federación de Partidos del Pueblo Mexicano was put down in three days, it may have killed over one hundred people and did lead to the ley fuga for a couple of officers and about one thousand political jailings, including Demetrio Vallejo's wife, miners from Nueva Rosita, and peasant leaders from the Laguna. Col. José Inclan to Governor of Veracruz, 11/29/1949, AHEV-1693/542/0; Bartra, *Guerrero bronco*, 115–16; Servín, "Hacía el levantamiento armado," in Oikión Solano and García Ugarte, *Movimientos armados*, 307–15; Knight, "The Peculiarities of Mexican History," 101; Carlos Loret de Mola, *Manos sucias: crónicas verdaderas del poder* (Mexico City: Editorial Océano de México, 1996), 15–16, 181.

145. Massey to Secretary of State, 10/20/1948, NARG-812.00/10-2048.

146. Codoner to State Department, July 1945, NARG-812.00/Guerrero/7-3145; Third Secretary Massey to State Department, 09/28/1948, NARG-812.00/9–2848; PS-19 to Gobernación, 08/03/1945, AGN/DGIPS-132/2-1/302.4(0.11)/2.

147. Carlos R. Martínez Assad, *El henriquismo, una piedra en el camino* (Mexico City: Martín Casillas Editores, 1982), 19.

148. For an example of abject failure, see henriquismo in Guerrero. Assorted reports, January–June 1952, AGN/DFS-Guerrero-100-10-14-51H194L4, H203L4, H219L4, AGN/DFS-Guerrero-100-10-14-52H247L4, H264L4, H302L4, H313L4, H319L4, H2L5.

149. Martínez Assad, *El henriquismo,* 9–10. The concern of the government and the endurance of strong support for Henríquez Guzmán past July 1952 have been underestimated. See the reports of the six inspectors assigned to the case in AGN/DGIPS-104/2-1/131/1062.

150. Reports, 11/16/1952, AGN/DGIPS-104/2-1/131/1062.

151. Mónica Serrano, "The Armed Branch of the State: Civil–Military Relations in Mexico," *Journal of Latin American Studies* 27, no. 2 (May 1995): 439.

152. Rath, *Myths of Demilitarization,* 97.

153. Suggestively there was simultaneously a reorganization. *Foreign & Commonwealth Office Confidential Print for 1956,* 16.

154. In the early 1950s Mexico's military absorbed some 0.6 percent of GDP and consisted of 2.1 soldiers per 1,000 population. In the heyday of bureaucratic authoritarianism Argentina's military took 3.6 percent of GDP and numbered 5.6 soldiers per 1,000 population; Chile spent 3.6 percent of GDP and had 10.5 soldiers per 1,000 population. INEGI, *Estadísticas históricas* CD-ROM; Alfred C. Stepan, *Rethinking Military Politics: Changing Patterns in Brazil* (Princeton: Princeton University Press, 2015), 73–74.

155. See, for example, Sullivan to Foreign Office, 04/18/1955, FO371-AM1015/14 for the 1955 very public meeting between Ruiz Cortines and Cárdenas; for meetings of Cárdenas, Abelardo, and Avila Camacho during the formation of the henriquista campaign, see Laidlaw, US Embassy, to State, 04/18/1950, NARG-712.00/4-1850; the *Buró de Investigación Política* for "the mere coincidence" of the posting of Cárdenas and Avila Camacho's brothers to command the two most powerful zones flanking Mexico City in 1952, cited in Thomas Rath, "Camouflaging the State: Soldiers, Politics and the Myth of Demilitarization," in Gillingham and Smith, *Dictablanda,* 96.

156. "Annual Report on Mexico, 1946," FO371/60940/AN397.

157. Walter Washington to Secretary of State, 05/19/1948, NARG-812.00/5–1948; Massey to Secretary of State, 05/11/1949, NARG-812.00/5–1149.

158. Rapp to Bevin, 08/12/1948, FO486/2; *Foreign & Commonwealth Office Confidential Print for 1948,* 45.

159. Monthly political report, 04/18/1949, FO371/74077/AN1223.

160. JCB to Gobernación, 04/03/1950, memorandum, 05/23/1950, assorted press, all AGN/DGIPS-803/1.

161. Burrows to State Department, 06/06/1950, NARG-712.00/6–650; Alemán, *Remembranzas,* 388.

162. *El Universal,* 09/08/1952.

163. Lázaro Cárdenas, *Obras,* 4 vols. (Mexico City: UNAM, 1973), 2:417, 440–41.

164. JNM to Gobernación, 12/09/1950, AGN/DGIPS-102/JNM.

165. Burrows to State Department, 04/18/1950, NARG-712.00/4-1850.

166. Santos, *Memorias,* 862–64; Wilkie and Wilkie, *México visto en el siglo XX,* 369.

167. Alemán, *Remembranzas,* 388–89; "El presidente—extensión periodo," AGN/MAV-544.1/44.

168. JNM to Gobernación, 12/09/1950, AGN/DGIPS-102/JNM; Rogelio Hernández Rodríguez review of Ryan M. Alexander, *Sons of the Mexican Revolution: Miguel Alemán and His Generation, Historia Mexicana* 68, no. 2 (2018): 855.

169. Memorandum, Dir. DFS Castillo Venegas, 08/19/1955, AGN/DFS-VP Alemán Velasco, Miguel, tomo 1 11. The two met again with Abelardo Rodríguez in 1957 to discuss the politics of Baja California with its governor, PS-30 to Gobernación, 01/24/1957, AGN/DGIPS-1989A-103.

170. Serrano, "The Armed Branch of the State," 448.

171. Villalpando, "Política y ejército, 1945–1994," 321.

172. Servín, *La oposición política,* 56.

173. Unlike later, when drugs profits moved up several orders of magnitude. Navarro, *Political Intelligence,* 10, 155–56.

174. Camp, *Generals in the Palacio,* cited in Navarro, *Political Intelligence,* 107.

175. Frank Brandenburg, *The Making of Modern Mexico* (Englewood Cliffs, NJ: Prentice Hall, 1964), 32, 151. For the estimate of senatorial cuota de poder, lists of senators from the first legislatures of Ruiz Cortines and López Mateos were examined for military records, revealing twelve officers in the first and eleven in the second case. Senators, unlike deputies, were of some consequence in federal politics, serving as checks and balances to their state's administration. Hernández Rodríguez, *El centro dividido,* 64–65.

176. American consul Mérida to embassy, 08/29/1966, NARG-63-66 microfilm roll 1 237.

177. Rath, *Myths of Demilitarization,* 124.

178. Diane E. Davis, "Policing and Regime Transition: From Postauthoritarianism to Populism to Neoliberalism," in Pansters, *Violence, Coercion, and State-Making,* 73.

179. Cuartel General to Comdte 119 Regiment, 04/05/1951, SDN-1-356/X-2325.

180. López to Daniels, 03/05/1934, NARG-812.114 narcotics/370 roll 34.

181. Región Militar commands were not the only institutional means of pacifying politically ambitious young generals. In a deeply Tocquevillian transaction, Luis Alamillo Flores, the leader of one of those juntas, was removed from the Military College and given control of a 70-million-peso budget as head of the National Diesel Motor Factory. Memos, 09/27/1948, 10/25/1948, AGN/DGIPS-24/3; *La Prensa,* 10/07, 22/1948.

182. The interpretation that postings to regiones militares constituted an incentive to acquiescence in civilian rule is reinforced by some subsequent appointments. Miguel Z. Martínez, for example, was one of the powerful generals at the heart of the 1948 juntas; in 1952 he was given command of the 10th Región Militar. *La Prensa,* 09/06/1948; *El Universal,* 01/30/1952. For narcotrafficking see Nicole Mottier, "Drug Gangs and Politics in Ciudad Juárez: 1928–1936," *Mexican Studies/Estudios Mexicanos*

25, no. 1 (2009), 26–41; Pansters and Smith, "Writing Twentieth Century Mexico's Drug Histories."

183. Telegram, RPTE-XA 1 to "Mi General," 10/05/1956, SDN-P/111/1-109; telegram, anonymous to "Mi Mayor," 02/09/1960, SDN-P/111/1-109.

184. IPS report of P.L.L., 03/24/1973, AGN/DFS-VP Bonifacio Salinas León; assorted documents, SDN-A/111/1-58/11.

185. Alongside, among others, two governors and assorted members of the Terrazas family. Elizabeth Henson, "Madera 1965: Primeros Vientos," in Herrera Calderón and Cedillo, *Challenging Authoritarianism,* 25.

186. Rath, *Myths of Demilitarization,* 86.

187. Ireta stayed put from 1954 to 1969, López 1953 to 1966, Díaz Dávila 1936 to 1953. Rath, *Myths of Demilitarization,* 103, 93.

188. SEDENA, *Memoria de la Secretaría de la Defensa Nacional Septiembre 1949–Agosto 1950,* 21.

189. Assorted telegrams, Ometepec, to Alemán, August to September 1950, AGN/MAV-840/5503; sworn statement, Flores, Ixcateopan, 12/24/1969, AMI-post-1952/II.

190. Lieuwen, *Mexican Militarism,* 119.

191. General Limón to Dir. General Personal, 05/24/1950, SDN-1-356/X/2264; Jefe del EMP Santiago Piña Soria to SEDENA, 06/22/1950, SDN-1-356/X/2422; Limón to Dir. Justicia y Pensiones, 06/24/1950, SDN-1-356/X/2173.

192. General Anaya to Dir. General Personal, 08/07/1950, SDN-1-356/X/2288.

193. Coronel Heliodoro E. Cabrera Jiménez to Dir. General de Personal, 01/17/1951, SDN-1-356/X/2304.

194. Corzo Ramírez et al., *Cándido Aguilar,* 328.

195. Departamento del retiro y pensiones to departamento de hojas y servicio, 05/09/1959, SDN-1-356/XII.

196. Dir. General de justicia to Jefe del departamento de Archivos, 05/09/1959, SDN-1-356/XII/2798; Dir. general de personal to comandante de la 1a zona militar, 08/07/1959, SDN-1-356/XII/2804; Mange to SEDENA, 12/29/1958, SDN-1-356/XII/2856; Pérez to SEDENA, 01/07/1959, SDN-1-356/XII.

197. Literally, "they took his breast away." Pérez to SEDENA, 01/07/1959, SDN-1-356/XII.

198. Sullivan to Eden, 01/12/1955, FO371/AM-1015/2, in *Foreign & Commonwealth Office Confidential Print for 1955,* 5; Rath, *Myths of Demilitarization,* 105; Davis, "Policing and Regime Transition," 80; Consul General Richard Johnson, Monterrey, to State Department, 09/08/1963, NARG 1963–66 reel 3 121.

199. General Alejandro Mange Toyos, *hoja de servicios,* SDN-1-356/XI.

200. The FBI believed Alemán to have left some forty-five bodies behind him in his political ascent; the British ambassador wondered whether his predecessor in the governorship had been among them, as one of the Armentas claimed. Alejandro Quintana, *Maximino Avila Camacho and the One-Party State: The Taming of Caudillismo, and*

Caciquismo in Post-Revolutionary Mexico (Lanham, MD: Lexington Books, 2010), 120; Rapp to Bevin, 03/17/1948, *Foreign & Commonwealth Office Confidential Print for 1948*, 15.

201. López vda. de Pampín to Alemán, 1950, AGN/MAV-001/4232.

202. Pérez to SEDENA, 01/07/1959, SDN-1-356/XII.

203. Jefe del EMP Santiago Piña Soria to SEDENA, 06/22/1950, SDN-1–356/X/2422.

204. Ferrocarriles Nacionales de México to SEDENA, 03/31/1959, SDN-1-356/XII.

205. Benítez Manaut, "Avances y límites de las relaciones civiles–militares," 414.

206. See, for example, the 1949 report on Pablo Díaz Dávila in Ríos Thivol to Gobernación, 10/11/1949, AGN/DGIPS-84/2-1/131/655/IV.

207. Díez, "Civil–Military Relations," 274.

208. And saw that power reinvigorated in the 1990s, Ferreyra and Segura propose, arguing that "while the military has contributed to a consolidation of democratic transformations at the national level, it has acted against it in the local sphere." Ferreyra and Segura, "Examining the Military in the Local Sphere: Colombia and Mexico," in *Latin American Perspectives* 27, no. 2 (March 2000): 19, 32–33.

Conclusion

1. Among many other places. Santos, *Memorias*, 720, 723.

2. Over six hundred thousand people migrated to the city between 1940 and 1950. "Migración neta intercensal por sexo 1930–1970," INEGI *Estados Históricos de México*, http://torrelatinoamericana.com.mx/historia/.

3. Although the decision to go to war was preceded by widespread reluctance, from Cárdenas to the PAN, and some lurid missteps, including, US intelligence believed, assorted cabinet members sleeping with the same German spy, Hilda Kruger. Miguel Alemán paid her rent. Jones, *The War Has Brought Peace*, 62–81; Juan Alberto Cedillo, *Los Nazis en México* (Mexico City: Debolsillo, 2017), 14–15, 35–39.

4. Bateman to Bevin, 01/21/1947, FO371/60940.

5. Daniel Cosío Villegas, "La Crísis de México," *Cuadernos Americanos* 6, no. 32 (1947): 15. The "family" tried to make sure he didn't either, threatening to publish rumors concerning his love life if he didn't desist. Smith, "The Year Mexico Stopped Laughing," 110.

6. In 1946; the comparison between court and registro civil counts comes from 1950, when courts were more effective and homicides probably decreasing. Pablo Piccato, "Estadísticas del crimen en México: Series históricas, 1901–2001," http://www.columbia.edu/estadisticascrimen/EstadisticasSigloXX.htm; "Defunciones por homicidio según entidades federativas," AQC-14.

7. De la Peña, *Guerrero económico*, 1:417–18.

8. PS-12 to Gobernación, 02/16/1945, AGN/DGIPS-788/2-1/45/374.

9. In September 1943 one flying column was attacked near Copala; in September 1944 another near San Luis Loma; in both cases General Ramos held local authorities and agraristas responsible. Report, oficial mayor 27a zona militar to presidency, 09/09/1943, AGN/MAC-542.1/822; letter, Ramos to president, 09/28/1944, AGN/MAC-542.1/579.

10. Leyva Mancilla married a Neri, a family whose power stretched back well into the nineteenth century, and continued as the elder statesman of Guerrero politics for decades after the end of his governorship.

11. Even if the court system worked better, with only a 56 percent rate of impunity for homicides. Piccato, "Estadísticas del crimen en México: Series históricas, 1901–2001."

12. More than half the taxes on rural properties went unpaid in 1945. Informes de tesorería, AHEV-1229/024/0; De la Peña, *Veracruz Económico,* 2:503, 507; Ruiz Cortines report 1945, BD-XIII/7336.

13. On the link between "secondary," imported land reform and violence, see Knight, "The End of the Mexican Revolution?" 57.

14. The Southeast stretched here to encompass Yucatán and Quintana Roo, likewise comparatively unmurderous. "Defunciones por homicidio según entidades federativas," AQC-14.

15. Frans J. Schryer, *The Rancheros of Pisaflores: The History of a Peasant Bourgeoisie in Twentieth-Century Mexico* (Toronto: University of Toronto Press, 1980), 70, 96–100; Friedrich, *The Princes of Naranja,* 23.

16. Smith, *Pistoleros and Popular Movements,* 289–302.

17. Padilla, *Rural Resistance,* 91, 141–47.

18. Kloppe-Santamaria, "Lynching and the Politics of State Formation," 7; Rath, "Camouflaging the State," 99.

19. Claudia Agostoni, *Médicos, Campañas y Vacunas: La viruela y la cultura de su prevención en México, 1870–1952* (Mexico City: UNAM/Instituto Mora, 2016), 172.

20. Aboites Aguilar, "The Illusion of National Power," 228.

21. See above, chapter seven.

22. Wasserman, *Persistent Oligarchs,* 10.

23. In Veracruz murders declined by 9 percent in the first half of the 1950s; in Guerrero they increased by 10 percent. Piccato, "Estadísticas del crimen en México: Series históricas, 1901–2001"; Quiroz Cuarón, "Defunciones por homicidio según entidades federativas," ORC libros de defunciones, 1950–52.

24. Proverbially living and dying by the sword, Joaquín Salmerón of Tlacoachistlahuaca, accused of numerous murders of agrarista leaders, including a mayor, a police commander, and a tax collector, was himself shot dead. In an example of the tangled loyalties of the region, his family had come to prominence as Zapatistas. His brother Marino and his father, Vicente, both ended up operating from exile. Vázquez Añorve,

El ayer de mi costa, 394; letter, Vicente O. Salmerón to President, 02/21/1947, AGN/MAV-541/93.

25. Letter, Pérez Olivares to Maximino Viveros, 06/08/1955, in Pérez Olivares, *Memorias,* Anexo VI doc 13.

26. Piccato, *A History of Infamy,* 180–82; Torres to de la Selva, 09/24, 25/1952, AGN/MAV-742/39535.

27. Gómez Galeana to Alemán, 04/25/1947, AGN/DGIPS-12/2/389(9)38; letter, José Bernardo Domínguez and three hundred others to Cárdenas, 07/26/1935, AGN/DGG 2.012.8(9)/43; letter, Nicolas Parra et al. to Cárdenas, 02/16/1940, AGN/LCR 555.1/149; Vázquez Añorve, *El ayer de mi costa,* 153; Encarnación Ursúa, *Los copreros,* 44–48.

28. Aviña, *Specters of Revolution,* 49.

29. Alexander Aviña, "Seizing Hold of Memories in Moments of Danger: Guerrillas and Revolution in Guerrero, Mexico," in Herrera Calderón and Cedillo, *Challenging Authoritarianism,* 50.

30. Bernal, *El complot mongol,* 9.

31. Moreno to Carvajal, 08/13/1949, AHEV-1696/549/0 1; Dormady, *Primitive Revolution,* 88.

32. Whetten, *Rural Mexico,* 501–9.

33. Fallaw, *Religion and State Formation,* 101, 111–12; Jocelyn Olcott, *Revolutionary Women in Post-revolutionary Mexico* (Durham: Duke University Press, 2005).

34. Alonso, *El rito electoral,* 28.

35. In the 1961 local elections in Veracruz's 202 municipios there were four women candidates for mayor; in 1964, none at all. Fowler-Salamini, *Working Women,* 175, 194, 252, 258; *El Informador,* 07/04/1955; "Presidentes municipales Veracruz 1961" AGN/DGIPS-1980A; "Relación de candidatos a Presidente Municipales del PRI en los 202 municipios del estado de Veracruz," AGN/DGIPS-1997A/2-1/010(18)"64"/52.

36. María Teresa Fernández Aceves, "Advocate or Cacica? Guadalupe Urzúa Flores: Modernizer and Peasant Political Leader in Jalisco," in Gillingham and Smith, *Dictablanda,* 247–49.

37. *El Universal,* 11/01/1952, 01/09/1953; vecinos of Citlaltepec to President, 12/10/1952, AGN/DGG 2.311 M(26)-79/30.

38. President PRM Igualapa Eduardo González to Chilpancingo, 12/06/1944, AGN/DGG-2.311 M(9)12.

39. From 1959. Almond and Verba, *The Civic Culture,* 39.

40. Joseph, Rubenstein, and Zolov, "Assembling the Fragments," 11–12.

41. On the "cognitive boundaries" of the revolution as central to regime longevity, see Randal Sheppard, *A Persistent Revolution: History, Nationalism, and Politics in Mexico since 1968* (Albuquerque: University of New Mexico Press, 2016), 11, 134, 256.

42. Memorandum, 04/19/1956, AGN/DGIPS-1993/1958–1962B.

43. *Ovaciones,* 01/26/1953.

44. Adán Aguirre Benítez, "L'économie paysanne, le capitalisme et les mouvements sociaux dans l'état de Guerrero (Mexique): 1960–1985" (Ph.D. diss., Sorbonne, 1988), 598.

45. Libros de defunciones 1930, 1940, 1946–52, IRC, Libro de defuncion 1949–52, ORC.

46. Agostoni, *Médicos, Campañas y Vacunas,* 201, 205.

47. From 34.9 to 20.7 per 100,000.

48. Although teachers were not necessarily technocrats, Weberians, or reliable priista centrists. Gillingham, "Ambiguous Missionaries"; Padilla, "Rural Education."

49. Emigdio Martínez Adame. The other senator, Alfonso G. Alarcón, was a doctor and academic whose works included *Bajo el régimen vagal: el vagotonismo fisiológico del lactante, estudio clínico acerca de la fisiopatología de la primera edad.* FFM to Gobernación, 03/16/1950, DGIPS-129/26; Camp, *Mexican Political Biographies,* 594; Roderic Ai Camp, *Intellectuals and the State in Modern Mexico* (Austin: University of Texas Press, 2014), 187.

50. José Fernández Clavería.

51. Reports on presidentes municipales and state congress for 1961, AGN/DGIPS-1450A/6; Hernández Rodríguez, *El centro dividido,* 41–42.

52. Municipal Elections in Veracruz 1961, AGN/DGIPS-1980A.

53. Camp, *Mexican Political Biographies,* 166.

54. From thirty-eight in 1936–45 to sixteen between 1946 and 1955. Friedrich, *The Princes of Naranja,* 272–74; Piccato, http://www.columbia.edu/estadisticascrimen/EstadisticasSigloXX.htm.

55. "Leading personalities in Mexico, 1953," Hadow to Churchill, 01/01/1953, FO-371-AM1012/1, *Confidential Print of the Foreign Office for 1953,* 8.

56. Smith, *Pistoleros and Popular Movements,* 229.

57. Hernández Rodríguez, *El centro dividido,* 31.

58. Report on Senguio jacquerie, 09/01/1947, AGN/DGIPS-84/MRT; Paxman, *Jenkins of Mexico,* chap. 9.

59. Smith, "Who Governed?" 241, 253; Hernández Rodríguez, *El centro dividido,* 48–49, 71.

60. Fernández Aceves, "Advocate or Cacica?" 393–95.

61. Riots that originated in competitive municipal elections and increased bus fares in Villahermosa. Moncada, *¡Cayeron!,* 241.

62. Ibid., 243–45.

63. Rath, *Myths of Demilitarization,* 207.

64. British ambassador to Slater, Foreign Office, 01/25/1963, FO371/AM1015/13.

65. The government broke the 1965 doctors' strike by firing five hundred civilians and replacing them with army medics. Gabriela Soto Laveaga, "Shadowing the Professional Class: Reporting Fictions in Doctors' Strikes," *Journal of Iberian and Latin American Research* 19, no. 1 (2013): 31; Pensado, *Rebel Mexico;* Hernández Rodríguez, *La*

formación del político mexicano, 95–96; Padilla, *Rural Resistance*, 207–9; Crockett, Tijuana, to State, 09/24/1962, NARG-712.00/9-2462.

66. Subsecretario Dirrección General del Servicio Diplomático to Gobernación, 10/31/1957, AGN/DGIPS-1993/1958–1962B.

67. For oligarchy, see Hughes, Juárez to State, 04/16/1963, NARG-63-66 microfilm roll 3 192–5; on ixtleros, EAC and JNM to Gobernación, 02/09/1950, AGN/DGIPS-112/2-1/260/106; Warner, Tampico, to State, 02/27/1963, NARG-63-66 microfilm roll 3, 8.

68. Rath, *Myths of Demilitarization*, 97, 100–106.

69. Rodríguez Munguía, "The Invisible Tyranny," 183, 190–91; "Memorandum relativo al problema político del Estado de Guerrero," undated (probably early 1961) AGN/DGIPS.1447A.

70. Arturo Valenzuela and J. Samuel Valenzuela, "Party Oppositions under the Chilean Authoritarian Regime," in J. Samuel Valenzuela and Arturo Valenzuela, eds., *Military Rule in Chile: Dictatorship and Oppositions* (Baltimore: Johns Hopkins University Press, 1986), 209–10; James P. Brennan, *Argentina's Missing Bones: Revisiting the History of the Dirty War* (Oakland: University of California Press, 2018), 91–95.

71. To Arnaldo Córdova, Cárdenas was "the most inspired prophet . . . of the capitalist counter-insurgency" that created a "Mexican Leviathan." Arnaldo Córdova, *La política de masas del Cardenismo* (Mexico City: Ediciones Era, 1989). The main works of postrevisionism on the theme are Bantjes, *As If Jesus Walked on Earth;* Hernández Rodríguez, *El centro dividido;* Fallaw, *Cárdenas Compromised;* Alan Knight, "Cardenismo: Juggernaut or Jalopy?" *Journal of Latin American Studies* 26, no. 1 (1994); Rubin, *Decentering the Regime;* and Smith, *Pistoleros and Popular Movements.*

72. And at least once while in office, against the jefe máximo Plutarco Elías Calles. There may be more of which we are less aware: Cárdenas's 1955 speech backing Ruiz Cortines as midterm elections neared and some generals grumbled, an "impromptu" delivery—the ironic punctuation is that of the reporting ambassador—was probably indicative of another. These vetoes were considerably more salient than his better-known involvement in the Movimiento de Liberación Nacional and the Central Campesina Independiente. *Foreign & Commonwealth Office Confidential Print for 1956*, 4, 6.

73. Krauze, *La Presidencia Imperial*, 183.

74. "Ils adoraient l'égalité jusque dans la servitude." Alexis de Tocqueville, *L'ancien régime et la révolution* (Paris: Gallimard, 1991 [1967]), 319. González Casanova thought Mexicans had similar but frustrated aims: "The poorer strata have democratic tendencies in the economic sphere and authoritarian tendencies in the political sphere." González Casanova, *Democracy in Mexico*, 182, 215–60, 303–24.

Bibliography

Archives

Archivo Alfonso Quiroz Cuarón, Centro Cultural Isidro Fabela (AQ)
Archivo General Agraria (AGA)
Archivo General de la Nación, Fondo Bienes Nacionalizados (AGN/BN)
Archivo General de la Nación, Fondo Dirección Federal de Seguridad (AGN/DFS)
Archivo General de la Nación, Fondo Dirección General de Gobierno (AGN/DGG)
Archivo General de la Nación, Fondo Dirección General de Investigaciones Políticas y Sociales (AGN/DGIPS)
Archivo General de la Nación, Fondo Presidente Adolfo Ruiz Cortines (AGN/ARC)
Archivo General de la Nación, Fondo Presidente Lázaro Cárdenas del Rio (AGN/LCR)
Archivo General de la Nación, Fondo Presidente Manuel Avila Camacho (AGN/MAC)
Archivo General de la Nación, Fondo Presidente Miguel Alemán Valdés (AGN/MAV)
Archivo Histórico del Estado de Guerrero, Chilpancingo (AHEG)
Archivo Histórico del Estado de Veracruz, Xalapa (AHEV)
Archivo Municipal de Ixcateopan, Guerrero (AMI)
Archivo Municipal de San Andrés Tuxtla, Veracruz (SATAM)
Archivo Paucic, Chilpancingo (AP)
Carmen Blázquez Domínguez, *Estado de Veracruz: informes de sus gobernadores, 1826–1986* (20 volumes, Xalapa, 1986) (BD)
Central Intelligence Agency (CIA)
Instituto Nacional de Antropología e Historia, Archivo Sónoro (INAH/AS/PHO)
Ixcateopan Registro Civil (IRC)
The National Archives, London, Papers of the Board of Trade (BT)
The National Archives, London, Papers of the Foreign Office (FO)
The United States National Archives Record Group (NARG)
Ometepec Registro Civil (ORC)
Private Papers of Baltasar Leyva Ventura, Chilpancingo (PPBLV)

Private Papers of Manuel Turrent, San Andrés Tuxtla (PPMT)
Secretaría de Educación Pública, Dirección General de Educación Primaria (SEP/DGEP)
Secretaría de la Defensa Nacional, Hojas de Servicio (SDN)

Periodicals

Acapulco Gráfico
El Adelante, semanario de información general (San Andrés Tuxtla)
Así Somos . . . (Chilpancingo)
Diario de Guerrero (Chilpancingo)
Diario del Hogar
Diario de Xalapa
Diario Oficial de la Federación
El Dictamen (Veracruz)
Excélsior
Foreign Affairs
Gaceta Oficial del Estado de Veracruz
El Informador (Guadalajara)
El Nacional
Novedades
Periódico Oficial del Gobierno del Estado de Guerrero
El Popular
La Prensa
El Sol de Acapulco
El Suriano (Iguala)
Todo (Mexico City)
La Tribuna de Túxpam
Trópico, semanario independiente de información (Acapulco)
Últimas Noticias de Excélsior
El Universal
La Verdad, agil, audaz, dinámico, un diario al servicio del estado de Guerrero (Acapulco)
La Verdad de Minatitlán

Books and Articles

Luis Aboites Aguilar. *Excepciones y privilegios: Modernización tributaria y centralización en México, 1922–1972*. Mexico City: Colegio de México, 2003.

———. "The Illusion of National Power: Water Infrastructure in Mexican Cities, 1930–1990." In Christopher R. Boyer, ed., *A Land Between Waters: Environmental Histories of Modern Mexico*. Tucson: University of Arizona Press, 2012.

Claudia Agostoni. *Médicos, Campañas y Vacunas: La viruela y la cultura de su prevención en México, 1870–1952*. Mexico City: UNAM/Instituto Mora, 2016.

Sergio Aguayo Quezada. *El 68: Los estudiantes, el presidente y la CIA*. Mexico City: Ideas y Palabras, 2018.

———. *La Charola: una historia de los servicios de inteligencia en México*. Mexico City: Grijalbo, 2001.

Hector Aguilar Camín. "Nociones presidenciales de cultura nacional de Alvaro Obregón a Gustavo Díaz Ordaz, 1920–1968." In José Emilio Pacheco, ed., *En torno a la cultura nacional*. Mexico City: Secretaría de Educación Pública, 1982.

Octavio Aguilar de la Parra. *Mi tío, el cacique . . . ensayo político anecdótico*. Mexico City: Corporación Editorial, 1985.

Martín Gerardo Aguilar Sánchez. *Los conflictos ferrocarrileros en Veracruz: 1910–1927*. Mexico City: Colofón Ediciones Académicas Sociología, 2017.

Gonzalo Aguirre Beltrán. *Cuijla: esbozo etnográfico de un pueblo negro*. Mexico City: Universidad Veracruzana; Instituto Nacional Indigenista; Gobierno del Estado de Veracruz; Fondo de Cultura Económica, 1995 [1958].

Adán Aguirre Benítez. "L'economie paysanne, le capitalisme et les mouvements sociaux dans l'état de Guerrero (Mexique): 1960–1985." D.Phil. thesis, Sorbonne, 1984.

Fernando Saúl Alanís Enciso. *They Should Stay There: The Story of Mexican Migration and Repatriation during the Great Depression*. Translated by Russ Davidson. Foreword by Mark Overmyer-Velázquez. Chapel Hill: University of North Carolina Press, 2017.

Roberto Alegre. *Railroad Radicals: Gender, Class, and Memory in Cold War Mexico*. Lincoln: University of Nebraska Press, 2013.

Miguel Alemán Valdés, *Miguel Alemán contesta. . . .* Austin: University of Texas Press, 1975.

———. *Remembranzas y testimonios*. Mexico City: Grijalbo, 1987.

Alberto Alesina, Salvatore Piccolo, and Paolo Pinotti. "Organized Crime, Violence, and Politics." Working paper, Department of Economics, Harvard University, 2016, A8. http://nrs.harvard.edu/urn-3:HUL.InstRepos:27760119.

Ryan M. Alexander. "Alemán before Alemán." In Andrew Paxman, *Los Gobernadores: Caciques del pasado y del presente*. Mexico City: Grijalbo, 2018.

Ryan M. Alexander. *Sons of the Mexican Revolution: Miguel Alemán and His Generation*. Albuquerque: University of New Mexico Press, 2016.

Gabriel A. Almond. "The Intellectual History of the Civic Culture Concept." In Almond and Verba, *The Civic Culture Revisited*.

Gabriel A. Almond and Sidney Verba. *The Civic Culture: Political Attitude and Democracy in Five Nations*. Newbury Park, CA: Sage Publications, 1989.

———. *The Civic Culture Revisited*. Boston: Little, Brown, 1980.

Ryan M. Alexander. *Sons of the Mexican Revolution: Miguel Alemán and His Generation*. Albuquerque: University of New Mexico Press, 2016.

Jorge Alonso. *El rito electoral en Jalisco, 1940–1992*. Guadalajara: CIESAS, 1993.

V. de Paúl Andrade. "Un viaje a Chilapa leído en la sesión del 22 de abril de 1911." In Carlos Illades, ed., *Guerrero: una historia compartida*. Mexico City: Instituto de Investigaciones Dr. José María Luis Mora, 1989.

Catherine Andrews, ed. *La tradición constitucional en México (1808–1940)*. Mexico City: Librería CIDE, 2018.

Dudley Ankerson. *Agrarian Warlord: Saturnino Cedillo and the Mexican Revolution in San Luis Potosí*. DeKalb: Northern Illinois University Press, 1984.

Mario Appelius. *El Aguila de Chapultepec*. Barcelona: Maucci, 1931.

Francisco Arce. *Memoria presentada al X Congreso Constitucional del Estado*. Chilpancingo: Gobierno del estado de Guerrero, 1888.

Carlos R. Martínez Assad. *El henriquismo, una piedra en el camino*. Mexico City: Martín Casillas Editores, 1982.

Alexander Aviña. "Seizing Hold of Memories in Moments of Danger: Guerrillas and Revolution in Guerrero, Mexico." In Fernando Herrera Calderón and Adela Cedillo, eds., *Challenging Authoritarianism in Mexico: Revolutionary Struggles and the Dirty War, 1964–1982*, 40–59. New York: Routledge, 2012.

———. *Specters of Revolution: Peasant Guerrillas in the Mexican Cold War Countryside*. Oxford: University of Oxford Press, 2014.

David C. Bailey. "Revisionism and the Recent Historiography of the Mexican Revolution." *Hispanic American Historical Review* 58, no. 1 (February 1978).

John J. Bailey. *Governing Mexico: The Statecraft of Crisis Management*. Hampshire: Macmillan, 1988.

Antonio Balderas Cañas. "El sector privado." In Max Arturo López Hernández et al., eds., *La formación del poder en el estado de Guerrero*, 83–97. Chilpancingo: Universidad Autónoma de Guerrero, 1997.

Adrian Bantjes. *As If Jesus Walked on Earth: Cardenismo, Sonora, and the Mexican Revolution*. Wilmington, DE: Scholarly Resources, 1998.

Luis Barrón. "La construcción del cargo público." Paper presented at symposium. Mexico City: CIDE/University of Warwick/AHRC Conference, November 2017.

Armando Bartra, ed., *Crónicas del Sur: utopías campesinas en Guerrero*. Mexico City: Ediciones Era, 2000.

———. *Guerrero bronco: campesinos, ciudadanos y guerrilleros en la Costa Grande*. Mexico City: Ediciones Era, 2000.

Marc Becker. *The FBI in Latin America: The Ecuador Files*. Durham: Duke University Press, 2017.

Caroline C. Beer. *Electoral Competition and Institutional Change in Mexico*. South Bend: University of Notre Dame Press, 2003.

Mónica Beltrán Gaos. *La Comisión Nacional de los Derechos Humanos de México*. Valencia: Editorial de la UPV, 2005.

Raúl Benítez Manaut. "México: Avances y límites de las relaciones civiles–militares ante la democratización: Los retos de 2013." In Javier Garciadiego, coord., *El Ejército Mexicano 100 años de historia*. Mexico City: El Colegio de México, 2014.

Thomas Benjamin. *La Revolución: Mexico's Great Revolution as Memory, Myth, and History*. Austin: University of Texas Press, 2000.

———. "Laboratories of the New State, 1920–1929: Regional Social Reform and Experiments in Mass Politics." In Thomas Benjamin and Mark Wasserman, eds., *Provinces of the Revolution: Essays on Regional Mexican History, 1910–1929*. Albuquerque: University of New Mexico Press, 1990.

Roger J. Bergeret Muñoz et al. "Evolución y mutación del modelo turístico de Guerrero: Caso Acapulco 1945–2000." In Tomás Bustamante Alvarez and Sergio Sarmiento Silva, eds., *El Sur en movimiento: la reinvención de Guerrero del siglo XXI*. Mexico City: Consejo de Ciencia y Tecnología del Estado de Guerrero, 2001.

José López Bermúdez. *Canto a Cuauhtémoc*. Tuxtla Gutierrez, Chiapas: Edición del gobierno del estado de Chiapas, 1951.

Rafael Bernal. *El complot mongol*. Mexico City: Grupo Planeta, 2013.

Michael Bess. *Routes of Compromise: Building Roads and Shaping the Nation in Mexico, 1917–1952*. Lincoln: University of Nebraska Press, 2017.

Leslie Bethell, ed. *The Cambridge History of Latin America*, 10 vols. Cambridge: Cambridge University Press, 1994.

———. *Mexico since Independence*. Cambridge: Cambridge University Press, 1991.

——— and Ian Roxborough. "Latin America between the Second World War and the Cold War: Some Reflections on the 1945–1948 Conjuncture." *Journal of Latin American Studies* 20, no. 1 (1988): 167–89.

Ashley Black. "The Politics of Asylum: Caribbean Revolutionaries, Humanitarianism, and Foreign Policy in Mexico, 1944–1961." Ph.D. diss., Stony Brook University, 2018.

Roberto Blancarte. "Intransigence, Anticommunism, and Reconciliation: Church/State Relations in Transition." In Gillingham and Smith, *Dictablanda*.

Roberto Blanco Moheno. *Memorias de un reportero*. Mexico City: Libro Mex, 1965.

Eduardo Blanquel. "Esquema de una Periodización de la Historia Política del México Contemporáneo." In Wilkie et al., *Contemporary Mexico*.

Aaron Bobrow-Strain. *Intimate Enemies: Landowners, Power, and Violence in Chiapas*. Durham: Duke University Press, 2007.

Christopher Boehm. *Blood Revenge: The Enactment and Management of Conflict in Montenegro and Other Tribal Societies*. Philadelphia: University of Pennsylvania Press, 1987.

John A. Booth and Mitchell A. Seligson. "The Political Culture of Authoritarianism in Mexico: A Reexamination." *Latin American Research Review* 19, no. 1 (1984): 106–204.

Jeffrey Bortz and Marcos Aguila. "Earning a Living: A History of Real Wage Studies in Twentieth-Century Mexico." *Latin American Research Review* 41, no. 2 (2006).

Jeffrey L. Bortz and Stephen H. Haber, eds. *The Mexican Economy, 1870–1930: Essays on the Economic History of Institutions, Revolution and Growth*. Stanford: Stanford University Press, 2002.

Pierre Bourdieu. *Outline of a Theory of Practice*. Cambridge: Cambridge University Press, 1977.

Marguerite P. Boyce. *Yo oí a los burros rebuznar: 30 años en el campo misionero*. Mexico City: CUPSA, 1996.

Christopher R. Boyer, ed. *A Land between Waters: Environmental Histories of Modern Mexico*. Tucson: University of Arizona Press, 2012.

———. "Community, Crony Capitalism, and Fortress Conservation." In Gillingham and Smith, *Dictablanda*.

Frank Brandenburg. *The Making of Modern Mexico*. Englewood Cliffs, NJ: Prentice Hall, 1964.

James P. Brennan. *Argentina's Missing Bones: Revisiting the History of the Dirty War*. Oakland: University of California Press, 2018.

Ellen Brennan-Galvin. "Crime and Violence in an Urbanizing World." *Journal of International Affairs* 56, no. 1 (Fall 2002): 123–45.

John Brewer, Bill Lockhart, and Paula Rodgers. "Crime in Ireland since the Second World War." *Journal of the Statistical and Social Inquiry Society of Ireland* 27, no. 3 (1996).

Jonathan C. Brown and Alan Knight, eds. *The Mexican Petroleum Industry in the Twentieth Century*. Austin: University of Texas Press, 1992.

Samuel Brunk. "Remembering Emiliano Zapata: Three Moments in the Posthumous Career of the Martyr of Chinameca." *Hispanic American Historical Review* 78, no. 3 (August 1998).

Jürgen Buchenau. *The Last Caudillo: Alvaro Obregón and the Mexican Revolution*. Somerset: Wiley-Blackwell, 2011.

———. "The Arm and Body of a Revolution: Remembering Mexico's Last Caudillo, Alvaro Obregón." In Lyman L. Johnson, ed., *Death, Dismemberment and Memory: Body Politics in Latin America*, 198–99. Albuquerque: University of New Mexico Press, 2004.

Tomás Bustamante Alvarez. "La reforma agraria en Guerrero durante el gobierno de Lázaro Cárdenas." In Jaime Salazar Adame, *Historia de la cuestión agraria mexicana: Estado de Guerrero, 1867–1940*. Mexico: Gobierno del Estado de Guerrero, 1987.

———. *Las transformaciones de la agricultura o las paradojas del desarrollo regional: Tierra Caliente, Guerrero*. Mexico City: Procuradoría Agraria, 1996.

———, Gil Arturo Ferrer Vicario, and Joel Iturio Nava, eds. *Guerrero en el contexto de las revoluciones en México*. Mexico City: Editorial Fontamara, 2010.

——— and Sergio Sarmiento Silva, eds. *El Sur en movimiento: la reinvención de Guerrero del siglo XXI*. Mexico: Consejo de Ciencia y Tecnología del Estado de Guerrero, 2001.

José Antonio Caballero. "Amparos y *abogángsters:* La justicia en México entre 1940 y 1968." In Elisa Servín, ed., *Del nacionalismo al neoliberalismo, 1940–1994*. Mexico City: Colegio de México, 2010.

Fanny Calderón de la Barca. *Life in Mexico*. Berkeley: University of California Press, 1982.

Roderic Ai Camp. *Mexican Political Biographies*. Austin: University of Texas Press, 1995.

———. *Intellectuals and the State in Modern Mexico*. Austin: University of Texas Press, 2014.

Frank Cancian. *The Decline of Community in Zinacantán: Economy, Public Life, and Social Stratification, 1960–1987*. Stanford: Stanford University Press, 1992.

Enrique Cárdenas. "A Macroeconomic Interpretation of Nineteenth-Century Mexico." In Stephen H. Haber, ed., *How Latin America Fell Behind: Essays on the Economic Histories of Brazil and Mexico, 1800–1914*. Stanford: University of Stanford Press, 1997.

Lázaro Cárdenas. *Obras*, 4 vols. Mexico City: UNAM, 1973.

Ivonne Carillo Dewar. *Industria petrolera y desarrollo capitalista en el norte de Veracruz, 1900–1990*. Xalapa: Universidad Veracruzana, 1993.

E. H. Carr. *The Twenty Years' Crisis, 1919–1939: An Introduction to the Study of International Relations*. London: Palgrave Macmillan, 2016 [1939].

Laura Castellano. *México armado, 1943–1981*. Mexico City: Ediciones Era, 2007.

J. Justin Castro. *Radio in Revolution: Wireless Technology and State Power in Mexico, 1897–1938*. Lincoln: University of Nebraska Press, 2016.

Juan Alberto Cedillo. *Los Nazis en México*. Mexico City: Debolsillo, 2017.

François Chevalier and Javier Pérez Siller. *Viajes y pasiones: imágenes y recuerdos del México rural*. Mexico City: Instituto Francés de América Latina/Fondo de Cultura Económica, 1998.

Margaret Chowning. "Reassessing the Prospects for Profit in Nineteenth-Century Mexican Agriculture from a Regional Perspective: Michoacán, 1810–1860." In Stephen H. Haber, ed., *How Latin America Fell Behind: Essays on the Economic Histories of Brazil and Mexico, 1800–1914*. Stanford: University of Stanford Press, 1997.

Carlos Contreras Cruz and Claudia Patricia Pardo Hernández, eds. *De Veracruz a Puebla: un itinerario entre la colonia y el porfiriato*. Mexico City: Instituto de Investigaciones Dr. José Maria Luis Mora, 1999.

Frederick Cooper. *Africa since 1940: The Past of the Present*. Cambridge: Cambridge University Press, 2002.

Ricardo Corzo Ramírez, José González Sierra, and David Skerritt. *. . . nunca un desleal: Cándido Aguilar (1889–1960)*. Mexico City: Colegio de México, 1986.

Daniel Cosío Villegas. "La Crísis de México." *Cuadernos Americanos* 6, no. 32 (1947).

———. "El Porfiriato, era de consolidación." *Historia Mexicana* XIII (1963).

———. *El Porfiriato: la vida política interior primera parte*. Mexico City and Buenos Aires: Editorial Hermes, 1960.

———. *La Constitución de 1857 y sus críticos*. Mexico City: Secretaría de Educación Pública, 1973.

Michael P. Costeloe. "Generals versus Politicians: Santa Anna and the 1842 Congressional Elections in Mexico." *Bulletin of Latin American Research* 8, no. 2 (1989).

Raymond B. Craib. *Cartographic Mexico: A History of State Fixations and Fugitive Landscapes*. Durham: Duke University Press, 2004.

Ann L. Craig and Wayne A. Cornelius. "Political Culture in Mexico: Continuities and Revisionist Interpretations." In Almond and Verba, *The Civic Culture Revisited*.

James Creelman. "President Díaz: Hero of the Americas." *Pearson's Magazine* 19, no. 3 (March 1908).

Marcos Cueto. "Appropriation and Resistance: Local Responses to Malaria Eradication in Mexico, 1955–1970." *Journal of Latin American Studies* 37, no. 3 (August 2005): 533–59.

Robert Dahl. *On Democracy*. New Haven: Yale University Press, 1998.

———. *Polyarchy: Participation and Opposition*. New Haven: Yale University Press, 1971.

Diane E. Davis. "Policing and Regime Transition: From Postauthoritarianism to Populism to Neoliberalism." In Wil G. Pansters, ed., *Violence, Coercion and State-Making in Twentieth-Century Mexico: The Other Half of the Centaur*. Stanford: Stanford University Press, 2012.

Danièle Dehouve. *Cuando los banqueros eran santos: historia económica y social de la provincia de Tlapa, Guerrero*. Chilpancingo: Universidad Autónoma del Estado de Guerrero, 2002.

Klaus Deininger and Lyn Squire. "A New Data Set Measuring Income Inequality." *World Bank Economic Review* 10, no. 3 (September 1996): 565–91.

Moisés T. de la Peña. *Chihuahua económico*. 3 vols. Mexico City: Adrián Morales, 1948.

———. *Guerrero económico*. 2 vols. Chilpancingo: Gobierno de Estado de Guerrero, 1949.

———. *Veracruz económico*. 2 vols. Veracruz-Llave: Gobierno del Estado de Veracruz, 1946.

Mike Dennis. *The Stasi: Myth and Reality*. London: Routledge, 2003.

Departamento de la Estadística Nacional. *Anuario estadístico 1923–1924*. Mexico City, 1925.

Dirección General de Estadística. *Censo y división territorial de población del estado de Guerrero verificados el 28 de octubre de 1900*. Mexico City: Dirección General de Estadística, 1905.

———. *Censo de población 1950 Estado de Veracruz*. Mexico City: Dirección General de Estadística, 1953.

———. *Séptimo censo general de población 6 de junio de 1950 Estado de Guerrero*. Mexico City: Dirección General de Estadística, 1953.

———. *Séptimo censo general de población 6 de junio de 1950 resumen general*. Mexico City: Dirección General de Estadística, 1953.

———. *Tercer censo de población de los Estados Unidos Mexicanos verificado el 27 de octubre de 1910*. Mexico City: Dirección General de Estadística, 1918–20.

Adolfo Dollero. *México al día (impresiones y notas de viaje)*. Mexico: Vda. de C. Bouret, 1911.

Jason H. Dormady. *Primitive Revolution: Restorationist Religion and the Idea of the Mexican Revolution, 1940–1968*. Albuquerque: University of New Mexico Press, 2011.

Susana Draper. *1968 Mexico: Constellations of Freedom and Democracy*. Durham: Duke University Press, 2018.

John Foster Dulles. *Yesterday in Mexico: A Chronicle of the Revolution, 1919–1936*. Austin: University of Texas Press, 1961.

Robert H. Duncan. "Embracing a Suitable Past: Independence Celebrations under Mexico's Second Empire, 1864–1866." *Journal of Latin American Studies* 30 (1998).

James Dunkerley, ed. *Studies in the Formation of the Nation State in Latin America*. London: Institute of Latin American Studies, 2002.

Rebecca Earle. *The Return of the Native: Indians and Myth-making in Spanish America, 1810–1930*. Durham: Duke University Press, 2007.

Todd A. Eisenstadt. *Courting Democracy in Mexico: Party Strategies and Electoral Institutions*. Cambridge: Cambridge University Press, 2004.

Florencio Encarnación Ursúa. *Las luchas de los copreros guerrerenses*. Mexico City: Editoria y Distribuidora Nacional, 1977.

Laura Espejel López and Salvador Rueda Smithers. *Reconstrucción histórica de una comunidad del norte de Guerrero: Ichcateopan*. Mexico City: Dirección de Estudios Históricos, Instituto Nacional de Antropología e Historia, Seminario de Movimientos Campesinos del Siglo XX, 1979.

Alba Teresa Estrada Castañon. *Guerrero: sociedad, economía, política, cultura*. Mexico City: UNAM, 1994.

Romana Falcón. *El agrarismo en Veracruz: la etapa radical (1928–1935)*. Mexico City: Colegio de México, 1977.

——— and Soledad García Morales. *Adalberto Tejeda y el radicalismo en Veracruz (1883–1960)*. Mexico City: Colegio de México, 1986.

Ben Fallaw. *Cárdenas Compromised: The Failure of Reform in Postrevolutionary Yucatán*. Durham: Duke University Press, 2001.

———. *Religion and State Formation in Postrevolutionary Mexico*. Durham: Duke University Press, 2013.

———. "Praetorian Politics, Militant Jacobinism and Generalized Corruption: Francisco J. Múgica in Campeche and Yucatan (1934–35) and José Domínguez Cota in Guanajuato (1938–1940)." Paper delivered at the Southern Conference of Latin American Studies, Albuquerque, 2006.

Ben Fallaw and Terry Rugeley, eds., *Forced Marches: Militaries, Cacicazgos, and the Uneven Development of Mexican Politics* (Tucson: University of Arizona Press, 2012).

Claudia Fernández and Andrew Paxman. *El Tigre: Emilio Azcárraga y su imperio Televisa*. Mexico City: Grijalbo, 2000.

Gil Arturo Ferrer Vicario. "Guerrero, un trozo de su historia Porfiriato y Revolución." In Bustamante Alvarez et al., *Guerrero en el contexto de las revoluciones*.

Aleida Ferreyra and Renata Segura. "Examining the Military in the Local Sphere: Colombia and Mexico." *Latin American Perspectives* 27, no. 2 (March 2000): 18–35.

Fiscal Especial para Movimientos Sociales y Políticos del Pasado (FEMOSPP). "Concentrado General Desaparecidos," draft report, 2006, https://nsarchive2.gwu.edu//NSAEBB/NSAEBB180/index2.htm,

Charles M. Flandrau. *¡Viva México!* London: Eland Books, 1985.

Véronique Flanet. *Viviré si Dios quiere: un estudio de la violencia en la mixteca de la costa*. Mexico City: Consejo Nacional para la Cultura y las Artes, Dirección General de Publicaciones, Instituto Nacional Indigenista, 1990.

Joe Foweraker and Ann L. Craig, eds. *Popular Movements and Political Change in Mexico*. Boulder: Lynne Rienner Publications, 1990.

Heather Fowler. "The Agrarian Revolution in the State of Veracruz, 1920–1940: The Role of Peasant Organizations." Ph.D. thesis, University of Washington, 1970.

Heather Fowler-Salamini. *Agrarian Radicalism in Veracruz, 1920–1938*. Lincoln: University of Nebraska Press, 1978.

———. *Working Women, Entrepreneurs and the Mexican Revolution: The Coffee Culture of Córdoba, Veracruz*. Lincoln: University of Nebraska Press, 2013.

Vanessa Freije. *Scandalous Democracy: Journalists and the Politics of Corruption in Mexico*. Durham: Duke University Press, 2019.

Paul Friedrich. *Agrarian Revolt in a Mexican Village*. Chicago: University of Chicago Press, 1970.

———. *The Princes of Naranja: An Essay in Anthrohistorical Method*. Austin: University of Texas Press, 1986.

Vicente Fuentes Díaz. *Guerrero: un pasado aciago, un porvenir promisorio*. Mexico City: Cámara de Diputados, 2000.

François Furet. *Marx and the French Revolution*. Chicago: University of Chicago Press, 1966.

Bernardo García Díaz. *Un pueblo fabril del Porfiriato: Santa Rosa, Veracruz*. Mexico City: Fondo de Cultura Económica, 1981.

Jaime García Leyva. "Revoltosos, Bandidos y Rebeldes en la Montaña de Guerrero: 1850–1900." In Bustamante Alvarez et al., *Guerrero en el contexto de las revoluciones*.

Soledad García Morales and José Velasco Toro, eds. *Memorias e informes de jefes políticos y autoridades del régimen porfirista 1883–1911 Estado de Veracruz*. Xalapa: Universidad Veracruzana, 1997.

Josefina García Quintana. *Cuauhtémoc en el Siglo XIX*. Mexico City: Universidad Autónoma de México, 1977.

Livia García Quinto. "Breve Historia del Ingenio 'El Modelo' 1900–1974." MA thesis, Universidad Veracruzana, 1975.

Javier Garciadiego, coord. *El Ejército Mexicano 100 años de historia*. Mexico City: El Colegio de México, 2014.

Ernest Gellner. *Nations and Nationalism*. Ithaca: Cornell University Press, 2009.

George A. Genz. "Entrepreneurship and Caciquismo: A Study of Community Power in a Mexican Gulf Coast Village." Ph.D. thesis, Michigan State University, 1975.

Mario Gill. "Los Escudero, de Acapulco." *Historia Mexicana* 3, no. 4 (October–December 1953).

Paul Gillingham. "Ambiguous Missionaries: Rural Teachers and State Façades in Guerrero, 1930–1950." *Mexican Studies/Estudios Mexicanos* 22, no. 2 (Summer 2006): 331–60.

———. *Cuauhtémoc's Bones: Forging National Identity in Modern Mexico*. Albuquerque: University of New Mexico Press, 2011.

———. "Maximino's Bulls: Popular Protest after the Mexican Revolution." *Past and Present* 206 (February 2010): 145–81.

———. "Military Caciquismo in the Priista State." In *Forced Marches: Militaries, Cacicazgos, and the Uneven Development of Mexican Politics*, eds. Ben Fallaw and Terry Rugeley. Tucson: University of Arizona Press, 2012.

———. "Who Killed Crispín Aguilar? Violence and Order in the Post-revolutionary Countryside." In Wil Pansters, ed., *Violence, Coercion and State-Making in Twentieth-Century Mexico: The Other Half of the Centaur*. Stanford: Stanford University Press, 2012.

———, Michael Lettieri, and Benjamin T. Smith, eds. *Journalism, Satire, and Censorship in Mexico*. Albuquerque: University of New Mexico Press, 2018.

———, Michael Lettieri, and Benjamin Smith. "Journalism, Satire, and Censorship in Mexico." In Paul Gillingham, Michael Lettieri, and Benjamin Smith, *Journalism, Satire, and Censorship in Mexico*, 1–32. Albuquerque: University of New Mexico Press, 2018.

——— and Benjamin T. Smith, eds. *Dictablanda: Politics, Work, and Culture in Mexico, 1938–1968*. Durham: Duke University Press, 2014.

——— and Benjamin T. Smith. "Introduction: The Paradoxes of Revolution." In Gillingham and Smith, *Dictablanda*.

John Gledhill. *Casi Nada: A Study of Agrarian Reform in the Homeland of Cardenismo*. Austin: University of Texas Press, 1991.

Aurora Gómez-Galvarriato. "The Impact of Revolution: The Evolution of Prices, Real Wages, and Productivity Levels in a Mexican Textile Mill from 1900 to 1929." Paper presented at the Economic History Association Meeting, 1998.

———. *Industry and Revolution: Social and Economic Change in the Orizaba Valley, Mexico.* Cambridge: Harvard University Press, 2013.

———. "Measuring the Impact of Institutional Change in Capital–Labor Relations in the Mexican Textile Industry." In Jeffrey L. Bortz and Stephen H. Haber, eds., *The Mexican Economy, 1870–1930: Essays on the Economic History of Institutions, Revolution and Growth.* Stanford: Stanford University Press, 2002.

Pablo González Casanova. *Democracy in Mexico.* New York: Oxford University Press, 1970.

———. "Democracia en tiempos de crisis." In Pablo González Casanova, ed., *Las elecciones en México: evolución y perspectiva.* Mexico City: Siglo XXI, 1985.

Francisco González de Cossío et al. *Legislación indigenista de México.* Mexico City: Instituto Indigenista Interamericano, 1958.

Moisés González Navarro. *El Porfiriato: la vida social.* Mexico City: Editorial Hermes, 1957.

———. *Estadísticas sociales del Porfiriato 1877–1910.* Mexico City: Dirección General de Estadística, 1956.

José González Sierra. "Genesis y consolidación de un proyecto de historia regional." *Anuario* 5, no. 9. Xalapa: Universidad Veracruzana, n.d.

———. *Los Tuxtlas.* Xalapa: Universidad Veracruzana, 1991.

———. *Monopolio del humo (elementos para la historia del tabaco en México y algunos conflictos de tabaqueros veracruzanos: 1915–1930).* Xalapa: Universidad Veracruzana, 1987.

Antonio Gramsci. *Selections from the Prison Notebooks.* London: Lawrence and Wishart, 1996.

Ernest Gruening. *Mexico and Its Heritage.* New York: D. Appleton, 1940.

Peter Guardino. *Peasants, Politics and the Formation of Mexico's National State: Guerrero, 1800–1857.* Stanford: Stanford University Press, 1996.

———. *The Time of Liberty: Popular Political Culture in Oaxaca, 1750–1850.* Durham: Duke University Press, 2005.

Jesús Guzmán Urióstegui. *Evila Franco Nájera, a pesar del olvido.* Mexico City: Instituto Nacional de Estudios Históricos de la Revolución Mexicana, 1995.

Miguel Angel Gutiérrez Avila. *Corrido y violencia entre los Afromestizos de la Costa Chica de Guerrero y Oaxaca.* Chilpancingo: Universidad Autónoma de Guerrero, 1988.

———. *Derecho consuetudinario y derecho positivo entre los mixtecos, amuzgos y afromestizos de la costa chica de Guerrero.* Mexico City: Comisión Nacional de Derechos Humanos, 1997.

———. *Nabor Ojeda Caballero, el Batallador del Sur.* Mexico City: Centro de Estudios Históricos del Agrarismo en México, Confederación Nacional Campesina, 1991.

Stephen H. Haber. *Industry and Underdevelopment: The Industrialization of Mexico, 1890–1940*. Stanford: Stanford University Press, 1989.

———, ed. *How Latin America Fell Behind: Essays on the Economic Histories of Brazil and Mexico, 1800–1914*. Stanford: Stanford University Press, 1997.

David Halberstam. *The Best and the Brightest*. New York: Modern Library, 2001.

Christine A. Hastorf. "Rio Balsas Most Likely Region for Maize Cultivation." *Proceedings of the National Academy of Sciences of the United States of America* 106, no. 13 (March 2009).

Joy Elizabeth Hayes. *Radio Nation: Communication, Popular Culture, and Nationalism in Mexico, 1920–1950*. Tucson: University of Arizona Press, 2000.

Karl Bartolomeus Heller. *Alone in Mexico: The Astonishing Travels of Karl Heller, 1845–1848*. Translated and edited by Terry Rugeley. Tuscaloosa: University of Alabama Press, 2007.

James D. Henderson. *When Colombia Bled: A History of the Violencia in Tolima*. Tuscaloosa: University of Alabama, 1985.

Timothy J. Henderson. *The Worm in the Wheat: Rosalie Evans and Agrarian Struggle in the Puebla–Tlaxcala Valley of Mexico, 1906–1927*. Durham: Duke University Press, 1998.

Elizabeth Henson. "Madera 1965: Primeros Vientos." In Fernando Herrera Calderón and Adela Cedillo, eds., *Challenging Authoritarianism in Mexico: Revolutionary Struggles and the Dirty War, 1964–1982*. New York: Routledge, 2012.

Erasmo Hernández García. "Redes políticas y sociales: consolidación y permanencia del régimen posrevolucionario en Veracruz, 1920–1970." D.Phil. diss., Universidad Veracruzana, 2010.

Rogelio Hernández Rodríguez. *El centro dividido: La nueva autonomía de los gobernadores*. Mexico City: Colegio de México, 2009.

———. *Historia mínima del PRI*. Mexico City: Colegio de México, 2016.

———. *La formación del político mexicano: el caso de Carlos A. Madrazo*. Mexico City: Colegio de México, 1991.

———. Review of Ryan M. Alexander, *Sons of the Mexican Revolution: Miguel Alemán and His Generation*. *Historia Mexicana* 68, no. 2 (October–December 2018).

Luis Herrán Avila. "Rebels, Outlaws and Enemies." In Gema Santamaria and David Carey Jr., eds., *Violence and Crime in Latin America: Representations and Politics*. Norman: University of Oklahoma Press, 2017.

Fernando Herrera Calderón and Adela Cedillo, eds. *Challenging Authoritarianism in Mexico: Revolutionary Struggles and the Dirty War, 1964–1982*. New York: Routledge, 2012.

Reginald Hibbert. "Intelligence and Policy." *Intelligence and National Security* 5, no. 1 (January 1990).

Manuel Hinojosa Ortiz. *Los bosques de México: relato de un despilfarro y una injusticia*. Mexico City: Instituto Mexicano de Investigaciones Económicas, 1958.

Thomas Hobbes. *Leviathan*. London: Penguin, 1987.

Eric Hobsbawm. *Age of Extremes: The Short Twentieth Century*. London: Joseph, 1994.

Alexander von Humboldt. *Political Essay on the Kingdom of New Spain*, 3 vols. Translated by John Black. London, 1814.

Samuel P. Huntington. *Political Order in Changing Societies*. New Haven: Yale University Press, 1968.

Jorge Ibargüengoitia. *Los relámpagos de agosto*. Mexico City: Joaquín Mortiz, 2003 [1964].

Patrick Iber. *Neither Peace nor Freedom: The Cultural Cold War in Latin America*. Cambridge: Harvard University Press, 2015.

Carlos Illades and Martha Ortega. *Guerrero: textos de su historia*. Mexico City: Instituto de Investigaciones Dr. José Maria Luis Mora, 1989.

Instituto Nacional de Economía, Geografía e Informática. *Censo del estado de Veracruz 1950*. Mexico City, 1953.

———. *Estadísticas históricas de México* CD-ROM. Mexico City, 2000.

Elena Jackson Albarrán. *Seen and Heard in Mexico: Children and Revolutionary Cultural Nationalism*. Lincoln: University of Nebraska Press, 2014.

Ian Jacobs. *Ranchero Revolt: The Mexican Revolution in Guerrero*. Austin: University of Texas Press, 1982.

Lyman L. Johnson, ed. *Death, Dismemberment and Memory: Body Politics in Latin America*. Albuquerque: University of New Mexico Press, 2004.

Halbert Jones. *The War Has Brought Peace to Mexico: World War II and the Consolidation of the Post-Revolutionary State*. Albuquerque: University of New Mexico Press, 2014.

Gilbert M. Joseph and Daniel Nugent, eds. *Everyday Forms of State Formation: Revolution and the Negotiation of Rule in Modern Mexico*. Durham: Duke University Press, 1994.

———, Anne Rubenstein, and Eric Zolov, eds. *Fragments of a Golden Age: The Politics of Culture in Mexico since 1940*. Durham: Duke University Press, 2001.

Abel Juárez Martínez. "Reacomodo de las fuerzas sociales en el Valle de Perote, 1910–1920." *Anuario* 8. Xalapa: Universidad Veracruzana, n.d.

Friedrich Katz. *The Life and Times of Pancho Villa*. Stanford: Stanford University Press, 1998.

——— and Jane-Dale Lloyd, eds. *Porfirio Díaz frente al descontento regional (1891–1893)*. Mexico City: Universidad Iberoamericana, 1986.

Renata Keller. *Mexico's Cold War: Cuba, the United States, and the Legacy of the Mexican Revolution*. Cambridge: Cambridge University Press, 2015.

Gema Kloppe-Santamaria. "Lynching and the Politics of State Formation in Post-Revolutionary Puebla (1930s–50s)." *Journal of Latin American Studies* 50, no. 4 (November 2018).

Alan Knight. *The Mexican Revolution.* 2 vols. Lincoln: University of Nebraska Press, 1990.

———. "Corruption in Twentieth Century Mexico." In Walter Little and Eduardo Posada-Carbó, eds., *Political Corruption in Europe and Latin America.* London: Palgrave Macmillan, 1996.

———. "Weapons and Arches in the Mexican Revolutionary Landscape." In Gilbert M. Joseph and Daniel Nugent, eds., *Everyday Forms of State Formation: Revolution and the Negotiation of Rule in Modern Mexico.* Durham: Duke University Press, 1994.

———. "Cardenismo: Juggernaut or Jalopy?" *Journal of Latin American Studies* 26, no. 1 (February 1994).

———. "Peasants into Patriots: Thoughts on the Making of the Mexican Nation." *Mexican Studies/Estudios Mexicanos* 10, no. 1 (Winter 1994).

———. "México bronco, México manso: una reflexión sobre la cultura cívica mexicana." *Política y Gobierno* 3, no. 1 (1996).

———. "The Peculiarities of Mexican History: Mexico Compared to Latin America, 1821–1992." *Journal of Latin American Studies* 24: Quincentenary Supplement (1992): 99–144.

———. "The Weight of the State in Modern Mexico." In James Dunkerley, ed., *Studies in the Formation of the Nation State in Latin America.* London: Institute of Latin American Studies, 2002.

———. "Historical Continuities in Social Movements." In Joe Foweraker and Ann L. Craig, eds., *Popular Movements and Political Change in Mexico.* Boulder: Lynne Rienner Publications, 1990.

———. "Hegemony, Counterhegemony and the Mexican Revolution." In J. Chalcraft and Y. Noorani, eds., *Counterhegemony in the Colony and Postcolony.* London: Palgrave Macmillan, 2007.

———. "The End of the Mexican Revolution? From Cárdenas to Avila Camacho, 1937–1941." In Gillingham and Smith, *Dictablanda.*

———. "The Mexican State, Porfirian and Revolutionary, 1876–1930." In Miguel A. Centeno and Agustín E. Ferraro, eds., *State and Nation Making in Latin America: Republics of the Possible,* 116–38. Princeton: Princeton University Press, 2013.

———. "The Myth of the Mexican Revolution." *Past and Present* 209 (November 2010).

Karl B. Koth. "Teodoro A. Dehesa and Veracruz in the Porfiriato 1892–1913: A Case Study of Mexican Federal–State Relations." D.Phil. thesis, University of Manitoba, 1987.

Emilio Kourí. *A Pueblo Divided: Business, Property and Community in Papantla, Mexico.* Stanford: Stanford University Press, 2004.

Enrique Krauze. *La Presidencia Imperial: ascenso y caída del sistema político mexicano (1940–1996).* Mexico: Tusquets Editores, 1997.

———. *Por una democracia sin adjetivos.* Mexico City: Joaquín Mortiz Planeta, 1986.

Joy K. Langston. *Democratization and Authoritarian Party Survival: Mexico's PRI.* Oxford: Oxford University Press, 2017.

T. J. Jackson Lears. "The Concept of Cultural Hegemony: Problems and Possibilities." *American Historical Review* 90, no. 3 (June 1985).

Louis Lejeune. *Tierras mexicanas.* Mexico City, 1995.

Victoria Lerner. "Historia de la Reforma Educativa, 1933–1945." *Historia Mexicana* 29, no. 1 (1979).

Michael Lettieri. "A Model Dinosaur: Power, Personal Networks and the Career of Rubén Figueroa." *Mexican Studies/Estudios Mexicanos* 31, no. 2 (Summer 2015).

———. *The Motor of the PRI: Political Entrepreneurs and Authoritarian Rule, 1927–1985.* Albuquerque: University of New Mexico Press, forthcoming.

———. "In the Service of the *Gremio:* Bus Industry Magazines, PRI Corporatism, and the Politics of Trade Publications." In Gillingham, Lettieri, and Smith, *Journalism, Satire, and Censorship.*

Steven Levitsky and Lucan A. Way. *Competitive Authoritarianism: Hybrid Regimes after the Cold War.* Cambridge: Cambridge University Press, 2010.

Edwin Lieuwen. "Depoliticisation of the Mexican Revolutionary Army, 1915–1940." In David F. Ronfeldt, ed., *The Modern Mexican Military: A Reassessment.* La Jolla: Center for U.S.–Mexican Studies, University of California San Diego, 1984.

———. *Mexican Militarism: The Political Rise and Fall of the Revolutionary Army, 1910–1940.* Albuquerque: University of New Mexico Press, 1968.

José Yves Limantour. *Apuntes sobre mi vida política.* Mexico City: Editorial Porrúa, 1965.

Soledad Loaeza. *El Partido de Acción Nacional: La larga marcha, 1939–1994.* Mexico: Fondo de Cultura Económica, 2000.

———. "Sobre Paul Gillingham y Benjamin T. Smith (eds.), Dictablanda. Politics, Work, and Culture in Mexico 1938–1968." *Historia Mexicana* 65, no. 3 (January–March 2013).

Claudio Lomnitz-Adler. *Exits from the Labyrinth: Culture and Ideology in the Mexican National Space.* Berkeley: University of California Press, 1992.

Rick A. López. *Crafting Mexico: Intellectuals, Artisans, and the State after the Revolution.* Durham: Duke University Press, 2010.

Epigmenio López Barroso. *Diccionario geográfico, histórico y estadístico del distrito de Abasolo, del Estado de Guerrero.* Mexico City: Ediciones Botas, 1967.

Max Arturo López Hernández et al. *La formación del poder en el estado de Guerrero.* Chilpancingo: Universidad Autónoma de Guerrero, 1997.

Alvaro López Miramontes. "Panorama historiográfica del estado de Guerrero." In Alvaro López Miramontes et al., eds., *Ensayos para la historia del estado de Guerrero.* Chilpancingo: Instituto Guerrerense de la Cultura, 1985.

Malcolm Lowry. *Under the Volcano.* New York: Harper Collins, 2007.

Rafael Loyola Díaz. *El ocaso del radicalismo revolucionario: ferrocarrileros y petroleros: 1938–1947.* Mexico City: UNAM, 1991.

Beatriz Magaloni. *Voting for Autocracy: Hegemonic Party Survival and Its Demise in Mexico*. Cambridge: Cambridge University Press, 2006.

Florencia Mallon. *Peasant and Nation*. Berkeley: University of California Press, 1995.

Gela Manzano and Isaías Alanís. *Ometepec: historia y cultura*. Mexico City: Grupo Editorial Eón, 1996.

Stefano Manzocchi. *Foreign Capital in Developing Economies: Perspectives from the Theory of Economic Growth*. London: Macmillan, 1999.

Robert H. K. Marett. *An Eye-witness of Mexico*. London: Oxford University Press, 1939.

Ignacio Marquina. *Memorias*. Mexico City: Instituto Nacional de Antropología e Historia, 1994.

Gerard Martin. "The 'Tradition of Violence' in Colombia." In Göran Aijmer and Jon Abbink, eds., *Meanings of Violence: A Cross-Cultural Perspective*. Oxford: Oxford University Press, 2000.

María Antonia Martínez. *El despegue constructivo de la Revolución: Sociedad y política en el alemanismo*. Mexico: CIESAS, Miguel Angel Porrua, 2004.

Paulino Martínez. *La Hecatombe de Veracruz: Corona funebre en memoria de las víctimas sacrificadas la noche del 24 al 25 de Junio de 1879*. Mexico City: Fiat Lux, 1910.

Juana Martínez Alarcón. *San Cristóbal: un ingenio y sus trabajadores, 1896–1934*. Xalapa: Universidad Veracruzana, 1986.

Bertha Beatriz Martínez Garza et al. *Historia de las Ligas de Comunidades Agrarias y Sindicatos Campesinos*. Mexico City: Confederación Nacional Campesina, Centro de Estudios Históricos del Agrarismo en México, 1988.

Santiago Martínez Hernández. *Tiempos de Revolución: la Revolución en el Sur de Veracruz vista por un campesino zoque-popoluca*. Mexico City: Premia Editora, 1982.

Alvaro Matute. *Historia de la Revolución Mexicana, 1917–1924: la carrera del caudillo*. Mexico City: Colegio de México, 1980.

Gladys McCormick. *The Logic of Compromise in Mexico: How the Countryside Was Key to the Emergence of Authoritarianism*. Chapel Hill: University of North Carolina Press, 2016.

León Medel y Alvarado. *Historia de San Andrés Tuxtla (1525–1975)*. Xalapa: Gobierno del Estado de Veracruz, 1993.

Tzvi Medin. *El Minimato presidencial: historia política del maximato*. Mexico City: Colegio de México, 1982.

Luis Medina. *Historia de la Revolución Mexicana, 1940–1952: Del cardenismo al avilacamachismo*. Mexico City: Colegio de México, 1978.

———. *Historia de la Revolución Mexicana 1940–1952: Civilismo y modernización del autoritarismo*. Mexico City: Colegio de México, 1979.

Peter Metcalf and Richard Huntingdon. *Celebrations of Death: The Anthropology of Mortuary Ritual*. Cambridge: Cambridge University Press, 1991.

Jean Meyer. *Le Sinarquisme: un fascisme mexicain? 1937–1947*. Paris: Hachette, 1977.

Lorenzo Meyer, Rafael Segovia, and Alejandra Lajous. *Historia de la Revolución Mexicana, 1928–1934: los inicios de la institucionalización*. Mexico City: Colegio de México, 1978.

Albert L. Michaels. "Las elecciones de 1940." *Historia Mexicana* 21, no. 1 (1971).

Kevin J. Middlebrook. *The Paradox of Revolution: Labor, the State and Authoritarianism in Mexico*. Baltimore: Johns Hopkins University Press, 1995.

Joel Migdal. *Strong Societies and Weak States: State–Society Relations and State Capabilities in the Third World*. Princeton: Princeton University Press, 1988.

Marcela Mijares Lara. "Juan Andreu Almazán y la compañía Constructora Anáhuac: Negocios y política durante la posrevolución (1927–1932)." In Marco Palacios, ed., *Negocios, empresarios y entornos políticos en México, 1827–1958*. Mexico City: Colegio de México, 2015.

Ministerio de Fomento. *Censo del Estado de Guerrero (1895)*. Mexico City, 1899.

———. *Censo del Estado de Veracruz*. Mexico City, 1899.

———. *Censo y división territorial del Estado de Veracruz, verificados en 1900*. Mexico City, 1904.

Eduardo Miranda Arrieta. *Economía y comunicaciones en el Estado de Guerrero, 1877–1910*. Michoacán: Universidad Michoacana de San Nicolás de Hidalgo, 1994.

Iván Molina and Fabrice Edouard Lehoucq. "Political Competition and Electoral Fraud: A Latin American Case Study." *Journal of Interdisciplinary History* 30, no. 2 (Autumn 1999).

Daniel Molina Álvarez. "Período 1920–1934." In Salazar Adame, *La Cuestión Agraria Mexicana*.

Carlos Moncada. *¡Cayeron! 67 Gobernadores derrocados (1929–1979)*. Mexico City: C. Moncada, 1979.

Carlos Montemayor. *Violencia del estado en Mexico: Antes y después del 1968*. Mexico City: Random House Debate, 2010.

Nathaniel Morris. "Heroin, the Herreras and the 'Chicago Connection': The Drug Trade in Durango, 1950–1985." In Pansters and Smith, *Histories of Drug Trafficking in Twentieth-Century Mexico*.

Nicole Mottier. "Drug Gangs and Politics in Ciudad Juárez: 1928–1936." *Mexican Studies/Estudios Mexicanos* 25, no. 1 (Winter 2009).

Marcos Muñoz. "Mixteca-Nahua-Tlapaneca." In *Memorias del Instituto Nacional Indigenista*, vol. 9. Mexico City: Instituto Nacional Indigenista, 1963.

Aaron W. Navarro. "El ejército mexicano en la época de la posguerra: el argumento égida." In Javier Garciadiego, coord., *El Ejército Mexicano 100 años de historia*. Mexico City: El Colegio de México, 2014.

———. *Political Intelligence and the Creation of Modern Mexico, 1938–1954*. University Park: Pennsylvania State University Press, 2010.

Edward William Nelson. "A Winter Expedition in Southwestern Mexico." *National Geographic Magazine* 15, no. 9 (September 1904).

J. P. Nettl. *Political Mobilization: A Sociological Analysis of Methods and Concepts.* London: Basic Books, 1967.

Daniel Newcomer. *Reconciling Modernity: Urban State Formation in 1940s León, Mexico.* Lincoln: University of Nebraska Press, 2004.

Stephen R. Niblo. *Mexico in the 1940s: Modernity, Politics and Corruption.* Wilmington, DE: Scholarly Resources, 1999.

——— and Diane M. Niblo. "Acapulco in Dreams and Reality." *Mexican Studies/Estudios Mexicanos* 24, no. 1 (Winter 2008).

Salvador Novo. "Este y otros viajes." In Poblett Miranda, *Cien viajeros en Veracruz.*

Daniel Nugent. *Spent Cartridges of the Revolution: An Anthropological History of Namiquipa, Chihuahua.* Chicago: University of Chicago Press, 1993.

María Cristina Núñez Madrazo. "Entre patrones, caciques y líderes: Procesos políticos locales en una comunidad cañera del centro del estado de Veracruz." *Sotavento,* no. 5 (2000).

Guillermo O'Donnell and Philippe C. Schmitter. *Transitions from Authoritarian Rule: Tentative Conclusions about Uncertain Democracies.* Baltimore: Johns Hopkins University Press, 2013.

Frank O'Gorman. "The Culture of Elections in England: From the Glorious Revolution to the First World War, 1688–1914." In Eduardo Posada Carbó, ed., *Elections before Democracy: The History of Elections in Europe and Latin America.* London: Institute of Latin American Studies, 1996.

Verónica Oikión Solano and Marta Eugenia García Ugarte, eds. *Movimientos armados en México, siglo XX.* 3 vols. Mexico City: Colegio de Michoacán/CIESAS, 2008.

Alberto J. Olvera R. "La estructura económica y social de Veracruz hacia 1930: Un análisis inicial." *Anuario* vol. 3. Xalapa: Universidad Veracruzana, 1983.

———. "The Rise and Fall of Union Democracy at Poza Rica." In Brown and Knight, *The Mexican Petroleum Industry in the Twentieth Century.*

Ilene V. O'Malley. *The Myth of the Revolution: Hero Cults and the Institutionalization of the Mexican State, 1920–1940.* New York: Greenwood Press, 1986.

Sarah Osten. *The Mexican Revolution's Wake: The Making of a Political System, 1920–1929.* Cambridge: Cambridge University Press, 2018.

José Emilio Pacheco, ed. *En torno a la cultura nacional.* Mexico City: Secretaría de Educación Pública, 1982.

Tanalís Padilla. *Rural Resistance in the Land of Zapata: The Jaramillista Movement and the Myth of the Pax Priista, 1940–1962.* Durham: Duke University Press, 2008.

———. "Rural Education, Political Radicalism, and Normalista Identity in post-1940 Mexico." In Gillingham and Smith, *Dictablanda.*

——— and Louise E. Walker. "In the Archives: History and Politics." *Journal of Iberian and Latin American Research* 19, no. 1 (2013): 1–10.

Cándido Donato Padua. *Movimiento Revolucionario—1906 en Veracruz: relación cronológica de las actividades del PLM en los ex-cantones de Acayucpan, Minatitlán, San Andrés Tuxtla y centro del país.* Mexico City: n.p., 1936.

Julia del Palacio Langer. "Agrarian Reform, Oil Expropriation, and the Making of National Property in Post-revolutionary Mexico." Ph.D. thesis, Columbia University, 2014.

Claudia del Palacio Montiel. *Indice del fondo hemerográfico veracruzano del IEHS.* Xalapa: Universidad Veracruzana, 1999.

Alberto J. Pani. *El retroceso democrático del nuevo regimen.* Mexico City: A. J. Pani, 1947.

Erika Pani. *Para pertenecer a la gran familia mexicana: procesos de naturalización en el siglo XIX.* Mexico City: Colegio de México, 2015.

Wil G. Pansters, ed. *Citizens of the Pyramid: Essays on Mexican Political Culture.* Amsterdam: Rijksuniversiteit te Utrecht, 1997.

———. "Citizens with Dignity: Opposition and Government in San Luis Potosí, 1938–1993." In Aitken et al., *Dismantling the Mexican State?*

———. *Politics and Power in Puebla: The Political History of a Mexican State, 1937–1987.* Amsterdam: Rijksuniversiteit te Utrecht, 1990.

———. "Tropical Passion in the Desert: Gonzalo N. Santos and Local Elections in Northern San Luis Potosí, 1943–1958." In Gillingham and Smith, eds., *Dictablanda.*

———. "Zones of State-making: Violence, Coercion and Hegemony in Twentieth-Century Mexico." In Wil G. Pansters, ed., *Violence, Coercion and State-Making in Twentieth-Century Mexico.* Stanford: Stanford University Press, 2012.

——— and Benjamin T. Smith. "Writing Twentieth-Century Mexico's Drug Histories." In Pansters and Smith, *Histories of Drug Trafficking in Twentieth-Century Mexico.* Albuquerque: University of New Mexico Press, 2021.

Román Parra Terán. "Ixcateopan en el Siglo XIX." MA thesis, Universidad Autónoma de Guerrero, Chilpancingo, 1997.

Edgar Pavía Guzmán. *Acciones políticas ganaderas en Guerrero.* Chilpancingo: Asociación de historiadores de Guerrero, 1997.

María Teresa Pavía Guzmán. "Hacia una nueva historia de la economía suriana del siglo XIX." In Bustamante and Sarmiento Silva, *El Sur en Movimiento.*

Andrew Paxman. *Los Gobernadores: Caciques del pasado y del presente.* Mexico City: Grijalbo, 2018.

———. *Jenkins of Mexico: How a Southern Farm Boy Became a Mexican Magnate.* Oxford: Oxford University Press, 2017.

———. "Cooling to Cinema and Warming to Television: State Mass Media Policy, 1940–1964." In Gillingham and Smith, eds., *Dictablanda.*

Octavio Paz. *Posdata.* Mexico City: Siglo XXI, 1970.

———. *El laberinto de la soledad.* Mexico City: Fondo de Cultura Económica, 1972.

Lorena Paz Paredes and Rosario Cobo. "Café caliente." In Armando Bartra (ed.), *Crónicas del Sur: utopías campesinas en Guerrero* (Mexico City: Ediciones Era, 2000).

Antonio Peñafiel. *Anuario estadístico de la República Mexicana 1907*. Mexico City: Dirección General de Estadística, 1912.

Jaime M. Pensado and Enrique C. Ochoa. *México Beyond 1968: Revolutionaries, Radicals, and Repression during the Global Sixties and Subversive Seventies*. Tucson: University of Arizona Press, 2018.

———. *Rebel Mexico: Student Unrest and Authoritarian Political Culture during the Long Sixties*. Stanford: Stanford University Press, 2013.

Porfirio Pérez Olivares. *Memorias de un dirigente agrario de Soledad de Doblado*. Xalapa: Universidad Veracruzana, 1992.

Pablo Piccato. *City of Suspects: Crime in Mexico City, 1900–1931*. Durham: Duke University Press, 2001.

———. "Estadísticas del crimen en México: Series históricas, 1901–2001." http://www.columbia.edu/estadisticascrimen/EstadisticasSigloXX.htm.

———. *A History of Infamy: Crime, Truth and Justice in Mexico*. Oakland: University of California Press, 2017.

———. "*Pistoleros, ley fuga* and Uncertainty in Public Debates about Murder." In Gillingham and Smith, eds., *Dictablanda*.

———. "Murders of Nota Roja: Truth and Justice in Mexican Crime News." *Past and Present* 223, no. 1 (April 2014): 195–231.

Jeffrey M. Pilcher. *Cantinflas and the Chaos of Modernity*. Wilmington, DE: Scholarly Resources, 2001.

Martha Poblett Miranda. *Cien viajeros en Veracruz: crónicas y relatos*. 11 vols. Xalapa: Universidad Veracruzana, 1992.

Abel Quezada. *El mejor de los mundos imposibles*. Mexico City: CNCA, 1999.

———. *El Sistema: los mejores cartones, 1943–1988*. Mexico City: Planeta, 1999.

Sam Quinones. *True Tales from another Mexico: The Lynch Mob, the Popsicle Kings, Chalino, and the Bronx*. Albuquerque: University of New Mexico Press, 2001.

Alejandro Quintana. *Maximino Avila Camacho and the One-Party State: The Taming of Caudillismo, and Caciquismo in Post-Revolutionary Mexico*. Maryland: Lexington Books, 2010.

Emilio Rabasa. *La organización política de México: la constitución y la dictadura*. Madrid: Editorial América, 1917.

Rand McNally. *1938 Auto Road Atlas of the United States, Canada, and Mexico*. Chicago: Rand McNally, 1938.

———. *1950 Auto Road Atlas of the United States, Canada, and Mexico*. Chicago: Rand McNally, 1950.

Thomas Rath. "'*Que el cielo un soldado en cada hijo te dió . . .*': Conscription, Recalcitrance and Resistance in Mexico in the 1940s." *Journal of Latin American Studies* 37, no. 3 (August 2005).

———. *Myths of Demilitarization in Postrevolutionary Mexico, 1920–1960*. Chapel Hill: University of North Carolina Press, 2013.

Renato Ravelo Lecuona. "Periodo 1910–1920." In Salazar Adame, *La cuestión agraria mexicana.*

——— and Tomás Bustamante. *Historia general de Guerrero*. 4 vols. Mexico City and Chilpancingo: INAH, Gobierno del Estado de Guerrero, 1998.

Luis Reyes García. *Documentos manuscritos y pictóricos de Ichcateopan, Guerrero*. Mexico City: UNAM, 1979.

José Luis Reyna. "Redefining the Authoritarian Regime." In Reyna and Weinert, *Authoritarianism in Mexico.*

José Luis Reyna and Richard S. Weinert, eds. *Authoritarianism in Mexico*. Philadelphia: Institute for the Study of Human Issues, 1977.

Eulalia Ribera Carbó. "Traza, ocupación del espacio y segregación: La morfología urbana de Orizaba en el siglo XIX." In Contreras Cruz and Pardo Hernández, *De Veracruz a Puebla.*

Alan Riding. *Distant Neighbors: A Portrait of the Mexicans*. New York: Knopf, 1989.

L. Roberts, R. Lafta, R. Garfield, J. Khudhairi, and G. Burnham. "Mortality before and after the 2003 Invasion of Iraq: Cluster Sample Survey." *The Lancet* 364, no. 9448 (2006): 1857–64.

Marie Robinson Wright. *Picturesque Mexico*. Philadelphia: J. B. Lippincott, 1897.

Dennis Rodgers. "Living in the Shadow of Death: Gangs, Violence and Social Order in Urban Nicaragua, 1996–2002." *Journal of Latin American Studies* 38, no. 2 (May 2006).

Ariel Rodríguez Kurí. "Los años maravillosos: Adolfo Ruiz Cortines." In Will Fowler, ed., *Gobernantes mexicanos*, 2:263–86. Mexico City: Fondo de Cultura Económica, 2008.

Jacinto Rodríguez Munguía. "'The Invisible Tyranny'; or, the Origin of the 'Perfect Dictatorship.'" In Gillingham, Lettieri, and Smith, eds., *Journalism, Satire, and Censorship in Mexico.*

Marcial Rodríguez Saldaña. *La desaparición de poderes en el estado de Guerrero*. Chilpancingo: Universidad Autónoma de Guerrero, 1992.

Mary Roldán. *Blood and Fire: La Violencia in Antioquia, Colombia, 1946–1953*. Durham: Duke University Press, 2002.

Patricia Romero Lankao. "Coatzacoalcos-Minatitlán: el proceso histórico de transformación de la región y sus consecuencias socio-ambientales." B.A. thesis, UNAM 1986.

David F. Ronfeldt. "The Mexican Army and Political Order since 1940." In Wilkie, Meyer, and Monzón de Wilkie, *Contemporary Mexico.*

———, ed. *The Modern Mexican Military: A Reassessment*. San Diego: University of California, Center for U.S.–Mexican Studies, 1984.

William Roseberry. "Hegemony and the Language of Contention." In Joseph and Nugent, *Everyday Forms.*

Stanley Ross. "El historiador y el periodismo mexicano." *Historia Mexicana* 14, no. 3 (January–March 1965).

Anne Rubenstein. *Bad Language, Naked Ladies and Other Threats to the Nation: A Political History of Comic Books in Mexico.* Durham: Duke University Press, 1998.

Jeffrey W. Rubin. *Decentering the Regime: Ethnicity, Radicalism, and Democracy in Juchitán, Mexico.* Durham: Duke University Press, 1997.

———. "Popular Mobilisation and the Myth of State Corporatism." In Foweraker and Craig, *Popular Movements.*

Edward W. Said. *Reflections on Exile and Other Literary and Cultural Essays.* London: Granta, 2000.

Jaime Salazar Adame. "Alejandro Wladimir Paucic Smerdau: Un investigador anónimo del Estado de Guerrero." Paper given at the Seminario de estudios sobre Guerrero, Universidad Autónoma de Guerrero, Mexico City, 8/4/2009.

Jaime Salazar Adame, ed. *Historia de la cuestión agraria mexicana: estado de Guerrero, 1867–1940.* Mexico: Gobierno del Estado de Guerrero, 1987.

———. "Movimientos populares durante el Porfi riato en el Estado de Guerrero (1885–1891)." In Friedrich Katz and Jane-Dale Lloyd, eds., *Porfi rio Diaz frente al-descontento regional (1891–1893)*, 97–121. Mexico City: Universidad Iberoamericana, 1986.

———. "Período 1867–1910." In Jaime Salazar Adame, *Historia de la cuestión agraria mexicana, 1867–1940.* Mexico: Gobierno del Estado de Guerrero, 1987.

Richard J. Salvucci. "Mexican National Income in the Era of Independence, 1800–40." In Haber, *How Latin America Fell Behind.*

Gonzalo Sánchez. "The Violence: An Interpretative Synthesis." In Bergquist, Peñaranda, and Sánchez, eds., *Violence in Colombia.*

Jorge Alberto Sánchez Ortega. "Los escenarios y los actores sociales actuales: De la metáfora a la cultura: la invención política del Guerrero bronco." In Bustamante and Sarmiento, *La reinvención de Guerrero.*

Gema Santamaria and David Carey Jr., eds. *Violence and Crime in Latin America: Representations and Politics.* Norman: University of Oklahoma Press, 2017.

Gema Kloppe-Santamaria. "Lynching and the Politics of State Formation in Post-Revolutionary Puebla (1930s–50s)." *Journal of Latin American Studies* 51, no. 3 (August 2019).

Isela Myrna Santiago. "Huasteca Crude: Indians, Ecology, and Labor in the Mexican Oil Industry, Northern Veracruz, 1900–1938." Ph.D. diss., University of California Berkeley, 1997.

Gonzalo N. Santos. *Memorias.* Mexico City: Grijalbo, 1984.

Antonio Santoyo. *La mano negra: Poder regional y Estado en México (Veracruz, 1928–1943).* Mexico City: Consejo Nacional para la Cultura y las Artes, 1995.

Derek Sayer. "Everyday Forms of State Formation: Some Dissident Remarks on 'Hegemony.' " In Joseph and Nugent, *Everyday Forms.*

Arthur P. Schmidt. "Making It Real Compared to What? Reconceptualizing Mexican History since 1940." In Joseph, Rubinstein, and Zolov, eds., *Fragments of a Golden Age.*

———. *The Social and Economic Effects of the Railroad in Puebla and Veracruz, Mexico, 1867–1911.* New York: Garland, 1987.

Bettina E. Schmidt and Ingo W. Schröder, eds. *Anthropology of Violence and Conflict.* London: Routledge, 1995.

Samuel Schmidt. *The Deterioration of the Mexican Presidency: The Years of Luis Echeverría.* Tucson: University of Arizona Press, 1991.

Frans J. Schryer. *The Rancheros of Pisaflores: The History of a Peasant Bourgeoisie in Twentieth-Century Mexico.* Toronto: University of Toronto Press, 1980.

James C. Scott. *Domination and the Arts of Resistance.* New Haven: Yale University Press, 1990.

Secretaría de Agricultura y Fomento. *División territorial de los Estados Unidos Mexicanos correspondiente al censo de 1910.* Mexico, 1918.

Secretaría de Educación Pública. *Memoria de la SEP de septiembre de 1936 a agosto de 1937.* Mexico: Secretaría de Educación Pública, 1937.

———. *Memoria que indica el estado que guarda el ramo de educación pública el 31 de agosto de 1930.* Mexico: Secretaría de Educación Pública, 1930.

Ana María Serna. *Manuel Peláez y la vida rural en la Faja de Oro: Petróleo, revolución y sociedad en el norte de Veracruz, 1910–1928.* Mexico City: Instituto de Investigaciones Dr. José Luis Mora, 2008.

Mónica Serrano. "The Armed Branch of the State: Civil–Military Relations in Mexico." *Journal of Latin American Studies* 27, no. 2 (May 1995).

Elisa Servín. "Hacia el levantamiento armado: Del henriquismo a los federacionistas leales en los años cincuenta." In Oikión Solano and García Ugarte, eds., *Movimientos armados.*

———. *La oposición política: la otra cara del siglo XX mexicano.* Mexico City: Fondo de Cultura Económica, 2006.

———, ed. *Del nacionalismo al neoliberalismo, 1940–1994.* Mexico City: Colegio de México, 2010.

Randal Sheppard. *A Persistent Revolution: History, Nationalism, and Politics in Mexico since 1968.* Albuquerque: University of New Mexico Press, 2016.

Andrei Shleifer and Robert W. Vishny. *The Grabbing Hand: Government Pathologies and Their Cures.* Cambridge: Harvard University Press, 1998.

Alfred H. Siemens. *Between the Summit and the Sea: Central Veracruz in the Nineteenth Century.* Vancouver: University of British Columbia Press, 1990.

Jorge Luis Sierra Guzmán. *El enemigo interno: contrainsurgencia y fuerzas armadas en México.* Mexico City: Plaza y Valdés and Universidad Iberoamericana, 2003.

David Skerritt. "*¿Qué es la mano negra?*" In *Anuario del Centro de Estudios Históricos de la Universidad Veracruzana,* 3:129–38. Xalapa: Universidad Veracruana, 1980.

———. "Peasant Organisation in Veracruz, Mexico: 1920 to the Present." D.Phil. thesis, Oxford University, 1996.

———. *Rancheros sobre tierra fértil*. Xalapa: Universidad Veracruzana, 1993.

———. Review of A. Santoyo, *La mano negra: poder regional y estado en Mexico (Veracruz 1928–1943)*. *Sotavento* no. 2. Xalapa: Universidad Veracruzana, 1997.

Kathryn A. Sloan. *Death in the City: Suicide and the Social Imaginary in Modern Mexico*. Oakland: University of California Press, 2017.

Shawn C. Smallman. *Fear and Memory in the Brazilian Army and Society, 1889–1954*. Chapel Hill: University of North Carolina Press, 2002.

Benjamin T. Smith. "Building a State on the Cheap: Taxation, Social Movements, and Politics." In Gillingham and Smith, *Dictablanda*.

———. "Heliodoro Charis Castro and the Soldiers of Juchitán: Indigenous Militarism, Local Rule, and the Mexican State." In Fallaw and Rugeley, eds., *Forced Marches*.

———. *The Mexican Press and Civil Society, 1940–1976: Stories from the Newsroom, Stories from the Street*. Chapel Hill: University of North Carolina Press, 2018.

———. *Pistoleros and Popular Movements: The Politics of State Formation in Postrevolutionary Oaxaca*. Lincoln: University of Nebraska Press, 2009.

———. "The Rise and Fall of Narcopopulism: Drugs, Politics, and Society in Sinaloa, 1930–1980." *Journal for the Study of Radicalism* 7, no. 2 (Fall 2013).

———. *The Roots of Conservatism in Mexico: Catholicism, Society, and Politics in the Mixteca Baja, 1750–1962*. Albuquerque: University of New Mexico Press, 2012.

———. "The Year Mexico Stopped Laughing." In Gillingham, Lettieri, and Smith, eds., *Journalism, Satire, and Censorship in Mexico*.

———. "Who Governed? Grassroots Politics in Mexico under the Partido Revolucionario Institucional, 1958–1970." *Past and Present* 225, no. 4 (November 2014).

Peter H. Smith. "Mexican Democracy in Comparative Perspective." In Roderic Ai Camp, ed., *The Oxford Handbook of Mexican Politics*. Oxford: Oxford University Press, 2012.

———. *Labyrinths of Power: Political Recruitment in Twentieth-Century Mexico*. Princeton: Princeton University Press, 1979.

———. "Mexico since 1946: Dynamics of an Authoritarian Regime." In Bethell, *Mexico since Independence*.

Susana Sosenski Correa. "El niño consumidor: Una construcción publicitaria de la prensa mexicana en la década de 1950." In Ariadna Acevedo Rodrigo and Paula López Caballero, eds., *Ciudadanos inesperados: espacios de formación de la cuidadanía ayer y hoy*. Mexico City: Colegio de México, 2012.

Gabriela Soto Laveaga. "Shadowing the Professional Class: Reporting Fictions in Doctors' Strikes." *Journal of Iberian and Latin American Research* 19, no. 1 (2013).

John R. Southworth. *El Estado de Veracruz-Llave: su historia, comercio, agricultura e industrias, en inglés y español*. Liverpool: Blake and Mackenzie, 1900.

Matthew W. Stirling. "Discovering the New World's Oldest Dated Work of Man." *National Geographic Magazine* 76 (1939).

Frank Tannenbaum. *Peace by Revolution: Mexico after 1910*. New York: Columbia University Press, 1966.

T. Philip Terry. *Terry's Guide to Mexico*. New York, 1947.

Guy P. C. Thomson. "Bulwarks of Patriotic Liberalism: The National Guard, Philharmonic Corps and Patriotic Juntas in Mexico, 1847–88." *Journal of Latin American Studies* 22, no. 1 (February 1990).

——— and David G. LaFrance. *Patriotism, Politics, and Popular Liberalism in Nineteenth-Century Mexico: Juan Francisco Lucas and the Puebla Sierra*. Wilmington, DE: Scholarly Resources, 1998.

Rosemary Thorp. *Progress, Poverty and Exclusion: An Economic History of Latin America in the 20th Century*. Baltimore: Johns Hopkins University Press, 1998.

Alfred P. Tischendorf. *Great Britain and Mexico in the Era of Porfirio Díaz*. Chapel Hill: University of North Carolina Press, 1961.

Alexis de Tocqueville. *L'ancien régime et la révolution*. Paris: Gallimard, 1991 [1967].

Blanca Torres. *Hacia la utopía industrial*. Mexico City: Colegio de México, 1984.

Georgina Trigos. *El corrido veracruzano (una antología)*. Xalapa: Universidad Veracruzana, 1990.

George Tsebelis. "Decision Making in Political Systems: Veto Players in Presidentialism, Parliamentarism, Multicameralism and Mutipartyism." *British Journal of Political Science* 25 (July 1995).

Julius Turner. "Primary Elections as the Alternative to Party Competition in 'Safe' Districts." *Journal of Politics* 15, no. 2 (May 1953).

Rodolfo Usigli. *Teatro completo*. 4 vols. Mexico City: Fondo de Cultura Económica, 1996–97.

Norberto Valdéz. *Ethnicity, Class and the Indigenous Struggle for Land in Guerrero, Mexico*. New York: Routledge, 1998.

Alfonso Valencia Ríos. *Historia de El Dictamen*. Xalapa: Editorial del Gobierno del Estado, 1979.

Arturo Valenzuela and J. Samuel Valenzuela. "Party Oppositions under the Authoritarian Regime." In J. Samuel Valenzuela and Arturo Valenzuela, eds., *Military Rule in Chile: Dictatorship and Oppositions*. Baltimore: Johns Hopkins University Press, 1986.

Paul J. Vanderwood. *Disorder and Progress: Bandits, Police, and Mexican Development*. Lincoln: University of Nebraska Press, 1981.

Pablo Vargas González. "Estado y reivindicaciones agrarias: La guerra sofocada en la Huasteca hidalguense, 1974–1987." In Oikión Solano and García Ugarte, eds., *Movimientos armados*.

Mario Vargas Llosa. *Desafíos a la libertad*. Madrid: El País, 1994.

Various authors. *Alemán y la comisión del maíz*. Mexico City: Editorial Ruta, 1951.

———. *Enciclopedia Municipal de Veracruz: Chicontepec.* Mexico City: Secretaría de Gobernación y Gobierno del Estado de Veracruz-Llave, 1998.

———. *Enciclopedia Municipal de Veracruz: Perote.* Mexico City: Secretaría de Gobernación y Gobierno del Estado de Veracruz-Llave, 1998.

———. *Historia documental del Partido de la Revolución, tomo V: PRM-PRI, 1945–1950.* Mexico City: Partido Revolucionario Institucional, 1982.

———. *Montevideo–Oxford Latin American Economic History Database. http://moxlad.cienciassociales.edu.uy/en.*

Mary Kay Vaughan. *Cultural Politics in Revolution: Teachers, Peasants, and Schools in Mexico, 1930–1940.* Tucson: University of Arizona Press, 1997.

Emilia Vázquez. "De la intermediación política a la construcción local del Estado: distintos abordajes teóricos en el análisis de procesos políticos en una región del Istmo veracruzano." Paper presented at the coloquio internacional CIESAS-IRD, Xalapa, November 2006.

Francisco Vázquez Añorve. *Un recorrido interesante, o El ayer de mi costa.* Puebla: Epipsa, 1974.

Alfonso Luis Velasco. "Los recursos materiales." In Illades and Ortega, *Guerrero.*

Salvador Velazco. "*Rojo amanecer* y *La ley de Herodes:* cine político de la transición mexicana." *Hispanic Research Journal* 6, no. 1 (February 2005).

José Manuel Villalpando. "Política y ejército, 1945–1994." In Garciadiego, *El Ejército Mexicano.*

Rogelio Vizcaíno and Paco Ignacio Taibo II. "Acapulco en los tiempos de Juan Escudero." In Illades and Ortega, *Guerrero.*

Vadim Volkov. *Violent Entrepreneurs: The Use of Force in the Making of Russian Capitalism.* Ithaca: Cornell University Press, 2002.

Louise E. Walker. Review of Gillingham and Smith, "Dictablanda." *Hispanic American Historical Review* 95, no. 4 (2015).

Mark Wasserman. *Persistent Oligarchs: Elites and Politics in Chihuahua, Mexico, 1910–1940.* Durham: Duke University Press, 1993.

John W. Webber. "Down Mexico's Río Balsas." *National Geographic Magazine* 90, no. 2 (August 1946).

Nathan L. Whetten. *Rural Mexico.* Chicago: University of Chicago Press, 1948.

Laurence Whitehead. "State Organization in Latin America since 1930." In Bethell, *The Cambridge History of Latin America.*

Robert S. Wicks and Roland H. Harrison. *Buried Cities, Forgotten Gods: William Niven's Life of Discovery and Revolution in Mexico and the American Southwest.* Lubbock: Texas Tech University Press, 1999.

James W. Wilkie, "El complejo militar–industrial en México durante la década de 1930; diálogo con el General Juan Andreu Almazán." *Revista Mexicana de Ciencia Política* 20, no. 77 (1974).

——— et al. *Contemporary Mexico: Papers of the IV International Congress of Mexican History*. Berkeley: University of California Press, 1973.

——— and Edna Monzón de Wilkie. *México visto en el siglo XX: entrevistas de historia oral*. Mexico City: Instituto Mexicano de Investigaciones Económicas, 1969.

John Womack Jr. *Zapata and the Mexican Revolution*. London: Thames and Hudson, 1969.

Andrew Grant Wood. " 'The Proletarian Women Will Make the Social Revolution': Female Participation in the Veracruz Rent Strike, 1922–1927." In Stephanie Mitchell and Patience A. Schell, eds., *The Women's Revolution in Mexico, 1910–1953*. Lanham, MD: Rowman and Littlefield, 2007.

———. *Revolution in the Street: Women, Workers, and Urban Protest in Veracruz, 1870–1927*. Wilmington, DE: Scholarly Resources, 2001.

Desmond Young. *Member for Mexico: A Biography of Weetman Pearson, First Viscount Cowdray*. London: Cassell, 1966.

Index